THE BEST PLAYS OF 1936-37

EDITED BY

BURNS MANTLE

THE BEST PLAYS OF 1909-19
(*With Garrison P. Sherwood*)
THE BEST PLAYS OF 1919-20
THE BEST PLAYS OF 1920-21
THE BEST PLAYS OF 1921-22
THE BEST PLAYS OF 1922-23
THE BEST PLAYS OF 1923-24
THE BEST PLAYS OF 1924-25
THE BEST PLAYS OF 1925-26
THE BEST PLAYS OF 1926-27
THE BEST PLAYS OF 1927-28
THE BEST PLAYS OF 1928-29
THE BEST PLAYS OF 1929-30
THE BEST PLAYS OF 1930-31
THE BEST PLAYS OF 1931-32
THE BEST PLAYS OF 1932-33
THE BEST PLAYS OF 1933-34
THE BEST PLAYS OF 1934-35
THE BEST PLAYS OF 1935-36
THE BEST PLAYS OF 1936-37

Photo by Vandamm Studio, New York.

"HIGH TOR"

Van: . . . Maybe I'm cloud and maybe I'm dust. I might be old as time. I'd like to think knew. A man gets that way standing staring at darkness.

Lise: Then—you do know. It's better now. Somewhere along a verge where your life dips dusk and my gray days lift to the light a moment, we walk there and our eyes meet.

(*Burgess Meredith, Peggy Ashcroft*)

THE BEST PLAYS OF 1936-37

AND THE

YEAR BOOK OF THE DRAMA

IN AMERICA

EDITED BY

BURNS MANTLE

With Illustrations

DODD, MEAD AND COMPANY

NEW YORK - - - 1937

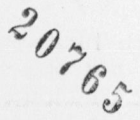

INTRODUCTION

DURING the publication of these records of the American theatre the number of new plays produced each season in the theatre's capital city, which would be New York, has ranged from this year's low of ninety to a peak of something like two hundred and sixty in the late nineteen-twenties.

Just why this particular season, the third in recovery rating following the great slump, should fall below the record in output the editor is neither in a position nor of a mind to say. There are those who have attributed it to the withdrawal of the huffers of Hollywood who, after a row with the dramatists over percents and profits, picked up their tin boxes and went home to resume their respective places in the California sun, vowing never again, so help them Goldwyn, to have anything to do as partners with the play producers of Broadway. Last season they furnished backing for some twenty-odd productions.

There are others who insist the shortage of new plays was due to the absence, not alone of investing capital, but more particularly to the absence of the better playwrights. Many of these were employed in Hollywood and were too busy or too tired to write plays. Many also gave up the first months of the season to battling with the producers over the terms of a Dramatists' Guild contract.

Personally I am inclined to think that, as is the case with most such mysteries, the simplest explanation is the sanest. There was both a lack of money and a lack of good plays. There was also quite frequently a lack of actors of sufficient experience and talent to be trusted in the casting of plays. The cinema has taken away a goodly crowd of those players upon whose talent and personal popularity the play producers have been accustomed to rely.

However, there were ninety new plays, and from these ninety ten have been selected that, again in the estimation of the editor, seem to reflect the greatest credit upon both the playwrights and the playgoers in representing the season.

These ten include Maxwell Anderson's "High Tor," voted by the New York Drama Critics' Circle as the best play by an American author to have been produced during the theatre year. The award, as usual, caused some discussion. "High Tor" enjoyed a positive rather than a general popularity. Being written largely in verse, and making free use of both fantasy and realism, employed in fairly violent combination, the comedy put some strain upon the quality of its auditors' imagination. As half its *dramatis personae* included the ghostly crew of the late Henrik Hudson's lost ship, the "Onrust," which went down in the Tappan Zee two hundred years ago, and as its romance was tied in with a legend of the Catskills such as Washington Irving might have dreamed, it was not an easy comedy for many patrons to assimilate. Those who did approve, however, were extravagant in their enthusiasm and "High Tor" was played successfully for many months.

The second prize winner of the season was Moss Hart's and George Kaufman's "You Can't Take It with You," a mildly riotous domestic farce that caught the fancy of that huge public usually loudest in announcing that it goes to the theatre for entertainment and nothing else. "You Can't Take It with You" provides entertainment for all groups, being the history of a family of mad hatters who followed their hobbies en masse, yet someway made a success of living.

A third winner of minor awards, though not a popular success, was Paul Green's "Johnny Johnson," a lightly ironic social problem drama presenting the case of a simple but completely honest man struggling to make reasonable adjustments in a dishonest, or at least hopelessly maladjusted, world.

Two of the plays in this list of ten were not in any sense popular successes. These were Robert Sherriff's and Jeanne de Casalis' "St. Helena" and Robert Turney's "Daughters of Atreus." It has been the custom, as you know, for the editor of the Best Play selections to collaborate as closely as possible with the selections of the public that supports the theatre. Not because he believes the will of the majority should always rule, even in matters of art, but because he is convinced that a Year Book of the theatre should honestly reflect not only the record of the season it covers but the tastes and preferences of the play patrons who made it possible. However, in this instance he feels that a considerable number of serious-minded play patrons were outvoted and in a way overwhelmed by this particular season's rush of highly amusing but essentially trivial comedies.

"St. Helena" was a thoughtfully, carefully, intelligently written biographical drama, made vivid in performance by the acting of the English actor, Maurice Evans, who played the role of Napoleon through the last seven years of his exile. "Daughters of Atreus" combined in felicitous verse and prose the tragedies of the House of Atreus, as approached through feminine motivation. They were two of the comparatively few plays of quality the season produced.

Edna Ferber's and George Kaufman's "Stage Door" brings into focus the timely problem of the young actress torn between stage and screen careers. It resolves the problem into typical and, in a sense, conventional Broadway drama, but does so with an intelligent and revealing overlay of character comedy.

Clare Boothe's "The Women" is a bright and bitter satire that has had a prominent place among the successes of the season. Its reading, like its playing, is destined to make its targets curl with resentment even as its masculine observers shake with satisfaction over its exposures. The frequent and vociferous assertions that "women are not like that" have been followed by an amazing assortment of nods of recognition in the play's New York audiences, which were largely feminine and of capacity size all Winter.

Mark Reed's "Yes, My Darling Daughter," is another brightly revealing type of sophisticated comedy. A significant work, I feel, not only for what it is, but also as an indication of what we have reason to expect from its newly arrived author in the future. So much is true, also, of Victor Wolfson's "Excursion," as heart-warming and as stimulatingly imaginative a comedy as has been recently brought to the stage.

The French Jacques Deval's "Tovarich," coming to us through the English version fashioned by Robert Sherwood, is another play that represents nothing more important than a very definite and quite general approval on the part of playgoers. It has been the sensational comedy success of every European capital the last two years and a record of the past season in New York would, I feel, be quite incomplete without it.

Otherwise "The Best Plays of 1936-37" goes to you with its established features intact and as correctly checked as it has been found humanly possible to check them. It is the eighteenth volume in the annual series begun in 1919-20; the nineteenth volume when we include "The Best Plays of 1909-19," the volume added in 1933 covering the ten years preceding the first issue. For his readers' support and continued interest the editor is again moved to record his gratitude and his heartfelt appreciation.

B. M.

Forest Hills, L. I., 1937.

CONTENTS

ILLUSTRATIONS

THE BEST PLAYS OF 1936-37

THE BEST PLAYS OF 1936-37

THE SEASON IN NEW YORK

TO a greater degree than usual this particular theatre season was a direct continuation of last season. That is to say it furnished a testing period for several enterprises and one or two trends that had been formally inaugurated a year ago.

It was, for example, the season during which the motion picture capitalists had sworn to make no cash advances for the production of such Broadway drama as they might later care to put into pictures. And it was the second season in which the WPA Federal theatre had operated. These were continuing problems of some speculation and considerable importance.

As for the withdrawal of motion picture capital, that appears to have had the result of reducing the number of plays presented for trial performances. At least the season was some ten or twelve plays short in volume compared with last season's record. Neither were there any extravagantly staged productions, save that of "White Horse Inn" at the Rockefeller Center theatre, and this, as it happens, was partly financed by picture money under an old contract.

From such facts and figures as are available the strenuously debated Dramatist Guild contract, limiting the motion picture tycoons' advantage in the purchase of the screen rights to plays for which they might furnish production costs, was working out to the general satisfaction of the playwrights. The irritation of the motion picture producers was, however, still acute. Another season or two of adjustment will probably be necessary before the new arrangement is thoroughly tested.

The second year of the WPA Federal theatre was, it seems to me, surprisingly successful for an enterprise growing out of an economic crisis and totally without precedents from which to chart a course or draft a plan of procedure. The Federal theatre project moved steadily forward, under the direction of Hallie Flanagan, kept itself reasonably free from political influences, hewed close to the line of providing work for able and enthused workers and developed such loyalties and enthusiasm as only an honest and worth while co-operation can breed.

I have a feeling that if it had been possible for one group or another to have taken advantage of what the government had established in the way of Federal theatre units, which were in effect national theatre bases, something fine and enduring could have been built upon them. But there was no time to organize and to propagandize individual communities. When the unscrambling of the art projects was ordered the Federal theatre was of necessity included and the beginning of the end was at hand.

We can agree, I think, that at least a start has been made, and a more promising start than ever has been made before, toward the eventual founding of such a national theatre as we have been dreaming about for many years. Out of the miseries and the needs of the depression a national theatre of a sort was born to live and function to the benefit of the theatre, the entertainment and mental stimulation of hundreds of thousands of citizens, many of whom were thus provided contact with a living theatre for the first time in their lives, and to the great credit of the workers who had made the contact possible.

I hold the hope, lightly visionary, it may be, that at some time in the future the chambers of commerce of those Western centers that have realized the great good community theatres and amusement centers have accomplished, and can accomplish, either for their own or neighboring cities, will start a movement that shall lead to co-operation with the government in the establishment of partially subsidized national theatre units. A chain of such units, stretching from coast to coast, could be made practically self-supporting within a decade. They would pay dividends in civic, social and cultural returns from the day of their establishment. It will be a great pity if some proper and promising use cannot be made of the organization Mrs. Flanagan has set up and directed these last two years.

Perhaps the outstanding achievement of the Federal WPA theatre season was the simultaneous production by eighteen units of the Sinclair Lewis-John C. Moffitt dramatization of Mr. Lewis' novel, "It Can't Happen Here." The play proved a slightly jittery drama of warning. It could be absurdly easy to Hitlerize America under the very noses of our smugly protesting patriots, Mr. Lewis argued, devoting his play to showing how it might happen. Both performances and reactions were varied, as suited the different sections of the country in which the producing units were located. A majority of the runs achieved by the play were long, that of the New York unit covering 95 performances.

A second WPA triumph in the local sector was the Orson Welles production of the seventeenth century Christopher Marlowe's "Dr. Faustus." This proved an attractive novelty, ran for 128 performances, and could have continued indefinitely at the 55-25-cent prices of the WPA had not other productions and producing complications crowded it off the stage.

The rest of the Federal theatre list offered a variety of drama, some good, some ordinary, very little that was downright bad. The outstanding living newspaper production was one called "Power." In this the history of electricity as a need and a power, the struggle for its control, the development of power monopolies and the recent efforts of the government to adjust and rationalize monopolistic tendencies and abuses through the formation of the TVA and other similar enterprises, was vividly sketched in a series of dramatic scenes. Another living newspaper issue was devoted to the use and abuse of the injunction privilege called "Injunction Granted." A drama by Friedrich Wolf, translated by Anne Bromberger, exposing the Nazi reign in Germany and called "Prof. Mamlock" was produced by the Jewish unit and proved popular. The Negro theatre, which had begun sensationally with a Haitian "Macbeth," progressed to the authorship and production of "The Case of Philip Lawrence," a drama of Harlem life.

A great number of free performances were given by the dramatic, musical, marionette and vaudeville units. Five Caravan, or portable, theatres operated during the Summer, one in each of the five boroughs of New York. It was estimated that Federal theatre audiences, gathered in twenty-seven states, numbered 350,000 weekly on the average.

A third feature of the season of 1936-37 was the quite unexpected revival in popularity of a poetic dramatist named William Shakespeare. Long neglected on Broadway, save in those exceptional revivals dominated by a reigning personality, it was not expected that the importation of John Gielgud of England to play with a supporting company organized in America would materially change the attitude of the playgoing crowd toward Shakespearean drama. It did, however. Mr. Gielgud's reception was enthusiastic and his stay was repeatedly lengthened until he had achieved a new record for Shakespeare, Hamlet and Broadway amounting to 132 performances.

Leslie Howard, who had been preparing a production of "Hamlet" for a year or more, elected to test comparisons with the Gielgud performance. The result was in no sense discreditable to the Howard confidence, nor to the Howard art. It was a test rather of a thoughtful and subdued modern Hamlet contrasted with a Hamlet conceived and brilliantly played in the Hamlet tradition. In New York both critics and the larger public preferred the tradition-inspired performance of Mr. Gielgud. After a season of five weeks Mr. Howard took his handsome production on tour and recovered a good part of both his professional poise and his financial investment.

A second, and even more sensational Shakespearean success, was that of Maurice Evans who, after achieving personal triumphs as an interpreter of stage character by playing the Dauphin to Katharine Cornell's Saint Joan in the Bernard Shaw drama of that title, and the Napoleon of "St. Helena," personally raised the money for a revival of "Richard II," which had not been presented in New York since Edwin Booth played the young King in 1878. Mr. Evans recruited his own company, bringing Margaret Webster from England to take charge of the play's staging and importing one or two players for his cast. Ian Keith was his Bolingbroke and the veteran Augustin Duncan the John of Gaunt. The first night of "Richard II" was emotionally stirring in the spontaneity and sweep of audience enthusiasm. The reports of the reviewers the following day were rapturous and "Richard II" was continued for 133 performances to a succession of capacity and near-capacity audiences in the fairly roomy St. James theatre.

The progress of the social drama of propagandic purpose was normal but less exciting than was promised by recent indications. Paul Green's "Johnny Johnson," a digest of which is included in this volume, was the most warmly debated of the half dozen or more plays of similar motivations. John Howard Lawson's "Marching Song" stirred comment, but could not seem to get really started. Sinclair Lewis' "It Can't Happen Here" was in a measure both helped and handicapped by its tie-up with the Federal theatre. Sidney Kingsley's "Ten Million Ghosts" was impressively produced, but veered so sharply to the left in argument as to limit its appeal. E. P. Conkle's "Two Hundred Were Chosen," a human and understanding picture of the settlement of the Mantanuska valley in Alaska under government direction, also failed of the support many felt it deserved.

The Summer season, picking up the theatre record where we left it last June 15, offered nothing worth calling attention to from last season's closing until mid-August, and then nothing more important than the resumption of the run of Helen Hayes in "Victoria Regina" and that of Alfred Lunt and Lynn Fontanne in "Idiot's Delight," and a return of the D'Oyly Carte Opera company for a renewal of its ever popular Gilbert and Sullivan revivals. The D'Oyly Cartes had been away for two years and were welcomed back with great heartiness, their frequently extended engagement continuing for a total of 266 performances.

Early September was also barren of new plays. On the fourteenth a Ziegfeld "Follies," under the Shubert direction, went into the Winter Garden with a new line of principals, "Bobby" Clark working with Fannie Brice in place of Herb Williams and Hugh O'Connell, who were prominent in the same revue the previous season. Gypsy Rose Lee, a strip-tease queen of the Minsky dynasty, a form of burlesque which was later to be barred from the Broadway theatres, made her debut in what is smilingly referred to as the higher-class revue field, continuing her disrobing in public with a Gypsy Rose Lee touch that caused more smiles than blushes.

The first drama to brighten the season was George Kelly's "Reflected Glory," which had been produced on the coast and brought East with Tallulah Bankhead in the star role, that of an actress with a domestic urge but insufficient courage to indulge it. Two military school dramas, Joseph Viertel's "So Proudly We Hail," a somewhat embittered exposure of what the author believes with passionate honesty are the character-weakening influences of such institutions, and Henry Misrock's "Bright Honor," a less prejudiced but also less effective drama written along similar lines, were comparatively quick failures. Two psychopathic murder mysteries from London, Emlyn Williams' "Night Must Fall," and Frank Vosper's "Love from a Stranger," also failed to live up to their London records. The Williams drama, with the author playing the chief role, lasted for sixty-four performances. Mr. Vosper's play, also with the author featured, achieved half that number of showings. It was while returning to England that actor Vosper met his death on shipboard as mysteriously as any of the victims of the Vosper plays. Weeks later his bruised body was washed up on the shores of France.

The Rockefellers' second adventure in show business, their partners on this occasion being the Warner Brothers of pictures and Rowland Stebbins (Laurence Rivers, Inc.) of New York, was "White Horse Inn." This production was made elaborately and expensively at the Center theatre the first evening of October and ran through until April. It did not reach the same popularity as that enjoyed by the first Rockefeller enterprise, which was "The Great Waltz," but often reported even larger weekly totals in box office receipts.

October first nights, frequently the most exciting of the theatre year, also included the Sherriff-De Casalis "St. Helena," with Maurice Evans featured; "Hamlet," with John Gielgud of England starred and enthusiastically acclaimed; the Jacques Deval-Robert Sherwood "Tovarich," a popular hit from London and the continent, played here by John Halliday and Marta Abba, Italy's leading actress; and Edna Ferber's and George Kaufman's "Stage Door," which brought Margaret Sullavan back from Hollywood to play a Broadway heroine who refuses to be lured to Hollywood.

These four were all highly successful. Interesting failures of the month were the first Theatre Guild production, a comedy by Julius and Philip Epstein called "And Stars Remain," and Robert Turney's "Daughters of Atreus," a rewriting of the dramas of Aeschylus and Euripides having to do with the Atreus legends. George Abbott, later to consolidate his gains as the first man of the theatre in the production of light comedy, suffered a quick failure with "Sweet River," a rewriting of the "Uncle Tom's Cabin" story that revealed more honest sentiment than appealing entertainment. Sidney Kingsley went down with a part of his profits from "Dead End" with the unsuccessful "Ten Million Ghosts," and Norman Bel Geddes suffered a similar adventure with "Iron Men," a story of steel construction workers impressively staged. Geddes, too, had invested profits from the same "Dead End," of which he was the fortunate producer. The first musical hit of the season was scored by "Red, Hot and Blue," a sort of sequel to "Anything Goes," written by Howard Lindsay and Russel Crouse, with music by Cole Porter. Vinton Freedley was the producer and Ethel Merman, Jimmy Durante and Bob Hope a trio of stars. This one ran through till Spring.

Following the season progressively, November was a month of disappointments, with the exception of Noel Coward's arrival with an assortment of nine one-act plays grouped under the inclusive title of "Tonight at 8.30." Mr. Coward brought Gertrude Lawrence with him as a co-star, and Miss Lawrence rewarded her patron with a succession of splendid characterizations.

Otherwise this was the month in which Leslie Howard courageously matched Hamlets with John Gielgud and won more sympathy than acclaim. It was the month in which two labored but well played biographical dramas, Sophie Treadwell's "Plumes in the Dust," emphasizing the sadness and the frustrations of Edgar Allan Poe's hectic existence, and William McNally's "Prelude to Exile," extracting and romanticizing the Mathilde Wesendonck episode from the life of Richard Wagner, regrettably met defeat.

They were not holding plays, as entertainment for the general public, but they were intelligently written, well acted and of real interest to those specific publics interested in their subjects.

The holiday period, which usually furnishes a new impetus to playgoing, had a few outstanding productions to its credit, but not many. Gilbert Miller, who had been grooming a revival of Wycherley's "The Country Wife" for several weeks, and had gone so far as to send Ruth Gordon to England for intensive training with an English company headed by Edith Evans at the famed Old Vic theatre, brought the seventeenth century comedy to production at the Henry Miller theatre early in the month. Miss Gordon's personal success fully equaled expectations, but the boldnesses of the Restoration classic, albeit considerably modified, appealed to a comparatively small public only. Nearing Christmas the immensely popular Moss Hart-George Kaufman "You Can't Take It With You" was produced, achieving immediate popularity, and was followed a few days later by "Brother Rat," written by John Monks and Fred Finklehoffe, two graduates of the Virginia Military academy. This, being the third of the military school plays, approaching the problem of the plebes from an exclusively comedic angle, proved the one success of the three and ran the season out.

Katharine Cornell, having toured the early part of the season with "Romeo and Juliet," made her first New York bid in a new play as a Malay Princess in Maxwell Anderson's "The Wingless Victory." She scored the expected personal success for Miss Cornell and a sort of half-hearted success for Mr. Anderson's drama. The day after Christmas Clare Boothe's frank exposure of the common character weaknesses of her sex, a comedy called "The Women," with a cast of thirty-five women and nary a man in sight, startled, shocked and convulsed its first audience, wavered uncertainly for a few weeks and then found a public, largely feminine, that loved it so it was sensationally successful the rest of the season. Important failures of the holiday period included "Days to Come," a thoughtful and provocative study of the labor versus capital problem as it afflicted the descendants of a family of stalwart American manufacturers, written by the Lillian Hellman who had skyrocketed into prominence the season before with "The Children's Hour," and "Aged 26," a human and sympathetic biographical drama having to do with the romance of the poet John Keats, sensitively written by Anne Crawford Flexner. A new revue, "The Show Is On," with Beatrice Lillie and Bert Lahr its leading comedians, was also a popular Christmas bill at the

Winter Garden.

Early in the new year Maxwell Anderson's "High Tor" charmed the critical fraternity and the Anderson following, which has grown apace these last few seasons. Being a mixture of fantasy and realism the play also left large sections of the general playgoing crowd a little mystified and unsatisfied. Walter Huston brought his revival of "Othello" to Broadway, after a considerable tour, and met a disappointing reception at the hands of the reviewers. This served to retard such enthusiasm as the "Dodsworth" star's adherents might conceivably have worked up for their favorite American actor had they been given a chance. Mr. Huston withdrew his revival after three weeks.

"The Eternal Road" also came to production at this time, revealing a spectacle that had cost, in good, round figures, nearly a half million dollars. For its setting the huge Manhattan opera house, built originally by Oscar Hammerstein, was literally torn apart from orchestra pit to rear wall and rebuilt to disclose a mountainside of five levels, rising from a winding road below a Jewish synagogue situated in a small town in Central Europe, to the very portals of Heaven itself. With a cast of several hundred, "The Eternal Road" related the story of the Old Testament in dramatic action. The physical impact of the production was tremendous. On the artistic side there was generous praise for the story woven from the Biblical legends by Franz Werfel; for the musical setting written by Kurt Weill and for the majestic setting fashioned by Norman Bel Geddes. Max Reinhardt staged the spectacle and a large cast performed admirably. After three months, during which attendance was heavy, interest slackened somewhat. A road tour is possible but uncertain.

Proving the wide contrast and complete democracy of taste represented in a theatre season, a few days after "The Eternal Road" got under way a little something written by the late Samuel Shipman and Beth Brown called "Behind Red Lights" was shown. This was the story of a harlot with a heart of gold who was framed by a vice crusade and nearly married the public prosecutor. It continued for 177 performances, which was 24 more than the Bible spectacle was given.

February, a little to everyone's surprise, turned out more substantial successes than any other one month of the season. This was the month Maurice Evans revived "Richard II" and scored a resounding hit, and the month Maxwell Anderson's "The Masque of Kings," with Dudley Digges and Henry Hull, gave the Theatre Guild the first near-success of its season. A bright new comedy by

Mark Reed, "Yes, My Darling Daughter," also proved an overnight hit and a few weeks later Arthur Kober's "Having Wonderful Time" delighted its first audience and all its reviewers. There was also a pleasant Franz Lehar musical comedy with operetta trimmings, "Fredericka," with Dennis King and Helen Gleason featured, and an amusing little piece called "Fulton of Oak Falls," which George M. Cohan had adapted from an original script by Parker Fennelly. "Fulton" was in the same general atmosphere as "Ah, Wilderness," putting an adolescent daughter in the place of a son, but the Cohan following did not respond as quickly nor as generously as had been hoped.

An incident of the month was the arrival of Ethel Barrymore Colt with a revival of Bouccicault's "London Assurance" which she had newly adapted. It served to show that Ethel Barrymore's daughter is making progress as an actress director, but was definitely not in the Broadway competition.

Sir Cedric Hardwicke, frequently spoken of as London's first actor, had arrived earlier in the season with Gilbert Miller's production of "Promise," a light domestic problem drama from the French of Henri Bernstein. Sir Cedric's opportunities in this play were distinctly limited. His supporting cast included Jean Forbes-Robertson, daughter of Sir Johnstone Forbes-Robertson and Gertrude Elliott, favorites of another generation of playgoers, and one or two other distinguished players, but even a perfect performance could not save it for long.

A month later Sir Cedric was returned to the stage in a detective-story melodrama reminiscent of "Sherlock Holmes," called "The Amazing Dr. Clitterhouse." Barre Lyndon wrote it and it had been a great success in London. "Clitterhouse" started off very well in New York, but as Spring approached the amazing doctor, who had taken up crime as a part of his laboratory research work, had some little difficulty gathering audiences and decided to leave the field. A run of eighty performances, however, which isn't bad.

The Theatre Guild, which had had a disappointing season, now came upon another semi-failure, "Storm over Patsy." This was a lightly amusing comedy of Scotch home life, adapted from the German of Bruno Frank by James Bridie, the amiable Scot who wrote "A Sleeping Clergyman." It amused but it did not enthuse the Theatre Guild subscribers and was all through in five weeks.

Katharine Cornell, having worked herself into a state of some weariness in Maxwell Anderson's "The Wingless Victory," determined to revive Bernard Shaw's "Candida." She could play this part two or three times a week and the change should prove stimulating. It did. But as it turned out "Candida" proved much too popular for a few casual performances, and Miss Cornell was forced, before going on tour, to substitute it for the Anderson drama as a full week's bill.

Warden Lawes of Sing Sing, in collaboration with Jonathan Finn, wrote a lively and interesting drama revealing the influences that develop criminals and the adventures they are likely to encounter in prison. It was called "Chalked Out" and Brock Pemberton negotiated an excellent production for it. There had been a gradual recoiling from gangster and criminal plays the last several months, however, and the Warden Lawes opus failed to interest enough playgoers to make it pay. In two weeks it was gone. Then Mr. Pemberton tried an equally well written drama relating the documented adventures of a Red Cross unit in the Great War. This was called "Red Harvest" and Walter Charles Roberts was the author. Again the temper of the times was against the play, and again, despite an excellent production and performance, "Red Harvest" was not strong enough nor appealing enough to beat down its handicaps.

Constance Cummings, coming back to America hoping to capitalize the fine record she had made as the heroine of "Accent on Youth" the season before, was presented in a trial-scene melodrama called "Young Madame Conti." Bruno Frank of Germany wrote the play originally, and it was adapted by Hubert Griffith and Benn W. Levy. It proved a well-written, well-staged and well-acted drama, but it was a shade too synthetic to excite audiences. Three weeks and it was gone.

The end of the season was in sight. There was a sudden depression of interest all along the line. Playgoers were still eager to buy entertainment, but unusually selective in their purchasing. Nothing old and nothing new, unless it had at least a trace of novelty. April produced two such plays—a nicely imaginative comedy by Victor Wolfson, called "Excursion," which is included in this book, and a musical comedy, "Babes in Arms," which brought in a carload of talented youngsters, led by Mitzi Green, once of the cinema, Ray Heatherton, Wynn Murray and Duke McHale.

Peggy Wood, becoming interested in a pleasant little comedy about a middle-aged Cinderella called "Miss Quis," helped the author, Ward Morehouse, in the staging of the play and carried it through five weeks at Henry Miller's theatre. "Penny Wise," a bright and inconsequential comedy by the Jean Ferguson Black who had dramatized Morley's "Thunder on the Left," the season before, ran briefly, and a biographical comedy having to do with the Duse-D'Annunzio romance called "Curtain Call" died quickly.

The season went out with a shout when George Abbott produced John Murray's and Allen Boretz's "Room Service" at the Cort on May 19. This comedy of the shoe-stringers of show business trying to negotiate the production of a promising play, and to stave off eviction from a typical Times Square hotel until after the production, was, next to the prize-winning "You Can't Take It with You," the laughing success of the season. It gave Abbott a record of four straight comedy hits—"Boy Meets Girl," "Three Men on a Horse," "Brother Rat" and "Room Service," and sent him to Hollywood at a maharajah's salary to see if he can repeat in pictures.

Nothing else interesting happened before the ides of June closed in. There was a revival of "Abie's Irish Rose" which got five weeks in place of five years this time; a revival of "The Bat," which played for two weeks; a revival of "Damaged Goods" which closed after eight performances. And that was all.

THE SEASON IN CHICAGO

By Charles Collins

Dramatic Critic of the *Chicago Tribune*

THE omens are more favorable than they have been for several years. A survey of the stage year in Chicago, with June 1 as the point of chronological division, reveals an increase in the number of bookings, an improvement in the quality of productions, and an acceleration of patronage. In other words, more shows, better shows, bigger business. The upturn has not been extraordinary, but it has been definitely satisfying to well-wishers of the legitimate theatre who are now persuaded that their favorite art is not doomed to vanish from this metropolitan area.

The professional stage offered 26 engagements or runs, many of them affairs of distinction. This total may be increased to 29 by the addition of two excellent Yiddish companies from New York and one hold-over, of brief duration, from the preceding year. The Federal Theatre Project [WPA] added 9 productions, and carried over two. Thus it will be seen that first-nighters had 37 opportunities to attend premières during the year and that dramatic critics had some reason for believing that they had not fallen into the class of forgotten men.

The story of the year may be read, in condensed form, in the following catalogue of activities:

Katharine Cornell in Shaw's "Saint Joan"; Grand Opera House, opened June 9; two weeks.

"Broken Dishes," WPA revival; Blackstone theatre, opened June 15; eighteen weeks.

"The Old Maid," semi-professional revival; Chicago Woman's club theatre, opened June 22; eighteen weeks.

"Triple A Ploughed Under," WPA production, Great Northern theatre, opened July 6; moved to Civic theatre; eight weeks.

"Macbeth" adapted for Negro players, WPA production, Great Northern theatre; two weeks.

George White's "Scandals," with Helen Morgan, Willie and Eugene Howard; Grand Opera House, opened June 28; eleven weeks.

"Dead End," Studebaker theatre, opened September 13; ten

weeks.

"Blossom Time," operetta revival, Grand Opera House, opened September 19; two weeks.

"The Night of January 16," Selwyn theatre, opened September 20; nine weeks.

"Lady Precious Stream," Harris theatre, opened September 28; two weeks.

"Pride and Prejudice," Harris theatre, opened October 12; six weeks.

"Naughty Marietta," operetta revival with Ilse Marvenga; Grand Opera House, opened October 18; three weeks.

"End of Summer," with Ina Claire and Osgood Perkins; Erlanger theatre, opened October 26; four weeks.

"It Can't Happen Here," WPA production; Blackstone theatre, opened October 27; twelve weeks.

"Call It a Day," with Philip Merivale and Gladys Cooper; Grand Opera House, opened November 9; four weeks.

Charlotte Greenwood in "Leaning on Letty" [adaptation of "The Post Road"]; Selwyn theatre, opened November 22; twenty weeks.

"O, Say Can You Sing," revue, WPA production; Great Northern theatre, opened December 11; fourteen weeks.

Leslie Howard in "Hamlet," Grand Opera House, opened December 25; one week.

"Mulatto," with James Kirkwood, Studebaker theatre, opened December 25; three weeks.

Jane Cowl in "First Lady," Harris theatre, opened December 26; six weeks.

Alla Nazimova in Ibsen's "Ghosts" and "Hedda Gabler," Erlanger theatre, opened December 28; two weeks.

Katharine Hepburn in "Jane Eyre," Erlanger theatre, opened January 11; four weeks.

"Ziegfeld Follies," with Fannie Brice and Bobby Clark; Grand Opera House, opened January 4; ten weeks.

"Within These Walls," WPA production, Blackstone theatre, opened January 28; two and a half weeks.

"The Great Waltz," return engagement, Auditorium theatre, opened January 29; one week.

"You Can't Take It with You," Harris theatre, opened February 7, sixteen weeks until May 31; continued indefinitely.

D'Oyly Carte Opera Company of London in seven Gilbert and Sullivan operettas; Erlanger theatre, opened February 8; five weeks.

"The Good Old Summer Time," WPA production [called "Around the Corner" in New York]; Blackstone theatre, opened February 19; seven weeks.

"Mississippi Rainbow," WPA production for Negro players, Princess theatre, opened March 7; fourteen weeks.

Tallulah Bankhead in "Reflected Glory," Grand Opera House, opened March 15; three weeks.

"Idiot's Delight," with Alfred Lunt and Lynn Fontanne, Erlanger theatre, opened April 12; four weeks.

"Red, Hot and Blue," revue with Ethel Merman, Jimmy Durante, Bob Hope, Grand Opera House, opened April 14; three weeks.

Maurice Schwartz in "The Water Carrier," Yiddish comedy with songs; Selwyn theatre, opened April 12; one week.

"Close Quarters," with Philip Merivale and Gladys Cooper, Selwyn theatre, opened April 26; two weeks.

"Take It Easy," comedy of Chicago authorship and management; Studebaker theatre, opened May 1; two weeks.

Artef company of New York [Yiddish] in two plays, "200,000" and "Recruits"; Civic theatre, opened May 6; five performances.

"The Lonely Man," WPA production, Blackstone theatre, opened May 16; two weeks; continued into summer.

Katharine Cornell in "The Wingless Victory" and Shaw's "Candida," Grand Opera House, opened May 17; two weeks, continued one week in June.

A study of the above summary discloses the fact that stage activities in Chicago are largely confined to four theatres—the Grand Opera House, the Harris, the Selwyn and the Erlanger. These are the houses favored by the United Booking Office in New York when routes and schedules for touring companies are prepared. They form a "bottle neck" which occasionally obstructs traffic. Other available theatres of the first rank, with desirable locations, are the Blackstone and the Studebaker; but the former is occupied by the Federal Theatre Project and the latter is handicapped by life insurance company control, which appears to prevent it from booking companies on the customary sharing basis.

The longest run of the year was the twenty weeks of Charlotte Greenwood in "Leaning on Letty," at the Selwyn. This success came as a surprise which should have disturbed the complacency of New York producers who have regarded Chicago, for generations, as part of their own domain, to be cultivated or neglected as they chose. The production, a comedy with a melodramatic background, came from the Pacific Coast under the auspices of

Henry Duffy, without exploitation of the play's Broadway record under the title of "The Post Road." The original piece had been adapted to fit Miss Greenwood's personality, and the performance had an epilogue in which the star appeared as her old song-singing, leg-waving self. Chicago accepted it as an engaging novelty in entertainment, and the box-office boys at the Selwyn had a happy, old-fashioned winter.

Second to Miss Greenwood in length of run was "You Can't Take It with You," specially cast for Chicago with all the care that Sam H. Harris and George S. Kaufman could bestow upon it. The "second company" haters, who are numerous and undiscriminating in Chicago, were baffled by the admirable performance of this ingenious and amiable whimsy, in which Aldrich Bowker had the central role [the grandfather of the happy-go-lucky family], and the play's success was immediate. Its sixteen weeks up to June 1 are only a part of its Chicago history, for the run has contniued into an otherwise vacant summer and is expected to last until Thanksgiving Day.

The year was notable for containing two visits from Katharine Cornell—in Shaw's "Saint Joan," early in June, 1936; in "The Wingless Victory" and Shaw's "Candida," late in May, 1937. Her plans for a professional tour of the world, announced in the latter engagement, probably mean that she will not be able to return to Chicago again for two or three years. Other dramatic stars of the year were Ina Claire, Charlotte Greenwood, Philip Merivale and Gladys Cooper [two appearances for these co-stars], Leslie Howard, Alla Nazimova, Katharine Hepburn, Tallulah Bankhead [her début in Chicago], Alfred Lunt and Lynn Fontanne.

Mr. Howard came to Chicago with his notable production of "Hamlet" immediately after his unhappy experience in New York, where unfavorable comparisons with John Gielgud's interpretation of the great tragic role had obscured the values of his achievement as an actor-manager. The Chicago verdict served to iron the wrinkles of care from his sensitive brow and to encourage him to continue his tour. The production as a whole was highly praised; many veterans, in fact, regarded it as the finest staging of "Hamlet" in their experience. Mr. Howard's Prince of Denmark was not extolled, but neither was it derided; it was accepted as a laudable adventure by a thoughtful and graceful actor whose Shakespearean experience has been brief. The critics were kindly; the audiences were enthusiastic. The final curtain at every performance brought demonstrations of appreciation that recalled the theatre of forty and fifty years ago. These ovations, moreover, did not suggest celebrity-hunters admiring a motion picture star; they seemed to be a frank response to the play and its interpretation.

The glamour of cinema fame also brightened the theatrical scene when Katharine Hepburn arrived as star of the Theatre Guild's production of a new version of "Jane Eyre," with Helen Jerome, adaptor of "Pride and Prejudice," as its author. This was the first time that the Theatre Guild had ever sent a play to Chicago before submitting it to New York. The occasion had a double edge of novelty, for Miss Hepburn herself had never acted here. The critical opinion was mixed as far as the star's talent is concerned, but her personal charm and suitability for the role of Charlotte Brontë's heroine were undeniable. The audiences reacted to the old-school sentimentality and rhetoric of the play in a manner which suggested that "sophistication" is passing out of fashion. Altogether, Miss Hepburn's Chicago début was a definite success and a stimulating event in the history of the theatrical year.

Five weeks of the D'Oyly Carte revivals of Gilbert and Sullivan also served to arouse play-going enthusiasm. For many, this rich repertory of lyric classics was the happiest period of the season's play-going. The bills which the visiting Londoners offered with Savoyard authority and unction were: "The Mikado," "Iolanthe," "The Gondoliers," "The Yeomen of the Guard," "The Pirates of Penzance" with "Trial by Jury," "Patience," and "H. M. S. Pinafore" with "Cox and Box."

The fact that Tallulah Bankhead, who is nearly twenty years old as an actress, made her Chicago début on March 15, 1937, may not be important, but it suggests the familiar story of the drama's withdrawal from "the road" during the past generation. At any rate, Miss Bankhead arrived at last, acted in a vigorous and picturesque manner in "Reflected Glory," and aroused an interest in her plans for the future.

Musical shows of the opulent Broadway type, for which Chicago has a voracious appetite, were scarce. George White's "Scandals," with Helen Morgan and the Howard brothers as stars, had a satisfactory summer run, and the "Ziegfeld Follies," with Bobby Clark recruited as Fannie Brice's co-star, kept the town amused through January and February. "Red, Hot and Blue," fresh from its Broadway popularity, arrived in the spring with ambitions for a run, but was withdrawn and permanently closed after three weeks because its box-office takings, although handsome, were not quite enough to pay its expenses of $20,000 a week. The opening of this frolic was an eccentric occasion which had no precedent in Chicago stage history. The audience assembled in festive mood and attire, waited until fifteen minutes after curtain time, and then was informed by Jimmy Durante [in costume] that no performance would be given that night because the stage crew could not untangle the scenery. Therefore the show's première was twenty-four hours late. The incident caused some people to wonder if the American stage had not emerged from the depression minus its favorite slogan: "The show must go on."

In the green pastures of the musical arts, Chicago bravely upheld its metropolitan status. The city opera company behaved handsomely during a season of six weeks and nine postscript performances. Basil's Ballet Russe remained for two weeks in mid-season and returned for a supplementary engagement of five performances.

The year ended with no plans for summer theatricals, formerly a Chicago tradition. The schedule from June 1 to mid-August, 1937, is the blankest in the memory of the oldest inhabitant.

THE SEASON IN SAN FRANCISCO

By Fred Johnson

Drama Editor of *The Call-Bulletin*

SAN FRANCISCO became the proving ground of two New York-bound play productions within the year ending in June, one falling not quite inside the theatrical season of Broadway reckoning.

The summer premières of Tallulah Bankhead's "Reflected Glory," and "Amphitryon 38," starring Alfred Lunt and Lynn Fontanne, were reminiscent of Henry Miller's annual visits during the eastern heated term, when he tried out at least one new play as part of his yearly touring repertoire.

The Lunts, who climaxed the pre-vacation if not the show season of 1936-37 in San Francisco's accounting, found the west coast so profitable a field on their first joint visit that they pledged future appearances and the testing of another new production. This promise was made more emphatic after the first-night acclaim for "Amphitryon." The Jean Giraudoux play, adapted from the French by Samuel N. Behrman, was heralded as a world première, due to its virtually new form. Behrman was present for the final rehearsals, as were Lee Simonson, Theatre Guild stage designer; Samuel L. M. Barlow, composer of the special music; Guild Directors Theresa Helburn and Lawrence Langner and Business Manager Warren P. Munsell.

The preceding engagement of "Idiot's Delight," beginning early in June, drew capacity audiences at the Curran Theatre for two weeks and might have prospered for another fortnight. While playing in the Robert E. Sherwood drama for the season's last performances, many of the cast were rehearsing in the new piece.

The Lunts' initial coast success was equaled by Katharine Cornell's engagement of two weeks at the same theatre in "Saint Joan," a red-letter event of the early season. As usual, she ended the run to sell-out patronage for the start of her annual vacation.

Tallulah Bankhead followed Miss Cornell in the première of "Reflected Glory," exceeding the latter's run by one week for receipts labeled "good" at the boxoffice. The new George Kelly play was awarded the initial verdict of suitability as a showcase for the Bankhead personality. Lee Shubert made the coast production in association with Homer Curran and the same partnership was committed to the staging of a new musical by the same author, called "Summer Breezes," for the 1937-38 season.

George White personally presented his "Scandals," headed by Willie and Eugene Howard and Helen Morgan, for the first time in San Francisco. An autumn attraction, it drew heavy profits for two weeks and could have fared well for a third.

The reign of "big time" in the legitimate suffered a let-down with the appearance of James Kirkwood in "Mulatto." The drama of racial conflict was given its full opportunity over a two weeks' stretch, but had few takers.

Early in 1937 came "The Great Waltz," minus four chandeliers but with Guy Robertson in his original role of Johann Strauss Jr. and with support by Lee Whitney, Ruth Altman and Charles Romano. The current shipping strike had its effect upon patronage, but the town and hinterland backed the show for three weeks of fair profit.

Balm in Gilead to Leslie Howard was the applauding response to his "Hamlet." Moved to nightly curtain talks by full houses and repeated ovations, he replied to his New York critics to the extent of claiming his performance and the entire presentation had benefited by seasoning since he had left Broadway. There were demands for more than a fortnight's engagement, but the star was pressed by assignments in Hollywood.

Honors for the season's longest run, four weeks, were awarded Jacques Deval's "Tovarich," as adapted by Robert Sherwood, with Eugenie Leontovich in the role of Archduchess Tatiana Petrova, which she created in London. Osgood Perkins, Melville Cooper and Bela Lugosi shared in the plaudits.

The succession of Broadway hits to reach the coast was continued with Jane Cowl in "First Lady," which fared well for three San Francisco weeks. The same period was rounded out by "Dead End," which coincided with the Golden Gate bridge opening fiesta, but with the balancing effect of a hotel strike upon out-of-town visitors. Publicity that attended the drama's long Broadway run was enough to offset the lack of "names" in its cast.

Louis Lurie's Geary Theatre, adjoining the Curran, filled out its year with road-show films to the point where its stage attractions were advertised as "not a motion picture." Beginning its season with "Personal Appearance," starring Gladys George and others of the original cast, the theater housed "Russet Mantle" for three lean weeks, with Martha Sleeper and Hardie Albright in the principal roles. Then Alexander Leftwich staged a new operetta comique called "Cocktail Bar," authored by Lloyd Chase and aimed for a Broadway showing, which fell 3,000 miles short in distance and much further in other respects. It was, in fact, never heard of again.

There was also talk of giving Broadway a glimpse of "The Return of Hannibal," a new play by Amory Hare, which lasted but one week at the same theatre. Ralph Kettering, manager for Farmor Inc., the producers, had trusted too completely in the publicity value of one name in the cast, that of Elaine Barrie, who on the same week sued John Barrymore for divorce.

A George Abbott vogue improved legitimate business. The coming of "Boy Meets Girl" and "Brother Rat" proved that an Abbott laugh carnival may reach its objective without benefit of players known to the coast. Success of these two inspired the summer booking of a "Room Service" touring company.

With Homer Curran's disappearance for a season as coast producer, the legendary "Henry Duffy presents" dropped from local theatre announcements upon his shuttering of the Alcazar Theatre. For years his important base, it was later taken over by the Federal Theatre Project. Duffy's final offerings here were ironically among his most lustrous, with Otto Kruger in "Parnell" and Walter Slezak in his original role of "Meet My Sister," a continental musical play.

The Federal Theatre's healthiest season since its inception ended with the official elimination of 115 members from its rolls, including William E. Watts, drama supervisor and director. Approximately 215 persons, including actors, were sufficient to continue the group's scheduled attractions, with the postponement until August of a production of "Power," already in rehearsal when the Washington curtailment order arrived.

Within a year the Project had become a vital institution in the city's amusement life. Its audiences and length of runs had increased with such productions as "The Farmer's Wife," "Old Orpheum Days," Director Max M. Dill's revival of two-a-day vaudeville; "The Fool," "It Can't Happen Here," "The Devil Passes," "Battle Hymn," a drama of the John Brown tragedy; "A Touch of Brimstone," "Help Yourself," an FTP road show; "Swing Parade," a musical revue, and "Blind Alley," with another touring company.

The San Francisco Theatre Union, a prototype of the New York Group Theatre, revived its activities late in the season with a first staging anywhere of John Steinbeck's novel, "Of Mice and Men," and a production of "Bury the Dead."

The University of California "Little Theatre Without a Theatre" continued its schedule of old and new plays under the limitations of a miniature stage in Wheeler Auditorium. While at Stanford the third summer drama festival was programmed to take place in a perfectly equipped experimental theatre, a section of the new million-dollar Memorial Hall. The scheduled festival production was "Twelfth Night."

The 1936-37 season in San Francisco brought virtually the same number of visiting attractions as the preceding period. Long known as a "good show town," it continued the generous support of amusements of recognized merit and a knowing neglect of most of the shoddier offerings. Linked with the proximity of Hollywood, the allure of motion picture names has infected potential patrons of the legitimate, as in other communities. But there is a sizeable coterie of the old guard, or coast defenders of the drama, although some of their progeny are charged with never having witnessed a stage play. The balconies at such entertainments, however, have made a comeback of bulging proportions. This is taken as a hopeful sign.

THE SEASON IN SOUTHERN CALIFORNIA

BY EDWIN SCHALLERT

Drama Editor of the *Los Angeles Times*

WITH hopes for betterment happily crowned by the late spring visit of Alfred Lunt and Lynn Fontanne in "Idiot's Delight," first stirrings and rustlings of a new day in the theatre were felt during the 1936-37 season in Southern California. Still far short of the best years of the past in commercial theatre activity, the twelve months period ending June 30 displayed certain definite improvements. Not the least of these was the increase in road attractions. While Coast production was a little below normal, Federal and community play-giving showed progress.

The Lunt-Fontanne visit was significant, as besides "Idiot's Delight" it also brought the initial presentation of "Amphitryon 38," consideration of which properly belongs to the 1937-38 season. The Los Angeles première followed the San Francisco. However, this try-out of the play promised a far-reaching effect, in that it portends other first performances by the New York Theatre Guild on the Coast. This would mean the most important impetus given to such activity in this section in many years, and also possibly reawaken a lagging interest in the stage on the part of many noted actors now identified with motion pictures. Doubtless the guild itself foresees that development.

Touring attractions kept the Biltmore Theatre open practically the entire first six months of 1937. "Hamlet," starring Leslie Howard, "Boy Meets Girl," "First Lady" with Jane Cowl, Ruth Draper in her repertoire, "Tovarich," Coast staging of the play with Eugenie Leontovich and Osgood Perkins; "Idiot's Delight" and "Dead End" were attractions at the main showhouse for road companies. Late in 1936 George White's "Scandals" played a short engagement, while "Mulatto" with James Kirkwood was offered, though it drew little attention.

At El Capitan Theatre Henry Duffy produced "Call It a Day," with Conway Tearle and Violet Heming; "Parnell," with Otto Kruger, Edith Barrett, Effie Shannon and John Emery; "The Distaff Side," with a cast including Blanche Yurka, Estelle Winwood, Henrietta Crosman, Margalo Gillmore, Hardie Albright and Tom Moore; "Meet My Sister," with Walter Slezak and Nancy McCord; "The Petrified Forest," with Conrad Nagel, Jean Rouverol and Harland Tucker; "Tomorrow We Live" (new) by Michael Sheridan, with Genevieve Tobin, Minor Watson, Helen Mack and Douglas Walton; "Boy Meets Girl," with Helen Chandler.

Homer Curran sponsored "Reflected Glory," with Tallulah Bankhead starred, which subsequently ran in New York, and "Tovarich." Other leading offerings were "Everyman," produced in the Hollywood Bowl as a festival play with Johannes Poulsen from the Royal Theatre of Copenhagen directing, and George Houston, Fritz Leiber, Mrs. Leslie Carter and Peggy Wood among those in the cast; "The Great Waltz," touring company; "Russet Mantle," with Taylor Holmes, Martha Sleeper, Hardie Albright and Evelyn Varden. Also the "Pilgrimage Play; Life of the Christ" was given at the outdoor theatre dedicated to this biblical pageant-drama for about six or seven weeks during the summer of 1936.

Hardly any engagement of the commercial theatre plays lasted more than four weeks, and the majority were briefer. Road companies of the first water generally risked no more than ten days, or at the outside two weeks, but this policy worked with charm in the instance of Lunt and Fontanne, for they were selling standing room during the later days of their short stay.

In spite of this curtailment of runs, "The Drunkard," the celebrated hardy perennial, was about to enter its fifth year June 30, with a record of more than 1,400 performances, unsurpassed by any stage offering playing a continuous engagement in a single city, except the famous "Abie's Irish Rose" with its plus-2,000. Ultimately it is surmised that "The Drunkard," which is still going strong, will surpass that. Predictions are that the play will last three more years, provided the supply of brew also keeps up, which brew is imbibed by a majority of those attending the performances. The play has made a living for those concerned, despite the small capacity of the showhouse, the Theatre Mart, which is its home. Estimated possible gross per week is $2,500, and the play has long been in the class of a phenomenon.

Of the stage creations selected by Mr. Mantle as the best during the 1936-37 season only "Tovarich" and "Johnny Johnson," under Federal auspices, have been seen. "Stage Door," it is true, was played, but only at a private unpublicized performance. At the close of the fiscal year there seemed no immediate prospect of the other eight Mantle selections being viewed. However, most of the 1935-36 group were performed in one fashion or another. "Ethan Frome" was staged by the Pasadena Community Playhouse and "Winterset" by another group with John Carradine and Philippe de Lacey in leading parts. Helen Hayes is expected to visit with "Victoria Regina" during the 1937-38 season.

Attitude of audiences during the year was severely discriminating. In road productions they demanded the best. Howard was appreciated for his "Hamlet," because of his modernized conception of the play. Southern California, naturally, did not see John Gielgud's Melancholy Dane, and Howard is a favorite star because of his motion picture background. His Hamlet was genuinely liked by many people. Jane Cowl was very popular, and, as previously suggested, Lunt and Fontanne triumphed in respect to size of audiences, despite the fact that reactions to their plays were not uniformly enthusiastic.

Productions like "Dead End" and "Boy Meets Girl" (road company) did not fare very well, because both had inferior troupes. Through the years this same objection has been raised, but little seems to be done about it, though it is futile for New York managers to send second-rate organizations to the Southern California district. "Scandals" missed out somewhat in this regard, although attendance was good.

Toward the season's close producer Duffy's experiment with "Tomorrow We Live" was interesting as one of his few ventures with a new stage piece. This one unfortunately lacked the bigger values—a sort of miniature very pleasingly enacted by the efficient Miss Tobin, Watson, Miss Mack and others. Duffy now contemplates development of a school of the drama, with Mary Pickford as one of his principal associates. Necessity for an important institution of this type has long existed on the Coast, where new people must receive training to equip them for film work, and where the stage also lacks qualified new blood.

"Reflected Glory" was in a majority of aspects the most interesting new play produced on the Pacific Coast, while "Tovarich" was the most effective, bringing, as it did, Miss Leontovich, who had played the leading feminine role for a long time in London. Osgood Perkins adeptly enacted the exiled prince, while Bela Lugosi was the Commissar. In brilliance of attendance the première rivaled "Idiot's Delight," and for the first time the theatre made use of that exploitation feature of film openings, the radio, broadcasting the news of movie stellar arrivals at the performance.

Much talk about summer theatres in Southern California crystallized in plans for the inauguration of this enterprise at the Lobero, often used as a try-out playhouse, in Santa Barbara. There the performance of excerpts from "Tonight at 8.30" was to be an early July event. Mary Astor and Vivian Tobin were listed for the first presentation, while Genevieve Tobin, who resides at that seaside city, and Karen Morley were mentioned for subsequent performances. A remote summer theatre like that —for Santa Barbara is 100 miles from Los Angeles—has, perhaps, more chance of interesting film celebrities, who dread the ordeal of a Hollywood first night, with all its swank and réclame, and often condemnatory critical asides during the intermissions. The informality of the entire summer theatre idea has possibilities, and in attractive locations such projects might thrive in spots closer to the Southern California metropolis. While very successful screen players are lured to the stage only with great difficulty, an exhibition of greater interest may be foreseen in the future, and would help the upbuilding of the theatre on the Coast. Good direction will go far to aid this cause.

Pasadena Community Playhouse still remains the stronghold of creative theatre in Southern California. The third summer festival season, detailing "The Story of the Great Southwest" began uniquely with the mystical "Montezuma" by Gerhart Hauptmann, and was to be followed by "Miracle of the Swallows" by Ramon Romero, a first performance; "Night over Taos," Maxwell Anderson; "Juarez and Maximilian," Franz Werfel; "Girl of the Golden West," David Belasco; "Rose of the Rancho," David Belasco and Richard Walton Tully, and "Miner's Gold" by Agnes E. Peterson. A heterogeneous assemblage, to say the least. Gilmor

Brown and Onslow Stevens were in the introductory play.

The same theatre's Greco-Roman Shakespearean cycle of 1936 (summer) did not impress as much as the English chronicle plays, though "Timon of Athens," the rarely given "Pericles, Prince of Tyre," "Coriolanus" and "Antony and Cleopatra" were perhaps to be remarked. The only really familiar Shakespearean play was "Julius Caesar."

More first performances were staged at the Community theatre than usual, including the interesting "Money" by Aurania Rouverol —much more serious than her "Skidding"; "Emma" by Jane Austen, as attractively adapted by DeWitt Bodeen, the dynamic "Deadline" by Robert Payne White and Gerald Burtnett; "Periphery," from a Frantisek Langner original, as dramatized by Blanche Yurka and Libby Holman; "God Save the Queen" by Ladislaus Fodor, adapted by Frederick Jackson; Gilmor Brown's dramatization of "A Christmas Carol" by Charles Dickens; "Beach House" by Robert Chapin, and "We Dress for Dinner" by Aben Kandel. Other plays included "Paths of Glory" by Sidney Howard from Humphrey Cobb; "The Chalk Circle" (Klabund), translated by I. S. Richter; "Murder in the Cathedral," T. S. Eliot; "Tobias and the Angel," James Bridie; "Ethan Frome" (Edith Wharton), dramatized by Owen and Donald Davis; "Nude with Pineapple," Fulton Oursler and Aubrey Kennedy; "Lost Horizons," John Hayden; "Libel," Edward Wooll; "The Bishop Misbehaves," Frederick Jackson; "Wind and the Rain," Merton Hodge; "Madame Sans-Gene," Sardou and Moreau, in the C. H. Meltzer translation. A worthy roster.

The Federal theatres seem to be finding a wider and a better audience, although the project moves still in an uncertain way. It is drawing the attention of many people to the stage again, and in certain productions this movement quite outdoes itself. Notably was this true of "Johnny Johnson," which was well performed, and critically approved. This and "It Can't Happen Here" were among the most forward-looking enterprises of the past year, both having good runs.

Figures on the amount invested during the year show in excess of $1,500,000, the main object being employment. In fact, the restrictions are, if anything, to be more severe on the relief nature of the Federal activity.

Very popular were some of the revivals, like "East Is West," "Three Wise Fools," "Potash and Perlmutter," "Cradle Snatchers," "Help Yourself," "Smilin' Through," "Warrior's Husband," and "A Texas Steer," the old Hoyt farce. Aside from Shakespeare and

Morality Plays the most ancient of revivals was "The Black Crook," thought to be quite scandalous in its day, but mild and unimpressive in this era. Noteworthy were "Blind Alley," "Censored," "Follow the Parade," "Revue of Reviews," "Purple Is as Purple Does," "Rachel's Man," "The Wisdom Tooth," "The Merchant of Venice" with Estelle Winwood as Portia and Gareth Hughes as Shylock, "Class of '29," and various others. "Macbeth" was given by Negro actors. "Pinocchio" was a favorite with the younger audience. In all, some seventy productions were staged during the Federal season. The program was comprehensive, and occasionally a bit exciting.

The feeling in Southern California is that many actors in the films, and perhaps also playwrights, are going to find their way back to the theatre. Various New York producers are trying to crusade for this, among them Arch Selwyn, William Brady, Lee Shubert and a few others. However, it is going to be difficult to intrigue those who are active, away from Hollywood. Concentration of more play-producing on the Coast, should help a situation that is vexed at both extremes of the continent—namely reawakening the experienced dramatists and stars to the importance of the legitimate drama.

HIGH TOR

A Comedy in Three Acts

By Maxwell Anderson

THE second of three Maxwell Anderson plays to adorn the season, the first having been "The Wingless Victory," with Katharine Cornell, was a romantic fantasy called "High Tor." It reached New York in early January, with Burgess Meredith, the personable young actor who had gained stardom in "Winterset" the season before, playing the lead.

"High Tor" proved a pleasant surprise to many of the Anderson following. This playwright has rarely been credited with a definite sense of comedy. Most of his plays have been in serious vein, several, in fact, standing forth as vigorously spoken protests against this or that social injustice. There was a rough line of comedy in "Outside Looking In," and a nice vein of gentle raillery and satire in "Both Your Houses," but these exceptions were still dominated by a seriousness of both purpose and expression.

In "High Tor," however, all those episodes having to do with the realistic present, in contrast to the gentle romance of a misty and legendary past that is woven with them, are conceived and played in a spirit of broad fun. The combination provides a unique and fascinating form of entertainment. Particularly for those susceptible to the charm of fantasy when it is intelligently conceived and written.

We stand, as Mr. Anderson begins his play, on "a section of the broad flat trap-rock summit of High Tor, from which one looks out into sky and from which one might look down a sheer quarter mile to the Tappan Zee below." There are high, pillared rocks masking the view at either side. Light from the setting sun pours in from the left, and in its rays stands an ancient Indian "wearing an old greatcoat thrown round him like a blanket." He is making his prayer to the sunset. Listen as he speaks—

"I make my prayer to you, the falling fire,
bearing in mind the whisper in my ears
from the great spirit, talking on the wind,

whispering that a young race, in its morning,
should pray to the rising sun, but a race that's old
and dying, should invoke the dying flame
eaten and gulfed by the shark-toothed mountain-west,
a god that dies to live. As we have died,
my race of the red faces and old ways,
and as we hope to rise. I give you thanks
for light, for the coming summer that will warm
my snake's blood, cold and crawling; for the rain
that fed the ripe May apples in the woods·
in secret for me; for the waterfall
where the trout climb and pause under my hand,
taken in silence; for quiet on the hills
where the loud races dare not walk for fear
lest they be lost, where their blind hunters pass
peering with caps and guns, but see no game,
and curse as they go down—"

The Indian has finished his prayer and moved from the spot he held when Van Van Dorn and Judith come up the mountain path and break the solitude. They are young people and personable, he in hunter's garb, she becomingly but modestly gowned.

Van Dorn knows the Indian well. His name is John. At least that is his name to Van Dorn. He is a very old Indian and there is an understanding between them. When it shall come time for John to die, and he has chosen the place he would have them make his grave, Van has promised to dig the old fellow in so the crows and foxes cannot get him.

"But you couldn't, Van, without a permit," protests Judith.

"I guess you could," Van answers, with conviction. "This getting old and dying and crawling into the ground, that was invented back before medical examiners and taxes and all that. The old boy's clean. He'll go right back to dirt."

Judith has produced a lunch box and they are soon eating their dinner. Van is also committing the social error of reading at table. Reading the paper that was wrapped around the lunch. There is news in it, too. The Nanuet bank has been robbed of twenty-five thousand dollars! To Van it's against nature that there should ever be that much money in Nanuet.

"Maybe it wasn't real," suggests Judith.

"Federal money, that's it," agrees Van. "Some of the stuff Jim Farley prints in Washington with the stamps to pay you for voting straight. Only now you see it and now you don't." . . .

Judith would like to have a serious talk with Van. His free and easy way of living distresses her. Van is an expert mason, according to Judith, and yet he has consistently refused to work more than three weeks in any one year. The rest of the time he puts in hunting and fishing and sleeping. That's no way to live!

Maybe not, Van is agreed, but it is a lot of fun. He knows what Judith wants. She wants him to take a job. There's one been offered—

"Porter in a hotel, lugging up satchels, opening windows, maybe you get a dime," sneers Van. "I'd choke to death."

"I'd see you every day."

VAN—Yeah, I could see you on the mezzanine,
taking dictation from the drummer boys,
all about how they can't get home. You can stand it,
a woman stands that stuff, but if you're a man
I say it chokes you.

JUDITH—We can't live in your cabin
and have no money, like the Jackson Whites
over at Suffern.

VAN—Hell, you don't need money.
Pap worked that out. All you need's a place to sleep
and something to eat. I've never seen the time
I couldn't find a meal on the mountain here,
rainbow trout, jugged hare, something in season
right around the zodiac.

JUDITH—You didn't like the Chevrolet factory, either?

VAN (*walking toward the cliff edge*)—Look at it, Judy.
That's the Chevrolet factory, four miles down,
and straight across, that's Sing Sing. Right from here
you can't tell one from another; get inside,
and what's the difference? You're in there, and you work,
and they've got you. If you're in the factory
you buy a car, and then you put in your time
to pay for the goddam thing. If you get in a hurry
and steal a car, they put you in Sing Sing first,
and then you work out your time. They graduate
from one to the other, back and forth, those guys,
paying for cars both ways. But I was smart.
I parked at a polis station and rung the bell
and took to the woods. Not for your Uncle Dudley.
They plugged the dice.

JUDITH—But one has to have a car.

VAN—Honest to God, now, Judy, what's the hurry?
where in hell are we going?
JUDITH—If a man works hard,
and has ability, as you have, Van,
he takes a place among them, saves his money,
works right out of the ruck and gets above
where he's safe and secure.
VAN—I wouldn't bet on it much.
JUDITH—But it's true.
VAN—All right, suppose it's true. Suppose
a man saves money all his life, and works
like hell about forty years, till he can say:
good-by, I'm going, I'm on easy street
from now on. What's he do?
JUDITH—Takes a vacation.
VAN—Goes fishing, maybe? I'm on vacation now.
Why should I work forty years to earn
time off when I've got it?

It is true, Van admits, that he had been offered money for High Tor. Seven hundred dollars they offered him. And his father had refused ten thousand.

"They want to chew the back right off this mountain, the way they did across the cove there," Van explains. "Leave the old palisades sticking up here like billboards, nothing left but a false front facing the river. Not for pap, and not for me. I like this place."

"But, Van Van Dorn! Ten thousand dollars!"

"Well, it's Federal money.
Damn stuff evaporates. Put it in a sock
along with moth balls, and come back next year,
and there's nothing left but the smell. Look, Judy, it's
a quarter mile straight down to the Tappan Zee
from here.—You can see fifteen miles of river
north and south. I grew up looking at it.
Hudson came up that river just about
three hundred years ago, and lost a ship
here in the Zee. They say the crew climbed up
this Tor to keep a lookout for the fleet
that never came. Maybe the Indians got them.
Anyway on dark nights before a storm,
they say you sometimes see them."

"Have you seen them?"

"The Dutchmen? Maybe I have. You can't be sure.
It's pretty wild around here when it storms.
That's when I like it best. But look at it now.
There was a Jaeger here from Switzerland
last year. He took one squint at this and said
they could keep their Alps, for all him. Look at the willows
along the far breakwater."

"It's beautiful," admits Judith.

"Every night I come back here, like the Indian, to get a fill of it," Van goes on. "Seven hundred dollars and tear it down? Hell, no!"

Art J. Biggs and Judge Skimmerhorn have appeared, coming up the trail at the right. Biggs is a realtor, broad and blustery. Skimmerhorn, of the probate court, is a smaller man of somewhat greater dignity. Biggs and Skimmerhorn are looking for a house and a fellow who lives in it named Van Dorn. Van has heard of such a place and such a man. If they will climb down the face of the cliff and keep left along the ledge a hundred yards and then turn sharp left through a cleft up the ridge—

"A monkey couldn't go down there hanging on with four hands and a tail," protests Judge Skimmerhorn, taking a peek over the edge of the cliff. He'll go down the other way, he decides. So will Biggs.

Judith can't understand why Van should have been so mean as to fool the visitors that way, but Van has his reasons. He knows those two. He has communicated with them by mail—

"I've got a dozen letters stacked up from the firm," says Van; "Skimmerhorn, Skimmerhorn, Biggs and Skimmerhorn, and maybe two or three Skimmerhorns I left out printed across the top. They're realtors, whatever that is, and they own the trap-rock company, and one of the Skimmerhorns, he's probate judge, and goes around condemning property when they want to make a rake-off."

Judith is excited. She would call the trap-rock men back if Van would let her. She is pretty disgusted when he won't. This, to Judith, is the end. He thinks because she said once she loved him; he thinks because a girl's been kissed she stays kissed, and after that the man does her thinking for her—

"If we're married I'll have to live the way you want to live. You prefer being a pauper!"

"Get it straight," Van answers, matching her show of spirit. "I don't take money nor orders, and I live as I damn well please."

Nor can any of her arguments move him. He is determined not to sell. He just can't.

"They'll get it anyway," protests Judith. "They've worked right up to where your land begins, and they won't stop for you. They'll just condemn it and take it."

"They'll be in trouble."

"You can't make trouble for companies. They have a dozen lawyers and ride right over you. I've worked for them. It's never any use."

"Well, I won't sell."

That, then, is the end so far as Judith is concerned. She can see no hope for their love or for their future. And she had better be going. . . .

Biggs and Skimmerhorn are back. They would like to hire our young man to take a paper around to Van Dorn. Offer him two dollars. But Van will serve no paper for them.

"My rule in life is keep away from skunks!" he says.

There might have been trouble if Judith had not spoken up and told the visitors who Van is. They are all interest and apologies now and eager to make an impression. Van is just the boy they want to see. They want to buy High Tor. They like it. They like the view.

"You wouldn't spoil it, of course?" sneers Van. "You wouldn't move in with a million dollars worth of machinery and cut the guts out of the mountain, would you?"

"We always leave the front—the part you see from the river," promises Skimmerhorn.

VAN—But you take down all the law allows.

SKIMMERHORN—Well, we're in business.

VAN—Not with me.

JUDITH—Do you mind if I ask how much you're offering?

BIGGS—We said seven hundred, but I'll make it a thousand right here and now.

SKIMMERHORN—As a matter of fact, we'll make it two thousand.

BIGGS—Yeah, all right. Two thousand for the hundred and seven acres.

JUDITH—But you offered Mr. Van Dorn's father ten thousand before he died.

SKIMMERHORN—His father had a clear title, right down from the original Dutch patroon to the original Van Dorn. But unfortunately the present Mr. Van Dorn has a somewhat clouded claim to the acreage.

VAN—My father's title was clear, and he left it to me.

SKIMMERHORN—The truth is he should have employed a lawyer when he drew his will, because the instrument, as recorded, is faulty in many respects. It was brought before me in my capacity as probate judge at Ledentown.

VAN—And in your capacity as second vice-president of the trap-rock company you shot it full of holes.

SKIMMERHORN—Sir, I keep my duties entirely separate.

VAN—Sure, but when your left hand takes money your right hand finds out about it. And when there's too much to carry away in both hands you use a basket. You're also vice-president of the power company, and you stole right-of-ways clear across the county north and south—

SKIMMERHORN—We paid for every foot of land—

VAN—Yes, at your own price.

BIGGS—Let's not get in an argument, Mr. Van Dorn, because the fact that your father's will was improperly drawn means he died intestate and the land goes to his heirs. Now we've found twenty-seven Van Dorns living at Blauvelt, all claiming relationship and all willing to sign away their rights for a consideration.

VAN—The best you can do you'll need my name in your little paper, and you won't have it.

Skimmerhorn has still another proposition. If Van will sign now they will give him $3,000. If he won't take this there is a chance he may be haled into court and adjudged incompetent. That doesn't frighten Van either. If they would take a little advice from him they would be pretty careful as to how they proceed. Both against him and the land. A Dutchman is poison when he doesn't like you, and Van is Dutch. What's more, there is something funny about this mountain top. It draws fire. Every storm on the Tappan Zee climbs up and wraps itself around High Tor. "It smashed the beacon twice," says Van. "It blew the fuses on your shovel and killed a man only last week. I've got a premonition something might happen to you."

There is a sudden rumbling roar of falling rock and they are frightened. "What's that?" demands Biggs.

VAN—That's nothing much. That's just a section of the cliff come down across the trail. I've been expecting it this last two years. You'd better go down this way.

BIGGS—This way?

VAN—Yeah.

BIGGS—No, thanks.

VAN—Just as you say. But there's something definitely hostile here toward you two pirates. Don't try that trail in the dark. Not if you want to be buried in your vaults in Mount Repose. Your grieving families might have to move two thousand tons of rock to locate your remains. You think High Tor's just so much raw material, but you're wrong. A lot of stubborn men have died up here and some of them don't sleep well. They come back and push things round, these dark nights. Don't blame me if anything falls on you.

SKIMMERHORN—Oh, what the hell! Let's get out of here. (*Another long rumble of falling rock.*)

VAN—Another rock-fall. Once they start there's likely to be more. Something hanging round in the dark up here doesn't like you boys. Not only me. Better go down this way.

BIGGS—Thanks. (BIGGS *and* SKIMMERHORN *leave.*)

JUDITH—What do you mean?

VAN—I don't know.

JUDITH—They'll say you threatened them. Good-by, Van.

VAN—You'll be up tomorrow?

JUDITH—No. (*She steps down into a cleft.*)

VAN—You'd better let me see you down.

JUDITH—Oh, no. I can climb. Stay here and guard your rock —you think so much of it.

VAN—When will I see you?

JUDITH—Never. We'll forget about it. You had a choice and you chose High Tor. You're in love with your mountain. Well, keep your mountain.

VAN—All right.

JUDITH—Good night.

VAN—Good night.

"She disappears down the rocks. Van sits in the shadow, looking into darkness. After a moment a barely perceptible *Figure* enters from the gloom and crosses toward the rocks. At the foot of the climb he pauses and his face is caught in the light of the beacon. He is seen to be young or middle-aged, bearded, and wearing the costume of a Dutch sailor of the sixteen hundreds. He climbs the rocks, and *Another Sailor,* a small cask strapped to his shoulders, follows. *Three More* cross the stage similarly, then the *Captain* and *His Wife* pause, like the others in the light of the beacon. The *Captain* is like his men, only younger perhaps; *His Wife* is a tiny figure with a delicate girlish face looking out from under the Dutch bonnet. They too pass up the rocks, and are followed by a rolling Silenus in the same garments. As they vanish Van rises, looking after them."

VAN—Uh—huh—going to rain.

The curtain falls.

There is complete darkness at the summit of High Tor pierced by a "long cumbrous rolling, as of a ball going down a bowling alley." Only by the flash of the airplane beacon do we make out the outline of the mountain, and after that several dark gray shadowy figures of a Dutch crew in sailor costume and broad hats. Some are at the game of bowls. Some are gathered around a keg. Sitting apart from the rest is Lise, the Captain's wife, a fragile little lady with a wide bow at the back of her head.

It is Lise who is speaking, with a gentle querulousness. She is wearied and anxious. When they drink they frequently forget to post a watch to let them know should their ship return. It might come and pass again and they would be left to haunt the dark another year.

Captain Asher posts the guard. He is inclined to be gruff about it. He, too, is restless at the thought of that Texel town across the Zuyder Zee from whence they hail, but he would not be constantly reminded of what is lost. He would have Lise be quiet. She was so much in love she must come with him, and he has been patient with her, but now she is fast becoming a carping wife. That he does not like.

But Lise will have her say. It has been too long since they were set down upon this alien shore. At first the days were years, but now the years are days and there is no sign of the returning ship. Lise has begun to doubt that there ever was a ship or even a sailor-city called Amsterdam, or that they will ever again see the Netherlands.

"Aye, there was a ship, and we wait here for her," answers Captain Asher. "But she's long away, somewhere up-river."

"And now you drink and drink," says Lise—
distill your liquor on the mountain-top
and bowl against the light. But when you break it
these new strange men come build it up again;

and giant shovels spade the mountain down,
and when you break them still the new strange men
rig them afresh and turn them on the rock,
eating the pillared stone. We must go back.
There's no safety here."

A Sailor—We must go back.
Asher—These muttering fools!
Lise—Oh, Asher, I'm afraid!
For one thing I have known, and never told
lest it be true, lest you be frightened, too,
lest we be woven of shadow! As the years
have gone, each year a century, they seem
less real, and all the boundaries of time,
our days and nights and hours, merge and are one,
escaping me. Then sometimes in a morning
when all the crew come down the rocks together,
holding my breath, I see you in the light,
and back of you the gray rock bright and hard,
seen through figures of air! And you, and you,
and you were but cloud-drift walking, pierced by the light,
translucent in the sun.
DeWitt—Now damn the woman!
Lise—Love, love, before our blood
be shadow only, in a dark fairyland
so far from home, we must go back, go back
where earth is earth, and we may live again
and one day be one day!
Asher—Why, then, I knew it,
and I have known it, now that you know it, too.
But the old Amsterdam of our farewells
lies in another world. The land and sea
about us on this dark side of the earth
is thick with demons, heavy with enchantment,
cutting us off from home.
Lise—Is it enchantment?
Yes, it may be. At home there were tulips growing
along my bordered path, but here the flowers
are strange to me, not one I knew, no trace
of any flower I knew; no, seedlings set
upon a darkened, alien outer rim
of sea, blown here as we were blown, enchanted,
drunken and blind with sorcery.

ASHER—And yet
What we're to have we shall have here. Years past
the demons of this air palsied our hands,
fixed us upon one pinnacle of time,
and on this pinnacle of stone, and all
the world we knew slid backward to the gulf,
stranding us here like seaweed on the shingle,
remembering the sea. In Texel town
new houses have gone up, after new fashions;
the children of the children of our days,
lying awake to think of what has been,
reach doubtfully beyond the clouds of years
back to our sailing out of Texel. Men
are like the gods, work miracles, have power
to pierce the walls with music. Their beacon light
destroys us. You have seen us in the sun,
wraithlike, half-effaced, the print we make
upon the air thin tracery, permeable,
a web of wind. They have changed us. We may take
the fire-balls of the lightning in our hands
and bowl them down the level floor of cloud
to wreck the beacon, yet there was a time
when these were death to touch. The life we keep
is motionless as the center of a storm,
yet while we can we keep it; while we can
snuff out to darkness their bright sweeping light,
melt down the harness of the slow machines
that hew the mountains from us. When it goes
we shall go too. They leave us this place, High Tor,
and we shall have no other. You learn it last.
A long while now we've known.
A SAILOR—Aye, aye, a long while.
ASHER—Come, we'll go down.

The men of the crew follow their Captain down the mountain. Only DeWitt and Lise are left. DeWitt is a rugged sailor who holds his gin, considering the quantity he drinks, with good success. There is little contentment in DeWitt. This being "marooned somewhere on the hinder parts of the earth and degenerating hourly to the status of a flying Dutchman, half-spook and half God-knows-what," is enough to drive any man to drink.

"A pewter flagon of Hollands gin puts manhood into the remnants and gives a sailor courage to look out on these fanciful new devils that ride sea, land and air on a puff of blue smoke," declares DeWitt.

DeWitt completely agrees with Lise that something should be done about their inactive state. They should be getting back to where they came from. But how? And where would they go?

"The very points of the compass grow doubtful these latter years," insists DeWitt; "partly because I'm none too sober and partly because the great master devil sits on top of the world stirring up north and south with a long spoon to confuse poor mariners." . . . "We'll see the time, if they continue to work on us, when we'll be apparent in a strong light only by the gin contained in our interior piping. The odor itself, along with that of church-warden tobacco, should be sufficient to convince a magistrate of our existence.—You tremble, little Lise, and you weep, but look now, there's a remedy I've had in mind. Fall in love with one of them. Fall in love with one of these same strange new-world magicians. I shall choose me out one of their female mermaid witches, and set my heart on her, and become a man again. And for God's sake let her love me strongly and hold on, lest I go down the brook like a spring freshet in the next pounding rain."

LISE—I gave my love long ago, and it's no help.
I love enough.

DEWITT—Aye, but he's in a worse case than you are, the
Captain. Saving his captaincy, there's not enough
belief in him to produce half a tear in a passion
of sobbing. You'll make me weep, little one, and what
tears I have I shall need, lest my protestation turns out
to be a dry rain.

LISE—Aye, we were warned before we came away
against the cabalistic words and signs
of those who dwell along these unknown waters;
never to watch them dance nor hear them sing
nor draw their imprecations—lest their powers
weave a weird medicine throughout the air,
chilling the blood, transfixing body and mind
and we be chained invisibly, our eyes darkened,
our wrists and breasts pulseless, anchored in time,
like birds blown back in a wind. But we have listened,
and we are stricken through with light and sound,
empty as autumn leaves, empty as prayers
that drift in a godless heaven. Meaningless,

picked clean of meaning, stripped of bone and will,
the chrysalids of locusts staring here
at one another.

DEWITT—If it's true it's enough to make a man weep for himself, Lise, and for all lost mariners, wherever they are, and for us more than any, here on these spell-bound rocks, drawing up water from time past—the well growing deeper, and the water lower, till there be none. (*He turns to go down the path.*)

The curtain falls.

We are in another section of the Tor now. It is dark, save for the rays of the airplane beacon. A large steam shovel, swung in from an adjacent excavation, hangs overhead. Van Dorn is looking at the machinery when Biggs and Skimmerhorn come in. They've found one trail gone out, as Van had predicted, and they're looking for another. But Van can show them none. Let them spend the night on the mountain. There'll be no charge for that. He leaves them pondering that suggestion.

Biggs and Skimmerhorn are weary and hungry and quarrelsome as well. They are already counting on the twenty-two thousand dollars they hoped to make from the Van Dorn deal, but Skimmerhorn is tired of taking forty percent as his share. He wants fifty percent after this. Biggs will have none of that. Shyster lawyers are too numerous. He thinks he will be slipping another probate judge into Ledentown next election.

"Oh, no, you won't, Art," Skimmerhorn warns. "Oh, no, you won't. You wouldn't do that to an old friend like me; because if you did, think what I'd do to an old friend like you."

They have gone to examine the cables on the steam shovel engine when three young fellows climb in over the rocks at the left. One of them carries a black zipper bag. They are all tired from the climb and sore at having been chased by State troopers. They had been obliged to abandon their car and run it over an embankment when the pursuit got close. The three are the young men who have just robbed the Nanuet bank. Their names are Elkus, Buddy and Dope and their nerves are on edge. They've got twenty-five thousand dollars in the zipper bag. It's the Orangeburg payroll and—

Buddy has looked off left and goes white with fright. Judge Skimmerhorn is coming round the rocks and the Judge knows him. There's no time for them to get away. Elkus drops the bag back of the rocks. The next minute all three are explaining to the Judge and Biggs that they have been hiking. They climbed Tor on a bet. No, they didn't bring anything to eat, because they had had something before they left.

The Judge is saddened by the knowledge that they have no food. He would hire Buddy to go back down and buy him some sandwiches. And while he's down he might call up the State troopers and send them up to make an arrest. The Judge is looking for someone.

Elkus is trembling with suspicions, but he gives Buddy the word to take the Judge's money and go for the sandwiches and follows him out for further instructions. Skimmerhorn, starting to rise, puts his hand behind him and touches the satchel. He thinks it a snake and flips it wildly into the rocks.

Elkus is back, looking furtively about for the satchel. He has decided that they will all three go back to town with Buddy. He can't find the satchel, and Dope, searching the rocks, catches sight of Sailor DeWitt's broad hat and yells a warning. It's the troopers! Elkus draws a gun. Then thinks better of it and runs out the trail, followed by Dope.

Now Biggs and Skimmerhorn have also gone in search of the trooper Dope reported. They find no one. Nor get any answer to their calls. They may as well make the best of their situation, they decide. They will have to spend the night there. After some figuring they decide to take one of their overcoats and use it for a pillow, and pull the other over them as covering. . . .

DeWitt has found the satchel and is examining its contents. Biggs and Skimmerhorn are trying to find a comfortable position on the rocks. There are packages of bills in the satchel, which mean nothing to the sailor. And a roll of pennies in one of the inner pockets. The copper pieces he might use to buy a new wig, DeWitt thinks, if he ever got back to a place where money was useful.

"A counting-house full of them wouldn't buy a ship from one of these semi-demi-demi-semi-devils, so that's no good," he mutters, noticing for the first time the strange bundle that is Skimmerhorn and Biggs under the coat. "What kind of demi-semi-devil do you think you are, with four legs and two faces, both looking the same direction? Jesu Maria, it's a kind of centaur, as big one way as another, no arms, and feet the size of dish-pans."

Biggs sits up, staring into the gloom. He demands to know who's there. The sight is amusing to DeWitt—

"It's the rear end that talks, evidently, the front being fast asleep in the manner of a figure-head."

BIGGS—Who's there? Did somebody speak?

DEWITT—None too clear in the back thinker, I should say, which would be a natural result of lugging two sets of brains, fore and aft. I'd incline to communicate with the front end, but if necessary I'll converse with the posterior.

BIGGS (*sitting up, looking at* DEWITT)—Skimmerhorn!

SKIMMERHORN—What's the matter?

BIGGS—I'm damned if I know.

SKIMMERHORN—Go to sleep, then.

BIGGS—Do you believe in apparitions?

SKIMMERHORN—No.

BIGGS—Well, there's a figure of fun sitting talking to me, right out of a masquerade ball.

SKIMMERHORN—You been drinking?

BIGGS—What would I find to drink?

DEWITT—If the forecastle wakes now I shall play both ends against the middle, like a marine auctioneer. I want to buy a boat.

BIGGS—You've come to the wrong shop, sailor. I'm in the real-estate business, and it's a long mile down to sea level.

DEWITT—You have no boats?

BIGGS—No boats.

SKIMMERHORN (*sits up suddenly*)—What in the hell?—

BIGGS—I told you I'm damned if I know.

DEWITT—And the front end has no boats?

BIGGS—You're the front end, see. He wants to know if you've got boats.

SKIMMERHORN—No, stranger, no boats.

DEWITT—Ah. (*Shakes his head mournfully, turns him about and goes to the right, still muttering.*) The great plague on them, the lying, two-headed fairies out of a witch's placket. What chance has an honest man against a two-faced double-tongued beast, telling the same tale— (*He disappears through the rocks.*)

BIGGS—Did you see what I saw?

SKIMMERHORN—Not if you saw what I saw. What I saw wasn't possible.—Did you fake that thing?

BIGGS—Fake it? I saw it.

SKIMMERHORN—Oh, no—! Nobody saw that—what I saw.

I didn't either. I've got a family to support. They aren't going to put me away anywhere.

Biggs has spied the bag. Probably the apparition's lunch. But it isn't lunch. It's a package of money! And there are other packages! All fives and tens! It's the bank's money! So the funny little Dutchman was a bank robber!

Now Skimmerhorn has confirmed the find. It is money, all right, and none of it marked. Biggs can vouch for that, having talked with the President of the bank after the robbery. It should be returned—for the reward—thinks Skimmerhorn. And yet if it weren't returned the bank wouldn't lose anything, being insured. And nobody in the world would ever know who had it.

"What do you say?" ventures Biggs.

"I say fifty-fifty," promptly answers Skimmerhorn.

"Damn you, Skimmerhorn, if I hadn't been in business with you for twenty years I'd say you were a crook!"

"If I wasn't a crook after twenty years with you I'd be slow in the head and hard of hearing!"

They are still arguing about the division when Van Dorn suddenly reappears. Biggs and Skimmerhorn have a time of it stuffing the bills into their pockets.

Van has come only to suggest that, although they are not friends of his, he is willing to show them where they can keep dry under a ledge when the approaching storm comes, but they are not interested. They will find their own cover. . . .

Van has picked up a discarded envelope from the bag and is studying it curiously when Lise comes up the rocks in the rear and stands for a moment looking out upon the river, shading her hands against the rays of the beacon. Her voice is raised in gentle lament for the ship that she fears will never come again.

Presently Van Dorn rises and they face each other, fascinated and doubtful. Now they have spoken, and been heard and understood by each other. Lise has seen Van before. She knows him to be kind. Had she not watched him the time she had, in her loneliness, built a wild flower garden and he had come upon it and had not laughed nor trampled it? Rather he had set a new flower growing in her garden. This, he tells her, was a wild orchid. They talk of flowers, and of the names they bear which are strange to her. And, speaking of flowers, Van would know her name, too.

"It's Lise, or used to be," she says, simply.

"Not now?" he asks.

Lise—I'm weary of it,
and all the things that I've been. You have a lover?

She'll be angry?

VAN—She's angry now. She's off
and gone. She won't come back.

LISE—Love me a little,
enough to save me from the dark. But if
you cannot give me love, find me a way!
The seas lie black between your harbor town
and mine, but your ships are quick. If I might see
the corner where the three streets come to end
on sundial windows, there, a child by a fire—
no, but it's gone!

VAN—I've seen you on the hills
moving with shadows. But you're not shadow.

LISE—No.
could one live and be shadow?

VAN—Take my hand.

LISE—I dare not.

VAN—Come, let me see your garden.

LISE—No.
I dare not. It is your race that thins our blood
and gathers round, besieging us with charms
to stay the feet of years. But I know you kind.—
Love me a little. Never put out your hand
to touch me, lest some magic in your blood
reach me, and I be nothing. What I am
I know not, under these spells, if I be cloud
or dust. Nor whether you dream of me, or I
make you of light and sound. Between this stone
and the near constellation of the stars
I go and come, doubting now whence I come
or when I go. Cling to me. Keep me still.
Be gentle. You were gentle with the orchid—
Take my hand now.

VAN—You're cold.

LISE—Yes.

VAN—Here on the Tor
the sun beats down like murder all day long
and the wind comes up like murder in the night.
I'm cold myself.

LISE—How have I slipped so far
from the things you have? I'm puzzled here and lost.
Is it so different for you? Keep my hand
and tell me. In these new times are all men shadow?

All men lost?

VAN—Sometimes I stand here at night
and look out over the river when a fog
covers the lights. Then if it's dark enough
and I can't see my hands or where the rock
leaves off against the cloud, and I'm alone,
then, well, I'm damned if I know who I am,
staring out into that black. Maybe I'm cloud
and maybe I'm dust. I might be old as time.
I'd like to think I knew. A man gets that way
standing staring at darkness.

LISE—Then—you do know.
It's better now.—Somewhere along a verge
where your life dips in dusk and my gray days
lift to the light a moment, we walk there
and our eyes meet.—Look, when the wizards come
to tear the mountain down, I'll have no place.
I'll be gone then.

VAN—Child, they won't get our mountain!
Not if I have to shoot them as they come
they won't get our mountain! The mountain's mine,
and you're to make your garden where you like;
their feet won't step across it! All their world's
made up of fat men doing tricks with laws
to manage tides and root up hills. The hills
can afford to laugh at them! A race of grubs
bred down from men!

LISE—Is it the light I feel
come flooding back in me? Light or their charms
broken here, seeing your face?

VAN—Your hands are warm.

LISE—I'm not cold now; for an instant I'm not cold,
seeing your face. This is your wizardry.
Let me stand here and see you.

On the trail outside, the voices of the bank robbers can be heard. Elkus and Dope are coming back to pick up the satchel. Van and Lise slip quietly out through the rocks, while the hunt goes on. There is no satchel, but there is scattered evidence that it has been found. Elkus is furious. He'll send Buddy back with the sandwiches to see if the Judge got the money. If he did Elkus will stick him up and take it away from him. . . .

Biggs and Skimmerhorn are back, bulging with bills and still hunting a way to get off the mountain. Suddenly it occurs to them that if there were anyone around who could run the engine, they could get in the steam shovel and be swung over to the dump below. It would be easy to slide the rest of the way.

They are sitting on the rocks, their backs to the river, ruminating on the possibility of finding an engineer, when the Dutch sailor crew begins closing in from the back, led by DeWitt. Suddenly a chill effects both Biggs and Skimmerhorn. They pale with the shock of it. Each would have the other turn around and face whatever it is that effects them so. They are on their hands and knees, crawling forward, when they agree to face the dread simultaneously. They whirl in concert and face the crew, trying bravely to deny that there is anything there.

"You're crazy!" says Biggs.

"I certainly am. And so are you," answers Skimmerhorn, trying a laugh.

BIGGS—That isn't there at all. There's nothing there.

SKIMMERHORN—All right, you go up and hit it. I'll stay right here, and you go punch it in the nose.

BIGGS (*standing up*)—Uh—how do you do?—Maybe you—wanted to give us something, huh? Uh—I see you brought your friends with you.—If you want the money back you can have it, you know. We don't want the money. How much was it now? Anything we could do, you know, we'd be glad to do. We're just trying to get down off here.

SKIMMERHORN—You know what it is, Art; it's a moving picture company. And have they got the laugh on us? Thinking they're real. It's all right, boys, we're onto you.

BIGGS—Is that so? Say, I guess that's so. Was that moving picture money, you gave us, you fellows? We thought that was real. Ha, ha! That's a good one. I guess you must have thought we were pretty funny, backing up that way and jumping around. You had us scared stiff! (THE CREW *shake their heads at each other.*)

SKIMMERHORN—Come on, now, you aren't bluffing us at all. We've seen the pictures work over at Suffern. We were right out on location there with actors and producers and everything. Some of those girls didn't care whether they wore clothes or not. You're probably used to that where you come from, but I certainly got a kick out of pictures. Fifty chorus girls changing clothes in the bushes over there.

ASHER (*a silence.* DEWITT *goes over to the* CAPTAIN *and whis-*

pers in his ear.)—Lay a hand to it.

DEWITT (*catching hold of the dangling cable*)—Lay a hand to it, lads. Heave.

THE CREW (*catching the rope and hauling on it, sailor-fashion, the shovel beginning to descend*)—Heave! Heave! Heave! Heave!

Coming a blow, coming a blow;
Sea runs black; glass runs low;
Heave! Heave!
Yardarm dips; foam's like snow!
Heave!

BIGGS (*as shovel touches ground*)—Say, that's an act if I ever saw one. What kind of picture are you putting on? (*The* CAPTAIN *points to the interior of the shovel, looking at* BIGGS *and* SKIMMERHORN.) What's up, anyway? Want us to go aboard? You know, we were just saying if somebody could run that thing we might get across to the dump and slide down out of here. Think you could swing it across there? (*The* SAILORS *maneuver behind the two, edging them into the machine.*) You might haul us up there and not be able to get us down, you know. It's mighty friendly of you to try it, but you'll have your work cut out. Sure, I'll get in. I'll try anything once. (*He steps in,* SKIMMERHORN *follows reluctantly. The* CAPTAIN *and* DEWITT *guard their retreat. The* SAILORS *catch hold of the cable.*) Take it easy, now.

THE CREW—Hoist! Hoist! Hoist! Hoist!

Tar on a rope's end, man on a yard.
Wind through an eye-bolt, points on a card;
Hoist! Hoist!
Weevil in the biscuit, rats in the lard,
Hoist!

Now the shovel is dangling over the abyss and the Dutch crew has lost interest. The louder Biggs and Skimmerhorn shout instructions as to what they want done the harder the Dutchmen stare. Now there is danger that the Judge is going to be sick if Biggs doesn't stop rocking the boat. Nor is Biggs feeling any too well. And now the crew has slowly walked away for a game of bowls, leaving Biggs shouting lustily that they (the Dutch) will be held responsible for whatever happens. "There's such a thing as laws in this country!" yells Biggs. But if Captain Asher and his men care anything about that they give no sign.

The wrangling in the shovel goes on. There are even charges and counter charges of pocket picking when Skimmerhorn thinks he has lost his billfold. They have decided to count their money again when the storm breaks. The lightning flashes, the thunder rolls, the shovel sways uncertainly. One crash signalizes the collapse of the airplane beacon and darkness follows. A bolt of lightning runs directly down the crane from which the steam shovel is suspended. It is enough to make Biggs and Skimmerhorn think of God and a possible bargain. But neither is very good at praying. Skimmerhorn is the only one who can think of a prayer. He tries it:

"Matthew, Mark, Luke and John
Bless the bed that I lie on—"

It doesn't seem to do much good. In addition to their fright Skimmerhorn has just dropped fourteen ten-dollar bills.

"Will you quit counting money? We're going to be killed!" shouts Biggs. "We're going to die right here in our own steam shovel!"

SKIMMERHORN—Oh, no. I can't die now. I'm not ready to die!

BIGGS—I wish you'd put up your money, then, and pray!

SKIMMERHORN—I don't know how to pray. (*A crash.*)

BIGGS (*on his knees*)—Oh, God, I never did this before, and I don't know how, but keep me safe here and I'll be a better man! I'll put candles on the altar, yes, I'll get that Spring Valley church fixed up, the one that's falling down! I can do a lot for you if you'll let me live! Oh, God— (*A crash.*)

SKIMMERHORN (*on his knees, his hands full of money*)—Oh, God, you wouldn't do a thing like that, hang us up in our own steam shovel, wet through, and then strike us with lightning! Oh, God, you've been kind to us tonight, and given us things we never expected to get so easy; don't spoil it now!—God damn it, there goes another batch of bills! (*He snatches at the falling money, and is hauled back by* BIGGS.) I don't know how to pray! What makes you think there's anyone up there, anyway? (*Another crash.*)

BIGGS—Say the one you know then, for God's sake—say it!

SKIMMERHORN—Matthew, Mark, Luke and John,
Bless the bed that I lie on!

BIGGS—Matthew, Mark, Luke and John, Bless the bed— Oh, God, I've got an old mother dependent on me; please let me live! Why don't you tell him you'll give the money back?

SKIMMERHORN—Because I won't! And you won't, either! (*A crash.*)

BIGGS—Now you've done it! Can't you keep anything to yourself? There's such a thing as being politic, even when you're talking to God Almighty! (*Thunder again.*)

The curtain falls.

ACT II

It is some five or six hours later. We are still at that part of the Tor where the steam shovel is suspended. Biggs and Skimmerhorn, from an occasional sound of snoring, would appear to be asleep in the shovel. No sight of their heads appears above the rim.

Beneath the shovel, partly shrouded in mist, sits the sailor DeWitt. He has found some of the bills that Skimmerhorn dropped. The sight of them interests him. He smooths a bill out on his knee, as the light from the beacon swings around.

"These will be tokens and signs, these will," mutters DeWitt; "useful in magic, potent to ward off evil or put a curse on your enemies. Devil's work or not, I shall carry them on me, and make myself a match for these fulminating latter-day spirits. (*He pouches the bills.*) I'm hanged if it's not noticeable at once, a sort of Dutch courage infused into the joints and tissues from the mere pocketing up of their infernal numbered papers."

They have made a new man of DeWitt, these curious "numbered papers." He feels an urge for snuff, which, as best he can remember, he has not felt these two hundred years. He would have feminine companionship, too, "even one of these new female furies of theirs, wearing pants like a man." "Let my woman appear, god of the numbered papers," calls the sailor, "and let her wear what she likes, so long as a man can make out how she's made. Let her appear within this next three minutes, for God knows how long this mood will last in an old man!"

The god of the numbered papers is evidently out of sympathy with the Dutchman. The only one to appear is Buddy of the robber trio. He has brought a bag of sandwiches and he is impatient to find Biggs and Skimmerhorn. DeWitt thinks it funny that Buddy, being of the wizard race and practically in the presence of the fat men in the shovel, should not sense their presence. In a way he is ready to substitute for them. Now that he has their paper bearing the mystic countersign he feels that he is one of them. He waves a sheaf of bills in the face of the startled Buddy, nor is he at all startled when the boy draws a revolver and threatens to take the numbered papers away from him. Rather, drawing his own ancient artillery he is prepared to blast this foolish cabin boy halfway to the river. The sight of the flintlocks is frightening to Buddy. He drops gun and sandwiches and takes to his heels down the trail.

"Why, this new world is not so bad," cries DeWitt, exultantly. "I am left in possession of the field." He has picked up Buddy's discarded automatic and the bag and retreated to the rocks. "They fight with the weapons of children," ruminates DeWitt, examining the revolver, as he settles to the food. "Why, this new world begins to be mine, to do as I please with. Whatever kind of witch a sandwich may be come out and let me interrogate you. (*He takes out the sandwiches.*) If it be the food eaten by witches and wizards so much the better, for I am now a wizard myself, and by the great jib boom I haven't tasted food in God knows when. (*He eats.*) A sweet and excellent morsel, very strong with garlic and salami, medicinal for the veins and bladder."

DeWitt has eaten the sandwiches, pausing long enough to re-prime his pistols, but he will have none of the beer. "As Pastor Van Dorf observed very wisely before we sailed; you may eat the food of the salvages, said he, when you have voyaged to the new lands overseas; you may share their rations; you may even make up to their females after the fashion of sailors when the flesh is weak, but drink none of their drink, said he, lest it prove to be Circe's liquor and turn you all to hogs."

There is a sound of footsteps down the trail and presently Judith appears. Judith has come in search of Van and is a little startled to find DeWitt. The sailor is quick to acquaint her with his status. "I'm a poor bosun, ma'am, but grown, God knows how, to something of a person this last quarter hour." He is also pleased to report that he knows Van Dorn.

"You have seen him?" queries Judith, anxiously.

"God help him, I have," answers DeWitt; "and in none too sanctified an attitude, saving your ladyship, for the lad was obviously a bit taken with the Captain's wife, and she a married woman of some years' standing, young though she appear."

"Where was he?"

"I was never one to break in on a budding romance, sweetheart, and out of sheer delicacy I looked the other way."

"No, but where was he, please? I can show you the path."

"If you hunt out a very pretty little mistress in a bonnet somewhat behind the fashion, and look under the bonnet, you may chance to find him there."

It might be, reasons DeWitt, that not finding the man she is looking for, Judith could be induced to accept a substitute. If she could love him a little—"This is a kindly face, this of mine," suggests the sailor; "and a kindly heart under a worn jerkin. These are real tears on my cheeks, too, and I weep them for you, lady."

But Judith is not interested. DeWitt, to her, is a stranger and the face with which he is so satisfied is, to Judith, "ancient and terrible and horrible!" This is a great surprise to the sailor. "I'm a sad and broken man, lady, lost here among the lesser known peaks on the west side of the world, and looking only for a hand to help me."

Still Judith is unmoved. When there is a rustling, as of some-one approaching on the trail, she slips quietly out, leaving DeWitt with his flintlocks drawn and facing the coming intrusion.

It is Elkus and Dope, the robber boys, who are back. They approach guardedly, their automatics drawn, and with the command that DeWitt "Stick 'em up!" DeWitt is impatient. Let these "cheap new devils" stand back or— The gunmen open fire. There is a fusillade of shots, but the sailor remains untouched. He will, he fears, be obliged to blow them both into the Tappan Zee.

Dope, advancing on Elkus' orders to take the money off the sailor, is startled to find that he can see right through DeWitt. What kind of thing is he?

"I'm not a man to be daunted by loud noises and firecrackers, Beelzebub!" shouts DeWitt. "Go seek your place with the new father of hell before I send you there! Wizards!"

"Where's the money?"

"I have a talisman and I ate a sandwich, devils!" The sailor is defiant.

Now Dope has rushed in and shot DeWitt straight through the head and then retreated rapidly.

"I warn you I begin to be annoyed," warns DeWitt.

"It's no use, chief," reports the disgusted Dope. "I blew his brains out and he's standing right there!"

There is a movement in the steam shovel. Biggs and Skimmer-horn are again leaning over the edge.

"It's a war!" comments Biggs.

The sound of a voice is further proof to Elkus and Dope that something decidedly is wrong. They care for no more of it. With a rush and an intimation that Canada is the place for them the robbers are gone.

DeWitt is triumphant. Now is he "master of the world of things, a buccaneer, a devil and a rake!" He turns to receive the affirmations of Judith, but she is gone. Excitedly he follows down the trail. . . .

Biggs and Skimmerhorn are feeling fairly poisonous after their night in the shovel. The sight of the bag of sandwiches below is no help. Soon they are quarreling, and now they have grabbed each other and are struggling for some sort of mastery of the situation. Then it occurs to Biggs that if one does push the other out, the other will surely fall with him. It isn't a pleasant thought—that of splashing on the rocks a thousand feet below. So they mutually agree to call off their holds. They have resumed looking disconsolately at the sandwiches when Van and Lise return. The young people have been talking of the ways of Nature and the characteristics of the animals that inhabit the mountain, Van being teacher and Lise a fascinated listener.

Now Van, looking up, has discovered the men in the shovel and is pleased. Let them down? Not Van. He considers the situation perfect. Even after Judge Skimmerhorn has offered to give him the validation that will make him sole owner of the mountain as the price of their release, and tossed the paper to him, he is not interested. He knows there is a bond signed by the court that goes with the validation. Skimmerhorn is craftily holding that back until he is on the ground.

Van thinks perhaps the Judge might change his mind if he had even a little reminder of what might happen if the cable that holds the shovel should be released. To make his point clear Van pulls upon the cable, tilting the shovel dangerously. Biggs is petrified with fright and yelling to Skimmerhorn to give up the damned bond. Another tip of the shovel and Skimmerhorn sails the bond down to Van.

Now the unhappy shovel prisoners would try another offer. Biggs will give Van five thousand dollars cash for his land.

"Bid against them, Lise," shouts Van. "It's a game. What would you say, Lise? They offer me five thousand."

"Pieces of silver?"

"Pieces of silver."

LISE (*smiling*)—But I'll give you more!
Only five thousand for this crag at dawn
shedding its husk of cloud to face a sunrise
over the silver bay? For silver haze
wrapping the crag at noon, before a storm
cascading silver levin? For winter rains
that run in silver down the black rock's face

under a gray-sedge sky? For loneliness
here on this crag? I offer you nine thousand!
To be paid in silver!

VAN—You hear? I've got nine thousand;
what am I offered?

BIGGS—Make it ten thousand—
and let us down in the bargain!

VAN—Yes? Ten thousand?
A mountain for ten thousand? Hear them, Lise,
In their despair they lift it by a grand!
Should it go for ten?

SKIMMERHORN—We'll never get it back—
but that's all right.

VAN—Yes, Lise?

LISE—Will they pay
no more then for the piling of this stone,
set in its tall hexagonals by fire
before men were? Searching a hundred kingdoms
men will not find a site for lodge or tower
more kingly! A hundred thousand, sir, in silver,
this is my offer!

VAN—Come now, meet it boys—
I have a hundred thousand!

BIGGS—She's a fraud!
She's no dealer; she's a ringer, primed
to put the price up! What do you mean by silver?
She won't pay silver!

VAN—Coinage of the moon,
but it's current here!

SKIMMERHORN—Ten thousand, cash, and that's
the last. Five thousand out of my pocket, see
and five from Biggs! (*He pulls out a bundle of bills.* BIGGS *does the same.*)
Take a good look at cash,
see how that operates! (*He tosses down the roll.* BIGGS *follows suit.*)

VAN—You go well-heeled
when you go mountain-climbing. Is it real?

SKIMMERHORN—Well, look it over. Count it.

VAN (*taking up one packet, then another*)—Where did this come from?

SKIMMERHORN—Where would you think?

VAN—I'll say I got a shock. (*He studies the bills again.*)

I don't want your money.

BIGGS—What's wrong with it?

VAN—Didn't I tell you I had a hundred thousand?
Take the stuff back. We reckon in moonlight here!

Biggs and Skimmerhorn are yelling frantically as Van and Lise start out. They will pay ten thousand now! Fifteen! Twenty! Still Van is not interested. He stops long enough to throw them up the soggy sandwiches. Then he and Lise disappear.

Biggs and Skimmerhorn are left with the sandwiches and the money they found. There is some little satisfaction in remembering the money. They hear someone coming. It is, if Biggs can believe his eyes, their mascot: "Our little rabbit's foot, little good-luck token, little knee-high with the big heart." DeWitt strolls in. He notices that the sandwiches have disappeared, a further mystery that causes him to mutter—

DEWITT—Magic again! More devil's work! And the woman
gone, slipped round a turn, and the scent was cold
for an old dog like me. By the mizzen yards,
it's wearing to the temper of a man
even if he's not choleric!—And those two,
those buzzards of evil omen, brooding there
on how they'll cut the mountain like a pie
and sell it off in slices! (*He looks at his pistols.*)
One apiece.
It should be just enough, and it's a wonder
I never thought of it. (*He lifts his pistols, the two drop their sandwiches into the void, and cower down; he clicks the hammers.*)
Damp again! Well, boys,
we'll fix that. (*He sits down to freshen the priming.*)
They'll brood over us no more,
those two sea-lions. Damn the rain and mist;
it penetrates the priming! Damn the flint,
and damn the spring! A brace of fine horse-pistols,
that's what the Jew said back in Amsterdam;
it takes a horse to cock 'em. Now then, damn you,
blow 'em off their perch! (*As he rises his eye catches something out on the Zee. He stands transfixed for a moment, watching.*)
It can't be there!
It's there! It's gone! I saw it! Captain Asher!

Captain! Captain! Captain! Captain Asher! (BIGGS *and* SKIMMERHORN *have ducked down again.* DEWITT *rushes out firing his pistols in the air in his excitement.* BIGGS *sits up, then* SKIMMERHORN.)

SKIMMERHORN—Am I hurt? Do you see blood anywhere?

BIGGS—It seems there was nothing there. (*They contemplate the place where* DEWITT *stood.*)

The curtain falls.

At another part of the Tor, where the foreground is a little less precipitous, and where the mists float idly in from the Tappan Zee, Lise is sitting high up on a ledge. It is almost morning. The light of the airplane beacon throws Lise's face into relief. Van stands near, fascinated as she talks of the wreath of dandelions she has woven for his old felt hat. There is, thinks Lise, something a little pathetic about dandelions. Nobody likes them. And yet—"Where will you find another prodigal so merry or so golden or so wasteful?" she wants to know.

There are other things that Lise would know, too. When did Van part from Judith? And did he love her very much? Lise had loved someone, too. And still did.

"No, you're mine now," corrects Van, as he comes to sit beside her.

"See that great gulf that lies
between the heavy red star down the west
and the star that comes with the morning? It's a long way.
There's that much lies between us," answers Lise.

"Not for me," protests Van.

Van is weary and should rest, counsels Lise. Let him lay his head on her knees and rest. She would sing to him if she could, but all the songs she used to know are gone from her. All she knows now are the birds' songs, and she is not sure of them. Now she has forgotten the birds and would have Van tell her something of the men of his world—

LISE—There's so much that's changed now men can fly
and hear each other across seas, must men
still die—do they die still?

VAN—Oh, yes, they die.

Why do you ask?
LISE—Because I'm still so young,
and yet I can't remember all the years
there must have been.—In a long night sometimes
I try to count them, but they blow in clouds
across the sky, the dancing firefly years,
incredible numbers.—Tell me how old you are
before you go to sleep.
VAN—Lying here now
there's not much logic in arithmetic.
Five, or six, maybe. Five or six thousand, maybe.
But when I'm awake I'm twenty-three.
LISE—No more?
VAN—No more.
LISE—Tell me why it is I am as I am
and not like you?
VAN—I don't know, Lise.
LISE—But tell me.
Have I been enchanted here? I've seen
the trap-rock men, there in the shovel, seeming
so stupid and so pitiful. Could these
use charms and rites to hold wrecked mariners
forever in a deep cataleptic spell
high on a mountain-fringe?
VAN—The trap-rock men?
They're no more wizards than I am. They buy
and sell, and when they've had their fill of dust
they die like the rest of us.
LISE—But they laid spells
about us?
VAN—There are no wizards and no spells.
Just men and women and money and the earth
the way it always was. The trap-rock men
don't know you're here.
LISE—It's not sorcery then. If I had died
and left my bones here on the mountain-top
but had no memory of it, and lived on
in dreams, it might be as it is. As children
sure we were told of living after death,
but there were angels there, and onyx stone
paving an angel city, and they sang
eternally, no darkness and no sun,

nothing of earth. Now can it be men die
and carry thence no memory of death,
only this curious lightness of the hands,
only this curious darkness of the mind,
only to be still changeless with the winters
passing; not gray, not lined, not stricken down,
but stamped forever on the moving air,
an echo and an image? Restless still
with the old hungers, drifting among men,
till one by one forgotten, fading out
like an old writing, undecipherable,
we lose our hold and go? Could it be true?
Could this be how men die?

VAN (*half asleep*)—It may be, Lise.
I love you when you speak.

LISE—And I love you.
But I am dead, and all the crew is dead;
all of the "Onrust" crew—and we have clung
beyond our place and time, on into a world
unreal as sleep, unreal as this your sleep
that comes upon you now. Oh, you were cruel
to love me and to tell me I am dead
and lie here warm and living! When you wake
we shall be parted—you will have a world
but I'll have none! There's a chill falls on me,
the night-dew gathering, or my mind's death chill—
knowing at last I know.—You haven't heard.
You told me this in a half-dream. You've been kind.
You never thought to hurt me. Are you asleep?

VAN—I think I was.

LISE—Sleep, sleep. There was once a song,
if only I could call back air and words,
about a king who watched a goblet rising
and falling in the sea. It came to land
and on the rim the king's name was inscribed
with a date many years before. Oh, many years,
a hundred or three hundred. Then he knew
that all his life was lived in an old time,
swept out, given to the waters. What remained
was but this goblet swimming in the sea,
touching his dust by chance.—But he's asleep.
And very well he might be with dull stories
out of old songs.—Sleep, sweet; let me have

your head here on my knees, only this night,
and your brown hair round my finger.

A girl's shadowy figure has appeared at the head of the trail. It is Judith. Mistily she sees Lise and Van and turns to go, but Lise calls to her—

"The lad's asleep, but when he wakes you'll have him back."

"Do you dispose of him just as you please?" demands Judith.

"No. It's not what I please. It's what will happen."

Lise is but Van's friend, she would explain. Judith had left him bitter and she (Lise) was bitter, and they had tried to play at being lovers. But, when Van awakes he will be Judith's again, and Lise, too, will be happier, even though now there seem to be tears in her eyes. They are tears not for love or longing but shed for something far away.

"Only when you have him," Lise counsels, "love him a little better for your sake, for your sake only, knowing how bitterly I cried for times past and things done—"

Two or three of the sailors have appeared on the rocks above. They are looking anxiously out over the Zee. There is excitement among them. It's a ship they see. A ship with square top-yards! A brigantine! The "Onrust" tacking in shore! Now the voice of Captain Asher is heard above the others. He is calling Lise. The ship's on the river! They must hurry! The "Onrust" must catch the tide downstream.

But Lise would have him make less noise. He will waken the boy. And there is no ship—"Only a phantom haunting down the Zee as we still haunt the heights," she says.

Van is awake now, and worried. The ship's come, Lise tells him, and she and the others must hurry to catch the tide. She will go back with Asher—

VAN—And was nothing meant of all we said?

LISE—What could we mean, we two? Your hurt's quite cured
and mine's past curing.

VAN—Let me go with you then.

LISE—I should have told you if I'd only known
how we stood at the tangent of two worlds
that touched an instant like two wings of storm
drawn out of night; touched and flew off, and, falling,
fall now asunder through a wide abyss,
not to touch again. (*She steps back among the rocks.*)

VAN—Let them go if they like!

What do I care about worlds? Any world you have
I'll make it mine!

LISE—You told me in your sleep.
There is no witchcraft. Men are as they were;
we're parted now.

VAN—Give me your hand again!
They dare not take you from me, dare not touch you
no matter who they are, or where they come from—
they have no hold on us!

LISE—If I could stay!
If I could stay with you. And tend my garden
only a little longer!

VAN—Put out your hand!

LISE—There were too many, many, many years.

VAN—I'll be alone here—

LISE—No, not alone. When you must walk the air,
as all must walk it sometime, with a tread
that stirs no leaf, and breathe here with a breath
that blows impalpable through smoke or cloud,
when you are as I am, a bending wind
along the grain, think of me sometimes then
and how I clung to earth. The earth you have
seems now so hard and firm, with all its colors
sharp for the eye, as a taste's sharp to the tongue,
you'll hardly credit how its outlines blur
and wear out as you wear. Play now with fire
while fire will burn, bend down the bough and eat
before the fruit falls. For there comes a time
when the great sun-lit pattern of the earth
shakes like an image under water, darkens,
dims, and the clearest voices that we knew
are sunken bells, dead sullen under sea,
receding. Look in her eyes. (VAN *looks at* JUDITH.)

ASHER—Come!

LISE—See, the dawn
points with one purple finger at a star
to put it out. When it has quite gone out
then we'll be gone. (VAN *looks at the dawn, then turns back toward* LISE.)

VAN—Lise! Lise! (*But even as he speaks* LISE *and* THE CREW *have disappeared.*)

LISE (*unseen*)—This is your age, your dawn, your life to live.
The morning light strikes through us, and the wind

that follows after rain tugs at our sails—
and so we go.

DeWitt is the last to disappear, calling back a slighting impression of the age he is leaving, "an age of witches and sandwitches," "an age of paper money and paper men." Van stands wondering and silent. Judith can see the ship now, "Tiny, with black square sails; low and small." And there is just the breath of an echo of the sailors' song.

"There are no ghosts," protests Judith.

"I know," admits Van, dreamily; "but these were ghosts or I'm a ghost, and all of us. God knows where we leave off and ghosts begin. God knows where ghosts leave off and we begin."

Judith is a little troubled. It was for Lise that Van was calling, not for her. It was Lise Van loved. They may be ghosts and they may never come again, but Judith is not sure.

VAN—There's no ship at all.
It faded in the dawn. And all the mists
that hung about the Tor, look how they lift,
pouring downstream with the wind. Whatever it was,
was said, or came between us, it's all gone
now it's daylight again.
JUDITH—I came to say
if only I could keep you, you should keep
the Tor, or what you wished. I'm sorry I went.
I'm sorry this has happened. But it has.
And so—
VAN—Should I keep the Tor?
JUDITH—Yes, if you like.
VAN—God knows they haven't left me much of it.
Look, where the new road winds along the ledge.
Look at the jagged cut the quarries make
down to the south, and there's a boy scout trail
running along the ridge Mount Ivy way,
where they try out their hatchets. There's the light,
and steps cut into stone the linesmen blew
for better climbing. The crusher underneath
dumps road rock into barges all day long
and sometimes half the night. The West Shore tunnel
belches its trains above the dead lagoons
that line the brickyards. Their damned shovel hangs
across my line, ready to gouge the peak

we're standing on. Maybe I'm ghost myself
trying to hold an age back with my hands;
maybe we're all the same, these ghosts of Dutchmen
and one poor superannuated Indian
and one last hunter, clinging to his land
because he's always had it. Like a wasp
that tries to build a nest above your door—
and when you brush it down he builds again,
then when you brush it down he builds again—
but after a while you get him.

JUDITH—Then you'll sell?

VAN—I guess if you were with me then we'd sell
for what we could, and move out farther west
where a man's land's his own. But if I'm here
alone, I'll play the solitary wasp
and sting them till they get me.

JUDITH—If it's your way
then it's your way.

VAN—I'll sell it if you'll stay.
Won't you stay with me, Judith?

JUDITH—I think I'd always hear you calling Lise
while I was standing by. I took a wrong turning
once, when I left you and went down the hill,
and now it may not ever be the same.

The curtain falls.

ACT III

The level rays of a rising sun light up the faces of Biggs and Skimmerhorn as they hang over the edge of the steam shovel. Biggs has torn a handkerchief into strips, tied the strips together and is fiishing for a bottle of beer on the rocks below. Despite the voluble and irritating advice of Skimmerhorn, Biggs manages finally to hook the beer, but loses it before he can land it in the shovel.

There is some excitement below when Patsy, a State trooper, and A. B. Skimmerhorn, Sr. appear. They have climbed the mountain this early in a search for the missing Biggs and Skimmerhorn, whose wives in Ledentown have been pretty worried. The elder Skimmerhorn, after being threatened with a collapse at sight of his nephew and his partner in the shovel, feared they had been caught by the rock slide of the night before. Now he is convinced they have been on a bat, and no amount of explaining has the least effect on that conclusion. Senior is also pretty mad about it, and of no mind to help Patsy at the ropes when he would let them down.

"What were you doing?" demands Senior. "You came up here to buy Van Dorn's property; you're gone all night, and the whole damn town's up all night hunting for you! And we find you up in a steam shovel enjoying a hang-over!"

"I tell you we didn't even have a drink of water," protests Biggs.

"I can believe that. . . . Well, if you weren't drunk how did you get there?"

"Well, you see, first we tried to negotiate with Van Dorn."

"And he wouldn't take the money?"

"That's right." . . .

"Did you tell him you could take the land away from him?"

SKIMMERHORN—Oh, yes.

SENIOR—And you offered him the twenty-five thousand?

BIGGS—We offered him a fair price.

SENIOR—You were authorized to say twenty-five thousand.

BIGGS—We didn't quite get to that. We offered ten.

SKIMMERHORN—You see, we thought we'd save the company some money.

SENIOR—I'll bet you did. You thought you'd make a little on the side, and I'd never know.

SKIMMERHORN—Oh, no.

BIGGS—Oh, no.

SENIOR—All right, you offered ten and he wouldn't take it. Then what happened?

SKIMMERHORN—Well, we couldn't get down because of the slide, so some sailors offered to let us down in this thing.

SENIOR—Sailors—up here?

SKIMMERHORN—Little men, in big hats.

BIGGS—Might have been a moving picture company.

SENIOR—Yeah? Any elephants? Or snakes?

SKIMMERHORN—We're trying to tell you the truth!

PATSY—Certainly sounds like delirium tremens, boys.

SENIOR—Never mind, you were hauled up by pink elephants, and then what?

SKIMMERHORN—Van Dorn came along and started to dump us down the cliff.

SENIOR—What's Van Dorn look like? Kind of an octopus, with long feelers?

SKIMMERHORN—Are you going to let us down out of this basket?

SENIOR—No. Not till you come across with what's been going on.

SKIMMERHORN—All right. I'll talk when I'm down.

SENIOR—Can a grown man get pie-eyed on beer?

PATSY—Must have been something stronger.

Now Van has arrived and taken in the scene with interest. The senior Skimmerhorn introduces himself. He would also explain his connection with the firm of Skimmerhorns and their offer of twenty-five thousand dollars which they had delegated their agents to make. Hearing that Van already has the validation papers, he would now raise that offer to fifty thousand dollars. And still Van is not interested. . . .

Judith has come up the trail leading John, the Indian. John has come looking for Van, but his eyes are bad now, and he could not find the way alone. . . .

The senior Skimmerhorn has returned to his bargaining. Every man has his price. Even God, 'tis said, has his price. Let Van set a price for the land. Or, if he'll not do that, will he take a partnership in the company? To all of which Van's answer is No.

"Good God, what do you want?" demands the flushed Senior.

VAN—I want to have it back the way it was
before you came here. And I won't get that. I know
what kind of fool I look to all of you,
all but old John there. But I'll be a fool
along with John, and keep my own, before
I let you have an inch. John, fifty thousand
or this old hill-top. Is it worth keeping?

THE INDIAN—No.

VAN—No?

THE INDIAN—It's gone already. Not worth keeping.

VAN—I thought you'd say it was. I counted on you
to be my friend in that.

THE INDIAN—It's an old question,
one I heard often talked of round the fire
when the hills and I were younger. Then as now
the young braves were for keeping what was ours
whatever it cost in blood. And they did try,
but when they'd paid their blood, and still must sell,
the price was always less than what it was
before their blood was paid.

VAN—Well, that may be.

THE INDIAN—I wish now I had listened when they spoke
their prophecies, the sachems of the tents;
they were wiser than I knew. Wisest of all,
Iachim, had his camp here on this Tor
before the railroad came. I saw him stand
and look out toward the west, toward the sun dying,
and say, "Our god is now the setting sun,
and we must follow it. For other races,
out of the east, will live here in their time,
one following another. Each will build
its cities, and its monuments to gods
we dare not worship. Some will come in ships,
and some with wings, and each will desecrate
the altars of the people overthrown,
but none will live forever. Each will live
its little time, and fly before the feet
of those who follow after." Let them come in
despoiling, for a time is but a time
and these will not endure. This little hill,
let them have the little hill, and find your peace
beyond, for there's no hill worth a man's peace
while he may live and find it. But they fought it out
and died, and sleep here.

SENIOR—Why, this is a wise Indian.
A little pessimistic about the aims
of civilization, but wise anyway.
What do you say, Van Dorn?

THE INDIAN—You too will go
like gnats on the wind. An evening and a day,
but still you have your day. Build monuments
and worship at your temples. But you too will go.

SENIOR—You're on my side, so I don't mind,
but you have a damned uncomfortable way
of speaking. I'm a Republican myself,
but I don't go that far! What do you say, Van Dorn?
Can we do business?

VAN—Judith?

JUDITH—I'm out of it.
It's your decision. I'd say keep it though
if you want to keep it.

VAN—I'll sell it. Fifty thousand.
On one condition. There's a burying ground
I want to keep.

SENIOR—Sure. That can be arranged.
It's settled, then. Come down to Ledentown
tomorrow and get your money.
VAN—Yes, I'll come.
SENIOR—Why, three cheers, boys. We're out of the woods.
Take hold,
Van Dorn, and swing these topers off the limb.
Then they can sign the pledge.

A second trooper, Budge, has come in with the robber boys, Elkus and Dope. He has picked them up below and got a confession from them. But the boys insist the money from the Nanuet bank robbery is there on the mountain in a satchel. They saw either Biggs or Skimmerhorn, "one of those birds," sit down on it.

Biggs and Skimmerhorn wax indignant and lean far out of the steam shovel in their eagerness to impress their accusers that they are men of standing in the community. There was a third fellow, Elkus admits. A little guy in a big hat, "Short and fat, had two sawed-off shotguns and wore knee pants."

"And you could see right through him," chimes in Dope.

Budge is disgusted. "You expect me to send that out over the country: 'Look for a short, fat man with a big hat and two sawed-off shotguns. Dangerous. You can see right through him.'"

"They buried the money, Budge. Or else they're screwy." That's Patsy's opinion. They're nuts, the three of them.

But when they question Van, he, too, heard a lot of shooting during the night, and he had seen not only one little fellow in a big hat, but six or seven of them.

"I suppose you could see right through them?" smiles the incredulous Budge.

"Once in a while."

That's too much for Budge. "I'm going to quit writing this down," he declares. "There's enough here to get me fired already."

The examination goes on. Van can tell them where some of the missing bills are—on the ledge below. Three ten dollar bills. They might belong to the gentlemen in the scoop. But neither Biggs nor Skimmerhorn can recall having dropped any money. They did, however, see the little fellow in the big hat. He was fighting with those other two, Elkus and Dope. He probably took something out of the satchel, too.

Van suggests that the trooper help Biggs and Skimmerhorn down from the shovel before he goes. The boys are suddenly quite satisfied with their perch. Everything's all right with them.

They are in no hurry to get down. No, sir. But Van insists, and the shovel is lowered.

When the two are down from the shovel their pockets are noticeably bulging. It might be their lunch, but it happens, on investigation, to be money. Which reminds Biggs that they did bring up quite a lot of cash to pay Van Dorn for his farm. Twenty-five thousand dollars, in fact. How it ever got the Orangeburg pay roll stamp on it they haven't the least idea. Probably a mistake at the bank.

The troopers decide the mistake, if any, can be checked in Nanuet. Meantime, things being as they are, it will be necessary for the troopers to take over the cash and to put the realtors under arrest. Only temporarily, of course; just for an examination. Biggs and Skimmerhorn are of a mind to protest. They wouldn't like to have a thing like that get into the newspapers. And Skimmerhorn, for one, doesn't propose submitting to an examination. He—

But Budge happens to have an extra pair of handcuffs and Skimmerhorn decides perhaps he had better go along with the troopers.

They've all gone now—all save Van, Judith and John, the Indian. Suddenly Van remembers that he has sold Tor. It may be better so—better than living on a grudge, he decides. There's wilder land—and higher mountains—in the West, the Indian reminds him.

"He came to tell you, Van—this is his death day," Judith explains. "I'll go now."

John has reached for Judith's hand. He would hold it a little, if she doesn't mind. "It's a new thing, being blind, when you've had an Indian's eyes," he says.

"I'll stay a while," agrees Judith, giving him her hand.

THE INDIAN—When I had lost the path
halfway along the ridge, there at my feet
I heard a woman crying. We came on
together, for she led me. There'll be time
for crying later. Take her west with you.
She'll forget the mountain.

VAN—Will you come?

JUDITH—I'd remember Lise!

VAN—Was there a Lise?
I think she was my dream of you and me
and how you left the mountain barren once

when you were gone. She was my dream of you
and how you left the Tor. Say you'll come with me.

JUDITH—Yes.

THE INDIAN—It's a long day's work to dig a grave
in stony ground. But you're young and have good shoulders.
It should be done tonight.

VAN—I'll have it done
even if you don't need it. Tell me the place.

THE INDIAN—There's still an Indian burying ground that lies
behind the northern slope. Beneath it runs
a line of square brown stones the white men used
to mark their dead. Below still, in a ring,
are seven graves, a woman and six men,
the Indians killed and laid there. In the freshet,
after the rain last night, the leaf-mold washed,
and the seven looked uncovered at the sky,
white skeletons with flintlocks by their sides,
and on the woman's hand a heavy ring
made out of gold. I laid them in again.

VAN—Seven graves—a woman and six men—
Maybe they'll rest now.

THE INDIAN—Dig them in deeper, then.
They're covered only lightly.

VAN—I'll dig them deeper.

THE INDIAN—But you must make my grave with my own people,
higher, beneath the ledge, and dig it straight,
and narrow. And you must place me in the fashion
used by the Indians, sitting at a game,
not fallen, not asleep. And set beside me
water and food. If this is strange to you,
think only I'm an Indian with strange ways,
but I shall need them.

VAN—Don't worry. You shall have it
just the way you want it.

THE INDIAN—Shall we go?

VAN—One last look at the rock. It's not too late
to hold out on the bargain. Think of the gouge
they'll make across these hills.

JUDITH—If it's for me
you sell, we'll have enough without it, Van.
We'll have each other.

VAN—Oh, but you were right.
When they wash over you, you either swim

or drown. We won't be here.
THE INDIAN—And there's one comfort.
I heard the wise Iachim, looking down
when the railroad cut was fresh, and the bleeding earth
offended us. There is nothing made, he said,
and will be nothing made by these new men,
high tower, or cut, or buildings by a lake
that will not make good ruins.
JUDITH—Ruins? This?
THE INDIAN—Why, when the race is gone, or looks aside
only a little while, the white stone darkens,
the wounds close, and the roofs fall, and the walls
give way to rains. Nothing is made by men
but makes, in the end, good ruins.
VAN—Well, that's something.
But I can hardly wait.

THE CURTAIN FALLS

YOU CAN'T TAKE IT WITH YOU

A Comedy in Three Acts

By Moss Hart and George S. Kaufman

THIS was scheduled as one of the early season productions in the Fall of 1936. Thanksgiving time was the date set. But there were delays that kept it out of town until near Christmas. Whether the added weeks of tinkering and revising were responsible for the perfect timing and the steady barrage of laughter resulting when the play was produced no one will ever know. But the fact is patent that "You Can't Take It with You" came to Broadway a highly perfected comedy production.

The result was an overnight success of expansive proportions. Within three months seats were selling a good four months ahead. There was not, according to the statistical records, an empty seat in the theatre until the hot waves of July and August completely discouraged playgoing, and even then the vacant places had been bought and paid for in advance.

"You Can't Take It with You" proved a popular success of the purest type. Critical endorsement was generous but far from fulsome. The professional playgoers admitted that Moss Hart and George S. Kaufman, the wily collaborators, had written a completely mad farce with greater skill than any other two writers known to the theatre could have written it, and that there was magic in the direction of Mr. Kaufman.

But they were also free to confess that there was precious little body to the fantastic yarn which is the comedy's story, and no more than a trace of acceptable philosophy to justify the incredible goings on.

"There is not a fleck of satire in 'You Can't Take It with You,' " wrote Richard Lockridge, "but only gargantuan absurdity, hilariously preposterous antics and the rumble of friendly laughter with madly comic people." Which, as it turned out, was exactly what thousands of playgoers appeared to be hungering for in this particular recovery year.

The home of the Martin Vanderhofs, the authors of "You Can't Take It with You" are frank to confide, is just around the corner from Columbia University, but advise against a search for it. Also the room into which we are ushered as the play opens is "what is customarily described as a living room, but in this house the term is something of an understatement."

"Here meals are eaten, plays are written, snakes collected, ballet steps practiced, xylophones played, printing presses operated—if there were room enough there would probably be ice skating. In short the brood presided over by Martin Vanderhof goes on about the business of living in the fullest sense of the word. This is a house where you do as you like, and no questions asked."

At the moment Penelope Vanderhof Sycamore, Grandpa Vanderhof's daughter, "a round little woman in her early fifties, comfortable looking, homey, gentle," is seated at a typewriter, writing her eleventh play. On the table with the typewriter are a couple of kittens lapping milk from a saucer which tops a pile of completed manuscript.

Mrs. Sycamore, "Penny" to her intimates, is permitted to continue with her inspiration for a moment before she is interrupted by her eldest daughter, Essie, "a girl of about twenty-nine, very slight, a curious air of the pixie about her," who, so far as we know, never wears anything on her feet but ballet slippers.

Essie has been in the kitchen making candy, and has found it hot work. Still, she feels that she has to keep on with it so long as the sale continues good. Dancing is Essie's real ambition, but candy making may prove a profitable side line.

The family and its activities gradually take form. Rheba, the black girl from the kitchen, is in to lay the table. Rheba is in her thirties and is greatly interested in the progress Mrs. Sycamore is making with her play. A little surprised, she admits, to learn that Penny has taken her heroine out of El Morocco and put her in a monastery, but that is the way Penny writes.

Paul Sycamore, Penny's husband, "in his middle-fifties, but with a kind of youthful air," comes up from the cellar. Paul, whose chief interest is the manufacture of fireworks, is anxious that his wife should see what he has done with a midget firecracker and proceeds to set one off on the center table. He can sell those at five strings for a nickel. There is also a new sky rocket of which Paul is pretty proud. He has asked his associate, Mr. De Pinna, "a bald-headed little man with a serious manner," to bring one of these up from the basement for inspection. Mr. De Pinna is a helpful assistant. It is he who has thought of adding a balloon to the skyrocket, to follow a succession of gold stars, blue stars and bombs, but he is a little doubtful as to its spacing. The only way to determine that, declares Mr. Sycamore, is to try it, and Mr.

De Pinna returns to the cellar for the experiment.

It is while Rheba is trying to figure on the number that can reasonably be expected to be home for dinner (six counting Alice, who hasn't had dinner at home for a week, and eight if Mr. De Pinna and Mr. Kolenkhov are included) that the skyrocket goes off with a hiss and roar "lightly reminiscent of the Battle of the Marne." Neither Penny nor Rheba, however, pays the slightest attention to the interruption. Rheba goes on with setting the table and Penny falls to musing on the advisability of completing the monastery play. She thinks perhaps she had better give it up for the present and return to her war play. She finds getting out of the monastery a little difficult, though, as Essie reminds her, she once had the same trouble with a brothel and got out of there all right.

Ed Carmichael, Essie's husband, "a nondescript young man in his mid-thirties," has been upstairs working out a melody which he now comes to try on his xylophone. This sets Essie on her toes immediately. It is a nice melody. Mostly Beethoven's, but with a Carmichael touch. Essie finds steps to fit it and decides to try it for Kolenkhov when he comes.

It occurs to Penny, still searching for her war play, that Ed and Essie should have a baby. Ed's willing, if Essie is. Essie wouldn't mind, if Grandpa didn't. So that seems temporarily settled.

Now Donald, "a colored man of no uncertain hue," has arrived. Donald is Rheba's friend and helper and he brings a box of flies for Grandpa Vanderhof's pet snakes, which are kept in a converted aquarium on a back table.

Paul Sycamore is just telling Penny his new idea for putting the Russian revolution into an hour's fireworks display, like "The Last Days of Pompeii," when Grandpa Vanderhof arrives home from the commencement exercises at Columbia. Snakes and commencements are perhaps his greatest hobbies. "Grandpa is about seventy-five, a wiry little man whom the years have treated kindly. His face is youthful despite the lines that sear it. His eyes are very much alive. He is a man who made his peace with the world long, long ago, and his whole attitude and manner are quietly pursuasive of this."

As soon as he is in the house things sort of revolve around Grandpa. Everybody reports to him. Everybody is anxious to know how his day has gone. This time Grandpa has had a good day at the commencement. There must have been two acres of people. Everybody graduated and the speeches were much funnier than they had been the year before.

Now, at Grandpa's suggestion, Ed has started playing a little something on the xylophone. This brings Essie up on her toes again. Drifting through the mazes of a toe dance does not, however, interfere materially with Essie's conversation.

"There was a letter came for you, Grandpa. Did you get it?"

"Letter for me? I don't know anybody."

ESSIE—It was for you, though. Had your name on it.

GRANDPA—That's funny. Where is it?

ESSIE—I don't know. Where's Grandpa's letter, Mother?

PENNY (*who has been deep in her work*)—What, dear?

ESSIE (*dancing dreamily away*)—Where's that letter that came for Grandpa last week?

PENNY—I don't know. (*Then, brightly.*) I remember seeing the kittens on it.

GRANDPA—Who was it from? Did you notice?

ESSIE—Yes, it was on the outside.

GRANDPA—Well, who was it?

ESSIE (*first finishing the graceful flutterings of the Dying Swan*) —United States Government.

GRANDPA—Really? Wonder what *they* wanted.

ESSIE—There was one before that, too, from the same people. There was a couple of them.

GRANDPA—Well, if any more come I wish you'd give them to me.

ESSIE—Yes, Grandpa. (*A fresh flurry of dancing; the xylophone grows a little louder.*)

GRANDPA—I think I'll go out to Westchester tomorrow and do a little snake-hunting.

Ed has decided on a quotation from Trotsky: "God is the state; the state is God," for the next card he slips in the boxes of Essie's candy when he delivers them. This is a novelty Ed is developing.

Then Alice Sycamore arrives. Alice is "a lovely, fresh young girl of about twenty-two. She is plainly Grandpa's granddaughter, but there is something that sets her apart from the rest of the family. For one thing, she is in daily contact with the world; in addition she seems to have escaped the tinge of mild insanity that pervades the rest of them. But she is a Sycamore for all that, and her devotion and love for them are plainly apparent. At the moment she is in a small nervous flutter, but is doing her best to conceal it."

For one thing Alice is appearing in a brand new white dress, the second of the week. For another she wishes to announce that she is not home for dinner, but is expecting a young gentleman to call for her.

"I did everything possible to keep him from coming here, but he's calling for me," explains Alice.

"Why don't you both stay to dinner?" Penny suggests, a little excitedly.

"No, I want him to take you in easy doses. I've tried to prepare him a little, but don't make it any worse than you can help. Don't read him any plays, Mother, and don't let a snake bite him, Grandpa, because I like him. And I wouldn't dance for him, Essie, because we're going to the Monte Carlo ballet tonight."

"Can't do *anything,*" grumbles Grandpa. "Who *is* he—President of the United States?"

"No, he's vice president of Kirby & Co. Mr. Anthony Kirby, Jr."

"The Boss' son?"

"The Boss' son. Just like the movies."

Now there is more excitement, with everybody interested in Alice's young man. Is she going to marry him? Penny wants to know. Is he good looking? demands Essie. Alice stands up under the questioning with good humor and begs them to let her know the moment Mr. Kirby arrives. When she has gone to dress the buzz of interest multiplies and speculation is at least rife. During which the bell rings and Penny, all a-flutter, goes smartly to the door to admit the young man.

There is a young man at the door, but, as it turns out after Penny has smiled and bowed and welcomed him with enthusiasm, he is not Alice's young man. He is Wilbur C. Henderson, an agent from the Internal Revenue department. He has come to talk to Mr. Martin Vanderhof about a little matter of income tax. Grandpa is the Martin Vanderhof named, and he is quite willing to talk to Mr. Henderson, but he hasn't the least idea what it is all about.

Mr. De Pinna and Paul would like to demonstrate a new bomber for Grandpa, but give way when they see he is busy. Mr. Henderson is therefore privileged to proceed.

"According to the records, Mr. Vanderhof, you have never paid an income tax."

"That's right."

"Why not?"

"I don't believe in it."

"Well—you own property, don't you?"

oto by Vandamm Studio, New York.

"YOU CAN'T TAKE IT WITH YOU"

Henderson: You'll pay every cent of it, like everybody else. And let me tell you something else! ou'll go to jail if you don't pay, do you hear that?

(*Henry Travers, Josephine Hull, Hugh Rennie*)

"Yes, sir."

"And you receive a yearly income from it?"

"I do."

"Of—between three and four thousand dollars?"

"About that."

"You've been receiving it for years?"

"I have. 1901 if you want the exact date."

"Well, the Government is only concerned from 1914 on. That's when the income tax started."

"Well?"

"Well—it seems, Mr. Vanderhof, that you owe the government twenty-two years' back income tax."

There is, Mr. Henderson points out, a penalty for not filing an income tax return, but Grandpa is not at all frightened. What he would like to know is what the Government does with the money after it gets it. What does he get for his money? Protection? Grandpa doesn't think any foreigners are going to invade America. The Army and Navy? Last time we used battleships was in the Spanish-American war, notes Grandpa. And what did we get for that? Cuba. And gave it back. Who's going to pay for Congress? The Supreme Court? The President? Not Grandpa. As for the Constitution, that was paid for long ago.

"Well, I might pay about seventy-five dollars, but that's all it's worth," reluctantly agrees Grandpa.

"You'll pay every cent of it, like everybody else," shouts Mr. Henderson, trying to top the xylophone music Ed is playing for Essie's dance. "And let me tell you something else! You'll go to jail if you don't pay, do you hear that? There's a law, and if you think you're bigger than the law you've got another think coming. You'll hear from the United States Government, that's all I can say!"

Mr. Henderson is backing out of the room when Grandpa warns him to look out for the snakes. He has no more than jumped away from the snakes than the firecracker boys let go with their new bomber and Mr. Henderson jumps a full foot. He is out the door in no time, leaving a Panama hat behind him. Fortunately it is exactly Grandpa's size.

Another ring at the doorbell announces Mr. Kirby. And this time it is Mr. Kirby, "a personable young man not long out of Yale. . . . Although he fits all the physical requirements of a Boss' son, his face has something of the idealist in it. All in all a very nice young man."

Penny manages the family introductions and then calls Alice, contributing for her daughter's information that her young man is lovely. Alice probably hurries, but she doesn't get there before Grandpa has done what he could to be friendly by offering Mr. Kirby a tomato, and Penny has passed him the candy from one of those plaster skulls usually used for an ash tray. Mr. De Pinna, on being introduced, thinks he remembers having read that the young man's father was recently indicted.

The family has taken Mr. Kirby pretty thoroughly over the jumps before Alice does come. They have discovered that though he is a vice president it doesn't mean much; that he did a bit of traveling after leaving college; that he had a year at Cambridge; that the English commencements are very impressive, and that he supposes, as Penny suggests, that he now is ready to settle down and get married. Then Alice rescues Mr. Kirby. She would also escape with him as soon as possible, but there are other interruptions. Among them the arrival of Kolenkhov, Essie's dancing teacher. Kolenkhov "is enormous, hairy, loud, and very, very Russian." He greets the family with a series of short bows and frequently a clicking of heels. He is pleased to meet Mr. Kirby but a little distressed when he hears that he and Alice are going to the Monte Carlo ballet. The Monte Carlo ballet, in the estimation of Mr. Kolenkhov, "stinks."

Alice and Tony Kirby are able at last to negotiate their good-bys and are gone. There is immediately considerable family discussion as to their future.

"I think if they get married here, I'll put the altar right where the snakes are," announces Penny. "You wouldn't mind, Grandpa, would you?"

Essie—Oh, they'll want to get married in a church. His family and everything.

Grandpa (*tapping on a plate for silence*)—Quiet, everybody! Quiet! (*They are immediately silent—Grace is about to be pronounced.* Grandpa *pauses a moment for heads to bow, then raises his eyes heavenward. He clears his throat and proceeds to say Grace.*) Well, Sir, we've been getting along pretty good for quite a while now, and we're certainly much obliged. Remember, all we ask is just to go along and be happy in our own sort of way. Of course we want to keep our health, but as far as anything else is concerned, we'll leave it to You. Thank You. (*The heads come up as* Rheba *comes through the door with a steaming platter.*) So the Second Five Year Plan is a failure, eh, Kolenkhov?

KOLENKHOV (*booming*)—Catastrophic! (*He reaches across the table and spears a piece of bread.*)

The family is busily plunging in. The curtain is down.

Later that night the Vanderhof living room is in darkness, save for a light in the hall. Faintly, the tuneful whine of an accordion can be heard. When this ceases there is quiet for a moment, and then a loud BANG from the cellar breaks the silence. Some of the Sycamores are evidently still at work.

The sound of a key in the lock of the front door signalizes the arrival of Alice and Tony. They have had a wonderful evening at the ballet. Tony is reluctant to end it. With practically no urging at all he is induced to stay while Alice conducts an icebox search for something they might eat. The icebox is full of cornflakes and ginger ale.

The conversation turns to vacations. Alice's is in August. Tony thinks perhaps he could take August, too. Alice likes it in New York in the Summer. Tony thinks it would be great—especially with Alice there. In fact Tony is convinced it would be great any place, and all year 'round, if Alice were there.

Now Penny comes down the stairs, wrapped in a bathrobe. She is suddenly embarrassed to find Mr. Kirby. Really, she had no intention of interrupting anything. She has come in search of a manuscript, and here it is: "Sex Takes a Holiday." And so, good-night.

BANG goes another experiment in the cellar. That would be father, Alice explains. This time of night? Any time of night! Any time of day! Alice is plainly disturbed. But not Tony. He is standing gazing fondly at her—

"You're more beautiful, more lovely, more adorable than anyone else in the whole world," he says, with fervor, seeking to embrace her.

"Don't, Tony; I can't."

"What?"

"I can't, Tony."

"My dear, just because your mother—all mothers are like that, Alice, and Penny's a darling. You see, I'm even calling her Penny."

"I don't mean that." Alice has turned and is facing him squarely. "Look, Tony. This is something I should have said a long time ago, but I didn't have the courage. I let myself be swept away because—because I loved you so."

"Darling!"

"No, wait, Tony. I want to make it clear to you. You're of a different world—a whole different kind of people. Oh, I don't mean money or socially—that's too silly. But your family and mine—it just wouldn't work, Tony. It just wouldn't work."

There is another interruption. Ed and Essie are home from the movie and Essie doesn't care what Ed says, Ginger Rogers can't dance. At least Essie doesn't call it dancing. She is willing to demonstrate with Tony, if Alice will loan him for a minute. And she does—her arms around Tony's neck, her cheek against his cheek—until Alice manages to discourage the demonstration.

Now the Carmichaels have said their good-nights and are going up the stairs when a thought comes to Ed. "Essie, did you ask Grandpa about us having a baby?" "Yes," answers Essie; "he said go right ahead."

This to Alice is practically the last straw. She turns hopelessly to Tony. "You see? That's what it would be like, always."

"But I didn't mind that," insists Tony. "Besides, darling, we're not going to live with our families. It's just you and I."

ALICE—No, it isn't. It's never quite that. I love them, Tony—I love them deeply. Some people could cut away, but I couldn't. I know they do rather strange things—I never know what to expect next—but they're gay, and they're fun, and—I don't know—there's a kind of nobility about them. That may sound silly, but I mean—the way they just don't care about things that other people give their whole lives to. They're—really wonderful, Tony.

TONY—Alice, you talk as though only you could understand them. That's not true. Why, I fell in love with them tonight.

ALICE—But your family, Tony. I'd want *you*, and everything about you, everything about *me*, to be—one. I couldn't start out with a part of me that you didn't share, and a part of you that I didn't share. Unless we were all one—you, and *your* mother and father—I'd be miserable. And they never can be, Tony—I know it. They couldn't be.

TONY—Alice, every family has got curious little traits. What of it? My father raises orchids at ten thousand dollars a bulb. Is that sensible? My mother believes in spiritualism. That's just as bad as your mother writing plays, isn't it?

ALICE—It goes deeper, Tony. Your mother believes in spiritualism because it's fashionable. And your father raises orchids because he can afford to. My mother writes plays because eight years ago a typewriter was delivered here by mistake.

TONY—Darling, what of it?

Alice—And look at Grandpa. Thirty-five years ago he just quit business one day. He started up to his office in the elevator and came right down again. He just stopped. He could have been a rich man, but he said it took too much time. So for thirty-five years he's just collected snakes and gone to circuses and commencements. It never occurs to any of them—

Donald has come drifting in from the kitchen. He is wearing a long white nightgown, exposing a couple of very black shins. He carries his accordion slung across his shoulder. Donald obviously did not expect to meet any midnight visitors and is somewhat taken aback, though not much. He has come for the candy, Essie having a fancy for candy, and he gets out as gracefully as may be when he has found it.

"Now! Do you see what I mean?" demands Alice, still pressing her argument. "Could you explain Donald to your father? Could you explain Grandpa? You couldn't, Tony, you couldn't! I should have known. I did know! I love you, Tony, but I love them, too! And it's no use, Tony! It's no use!"

Alice is weeping now, but Tony is master of both the situation and himself. There is only one thing she has said that matters, and that is that she loves him. Everybody's got a family. And family problems.

"That's doesn't stop people who love each other. . . . Darling! Darling, won't you trust me, and go on loving me, and forget everything else?"

"How can I?"

"Because nothing can keep us apart. You know that. You must know it. Just as I know it."

And now she is in his arms. Soon she is happy and smiling again. It is time for Tony to go now, but it's grand to think they work in the same office. As a vice president Tony can spend the day dictating to her: "Miss Sycamore: I love you, I love you, I love you!" And they can meet in the drugstore in the morning before they go to the office.

Alice and Tony are out of sight in the hallway when Mr. De Pinna and Paul Sycamore come up from their cellar laboratory. They have done a good day's work—"five hundred Black Panthers, three hundred Willow Trees, and eight dozen Junior Kiddie Bombers."

There is just one thing more: Paul would like to have Alice take a look at a new red fire they've discovered. If Mr. De Pinna will turn out the lights Paul will light the red fire, and does. It sheds a soft glow over the room.

"There! What do you think of it? Isn't it beautiful?" demands Paul, rapturously.

"Yes, Father," agrees Alice, her face aglow, her voice soft. "Everything is beautiful. It's the most beautiful red fire in the world!"

She has rushed to her father and thrown her arms about his neck, "almost unable to bear her own happiness," as the curtain falls.

ACT II

It is a week later. The Sycamores have finished their dinner and are scattering. There is, however, a newcomer present. She is Gay Wellington, "an actress, a nymphomaniac, and a terrible souse." Gay at the moment is drinking gin. Hovering over her is Penny Sycamore with a play manuscript in her hand. Standing back of Gay is Donald who has paused in his job of clearing the table to note whether or not Gay will be able to drink the last gin she has poured. Miss Wellington has no difficulty with the poured drink nor with the next one. But a moment later she catches a glimpse of Grandpa's snakes and that's the finish.

"When I see snakes it's time to lay down," announces Miss Wellington, starting uncertainly for the couch. She is no sooner sprawled on that than she is, as Ed says, "out like a light."

"Next time you meet an actress on top of a bus, Penny, I think I'd *send* her the play, instead of bringing her home to read it," suggests Grandpa.

Essie suggests that Ed finish printing circulars and start taking her Love Dream candies around. He will have to come back to play for her when Kolenkhov comes. This isn't Essie's regular lesson night, but Alice is giving a party for the Kirbys the next night and a change was necessary. There is a good deal of deck clearing for the Kirbys' party. Ed must deliver his candies a day ahead. Mr. De Pinna and Paul must get a consignment of fireworks packed ready to take to Mt. Vernon in the morning and Alice is set for a last conference with Rheba. . . .

Ed has left with the candies and the circulars he packs with them, vaguely convinced that recently he has been followed by a strange-looking man. Mr. De Pinna and Paul are in the cellar and Alice is issuing her final orders—

"Look, Mother, I'm coming home at 3 o'clock tomorrow. Will you have everything down in the cellar by that time? The typewriter, and the snakes, and the xylophone, and the printing press. . . ."

"And Miss Wellington," adds Grandpa.

"And Miss Wellington. That'll give me time to arrange the table, and fix the flowers."

"The Kirbys are certainly going to get the wrong impression of this house," ventures Grandpa.

Alice is terribly worried, and Grandpa doesn't think she should be. Everything is pretty sure to go off all right. And, as Penny says, they are all going to do everything they can to make it a nice party.

"Oh, my darlings, I love you," sings Alice. "You're the most wonderful family in the world, and I'm the happiest girl in the world. I didn't know anyone could be so happy. He's so wonderful, Grandpa. Why, just seeing him—you don't know what it does to me."

"Just seeing him. Just seeing him for lunch, and dinner, and until four o'clock in the morning, and at nine o'clock *next* morning you're at the office again and there he is. You just see him, huh?"

"I don't care! I'm in love!" And Alice is away to have another word with Rheba in the kitchen. . . .

Packing fireworks in the basement Mr. De Pinna has found an old sketch of himself posed as a discus thrower. That was started in Penny's painting days. Mr. De Pinna wishes she might finish it, and Penny thinks perhaps she can.

"Who would have thought, that day I came to deliver the ice, that I was going to stay here for eight years?" says Mr. De Pinna.

"The milkman was here for five, just ahead of you," recalls Grandpa.

"Why did he leave, anyhow? I forget."

"He didn't leave. He died."

"He was such a nice man," Penny remembers. "Remember the funeral, Grandpa? We never knew his name and it was kind of hard to get a certificate."

"What was the name we finally made up for him?"

"Martin Vanderhof. We gave him *your* name."

"Oh, yes, I remember."

"It was a lovely thought, because otherwise he never would have got all those flowers."

"Certainly was. And it didn't hurt *me* any," agrees Grandpa. "Not bothered with mail any more, and I haven't had a telephone call from that day to this."

Penny thinks that she will do a little more work on the picture of Mr. De Pinna as the discus thrower, seeing Miss Wellington is not likely to awaken sufficiently to hear a play. She has gone in search of her palette and brushes and Mr. De Pinna is down cellar getting into his discus-throwing costume when Kolenkhov arrives.

The Russian is in a jolly mood but suffers a couple of minor shocks. He catches sight of Penny's picture of the discus thrower. "It stinks!" says he. He is less critical of the prostrate Gay, but is sadly reminded of the fate of Russia when Grandpa questions him about the Soviet.

"Donald, what do you think of the Soviet government?" Kolenkhov demands of the black boy as he comes from the kitchen.

"The what, Mr. Kolenkhov?"

"I withdraw the question. What do you think of *this* government?"

"Oh, I like it fine. I'm on relief, you know."

"Oh, yes. And you like it?"

"Yassuh, it's fine. Only thing is you've got to go around to the place every week and collect it, and sometimes you got to stand in line pretty near half an hour. Government ought to be run better than that—don't you think, Grandpa?"

Grandpa evades that issue, but he is convinced the Government should stop sending him letters. He has had another call to the United States Marshal's office. They probably want him to pay the tax so they can keep Donald on relief.

"Ah, Grandpa, what they have done to Russia," bursts out Kolenkhov. "Think of it! The Grand Duchess Olga Katrina, a cousin of the Czar, she is a waitress in Childs' restaurant! I ordered baked beans from her only yesterday. It broke my heart. A crazy world, Grandpa."

"Oh, the world's not so crazy, Kolenkhov. It's the people *in* it. Life's pretty simple if you just relax."

"How can you relax in times like these?"

"Well, if they'd relaxed there wouldn't *be* times like these. That's just my point. Life is simple and kind of beautiful if you let it come to you. But the trouble is, people forget that. I know I did. I was right in the thick of it—fighting and scratching and clawing. Regular jungle. One day it just kind of struck me. I wasn't having any fun."

"So you did what?"

"Just relaxed. Thirty-five years ago, that was. And I've been a happy man ever since."

Grandpa has found a colored target and a handful of feathered darts. He is throwing the darts at the target when Penny comes downstairs ready for painting. She has found her palette, her smock and a large black velvet tam-o'-shanter, which she wears at a rakish angle. Now Mr. De Pinna appears from the cellar in the traditional Roman costume. He is carrying Penny's easel, a discus and a small platform on which to pose.

Ed is back, quite certain this time that he has been followed. Gay Wellington has turned over on the couch, taken one hasty look at Penny and Mr. De Pinna in costume and passed right out again. And now Essie comes tripping down the stairs, very much the ballet dancer and also in full ballet costume. It being a hot night Kolenkhov, realizing the work before him, removes his coat and then his shirt—

"We have a hot night for it, my Pavlowa, but art is achieved only through perspiration," he observes, cheerily.

Grandpa has resumed his dart throwing, pausing only to consider changing targets as his eye travels to the bulging posterior of the prostrate Gay. Ed is at the xylophone ripping into the first movement of the "Scheherazade." Essie is entering the mazes of a pirouette and Penny is calling, a little nervously, to Mr. De Pinna to pull in his stomach when the front door bell tinkles and Rheba goes to answer it. In a moment she is back, her eyes popping as she calls wildly to Mrs. Sycamore. A moment later a reason for this state of panic is revealed. The three Kirbys, Mr. and Mrs. and Tony, in full evening dress, are standing in the archway!

There is a stifled gasp from Penny, and startled stares from the others, including the Kirbys. "Grandpa, alone of them all, rises to the situation. With a kind of old world grace he puts away his darts and makes the guests welcome."

It would appear to be Tony's mistake. He had thought the invitation to dinner was for tonight instead of tomorrow night. Mr. and Mrs. Kirby are terribly embarrassed and would withdraw if Grandpa were not so graciously persistent. The Sycamores, he assures them, were not doing a thing. "Just spending a quiet evening at home," Penny hastens to explain.

Mrs. Kirby is, with some further reluctance, laying aside her wrap when she suddenly spies the snakes and emits a healthy scream. Calmed by the removal of the snakes to the kitchen, Mrs. Kirby agrees with Mr. Kirby that they both would be perfectly happy with a little canned salmon and some beer, with frankfurters as an alternative. Penny compromises by ordering frankfurters, canned corn and Campbell's soup. Donald is to get them at the A & P.

And then Alice comes. "She is a step into the room before she realizes what has happened; then she fairly freezes in her tracks." Tony is profuse with his apologies. The Kirbys are as gracious as circumstances permit. But Alice is still dreadfully worried. What has her mother ordered? Did she know that Mr. Kirby, suffering from indigestion, could only eat certain things?

"Perhaps it is not indigestion at all, Mr. Kirby," suggests Kolenkhov, breezily helping things along. "Perhaps you have stomach ulcers."

"You mustn't mind Mr. Kolenkhov, Mr. Kirby," quickly injects Grandpa. "He's a Russian and Russians are inclined to look on the dark side."

"All right, I am a Russian," sputters Kolenkhov; "but a friend of mine, a Russian, died from stomach ulcers."

Things have quieted down and Grandpa has led Mr. Kirby into a discussion of the industrial situation when Gay Wellington, who has been pretty well covered on the couch, chooses this moment to come to life. "With a series of assorted snorts, she throws the cover back and pulls herself to a sitting position, blinking uncertainly at the assemblage. Then she arises and weaves unsteadily across the room. The imposing figure of Mr. Kirby intrigues her. 'Hello, Cutie!' she calls, playfully rumpling his hair as she passes."

"That may seem a little strange to you, but she's not quite accountable for her actions," explains Grandpa, quickly. "A friend of Mrs. Sycamore's. She came to dinner and was overcome by the heat."

Mr. Kirby, pacing the room, has come upon Paul Sycamore's Erector Set and the subject naturally turns to hobbies. Mr. Kirby raises orchids. Some of them take six years before they blossom and some longer than that. Mrs. Kirby agrees that probably everyone should have a hobby, but for herself she finds spiritualism a much greater solace. Which strikes Penny as being quite silly.

"I don't think it matters what the hobby is," speaks up Grandpa, trying to save another situation; "the important thing is to have one."

"To be ideal, a hobby should improve the body as well as the mind," puts in Kolenkhov, with a show of authority. "The Romans were a great people. Why? What was their hobby? Wrestling. In wrestling you have to think quick with the mind and act quick with the body."

"Yes, but I'm afraid wrestling is not very practical for most of us," protests Mr. Kirby, with a deprecating little laugh. "I wouldn't make a very good showing as a wrestler."

"You would be a *great* wrestler," insists Kolenkhov. "You are built for it. Look!"

With a quick movement Kolenkhov has pinioned Mr. Kirby's arms, knocked his feet out from under him and not only has him flat on the floor but is triumphantly sitting on him. At which moment Alice comes back into the room and is again completely astounded by what she sees. Tony and Paul have rushed to Mr. Kirby's assistance. He is considerably mussed up and very, very mad. His glasses have flown off and when Alice finds them they're broken.

"Oh, I am sorry," apologizes Kolenkhov. "But when you wrestle again, Mr. Kirby, you will, of course, not wear glasses."

"I do not intend to wrestle again, Mr. Kolenkhov," answers Mr. Kirby, coldly furious.

Donald is back and the food is in the kitchen, but again the Kirbys think they really had better be going. Again the pleading of Alice prevails upon them to stay. She has ordered some scrambled eggs and a plain salad for Mr. Kirby, and everything is going to be just fine. Which it is for a moment. Then Rheba comes to whisper hoarsely to Alice that the eggs have gone down the sink. There is nothing to do now but send Donald for more and explain that there will be a slight delay.

It is then that Penny, rising to another crisis, proposes that they play a game. (MR. KOLENKHOV *knows a trick with a glass of water, but* ALICE *successfully stops him trying it.*) Penny's game is called Forget-Me-Not. She used to play it at school. First everybody is to write his name on a piece of paper, then Penny is to call out five words and as she says each word everybody is to write down the first thing that comes into his mind—

"For instance, if I say 'grass' you might put down 'green'—just whatever you think of, see? Or if I call out 'chair' you might put down 'table.' It shows the reactions people have to different things. You see how simple it is, Mr. Kirby?"

Mr. Kirby sees, but he is not at all interested in playing. However, he submits. When everybody has paper and pencils poised Penny begins.

PENNY—Everybody ready? . . . The first word is "potatoes." (*She repeats it.*) "Potatoes." . . . Ready for the next one? . . . "Bathroom." (ALICE *shifts rather uneasily, but seeing that no one else seems to mind, she relaxes again.*) Got that?

KOLENKHOV—Go ahead.

PENNY—All ready? . . . "Lust."

ALICE—Mother, this is not exactly what you—

PENNY—Nonsense, Alice—that word's all right.

ALICE—Mother, it's not all right.

MRS. KIRBY (*unexpectedly*)—Oh, I don't know. It seems to me that's a perfectly fair word.

PENNY (*to* ALICE)—You see? Now, you mustn't interrupt the game.

KIRBY—May I have that last word again, please?

PENNY—"Lust," Mr. Kirby.

KIRBY (*writing*)—I've got it.

GRANDPA—This is quite a game.

PENNY—Sssh, Grandpa. . . . All ready? . . . "Honeymoon." (ESSIE *snickers a little, which is all it takes to start* PENNY *off. Then she suddenly remembers herself.*) Now, Essie! . . . All right. The last word is "sex."

ALICE (*under her breath*)—Mother!

PENNY—Everybody got "sex?" . . . All right—now give me all the papers.

GRANDPA—What happens now?

PENNY—Oh, this is the best part. Now I read out your reactions.

KIRBY—I see. It's really quite an interesting game.

PENNY—I knew you'd like it. I'll read your paper first, Mr. Kirby. (*To the others.*) I'm going to read Mr. Kirby's paper first. Listen, everybody! This is Mr. Kirby. . . . "Potatoes—steak." That's very good. See how they go together? Steak and potatoes?

KIRBY (*modestly, but obviously pleased with himself*)—I just happened to think of it.

PENNY—It's *very* good. . . . "Bathroom—toothpaste." Uh-huh. "Lust—unlawful." Isn't that nice? "Honeymoon—trip." Yes. And "sex—male." Yes, of course. . . . That's really a wonderful paper, Mr. Kirby.

KIRBY (*taking a curtain call*)—Thank you. . . . It's more than just a game, you know. It's sort of an experiment in psychology, isn't it?

Penny agrees with Mr. Kirby, and then turns to the replies of Mrs. Kirby. These, she finds, are a bit more subtle. "Potatoes—starch." Penny understands. "Bathroom—Mr. Kirby." Well, after all, Mr. Kirby does take a long time. "Lust—human." Mr. Kirby is annoyed at that one, and Alice thinks perhaps they had better stop the silly game, but now Mr. Kirby wants to go on. "Honeymoon—dull." Yes, that is what Mrs. Kirby meant—"old people sitting on the porch all afternoon and nothing to do at night." Penny resumes. "Sex—Wall Street." Mrs. Kirby doesn't quite know what she really did mean by that, except that Mr. Kirby was always talking about it. Anyway, now she has a headache and thinks they really should be going.

This time Kirby agrees. A postponement of the dinner would probably be better. Tony, however, is as strongly opposed as ever. He thinks they should stay. But he has lost Alice's support—

"We were fools, Tony, ever to think it would work," she says. "It won't. Mr. Kirby, I won't be at the office tomorrow. I—won't be there at all any more."

"Alice, what are you talking about?" demands the distressed Tony.

"I'm sorry, my dear—very sorry. . . . Are you ready, Miriam?"

"Yes, Anthony." Mrs. Kirby is enormously dignified.

"It's been very nice to have met you all," continues Mr. Kirby. "Are you coming, Anthony?"

"No, Father. I'm not."

"I see. . . . Your mother and I will be waiting for you at home. . . . Good-night."

The Kirbys have taken no more than a short step toward the door when they are stopped by "a quiet and competent-looking individual with a steely eye, and two more just like him loom up behind him."

These are the men who have been following Ed when he delivered candy. They are from the Department of Justice, which makes them, as Penny says, "J-men."

The chief of the squad has sent the two others to search the house, one the cellar, the other the upper rooms. He now gives some attention to Ed, who repeatedly insists that he hasn't done anything. It is true he has been printing circulars, of which the G-man has several samples. It is true that he has put them in the boxes of candy. Circulars reading: "Dynamite the Capitol!" "Dynamite the White House!" "Dynamite the Supreme Court!" "God Is the State; the State Is God." But these are not Ed's sentiments. He just liked to print.

"Now, Officer, the Government's in no danger from Ed," quickly interposes Grandpa. "Printing is just his hobby, that's all. He prints anything."

The man sent into the cellar is back with Mr. De Pinna, the latter loudly protesting that he has left his pipe and would like to get it.

"Shut up, you!" roughly answers Mr. De Pinna's captor, turning to his chief. "We were right, Chief. They've got enough gunpowder down there to blow up the whole city."

"Everybody in this house is under arrest," announces the chief.

KIRBY—What's that?

MRS. KIRBY—Oh, good heavens!

GRANDPA—Now look here, Officer—this is all nonsense.

DE PINNA—You'd better let me get my pipe. I left it—

THE MAN—Shut up, all of you!

KOLENKHOV—It seems to me, Officer—

THE MAN—Shut up! (*From the stairs comes the sound of drunken singing—"There was a young lady," etc.* GAY WELLINGTON, *wrapped in* PENNY'S *negligee, is being carried down the stairway by a somewhat bewildered* G-MAN.)

THE G-MAN—Keep still, you! Stop that! Stop it!

THE LEADER (*after* GAY *has been persuaded to quiet down*)—Who's that?

GRANDPA (*pretty tired of the whole business*)—That—is my mother. (*And then, suddenly, we hear from the cellar.* MR. DE PINNA *seems to have been right about his pipe, to judge from the sounds below. It is a whole year's supply of fireworks—bombs, big crackers, little crackers, sky rockets, pin wheels, everything. The house is fairly rocked by the explosion. In the room, of course, pandemonium reigns.* MRS. KIRBY *screams; the* G-MAN *drops* GAY *right where he stands and dashes for the cellar, closely followed by* MR. DE PINNA *and* PAUL; PENNY *dashes for her manuscripts and* ED *rushes to save his xylophone.* KOLENKHOV *waves his arms wildly and dashes in all directions at once; everyone is rushing this way and that. All except one. The exception, of course, is* GRANDPA, *who takes all things as they come.* GRANDPA *just says, "Well, well, well!"—and sits down. If a lot of people weren't in the way, in fact, you feel he'd like to throw a few darts.*)

The curtain falls.

ACT III

It is the following day. As Rheba sets the table for dinner Donald, "the Edwin C. Hill of the moment," reads to her a newspaper account of the arrest and incarceration of the Sycamores and their guests.

". . . After spending the night in jail the defendants, thirteen in all, were brought before Judge Callahan and given suspended sentences for manufacturing fireworks without a permit," reads

Donald, a little laboriously, but with great interest.

The police, Rheba reports, had put her in the same cell with Mrs. Kirby and a strip-teaser, who fought all the time.

Donald concludes his reading with the reporter's statement that the prominent Anthony W. Kirby of Kirby & Co., 62 Wall Street, had denied that he was in any way interested in the manufacture of fireworks, but refused to state why he was on the premises at the time of the raid. . . .

Alice Sycamore is determined to go away and no argument has been able to dissuade her. Family and friends are agreed that Alice is that way once her mind is set. Penny has put a sheet of paper in the typewriter and is trying to work out of her depression, but when Paul comes downstairs, after making a final plea to his daughter, and confirms the fixed state of Alice's determination, Penny begins to weep. Alice's father and mother are very unhappy. Each is prepared to take the blame. Perhaps if they had been different—instead of just happy—Alice might have been proud of them. Penny's last hope is set on Tony. Perhaps Tony, who is out walking around the block again, after repeated attempts to see Alice, can catch her as she goes out—

Grandpa is the only one who isn't worried. "Suppose she *goes* to the Adirondacks?" reasons Grandpa. "She'll be back. You can take just so much Adirondacks and then you come home."

"Oh, but it's all so terrible, Grandpa," wails Penny.

"In a way, but it has its bright side, too."

"How do you mean?"

"Well, Mr. Kirby getting into the patrol wagon, for one thing, and the expression on his face when he and Donald had to take a bath together. I'll never forget that if I live to be a hundred, and I warn you people I intend to. If I can have things like that going on."

"Oh, it was even worse with Mrs. Kirby," reports Penny. "When the matron stripped her. There was a burlesque dancer there and she kept singing a strip song while Mrs. Kirby undressed."

"I'll bet you Bar Harbor is going to seem pretty dull to the Kirbys for the rest of the summer," smiles Grandpa.

Alice has come downstairs and started for the kitchen to press a couple of dresses. As delicately as possible the family hovers about, hoping to think of something that will change her plans. But the plans hold—or might have held if everybody had not forgotten to call the cab Alice had asked them to call.

"Oh, I wish I lived in a family that didn't always forget *every-*

thing," sighs Alice. "That—that behaved the way other people's families do. I'm sick of cornflakes—and Donald—and everything! Why can't we be like other people? Roast beef and two green vegetables, and—doilies on the table, and—a place you could bring your friends to—without—"

She has burst through the kitchen door. A moment later Tony has come in the front way and, on the family's advice, followed after Alice. He no sooner gets to the kitchen than Alice comes bursting out, with Tony at her heels. He follows her right up the stairs, still insisting that she listen to what he has to say. But she won't.

Presently a subdued Kolenkhov appears. He has come to give Essie her usual lesson, but Essie is not up to dancing today. He also has come upon another mission. He would tell them more of his friend, the Grand Duchess Olga Katrina. "She has not had a good meal since before the revolution." Today is the Grand Duchess's day off and Kolenkhov thought possibly they would be willing to invite her to dinner.

The Sycamores would, of course, be delighted. Penny can hardly wait to meet the Grand Duchess. As it happens she does not have to wait long. The Grand Duchess is just outside pending a summons from Kolenkhov.

"The Grand Duchess Olga Katrina, wheat cakes and maple syrup out of her life for a few hours, sweeps into the room. She wears a dinner gown that has seen better days, and the whole is surmounted by an extremely tacky-looking evening wrap, trimmed with bits of ancient and moth-eaten fur. But once a Grand Duchess always a Grand Duchess. She rises above everything—Childs', evening wrap and all."

Introductions are accomplished with considerable show of form. Penny does a curtsey that is fairly sweeping but a little difficult to get out of. Essie, "starting on her toes, merges the Dying Swan with an extremely elaborate genuflection," and Mr. De Pinna, bowing to the floor, practically remains there.

The ceremonies over, and the Grand Duchess properly enthroned, the talk turns quickly to the dinner hour. Her Highness has no intention of being rude, but she will have to be back in the restaurant by eight to relieve another waitress. Penny is quite prepared to hurry things.

"Quite a lot of your family living over here now, aren't there?" queries Grandpa, affably.

"Oh, yes—many. My uncle, the Grand Duke Sergei—he is an

elevator man at Macy's. A very nice man. Then there is my cousin, Prince Alexis. He will not speak to the rest of us because he works at Hattie Carnegie's. He has cards printed—Prince Alexis of Hattie Carnegie. Bah!"

"When he was selling Eskimo Pies at Luna Park he was willing to talk to you," Kolenkhov recalls, a little bitterly.

"Ah, Kolenkhov, our time is coming," promises the Grand Duchess. "My sister Natasha is studying to be a manicure, Uncle Sergei they have promised to make floor-walker, and next month I get transferred to the Fifth Avenue Childs'. From there it is only a step to Schrafft's, and *then* we will see what Prince Alexis says!"

The question of meal time again arising, the Grand Duchess suggests that perhaps she could help in the kitchen. She is a very good cook, and loves it. "If they have got sour cream and pot cheese I will make you some blintzes," she promises Kolenkhov, as they go into the kitchen to see. . . .

Alice and Tony come downstairs. Alice is still preparing to depart. She is, reports Tony, the stubbornest daughter in forty-eight states. From the set of her expression Alice seems likely to confirm the charge.

A cab has driven up, but it is not for Alice. It has brought Mr. Kirby. Mr. Kirby has come for Tony. Tony, with one last plea to Alice to marry him, to which a firm No is again the answer, is ready to go. Then Grandpa takes a hand, even over Alice's protest. Grandpa knows what is happening: Alice loves Tony, but isn't marrying him because the Sycamores are the kind of people they are. She thinks the two families wouldn't get along, and perhaps they wouldn't—but who can say which of them is right and which wrong?

However she may feel about it, it is Grandpa's opinion that Tony is too nice a boy "to wake up twenty years from now with nothing in his life but stocks and bonds . . . mixed up and unhappy," the way his father is.

"I beg your pardon, Mr. Vanderhof, I am a very happy man," politely thunders the outraged Mr. Kirby.

GRANDPA—I don't think so. What do you think you get your indigestion from? Happiness? No, sir. You get it because most of your time is spent in doing things you don't want to do.

KIRBY—I don't do anything I don't want to do.

GRANDPA—Yes, you do. You said last night that at the end of

a week in Wall Street you're pretty near crazy. Why do you keep on doing it?

KIRBY—Why do I keep on—why, that's my *business.* A man can't give up his business.

GRANDPA—Why not? You've got all the money you need. You can't take it with you.

KIRBY—That's a very easy thing to say, Mr. Vanderhof. But I have spent my entire life building up my business.

GRANDPA—And what's it got you? Same kind of mail every morning, same kind of deals, same kind of meetings, same dinners at night, same indigestion. Where does the fun come in? Don't you think there ought to be something *more,* Mr. Kirby? You must have wanted more than that when you started out. We haven't got too much time, you know—any of us.

KIRBY—What do you expect me to do? Live the way *you* do? Do nothing?

GRANDPA—Well, I have a lot of fun. Time enough for everything—read, talk, visit the Zoo now and then, practice my darts, even have time to notice when spring comes around. Don't see anybody I don't want to, don't have six hours of things I *have* to do every day before I get *one* hour to do what I like in—and I haven't taken bicarbonate of soda in thirty-five years. What's the matter with that?

KIRBY—The matter with that? But suppose we *all* did it? A fine world we'd have, everybody going to zoos. Don't be ridiculous, Mr. Vanderhof. Who would do the work?

GRANDPA—There's always people that like to work—you can't *stop* them. Inventions, and they fly the ocean. There's always people to go down to Wall Street, too—because they *like* it. But from what I've seen of you, I don't think you're one of them. I think you're missing something.

KIRBY—I am not aware of missing anything.

GRANDPA—I wasn't either, till I quit. I used to get down to that office nine o'clock sharp, no matter how I felt. Lay awake nights for fear I wouldn't get that contract. Used to worry about the world, too. Got *all* worked up about whether Cleveland or Blaine was going to be elected President—seemed awful important at the time, but who cares now? What I'm trying to say, Mr. Kirby, is that I've had thirty-five years that nobody can take away from me, no matter what they do to the world. See?

KIRBY—Yes, I do see. And it's a very dangerous philosophy, Mr. Vanderhof. It's—it's un-American. And it's exactly why

I'm opposed to this marriage. I don't want Tony to come under its influence.

It is Tony who takes issue with that statement. What's wrong with the Sycamore family philosophy? His father did not always think it was communistic, Tony points out. There was a time in his youth when he wanted to be a trapeze artist. There was a time when he wrote quite bitterly to his father (Tony's grandfather) protesting his right to do what he wanted to do, including the playing of a saxophone. When he was twenty-one he had run away from home because they wanted to force him into the business. Tony knows these things because once he had come upon some old letters of his father's in the attic and had read them.

"I may have had silly notions in my youth, but thank God my father knocked them out of me," answers the elder Kirby. "I went into the business and forgot about them."

"Not altogether, Father. There's still a saxophone in the back of your clothes closet."

"That's enough, Tony. We'll discuss this later."

"No, I want to talk about it *now*. I think Mr. Vanderhof is right—dead right. I'm never going back to that office. I've always hated it and I am not going on with it. And I'll tell you something else. I didn't make a mistake last night. I knew it was the wrong night. I brought you here on purpose. I wanted to wake you up. I wanted you to see a real family—as they really were. A family that loved and understood each other. You don't understand me. You've never had time. Well, I'm not going to make *your* mistake. I'm clearing out."

Tony is not sure of what he is going to do, but he isn't going to be pushed into the business just because he is Mr. Kirby's son. He may be a bricklayer, but at least he will be doing something he wants to do.

"You know, Mr. Kirby, Tony is going through just what you and I did when we were his age," puts in Grandpa. "I think, if you listen hard enough, you can hear yourself saying the same things to *your* father twenty-five years ago. We all did it. And we were right. How many of us would be willing to settle when we're young for what we eventually get? All those plans we make . . . what happens to them? It's only a handful of the lucky ones that can look back and say that they even came close. . . . So, before they clean out that closet, Mr. Kirby, I think I'd get in a few good hours on that saxophone."

Mr. Kirby has turned to look at his son as though he were

seeing him for the first time. Then the kitchen door opens and the Grand Duchess, an apron over her evening dress, appears. She has come to learn how many there will be for dinner. She must know before she makes the blintzes.

There is a faint suggestion of social triumph in Grandpa's voice as he presents the Kirbys to the Grand Duchess, and more than a suggestion of awe in the expression of the elder Kirby as he acknowledges the introduction.

"Before I make the blintzes, how many will there be for dinner?" repeats the Grand Duchess Olga Katrina.

"Oh, I'd make quite a stack of them, Your Highness," advises Grandpa. "Can't ever tell."

"Good! The Czar always said to me, 'Olga, do not be stingy with the blintzes.' "

Now it occurs to Grandpa that the Kirbys ought to stay to dinner. Penny, too, is anxious to get some of the food in the house eaten up. Mr. Kirby decides that he would like to stay very much. Tony also thinks it would be fine—if Alice will send away her cab. For answer a radiantly happy Alice is now in Tony's arms and everything is fine.

But there is one thing more. Essie has just found a letter for Grandpa in the icebox and it is from the Government. That old Government again. But this time, it seems, the Government wants to apologize. It has just been discovered that Grandpa has been dead eight years and doesn't owe a cent.

"Remember Charlie, the milkman? Buried under my name? Well, I just told them they made a mistake and I was Martin Vanderhof, Jr. So they're very sorry and I may even get a refund."

"Why, Grandpa, you're an old crook," laughs Alice.

"Sure!"

Ed has gone to his xylophone and is playing. Essie is promptly on her toes. Kolenkhov is in from the kitchen, carrying his own chair and eager to get started on the blintzes. And now the Grand Duchess arrives to announce that everything will be ready in a minute. They can all sit down.

PENNY—Come on, everybody. Dinner! (*They start to pull up chairs.*) Come on, Mr. Kirby!

KIRBY (*still interested in the xylophone*)—Yes, yes, I'm coming.

PENNY—Essie, stop dancing and come to dinner.

KOLENKHOV—You will like Russian food, Mr. Kirby.

PENNY—But you must be careful of your indigestion.

KIRBY—Nonsense! I haven't any indigestion.

TONY—Well, Miss Sycamore, how was your trip to the Adirondacks?

ALICE—Shut your face, Mr. Kirby!

KOLENKHOV—In Russia, when they sit down to dinner . . .

GRANDPA (*tapping on his plate*)—Quiet! Everybody! Quiet! (*Immediately the talk ceases. All heads are lowered as* GRANDPA *starts to say Grace.*) Well, Sir, here we are again. We want to say thanks once more for everything You've done for us. Things seem to be going along fine. Alice is going to marry Tony, and it looks as if they're going to be very happy. Of course the fireworks blew up, but that was Mr. De Pinna's fault, not Yours. We've all got our health and as far as anything else is concerned, we'll leave it to You. Thank You.

"The heads come up again. Rheba and Donald come through the kitchen door with stacks and stacks of blintzes. Even the Czar would have thought there were enough."

THE CURTAIN FALLS

JOHNNY JOHNSON

A Fantastic Drama in Three Acts

BY PAUL GREEN

(Incidental Music by Kurt Weill)

THERE was a good deal of controversy aroused by the production of "Johnny Johnson." Written by Paul Green practically on order from the Group Theatre, Inc., one of the more progressive off-shoots of the New York Theatre Guild, it was fitted with a musical score by Kurt Weill, a German composer of standing whose continued residence in Germany had been discouraged by Hitler. It projected the cause of the average man in a legend that was a little fantastic but very earnest.

The divergence of opinion centered about the effectiveness of the play's statement rather than the quality of its writing. It was conceded that in intent and purpose Mr. Green, who had won a Pulitzer award with his "In Abraham's Bosom" and a sheaf of laudatory notices for his "House of Connelly," had been nobly actuated. But in neither direction nor casting had the Group lived up to previously acquired standards. The amateur spirit was a little too strongly in evidence.

Despite the controversy, "Johnny Johnson" was the most warmly supported of last season's social problem dramas. There was a strongly partisan group ready to fight for John Howard Lawson's "Marching Song," but the appeal of "Johnny" was wider. "Under the buffoonery of this fugacious satiric legend Mr. Green knows that Johnny is the most tragic figure in the world," wrote Brooks Atkinson. "The world has slapped him with its ultimate indignity. It can no longer find room for a completely honest man, for it has surrendered to the charlatans, opportunists and rogues who are the captains and kings of destruction."

It is a beautiful Spring day in April, 1917, when the curtain rises on "Johnny Johnson." We stand with a small crowd of village folk at the clean-swept top of a little hill. "In the middle background is a funereal obelisk-like monument about ten feet high and draped in a dark low-hanging cloth. At the left is a naive and homemade example of the Star-Spangled Banner hanging down from a hoe-handle staff which stands stuck in the ground."

The ten or twelve women at the edge of the crowd "are garbed in dark dresses and wear brown slat bonnets which shadow their faces, and each holds a little United States flag in her hand." An equal number of men in another group are similarly dressed in sober clothes, and each carries a tiny flag.

The Mayor is there. "He is an elderly fellow with a violet red nose, dressed in an antediluvian swallow-tail coat, wing collar, swollen black tie, baggy striped trousers and button shoes." Anguish Howington, "a gangling young man resembling the stage undertaker type," is prominent. So, too, are Minerva (Minny Belle) Tompkins, "a vision of loveliness with her golden hair, baby limpid eyes and doll-like face;" Johnny Johnson, "a quiet-mannered young fellow of twenty-five or six, dressed in a well-worn palm beach suit, soft checked shirt, blue tie, flat-topped straw hat and square-toed russet shoes;" Grandpa Joe, "an old man with a scraggly graying mustache, dressed in a shrunk-up faded blue-and-gray uniform of 1865," and the editor of the *County Argus*, "a nondescript middle-aged man in a dark, shiny-sleeved seersucker suit, with spectacles, a grimy collar and shoestring tie."

These friends and fellow citizens, about to be addressed with studied oratorical eloquence by the Mayor, have gathered to commemorate the founding of the town. On this hilltop two hundred years before, the forefathers had met to arbitrate and sign a treaty with the Indians which was to end all strife and war—

"And at this moment let me pay respect
To Johnny Johnson here,
Our gentle-hearted friend and artisan
And tombstone carver of the skillful hand—
'Twas through his kindly zeal
That we at this late date
Erect this monument of peace—
Our thanks to Johnny Johnson."

Johnny's acceptance is a shy and awkward "Thanks, folks, thanky." It is Minny Belle who gets the thrill and looks admiringly on as the Mayor continues—

"And now
Full meet it is that I speak forth my thoughts
Upon this vital subject—peace. (*Leaning forward.*)

These are parlous times— (*To the Editor.*)
Parlous times.
The war clouds belch and thunder over Europe's sky
As if to swallow up the solid earth—
Where Germany and France and half the world
Do battle unto death.
The question now before th' American people is
Shall we take part or not— (*After an emphatic pause.*)
I point you to our glorious president— (*He points in a general direction towards Washington.*)
Who stands unshaken like a rock
And tells us nay—
We are too proud to fight—
For peace it is that's made our nation great
And peace that's made our village likewise what she is
Where each man loves his neighbor as himself
And puts his money in the bank on Monday morn."

At this juncture the Mayor breaks suddenly into song in a "slightly cracked and nasal voice—"

"Over in Europe things are bad,
A great big war is going on,
And every day somebody's dad
Has shot and killed somebody's son.
—Turr—uble—turr—uble,
It's awful to think about,
Oh, frightful, oh, shameful,
America will stay out."

There are two verses, set to "a soft and teasing tune," and the villagers join uncertainly but earnestly in the chorus, bearing with especial emphasis upon the "Turr—uble—turr—uble!"

The Mayor's speech is resumed. He enlarges upon the theme of America's staying out. What said the immortal Washington? No entangling alliances. And James Monroe? People of Europe stay home. And now the great president of the United States—

"He says that neutral we must be to the last ditch.
And what do I your mayor say?
I say the same!"

Which is Minny Belle's cue to clear her throat preparatory to singing "Democracy Advancing," the words for which she had

oto by Bligh-Colbert, New York.

"JOHNNY JOHNSON"

McBray: Problem No. 2—If you fell into a river and couldn't swim, would you—one, yell for p and try to scramble out; two, dive to the bottom and crawl out; or, three, lie on your back d float until help came?

Johnny: How deep is the river?

(*Russell Collins, Lee Cobb*)

contributed to the *Argus*. There are three verses. One for Washington. One for Lincoln. And one for Wilson—

" 'Tis Wilson with the golden word
Of peace and liberty—" . . .

"Of peace—peace—peace,
And thus his flag is furled—
Wilson, great Wilson,
The leader of the world."

It is time to unveil the monument and have their pictures taken, but the Mayor would like to hear from Johnny first.

"Aw, shucks—I can't make a speech," insists the embarrassed Johnny. "I might say though, I think we've done a mighty good thing in putting up this monument. It's the biggest job I've ever done.—But then peace and arbitration's a big idea. I side with Woodrow Wilson on that."

"He'll be glad to hear of it, Johnny."

"I reckon he's already heard of it. I wrote him a letter—inviting him down to the unveiling—but he hasn't come—not yet—Well (*he twists his hat about in his hands*), that's about all. I am better at working with my hands than with my tongue."

The photographer is busy posing the group and attracting its attention to the little bir-dee, when, following a rumble of approaching hoof-beats "a lanky, barefoot boy with a tangle of grimy hair under a Coca-Cola cap," rides into the scene on a ramshackle bicycle and delivers to the Mayor an official-looking envelope. The Mayor, reading the contents hurriedly, is amazed. Suddenly he throws up his hands—

"War is declared!" he bellows.

It is difficult for the visitors to grasp. War? What war? Johnny is completely bewildered. They are there to unveil his monument. Let them—

But the Mayor has again commanded attention. He is about to read the Presidential proclamation—

"Now, therefore, I, Woodrow Wilson, by virtue of—and so on—so on—do hereby proclaim to all whom it may concern that a state of war exists between the United States and the Imperial German government—"

Excitement mounts. Grandpa Joe is for starting a spy hunt immediately. The Mayor is ready to call for volunteers. Let all who will go hold up their hands.

Practically everybody volunteers, men and women alike. All

except Johnny Johnson. Johnny is still bewildered. Johnny thought they were all for peace. Johnny—

"Follow me to the courthouse! War! War!" shouts the Mayor.

The parade starts, led by Minny Belle and the Mayor. Anguish Howington promptly takes his place with Minny Belle and sings lustily with the rest of them—

"And now the fateful hour has come
And millions strong we rise
To fight for France and Belgium
And crush their enemies! . . ."

They have marched off, singing and shouting. Johnny is left mournfully behind. A moment later Minny Belle has come rushing back to fetch him. Anguish has followed her. Minny Belle is fearfully excited. Johnny must come, now, at once. The Courthouse bell is calling. She gets between Johnny and Anguish and would march them off, but Johnny balks—

JOHNNY—I can't go just now. (*Calling off to the left.*) Heigh, you, Mr. Fink—we want our pictures took!

MINNY BELLE (*staring at him*)—Oh, Johnny, surely you'll be the first to fly to the defense of your flag.

JOHNNY—But—why, I got all my work to attend to (*Softly*) and—and— (*He touches her shyly and lovingly on the arm.*) I've got other things to arrange for—for you and me. I'll tell you Wednesday night.

MINNY BELLE (*hiding her face in her hands*)—He can't mean it. His country needs him, and now he talks of personal happiness.

JOHNNY—Goodness gracious, Minny Belle, you don't expect me to do that—go off and enlist—and we don't even know what it's all about.

MINNY BELLE—We've declared war on Germany, that's what.

JOHNNY—And it ain't like Woodrow Wilson to do that. Why, he's been our first leader for peace. And now— (*Shaking his head.*) I bet it's a false alarm.

ANGUISH (*swallowing manfully and then speaking out boldly, as he raises his clenched fist*)—I'll go—I'll be in No-Man's Land in a fortnight. Yes, that I will! (*His valor mounting.*) They'll get a taste of my smoke—them Huns and Boches that rape—mistreat French ladies. Let me at 'em.

MINNY BELLE—Ah, listen!

ANGUISH—Yeh, dod-rot their souls!

MINNY BELLE—Yes, Anguish, yes.

ANGUISH—Dod—dum 'em, I say. (*Letting out a bloodthirsty gr-r-r.*) Give me a gun and a bayonet—a gun and a bayonet is all I want.

MINNY BELLE (*rapturously*)—Hurrah!

JOHNNY (*growling*)—Yeh, hurrah! Anguish Howington won't ever see the sight of a German. He can run too fast.

ANGUISH—Here, now—

MINNY BELLE (*stamping her tiny foot*)—Stop it—stop it!

JOHNNY—Oh, Minny Belle, I'm sorry, but this buzzard here—(*Snapping at* ANGUISH.) Take your hand off her arm. (ANGUISH *instinctively jerks away from* MINNY BELLE, *and then reaches out to take her hand, but she denies him that. In the distance a trumpet begins blowing "The Star-Spangled Banner."* JOHNNY *calls out.*) All right, Mr. Fink, we're ready for the pictures! (*Reaching out and taking* MINNY BELLE'S *hand.*) You and me, Minny Belle, one on either side of the tombstone.

MINNY BELLE (*pulling her hand away*)—No—most emphatically no.

JOHNNY—But I need the pictures for advertising the business.

MINNY BELLE (*almost ready to weep with vexation*)—Business—business—and our country called to war.

ANGUISH (*taking his cue from* MINNY BELLE)—Yes, he talks of business—and at such an hour!

JOHNNY (*angrily again*)—Yeh? You may not be talking it right now but you're thinking it. (*Scornfully.*) And such a business!

ANGUISH (*likewise angry again*)—Well, selling mineral water is just as elevated as putting up tombstones. And there's a sight more money in it.

MINNY BELLE—Stop it! You boys promised not to quarrel over me again. (*She starts away and then turns back.*) I'm not engaged to either of you. Remember that.

Minny Belle has hurried tearfully away. Johnny stops Anguish from following her. Minny Belle is Johnny's girl. He'd have Anguish understand that. And this is one question he doesn't believe can be settled by arbitration. With a mighty lunge he is after Anguish, who escapes around the monument and darts away.

Johnny stands for a moment gazing queryingly at the ground. Now he walks over to the monument and pulls the drawstring hanging from the top. "The drape rolls up and reveals the single word 'Peace' engraved in large letters on the stone." The lights fade.

"KEEP THE HOME FIRES BURNING"

The living room of the Tompkins house is simple and typical of the American rural village home of 1917. There are the familiar combination day bed and sofa, made attractive in mail-order catalogues; an oval center table and a variety of heavy oak chairs of the same suite. Three framed poster portraits on the rear wall, however, give a personal and patriotic touch to the decorations. In the center is a large picture of Woodrow Wilson. To the right is a smaller one of Washington and to the left one of Lincoln. Under Washington is a cardboard slogan reading: "He saved the Colonies!" Under Lincoln: "He saved a nation!" And under Wilson, in larger letters: "Make the world safe for democracy!"

Grandpa Joe is present, in galluses, sleeve-supports, a collarless shirt and dark trousers, puttering with what appears to be a small Ferris wheel, an invention that Grandpa expects one day to solve the problem of perpetual motion.

Across the room Aggie Tompkins, "a stoutish, middle-aged woman with a strong-jowled face, a thundering ample bosom and a pair of capable arms," is sitting at the sewing machine. Aggie is about to fume, having worked up a feeling of disgust with Grandpa because he will hang around the house fooling with his inventions when he should be concerning himself about Minny Belle, a fanatical patriot if ever there was one. Grandpa certainly ought to talk to Minny Belle.

Failing to get any satisfaction from her appeals to Grandpa, Aggie returns to her sewing, breaking into a mournful song relating the death of her husband and the burden laid upon her by way of keeping herself company. She is not at all cheered by the arrival of Johnny Johnson, who has dropped in for a moment of gossip about the tombstone business and to bring Aggie a little birthday present he has made with loving hands—a miniature white tombstone with clasped hands and "Friendship" carved on it. Aggie, however, is depressed rather than elated by the thought that Johnny is carving her tombstone already, and flies into a passion. Johnny, Aggie shouts, as she flies from the room, is a fool.

"She don't like you, Johnny," ventures Grandpa Joe.

"Well, everybody to his own taste, as the goat said to the skunk," answers Johnny, with a doleful shrug.

"It's Anguish she likes, the rising young business man," Grandpa reports. "Come on now, don't worry about Aggie."

JOHNNY—I'm not worrying about her—especially. It's the war, Mr. Joe. I still can't make heads or tails of it.

GRANDPA JOE—I didn't understand the Civil War but I fought in it—just the same.

JOHNNY—Yeh, and suppose you had been killed—

GRANDPA JOE—Then they'd a-raised me up a fine tombstone the way you did to peace.

JOHNNY—But what good would it do you and you dead as a door-nail?

GRANDPA JOE—Whew—no good, that's certain. Say, you ain't afraid, are you, Johnny?

JOHNNY—No, but if I had to die I'd like to know what I was dying for— (*Emphatically.*) You're durn right I would.

GRANDPA JOE—You're getting sort of strong in your language, ain't you, Johnny?

JOHNNY—Yeh—I feel strong about it all, Mr. Joe. I tell you, it's plain as the nose on your—my face—war is about the low-downest thing the human race could indulge in. Add up all the good in it and it's still a total loss. There ought to be some way of settling it by discussion—the way we do over in the Adelphi Debating Society, and not by killing. The more you fight and kill the worse it gets. You may conquer your enemy for a while but he or his friends only wait to grow strong again to come back at you. That's human nature. And what I can't understand about Wilson is—why all of a sudden he's willing to go out and kill a lot of people for some idea about freedom of the seas.

GRANDPA JOE—The sea has got to be free, Johnny—it's got to be free.

JOHNNY—Well, maybe it has, though after all you could look on it as nothing but a big pond. Now if I was out in a pond and Anguish passed by—

GRANDPA JOE—Anguish?

JOHNNY—Well, take anybody you don't like. And he tried to come in and contaminate the water, I'd raise a little disturbance all right, but I wouldn't try to kill him. No, we'd get out on the bank and—

GRANDPA JOE—Arbitrate, Johnny?

JOHNNY—Anyhow, there wouldn't be any killing, at least I don't think so. (*Glumly.*) There must be some other idea in Wilson's mind—for him and me's been seeing eye to eye all along.

Maybe when *The Argus* come out—

GRANDPA—Well, you needn't worry so. You don't *have* to go fight, not yet you don't.

JOHNNY—Uh, that's just the trouble, Mr. Joe. I'm for peace and Minny Belle's for war. That's the long and short of it.

GRANDPA JOE (*thoughtfully*)—Uhm, you are in a kind of a jam, ain't you—in a manner of speaking? On the one hand—your principle, on the other—your—er—love?

JOHNNY (*fervently*)—Yes, sir.

GRANDPA JOE—I'd drop principle.

JOHNNY—But I can't do what I don't believe in.

GRANDPA JOE—Then you're sunk—like the "Lusitania."

If Johnny could find any reason for the war he wouldn't mind going. He'd go quick as scat, in fact. When it was all over all the democratic nations could unite for peace and that would mean something. But—

Minny Belle has come. Johnny is on his feet to hold a chair for her. Minny Belle, wearing a trim blue coat suit, her golden hair combed back into a becoming bob, is no more than mildly interested in the excitement her coming has stirred in Johnny. She is excessively formal. Even when he sheepishly lays a locket in her lap—a locket with a picture of Johnny inside—she hesitates before putting it on.

She cannot, however, long resist his pleading, or the utterly beatific smile with which his face is wreathed when she admits that she keeps the song book from which they often sing in her own room—the very room where she sleeps at night. Soon she is singing for him the song called "Longing," and he is supremely happy—

"Oh, heart of love,
The soul of all my yearning,
Come back to me,
My days are filled with pain.
My fondest thoughts
To you are ever turning—
Wild foolish hopes
To have you back again." . . .

The song is finished now and Johnny, still enraptured, is standing before Minny Belle, pouring out his love—

"Like the song says, Minny Belle, you are the—" The words stick, Johnny stutters, swallows hard and struggles on. "From that first day I saw you down there in the meat market—yes, my heart thumps like it will hurt when I think of you. When I'm carving my tombstones—my hammer going whick-whack—whick-whack—it's all in time to my heart beating out what I want to say— (*Pulling out his handkerchief and wiping his forehead.*) And I can't say it—"

"Beautiful—beautiful how you talk so," mutters Minny Belle, and is in his arms.

"My little—er—bird," whispers Johnny, bending to kiss her tenderly on top of the head, and then to reel stupefiedly away from her, completely overcome by the force of his happiness.

"We're engaged," shouts Johnny, spinning drunkenly about the room. "We're engaged. I'm the happiest man in all the world. Yay-eh! (*Turning ecstatically back to her.*) And now can I ask you—ask you that other question? (*A tiny nod of her bright head says he may.*) When are we to be— (*His voice trembling over the word.*) be married? What do you say to next week? We'll get his honor the Mayor to—to do it."

"But we can't do that," protests Minny Belle, moving ever so slightly away from him.

"Why not, Precious?"

"It's the war—you've got to enlist!"

"Great guns, I'd forgot all about the war!" Johnny's arms have dropped from Minny Belle with a thud. He stands moodily gazing at the floor.

Nor can she, with all her assurances of the loss she will feel with his going, rouse him from his moodiness.

Presently Minny Belle has broken into song again, "her face already touched with the pain of woman's renunciation." This is a song of farewell ("Alone I'll wait steadfast and true, my every thought a thought of you."), and at its conclusion Minny Belle buries her face tearfully against Johnny's shoulder. Johnny is practically on his way to camp, so far as Minny Belle is concerned.

Johnny, however, is still not convinced that he should go. He has a lot of thinking to do about that. Before he can explain himself Minny Belle, heartbroken at the thought of Johnny's not going, has stifled a sob with her handkerchief and rushed from the room, calling as she goes that everything is changed; they are no longer engaged. Johnny, hopelessly and completely crushed by the news, picks up his tombstone and walks slowly into the garden. . . .

Anguish Howington has come to bring Miss Aggie a bottle of mineral water. Also to announce the imminence of his enlisting, because of Minny Belle's urging. This does not fit in with Aggie's plans at all.

"In the Civil War my Uncle Heck didn't enlist," confides Aggie, in a low voice. "Why? He melted down a whole beeswax candle, got himself a hollow reed, and blew the stuff into a hole he'd cut into his arm. From then until Grant captured Lee at Appomattox he had a bad case of St. Vitus's Dance. He shook so bad that bringing the milk from the cowbarn he'd make the butter come. Yes, and Cousin Melchisidec, he hamstrung his left leg with a butcher knife."

ANGUISH (*staring at her in fearful amazement as he drops down in a chair*)—Lord upon me, you mean they done damage to theirselves with knives!

AGGIE—And Bud Lauderdale, an old sweetheart of Ma's, cut off his big toe with a grass hook. He limped bad the rest of his life and wore a special made shoe.

ANGUISH (*aghast*)—Merciful heavens!

AGGIE (*shaking her head reminiscently*)—Ah, they had nerve—Uncle Heck and Cousin Melchisidec, and Bud Lauderdale. Brave men all, they were. (*Consolingly.*) But you don't have to do damage to yourself to keep out of this war, Anguish. It's your eyes. Cataracts and scales—Anguish.

ANGUISH—Huh, Mis' Agnes?

AGGIE—You can hardly see from here to the door— Almost blind. I'll swear an affidavid for you. (*She gazes at him in silence.*)

ANGUISH (*a great ragged smile sliding around his slit of a mouth*)—I see—I see. (*Suddenly rising and grasping her hand in thankfulness.*) You've saved my life— Ever since last Sunday when that English hero preached in church I haven't slept a wink— (*Stiffening sharply and croaking in a hypnotic, sepulchral voice.*)

"In Flanders Fields the poppies blow
Between the crosses row and row
That mark *my* place—"

AGGIE (*rising*)—I got a pair of cross-eyed glasses I used when the flues settled in my eyes. You wear 'em and if you're not blind now you will be shortly. Come on into the kitchen. (*She starts out front,* ANGUISH *following; then suddenly she turns back, picks up the jug, and goes off drinking from it. For a moment the scene is empty except for a low note that scurries around in the orchestra like a mouse on the floor. Then there is a noise of thumping foot-steps in the hall at the rear. The door is opened and* JOHNNY *comes running in with a newspaper in his hand.*)

JOHNNY (*calling out wildly*)—Minny Belle! Minny Belle, say, I've got some wonderful news for you! (MINNY BELLE *comes in with her hair hanging down. Her eyes are red from weeping.* JOHNNY *runs over to her.*) Minny Belle, I'm going to enlist. Listen, it's all here in *The Argus*. Wilson's proclamation. And now I'm ready to go. (*Reading enthusiastically.*) "We have no quarrel with the German people. It's their leaders who are to blame. Drunk with military power and glory, they are leading the democratic people of Germany as well as the whole world into shameless slaughter." (*With deep finality.*) "This is a war to end war." Daggone, near 'bout my own words!

He sweeps Minny Belle into his arms and kisses her on the lips as the lights fade.

"YOUR COUNTRY NEEDS ANOTHER MAN—AND THAT MEANS YOU"

"Recruiting Office Number 18,659" is located in a medium-sized room of a small-town building. The walls are plastered with flaming signs and posters calling upon American manhood to go and fight for its country. There are two desks, one used by Private Jessel, a nervous lad of twenty, who is the stenographer, the other by the officer in charge; a bench; a tall white weighing and measuring scale; a small table on which a phonograph stands, with its horn disappearing through the wall toward the street.

At the moment Captain Valentine, "a handsome man some thirty years old, dressed in a spick and span uniform of the United States Infantry;" Sergeant Jackson, "with a scrubby bull-dog face and stubby upturned nose, about forty years old," and Private Jessel are in the room. The Captain and the Sergeant are reading a movie magazine together, Jessel is pounding away, hesitantly but confidently, at his typewriter. Presently from an inner room there issues a low, moaning sound. No one pays any attention to that. Captain Valentine hums a song, mumbling a verse or two of a barrack room ballad.

Suddenly the half silence is broken by a blood-curdling scream from the inner room. The Captain and the Sergeant continue reading, but Private Jessel stops typing and listens. Then he arises and starts the phonograph, spilling the brassy band notes of "Democracy's March" into the street.

Now the door of the room from which the screams have issued is opened and Dr. McBray, "a middle-aged, pot-gutted fellow wearing a medical corps major's uniform," comes in. The Doctor is carrying a stethoscope in one hand and mopping his head and neck with the other. He is shortly followed by two giant private soldiers of the regular army, stripped to the waist, "their muscular torsos tattooed most horribly, mostly with voluptuous women's figures." Between them is Anguish Howington, naked save for a hand-towel about his middle. Anguish is apparently on the verge of a collapse. "His swollen red eyes are almost closed, his face is bathed in cold sweat and he is panting hoarsely for breath." The soldiers drop him into a chair while Dr. McBray takes up with Private Jessel the dictation of his report.

He finds Anguish free of venereal diseases, very nervous and in need of nutritious food. "Teeth show candidate to be about twenty-eight. Sight moon-eyed, almost blind. Combination diseases—leucoma, incipient cataract, granular conjunctivitis and God knows what!" He turns to Anguish and yells: "Get out!" The private soldiers shove Anguish through a door and Dr. McBray sprawls exhausted upon the desk.

"It's all very well for you to turn down that fellow, Major, but I need another man to fill out my company," protests Captain Valentine, politely.

"And pursuant thereof to General Order thirty-four thousand oh—oh—six, we've got to have him today," responds McBray. "And let me tell you the next fellow comes in here better be a man."

Private Jessel has turned on the phonograph again. Going to the door he calls above the music: "Next man! Next man!" For a moment there is no response. Even the man who, the Private reports, has been walking up and down for an hour or more, continues to walk. But soon the music appears to get him and in he comes. He is Johnny Johnson.

Johnny is in smiling good humor. His new blue serge suit is all pressed for the occasion. A red poppy blooms in his lapel and a little United States flag is stuck in the band of his flat-topped straw hat. Johnny removes his hat and is prepared to shake hands with everybody.

Johnny—Well, folks, I've decided to do what Minny Belle said and enlist. Where's the paper I sign?

McBray—Come right in, sir, and make yourself at home.

Sergeant Jackson—We're tickled to death to see you.

JOHNNY—And I'm real glad to see you all. (*Turning toward the chair.*) I came here last night but the office was closed.

MCBRAY—Now ain't that too bad?

JOHNNY—Yes, sir. But if you don't succeed at first—you know. And so—since this is a war to end war, I'm in it a hundred percent strong.

MCBRAY—You are?

JOHNNY—You bet your tintype. But it's not against the common man I'm going to fight. No-siree. It's the German leaders. As Wilson says, drunk with military power and—

MCBRAY (*chortling*)—Good, good. (*Growling.*) Sit down. (*The two privates step forward and, lifting him suddenly from the floor, slam him down in the chair.* JOHNNY *looks up at them in pained surprise.*)

JOHNNY—Heigh, you fellows are kinder rough, ain't you?

MCBRAY (*chuckling in low malevolence*)—Don't mind them, son, it's just their little way.

JOHNNY (*sharply*)—Well, I don't like it.

SERGEANT JACKSON (*to the* CAPTAIN)—He don't like it.

CAPTAIN VALENTINE (*crooning*)—Says he don't like it, but he will—

JOHNNY—Still if that's the way you initiate folks into the army, then I suppose I'll have to stand it. It's all in the cause.

CAPTAIN VALENTINE (*languorous as always*)—And what cause is that, my friend?

JOHNNY—Why, democracy—world democracy—the biggest idea of modern times, including electricity. (*They all stare at him with some show of interest.* PRIVATE JESSEL *lifts a sort of tripod easel from the corner and sets it between* JOHNNY *and* MCBRAY *and slightly towards the rear, then stands waiting with his notebook in his hand.*)

MCBRAY (*in his barking manner again*)—What's your name?

JOHNNY—Johnny Johnson.

MCBRAY (*as* PRIVATE JESSEL *writes*)—Occupation?

JOHNNY—I'm an artist.

MCBRAY—Artist?

JOHNNY—At least that's what the Mayor called me. Artist in stone—I make tombstones—tombstones for both people and animals. You know we don't properly appreciate our pets. They are about the best friends man ever—

MCBRAY (*snapping*)—Place of birth?

JOHNNY—I don't know.

MCBRAY—Don't know?

JOHNNY—You see, my daddy and mammy were sort of worthless and wandered around all over—from one poorhouse to another. I don't know where I was born. I was dragged from pillar to post—

McBray (*to* Private Jessel)—Born—between pillar and post.

Johnny (*with a wide breaking laugh as he slaps his knee*)—Daggone my hide, that's good!

McBray—How old are you?

Johnny—Well, let me see.—According to the way my pappy figured it I ought to be about twenty-six come pumpkin time. He remembered there was a big frost on the ground—

McBray (*wagging his tired, shaggy head and speaking in a soft query to the* Captain)—My God, don't tell me he's crazy!

Captain Valentine (*bored*)—Let science decide it.

McBray (*loudly to* Private Jessel)—Army intelligence test number one—lowest grade. (Private Jessel *now throws back a wide sheet of paper from the easel and reveals the illustrated example in test number one.*)

Private Jessel—Look this way, Mr. Johnson. (Johnny *shifts himself around and stares at the easel. As* McBray *calls off the questions,* Private Jessel's *pencil points them out.*) First question—

McBray—Cats are useful animals because—one, they catch mice; two, they are gentle; and three, because they are afraid of dogs. (*Whirling on him.*) Quick, Mr. Johnson, which is correct—one, two or three?

Private Jessel (*looking at his wrist watch and counting off the seconds*)—One—two—three—four—

Sergeant Jackson and Captain Valentine (*in unison*)—Make it snappy, Mr. Johnson.

Johnny—Well, as a matter of fact, cats *ain't* useful. They're the worst pests in the world. Once I had a mocking-bird—

McBray (*controlling himself by grim will*)—Mr. Johnson, I want you to understand that we are trying to find out whether you've got sense enough to be a soldier.

Johnny—Sure I have. You ain't blind.

McBray (*loudly—as he strikes the table with his fist*)—Problem number two! (Private Jessel *turns another sheet.*) If you fell into a river and couldn't swim, would you—one, yell for help and try to scramble out; two, dive to the bottom and crawl out; or three, lie on your back and float until help came?

Johnny—How deep is the river?

Dr. McBray is ready to quit. Johnny is a little too much for him. These tests, prepared by the psychological experts of the

United States government, prove that he is either crazy or he isn't. At Captain Valentine's urging McBray tries another test: Why is wheat better for food than corn? That depends, according to Johnny. Mules like corn, Johnny prefers wheat and a hog'll eat anything—

The tattooed privates have started for Johnny, but he dodges them, protesting that he has come there to enlist and he doesn't intend to be turned down. He's just got to go and fight or Minny Belle won't ever speak to him again.

At a signal from McBray the privates have grabbed Johnny and thrown him through the door into the other room. A second later there is a hoarse cry from the room and one of the tattooed giants comes hurtling through the door into the office, followed by Johnny, carrying a torn blue serge coat.

"So you'd tear my blue serge, would you?" shouts Johnny. "Well, let me tell you I'm planning to get married in that coat—at least I was." A moan from the private on the floor inspires his sympathy. "I got a mighty hard fist from chiseling tombstones, and I didn't mean to hit you such a blow in the face," Johnny explains.

"Crazy or not crazy, he's our man!" announces Captain Valentine, with a courtly bow and a sweet smile, as the lights fade out.

"A LIGHT THAT LIGHTETH MEN THEIR WAY"

It is a few nights later. Looking across New York harbor the Statue of Liberty can be seen, the upper part of her figure bathed in flood lights. The shadow of a ghostly warship slips past, "its threatening guns stuck forward like the antennae of some strange primeval crustacean." The forward deck of a transport slides in through the dark. The sleeping forms of soldiers, "their pale upturned faces bathed in the radiance of the moon, and looking like recumbent figures on a great slow-moving catafalque," are to be seen on the deck.

Johnny Johnson stands by the rail, partly obscured by his hanging blanket. He is dressed in an army union suit, having just risen from sleep, and is staring "in dreamy and silent awe" at the faraway statue. Presently he begins to speak, softly—

> "Think of it—
> There you stand,
> Like a picture in that history book I read.
> Minny Belle said I'd see you so,

And now at last I have—
Your hand uplifted with a torch
Saying good-by to us,
Good luck and bless you every one.

"I swear that neither by a look, a thought, or word,
Will I fail either you or Minny Belle.
And I will keep my character clean
And come back as I went—
Without a smirch.
And furthermore I swear
That I will never see your light again
Until I've helped to bring back peace—
And win this war which ends all wars.

"And yet I'm not just sure
How it will come to pass,
But I will find a way,
And if the generals and the kings don't know
I'll show them how it's done,
For never yet has Johnny Johnson failed
To get an answer when he hunted for it.
I swear!
I swear!
And once an oath is made with me,
It's same as sealed and bound.
(*Murmuring*)
Farewell, Mother,
And peaceful be thy dreams."

His hand is still at salute as he sinks down upon the deck. "A murmurous groan seems to run among the sleepers; they turn in their hard beds and lie still again. Johnny's voice rises once more in falling drowsy syllables—"

"Starlight, star-bright—
Good-by, Minny Belle, my darling,
I sleep with your dear—picture—'gainst—my—heart."

The rail and the deck of sleeping soldiers has disappeared. In the dim distance the Statue remains silhouetted against the night, "lonely and aloof as she holds her beacon up, following with her sightless, stony stare the progress of the boat that carries Johnny Johnson out to sea." The curtain falls.

ACT II

"LEAD, KINDLY LIGHT"

Along a shadowy road somewhere in France, in the middle of the night, "a slow cortege of dark, twisted and anguished French soldiers is moving across the scene. These are the wounded men returning from the front."

As the French go slowly and painfully by, a file of American soldiers in full war gear, including gas masks, at the alert, come from the opposite direction. They are silhouetted against the brightening sky at the top of the road. These are the American troops coming into the front line trenches. Among them we recognize the form of Johnny Johnson. He has stopped for a little, watching the last of the French limp painfully away. Suddenly Johnny straightens and raises a clenched fist as though making another covenant.

"Lafayette, we are here!" he mutters, and starts running after his fellows. The lights fade.

"THERE IS ONE SPOT FOREVER ENGLAND"

It is an early autumn day in the front line trenches in France. Parapet and kneeling ledge zigzag across the scene. Over the parapet may be seen the tops of a few scattered and broken wooden crosses leaning awkwardly against the sky. On one cross a small bird is sitting. Corporal George and a squad of American soldiers have just taken over the trench from an English company, on its way out. The English are a bit fed up after waiting long for the big push, but the Yanks will get it, all right.

The whine of a bullet splits the air and ends in a plop in the soft dirt of the parapet. That's the calling card of a sniper who has been taking pot shots at the position for hours. Private Abie Goldberger digs the bullet out of the earth while it is still warm and puts it away as a souvenir. Private Goldberger, assumes Private Kearns, was a junkman at home.

A mixup of some character seems imminent between an English Sergeant and Private Pat O'Day of the Americans. They are of a mind to test again the superiority of race. The arrival of Johnny Johnson, staggering under a load that includes a huge bucket of steaming tea and a tow sack of biscuits, puts an end to that. It even sets the Sergeant singing:

"Now, England is, as we all know,
A great and mighty nation
With power big as half the world
And colonies galore.
Her army and her navy too
They quite befit her station,
The watchdogs of her flag unfurled
From Bath to Singapore. (*The English soldiers join in the chorus.*)
Then hail—hail—hail!
All hail Brittania and her crown!
We lift our cups to thee—
And drink thy health in bumpers down
Of tea, strong tea."

The chorus swells as the men drain their cups. Suddenly they are conscious of a faint echo of the song, though in a foreign tongue. The Heinies are answering them from the German trenches across No Man's Land.

"Last Christmas up here we were singing 'Holy Night,' and they done the same," reports the Sergeant, reminiscently.

"See there," cries Johnny, snapping his fingers as one who has found proof of a conviction, "good scouts like us, I been telling you."

"Well, good or bad, our business is to lick 'em."

The English have formed ranks and marched away, still singing the tea song chorus. It's like them to be leaving just as a good fight's coming on, according to O'Day. The American squad takes over, under Corporal George. The Corporal is a touchy lad, and given to riding Johnny, making sport of his homely expressions and his ideas for ending the war. Johnny takes the riding good-naturedly, though he is ready to fight if it gets too thick. . . .

Captain Valentine has drifted into the section. He is immaculately dressed as usual. He has come this time with an assignment. The company has orders to get that sniper—

"Right now he's more important to us than Hindenburg himself," admits the Captain. "He's got the provision train scared off of that road down there."

"I volunteer, sir," speaks up Johnny, at salute.

"That's very nice of you, Johnson, but you're too valuable a man to risk," answers the Captain. He takes a box of matches from his pocket and strikes one of them, reversing the ends of several others and holding them out to the men. "The fellow who draws the burnt match goes for the sniper at dawn."

"Can I draw, sir?" asks Johnson.

"Yes—last."

"I'm always lucky at such things," insists Johnny.

The others take their draws and the burnt match remains to the last. "I told you so," shouts Johnny.

"I'll say this for you, Johnson," smiles Captain Valentine, "whatever your drawbacks, cowardice is not one of them. . . . You can use your own judgment about the sniper."

The Captain has gone. All the men of the squad, save two, are settling down for the night. Private Fairfax is reading his Bible. Johnny has brought his old coat and spread it out close to the can of tea. Fairfax has fallen on his knees in an attitude of prayer.

"I'll tell you this, Johnson. If I were in your shoes I'd be praying, too."

"Human beings are funny, ain't they?" observes Johnny. "I was just think how the Germans are praying to the same God on their side too."

Soon they are all settled for the night save Private Harwood. Harwood is unwrapping his leggings and musing softly on the fact that back home in Texas the boys are just about rounding up the calves. The thought brings to mind a song, and he sings softly of the Rio Grande, where the wind blows free and the sun shines clear and bright. . . .

A foggy twilight creeps over the scene as Harwood lies down on the parapet. Gradually darkness settles. The men murmur in their sleep. "Far away, as if under the rim of the earth, the low growling of the mighty guns is heard."

In the half light the smiling, blissful face of Johnny Johnson may be seen. A faint recurrence of Minny Belle's love song is borne in on the breeze. "Minny Belle—my honey love," murmurs Johnny. The others are twisting and turning in the grip of an uneasy dream. "As if embodied forth by the restless sleepers' nightmare, the round muzzles of three great cannon push themselves slowly up over the parapet and then out and out until their long threatening necks stretch above the recumbent figures. Minny Belle's song has now died out and is supplanted by the growling croompy notes of the guns. They begin to sing in a queer outlandish trio harmony."

"Soldiers, soldiers—
Sleep softly now beneath the sky,
Soldiers, soldiers—
Tomorrow under earth you lie.
We are the guns that you have meant
For blood and death.—Our strength is spent
Obedient to your stern intent—
Soldiers, masters, men.

"Masters, masters,
Deep dark in earth as iron we slept,
Masters, masters,
Till at your word to light we leapt.
We might have served a better will—
Plows for the field, wheels for the mill,
But you decreed that we must kill—
Masters, soldiers, men."

"As the cannon song begins to die, the air is split by the musical tinkling of an alarm clock. As it continues to ring, the guns withdraw behind the parapet, their great muzzles slowly and sullenly sinking out of sight. The ringing of the clock stops, and Johnny sits up looking about him. Jerking his arms above his head, he yawns and gapes and then gets to his feet."

CORPORAL GEORGE (*mumbling*)—What time is it, Johnson?

JOHNNY (*looking up at the sky*)—About three-thirty—by the ell and the yard. Go on and get your sleep. (*He takes an old sock from his knapsack and begins to fit it over his face like a mask. Suddenly* PRIVATE FAIRFAX *lets out a scream, sits up and begins to beat wildly about him.*)

PRIVATE FAIRFAX—Catch him, catch him! (*The other soldiers sit up and beat at something in the trenches.*)

PRIVATE GOLDBERGER (*lunging off to the left*)—There he goes.

PRIVATE O'DAY—Whoo!—that bugger was big as a hog!

JOHNNY (*still working with his mask*)—Yeah, the rats get plenty to eat up here. I saw one yesterday squatted on a dead Australian's face. (*For a while they all sit in disconsolate silence.*)

CORPORAL GEORGE—What in the devil are you doing now, Johnson?

JOHNSON—Camouflage. (*Now pulling an old poncho over his shoulders, he picks up the bread knife and begins whetting it on his palm. Then he goes over to the parapet, pulls in part of the lariat and cuts it off. The soldiers stare at him.*)

CORPORAL GEORGE—Don't tell me you're going after that sniper without a gun.

JOHNNY—This piece of rope and bread knife ought to do.

PRIVATE GOLDBERGER—Do you know where he hangs out?

JOHNNY—I've got an idea.

PRIVATE KEARNS—He's got ideas. (PRIVATE SVENSON *clambers up and comes over to* JOHNNY.)

PRIVATE SVENSON (*grabbing his hand, his voice choked with emotion*)—Good-by, Yohnny. Be careful—uh— (*He gulps.*)

JOHNNY—I will, Slim. (*Jauntily.*) So long. I'll be back about sun-up. (*Stopping and calling back.*) Better have some breakfast for that sniper, he'll be hungry. (*He goes away.*)

PRIVATE SVENSON (*blubbering*)—He'll be killed!

CORPORAL GEORGE—I hope so. Go to sleep.

They all lie down again as the scene fades out.

"A NEW WAY TO PAY OLD DEBTS"

It is near dawn in a shell-battered churchyard. The grass is long, and at the back there stands a large wooden statue of the Christ, "leaning a bit awry and showing in its posture something of the beaten and agonized torture of an El Greco figure."

Johnny Johnson wriggles into the scene and conceals himself as well as he can in the rank grass. Presently, from the other side of the churchyard, the Sniper appears. He dodges behind gravestones and trees until he reaches the base of the statue. "He is a slender fellow with a rather large Kaiser Wilhelm mustache and an evil-looking helmet pulled low down over his forehead."

Convinced the way is clear the Sniper crawls up on the platform at the rear of the statue, opens a panel in the figure and lets himself in. As he worms his way into position the statue shakes and wriggles with his weight. "And now through a great wounded hole in the breast of Christ, where the heart should be, the ugly muzzle of a telescopic rifle with a silencer attached is pushed through." Soon a bullet has gone whinging on its way, and as the explosion subsides Johnny Johnson bounds forward, throws his rope around the statue and draws it tight. Immediately there is a great shaking and knocking inside the tottering wooden figure.

"Kamerad! Kamerad!" shouts the Sniper.

"Yeah, and I'll Kamerad you, you Proosian devil!" Johnny yells back. "Drop that gun! Drop it, I tell you! Pistol, too! You've got one!" Gun and pistol are shoved through the opening. "Come on out!"

Gingerly the Sniper crawls down. As he reaches the ground Johnny lays a knife against the back of his neck. "Ooh, um Gottes willen, tun Sie das nicht!" squeals the Sniper. Johnny cuffs him about the head.

"You dirty stinking rascal! I've a good mind to cut your throat," threatens Johnny. "Ain't you ashamed! Using Jesus Christ like that—and he a good man!" He gives him another slap.

"Du lieber Himmel!" gasps the Sniper. For which Johnny kicks him in the shins, exhibiting at the same time a hole in his helmet the Sniper had made the day before. "I ought to get me a switch and beat the lard out of you," says Johnny.

The Sniper is pleading piteously when Johnny discovers that he can speak English. Discovers, too, that without the mustache, which is stuck on, the German is only a beardless boy. A boy of sixteen, whose name is Johann Lang. His mother is living, too, and Johann would weep a little at the thought if Johnny didn't shut him up. He's in the war, Johann says, for Faterland and Kaiser—

"Nuts! As the monkey said!" exclaims Johnny with great impatience. "But never mind that— Don't you know it's for his own power and glory that the Kaiser sends such little boys as you out to die?" As the boy makes no answer—"Don't you believe that?"

"That's what Sergeant Mueller says," reports Johann with lowered voice. "But he only talks it among the soldiers—"

Sergeant Mueller, it appears, is Johann's English teacher. A kind and good man who hates the war. Which gives Johnny an idea. Suddenly he reaches out for Johann's hand. The boy pulls away. It isn't easy to convince him that Johnny has suddenly become friendly.

"But the generals tell us you Americans cut and kill and scalp and chop the German soldiers to pieces with knives," reports Johann. "Yes, sir, they all do—the generals and the colonels in their speeches—the newspapers, too. But Herr Mueller says he don't believe it—to us he says so. He says he thinks you soldiers are like us—in the heart good. But he don't know—he think so."

Johnny's idea continues to expand. He thinks perhaps he and the Miller fellow ought to get together on the war. Suppose Miller knew—

Johnny—Suppose he knew that we Americans deep down are the German people's friends—what do you think he'd want to do?

JOHANN—Stop fighting.

JOHNNY—He's a sensible man. (*Dumping some letters and folded papers from his pockets, he suddenly begins writing with a stub of a pencil, reading off some of the words as he does so.*) "Friend Miller, John Lang who brings this letter to you was captured by me, but I am sending him back—"

JOHANN (*with a cry*)—You let me go! (*He springs forward and hugs* JOHNNY'S *knees and then lies weeping on the ground, one of his hands touching* JOHNNY'S *foot.*)

JOHNNY (*smiling*)—Yeah, that's right— (*Looking around toward the flaming horizon.*) and we got to hurry. (*Reading aloud again as he writes.*) "—Sending him back with these messages—um—um— See the enclosed speeches of Woodrow Wilson, also some by me which come quicker to the point. You and me have the same ideas about being friends and ending this war. John will tell you more. I must close on account of the sun coming up— Yours in friendship, Johnny Johnson, Private soldier." (*Touching* JOHANN *on the shoulder.*) Get up, son. (JOHANN *rises and stands wiping the tears of happiness from his eyes.*)

JOHANN—You—you really let me go?

JOHNNY (*shoving several papers in an envelope and sticking them into* JOHANN'S *pocket.*)—I'm sending you back, son, and I hope we end the war before it ends you.

JOHANN (*grabbing his hand and kissing it with wild joy*)—Forgive me—the Colonel, he made me do it—

JOHNNY (*pulling his hand sheepishly away*)—Do what?

JOHANN (*with a gesture towards the figure of Christ*)—Hide in there and shoot at you Americans. All the time after this I shoot in the air.

JOHNNY (*quickly*)—That's the idea. Tell friend Miller to spread the news among his soldiers—his friends—make copies of the speeches, distribute them everywhere. You'll hear from me again—somehow. Now quick—run—we're going to save a lot of lives. (*He pushes him along.* JOHANN *grabs* JOHNNY'S *hand once more, then embraces him and dashes away.* JOHNNY *stares after him, waves his hand, and then picks up the rifle and the pistol and stands looking at the statue of Christ. He pulls off his helmet in humility and respect.* CAPTAIN VALENTINE *comes crawling in on his all-fours at the right. He is humming softly to himself.* JOHNNY *gives a last look at the statue, gazes at the rifle and pistol in his hands, then shrugs his shoulders in a vague comment on the world and comes toward the front.* CAPTAIN VALENTINE *calls out in a low admiring voice.*)

CAPTAIN VALENTINE—You killed him!

JOHNNY (*in good humor*)—No.

CAPTAIN VALENTINE (*standing quickly up*)—What! (*Looking off and then jerking out his pistol.*) Yonder—look out! (*Raging.*) Oh, you fool!

JOHNNY (*springing in front of him*)—Don't you shoot him! (CAPTAIN VALENTINE *tries to dodge this way and that around* JOHNNY, *and finally gets in a shot over his shoulder.*)

CAPTAIN VALENTINE (*raising his pistol as if to strike* JOHNNY *with the butt of it*)—I missed him. (*Suddenly a burst of machine gun fire rattles out from the direction of the German trenches. The air is filled with a medley of whinging sounds and the plop of bullets striking against the earth. The* CAPTAIN *throws himself flat on his belly.* JOHNNY *darts forward to drop down beside him, then suddenly slaps his hand to his rump with a howl.* CAPTAIN VALENTINE *laughs hysterically as* JOHNNY *sprawls down by him.*) Ha-Ha-Ha, got you, did they? There is a just God after all!

JOHNNY (*half-sobbing with anger and vexation, one hand still on his rump*)—Ain't that a hell of a place to get shot!

The Captain starts crawling off, Johnny crawling painfully after him. The lights fade.

" 'TIS NOT SO DEEP AS A WELL—BUT 'TIS ENOUGH, 'TWILL SERVE"

Johnny is in a hospital. At the moment he is lying on his side, listening to a young and attractive French nurse sing about Madelon of Paree who would do all she could to cheer the weary soldier back from the war. Even though she has lost her true love in the fighting, Madelon does not sit and grieve, but sings away her sorrow to cheer the soldier's leave—

"For life is short and funny,
And love must have an end.
An hour may be forever—
Oh—mon ami, my friend."

Johnny is not greatly interested in either the nurse or her song. He is more interested in getting out of there. Next to that he'd like another letter from Minny Belle. How can he love his nurse, even a little, when he is an engaged man? The nurse should know that, seeing he has read her Minny Belle's letter telling how she is praying for him and how Anguish is standing by. The Nurse doesn't like Anguish. Neither, agrees Johnny, does anybody else, certainly not Minny Belle. But there is nothing to do about that. . . .

The Doctor has arrived, wearing his goatee and carrying a black satchel. He is followed by an orderly carrying a small fifteen-inch tank of laughing gas. They think Johnny had better have a whiff, but Johnny won't take it. Let them go ahead and dress his wound and tell him how soon he can get back to his work in the trenches. They are attending to the dressing back of a screen when a lady leader of the Organization for the Delight of Disabled Soldiers appears. "She is a tall, rawboned, breezy woman of middle-age, over-dressed and slightly over-enthusiastic in her manner."

The visitor is arranging for a show in the hospital, which at present is accommodating four thousand wounded men, and more expected after the big battle. She would also say a cheering word to Johnny, but a peek back of the screen convinces her that Johnny must be a coward, else he could not have been shot where he was. . . .

The Doctor is enthused at the prospect of entertainment. He sends his orderly to notify the colonel with such haste that the orderly forgets the tank of laughing gas. Johnny is fooling with the tank and bewailing his idleness and the coming battle when the entertainment sister repeats her charge that he is a coward. The lady, suggests Johnny, is full of prunes. It makes him boil to think of all the fools that are running the world. Can't somebody do something to put off this fight?

"This is the most opportune time," explains the Doctor, as he turns to the sister. "From yesterday's prisoners we learn that a spirit of rebellion has begun to spread among the German soldiers."

"What! Say that again!" Johnny is half out of bed.

"And we must strike while the iron is hot," the Doctor continues.

"Hooray! Hooray! It's working," shouts Johnny, wildly. "Good for you, Sergeant Miller!" He gazes out at them in happy innocence. "He's a German friend of mine on the other side—thinks the same way I do. He and Johann."

"Not only a coward, but a—traitor!" sneers the sister, glaring at Johnny.

The next minute Johnny has pressed the control lever of the gas tank and given the sister a sprinkle right in the face. One whiff and a vacant look passes across her face. "With a low, infectious gurgle of fun" she emits a sudden whoop—

"I feel good!" she shouts. "I love everybody! I love you, my brave suffering hero."

Now she has grabbed Johnny and begun to manhandle him in an affectionate embrace. The Doctor and the Nurse finally pull her off Johnny. "I feel wonderful! I feel like flying!" the sister yells, grabbing the Doctor. "Come on, Doctor, the show's ready to start."

"Young man, I'll attend to you later!" The sister has pulled the protesting Doctor into the corridor. Johnny and the Nurse sit staring after them. Then Johnny has another idea.

"You see what happened? One minute she wanted to shoot me and the next minute eat me with love. Wonderful stuff this laughing gas. . . . Pity they don't use laughing gas in the war instead of poison gas." He snaps his fingers as the idea takes form. "Bring me my britches."

The Nurse will not let Johnny go. She tries to push him back in the bed. Johnny would protest, but sees it is no use. Now he becomes gentle and lets the Nurse pull up the covers and tuck him in. She kisses him on the forehead as she says good-night, and blows him a kiss from the doorway.

Now she has gone. Johnny cautiously throws aside the covers and gets his feet on the floor. As he does so the gas tank falls to the floor. He picks it up gingerly—

"Guess I'd better take you along—might meet another fool," he mumbles as he crawls out, pajamas and all, and through the open window at the right. The lights fade.

"IN THE MULTITUDE OF COUNSELORS THERE IS SAFETY"

The Allied High Command is meeting in the Château de Cent Fontaines somewhere back of the line in France. It is a magnificent hall, trimmed largely in glass and red plush, and there is a wide stairway of marble-columned stairs at the back.

Sitting around a long table in the middle of the room, to the right and left of the Chief of the Combined Allied Forces, who bears a striking resemblance to Marshal Foch, are the Commander of the American Expeditionary Forces, the Commander-in-Chief of the British Expeditionary Forces, a British Major-General, a French Major-General, two distinguished gentlemen in civilian garb at either end of the table, and a lonely figure in uniform. All these might easily be mistaken for officers and persons prominent in the war—General Pershing, Marshal Haig, General Rawlinson, General Petain, Lloyd George, Clemenceau and Alfred, King of the Belgians.

Standing in the rear is a group of Allied officers in resplendent uniforms and wearing all their medals and decorations. On the table is a huge war map which the three military leaders are studying. Presently the Chief of the High Command speaks, theoretically moving his forces about on the war map as he seeks confirmation of the plan from the various leaders present. The Flanders group of armies will march toward Brussels, announces the Chief. The Belgians agree. The British army's mission will be to hurl the invaders back toward Froidchapelle and Philippeville. The British Commander murmurs a characteristic "Ha-ha—quite so!" The American forces will move south, co-operating with the French armies and maneuvering with both wings to catch the Boches by surprise. The American Commander nods his head "in slothful agreement."

Now the chief has duly stamped the orders, as the others nod in agreement, and rises to address the assembly—

"And so, Messieurs,
The disposition of the Allied arms
Is—all—arranged,
And each man knows his task,
N'est-ce pas?
And now the saddest subject possible—
The necessary loss of life
In this oncoming drive—
Are we prepared to suffer it—
As we have done so many times before?"

There is a murmur of "Oui!" "We are!" Then the Chief proceeds to check the losses that may be counted on. He begins with the King, who passes the inquiry on to his Major-General.

BELGIAN MAJOR-GENERAL (*in a crisp mathematical voice*)—
The rivers, mud, concrete and wire,
Which Belgium's sons must struggle through
Force us to allow for heavy loss—
Some thirty thousand dead perhaps,
Some hundred and ten thousand wounded too.

CHIEF (*stamping an order with his seal*)—Your excellency of the British Isles? (*The* BRITISH COMMANDER *leans towards the* ENGLISH MAJOR-GENERAL, *who turns once more and looks to the left at the* ENGLISH BRIGADIER-GENERAL.)

BRIGADIER-GENERAL—More than a hundred thousand killed
And thrice as many wounded, sir.

CHIEF (*hollowly*)—Vive, vive!
Proud England's glory never shall grow dim
The while her sons can die so easily. (*Once more he stamps an order.*)

BELGIAN MAJOR-GENERAL—But Belgium, sir, is such a little land,
So tiny and so small— (*Beginning to figure on a piece of paper.*)
But tiny though she is, who knows?
We may enlarge that figure some—to say—
Er—fifty thousand dead.

CHIEF—Bravo!

OTHERS—Bravo!

CHIEF (*to the* FRENCH MAJOR-GENERAL)—Et vous, mon cher *brave camarade?*

FRENCH MAJOR-GENERAL (*rising and glancing about him*)—We bow before the mighty English nation.
(*Pounding the table.*) If we lose more than eighty thousand dead
Revolt will spread and anarchy break out in France!

CHIEF (*stamping another order with a bang*)—Vraiment!

FRENCH PREMIER (*standing up, his white mustache quivering*)—Non, non, I say and still say non!
If England gives her hundred thousand dead,
La Belle France, my native France,
Can give her hundred thousand so the same. (*He collapses suddenly in his chair.*)

VOICES—Vive la France!

FRENCH MAJOR-GENERAL—But England has more men to lose—
(*Loudly.*) —and why?— (*Now on his feet again.*)
Because the sons of France fell with their guns
The while the English let them fall—
At Ypres, Vimy Ridge and Mons they did.

ENGLISH PREMIER (*springing up*)—The English soldiers are no fools.
They know well when to die—
Unlike the French who at Verdun
Lost half a million wasteful dead—
Perhaps a million if the truth were known. (*And now the French and Belgian staff officers are on their feet and the* FRENCH PREMIER *sputters like a fire cracker in his chair.*)

OFFICERS—We protest!

BRITISH PREMIER—I see that's still a hornet's nest—

So let it lie—
I only wanted to make clear my point,
And no offense was meant.

CHIEF (*banging table with baton*)—As allies in a sacred cause
I ask you to forget what's past—
Please have no worry, mes amis,
The course of tactics and control
Is safely in French hands.
Be seated.
(*To the* AMERICAN COMMANDER.) Your estimated losses, sir?

AMERICAN COMMANDER (*curtly*)—Very few, I hope.
It seems we have right many trees
Along the sector where we fight—
I don't expect so many killed—
I say expect. (*The generals and officers look at him in querying displeasure.*)
There's nothing better than a tree
Between you and machine gun fire—
Especially if it's big.

CHIEF (*airily*)—Much so the poor benighted Indians used to fight.
Where are they now? (*With a shrug.*)

AMERICAN COMMANDER—I hear they're living peaceful in the West
And doing well with copper mines and oil.

The Chief has brought them all to their feet to "salute the coming of the early dawn that marks the zero hour of doom, the end of Germany!"

They are just about to adjourn for breakfast, when who should appear at the head of the stairway but Johnny Johnson. He is still in his pajamas, now muddy-legged, and under his arm he carries the gas tank wrapped in a hospital sheet. Cheerfully he calls to them, asking that they do not break up just yet.

The Command stands somewhat astounded at this appearance. The American Commander recognizes his fellow countryman from his accent and would save him from arrest, as ordered by the Chief. The American would have Johnny leave the room before it is decided to hang him. Johnny, however, does not want to leave. He has come to help them end the war. He has been in communication with the German soldiers, he tells them, and they, too, are about ready to quit. A rebellion is spreading!

"Yes, sir, I got direct news from the German sniper I captured," boasts Johnny. "He said the common soldiers wanted to be friends with us, and I sent him back with all kinds of messages saying we wanted to be friends too. And I tell you it's beginning to work. They're rebelling against their German war lords—already. What we got to do now is get millions of articles and speeches printed and—"

"Is your name by any chance—Johnson—Johnny Johnson?"

"Yes, sir, that's me, and you never did answer my letters," admits Johnny with a pleased grin.

"There's nothing to fear, gentlemen, he's harmless."

"The meeting is adjourned," thunders the Chief.

"But it's the truth, the truth I'm telling you," protests Johnny, springing frantically toward them. "You've got to hold up this battle. I'll make my way into the German lines—I'll prove it—I'll do anything! You and the other generals can sign an order right now stopping the offensive. Then we get busy with prop—propaganda—words—words.—Yessir, they're a lot more powerful than bullets if you speak them at the right time. And this is the right time. For the more the Germans read, the more they'll see the truth of what we say. And right now when they're worn out and sick of war they'll be glad to come to terms, and there won't be a dozen people killed."

The Chief would turn the staff officers upon Johnny, but as they approach Johnny faces them threateningly with his gas tank. They think it a bomb and back cautiously away. In no time at all they are plainly subdued and Johnny takes advantage of the situation to get over his point—

"Now then maybe you'll listen to me," he shouts. "I was standing there listening to you all right and you were speaking of a pile of dead men in tomorrow's battle higher'n that big tower in Paris—poor dumb guys like me you're sending out to die—to be blown to pieces! (*With sudden rage.*) All right, suppose I blow you to pieces with this—er—bomb."

The King of the Belgians has started forward but Johnny quickly orders him into his chair and the King collapses, calling piteously for his Gendarmes. All the others sink into their chairs, too, all except the American, who never takes his eyes off Johnny.

"So here you sit on your hind ends holy as God and make your plans," yells Johnny; "marking up your thousands of dead and dying like cold figures on a blackboard. Know what that means? I ask you—know what it means?—all these boys—young fellows like me—like what you used to be—going out to die—shot down—killed—murdered—to lie dead and stiff and rotten in a trench with rats and mud? We were meant for something better, I tell you. (*Vehemently.*) We want to live, and you could let us live! We want to be let alone to do our work in peace—to have our homes—to raise our families— We want to look back someday and say our life has meant something—we have been happy and it was good to be born into this world. (*Pleadingly to* AMERICAN COMMANDER *who has approached close to him.*) You see what I mean, don't you—don't you? (*More quietly as he controls the trembling in his voice.*) When you come right down to it, what sense is there in human beings trying to cut and tear and destroy one another like wild beasts in a jungle? There's no sense in it, is there? Is there! (*Stretching out his hands to all of them.*) You're our leaders—you're all-powerful over us—you tell us to die for freedom or a flag or our country or whatever crazy ideal it is—and we have to die. (*Half-sobbing as they look at him with cold authority-set faces.*) You'd rather live too, hadn't you? You'd rather be at home with your wives and children, hadn't you—living in peace the way men are meant to live? Then end this killing—end it now— (*Brokenly.*) Only a second's time—a movement of your hand—a written word—and you could stop this war. Do it! Do it! (*Staring at them aghast as they look at him with dull baleful eyes.*) But you don't listen. That Englishman was right. You don't want to end this war. (*A queer baffled grieving in his voice.*) There's something black and evil got into you—something blinded you—something—"

The American Commander, motioning to the others, closes in on Johnny. As they do Johnny quickly unscrews the tank of gas and begins shooting it at them. The expression of their faces suddenly changes. They begin to grimace queerly and to laugh loudly. The Generals at the back are stunned for a moment, but now they join the attack, only to be swept back in turn by Johnny and his gas tank.

"Ho—ho—ho!" shrieks the King of the Belgians.

"Whoops!—Wonnerful!—Merveilleux!" echo his dancing colleagues.

The American Commander has broken into a perfect roar of laughter. To the music of a lively tune that is floating in, the Polish Colonel dances a polonaise, the Scotch Colonel breaks into a hornpipe. The officers in the rear line are variously contributing waltzes, minuets and a little tap dancing. The British and French Premiers have locked arms and are swinging in an old-fashioned country dance. It is all quite wild. Soon the Frenchmen are kissing the Americans, and frequently vice versa. Now they have all joined hands and are circling the room, laughing and singing.

In one sweep of the circle the American Commander has drawn Johnny Johnson into the dance. A moment later he has put his own greatcoat around Johnny, his cap on his head, and saluted him as "General Johnny Johnson!"

"What can we do for you, General?" inquires the Chief, at salute.

"Stop this war!" shouts Johnny.

AMERICAN COMMANDER—Just as you say, General. Tee-hee-hee—so you want this fighting stopped? (*Turning around and calling to everybody.*) General Johnson's right. This war is foolish, there's nothing to it but blood and murder.

VOICES—War is foolish! Let's stop it!

AMERICAN COMMANDER (*embracing the* CHIEF)—Old boy, we're going to stop this war. What you say?

CHIEF (*clapping his hands*)—Stop the war! (*A great burst of applause and cheering follows.*)

AMERICAN COMMANDER—We'll sign the order right now. (*He hurries over to the table, writes something, signs it and hands the pen to the* CHIEF *who also signs and stamps it. Then he gives the paper to* JOHNNY, *and calls out in a loud voice.*) Silence! (*The laughter dies down once more to suppressed giggles.*) We have signed an order stopping the offensive! General Johnson, see that it is carried out!

THE ASSEMBLY—Vive—Hooray—Hip, Hip—Johnny Johnson! (*And now the orchestra resumes playing. The officers lift* JOHNNY *on their shoulders and march around the room, then place him on the table and stand applauding him.*)

VOICES—Speech, speech!

JOHNNY (*blinking and passing his hand across his forehead as if to clear his mind*)—There's not much to say, friends. Now that we're going to stop the war, we'll all be home in time for Christmas to see old Santa Claus. Ain't that fine?

VOICES—Christmas! Christmas! Merry Christmas! (*And now they all start marching around the table again and singing, with the exception of* JOHNNY, *who hops down and disappears up the stairs the way he came.*)

ALL (*singing as in a round*)—We'll all be home for Christmas—a merry, merry Christmas! (*A moment passes while the singing continues. The orchestra rises to a loud fortissimo and suddenly stops. Gradually the noise subsides, the generals and the others sink down in their seats and gaze about them in amazement. The* AMERICAN COMMANDER *looks at the* CHIEF'S *scattered and wind-blown hair and the* CHIEF *looks at his disarray.*)

CHIEF (*in a hollow dazed voice*)—What time is it?

AMERICAN COMMANDER (*staring at his wrist watch*)—Ten minutes till five.

CHIEF (*with a cry*)—The offensive!

AMERICAN COMMANDER (*springing out of his chair with a yell*) —My God!—We gave him an order stopping the offensive! Catch that man!

The American Commander and the Chief tear out through the door followed by the mad scramble of the others as the lights fade out.

"STILL STANDS THINE ANCIENT SACRIFICE"

It is near dawn. In a small dugout "opening into a raised eye-brow of the earth," are two liaison officers, a Captain, talking into a field telephone, and a young lieutenant checking the orders in a book. It is nearing the zero hour. The Captain's relayed orders dispose of the various units. In three minutes more they will be going over the top all the way from Calais to Sedan.

"May heaven help our enemies in such an hour," the Captain murmurs.

"Check—and help us all!" agrees the Lieutenant.

Suddenly from some distance up the line there is a ringing command of "Attenshun!" A second later it is repeated nearer. It continues coming nearer and nearer until it is at hand and Johnny Johnson, wrapped in the American Commander's overcoat and hat, enters the dugout. The Captain and the Lieutenant spring to their feet and stand at salute. They are surprised and worried to see their General thus exposed to danger, but their General isn't worried. He has come to learn if they are in touch with the different commanders.

They are in touch, the Captain reports, and there remain but two minutes before the barrage will begin—

"There will be no barrage—no bombardment either," General Johnson reports. "The war is called off."

"What!"

"Suspended until further orders— In the name of the Allied High Command."

Johnny produces the orders. The Captain reads. The Lieutenant murmurs a hearty "Thank God!" and goes into a dance that includes a pause while he kisses Johnny's hand and embraces his Captain.

"Quick—get the news on the wire!" orders Johnny.

Now the Captain is sputtering the order of cancellation into the field phone. "General offensive will not take place. Indefinite suspension of hostilities!" The Lieutenant is asking for orders to send up flares. "Send 'em up! Send 'em up!" shouts Johnny.

Now there is a great burst of music. The lights black out for a moment. When light returns, Johnny is at the top of the parapet waving his sheet in the air. From far down the line a sound of cheering is heard. It grows in volume. In the flares of light glimpses of No Man's Land may be seen. Soldiers are shouting across—

"Hooray, the war is over! War is over! Heigh, Heinie, where are you?"

"Come on out, you boys! We've quit fighting!"

"Kommt d'raus! Kein Krieg mehr!"

Presently the figures of several Germans, muddy and begrimed, can be seen coming across to meet the Americans. Now they are shaking hands, slapping each other on the back, yelling, singing, dancing, embracing each other affectionately, weeping with happiness.

The blast of a siren is heard. The Captain and the Lieutenant are struck dumb. Johnny Johnson pays no attention. He is out of the dugout and fraternizing with the Germans. Now three or four excited brigadier-generals and colonels rush in. Their pistols are drawn and their first command is directed at Johnny Johnson—

"Catch that man!"

"Get back to headquarters, you fellows, or I'll slap you under arrest," shouts Johnny.

SECOND BRIGADIER (*raising his pistol*)—Spy! Spy! Kill him!

LIEUTENANT (*stepping in front of him*)—My God, would you shoot the Commander-in-Chief? (*The soldiers spring protectingly around* JOHNNY.)

SECOND BRIGADIER—Commander-in-Chief!

JOHNNY (*pushing his way through the soldiers and turning towards them*)—Boys, do you want to stop this war?

SOLDIERS (*with some of the Germans crying, "Ja, Ja!"*)—Yes, General, great God, we say so! End it right now. And let's go home. Home—let's go home.

COLONEL (*springing suddenly over, jerking* JOHNNY'S *coat from him, another officer knocking off his cap*)—Look at him! (*The soldiers stare at him in silent astonishment.*)

FIRST BRIGADIER (*to the liaison* CAPTAIN)—Command the offensive to begin at once! (*He sticks an order into his hand. The* CAPTAIN *stares at the order, then springs to the telephone and begins cranking.* JOHNNY *whirls about as the officers and soldiers start towards him, jumps down into the trench and disappears. The* FIRST BRIGADIER *yells to the soldiers.*) Back into your trenches! The battle is beginning! (*The American soldiers look helplessly about. Both brigadiers now have their pistols drawn.*)

SECOND BRIGADIER—At "three" we fire. One—two— (*He raises his pistol. The American soldiers jump down into the trenches.*)

CAPTAIN (*at the telephone*)—G-O-eight-four-three-two-one canceled. Forged orders. Work of spies.

LIEUTENANT (*now weeping as he squats with his pad and pencil*)—Check. (*The German soldiers at the back turn and flee toward their trenches. But some of them never reach there, for the American machine guns now begin their rat-tat-tat-tat-tat-tat, and they are seen falling. The* CAPTAIN *continues yelling into the telephone.*)

CAPTAIN—At once! At once! (*As he looks at his watch.*) It is now exactly hours—0510— Open fire!—Fire! (*Somewhere far away and as if beneath the earth, a great gun is fired. There is an instant of pause, and then the battle begins, with the music in the orchestra portraying its fury and violence. The lights fade.*)

"THERE'S MANY A MANGLED BODY, A BLANKET FOR THEIR SHROUD"

It is dark. Somewhere an organ is playing the stately chant music of a church prayer. From afar come the heavy reverberations of battle. By the light of bursting shells different incidents of the carnage can be picked out. In one corner of the field a German priest stands above a praying flock. In another an American priest is similarly employed. Both are reading the prayer "In Time of War and Tumults"—one in German, the other in English. "Almighty God, the supreme Governor of all things—" Their intoning fills in the pauses between the deafening assaults of the guns.

Another flash reveals two squads of horrible creatures in gas masks fighting hand to hand. Another, a German and American tearing with bare hands at each other's throat. Another, a squad of Germans holding up their hands in surrender, an American machine gunner mowing them down. Another, a squad of American soldiers holding up their hands in surrender, while a German machine gunner mows them down.

Johnny Johnson is running wildly around No Man's Land, his pajamas all but shot off him. A German is praying at the foot of the figure of Christ. An American soldier runs him through with a bayonet. Johnny Johnson is holding the head of the dying German in his lap as the lights fade out.

"DULCE ET DECORUM EST PRO PATRIA MORI"

As dawn breaks over No Man's Land dozens of dead bodies are to be discovered in the feeble light. The figure of Christ in the background is torn and mutilated. At the edge of a shell hole Johnny Johnson is sitting. The head of a young German is resting in his lap. It is Johann Lang, the sniper. For a moment Johnny stares at the white face. Then he tenderly moves the helmet off the forehead and lays a hand upon the German's brow.

"Feel better now?"

There is no reply. Johnny bends closer, puts his hand on the soldier's mouth. For a moment he sits back and stares blankly ahead of him. When he speaks "his voice rises through his burnt, swollen lips in a hoarse broken monologue—"

"Two hundred thousand dead, five hundred thousand dead, a million dead.—And they have had their way, Johann. And all for what? And why? What for? (*Wagging his head.*) Nobody knows—nobody!"

The voice of a stricken man is heard. "Mother! Mother!" it calls, piteously.

"He'll quit calling soon, he'll quit calling and lie still—like you, Johann, lie still," mutters Johnny. "And they killed you. I saw it happen. One of my own squad did it. He stuck a bayonet through you. (*Gasping.*) I had the war stopped once. Maybe there's no sense in that. They said so. But you wouldn't say so —no, you wouldn't, would you? (*Stretching out his hands over the still figure with a loud cry.*) Would you?"

Out of the darkness two tall military police appear. Their hands are on their pistols. They approach Johnny Johnson cautiously.

"Are you Johnny Johnson?"

"He's dead," answers Johnny without looking around.

"Are you Johnny Johnson?"

Johnny's head sags on his breast.

"In the name of the armies of Europe and America we arrest you!" one soldier says. The lights fade.

"HAIL, MARY, FULL OF GRACE"

The Statue of Liberty is shrouded in shadow when the home-coming army sails up New York harbor. Liberty stands solemnly against the evening sky as the great gray warship that had passed out of the harbor months before now passes in, followed by the transport with Johnny Johnson and his fellows aboard.

"Johnny is sitting at the rail with his back to the Statue. A uniformed guard is standing at his side. The Guard salutes and then touches Johnny on the shoulder and points to the Statue. But Johnny keeps staring ahead of him. The rail and the deck pass out at the right and disappear into a great engulfing shadow without stopping."

The curtain falls.

ACT III

"IS THERE NO BALM IN GILEAD? IS THERE NO PHYSICIAN THERE?"

This is the psychiatrist's office in a State Hospital. There is a large, flat-topped table, cut slightly on the bias, if you see it that way; one or two cock-eyed chairs and several filing cabinets. These give the room a definite futuristic touch.

Dr. Mahodan, "a melancholy, middle-aged man," is in charge here. He is discovered going through a variety of reports and clippings. A call to the telephone irritates him. He listens briefly and then, with an angry: "You're crazy!" slams down the receiver. Perhaps to compose his nerves the Doctor begins presently to sing—

"Back in the ages primitive
When souls with devils were possess't,
The witch man came and did his best
With yell and blow and expletive
  And loudly beaten drum.
And up and down and round about
He whirled with fearful fetish rout
  And wild delirium.
But rarely did the patient live
Back in the ages primitive.

"Today psychologists agree
The insane man is only sick,
The problem is psy-chi-a-trick,
See Jung and Adler, Freud and me,
  And we will analyze.
And though it hurts, we probe the ruts
Of mental pain that drives men nuts
  And heal their lunacies.
And from the devils being free,
They all take up Psychiatry."

Dr. Mahodan is expecting Johnny Johnson. A hard case, the Doctor observes to the nurse. "Only once in a generation does such a diseased personality occur. According to his record, he appears to be one of those naturals born into the world at rare intervals. You may recall my monograph on Jesus, the rural prophet and will-less egocentric? Same type. Same type."

Johnny is still under guard when he arrives. His oversized army uniform has been cleaned, but otherwise he looks the same. He has a ready and simple answer for each of the Doctor's questions. His chief concern is Minny Belle. He had written her that he was back, and has been expecting she would come to see him.

The Doctor continues his examination. Johnny admits that he is the man who stopped the war, even if they wouldn't let it stay stopped. As for his experiences, Johnny had none. He didn't even fire his gun once.

"The superman complex through the technique of humility," the Doctor decides, but doesn't put it in the record. . . .

When Minny Belle arrives she is wearing a cute hat and a little blue coat suit and looks adorable. Johnny's eyes fill with tears at sight of her. He grabs her to him, hugs her close and kisses her reverently upon the brow. Minny Belle is a little embarrassed, but Johnny assures her that it is all right. Everybody knows they're engaged. Still Minny Belle is shy. She wonders, too, why Johnny is home before the war is over, and is plainly disappointed when he admits that he had not killed a single German.

It will not be possible for Johnny to go home with her, Dr. Mahodan explains to Minny Belle a moment later, after he has sent Johnny out of the room. The psychological experts of the United States Army have pronounced him a mental case and he will have to stay where he is for a time.

At which juncture the door at the rear is pushed open suddenly and Johnny reappears, followed by the orderlies. His uniform coat has been replaced by the blue denim blouse of an inmate. He is wild with anger. He proposes to leave immediately with Minny Belle, and resentment mounts when Anguish Howington appears to place a protecting arm around Minny Belle's shoulders.

"They're going to keep Johnny here, Anguish," sobs Minny Belle.

"Well, an asylum is where he belongs," says Anguish.

"An asylum!" Johnny is ready to fight Anguish. "Take your hand off her arm!"

Anguish backs away and the orderlies close in. Johnny turns to Minny Belle, pleadingly.

"They think I'm crazy. They're going to shut me up. You can't—you can't think—"

Anguish has led the sobbing Minny Belle away. Johnny stands staring at the floor like a man in a dream. Dr. Mahodan lays a kindly hand on his shoulder—

"I think you'll make a very interesting patient, Mr.—er—Mr. Mahodan," he says, as the lights fade out.

"OUT OF THE MOUTHS OF BABES AND SUCKLINGS"

It is ten years later. In a club room containing several rows of chairs and a small speaker's stand a variety of aging men are gathered. This, by the placard over a beflagged picture of Woodrow Wilson above the speaker's stand, is the "Adelphi Debating Society." The aging gentlemen resemble the ordinary type of American business men.

Brother Thomas, "a man who resembles a certain late vice-president of the United States," has the seat on the rostrum. Johnny Johnson, gray at the temples, wearing an old collarless white shirt and a dark sack suit too large for him, is seated below the rostrum. In his hand he holds a wooden toy, which he is painting.

Brother Thomas leads the brethren through the closing verses of a song proclaiming the brotherly love of the society and its feeling of good will for all the world. There are Hurrahs for the President of the United States, led by a bearded Dr. Frewd. Some of the brothers, though strong for the Hurrahs, are a little confused as to the Presidency. They insist Johnny Johnson is President. And if he isn't he should be. But Johnny, with a gentle firmness, declines the nomination.

When the roll is called it is discovered that Brother Henry, the gentleman from Massachusetts, is absent. He is, it appears, working on a speech. Brother Thomas has just called Brother Theodore, who is present with a big stick, and instructed the Secretary to proceed with the minutes of the last meeting, when Brother Henry arrives with the speech finished. It is a speech in opposition to the Society's endorsement of the League of World Republics—

"This infamous League cuts at the very base of our democratic institutions," shouts Brother Henry. "I am first and foremost an American. I love the American flag, a flag devoted to the principles of liberty and the pursuit of happiness—"

"And in this asylum we're all happy," shouts a brother.

"Not only did the great Washington tell us to keep ourselves aloof and inviolable in the service of—"

"Liberty—"

"I challenge these interruptions," explodes Brother Henry.

For a moment there is quiet, but not for long. Brother Henry has barely stated his conviction that if this country should become involved in responsibility "for any and every unimportant quarrel in Europe, we would find our strength wasted and the great principles of—" when his voice fails and he is forced to sit down.

There are excited calls for another vote. The society has already adopted the covenant of the World Republics, but a few of the brothers would like to adopt it again. Brother Thomas takes the floor—

THOMAS—Brethren, it is obvious that a majority of people everywhere want some sort of world co-operation which will bring peace and happiness to mankind—in place of wars and misery which we have had so long.

VOICES—Hear, hear!

THOMAS—The disorganized nations of the earth—frightened, suspicious, hating one another—are waiting for someone to show them the way out of their dilemma. (*Gesturing towards the ledger.*) And in this covenant we show them.

VOICES—We show them.

THOMAS—Every day the need for great statesmanship increases —(*Bowing to* JOHNNY.)—while the terrors of war hang in the air. Remember the pictures Johnny showed us yesterday?—horrible pictures—(*Some of the old gentlemen shudder.*)—Little children all over the world are leaving their toys and their playthings, their marbles and their maypoles, to learn to wear gas masks and sleep in shell and gas-proof dungeons. In this very town they're doing it.

SEVERAL BRETHREN (*covering their faces with their hands*)—Horrible! Horrible!

THEODORE (*waving his rubber stick*)—In time of peace prepare for war.

JOHNNY (*chuckling*)—Same old argument, Theodore. We answered that the other day, I thought.

SECRETARY (*intoning*)—Article nineteen, Section six—inviolability of noncombatants.

THOMAS—Silence, Johnny's going to speak.

VOICES (*eagerly*)—That's right, Johnny, tell us a story.

JOHNNY (*as they listen attentively*)—I'm no speaker. (*Lifting his hand as* THEODORE *starts to interrupt.*) And I've already said what I believe on the subject. But Brother Theodore's old argument about every country having to have a big show-off army and navy to keep peace reminds me of old Mr. Zollicoff's dog. Now that was a good dog—until one day Mr. Zollicoff dressed him up in a brass spiked collar. First thing you know that dog was showing off his spikes and fighting every other dog in the neighborhood. They finally had to kill him with a baseball bat. Now our constitution shows—

VOICES (*with gentle laughter*)—That's right, Johnny. He speaks straight to the point, don't he?

WILLIAM—We are not talking about dogs, but civilized men. (JOHNNY *smiles, shrugs his shoulders and resumes his work.*)

THOMAS—The chair feels that men are the same as dogs—when they start fighting one another. (*He looks at* JOHNNY *for confirmation.*) History shows it.

The vote is ordered and, with the exception of Brother Hiram of California, is unanimous. It is difficult to count Hiram on one side or the other in a standing vote, because he insists on maintaining a sort of crouch. He is lifted to his feet finally, and a unanimous vote is recorded for the League of World Republics. All the old gentlemen are quite excited. Johnny is greatly pleased.

The next question before the society is that of Capital and Labor, but before they can get started on this a visiting commission arrives. This is a group of hospital directors on a tour of inspection. They are headed by Anguish Howington, with cane and top hat, and guided by a young clinical-faced Doctor. Anguish is one of the asylum's most generous patrons and hopes to continue his donations. Anguish is also greatly interested in the Adelphians, seeing that as a young man he had once belonged to a debating society. A fellow named Johnson was always stirring that society up. Curious, the founder of this Adelphi society is named Johnson, too. Nice fellow, the Doctor reports, whose disease has been diagnosed as peace monomania. They are thinking of letting him out in a few days.

Anguish, after a long look at Johnny, doubts the wisdom of such a move. In fact he is convinced the window bars seem rather frail and old. They probably should be replaced.

In response to a distant musical gong the old gentlemen rise sleepily from their chairs and file past their attendants. Johnny is carrying his basket of toys. Suddenly he recognizes Anguish's voice, though he never would have known him in his present getup. The guards move forward, but Anguish waves them back. He is not afraid of Johnny.

"Tell me, have you got any news—about Minny Belle, I mean," Johnny asks, anxiously.

"She's—er—well—very well," answers Anguish with some hesitancy.

"Golly, I'm glad to hear that. It's been so long since—I heard. (*Staring off an instant as if caught in a vague worry and then smiling around at* ANGUISH.) She must be awful busy—yeh—tell her I will be seeing her—I hope—soon."

"You don't keep up with what is going on, do you?"

"Well, we get the *International Digest* and that gives us the world news."

"Miss Tompkins did me the honor some years ago of accepting my hand in marriage," says Anguish, bowing stiffly and rejoining his group.

Johnny is left staring at the floor as the others pass out. The attendant who comes to fetch him notices that he is looking kind of sick. Perhaps he should get a doctor—

"I've got some good news for you, Johnny," he says cheerfully. "You're going to be let out of here next week. It's a secret, but we know it. Don't it make you feel better?"

"No, I guess I'll—I'll stay here—now."

"What!"

"All my friends—are here—my work too."

"Yeh, but when they say you're ready to leave you got to leave. That's the law."

Johnny is still confused and silent as the attendant takes him by the arm and gently leads him away. The lights fade out.

"WHITHER HAVE YE MADE A ROAD?"

Some years later Johnny Johnson, a man of forty-five or fifty but looking much older, is leaning against a lightless iron lamp-post on a street corner. It is Winter and through the leafless trees the outlines of a great penanted stadium can be seen. In the stadium a leather-lunged orator is hysterically haranguing a multitude.

Johnny "is dressed in nondescript clothes, an old shapeless gray felt hat, a work shirt, dark coat and trousers and heavy well-worn walking shoes. Hung by a string around his neck and held in front of him is a little tray like that with which street hawkers pursue their calling." As people pass him Johnny holds out his wares, hoping to attract a sale, but no one pays any attention to him until a small boy in a Boy Scout uniform approaches with his mother. He is about twelve years old and he wants to give the toy man a nickel. His mother reminds him that his daddy says nickels make dollars, but the little boy would like to count giving this nickel to the old man as his good deed for the day.

"Nice little toy-ees for nice little girls and boy-ees!" calls Johnny.

There is a far-off remembrance in the voice that halts the little boy's mother. As she turns into the light it is seen she is Minny Belle, wrapped in furs and somewhat stouter. She decides suddenly that the old man should have a nickel. He looks cold.

JOHNNY—What do you want?—A monkey or a dove?—Maybe this little terrapin. See—he can wiggle his legs when you pull the string. Look.

BOY (*appraisingly*)—Hmn— Maybe I might take a toy soldier.

JOHNNY (*sternly*)—No—no—I don't make soldiers.

BOY—Then I don't want anything.

JOHNNY—Here's your nickel.

BOY—Oh, no, you must keep the nickel anyway. My daddy's rich.

JOHNNY (*smiling*)—Is he?—That's nice. What's your name, son?

BOY—Anguish Howington, Junior.

JOHNNY (*after a moment's silence*)—That's a nice name. (*And now as if conscious that* MINNY BELLE *is there in the distance he pulls up his coat collar and turns his face slightly away.*)

ANGUISH, JR.—I'm named after my father. He's mayor of the town, you know.

JOHNNY—Is he? That's wonderful. I'm a sort of stranger here— So he's mayor of the town? And you're a Boy Scout?

ANGUISH, JR.—Yes, sir. And some day I'm going to be a soldier.

JOHNNY (*quickly*)—No, I wouldn't be that.

ANGUISH, JR.—Why not?

JOHNNY—You could be—well, you could make things—or be a great doctor—or a good farmer—do something that would be of use to the world.

ANGUISH, JR.—But Daddy says that we're in for a terrible war and all the people have got to be ready to keep the enemy from destroying us.

JOHNNY (*staring out before him*)—Ah—

MINNY BELLE (*calling*)—Come on!

JOHNNY—And—and how is your mother, son?

ANGUISH, JR.—Why, she's all right. She's standing right over there. (*But* JOHNNY *keeps looking before him.*) Good-by.

JOHNNY (*in a muffled voice*)—Good-by, son.

Little Anguish has rejoined his mother and they have turned into the street and disappeared. Johnny gazes at the nickel in his hand and then takes up his sales cry—

"Toy-ees for sale! Nice little—"

His voice dies away. From the stadium comes the blaring sounds of a band playing the "Democracy March." A moment later an American Legion Fife and Drum Corps crosses the street. Young men and women follow with banners and placards—"America First!" "Be Prepared!" etc.

Twilight has deepened. Now the street light flashes on, throwing the motionless figure of Johnny Johnson into sharp relief. Suddenly Johnny begins to whistle the theme melody of the play. For a moment he continues whistling; then giving his shoulders the faintest touch of a shrug, he turns and starts down the long street.

"Toy-ees! Toy-ees—for nice little girls and boys!"

Nobody answers. No windows are opened. "No smiling, youthful faces appear, for all are gathered into the great stadium in the distance where the drear outlandish haranguer voice can still be heard continuing its queer clamor to the sky—'Gog-a-gog

—Magog-a-gog.' Yet even so, Johnny Johnson is not hushed by this strange voice booming through the world. As he disappears down the long street that leads from the great city into the country and beyond, he begins whistling his song again—a little more clearly now, a little more bravely."

THE CURTAIN FALLS

DAUGHTERS OF ATREUS

A Tragedy in Three Acts

By Robert Turney

THE theatre season of which this volume is a record was dominated largely by the production of comedy, and rather light comedy at that, as has been previously reported in these pages. Dramas of stature and distinction were rare indeed, and such of these as did find production were put aside with a fairly distressing promptness by a playgoing public that was as frankly interested in its recovery of a gaiety of spirit as it was in its recovery of profits in business.

In October one of the finer failures of the year was financed by Delos Chappell, a modern Maecenas of the theatre who frequently risks a sizable donation to art by backing a drama that pleases him. His choice on this occasion was called "Daughters of Atreus," a tragedy written in an eloquent and poetic prose by Robert Turney.

The professional critics of the drama acknowledged the beauty and aesthetic appeal of the drama as staged, but were pretty generally agreed that "Daughters of Atreus," without the support of a superlative cast, were better left in the library—their comments covering a range that swung from Arthur Pollack's "The coming of 'Daughters of Atreus' is an event," to Douglas Gilbert's "'Daughters of Atreus' is a thing of beauty and a bore forever."

There was, however, a considerable public that endorsed the play, though as usual it was much too laggard in its support to save it as a commercial venture. The inclusion of Mr. Turney's play in this volume in influenced by the editor's determination that these year books of the drama in America shall be entirely fair in representing the whole season as completely as possible. Added to which is his personal admiration for the scope and general excellence of the author's effort to adapt Greek dramatic forms to the modern theatre. There are passages of rare beauty in Mr. Turney's text. If the Greeks and their more famous translators had better words for the retelling of the tragedies of the House of Atreus, they also wasted a good deal of time and space in the use of them.

In the courtyard of Klytaimnestra's Palace the walls curve back to great bronze doors. Leading to these are steps and levels so arranged that at one side they form a seat. "The floor and walls of the entire set are covered in velours of a soft earthy rose color." The bronze doors are open. A brilliant sunlight pours through them. "Beyond is a sweep of cloudless sky above faint blue hills."

Presently a woman enters, followed by two slaves carrying a cradle between them. The woman, about whom a quiet radiance seems to settle, is Polymnia. The child in the cradle is Orestes, infant son of Klytaimnestra and Agamemnon. The cradle is placed in the sun that the royal infant may know its warmth.

Soon a group of young women, laughing and talking, gowned in flowing robes of pale green and yellow gold—the colors of Spring—enter the courtyard. They gather excitedly around the cradle, admiring the little Prince extravagantly, as women will, but Polymnia shortly sets them about their tasks, advising them that their Queen will not be pleased if she finds them idle.

The laughter of children in the adjoining garden reminds Polymnia that Elektra is playing there with her sister, Iphegeneia, and that too much sun is not good for her. Elektra, a child of ten, is inclined to be stubborn. She is plainly displeased when Polymnia bids her sit for a time in the shade. Iphegeneia, a slender, lovely girl, "half child, half woman," does her best to interest Elektra, but the child is determined to continue her play. Why, she demands, should she be different from other children.

"There are a good many things we'll never understand, and there's no good in our complaining of them," explains Polymnia. "Some of us are strong and some of us are weak and some of us are lucky while some of us are not. And nothing we can do will ever make it different in the least. The only thing we can do is to rule ourselves. If we learn to do that, then we're happy; if we don't we're not."

"Poor Nurse had little in her life to make her happy; yet see how good she is," adds Iphegeneia. . . . "She was a Princess once and had a son—a little boy like our brother there— (POLYMNIA *looks up swiftly, turns away her face, and sits with folded hands.*) Grandfather sacked her city, killed her husband and her son, and brought her here to be our mother's nurse."

"I hate him! I hate him!" cries Elektra, flinging her arms about Polymnia.

"Hush! Hush! You must not hate your mother's father," admonishes Polymnia.

"But he hurt you. He was wicked! Wicked!"

"He only did as all men do."

"I hate him for what he did."

"You mustn't hate, no matter whom or why. (*Then to* IPHEGENEIA.) Where did you learn that story, child?"

"My mother told me once. And how you brought her up as tenderly as though she were your own after her mother died."

"I don't see how you could. I should have hated everyone. To be a Queen and then be made a slave." Elektra is bitter.

"Polymnia is not a slave," protests Iphegeneia, spiritedly. "She is our own dear Nurse. Our mother's dearest friend."

They are still arguing when Klytaimnestra is seen approaching. Iphegeneia goes happily to meet her mother, arms outstretched in greeting. Elektra clings the closer to Polymnia. She will not leave. She knows her mother cares more for both Iphegeneia and Orestes than she does for her. Nor is she impressed by Polymnia's horrified denials. . . .

Klytaimnestra "is a thin woman of medium height, with clearly, magnificently defined features. Her tawny hair is confined with a bandeau and pins of gold. She is dressed in a robe of pale yellow gold. Her sandals are gold, and there is a gold bracelet upon her left wrist, yet the effect is one of simplicity and great dignity." She stands for a moment, her arm about the waist of Iphegeneia and notes that the wind is still an off-sea wind, which is bad for those at Aulis. Why should men be forever at war? There is much for them to do at home.

She passes now among the women, inspecting and approving their needle work, and now she is seated at the foot of the steps, listening to Iphegeneia and Elektra as they report the beauties of the early-blossoming Spring. . . .

A guard has brought Ambassadors from Egypt and the North, to petition Klytaimnestra. The Egyptian is "suave, dignified, aloof." The other, obviously a Barbarian, "is clad in wolfskins thrown about him and held in place by a silver girdle."

The Barbarian, at Klytaimnestra's invitation, is first to speak. He is Vortigern. He comes to demand in the name of his people, the Norse, that their warriors be permitted to pass through the land of Agamemnon, and that they be provisioned as they pass.

For answer Klytaimnestra walks to the door and calls to the Barbarian to stand beside her and see what she sees: "Look out upon the city at your feet," she commands. "Mark well its many battlements; its shining ways; its spacious market-places; its many-storied homes; their gardens, where are lofty trees; the vines about their roofs. Mark well their ancient look. These are the signs of long maintained peace—a peace we keep by right of prowess in all feats of war. Your father and their fathers came and went. Our Mycenaean battlements are high and golden still against the hills. Return and tell your chief what you have seen."

Vortigern is impressed, but still inclined to argue. He knows that Agamemnon is sworn to sail with the Grecian hosts. "Your sister, Helen, is his brother Menelaos' wife," craftily repeats Vortigern. "Her beauty was so great that all the Grecian Kings took oath before she wed not only to respect her husband's rights but to avenge him were she ravished from his home. And now she's fled across the sea with Paris, Priam's son and Prince of Troy. You see I know how matters stand. Your husband's oath compels him to the Trojan war. You'd best be friends with us."

For answer Klytaimnestra summons a tall and muscular guard, magnificently accoutered with shield and armor, and bids the Barbarian consider meeting an army of thirty thousand such before he grows too defiant. Vortigern is mumbling threateningly as he takes his leave.

"They are a constant menace at our gates," Klytaimnestra reports to Cheops, the Egyptian. "I would my lord went not upon this war."

"In Egypt, too, they menace us," admits Cheops. "Not these, but others from the desert and beyond the seas. We raise the glittering tower of civilization century after century while they sweep in against its base like tidal waters of the sea."

They have come now to the Egyptian's mission, which is to learn from Agamemnon if he will unite with Egypt against a common enemy, Crete. Again Klytaimnestra is doubtful—

KLYTAIMNESTRA—What gain is ours if we should grant this treaty? You have seen with what we are confronted here. These savages are ever at our gates. If I unite with Pharaoh in this Cretan matter, he must lend me aid against these Norse.

CHEOPS—I heard you tell him of your strength.

KLYTAIMNESTRA—I showed him but the shining front and not the thing it hid. To you I speak with freedom—for I feel we shall ally ourselves with you. There is a reason why we look suspiciously toward Crete and welcome an alliance that would strengthen us against the Cretan King. An ancient feud of blood divides our house. Aegisthos, Agamemnon's cousin, dwells in safety and in favor at the Cretan court. The leader of a faction that but bides its time to war upon my lord.

CHEOPS—And wherefore?

KLYTAIMNESTRA—You know that for a brother or a father's death the law of honor has from ancient time demanded like revenge.

CHEOPS—Such is the law that all men hold.

KLYTAIMNESTRA—And also that the duty of this vengeance goes from father down to son until it's paid.

CHEOPS—That also do I know, as all men know.

KLYTAIMNESTRA—Such is the feud between Aegisthos and my lord. They are the second generation of this hate.

CHEOPS—But surely there are rites by which atonement may be made and so the State be brought to peace at last.

KLYTAIMNESTRA—There's no atonement for the crime of Agamemnon's father, Atreus. In vengeance for his ravished wife, he slew his brother's children on the holy day of Artemis, upon which day all living things are sacred to the gods. Aegisthos only was not slain and fled to Crete. This is the feud betwixt Aegisthos and my lord. Such have no end but death.

CHEOPS—A feud sprung from a sacrilege. An evil heritage for those born of the House of Atreus.

KLYTAIMNESTRA—Father and son, this kindred blood must war upon itself until Aegisthos' house or ours has ceased to be. And therefore, since I fear what Crete may do to aid Aegisthos once the King has left our shore, I will ally myself with you.

Elektra, having overheard the compact, dashes to the cradle in which Orestes lies. She is broken by sobs. Their enemy will kill her brother, she cries, nor can she be comforted by Iphegeneia or her mother. Only the fear that the stranger may report her conduct to her father, thus shaming the King, serves to quiet Elektra.

A messenger has come from Aulis. The others have withdrawn while Klytaimnestra receives him. Now he is kneeling before the Queen and has handed her a tablet of wax on which is written a message from Agamemnon. As she reads, Klytaimnestra's face lights with amazed delight. Quickly she summons Iphegeneia—

"Here's tidings, child, and presage of great joy," she calls. "Your father sends for you to be a bride!" She has taken Iphegeneia in her arms. "Oh, baby, baby! And I had scarcely thought you grown. (*To the* MESSENGER.) You shall be rewarded for your news. (*Turning to* IPHEGENEIA.) What! Blushing silence and no joyous word! Have you no tongue to ask who shall be your lord? Come, kiss your mother, baby. So it's come, the

by Jerome Robinson, New York.

"DAUGHTERS OF ATREUS"

e is Vortigern, the Barbarian. He comes to demand in the name of his people, the Norse, that warriors be permitted to pass through the land of Agamemnon, and that they be provisioned ey pass."

(*Eleanora Mendelssohn, John Boruff*)

time when I must give you up and see you pass to make your place in other halls. Well, it's a woman's sweetest time—and yet another woman's saddest, too, I think. (*Holding* IPHEGENEIA *off at arm's length and looking at her as though she saw her for the first time.*) Why, you are not a woman yet! And still no questions, sweet, no wondering word?"

IPHEGENEIA—My father bids me to my bridal thus?

KLYTAIMNESTRA—No other way. Look, this is what he writes. (*She holds out the message for* IPHEGENEIA *to read; then suddenly changing her mind, she draws it back.*) But still you have not asked the bridegroom's name?

IPHEGENEIA—I think—I hope I know the name.

KLYTAIMNESTRA (*speaking to* POLYMNIA)—So? She thinks, she hopes she knows. Well, it might be worse. In time a woman, if she tried, might teach herself to love a man like Ajax.

IPHEGENEIA, POLYMNIA, AND WOMEN (*horrified*)—Ajax!

KLYTAIMNESTRA—Somewhat dark and hairy, perhaps, but none the less a man.

IPHEGENEIA—Ajax!

KLYTAIMNESTRA—And with prudence and hard work a girl well skilled in management might make improvements at his court. You know, I hear he isn't quite as poor as people say.

IPHEGENEIA—Ajax!

KLYTAIMNESTRA—Oh, love! love! love! Don't look so sad. It isn't Ajax, it's Achilles, sweet. (IPHEGENEIA *hides her face in sudden confusion.* KLYTAIMNESTRA *lifts her by the chin and looks tenderly down into her eyes.*) Oh! it's he she thinks she hopes she knows. (*To the* MESSENGER.) How was my lord when this was written?

MESSENGER—Well.

KLYTAIMNESTRA—How soon must we to Aulis? Here he sets no time.

MESSENGER—At once. They wait the ships upon her coming there.

KLYTAIMNESTRA—How wait on this? The winds blow still as they have blown two months or more; until they change no ship can sail from Aulis. Yet we will haste. (*To* MESSENGER.) Go to your master. Say we come as soon as it may be. The girl must be prepared.

MESSENGER—He bade me bring her back to Aulis straight; and further—to entreat that you remain, nor undertake the weary journey there.

KLYTAIMNESTRA—That was a kindly thought. But I will go. I am delivered of the child a month already.

MESSENGER—I beg you, lady, do not go.

KLYTAIMNESTRA—Indeed! And why?

MESSENGER—My master bade me say that he commanded you to guard yourself and bide at home.

KLYTAIMNESTRA—Isn't that just like a man? Not see my daughter wed, indeed!

MESSENGER—My lady—

KLYTAIMNESTRA—No more! (*She turns to the women.*) Go prepare the necessary bridal garments—they are folded in my chests—and fetch the parasol of state—we go to Aulis. (*She goes out followed by the women.* IPHEGENEIA *and* POLYMNIA *are alone.* IPHEGENEIA *starts to follow the others, then turns and throws herself into* POLYMNIA'S *arms.*)

IPHEGENEIA—Oh, dear Polymnia! I'm happy! Happy! Happy!

The lights fade.

The scene has changed to the rocky seashore at Aulis. Two warriors have entered. One a man in the prime of life, "an air of great dignity, an intangible sense of greatness in his bearing." The other "a younger and very handsome warrior."

Agamemnon, the older, is greatly agitated. He would, if he could, explain to Achilles, the younger, the cause of a present distress, but finds it difficult—

"You have no child. You cannot understand," he is saying. "Nor know how I am tortured thinking of my wife. Ours is no common marriage for the State alone. Though that is how it chanced. Let others worship Helen's beauty as they will— My Klytaimnestra's deeper beauty far outwears it day by day. Few men have found a wife so fashioned all of tenderness and dignity and warmth. Oh, God! And I must do this thing to her!"

"Hear me!" protests Achilles with spirit. "Secretly I sent an order to my men to arm. But say the word and Iphegeneia shall not die, no matter how the auguries may read."

There is no comfort for Agamemnon in Achilles' offer, nor in his prophecy of victory. Agamemnon cannot plunge all Greece into civil war. Too long has he striven for the unity of Greece. His only hope is that the High Priest Kalchas will accept some other expiation.

But there is no comfort in Kalchas' decision, which is shortly given by the High Priest "robed in a sacerdotal mantle which falls in stiff folds from his shoulders to the ground and is the color of blood."

"Blood must be washed away with blood," solemnly proclaims the High Priest, when Agamemnon offers to give all that is his, or like to be his. "The evil of your house too long has gone unpunished. What has its history been but one of lust and blood? To gratify unholy lust Thyestes cruelly defiled his brother's wife. Did Atreus, the King and fountain source of law, abide by ancient law? Ten years he brooded and at last into his own hands took the awful vengeance which is God's alone. Cunningly dissembling a forgiveness he could not feel, he tempted home from Crete his brother and his brother's sons. Trusting God where they could feel but little trust in Atreus, they came to Mycenae again upon the day most holy in our calendar. And on that day King Atreus avenged himself. Nor did he slay the brother who had sinned, but children innocent of guilt—as innocent as Iphegeneia is. Do not think that gold can wash away the horror of this act. I tell you I have gone upon the mountains in the night and wept because I could not find another way. But man must have belief and law by which to live. Without these things the State is sick, civilization falls, the race is ended. Patiently, step by step, our people raised a civilization that is great and deeply rooted. This is a heritage to treasure and defend. Our fathers died in doing so. Yet its foundations have been undermined and shaken by the very hand that should have guarded it most sacredly. Because of what your father did, religion is no longer vitally a part of life. The people must be shocked into a reawakened sense of right and wrong. They must be shown that none—no matter what his station—may defy the ancient laws by which our race has lived. Your house is tainted, Agamemnon, and it must be cleansed to purify the State. Blood must be washed away with blood."

"Then let me die."

"Well do you know the sacrifice must be unstained and pure."

A great shout is heard. It is an unseen army cheering the arrival of Klytaimnestra and Iphegeneia. They come now, preceded by a guard clad in lead-colored breast plates and tunics, against which the costumes of the women with Klytaimnestra show "like Spring leaves and flowers against a stormy sky."

Klytaimnestra is alive with anticipation of their greeting, and puzzled by the lack of joy shown by her husband and by Achilles. Apprehension stabs her as she notes their gloom. She draws the trembling Iphegeneia closer to her, and demands that her apprehension be set at rest.

"Since Agamemnon cannot speak, I will," says Kalchas. "For many weeks there have been adverse winds—"

"Do not tell me what I know, but what I fear."

"All sacrifice was vain. Despairing how to placate angry gods, we sent to Delphi's oracle."

"Go on. Go on."

"This was the answer of the oracle: no Troyward wind shall blow, no undertaking of the State shall prosper, till the State is purified. The house of Atreus has sinned."

"Ah!"

"Atonement must be made by one born of the house of Atreus."

"No!" Klytaimnestra has spoken as though to herself, her hands seeking Iphegeneia blindly.

"And on your daughter, Iphegeneia, falls the lot."

At these dread words the girl has thrown herself into her mother's arms and is held close while Klytaimnestra comforts her with such promise of protection as a mother gives. The Queen turns then to Kalchas, the priest, and to Agamemnon, and demands to know how they can think of such a horror. Nor can they quiet her. To the others she turns, to the lords, pleadingly, that they stop this thing that is threatened. To her women, begging them to gather closely about her child and shield her. From group to group she goes: "You would not slay my daughter?" And to the next, when there is no response: "You would not slay my daughter?" Until suddenly, stunned and unbelieving, she screams out wildly—

AGAMEMNON—Klytaimnestra, in God's name, this torture is without avail. We have no power to save our child.

KLYTAIMNESTRA—Have I gone mad that I should hear you speak these words?

AGAMEMNON—We are without power, without hope. (KLYTAIMNESTRA *goes to him swiftly and speaks almost in a whisper.*)

KLYTAIMNESTRA—There's hope beside you there. Take up that sword and bare it. Lift our cry—the war-cry of our house. These will not fight if you'll but play the man.

AGAMEMNON—I cannot plunge the State in civil war. Wife, you and I are bondsmen to the State. This strikes too sharply at your heart or you would see how I am bound.

KLYTAIMNESTRA—Agamemnon, even wolves defend their young, and birds—those same soft, sunlight-loving timid birds will fly upon a snake that seeks their nest. And yet you say she dies? And dies for what? If Menelaos would not keep his wife, what recks it you that you should win her back? Was she unwilling ravished from her home? She is my sister and I know her heart. And you would kill our child to bring this whore, this bawdy baggage, home again. Is Helen so supreme in womankind that you must slay a virgin for her lust? Are there no other breasts as fair, no other eyes as bright as hers? There's many a woman still with yellow hair!

KALCHAS—Peace, woman.

KLYTAIMNESTRA—Is there no one? No one? Oh, God! Is there no one here who will defend me?

ACHILLES—O gray-beards! You of old have made your wars for this or that; stirring with the threat of fire divine or moving with an equal empty hope of glory restless youths to hate and lust of blood; while women sit in grief at home, and there behind the burning veil of stars the very soul of God cries out in pain of it. This earth is wide and fair and rich. There is enough for every man that tills and sows and reaps, and garners what he reaps. What is this lust for storied towers of gold, for ocean-polished stones and earth-embedded gems? For this it is that draws you on and not your wounded honor, as you claim. Is there a quarrel, be it howsoever great, that justifies the countless dead who, living, might have ministered to men?

KALCHAS—Well do I know that from the start, Achilles, you opposed this holy war.

ACHILLES—No war is holy! I whom you know am unafraid to fight repeat no war is holy and no war is just.

AGAMEMNON—We are bound to Menelaos by our oath.

KLYTAIMNESTRA—What are you men, what are you men, what are you that take our children, all we have?

KALCHAS—Silence!

ACHILLES—There is no silence that can hush her cry! She is the flame of motherhood wind-fanned—the never-ending cry of womankind.

At a sign from Agamemnon the soldiers are closing in. Before they can advance beyond a step or two Klytaimnestra has grabbed the sword of Agamemnon and faced them, holding her daughter back of her. Let them come now, she cries; let them tear Iphegeneia from her; she will not yield. The men are taken aback. They hesitate; turn to the High Priest for further sign.

Kalchas is soft spoken now. There is a pleading note in his voice as he appeals, not to Klytaimnestra, but to Iphegeneia.

"To give yourself—a willing sacrifice is an heroic deed. No warrior who dies in battle for his people could do more. So doing shall you stand superbly poised upon the brink of time, a beacon for the lighting of the world. Even the baleful loveliness of Helen shall pale beside the white holiness you shall become."

Then brave Achilles would spring again to the girl's defense and bid his trumpeters call his men of war to arms. Both Agamemnon and Kalchas move to stop him. The soldiers close in upon Achilles with leveled spears. From the distance comes the cry: "To arms! To arms!"

It is Iphegeneia who stills the clamor. Clearly her voice rises above the pandemonium. "Peace! Peace! I say. Shame! My lords! For shame!" The shouting is stilled. Complete silence reigns. "I speak not as a simple maid, but as one already sanctified to Artemis," cries Iphegeneia. "Shall swords defile my eyes, and clamor make these last and awful moments hideous?" . . . "My feet are set upon the stony way, they must not falter now!" she says, ignoring her mother's cries. And to Agamemnon she speaks: "Dearest, do not pity me. Mine is the Spring that shall not wither into Summer, nor ever know hivernal snows. I, who might have gone immemorably to death, am wound immortally with garlands now. I, who die childless, gather all my people to my heart to be my children now. My death shall give them strength to live."

Kalchas, the light of exaltation in his face, kneels silently before Iphegeneia and kisses her robe. "To touch you is to sanctify myself," he says. "Give me your hand and I will guide you."

"I am a King's daughter," she says. "I have the strength to walk alone." Iphegeneia has mounted the steps slowly, and paused at the top. "How full—how full of sunlight the heavens are!" she says.

A low chanting begins as she moves out of sight. Kalchas has remained standing against the sky. "His mantle hangs motionless about him in the breathless air." Above the chanting rises the renewed cries of Klytaimnestra to Agamemnon to save their child.

Suddenly a terrible silence settles upon the scene. The chanting has ended. "Kalchas stretches higher his arms as though he would pluck the wind from the very sky." The silence again. And then "the garments of Kalchas lift again and winnow gently about him in the rising wind."

"The gods are vindicated! The Troyward wind!" the High Priest shouts.

In the distance trumpets begin to sound. The call to ship is heard, rising with the wind.

"Wife—see. The gods have answered us," shouts Agamemnon. "The curse is lifted from our house. Atonement has been made. (*Almost sobbing.*) My Iphegeneia! My Iphegeneia!"

KLYTAIMNESTRA (*her eyes fixed upon emptiness*)—May I have my daughter now?

AGAMEMNON—Wife—

KLYTAIMNESTRA—May I have my daughter now?

AGAMEMNON (*brokenly*)—You may claim her— In God's name, wife—

KLYTAIMNESTRA (*motionless with unseeing eyes. The women begin to sob as they go to her*)—Hush! No tears. No tears.

AGAMEMNON—Klytaimnestra—wife. In God's name, hear me! (*At gesture from* AGAMEMNON, *the women go out.*) Have you no god-speed for me, wife—no word of comfort—nothing to hearten me upon this bitter voyage? (*She lifts her burning eyes to his face, but remains silent. A trumpet sounds.* AGAMEMNON *bows his head and starts swiftly out. Then he turns for the last time.*) God knows when I will come to Mycenae again.

KLYTAIMNESTRA (*her voice terrible in its quietness, its intensity of smothered passion*)—I will await your coming.

"Kalchas stands triumphant above her, his arms still uplifted. As the wind strengthens into a gale, his blood-red mantle streams out and up against the sky until it is like some terrible wave curling above her." The curtain falls.

ACT II

Years have passed. In a room of Klytaimnestra's palace Polymnia is directing the activities of the Queen's women. The night is falling. They are to prepare the Queen's bed. The sea is calm, and the heat is great. A storm threatens.

With Polymnia gone the women gossip among themselves. They know for what the preparations are being made. And he who will come, they've heard, is Agamemnon's enemy—

Elektra is there. She is a tall girl now; almost a woman. She has not been home for hours, but out in a boat with her brother Orestes. Only the night has brought them back. Elektra did not want to come. She would, if she could, be forever free of that house and all it holds. When Polymnia comes again and dismisses the women, Elektra, weeping bitterly, casts herself at the nurse's feet—

POLYMNIA (*stroking* ELEKTRA'S *head*)—What is it, child? Nay, do not weep so sorely! Dear heart! What a tempest of feeling is always in your breast! What is it now?

ELEKTRA—Why is he here?

POLYMNIA—Why is who here?

ELEKTRA—Aegisthos! Why is Aegisthos honored in my father's halls and by my father's wife?

POLYMNIA—He is a guest, my love.

ELEKTRA—He is my father's enemy!

POLYMNIA—Now, who has told you that?

ELEKTRA—Don't try to hide the truth from me! I know! I know!

POLYMNIA—How quickly you believe whatever ill you hear!

ELEKTRA—My mother told me this.

POLYMNIA (*startled*)—Your mother?

ELEKTRA—Long ago. That day the strange Egyptian came. I heard her tell him that Aegisthos was our mortal foe—one sworn to kill my father and my brother, both.

POLYMNIA—Perhaps there's more than one Aegisthos, then.

ELEKTRA—O dear Polymnia! Don't turn against me as the others have. Don't be my enemy. I'm so alone.

POLYMNIA—How quick you are to search out pain! Have I not nursed you, cherished you, and brought you up? And still you use the name of enemy!

ELEKTRA—You try to hide the thing I know. The man was Cretan-reared and this Aegisthos came from Crete.

POLYMNIA (*uneasily*)—Perhaps your mother tricks him into tarrying where she can guard him best.

ELEKTRA (*with bitter laugh*)—Perhaps! Why do her women whisper, then, and hush them when I pass? Oh, I'm not blind.

POLYMNIA—When has this happened, child?

ELEKTRA—A thousand times! Oh, that there were someone! Someone to whom I might turn for help!

POLYMNIA—And what of me?

ELEKTRA—You love her best!

POLYMNIA—No heart is ever given wholly to a single love. A small heart indeed were such! I love you both. My love stands ready at your need. (ELEKTRA *goes to the window.*) Why can't you trust your mother? Women are ever quick to whisper over what seems strange. Suppose Aegisthos is an enemy? Perhaps your mother keeps him near herself so, should he plot against our house, her spies may learn more easily of it.

An attendant has brought Orestes. Elektra turns from Polymnia to gather her brother fiercely in her arms. He, at least, is one who loves her and she is grateful. Together they move back to a window to see if there is yet a light upon the distant hills, the light that is to be a signal that their father will soon be with them. For long months they have awaited its showing, and grown impatient from day to day.

"Is Father big?" Orestes would know of his sister.

"Our father is the greatest man on earth," proudly answers Elektra.

"I'm glad. When he comes home he'll kill the men that say bad things behind their hands," predicts the boy.

The words startle Elektra, but she dismisses them quickly. The children are still there when Klytaimnestra comes. She observes them coldly, chiding her son for not having been in bed an hour before and dismissing her daughter with little feeling.

Polymnia does not like this mood of her Queen, nor thinks it wise that she should act so. A constant brooding is not good, and a lack of interest in the conduct of her house is certain to be talked about among the women. These women are not the spies that Klytaimnestra thinks, but "they see the things they cannot help but see, and talk as women will." The King's away. What if he return?

Klytaimnestra, with darkened eyes, declares that she awaits that return impatiently. And let not Polymnia look upon her with prying eyes.

Now the nurse is gentle with her overwrought Queen, soothing and comforting her as though she were again a child and would ease her heart by telling all that worries her—

"There's naught to tell, I say," insists Klytaimnestra, brusquely. "There's naught."

"I did not seek to pry."

KLYTAIMNESTRA—Oh, Polymnia! Polymnia! Why are we born, and in our turn why do we women give our children life!

POLYMNIA—Let me take off this heavy robe. You'll rest more easily.

KLYTAIMNESTRA—Oh, there is in me such a hate of men!

POLYMNIA—And what of young Aegisthos, then?

KLYTAIMNESTRA—He is a thing that loves me—all my own.

And, too, there is in me at times some sudden need that cries aloud for love. I loathe, I loathe this flesh I am. (*She springs up and begins her restless pacing.*) Oh, to be free! Free! But all about us wind the lives of other men, like threads that make a web and in it woven—we—of destiny and men made captive here.

POLYMNIA—Each of us weaves and what we weave is but ourselves.

KLYTAIMNESTRA—We are not weavers of our lives, not we. But threads thrown back and forth by other hands.

POLYMNIA—What others do has power upon no soul but theirs. Our hearts are blinded by our minds, which see reflections in a shield, but fail to see the thing reflected there—ourselves.

KLYTAIMNESTRA—The deeds of others have made desolate my life.

POLYMNIA—Cast out this hate you nurse. It is a poisonous weed that, fed upon, distorts all things. Believe me, if you learn to love instead, then peace will fill your heart.

KLYTAIMNESTRA—Love comes not easy to the house of Atreus. I think the fountain source of all its life is hate. Hate stronger than love, hate stronger than fear, hate stronger than death or life. We draw it from the air, our mother's breast, the sun, the stars.

POLYMNIA—O child! Those who in the madhouse of their own emotions dwell go mad at last. Learn to bear those things you cannot mend.

KLYTAIMNESTRA—I am the daughter of my house. I cannot be like you.

POLYMNIA—And yet it is no work to free yourself of hate. Why, hate is but a shadow cast by self.—Now let me brush your hair.

Aegisthos has come. He is a young man, "tall and straight, yet with a hint of weakness; something broken within his finely proportioned body." An impetuous young man, Aegisthos would embrace Klytaimnestra as soon as Polymnia has been dismissed. He feels a right to be more warmly welcomed. But Klytaimnestra's thought is not on love—

KLYTAIMNESTRA—You must strengthen you and be a man, else how in time shall you avenge our wrongs? I love the softness in your nature, but your body must be strong and schooled to fight. You love your ease and banqueting too much.

AEGISTHOS—And so does Agamemnon, if what I hear be true.

KLYTAIMNESTRA—But not so daintily as you. Give him his

due, he is a man for men, and he has fought right valiantly of old and will return hard schooled from combat with the Trojan great. How shall we strike at him if you are weak?

AEGISTHOS—I sometimes think you do not love me.

KLYTAIMNESTRA—It was not love that sent to Crete to bring you here. It was our common hate. Who but you is bound as I am bound to hate the house of Atreus? This love of ours came last, the fruit of secret meetings thus alone. You must be schooled by me or go your way. If you are weak, a useless tool to me, I will not keep you here in ease. It's best that I should speak thus plainly. Look. (*She leads him to a window.*) Upon that middle hill some day will shine a light that tells me Agamemnon lands at Argos. Then we have a day or night in which to make us ready for his coming here. What would you do if now in red fire and in golden smoke it blazed across the night its tidings full of doom for us?

AEGISTHOS—He will not come these many years.

KLYTAIMNESTRA—In that, my friend, you judge but ill. The Greeks will tarry little longer there at Troy. They either win or turn them homeward soon. Then what, my friend?

AEGISTHOS—Why, even so, they will not quickly come.

KLYTAIMNESTRA—Perhaps already they are on the sea. From Troy I have but restless news of homeward longing eyes among the Argives there. You carry at your side a hunter's ax where you should wear a sword; and spend the time that should be spent at arms—in banqueting.

AEGISTHOS—Well, I will mend my ways. Come, kiss me now.

KLYTAIMNESTRA—I will not kiss you.

AEGISTHOS—For all my faults no other man has ever made you feel your womanhood as I have done. Kiss me.

Even as they seek each other's arms the voice of Elektra is heard calling wildly to her mother. She has burst in upon them now, and drawn back from what she sees. She had excuse to come. The light has appeared upon the mountain top! Let Klytaimnestra look from the window!

Klytaimnestra looks and sees with widened eyes, "an altar in the hills, and on it burns prophetic fire"—

"Sweep up across the sky, great beard of flame, and light him home!" she cries exultantly. "Let birds and beasts awake to tremble at this miracle of fear! Paint all the night with dun red splendor so and welcome him with pomp that well befits a king! Look on it from your ship and mark it well, for it's your funeral pyre."

"In God's name, hush! Polymnia's here," cautions Aegisthos.

"You know each detail—all we planned?" continues Klytaimnestra, giving no heed to caution.

"What is it you have planned?" demands Polymnia.

"The way that Agamemnon dies!" quickly answers the Queen.

Determination sits upon the darkening brow of Klytaimnestra. She is deaf now to the wild pleading of Polymnia. She turns now in rage upon Aegisthos who is weakly repeating that Agamemnon comes too soon. Let him collect his men.

"In God's name, think of what you will do," cries the distraught Polymnia. "Think, think how many crimes have sprung from one. This will not quit them all. In God's name, think—Elektra and your son!"

"Three thousand days and seven have I thought," thunders Klytaimnestra. "Iphegeneia! Iphegeneia! Iphegeneia! Like the beating of a maddened heart this name has rung within me, rung and rung three thousand days and seven. Go raise your men and come to me before the dawn. He travels not tonight; that gives us time. If we achieve the thing, the palace guard will not revolt. But that I may be doubly safe, at dawn I'll send forth to meet the King. But by the road he will not take. The citadel and palace ours, the city will not rise."

"Klytaimnestra! My baby! My child! Look at me! Hear me!" Polymnia pleads. "We women often have strange thoughts at such a time. Leave her; in God's name, leave her, Aegisthos. Come to bed. Oh, baby, baby, come to bed. You must not think."

"Blood cries for blood. Shall all have vengeance, yet my child have none?"

"He is your husband!"

"She was my child!"

It is little use for them to plead, or to reason. Klytaimnestra has no time for either. Even though Polymnia threaten to warn the King, and Aegisthos refuse to go on with the murder as planned, she will not be halted in her intent—

"Yes. It could be done that way!" she mumbles, not heeding what they do or say. "A bath—I will prepare a bath. When he is come, Aegisthos, I will take away his armor—somehow send away those who are close to him— Yes! Yes!—Go now! Fetch me a net—a fisher's net—one that's wide and strong—and bring it here. When he is naked in his bath, I'll cast it over him. So tangled he will be an easy prey. Then you can slay him with your ax."

AEGISTHOS—I tell you I will have no part in this.

KLYTAIMNESTRA—Then go, traitor! Go! Go! Go! Traitor! Traitor! Leave me here to die! You never loved me!

AEGISTHOS—Whatever you may think of me—whatever I have been—this at least is true: I loved you deeply once. I am no warrior. But I will do what part I can though it be no more than dying at your side.

KLYTAIMNESTRA—You will not go?

AEGISTHOS—I stay with you.

KLYTAIMNESTRA—You shall be king—my king. Go now and seek—

AEGISTHOS (*sadly*)—My Klytaimnestra, save your words. They are but mist that hides the steep abyss in which I fall. I'll seek my men—do what I can to keep you safe. But murder is no part of me.

KLYTAIMNESTRA—Coward! Coward! I will do the thing if you're afraid! Give me the ax! (*He looks at her in unbelieving horror.*) Give me the ax! (*She snatches it from him. The moment the ax is in her hands, she is a changed being. From a Fury she becomes a priestess of destruction lost in a terrible exaltation.* AEGISTHOS *gazes at her a moment almost in fear. Then he turns and goes blindly from the room. Slowly* KLYTAIMNESTRA *lifts the ax, gazing intently. Then she begins to mount the steps, seeming to grow taller and taller as she does so.*) Up! Klytaimnestra, up! Lay off your womanhood! Up. Mycenaean Queen! Up! Up! To vengeance up! (*She is before the great central portal now. Suddenly she clasps the ax to her bosom as though it were a child and throws back her head in a gesture of ecstatic abandon terrible to see. The lamps in the room cast enormous and distorted shadows of* KLYTAIMNESTRA *and the ax upon the walls about her.* KLYTAIMNESTRA, *in a voice like the pounding of a heart.*) Iphegeneia! Iphegeneia! Iphegeneia! (*She is engulfed in darkness.*)

It is morning. The guard has been summoned to join Agamemnon at Aulis, by order of the Queen. The Queen's women gossip of the excitements of the day. There is a rumor that Agamemnon has brought a Trojan Princess home with him—one Kassandra, Priam's daughter. Some have said that Kassandra is mad, and others that she is a prophetess. All that she foretells, they say, is sure to come to pass. This is news the Queen should know. . . .

Elektra has come, followed by Orestes and his attendant, to watch from their mother's door, from where they can command each of the city's gates. And now Polymnia, struggling nobly to conceal her misery of mind, has followed them. Together they watch the roads, and still can see no signs of marching men nor the glint of spears in the sunlight. Orestes is eager with excitement to see his father, to see the peacocks and the ivory elephants Elektra has told him Agamemnon will surely bring his son.

It is strange, thinks Elektra, that the Palace has been deserted by the guard—and at the Queen's orders. Strange that they should have been sent by the new road to Aulis. There is no satisfaction in Polymnia's tortured explanation. "Would God this day were done!" is all the distraught nurse can mutter.

And now Orestes has caught the flash of spears among far-off trees. Elektra sees them, too. "How brave the chariots sweep along the road and up the hill," she cries, a moment later.

"Where is my father?" demands the young Orestes.

"He's the one beneath the golden parasol, the noblest of them all, the one whose steeds are two-fold hued—one white between two blacks," proudly answers Elektra.

"God help us now!" mutters Polymnia.

At her mother's suggestion Elektra has taken Orestes to the gate to watch when Polymnia turns upon the Queen—

"In God's name, think before you do this thing," pleads the nurse.

"All is prepared. Go."

POLYMNIA—Think of Elektra and Orestes.

KLYTAIMNESTRA—Be silent!

POLYMNIA—In God's name, see the end you make.

KLYTAIMNESTRA—I see the sacrificial fire, the altar raised, the knife made sharp and bright. The victim laid upon the stone; the bloodless lips—the frightened eyes; the shriek still ringing in my heart shuts out all thought of mercy now. The ox is ready for the sacrifice!

POLYMNIA—In God's name, hear me!

KLYTAIMNESTRA—And the ax made clean and purified!

POLYMNIA—Klytaimnestra!

KLYTAIMNESTRA—The incense smokes upon the air! And I am purified by prayer and fasting for the sacred rite.

POLYMNIA—What shall I do! What shall I do!

KLYTAIMNESTRA—I'll pour libations to her now at last. Make ready now the bath of blood! Now, Klytaimnestra! Now! See! See! The torn fillets trailing, the dust-dragged hair! The hands, the hands!

ELEKTRA (*rushing in*)—My father comes!

KLYTAIMNESTRA (*changing almost instantaneously. In a moment she becomes the smiling Queen who welcomes her lord*)—I shall go forth to meet him now. (*Exits.*)

ELEKTRA (*throwing her arms about* POLYMNIA *and hiding her face against her shoulder*)—I cannot go to him. My heart will break with joy! O sweet Polymnia, O Nurse! All will be well at last. Dearest! How white and ill you look!

POLYMNIA—O death! Death! Death!

ELEKTRA—Fria!

POLYMNIA—Call no one here!

ELEKTRA—But you're in pain!

POLYMNIA—The eyes of God are on this place. Call no one here!

Agamemnon is carrying Orestes in his arms when he enters the Palace. Klytaimnestra walks beside him, her eyes, "burning with a strange and terrible light," fixed on his face. A guard of soldiers and Klytaimnestra's women follow.

Now Kassandra moves out from the crowd of attendants and Agamemnon explains to Klytaimnestra how he had taken Priam's daughter to save her from the brutalities of Ajax. Slowly, awesomely, the prophetess moves among them, frightening the young Orestes when first she stares wildly at him, but conquering him finally with a friendly smile. Then again is Kassandra worried at what she beholds for Orestes: "Oh, pitiful feet, destined to wander and never find peace," she wails.

And now Agamemnon, taking joy in his homecoming, would embrace the Queen, but she craftily avoids him. She would help him first with his armor that he may be comfortable in the mounting heat. When again Agamemnon would take his wife in his arms she is forced to submit. But she goes rigid under his caress and escapes him a moment later to bring Elektra forward to greet him.

Agamemnon finds the daughter who was no higher than his waist when he went away grown to a tall and straight young woman now, and with great affection holds her close to him.

"Now that you have come, all will be well at last," sighs the girl, happily. "All will be well."

"She has been ill and speaks a sick girl's words," quickly interjects Klytaimnestra. "My lord, I have so longed to see your face again! Yet you are waiting. Go and bathe."

Elektra would cling to her father and have him stay. The worried Polymnia would add her word of warning, too, did not Klytaimnestra stop her. Kassandra, the prophetess, roused from a trance-like state, stands suddenly before Elektra and is moved further to direful prophecy:

"O pitiful avenger of our wrongs! All hail! Trojan mothers, weep no longer for your children slain. Here their avenger stands." And as all those near stop to stare and listen in full amazement, Kassandra adds: "Thine is the heritage, the bloody hands, the tortured heart. You shall avenge us in the end! The veil is rent! All bloody! See—the end approaches here. The weary road is done. Apollo, healer and slayer! Thou, quickener and dealer of death! The fire! Swift Swift! This is the end!"

Elektra clings the closer to her father, who makes no move to stop Kassandra's dread words. She will be very gentle when the spell passes, he promises. And so the prophecy is continued:

"Endless! Endless cycle of despair!" wails Kassandra. "O, warriors and women, this once believe Kassandra. Inscrutably we move along the paths of destiny, surrounded by prophetic and unheeded echoes of the past. Even as Troy has fallen, so shall Mycenae fall; and all those who follow after her, drunk upon war's frantic wine—Egypt shall be a stillness upon the desert; and Nineveh depart beneath the patient grass. O Mycenaean people! O Queen and Queen's daughter! You above whom dark wings already hover—hear the voice of Kassandra now! (*Suddenly, across fifty centuries, her indescribable eyes look into the audience and through them down incalculable vistas of time.*) O men and women! All you countless generations yet to be born, who sweeping through the air or moving over the water and under it shall yet accomplish but this end! Put by your swords! It is yourselves you kill. Lift up your faces to the sky! It is your heritage! About your foreheads are the everlasting stars. Within you God himself has life. O men and women; O thorn tree and the small sweet-voiced birds; the surging ocean; the vast pulsation of the universe; all things living and unliving—you are the indivisible God. Even you whose bitter mouths proclaim war's glory for a tainted gain, even you most pitifully are gods self-exiled into darkness. O you who live and breathe now and all those who are yet to know the splendor of this universe! Hear me! The laws of the universe are implacable. Implore the wide arc of heaven, and silence shall answer you. Alas! Who shall love mankind if men love not each other?"

A tremor passes over the form of Kassandra and she stands motionless for a moment. Again Agamemnon would calm their fears of what they have heard. Again Klytaimnestra would quiet the prophetess as one too terrible to live, and send her husband toward the bath she has prepared for him.

Now Agamemnon has left them. Kassandra's words still ring through the hall, prophesying the death of Klytaimnestra and calling after the King: "So war finds here its futile end; its hero its inglorious reward!" She has moved now through the room and stands before Klytaimnestra. "With a smile of infinite compassion she lifts the Queen's face and kisses her:

"Oh, woman! How pitiful all mankind is!"

Klytaimnestra has left the room. A moment later she returns, clutching to her bosom a long, heavy fisher's net that clings around her and trails beside her as she moves. "Through its folds gleams the ax of Aegisthos." . . .

Polymnia has dragged the fascinated Elektra from the scene. Klytaimnestra approaches the door cautiously. She peers into the lighted space beyond and enters. Elektra has crept back, and again the anxious Polymnia follows to save her ward from what she fears. Now Agamemnon's daughter has found the doors bolted fast, and from beyond can hear her mother's words—

"With this same net I trap you both!" . . . "Do not struggle, my lord; the net that tangles you is strong!"

Elektra has flung herself in fury against the unyielding doors, crying pitifully that her father open. And again Klytaimnestra's voice is heard—

"Iphegeneia! Iphegeneia!" . . . "Blood cries for blood!" . . . And again: "Iphegeneia! Iphegeneia!"

Above the cries of Elektra for the help of the guard there is "the crash of metal on shattered bone, a choked cry, and behind the bolted doors something falls to the ground."

An attendant returns with the boy Orestes. The sight of her brother galvanizes the crushed Elektra to a quickened action.

"Quick, quick! Bear him away," she cries to the guard. "Nor question why. But bear him far from here. Then bring or send me word of him. And teach him this: his life is dedicated to avenge his father's death. Take these few things I have, this gold. They will buy food and aid your flight. Quick, love, one kiss. O God!"

Now the door is opening slowly and Klytaimnestra, "smiling,

almost gay, a horrible travesty of what she was before the sacrifice at Aulis," comes into the room. Her arms are outstretched toward Elektra. "Iphegeneia! Iphegeneia! You have come back to me!" she calls. "Don't be afraid, Iphegeneia. They cannot hurt you any more. I have avenged you now at last!"

"Don't! Don't touch me! Let me go to him!" cries Elektra, beating the air with her hands in a frenzy of fear.

Aegisthos and his men have burst into the room.

"The thing is done?" demands Aegisthos.

"It's done and done and done," solemnly answers Klytaimnestra, as suddenly her manner changes. She cries out now in a choked voice and staggers, pressing her hand to her side. "There are more dead than should have been!" she mutters, and falls in a swoon.

Elektra has darted past them now and through the door. Aegisthos has called to his men to help him bear the Queen to her bed. The gathering night has plunged the room in darkness, save for a single pool of light before the door. Slowly Elektra comes from the room. "Her hair and dress are disheveled and she is torn with grief. Her blood-stained hands lift high the ax. Her upturned face is touched with a dedicated light of ecstasy and suffering."

"Father! Father!" she cries.

"There is a low muttering of thunder. The light above Elektra fades. She is lost in the darkness." The curtain falls.

ACT III

In the Palace courtyard, eleven years later, it is midday in Spring. A group of girls are discussing the festival in which the Queen of Spring is to bear the sacred bough back through the city's streets. One, named Hero, would have another, Melissa, assume this honor. But Melissa cannot. She is attending the nurse, Polymnia, who is old and ill, and should not be left.

They are still arguing the matter when two young men enter at the side. One is Pylades, the other, his friend. It is the friend who is slowly refreshing a memory of these Palace scenes that has grown vague with years. Now they both turn to Klytaimnestra's women for information.

"There have been great changes and most strange events," Euterpe would tell them, drawing them apart lest she be overheard. "Aegisthos slew the King and took his Queen for wife."

"Not Klytaimnestra—not that Queen—not her?" mutters the

friend.

"Even her."

"Oh, shame! Foul shame!"

"And there is more besides. Some say she had a part herself—"

"Euterpe! Guard your tongue. It would go hard with you should you be overheard," cautions Fria.

"I will be calm," the young man assures them. "He was my father's friend. I cannot but be moved by what has passed. And her—Elektra—and that same Orestes I have named, what of them?"

"None knows of him. As for Elektra—"

"Here she dwells among her father's halls as though she were a conquered slave."

"She is not wed?"

"She is not wed."

"Think, Pylades, think! This is the end to which an ancient house goes down in shame!"

The young man is at some pains to control his emotion and his tongue. But he would see and talk with the brooding Elektra, and goes into the grounds in search of her. It is, as it happens, the hour at which Elektra comes to fetch water from the spring and thus they miss her. She crosses the courtyard now, a water jar resting against her hip. She is haggard and wan. When the girls suggest that she should join them in celebrating the festival of Spring she sadly touches her breast—

"For me the Spring is done. There's Winter here," she says. And as they urge her further she adds with finality: "I have no place among the customary revels of my town. Let be. I keep my ways. The bright, high Mycenaean halls are bright for all but me; and music rings among their cedared beams and gilded cornices; yet is no music tuned for me." . . . "I tend a sacred fire I will not leave. But do not think I scorn your kindness, friends— Friends! How strange that word is on my lips!"

Now, to the sound of trumpets and the call of heralds, Aegisthos and Klytaimnestra appear, followed by a crowd of citizens, as well as Pylades and his friend. Aegisthos "has become more self-assured and somehow acquired dignity. But beneath this there is an intangible sense of weariness and cynicism." Klytaimnestra, her hair a slightly more flaming red, suggests "a marionette that carefully moves where her own will-power directs, her youth and radiance laborious deceit."

Elektra, stirred to a furious activity at sight of her mother, suddenly darts to the top of the steps and turns to face the people below—

"Hear me, people of Mycenae!" she shouts. "Hear me now—though never have you heeded me before. Tonight you hold those ancient rites you deem shall purify your city and yourselves. And once again I cry to you. How can the State be purified while still the Palace is unclean. What of my father and your King?"

Aegisthos wearily orders the trumpets to sound, and the trumpets drown out the girl's voice. And again, as she would resume they sound again to drown her out again and then the King and Queen and the people following continue on their way, leaving the two young men and the defeated Elektra behind. And now Pylades' friend has stepped forward excitedly, exclaiming that Elektra is his sister. To the huddled figure he approaches quickly.

"Are you Elektra—daughter of this house?" he asks.

"I am Elektra, and was once a daughter here," she answers.

ORESTES—I have come with news of your brother.

ELEKTRA—Of him—Orestes—how? Nay, it is nothing. This sudden joy has made me faint. It's nothing. Where dwells he, far from here? How does he live? What happiness is his and what success?

ORESTES—He dwells—

ELEKTRA—And when returns to Argos here?

ORESTES—When that may be. He dares not come awhile.

ELEKTRA—And is he strong? Ah, God! he must be strong.

ORESTES—His form is something like my own, I think. Is it not so, Pylades?

PYLADES—You two are very like.

ELEKTRA—Ah, that is well. And has he friends somewhere?

ORESTES—A few he has—as exiles have—some few.

ELEKTRA—Oh, brother, brother!

ORESTES—He sent his love to you.

ELEKTRA—I who am loveless have some love at last!

ORESTES—But tell me something of yourself. He bade me ask and I have little time to stay. I must away tonight for distant Crete.

ELEKTRA—Then tell me all of him—all—all.—But that's a selfish thought. My lot is what you see.

ORESTES—But surely they have not made of you a slave?

ELEKTRA (*who has been gazing intently at him*)—Your years should match them with my brother's years.

ORESTES—There is some few months difference in our age.

ELEKTRA—Your eyes and hair are like what his should be.

ORESTES—Your thoughts already leap to that?

ELEKTRA—No, no. Hope lies—and I am mad to think it so. How little wisdom I have shown! You are but spies that they have set to probe my thoughts. Perhaps to learn my brother's hiding-place.

ORESTES—Your heart was wiser than your mind—and quicker.

ELEKTRA—No! It is not thus Orestes comes! But with an army for his father's sake.

ORESTES—Have exiles armies at their call?

ELEKTRA—Ah, me! I know not what I say! If it be true—If it be false, it was a cruel thing you did—to make me hope!

ORESTES—It is not false! Look on your brother's face and know his love!

ELEKTRA—Ah, God! Some proof! Some proof! I am so much beset with those that hate us!

ORESTES—Look on this chain. It is the one I wore when from this house you sent me forth.

ELEKTRA—It is the same! And yet—men often steal.

ORESTES (*he takes out the robe worn by the child* ORESTES)—I am no thief. This is the robe I wore. Your hand embroidered it.

ELEKTRA—True! True! This is my handiwork. Yet that's not proof enough. Some other thing. Some memory long forgotten in our minds—that both—and only we—could know.

ORESTES—There was a grove to which you often carried me.

ELEKTRA—Yes! Yes!

ORESTES—We played beside a spring and there was one tall tree among whose branches we were wont to climb.

ELEKTRA—A linden tree!

ORESTES—It was our favorite haunt, and hidden by the leaves we sometimes sat all day and watched the clouds, pretending we were sailors in a ship that sought strange, distant isles.

ELEKTRA—We did! And yet all children play such games. Where was the grove?

ORESTES—I cannot tell. It all seems strange about this place—and yet not strange.

ELEKTRA—Too soon I leapt at hope to fall. Go, sir, and cease to mock me. It was a cruel sport.

ORESTES—What further proof— There's yet another thing! I can remember when my father came from Troy. The day was hot and still. A storm brooded upon the sky's dim edge. There was a bird among the trees.

ELEKTRA—Oh, God!

ORESTES—I asked you would he bring me things. "White

elephants and ivory toys," you said. At last across the hills we saw him come. The steeds he drove were twofold hued—one white between two blacks—and as they neared the gates, they reared. You cried aloud.

ELEKTRA (*in a whisper*)—Just at the gates they reared.

ORESTES—I asked you which our father was.

ELEKTRA (*throwing herself into his arms*)—You! You! At last! Oh, God!

ORESTES—United now at last!

ELEKTRA—Oh, joy is sharper than a sword!

ORESTES—Sit here. Pylades! Water—quick!

ELEKTRA—I am myself again. This face! This face! These hands at last. The cruel vigil paid. The moment come! But have you come with arms on vengeance bent?

ORESTES—I come to learn what hopes there are for me. And more than that, I come divinely sent: the gods decree the murderer must die.

ELEKTRA—Say rather murderess.

ORESTES—Her hand was not— No, she could not!

ELEKTRA—Her hand alone it was. Within her stirred Aegisthos child, still-born the selfsame day that Agamemnon died. Aegisthos was her lover long before. I saw them at their tryst the very night the beacon, blazing across the ink-black sky, declared the fall of Troy.

ORESTES—My mother, she! For that offense the gods decree her death. And I, unhappy, am the instrument. But how make end of them?

ELEKTRA—As they made end of him.

The deed, concludes Elektra, must be done at once. That night, because of the confusion and excitement attending the Spring festival, would seem a time perfectly appointed. Let Orestes approach the King's banquet as one newly come from foreign parts and when the King makes offer of the cup of greeting, but before he has touched either bread or salt to bind him by the laws of hospitality, he shall strike.

It is while Elektra has gone to fetch one thing that Orestes must have before the deed is done that Agamemnon's son is torn with misgivings. It is Pylades' reasoning that he (Orestes) should harken to the oracle's command and kill the murderer of his father, but not his mother.

"You and Elektra both have made a wasteland of your minds and in the center nourish hate, a fungus-rotted tree," declares

Pylades. "Uproot it, friend! Let proper sun and rain make fruitful harvest there instead. It is your right to kill Aegisthos, thus avenge your father and reclaim your heritage. But in this other thing I can see more clearly than yourself. Your mother must be spared."

"But she's the very root of all our ill."

"Orestes, it began in this same headlong hate that marks your house from first to last."

"She slew my father, cast me forth, and keeps my sister like a slave."

"These broodings are like midnight shadows that a dying fire casts. They and reality are not akin. Accomplish what you must and then forget the bitter past."

They are still arguing thus when Elektra returns. She has brought the self-same ax that Klytaimnestra wielded and has it wrapped in that same net the Queen had used. Carefully Elektra sketches the manner in which she believes Orestes should proceed to Aegisthos' slaying. Let him be stricken even as he passes the cup of welcome, while both his hands are occupied. The deed accomplished, let Orestes proclaim himself, and the justice of the thing he has done to the people in the hall. Then let him proceed to the chamber of Klytaimnestra, the partner of Aegisthos' guilt—

Again Pylades protests. Let Orestes avenge his father's death, but let him spare his mother's life.

"Is she to live who slew our father then?" demands the tense Elektra. "Is all the waiting vain for that at last? Hers was the hand that slew! Is he, whose body they cast out to rot, to be denied his full revenge? Let both live, then—and Agamemnon lie dishonored in his grave, as he has lain eleven years. What, brother, are you feared? Then I will do the thing!"

"Pylades, both must die," repeats Orestes.

"There speaks my father's son!" cries Elektra, exultantly. "Go hide you in the city, then, but where you still can see the orchard wall. Upon it I will raise a torch three times tonight and then extinguish it. When you have seen this signal, seek Aegisthos out."

"I will."

"Then—the corridor leads from the banquet hall straight to our mother's room. To mark it, I will set two lamps beside the door. Go now and watch. May God be with you till it's done."

"And with you, sister."

"Farewell."

Orestes and Pylades have gone. Elektra mounts the steps and

stands beyond the door looking out to the sea, the net clasped to her bosom. The red light of the waning sunset envelopes her, and in the fading light the doors are slowly closed. The stage is dark.

We stand again inside a chamber in the Palace. The Queen's women are lighting the lamps. Aesculapios, the physician, has been visiting Polymnia, and Melissa, who has been constantly in attendance upon the good nurse, is saddened by the report that the end for her is near.

"It seems as though there should be solemn thoughts about a bed of death," muses Melissa. "It seems as though there should be stillness in the world—and yet the night lives with a thousand sounds. . . . The morning will come, and with it all the loveliness of dew on bud and leaf; but her feet nevermore shall brush its silver from the orchard grass, as with her jar upon her hip she passes to the well. Together we will sit and sew as we were wont to do—her needle still at last. . . . I had not understood before that I should die and all the world go on the same without me."

AESCULAPIOS—Is that so very terrible?

MELISSA—The sun will shine, the flowers grow, the birds—Why, other eyes that now are dead have seen the same sweet things that gladden me, and other eyes will see them still when mine are dust.

AESCULAPIOS—Come here, my child. (*He leads her to the window.*) Look out. The earth, the sea, the sky are full of light. The trees spread out their fragile spring-enchanted leaves to feel the wind. They have no winter's thought. They hear the laughter of waters among the hills and answer the sound of its joy with their delight. Their season of sleep is done and they have life again. Before them is the summer's rich, luxurious hope. They are content to live, and when, in time, the storms of autumn come, contented will they rain their beauty down in showers of gold and flaming leaves upon the breast of earth and give themselves to sleep. And so should you find joy of life and claim it for your own; nor fear a future time. These eyes shall gladden other eyes; these gentle hands clasp other hands; these lips find other lips to kiss; this heart give life to other hearts; before they pass at last to nothingness. My child, there is no fear in death. The next year's leaves sleep in the bud through all the winter's storms and blossom with the spring; the earth is not bereft of light because the glorious sun has for a season set. Death is a universal good like sleep, and is as sweet to our old age. For we are weary from the toil and joy of life and ready for our rest—

MELISSA—I could not weary of my happiness!

AESCULAPIOS—You will not weary of your happiness, but still be glad to rest. Take all the best from life; live kindly day by day and have no fear. Make every moment sweet with gentleness and so your life with beauty and with love will ripen to its end.

MELISSA—And yet what lies for us beyond this death? Will it be good or ill or dark or bright?

AESCULAPIOS—There are yet other lands upon the earth, beyond the oceans, that we know not of; in Babylon and Pandie far beyond the East; and further still strange lands where towering cities rise beside the shining sea. So even are there other lives that we in time shall live; yet other joys that we shall taste; yet other deaths that we shall find unbitter in the end.

Klytaimnestra and Aegisthos have come from a banquet in their robes of state, and in some agitation, to inquire the physician's report as to Polymnia. They, too, are saddened that the nurse's days are numbered, and eager to do all that may be done to assure her comfort.

Soon Polymnia herself, leaning on the arm of Melissa, has come to have her say about this tyranny the good Aesculapios would put upon her. And gains her point that she shall stay awhile, being weary of the bed. . . .

Aegisthos would return now to his banquet, and Klytaimnestra is worried about what may happen at that banquet. She has seen Aegisthos frequently in lengthy conference with Vortigern, the Barbarian, and would caution her lord about this—

"You do not heed the tenor of our times," insists Aegisthos. "Mingling with their race shall strengthen ours."

"We are the guardians, the treasurers, of generations yet to come," protests the Queen. "How shall we justify the thing we did unless we guard the treasure and the glory of our past as righteously as Agamemnon would?"

"You cannot pour me into Agamemnon's mold. Come, love, you must leave matters such as this to me. Being a woman, you see, is always near yourself. In that old time it was your child, and now it is your race alone. I see a distant future clearly and must labor to that end. These Northmen are our complement. If we accept them, we have conquered them and made their greatness part of ours. But if we do not make them brothers in our destiny, they conquer us. The destiny of man is somehow peace and love."

"Do those who fought at Troy love one another now?"

"Their bond was lust and hate at first, not love. But even so, we still must labor patiently to move mankind along that path though all a lifetime shall not gain more than a single step."

"O husband! ponder what you do. You heard tonight how Egypt is no more and Pharaoh's greatness shattered by barbarians."

"Such is the end of those who trust in war—to perish from the earth."

"Far better that than live ignobly. That's the greatness of our race, that we have stood unconquered age by age."

"The arts of peace alone are great and in them is our only immortality. Be not so troubled, love. I must return. Good night."

With Melissa's help Klytaimnestra puts off her robes of state. And when Melissa has gone she wearily removes her flaming wig as well. Her own hair is white, and must be hurriedly covered with a veil when Melissa returns to say that Hero and her attendants have arrived with flowers for their Queen, who will not be able to attend the festival. Hero has brought some verses, too, that Phaon wrote. She begs permission to say them, while her friends help with a ritual dance they have prepared.

Klytaimnestra follows the interlude with interest to the end. Then, as the priestesses of the dance approach Hero and set fillets of blossoms upon her head, the Queen suddenly starts up with a cry of horror. For an awful moment she has seen "another form and other fillets wound about another brow." Her face is covered by her hands as she struggles to control her emotion.

The maidens are dismissed and go wonderingly from the room. Sadly Klytaimnestra picks up the flowers that were on Hero's brow, and drops them with a sigh.

"Will memory never die?" she cries. "O universe! To all your glory what are we—who for a moment pause beneath the splendor of your suns; who for a moment know the agony of all your loveliness; and, passing, leave you still unchanged, nor add nor take away from you one single thing except ourselves?"

"But each of us must die," protests Polymnia. "Believe me, love, it is so simple and so good that it is so."

"I know my end for I have made it mine. The day Orestes stands within these halls, I die. Forth from my womb I brought a sword. I made a temple of my mind to hate and of my heart a tomb. My life has been a clamor and an emptiness. I am a woman meant for motherhood and yet no child is mine. Defeated I go down to that dim place where those who have loved lie loveless and those who have hated are still."

Her old nurse would comfort Klytaimnestra if she could, telling her of the defeat that was hers in the days when she was led away from the flaming city where she lived; of the bitterness and hate that had welled up within her heart; of the acceptance of that slavery that had been put upon her; of her pleading to be given charge of the infant Princess—

"You were a babe still at the breast and your mother had been stricken with a sickness," recounts Polymnia. "There came to me a fearful thought. I made my supplication to your father: 'Give me the child that I may be her nurse.' There were other women in the chamber as I bent above the cradle where you lay; but I thought: 'It can be swiftly done.' "

"I do not understand. What could be done?"

"You were so very small a babe. Both little fists were pressed against your cheeks. You waved your little legs the way that babies do. I lifted you, still thinking, in myself: 'It can be swiftly done.' I felt the soft, small body in my arms, warm, warm and sweet. You rolled your head and crowed and sought my breast beneath the robe. I did not move, but stood looking at the little hand that rested on my sleeve. I felt your head against my heart. Then suddenly I sat me down upon the floor and wept and held you close, kissing you and rocking you upon my breast. I called you by my dead child's name and loved you for his sake.—It is not clear. I cannot tell it as I should. You see something hard and bitter had gone out of me—I understood. One living thing had been taken from me, and another given in its place. I no longer hated men. I understood. I felt pity, pity and a kind of love. It was as though they were my children, too—I cannot say it as I should. I do not know—it is so hard to make it clear for someone else to see."

Klytaimnestra has risen. She stands now before Polymnia and solemnly kisses her cheek. "I understand!" she says.

"Let me hold you close against my heart. Poor child! Poor child! Be not confused. There is such peace beyond the world."

"There is such comfort here." . . .

Now Klytaimnestra's women come to be instructed in the next day's tasks and Polymnia refuses to be put back to bed. She'll take her part in these affairs of the household as she always has done, and stays on as Klytaimnestra checks the kitchen lists and the orders for the great banquet that is to come.

It is an orderly and prescribed routine, interrupted only briefly when Melissa is sure she sees signal lights above the garden walls. Some lover's signal, it may be. Yet at thought of it Polymnia goes suddenly faint, and now must be urged again to leave them for her bed. As Klytaimnestra and Polymnia pass the great door a glimmer of light shines through, as though someone were placing a lamp there, but their backs are turned and they do not see—

For a second the room is empty. Then the door is slowly opened and Elektra is revealed. "She is completely enveloped in a cloak of dull red copper that fastens at the throat and falls in stiff folds to the ground. On her head is a gold crown of thin spikes. She moves slowly to the center of the top step and stands gazing down into the room with burning eyes."

Klytaimnestra, returning from Polymnia's chamber, pauses startled as she sees Elektra. It is long since Elektra has come to this part of the Palace, and never before arrayed as a Princess of the house, as she has a right to be. She has come, Elektra explains, because she has heard that Polymnia will die, and she had loved Polymnia well—

"Besides is not today the day when all things must be purified, all hate be laid away?" asks Elektra. "So shall our hate be laid at rest and be forgotten now at last. And from tonight I'll love you, cut my hair and lay it on your tomb, pour out libations, tears upon your grave when you are dead. . . . Tonight I will empty my heart of words: I will empty it of hate and loathing—here—tonight. After tonight I mean to love you."

KLYTAIMNESTRA (*with resignation and despair*)—Well, say it, then. Why do you hate?

ELEKTRA—Shall I love my father's murderer?

KLYTAIMNESTRA (*a heart-pierced cry*)—Elektra! (*Then controlling herself and speaking very quietly.*) There are many things you would understand better were you a mother. Had you lost—

ELEKTRA—Who is it denied me that? Who condemned me to be the withered, sterile thing I am? Why have I nothing of my own to love, nothing that is mine, mine to love?

KLYTAIMNESTRA (*in a low, shaken voice*)—Oh, God! Cannot the past rest in the grave?

ELEKTRA—The past never dies. The past is our shadow, our little gray shadow that goes slipping along beside us, behind us, whispering, whispering, whispering: "Have you forgotten? Have you forgotten? Do you remember these steps and the stain upon them? Do you remember how I stood here and cried: 'Father!' Have you forgotten this door through which he came or this window where I waited for his coming home?" And at night when you crouch by the fire, when you want not to know, to never think, to never remember any more: it is all about you, leaping out from the corner of the room, waving over the walls and roof, plucking at you, pointing, pointing and shouting: "Have you forgotten? Can you forget?" (*Suddenly her voice breaks, goes shrill and wild as, confused, she answers herself.*) No! No! I have not forgotten. I have not changed! (*Her voice sinks to a despairing wail.*) O Father! Father!

KLYTAIMNESTRA—Go on. Talk it all out. Tell me everything that is in your heart; Mother will understand.

ELEKTRA (*momentarily confused and brought out of herself by the unexpected tone of her mother's voice*)—What was it? What was I saying? This is so much, and I cannot remember it all.

KLYTAIMNESTRA (*sitting on the steps*)—Come here, Elektra, sit beside me and let me stroke your head.

ELEKTRA—No! No! You must not touch me. I do not want you to touch me. (*In a whisper to herself.*) She must not touch me. No.

KLYTAIMNESTRA—Stay there, then, and go on. It is better that you should tell me all the things you have been feeding on in silence these long years.

ELEKTRA (*more and more confused, moving her head a little from side to side*)—There are so many things. So many things. But in my mind's dark labyrinth of pain all's lost and all confused.

KLYTAIMNESTRA—I understand. I brooded then as you brood now.

ELEKTRA—How can you understand, you who forgot him, even while he lived? Oh, these corridors, these long halls and empty rooms! How I have gone about them in the night, and wrung my hands and stifled the cries in my throat, knowing my mother in a strange man's bed!

KLYTAIMNESTRA—Elektra!

ELEKTRA—Oh, those nights when I have sat alone and heard strange feet among my father's halls and known a stranger held his place and all his state! Those nights when I was wont to choke my cries with teeth fast clenched upon my flesh, and sealed my tears within my heart, nor cried aloud, but sat—nor moved—alone within my rooms, until the night was peopled with strange sights and sounds. Such nights are not forgot. They wake me from my sleep with awful hands and walk beside me silently all day.

KLYTAIMNESTRA—Ah, God! Do I not know such memories too? Are there not cries I cannot silence, too? . . . Elektra, have you forgotten your sister? You who remember so well, have you forgotten Iphegeneia?

ELEKTRA (*suddenly taking fire*)—No! No! I have forgotten nothing. She died for him. How happy she must have been! Oh, that I had died for him, that I had gone out to him over the sea and died for him there!

KLYTAIMNESTRA—Go on, child. Ease your heart.

ELEKTRA (*her voice dull and empty*)—There was so much I meant to say.

Suddenly Klytaimnestra half starts up. She has heard a cry as though of one in pain. But there was no cry. Elektra heard none. If there was it must have been an owl in the orchard. Klytaimnestra is not satisfied. There was a cry. It could not have been Polymnia, she is too near. It may be those at the banquet have taken to brawls.

Again Elektra would free her mother's mind of apprehension. The cry was nothing, or at most an owl, or a dog baying the moon. Nor does she want Klytaimnestra to go searching the cause. She must stay there.

"Mother, you must not go away if you want me to love you again!" pleads Elektra. "See, I will sit here and we will talk."

"Call me Mother once again."

"Mother."

"O baby! Baby!"

Klytaimnestra has started toward Elektra as though to embrace her. Orestes slips stealthily through the door.

"Who are you?" demands Klytaimnestra.

"It is your son, Orestes, Mother, come home at last."

Klytaimnestra starts forward. She would embrace her son, but stops sharply at the sight of his sword.

"There is blood upon your sword!"

"It is Aegisthos' blood."

Klytaimnestra gives a faint cry and puts out a hand to support herself. Elektra is quick to note the weakness. "See! See!" she shouts. "She has tears for her paramour who had no tears for Agamemnon's sake!"

ORESTES—Mother, kneel down and prepare to die, for it is just that you should do so.

KLYTAIMNESTRA—O children! What fearful thing is it you plan to do? Stop now before it is too late. (ELEKTRA *makes a fierce, scornful movement of her body.*) It is not for myself I plead. It is for you—for you! O my unhappy children—my unhappy children. Hear me, Orestes—

ELEKTRA—No! You must not hear her. She is subtle and full of guile. She greeted him she slew with words of love. I heard her. When she speaks you see no longer clearly and forget what you must do. Strike! Strike!

KLYTAIMNESTRA—O God! Give me some power of words to sweep like flame across their minds and burn away this darkness and this hate. I *will* save you from yourselves. Oh, do not think it is because I fear to die. Death will be welcome when it comes. You must believe me, child. It *is* of you I think, and not myself. (ELEKTRA *bursts into a long, dreadful laugh.* KLYTAIMNESTRA *shudders and puts her hand to her head, bewildered and confused.*) O God! Make them believe me! Gladly would I die to ease your hearts, Orestes—gladly—but by your hands—no! No! You cannot know how terrible it is to kill what most you should have loved. O children! Children! Cast out this hate. For we who in the madhouse of our own emotions dwell go mad at last. I know! I know!

ELEKTRA—Do not hear her, Brother. Strike! Strike!

KLYTAIMNESTRA—I will save you! You shall hear me! I cry across the chasm of your hate, a mother's cry who sees her child about to wound itself. Oh, vengeance seems the sweetest cup! But tasted— Your body moves and bears you like a burden on your flesh. You have the faculties of one alive. But from within a silence hear all things and from behind a darkness see the sun. (ORESTES *is visibly shaken.*)

ELEKTRA—Orestes! Why do you stand there? Strike! Our father's blood cries for vengeance.

KLYTAIMNESTRA—O child! Child! What have you become?

ELEKTRA—A sword made keen in the hand of God for your destruction. Kill her, Brother! Kill her!

KLYTAIMNESTRA—Orestes, Agamemnon *is* avenged.

ELEKTRA—Because Orestes slew your lover, harlot? (ORESTES *grips his sword convulsively and takes a step toward his mother.*)

KLYTAIMNESTRA—For me there is no punishment more hideous than so to see you standing there. O son, how gladly by my own hand I would die to keep your hands unstained! But even so my death would wither both your lives, knowing you had willed it as you do.

ORESTES (*disturbed and uncertain*)—Could she not live in exile? Pylades said—

ELEKTRA—Orestes, close your mind to her! There's such sweet reason dwells between her lips, stone would be melted into honey. But I—I saw! (*Slowly* ELEKTRA *begins to rise as she speaks. Her cloak has become unfastened at the throat and, as she rises, slips from her shoulders and, still clinging tightly about her, drops to the floor. In the light from the lamps, her nether robe glows like incandescent metal—the most intense red that appears in the whole play. It is as though a thin bud of flame were bursting from its dull calyx.*) I saw our father, Agamemnon, the King before whom other kings bowed down when Troy fell, Orestes, I saw our father's body cast upon the dungheap—left to rot—I buried him. I washed the limbs in wine and sprinkled dust upon the broken head. O God! I saw— (*Her emotion overcomes her and for a moment she is incoherent.*)

KLYTAIMNESTRA—I beat upon the doors of Fate—but they are shut between us three!

ELEKTRA—I saw the grinning white of bone laid bare! The flies that I could scarcely brush from off the clotted wounds! And things—horrible—white—burrowing in the flesh that dogs had gnawed! And in his eyes—his eyes! O Father! Father! (*She rushes wildly toward* ORESTES.) If you are Klytaimnestra's bastard, I am not. Give me the sword!

Stung by Elektra's taunt Orestes lifts his sword and starts fiercely toward Klytaimnestra when she, peering into the darkness behind them, says calmly: "Bind them. But do them no hurt!" Orestes and Elektra turn to face a second danger. As they do Klytaimnestra darts for the doors. Realizing there is not time to go so far, she cowers in the shadows, hoping thus to conceal herself.

Elektra and Orestes, quickly realizing the trick, turn and follow, gropingly, after her.

"She shall not escape! She shall not escape!" Elektra is shouting as they prowl the gloom. Suddenly Klytaimnestra has darted out from under their reaching arms and dashed up the stairs to the doors.

"Klytaimnestra has reached the central portal. For a moment her arms flash palely against the brass as she beats upon the doors, but cannot open them. Her pursuers are almost upon her when with one last and terrible gesture of despair she hurls them open and the awful hunt disappears into a flood of clean, pure moonlight and delicate tree-shadows that streams down over the steps and ripples across the floor far into the room."

For a moment the room is empty and silent. Then Klytaimnestra's women come with little lamps that soften the gloom. A few pause on the steps to hear the nightingales that sing in the garden, and to note the moon that by now has cleared the walls. Deftly the women remove the toilet things their Queen will need no more that night. Wonderingly they debate as to what robe they should lay out for the morning. And now they are gone, leaving the great doors open that the night wind may sweeten the chamber.

Again the room is briefly empty. The rising moon throws a radiant light against its walls and these seem to become almost transparent—

"Through the doorway creep two trembling, broken figures. They stand one at either side of the opening, casting tortuous shadows that stretch thin and long down the steps and out across the floor of the room. They seem to cower away from each other in horror, loathing, even while they are impelled toward each other by their fear and suffering. A thin, far-away voice breaks the silence."

ELEKTRA—Now, now she can never love me.

ORESTES—She died as did befit a Queen!

ELEKTRA—Orestes, give me your hand. (*She stretches out her hands toward him, yet remains withdrawn from him. He is motionless, as though he had neither heard nor seen. Her arms drop to her side.*)

ORESTES—She was tall before me in the night.

ELEKTRA (*with growing terror in her voice*)—Come to me! The night frightens me.

ORESTES—She spoke strange, unexpected words. I could not understand.

ELEKTRA—We must not think, Orestes! Do not think!

ORESTES—My sword was a bright flame in the night. Then it was darkened. (*Then with a terrible cry.*) O God! Her hair was white!

ELEKTRA—We must not think, Orestes. Do not think!

ORESTES—Her hair was white.

ELEKTRA—We must not think. We must not think.

ORESTES (*in a changed faint voice*)—Why is the moonlight so far away? Behind darkness.

ELEKTRA (*moving toward him brokenly*)—O my brother!—

My brother!

ORESTES (*springing away from her with a terrible cry*)—Away from me!

ELEKTRA—I am your sister, Elektra; your sister.

ORESTES (*swinging his sword*)—Away from me!

ELEKTRA (*stands still and broken, looking up into his face pitifully*)—Do not drive me away, Brother. Where is there for me to go?

ORESTES—You shall not seize upon my soul! I will not be punished. I will not be tortured all my days. I did not know! I did not know!

ELEKTRA—I—I alone—am guilty.

ORESTES—How can we know anything, we mortals, poor blind things that grope and tremble in the dark?

ELEKTRA—Orestes, listen, listen to me.

ORESTES—Back and away, or you— (*He swings the sword above his head threateningly.*)

ELEKTRA (*closing her eyes wearily*)—I am not afraid to die—I that am without hope.

ORESTES (*hesitatingly*)—I am not frightened now. You are only a shadow that creeps in and out among the other shadows.

ELEKTRA (*still with closed eyes*)—Oh, to be deep in the grave! Oh, to be at peace among the swift forms and transparent shadows at the bottom of the sea!

ORESTES—Hush! Hush! (ELEKTRA *opens her eyes and looks at him.*) They slip away before my sword and hide among the shadows there. I cannot kill them! I must hide. Hush! (*He springs back and wheels about.* ELEKTRA *looks at him with growing horror.*) Away! Away! (*He strikes out with his sword.*) I am not afraid of you! Lie there, and there! Through and through and still not dead! I'm not afraid of you. I am Orestes, the mother-slayer!

ELEKTRA (*realization bursting over her*)—O God!

ORESTES—Who is that standing pale in the moonlight?

ELEKTRA (*in an emotionless voice*)—There is no one, Orestes. There is no one.

ORESTES—Mother! O Mother!

Elektra, "exhausted and like an old, old woman," has moved toward Orestes. Now she "puts her arms around him and, drawing his head up into the moonlight, rocks it upon her breast as though he were a sick child, the child she never is to have." . . .

The door of Polymnia's room is slowly opened. Elektra has

shrunk down, huddling over Orestes in the deep shadow. Melissa, still crowned with the flowers of the festival, moves into the moonlight.

"You are mistaken, Polymnia. You heard nothing. There is no one here," she calls back. "No—no. You must not fret. It is all right. The Queen? She is not here. The doors are open. I think she has gone out into the garden. (*She moves a little way up the steps. Her voice becomes ecstatic, thrilling.*) O Polymnia! It is the most beautiful night that ever was! The heavens are like soft transparent fire behind the stars. (*She lifts her arms wide in a gesture of sudden delight; then drops them again and half turns toward* POLYMNIA'S *door.*) What did you say? Yes, I hear them singing across the fields; far away and faint, but very sweet. (*Her voice grows more and more hushed as she becomes one with the night's magic.*) They are moving through the night now, under the great branches; up into the holy hills. (*Her face is lifted. She stands a moment, motionless and beautiful.*) How full of light the heavens are! (*Then, a radiant figure, moving serenely, she goes out through the great doorway into the shimmering light.*)"

THE CURTAIN FALLS

STAGE DOOR

A Comedy in Three Acts

BY EDNA FERBER AND GEORGE S. KAUFMAN

IT was not a new field that Edna Ferber and George Kaufman invaded when they took up the subject of "Stage Door." They had, in 1927, written "The Royal Family," which was quickly numbered among the successes of the 1927-28 season, and as quickly recognized as an illuminative and authoritative study of stage folk.

In "Stage Door" these collaborators take up the adventure of the struggling debutantes of the theatre, the ingénues, who move upon Broadway and the theatre each season in a fairly solid phalanx of young, eager, attractive femininity, ever so earnest and ever so brave. Once in a long while the accidental, overnight success of one of their number will thrill and encourage the lot of them. More often the repeated failure of the majority would depress them utterly if their spirits were not so perfectly and continuously buoyed by that self-confidence which sent them seeking a stage job in the first place.

In the playing, more noticeably than in the reading, "Stage Door" struggles against a slight handicap. Its authors, through their leading character, argue with great enthusiasm for a loyalty to the theatre as against a career in pictures. Their point is that, although an actress may achieve a sudden success in pictures and profit generously from the sale of her personal graces on the screen, she will shortly find herself thrown back on the theatrical market with the best of her youth wasted and little achieved in the way of a developed talent. It happens in the play that the heroine of the New York production was Margaret Sullavan, who had already quite successfully disproved that statement. At least for the present. She had enjoyed both a Broadway career as an actress and a Hollywood career as a screen star. Indicating that the two are not, in actual fact, at all incompatibly opposed, one to the other.

The setting chosen by Miss Ferber and Mr. Kaufman for their play is that of the Footlights Club of New York. It is a club exclusively for girls of the stage and occupies one of those old brownstone houses in the West Fifties in New York. Our first glimpse is of the common living room just off the front hall. The dining room opens at one side and a broad stairway at the back leads to sleeping rooms above.

Topping an old-fashioned marble mantel over the fireplace is a copy of a portrait of Sarah Bernhardt "at her most dramatic." "It is an October evening, just before the dinner hour. The girls are coming home from matinees, from job-hunting, they are up and down the stairs, and presently they will be out again on dinner dates, playing the evening performances, seeing a movie."

At the moment Olga Brandt, "a dark, intense, sultry-looking girl," is playing Chopin at the piano with surprisingly good technique. Bernice Niemeyer, "a young girl who is definitely not the ingénue type" (and a little proud of it), is writing at a desk and bothering the pianist from time to time with silly questions.

Frequent rings at the doorbell are answered by Mattie, a colored maid, and the goings and comings of club inmates shortly include the appearance of two known as Big and Little Mary—Big Mary scaling no more than four feet two and Little Mary running up within an inch or two of six feet. A chatty pair, given to answering for and in unison with each other.

Madeleine Vauclain, "a languid beauty," in search of mail, is also looking for a girl to go out with her. "I've got an extra man," Madeleine explains. Olga might be interested, but she has a rehearsal. She must play the piano for a lot of chorus girls to sing and dance. "And for that I studied fifteen years with Kolijinsky!" explodes Olga.

Judith Canfield is in. Judith is "hard, wise, debunked," and properly thrilled at finding a letter from home. Letters from home are so stimulating— "Mmmmm!" she hums as she reads. . . . "Pa got laid off. . . . My sister's husband has left her. . . . And one of my brothers slugged a railroad detective. . . . I guess that's all. Yes. Lots of love and can you spare fifty dollars."

Judith thinks she might fill in for Madeleine's extra man. If he's from Seattle he is pretty sure to be breezy, with a "Hello, Beautiful!" greeting. Judith feels like stepping out tonight.

"That's all right for you," admits Ann Braddock, hearing about the date as she comes down to dinner; "you're not working. But I can't go out to dinner, and run around, and still give my best to the theatre. After all, you never see Kit Cornell dashing around."

"Kit Cornell! What about Bernhardt! I suppose *she* was a home girl!" Judith calls after her, with a wave toward the Bernhardt portrait. . . .

Mrs. Orcutt, the House Matron, has been showing Kaye Hamilton, "a fragile and rather wispy girl whose eyes are too big for her face," the upstairs rooms. Mrs. Orcutt, about 46, is one in whose manner and dress "you detect the flavor of a theatrical past. Her dress is likely to have too many ruffles, her coiffure too many curls." She introduces Kaye to Judith, explaining that Kaye is planning to be one of them, and that if she does she will room with Jean and Terry, now that Louise is leaving.

With three in the room the cost will be $12.50 a week to Kaye. Her references, of course, will have to be confirmed. As to the house rules—

"As you know, this is a club for stage girls. I assume you are on the stage." There is a slight note of inquiry in Mrs. Orcutt's voice.

"Yes. Yes. I'm not working now, but I hope . . ."

"I understand. . . . Now about callers—men callers, I mean—"

"There won't be any men."

"Oh, it's quite all right. We like you to bring your friends here. But not after eleven-thirty at night, and—of course—only in this room."

"I understand."

"I try very hard to make the girls feel that this is a real home. I was one of them myself not many years back, before I married Mr. Orcutt. Helen Romayne? Possibly you remember?"

"I'm afraid I—"

"That's quite all right. I think that covers everything. If you wish to go and get your bags—Mattie! (*Peering toward the dining room.*) Will you come here a minute?"

"Yes, ma'am!"

"Now, each girl is given a door key," concludes Mrs. Orcutt, gently piloting Kaye toward the doorway, "and there's a little charge of twenty-five cents in case they're lost. Well, good-by, and I'll expect you in a very short time."

The telephone has rung. The call is for Jean Maitland, and the fact that it is from Mr. Kingsley of the Globe Picture Company is pretty exciting. Mrs. Orcutt is visibly impressed as she calls Jean, and Jean, a beautiful blonde, "an opportunist; good-natured enough when things go her way; of definite charm and appeal for men," is herself a little tremulous with excitement as she answers Mr. Kingsley—

"Hello! . . . Mr. Kingsley! . . . How wonderful! . . . Well, *I* think it's pretty wonderful! With all the thousands of people at that party I didn't think you'd remember *me*. . . . Yes, I know you said that, but in your business you must meet a million beautiful girls a day. . . . Well, anyhow, half a million."

Could Jean go to dinner? Tonight? Jean thinks she could. She'd love it. She—

As she hangs up the receiver heads pop out from a dozen vantage points. Big and Little Mary come cloppity-clopping down the stairs. There is a perfect barrage of questions. Is it really Mr. Kingsley? What does he want? When is he coming? Could they—

Jean hasn't had time to borrow half the evening things she will need before there is further excitement. Louise Mitchell is leaving. The houseman has brought down her bags and Louise, in traveling clothes, accompanied by three other girls, is following after. There are greetings and regrets. Louise hates to go. Especially without seeing Terry, who hasn't come in yet. But Louise thinks perhaps she had better get out before she busts out crying—

"You've all been just too darling for words, every single one of you—and no matter how happy I am, I'll never forget you, and thanks a million times for the perfume, Pat, and you, Susan, for the compact, and all of you that clubbed together and gave me the exquisite nightgown."

"Oh, that's all right," clowns Bernice.

"So—I hope I'll make a better wife than I did an actress. I guess I wasn't very good at that—"

"You were so!" protests Big Mary.

"You were swell!" echoes Little Mary.

"I guess I wasn't very swell or I wouldn't be getting mar—" Louise catches herself just in time; "—that is, any girl would be glad to give up the stage to marry a wonderful boy like Bob—anyway, I certainly am. Goodness, when I think that for two whole years he's waited back there in Appleton, I guess I'm pretty lucky. . . . Well, if any of you ever come out that way with a show, why, it's only a hundred miles from Milwaukee. Don't forget I'll be Mrs. Robert Hendershot by that time, and Wisconsin's beautiful in the autumn—the whole Fox River Valley—it's beautiful—"

It doesn't sound very convincing, even to Louise. Fortunately at that moment "the situation is miraculously saved by the slam of the street door and the electric entrance of a new and buoyant figure."

The newcomer is Terry Randall, a girl with "the vivid personality, the mobile face of the born actress." Terry "is not at all conventionally beautiful, but the light in her face gives to her rather irregular features the effect of beauty. High cheekbones, wide mouth, broad brow." Breathlessly she has greeted her friend—

"LOUISE! Dar—ling! I was so afraid you'd be gone. I ran all the way from Forty-sixth Street. Nothing else in the world could have kept me—look—what do you think! I've got a JOB!"

Immediately there is a chorused demand for particulars and Terry has some trouble answering. It's a short part. Not big, but good. It's with Berger and—

But the taxi has arrived and the excitement returns to Louise and her departure. There is considerable kissing, a good many good-bys and finally Louise has gone, followed by a handful of rice the giggling Mattie has brought from the kitchen to throw after her. Now the girls have got back to the attack on Terry.

"When do you go into rehearsal, Terry?" asks Kendall Adams.

"Yes, when?" Olga wants to know.

TERRY—Right away!

BERNICE—Gosh, Terry, you certainly got a break. Berger wouldn't even talk to me.

LITTLE MARY—Berger's an awful meany. How'd you get to him, anyway?

TERRY—I just stood there outside his door for a week.

PAT—And it did the trick?

BIG MARY—*I* tried that.

BOBBY—It never helped *me* any.

JUDITH—Me neither. I laid there for a whole afternoon once with "Welcome!" on me.

TERRY—I've had a longer run outside his office than I've had with most shows. This was my second week. I was just going to send out for a toothbrush and a camp chair when suddenly he opened the door. He was going. I said, "Mr. Berger!" That's practically all I've said for two weeks—Mr. Berger. (*She gives an assortment of readings of "Mr. Berger," ranging from piteous pleading to imperious command.*)

LITTLE MARY—What did he do?

SUSAN—What happened?

TERRY—He never even stopped. Suddenly I was furious. I grabbed his arm and said, "Listen! You're a producer and I'm an actress. What right have you got to barricade yourself behind closed doors and not see me! And hundreds like me! The greatest actress in the world might be coming up your stairs and you'd never know it."

o by Vandamm Studio, New York.

"STAGE DOOR"

erry: There was never any doubt in her mind—I was going to be an actress. It was almost a
itual thing, like being dedicated to the church.
aye: I never thought of the theatre that way. I just used it as a convenience, because I was
erate.

(*Margaret Sullavan, Frances Fuller*)

KENDALL—Terry! What did he say?

TERRY—He said, "Are you the greatest actress in the world?" I said, "Maybe." He said, "You don't look like anything to me. You're not even pretty and you're just a little runt." I said, "Pretty! I suppose Rachel was pretty. And what about Nazimova! She's no higher than this." (*Indicates a level.*) "But on the stage she's any height she wants to be."

JUDITH—P.S. She got the job.

TERRY—Yes. (*A deep sigh that conveys her relief at the outcome.*) And when I walked out on Broadway again it seemed the most glamorous street in the world. Those beautiful Nedick orange stands, and that lovely traffic at Broadway and Forty-fifth, and those darling bums spitting on the sidewalk—

A ring at the doorbell sends the girls flying for cover. Jean barely has time to tell Terry of her luck in having a dinner date with David Kingsley as they disappear up the stairs.

The man at the door is not the expected Mr. Kingsley, however, but a rather engaging young Westerner, Sam Hastings, who is calling for Bobby Melrose. Hastings has no more than found himself a seat than another caller arrives. This would be Jimmy Devereaux, who has come for Susan Paige. Soon the young men have introduced themselves. They both have stage connections. At least Hastings has played one or two small parts and Devereaux is just finishing up at the New York School of Acting. After that he will go on the stage.

"Did you ever try to get a job on the stage?" asks Sam.

"Not yet," admits Devereaux.

"That's more of a career than acting. I've been in New York two years. I'm from Texas. Houston Little Theatre. We came up and won a contest, and I stayed. I've had ten weeks' work in two years. Don't ask me how I live. I don't know."

"You could go back to Texas, couldn't you?"

"Go back! Oh, no! I'm an actor."

Susan has come and taken her Jimmy out, and the two business men who are to squire Madeleine Vauclain and her friend are waiting. They are Fred Powell and Lou Milhauser, "overhearty Big Business Men out for a holiday," and they find the adventure amusing. Milhauser, in particular, is impressed with this "home for girls." It's a handy place to know about.

"I—I always thought actresses lived in flats or—uh—hotel rooms," ventures Milhauser.

"Lot of 'em do."

"What about men actors—where do they live?"

"I don't know—Lambs' Club, I guess."

The Big Business men have not had time to dress, and that is something of a shock to Madeleine and Judith, who arrive in full evening regalia "gathered from the richest recesses of the club." But the girls are forgiving. Judith makes only one stipulation. "Little Italian places" are out. She wants a decent dinner. . . .

Outside the club a big Cadillac has driven up for Linda Shaw. That's a regular performance, too, and the girls are curious. No one ever comes with the Cadillac—except the chauffeur.

"Well, it's nice work if you can get it," admits Pat Devine.

"I think it's disgraceful," snaps Ann Braddock. "A nice girl wouldn't want a man to send for her that way. And if you ask me, it gives the club a bad name."

Linda, coming down the stairs, might have heard if the girls had not hissed a warning. She is beautifully dressed, her evening cape handsomely furred and she sweeps into the room. The girls are all admiration and envy. The fur, Linda explains, was sent her. It used to be on a coat of her mother's.

"Oh—Mother has a nice taste in orchids, too," sweetly murmurs Pat.

"Yes," Linda snaps back, sharply. "Don't you wish *you* had a mother like mine?" and sweeps out of the room.

There is further excitement when David Kingsley, "a man of decided charm and distinction," really does arrive. Every girl in the club is eager to have a peek at him, even if she can't meet him. They have heard he can spot picture material at a glance. He is said to have picked no less than three picture stars last season that nobody had ever heard of before. Even Mattie is impressed by the Kingsley presence.

"If you'll just rest yourself—I'll go right up," she tells him when he asks that Miss Maitland be told.

There is to be no rest for Mr. Kingsley. A second later Bernice backs out of the dining room, apparently addressing someone she has just left. Bernice is giving as perfect an imitation of a screen actress as she knows how.

"Yes, Mattie, an actress's life is such an interesting one," Bernice is saying as she sidles into the room, apparently quite unaware that anyone is there; "if you could only see the different types that I do in the course of a day, Mattie. For example, an English actress came into an office today." (*Goes suddenly very English.*) "'My dear Harry, how definitely ripping to see you. Definitely ripping!' And then, Mattie, a little girl from Brooklyn came in. 'Listen, I did write for an appurnment! You got a noive!' " (*She turns, and to her obvious embarrassment there is* MR. KINGSLEY. *She is a picture of pretty confusion.*) "Oh, I am so sorry! I didn't dream anyone was here."

"That's quite all right," smiles Kingsley.

A moment later Pat Devine, the jacket of her pajama suit missing, "her slim figure well revealed in the trousers and the scant short-sleeved top, comes carefully down the stairs looking for her book. She flutters prettily from table to book shelves in her search.

The girls are no sooner through than Mrs. Orcutt arrives, having "shed her workaday dress for something very grand in the way of a silk dinner gown." How well Mrs. Orcutt remembers "Little David Kingsley" who used to be a boy in Al Woods' office when she was—yes, Helen Romayne—

But now Jean has arrived to rescue Mr. Kingsley. The others, including Mrs. Orcutt, take the hint and fade away. Jean has one favor to ask before they go on—she wants Mr. Kingsley to meet Terry Randall, her roommate. He may remember her in "Cyclone" or "The Eldest Son." Of course she only had a tiny part, but—

Mr. Kingsley is quite sure he remembers. Even more sure when he sees Terry, who comes downstairs a little hesitantly, wearing a plain, dark dress. "If it were not for the glowing face she would seem rather drab in comparison with the dazzling Jean."

"*Well,* if you will come calling at a girls' club, Mr. Kingsley, what can you expect?" she says.

"I didn't expect anything as charming as this," admits Kingsley.

TERRY—Mm! You *are* in the moving-picture business, aren't you?

KINGSLEY—I am, Miss Randall. But my soul belongs to God.

JEAN—Don't you think she'd be good for pictures, Mr. Kingsley? Look. (*Turning* TERRY'S *profile to show to the best advantage.*)

TERRY—I think I'd be terrible.

JEAN—Don't talk like that. Of course she's rehearsing now in the new Berger play. That is, she starts tomorrow.

KINGSLEY—Good! I hear it's an interesting play.

TERRY—Do you know the first play I ever saw, Mr. Kingsley?

KINGSLEY—No, what?

TERRY—It was your production of "Amaryllis."

KINGSLEY—"Amaryllis!" You couldn't have seen that! That

was my first production. Ten years ago.

TERRY—I did, though. I was eleven years old, and I saw it at English's Opera House in Indianapolis. My mother took me. She cried all the way through it, and so did I. We had a lovely time.

KINGSLEY—But "Amaryllis" wasn't a sad play.

TERRY—Oh, we didn't cry because we were sad. Mother cried because it brought back the days when she was an actress, and I cried because I was so happy. You see, we lived seventy-five miles from Indianapolis, and it was the first time I'd ever been in a theatre.

JEAN—Now, really, I don't think it's tactful to talk about the theatre to a picture man.

TERRY—I'm afraid I'm kind of dumb about pictures. Mother used to say the theatre had two offsprings—the legitimate stage, and the bastard.

JEAN (*taking* KINGSLEY *by the hand and pulling him from the room*)—Come on! And forget I ever introduced her to you. (*He goes, calling, "Good-by, Miss Randall!"*)

TERRY (*calling after him*)—Oh, I hope I didn't—

KINGSLEY (*as the door closes on them*)—It's all right. I forgive you.

Suddenly Terry remembers she has had no dinner. She goes to the dining room, but dinner is over there. Mattie is there, however. Mattie will fix her up a plate of something. . . . And then Keith Burgess barges in.

Burgess "is the kind of young man who never wears a hat. Turtle-necked sweater, probably black; unpressed tweed suit; unshaven." He is looking for Jean Maitland—and Jean is out in a taxi with a big moving picture man. Keith can't understand that. Jean had a date with him. But his interest is quickly switched to Terry. He doesn't know her but she knows who he is—

"You're a playwright," says Terry, "and you wrote a play called "Blood and Roses" that was produced at the Fourteenth Street Theatre, and it ran a week and it wasn't very good."

"It was the best goddam play that was ever produced in New York! And the one I'm writing now is even better."

"Mm! *Two* weeks!"

"I don't think in terms of material success. Who cares whether a play makes money! All that matters is its message!"

"But if nobody comes to see it, who gets the message?"

Kaye Hamilton is back and Mrs. Orcutt, introducing her to

Terry in passing, has taken her to her room. The interruption has stopped Keith Burgess only briefly. He has been spending the time inspecting Terry rather carefully. Her hair is wrong, he decides. It hides her face. Her head's too big for her body. She's got pretty legs, but she shouldn't wear red.

"What do you live in this place for?" demands Keith suddenly. "Do you like it?"

"I love it," admits Terry. "We live and breathe theatre, and that's what I'm crazy about."

KEITH (*eagerly*)—Are you? So am I. What do you want to *do* in the theatre? What kind of parts do you want to play?

TERRY—I want to play everything I'm not suited for. Old hags of eighty, and Topsy, and Lady Macbeth. And what do I get? Ingénues—and very little of that.

KEITH—Don't take 'em. Wait till you get what you want.

TERRY—Well, it's a nice idea. But did you ever hear of this thing called eating?

KEITH—You mustn't think of that. Why, I've lived on bread and cocoa for days at a time. If you believe in something you've got to be willing to starve for it.

TERRY—I'm willing. But you don't know what it is to be an actress. If you feel something you can write it. But I can't act unless they let me. I can't just walk up and down my room, being an actress.

KEITH—It's just as tough for a writer. Suppose they won't produce his plays? I write about ironworkers and they want grand dukes. I could write potboilers, but I don't. The theatre shouldn't be just a place to earn a living in. It should be thunder and lightning, and power and truth.

TERRY—And magic and romance!

KEITH—No, no! Romance is for babies! I write about *today!* I want to tear the heart out of the rotten carcass they call life, and hold it up bleeding for all the world to see!

TERRY—How about putting some heart *into* life, instead of tearing it out?

KEITH—There's no place for sentiment in the world today. We've gone past it.

TERRY—I suppose that's why you never hear of "Romeo and Juliet."

KEITH (*turning away*)—That's a woman's argument.

TERRY—Well, I'm a woman.

KEITH (*once more surveying her*)—Why haven't I run into

you before? Where've you been all the time?

TERRY—Right here, in and out of every manager's office on Broadway.

KEITH—Me too. But I'm going to keep right on until they listen to me. And you've got to keep right on too!

TERRY—I will! I'm going to! (MATTIE *appears in the doorway.*)

MATTIE—You-all want your dinner now, Miss Terry? It's ready.

TERRY—Why, I'd forgotten all about it, Mattie.

KEITH (*taking control*)—Never mind, Mattie! . . . How about dinner with me? We'll go to Smitty's and have a couple of hamburgers.

TERRY (*not at all unwilling*)—With onions?

KEITH—Sure—onions! . . . Say, what the hell's your name, anyway?

The curtain falls.

The bedrooms in the Footlights Club are pleasant enough, but rather cramped. The one occupied by Terry, Louise and Kaye has three beds, three dressers and three small chairs. "Each dresser reflects something of the personality and daily life of its owner. Stuck in the sides of the mirrors are snapshots, photographs, newspaper clippings, telegrams, theatre programs."

There is a window at back, and through this the city lights are reflected. The room is dark and unoccupied until Kaye comes from the bathroom. She is wearing a bathrobe over her nightgown. Kaye's dresser, it is noticed, is conspicuously bare of ornaments. She pauses there to count the money in her purse. That doesn't take long either.

A knock at the door is followed by Judith Canfield's entrance. Judith is in sleeping pajamas and obviously doing her face for the night. She has come to borrow a few of Terry's frowners.

"Any sign of a job yet?"

"No, not yet."

"Something'll turn up. It always does," Judith goes on. Kaye makes no reply. "You know, you're a funny kid. You've been here a month, and I don't know any more about you than when you came in. The rest of us are always spilling our whole insides, but you never let out a peep. Nobody comes to see you, no phone calls, never go out nights, you haven't even got a picture on your dresser. Haven't you got any folks? Or a beau or something?" Still Kaye says nothing. "Sorry. My mistake," concludes Judith.

Big and Little Mary stop in on their way to a search for food. They've been to see the Breadline Players in "The Tunnel of Death" and they're hungry. Pat Devine stops on her way to the night club where she is dancing. Kaye wishes she had learned to dance.

Nor does Terry bring anything in the way of cheering news when she arrives. Terry has lost her job. Her show has closed. Four performances and the notice had been posted when she got to the theatre.

"We stood there for a minute and read it," reports Terry. "Then we sort of got together in the dressing rooms and talked about it in whispers, the way you do at a funeral. And then we all put on our make-up and gave the best damned performance we'd ever given."

"Any other job in the world, if you get canned you can have a good cry in the washroom and go home," says Judith, bitterly. "But show business! You take it on the chin and then paint up your face and out on the stage as gay as anything. 'My dear Lady Barbara, what an enchanting place you have here! And what a quaint idea, giving us pigs' knuckles for tea!' "

Judith is sure Terry will get something else. Perhaps in pictures. Wait until she hears from her tests. She's ten times the actress Jean is in Judith's estimation.

"Oh, how do you know who's an actress and who isn't!" demands Terry. "You're an actress if you're acting. Without a job and those lines to say, an actress is just an ordinary person, trying not to look as scared as she feels. What is there about it, anyhow! Why do we all keep trying?"

Bernice drifts in for a minute, looking as she probably thinks Modjeska might have looked in pink pajamas, with a long filmy black something draped about her head and shoulders. Bernice is planning to try out for Madame X at the Guild. . . .

Now they have all gone. Terry and Kaye are alone. Terry starts to undress. She is feeling pretty low. Not only about the play closing, but also because she had an appointment to meet Keith Burgess, which that young man evidently forgot. Kaye is hoping Terry isn't getting in the way of placing too much dependence on Keith. This isn't the first time he has let her down.

"One of the things that makes him so much fun is that he's different," says Terry. "If he forgets an engagement it is because he's working and doesn't notice. Only—I wish he had come tonight. I needed him so." Suddenly Terry's defenses are down. "Kaye, I'm frightened," she admits. "It's three years now. The first year it didn't matter so much. I was so young. Nobody was ever as young as I was. I thought, they just don't know. But I'll get a good part and show them. I didn't mind anything in those days. Not having any money, or quite enough food; and a pair of silk stockings always a major investment. I didn't mind because I felt so sure that that wonderful part was going to come along. But it hasn't. And suppose it doesn't next year? Suppose it—never comes?"

KAYE—You can always go home. You've got a home to go to, anyhow.

TERRY—And marry some home-town boy—like Louise?

KAYE—I didn't mean that, exactly.

TERRY—I can't just go home and plump myself down on Dad. You know what a country doctor makes! When I was little I never knew how poor we were, because Mother made everything seem so glamorous—so much fun. (*All this time* TERRY *has continued her preparations for bed. At one point in her disrobing she has gone to the clothes closet, hung up her dress, and slipped her nightgown over her head. Unseen there, for a moment, she has gone on talking.*) Even if I was sick it was a lot of fun, because then I was allowed to look at her scrapbook. I even used to pretend to be sick, just to look at it—and that took acting, with a doctor for a father. I adored that scrapbook. All those rep-company actors in wooden attitudes—I remember a wonderful picture of Mother as Esmeralda. It was the last part she ever played, and she never finished the performance.

KAYE—What happened?

TERRY—She fainted, right in the middle of the last act. They rang down and somebody said, "Is there a doctor in the house?" And there was. And he married her.

KAYE—Terry, how romantic!

TERRY—Only first she was sick for weeks and weeks. Of course the company had to leave her behind. They thought she'd catch up with them any week, but she never did.

KAYE—Didn't she ever miss it? I mean afterward.

TERRY—I know now that she missed it every minute of her life. I think if Dad hadn't been such a gentle darling, and not so dependent on her, she might have gone off and taken me with her. I'd have been one of those children brought up in dressing rooms, sleeping in trunk trays, getting my vocabulary from stagehands.

KAYE—That would have been thrilling.

TERRY—But she didn't. She lived out the rest of her life right in that little town, but she was stage-struck to the end. There never was any doubt in her mind—I was going to be an actress. It was almost a spiritual thing, like being dedicated to the church.

KAYE—I never thought of the theatre that way. I just used it as a convenience, because I was desperate. And now I'm using it again, because I'm desperate.

TERRY—Oh, now I've made you blue. I didn't mean to be gloomy. We're fine! We're elegant! They have to pay me two weeks salary for this flop. Eighty dollars. We're fixed for weeks. One of us'll get a job.

KAYE—I can't take any more money from you. You paid my twelve-fifty last week.

TERRY—Oh, don't be stuffy! I happened to be the one who was working.

KAYE—I'll never get a job. I—I'm not a very good actress.

TERRY—Oh, stop that!

KAYE—And there's nothing else I can do and nobody I can go back to. Except somebody I'll never go back to.

TERRY—It's your husband, isn't it?

KAYE (*looking at* TERRY *a moment, silently*)—I ran away from him twice before, but I had to go back. I was hungry, and finally I didn't even have a room. Both times, he just waited. He's waiting now.

TERRY—Kaye, tell me what it is! Why are you afraid of him?

KAYE (*turning her eyes away from* TERRY *as she speaks*)—To most people he's a normal, attractive man. But I know better. Nights of terror. "Now, darling, it wouldn't do any good to kill me. They wouldn't let you play polo tomorrow. Now, we'll open the window and you'll throw the revolver at that lamppost. It'll be such fun to hear the glass smash." And then there were the times when he made love to me. I can't even tell you about that. (*She recalls the scene with a shudder.*)

TERRY—Kaye, darling! But if he's as horrible as that, can't you do something legally?

KAYE (*with a desperate shake of her head*)—They have millions. I'm nobody. I've gone to his family. They treated me as though *I* were the mad one. They're united like a stone wall.

TERRY—But, Kaye, isn't there anybody—what about your own folks? Haven't you got any?

KAYE—I have a father. Chicago. I ran away at sixteen and went on the stage. Then I met Dick—and I fell for him. He was good-looking, and gay, and always doing sort of crazy things —smashing automobiles and shooting at bar-room mirrors. . . .

I thought it was funny, then.

TERRY (*reaching out wordlessly to extend a comforting hand*)—And I've been moaning about my little troubles.

Kaye had never intended telling that much of her story, but Terry has a feeling it will do her good. Now they are ready "to get those sheep over the fence." Terry has raised the window and a blast of street noises assails them. They both adjust eye-shades and turn off the light. With the room in darkness the need of the shades is made apparent. A huge electric advertising sign on a neighboring roof flashes on, and off, on and off.

For a moment the girls try shouting a parting observation or two at each other. The noise outside makes it difficult to hear. Then, quite suddenly, the door flies open and Jean bursts in. She is in dinner clothes and fairly quivering with excitement. Jean brings news. Let Terry wake up and know that she is in the movies. They are both in the movies! Mr. Kingsley has just had word! Hollywood liked their tests and they are to sign their contracts next day.

"Of course we'll only get little parts in the beginning," explains Jean, hardly able to contain herself. "But there's that beautiful check every week, whether you work or not. And the swimming and the sunshine and those little ermine jackets up to here. No more running around to offices and having them spit in your eye. And a salary raise every six months if they like us. So at the end of three years it begins to get pretty good, and after five years it's wonderful, and at the end of seven years it's more money than you ever heard of."

Terry doesn't like that seven year idea. Nor the idea of learning to act by way of the screen.

"That isn't acting; that's piecework," insists Terry, with considerable vehemence. "You're not a human being, you're a thing in a vacuum. Noise shut out, human response shut out. But in the theatre, when you hear that lovely sound out there, then you know you're right. It's as though they'd turned on an electric current that hit you *here*. And that's how you learn to act."

JEAN—You can learn to act in pictures. You have to do it till it's right.

TERRY—Yes, and then they put it in a tin can—like Campbell's soup. And if you die the next day it doesn't matter a bit. You don't even have to be alive to act in pictures.

JEAN—I suppose you call *this* being alive! Sleeping three in a room in *this* rotten dump! It builds you up, eh?

TERRY—I'm not going to stay here all my life! This is only the beginning!

JEAN—Don't kid yourself! You've been here three years, and then it's three years more, and then another three, and where are you? You can't play ingénues forever. Pretty soon you're a character woman, and then you're running a boarding house, like old Orcutt. *That'll* be nice, won't it?

TERRY—I don't know! You make me sound like a fool, but I know I'm not. All I know is I want to stay on the stage. I just don't want to be in pictures. An actress in the theatre—that's what I've wanted to be my whole life. It isn't just a career, it's a feeling. The theatre is something that's gone on for hundreds and hundreds of years. It's—I don't know—it's part of civilization.

JEAN (*screaming at her*)—All right, you stay here with your civilization, eating those stews and tapiocas they shove at us, toeing the mark in this female seminary, buying your clothes at Klein's! That's what you like, eh?

TERRY—*Yes,* I like it!

JEAN—And I suppose you like this insane racket going on all night! (*She throws open the window.*)

TERRY (*yelling above the noise*)—Yes, I *do!*

JEAN—And that Cadillac car sign going on and off like a damned lighthouse! (*She turns off the light. Again we see the flash of the electric sign, off, on, off, on.*) I suppose you've got to have *that* to be an actress!

TERRY—Yes! Yes! Yes! Yes! Yes!

JEAN (*not stopping for her*)—Well, not for me! I'm going out where there's sunshine and money and fun and—

TERRY (*shouting above her*)—And little ermine swimming pools up to here!

"The street noise, the flashing light, and their angry shouts are still going on as the curtain descends."

ACT II

It is 11 o'clock in the morning of a sunny day a year later. Frank and Mattie are cleaning up the living room of the Footlights Club, which is slowly coming to life. Ann Braddock is down for breakfast. Bobby Melrose stops on her way to the dining room to have a look at the mail. There is a letter from Madeleine.

Madeleine is trouping—Portland and Spokane this week; Seattle next week. Kendall Adams is in a rush, being late for rehearsal. Judith Canfield, up this half hour and through breakfast, is starting for a rehearsal of the nuns in something that is like a cross between a Ringling Circus and a religious festival.

Terry Randall is down and at the mail. She finds a letter from Mrs. Robert Hendershot of Appleton, Wis. That would be Louise and there is considerable excitement about it. Also there is a telephone call from Keith Burgess. Terry would remind Keith that her father is coming as planned and that Keith is to take them to dinner. Also for this occasion he is not to wear a black shirt and is to refrain from being one of the Masses.—

Back to the letter from Louise, Terry finds it written to all the girls. It is the first word they have had from Louise since she left. There was so much to do with getting settled, and all, Louise had not found time to write before. Now she is settled, has just given the last of the parties that pay up all her social obligations—a party in pink, this one, for the young married set, "with three tables of bridge, and one of mah jong and two people just talked."

Life in Appleton is pretty exciting, Louise would have them believe, what with an occasional trip to Milwaukee to the theatre. They had just seen Walter Hampden in "Cyrano."

"Well, if you girls think of me as much as I do about you, my ears would be about burned off," concludes Louise. "We have supper here around six o'clock, just as you all do at the club, and when it's over I always think, well, the girls are all beating it down to the show shop and making up to go on and just knocking the audience cold. Only I don't say it out loud any more because Bob says, 'Oh, for God's sake, you and your club!' Love to old Orcutt and for goodness' sakes, write, write, WRITE!"

There is a deep silence for a moment after Terry has finished reading. It is broken by a heavy sigh from Terry. "Well, I'll never complain again," she says. "This makes my eighteen a week on the radio look pretty wonderful." . . .

Judith is somewhat exercised over Terry's attitude toward Keith. "He's been coming around here for a year, taking all your time, talking about himself, never considering you for a minute," storms Judith, when Terry suggests that Keith may have sold his play. "Sold his play! Well, if he has he can thank *you* for it. It's as much your play as his."

"That isn't true," protests Terry, spiritedly.

"Don't tell *me*. It was nothing but a stump speech the way he wrote it. You made him put flesh and blood into it."

"You're talking about someone you don't understand," Terry answers, quietly. And Judith is stopped. She would apologize now. It is only because she thinks more of Terry than she does of anybody else in that whole menagerie that she couldn't keep her trap shut. . . .

Judith and the others have gone. The room is empty for a moment. Kaye Hamilton, "like a little wraith," comes quietly down the stairs. She is half way to the front door when Mrs. Orcutt, who may have been waiting, calls to her. Mrs. Orcutt would have a word with Kaye. She is, of course, reluctant to bring the subject up, but there is the matter of Kaye's indebtedness, which has grown rather large. If Kaye would take a little suggestion, perhaps it would be better if she were to find some place a little cheaper than the club. There is such a place, not a theatrical club, of course, but a nice place over on Tenth Avenue, near Forty-ninth—

"Now, now—we mustn't be upset by this," comforts Mrs. Orcutt as Kaye is visibly affected. "It's just a little talk. . . . Now, let's put it out of our minds. Shall we? And let me see a little smile. . . . There! . . . Well, we both have our day's work to do."

Pat Devine comes rushing down the stairs, stops to chuck Kaye under the chin with a gay "H'ya, baby?" and dances into the dining room. Terry, coming down for breakfast, is distressed to think that Kaye should be starting for rehearsal without food. But Kaye has gone. . . .

Linda's mother has arrived. Mrs. Shaw is "a rather cozy little woman of about fifty-five, plainly dressed, sweet-faced and inclined to be voluble."

Mrs. Shaw has come as a big surprise to Linda. And a big surprise it it. Linda is just tiptoeing in the front door and starting up the stairs when her mother spies her and calls. Linda is frozen on the stairs.

Presently she turns and comes down. She is wearing a camel's hair coat that is a little too large for her and a beret that might belong to either a man or a woman. Mrs. Shaw is puzzled. Linda explains that she went out in a hurry and just grabbed anything handy. It is the evening slippers that give her away. Now Mrs. Shaw has pulled the coat aside and revealed Linda in a black satin evening dress of extreme cut—"the narrowest of shoulder straps, bare shoulders, a deep décolletage, the bodice almost backless."

"I spent the night with a girl friend," Linda nervously explains. "Oh, Linda!" Mrs. Shaw cannot take that.

LINDA—Oh, Mother, don't make a scene!

MRS. SHAW (*with repressed emotion*)—Linda, go up and pack your things. You're coming home with me.

LINDA—Oh, no, I'm not.

MRS. SHAW—Linda Shaw!

LINDA—We can't talk here, Mother. And there's no use talking, anyhow. I'm never coming home. I'm twenty-two years old, and my life is my own.

MRS. SHAW—Who—who is this man? Are you going to marry him?

LINDA—He *is* married.

MRS. SHAW—I'm going to send for your father. He'll know what to do.

LINDA—Mother, if you make a fuss about this I'll have to leave the club. That girl knows already. And if I leave here I'll go and live with him, and the whole world will know it. Now take your choice.

MRS. ORCUTT (*entering, with apprehension in her face, steeled for an eventuality. Her quick eye goes from the girl to the mother*)—I'm Mrs. Orcutt, Mrs. Shaw. My maid just told me you were here.

MRS. SHAW—Oh, how do you do, Mrs. Orcutt?

MRS. ORCUTT—I understand you arrived unexpectedly.

MRS. SHAW—Yes, I came down to do a bit of shopping and surprise my little girl, here, and we practically came in together. She spent the night with my niece and her husband—Eighty-sixth Street—they had a rather late party and Linda just decided to—I don't see how these young people stand it. . . . (*A little laugh.*) Doesn't she look silly—this time of day—Linda darling, do run up and change. Why don't you meet me for luncheon at the hotel? Can you do that?

LINDA—Of course, Mother dear.

MRS. SHAW—I'm at the Roosevelt, darling. Shall we say one o'clock?

LINDA (*in quiet triumph*)—Yes, Mother darling. (*She goes upstairs.*)

MRS. SHAW—Oh, well, I must run along. I'm only going to be here a day or two and . . . Well, good-by.

MRS. ORCUTT (*accompanying her to the door*)—Good-by. It's been *so* nice. I'm always happy to meet the parents of our girls. And I hope that whenever you are in the city you won't fail to drop in on us. Well, good-by.

Terry's father arrives several hours earlier than expected. He is in the living room now, waiting for Mattie to summon Terry. Dr. Randall is a "gentle-looking, gray-haired man touching sixty. There is about him a vague quality—a wistful charm—that is not of the modern professional world." He finds the club interesting, but he is a little startled by the activity at the moment swirling about him. Olga has grabbed a few minutes to run through the finale of something she is to do at a recital. Big and Little Mary appear suddenly on the stairs reading dialogue to each other that is more or less blood-curdling. Pat, intent on a new dance step, comes hopping rhythmically out of the dining room before she sees there is a stranger present.

Fortunately Terry, with a glad shriek from the top of the stairs, arrives in time to help her father compose himself. They are very fond of each other, these two, and anxious for such intimate news as concerns both. Dr. Randall would know of Terry's health and her activities. Terry is anxious as to the way Aunt Lucy is taking care of him, and of his trip down.

The Doctor is ahead of time, it appears, because Stacey, the young fellow who had invited him to ride to New York, is that kind of a driver. "Turned out he's one of those fellows slows down to eighty going through a town. I dozed off a couple of minutes, once, and missed all of Pennsylvania."

It is planned that they will have lunch "way up on top of something;" that the Doctor will have time for a short visit to the Polyclinic; that they will spend the afternoon whirling all over town and then meet Keith for dinner. Dr. Randall is anxious to meet Terry's young man, and not at all worried to hear that Keith is quite unlike anyone else he ever met.

"He's brilliant, and he's written the most marvelous play, and he hates the government and won't wear evening clothes," warns Terry.

"Sounds as if he didn't have a nickel," concludes the Doctor.

TERRY—Oh, but he will have! This play will put him over. It's thrilling and beautiful! And oh, Dad, I'm going to play the lead.

DR. RANDALL—Why, Tress, that's wonderful. Your mother would have been very proud.

TERRY—Of course he hasn't sold the play yet. But he will. He's bound to.

DR. RANDALL—Say, I'm going to come back and see you in that if it takes my last nickel.

TERRY (*who has been eyeing him a little anxiously*)—Dad.

DR. RANDALL—Yes, Tress?

TERRY—You look as though you'd been working too hard. Have you?

DR. RANDALL—I wish I could say I had. But my waiting room looks pretty bleak these days.

TERRY—Isn't anybody sick at all? How about old Mrs. Wainwright?

DR. RANDALL—Yes, folks get sick, all right.

TERRY—Well, then!

DR. RANDALL—Well, it seems just being a medical man isn't enough these days. If you had a cold, we used to just cure the cold. But nowadays, the question is, why did you get the cold? Turns out, it's because, subconsciously, you didn't want to live. And why don't you want to live? Because when you were three years old the cat died, and they buried it in the back yard without telling you, and you were in love with the cat, so, naturally, forty years later you catch cold.

TERRY—But who tells them all this?

DR. RANDALL—Why—uh—young fellow came to town a few months ago; opened up offices.

TERRY—Oh!

DR. RANDALL—Sun lamps, X-ray machines, office fixed up like a power plant. He's the one looking after Mrs. Wainwright. She's bedridden with sciatica, arthritis and a heart condition, but, fortunately, it's all psychic.

TERRY—Dad, do you mean he's taken your whole practice away from you!

DR. RANDALL—Mm—not as bad as that. The mill folks still come to me.

TERRY—But they haven't any money?

DR. RANDALL—They still have babies.

TERRY—Never you mind. I'm going to buy you the biggest, shiniest, sun-lamp machine ever invented; and fluoroscopes and microscopes and stethoscopes and telescopes. You'll be able to sit in your office and turn a button and look right *through* Mrs. Wainright, six blocks away.

Dr. Randall—How about that new doctor? Will it go through him?

Terry—It'll *dissolve* him.

The front door slams and Keith Burgess strides in to the foot of the stairs. "The black sweater has given way to a black shirt. Otherwise his costume is about the same." Keith is excited. When he is introduced to Dr. Randall he is courteous and polite beyond words. This show of manners suggests an act to Terry, but Keith will go through with it. . . . Dr. Randall has left and now the news comes out. It is the play. Keith has a chance to sell it. To Gilman, too. Gilman, who is one of the best—but—Keith doesn't think he can let Gilman have it—

Terry knows. It is she who stands in the way. The thought is crushing, but Keith admits it is true—

"Well—you see—Gilman's got Natalie Blake under contract, and she *is* a big star," Keith explains. "It just happens to be the kind of part she's been looking for—"

"Did you tell him you thought I would be good in it?"

"Of course. I gave him a hell of an argument. But he just won't do it unless Blake is in it."

"Well, then, that's—that. I wouldn't do anything to— I bow out, Keith."

"Gosh, Terry! You mean you really would do that for me!"

"The play is the important thing, Keith. I love every line of it. You didn't think, after the way we've worked on it for a whole year, that I'd stand in the way, did you?"

"God, you're wonderful, Terry! You're a great kid! I'm crazy about you!"

He would embrace her but Terry evades him.

"There isn't one girl in a million would have taken it like this. And I love you for it. Love you, do you hear!"

"Yes, Keith."

"Well, look—"

Linda Shaw has appeared on the stairs. She is wearing a neat little mink cape, and carrying a costly looking dressing case. Linda is moving, and moving fast. Nobody, she says, will ever know where. Will Terry be good enough to tell Mrs. Orcutt and to give her the money she is leaving? Terry is a little stunned but accepts the commission.

Now Keith has to run. Gilman is waiting and he is going to meet Natalie Blake this evening— Dinner? No, of course he can't have dinner with Terry and her father—not with as important a meeting as this on. That would be silly. Now, look—

Terry has stopped him. The front door has opened quietly and Kaye, a pathetically subdued figure, is creeping up the stairs. Kaye is back from rehearsal. She has been fired. After seven days they have decided she will not do. They've already taken another girl—

"Darling, don't let it upset you," Terry calls, cheerily. "It happens to all of us. To me. It's part of this crazy business."

"Terry, I haven't a cent!"

"Who cares? I've still got my radio job. We'll get along."

Kaye can't see that. She can't take more from Terry. She already owes her more than a hundred dollars. And Terry can't wait to argue with her. It is time for her own radio rehearsal.

Kaye goes on up the stairs. And now Keith has barged out through the front door and Terry is left for a moment trying to pull herself together. So many things have been happening. Dully she asks Mattie where Mrs. Orcutt is, and starts back to find her. Mattie goes on with her tidying.

Suddenly a piercing scream is heard from upstairs. Susan Paige comes hurtling down the steps, her face distorted with terror. Terry has rushed back into the room.

"What is it? What is it?" Terry demands.

"Up in the hall! She drank something! She's—" Susan can say no more.

Terry rushes up the stairs. Mattie follows. Mrs. Orcutt and Frank hurry breathlessly into the room, and up the stairs. Susan has collapsed on the piano bench. From above stairs excited, hysterical voices can be heard: "Kaye, can you hear me?" "Oh, Lord, look at her!" "Kaye, darling, why did you do it?"—

Mrs. Orcutt has come down and dashed to the phone. She is starting to dial when Terry follows, slowly.

"It's—no use," she says.

Mrs. Orcutt hangs up the phone. Terry is staring straight in front of her. Mrs. Orcutt is whimpering.

"It'll be in all the papers," she is muttering. "I never should have let her stay here. I felt it from the start. There was something about her. She was—different from the rest of you."

"Don't say that!" Terry almost shouts. "It might have been any one of us. She was just a girl without a job, like— (*She is afraid to finish the sentence.*) It might have been—any one of us."

Frank and Mattie, huddling together, frightened, have started down the stairs as the curtain falls.

It is seven o'clock in the evening, two months later. Sam Hastings is calling again for Bobby Melrose, and Bobby, as usual, is still powdering her nose. Big and Little Mary have finished their dinner and are wondering where to go. They'd like to see Keith Burgess' play, but that is such a hit they probably couldn't get in, not even to stand.

A ring at the doorbell announces Keith Burgess himself. As she admits him Mattie is reduced to a smothered exclamation of surprise. Keith is resplendent in tails, white tie, top hat, white muffler and a beautifully tailored topcoat. He is smartly tapping a platinum-and-gold cigarette case and waiting for Terry when Judith Canfield, finishing a large banana, comes from the dining room. One look and Judith thinks something should be done about Keith. Quietly she approaches the playwright, carefully lifts the hand that holds the hat shoulder high, backs away, raises her skirts and is about to kick when Keith, outraged, backs away.

Defeated at that game Judith tries another. Dropping the peeling of her banana on the floor she gets the other side of it and enticingly beckons Keith to "come to mamma." But Keith is disgusted.

"You were more fun in the other costume," Judith tells him, frankly.

Terry is as completely taken by surprise as the others when she starts down the stairs and gets a good look at Keith. He had said on the phone that of course they would be dressing, but Terry thought he was spoofing. They had never dressed before, even for an opening. And never sat downstairs, third row, center. The gallery had always been good enough—

"Gallery?" explodes Keith. "We're through with the gallery! I've got a table at the Vingt-et-un for dinner, and after the theatre we're invited to a party at Gilman's penthouse. You can't go like that!"

"Give me just ten minutes. I'll go up and change—"

But Terry suddenly recollects: She has loaned her evening dress to Susan! And Olga's wearing Judy's pink—

"This is the god-damnedest dump I was ever in!" ejaculates Keith, disgustedly. "Wearing each other's clothes! I suppose you use each other's toothbrushes, too!"

TERRY (*quietly*)—Would you rather I didn't go, Keith?

KEITH—I didn't say that I—

TERRY (*still quietly*)—Yes—but would you rather?

KEITH—Now you're playing it for tragedy. What's the matter with you, anyhow!

TERRY—There's nothing the matter with me, Keith. I just can't see us as third-row first-nighters. We always went to see the *play,* Keith. That whole crowd—it makes the audience more important than the show.

KEITH—Listen, I don't like those people any better than you do. They don't mean anything to *me.*

TERRY—Then why do you bother with them?

KEITH—They can't hurt me. I watch them as you'd watch a hill of ants. Insects, that's what they are.

TERRY—Keith, you wrote your last play about people you understood and liked. You lived with them, and you knew them, and they gave you something. You'll starve to death in third-row center.

KEITH—I'm going back to them. I'm no fool. They're keeping my room for me just as it was.

TERRY—Keeping it? How do you mean?

KEITH—Oh, I don't want to talk about it now. Come on, let's get out of here.

TERRY—But I've got to know. Do you mean you've moved without even telling me?

KEITH (*deciding to face the music*)—Well, I was going to break it to you later. I knew you'd jump on me. But as long as you've gone this far—I'm going to Hollywood.

TERRY—Hollywood!

KEITH—Yes, to write for pictures.

TERRY—No, no, Keith!

KEITH—Now don't start all over again! If you don't watch yourself you'll turn into one of those nagging— . . . Let's get out of here!

TERRY—Keith, you can't go to Hollywood! I won't let you! You said you'd never go, no matter how broke you were, and now that your play's a big hit you're going.

KEITH—Well, they didn't want me before it was a hit!

TERRY—Keith, listen—

KEITH—I know what you're going to say. All that junk about its shriveling up my soul. Listen! I'm going to use Hollywood. It's not going to use me. I'm going to stay one year at two thousand a week. That's one hundred thousand dollars. I'll write their garbage in the daytime, but at night I'll write my own plays.

TERRY—But will you? That's what I'm afraid of. *Will* you?

KEITH—You bet I will! And in between I'll keep fit with sunshine, and swimming, and tennis, and—

TERRY—Little ermine jackets, up to here.

KEITH—Huh?

TERRY—It doesn't matter.

KEITH—Believe me, they'll never catch *me* at their Trocaderos or their Brown Derbies.

TERRY (*quietly*)—When are you going, Keith?

KEITH—I don't know. Next week.

TERRY—Well—good-by.

KEITH—What!

TERRY—Good-by, Keith, and good luck. It's been swell.

Terry has turned and run quickly up the stairs. Keith, stunned for a moment, goes to the foot of the stairs and calls to her. There is no answer. With a flirt of the topcoat he claps the top hat on his head and slams the door as he leaves.

Immediately heads pop out. Bernice and the two Marys have heard the row, and are all curiosity. There does not seem much chance of their curiosity being satisfied. Another ring of the doorbell and Frank ushers in David Kingsley.

A moment later Terry is with him. She is a little excited. He arrives, she explains, just in the nick of time. She had just faced one of those emotional crises that calls for a head buried in a pillow and a good cry—but the tears would not come. Instead there had been a curious feeling of relief—

Kingsley would apologize for the strangeness of the hour for a call, but this happens to be an emergency. He has just had word from Hollywood. They want Terry for a picture. They have been through dozens of tests in Hollywood and Terry seems the type they need for a particular character-comedy role they are trying to fill. But they must know in twenty minutes.

Terry is stunned. She doesn't know what to say. It's too fantastic. Her hesitancy surprises Mr. Kingsley. To him it doesn't seem reasonable. He has been watching her for several seasons. He has seen her in perhaps a half-dozen plays, and none of them worth much. Some didn't last out the week of their production.

"You've been doing a lot of detective work, haven't you?" laughs Terry.

"No, I didn't need to. I know all about you," Kingsley answers.

TERRY—You do! That's a little frightening.

KINGSLEY—It's part of my business—watching the good ones. And you are good. You've got fire and variety and a magnetic quality that's felt the minute you walk on the stage.

TERRY (*as he hesitates*)—Oh, don't stop!

KINGSLEY—But off stage you're nothing at all. (TERRY *wishes she had let well enough alone.*) When you walk into an office an average manager doesn't see anything there. You might be the little girl who's come to deliver the costumes. They wouldn't see that spark. If Elisabeth Bergner walked in on them unknown—or Helen Hayes—what would they see! Little anaemic wisps that look as if they could do with a sandwich and a glass of milk. But put them on a stage, and it's as if you had lighted a thousand incandescent bulbs behind their eyes. That's talent—that's acting—that's you!

TERRY—Now I—*am* going to cry.

KINGSLEY—But what if they don't see what's hidden in you? Suppose they never discover you. You might go tramping around for twenty years, and never get your chance. That's the stage.

TERRY—Twenty years!

KINGSLEY—But let's say you go to Hollywood. They'll know what to do with you out there. Light you so as to fill those hollows, only take your—(*He is turning her head this way and that to get the best angle.*)—right profile. That's the good one. Shade the nose a trifle. (*Opens her mouth and peers in as though she were a racehorse.*) Perhaps a celluloid cap over those two teeth. They'd make you very pretty. (TERRY *steals a quick look in the mirror. Her morale is somewhat shaken.*) Then you play in this picture. Fifty million people see you. Fan mail. Next time you get a better part. No tramping up and down Broadway, no worries about money. A seven-year contract, your salary every week whether you work or not. And if you make a really big hit, like Jean, they'll tear up your contract and give you a bigger one.

TERRY (*a sudden idea*)—Wouldn't they let me do just one or two pictures, instead of this seven-year thing?

KINGSLEY—I'm afraid not. If you make a big hit they don't want another studio to reap the benefit. That's not unreasonable, is it?

TERRY—No, I suppose not. Oh, dear! Everything you say is absolutely sound and true, but you see, Mr. Kingsley, the trouble with me is—I'm stage-struck. The theatre beats me and starves me and forsakes me, but I love it. I suppose I'm just that kind of girl—you know—rather live in a garret with her true love than dwell in a palace with old Moneybags.

KINGSLEY—But it looks as though your true love had kicked you out of the garret.

TERRY—Oh, dear, if there was only somebody. Mr. Kingsley, won't *you* help me? Won't you tell me what to do?

KINGSLEY—Me?

TERRY—Please!

KINGSLEY—But I work for the picture company.

TERRY—But if you didn't.

KINGSLEY (*quietly*)—I'd think you ought to tell them to go to hell.

TERRY—What!

KINGSLEY (*indignantly*)—Go out there and let them do all those things to you! (*Again he has a finger under the chin, raising her head as he scans her face.*) That lovely little face! And for what? So that a few years from now they can throw you out on the ash heap! The theatre may be slow and heartbreaking, but if you build solidly you've got something at the end of seven years, and seventeen years, and twenty-seven! Look at Katharine Cornell, and Lynn Fontanne, and Alfred Lunt. They tramped Broadway in their day. They've worked like horses, and trouped the country, and stuck to it. And now they've got something that nothing in the world can take away from them. And what's John Barrymore got? A yacht!

TERRY—You're wonderful!

KINGSLEY—Are you going to Hollywood?

TERRY—NO!

KINGSLEY—Will you go to dinner?

TERRY—YES!

KINGSLEY—That's really all I came to ask you.

The curtain falls.

ACT III

It is a Sunday morning in October, a day of heavenly rest at the Footlights Club. A majority of the membership is sprawled over the living room with the Sunday papers and remnants of a breakfast that, on the Sabbath, "is a late and movable feast."

Olga, at the piano as usual, is skimming over popular tunes, inspiring occasional vocal co-operation from one of the girls. Pat Devine, in rehearsal shorts, is sprawled on her back on top of the piano idly following a fairly elaborate dance routine with her legs in the air.

There are two girls new to the group the last year, but they are already completely a part of the picture. The conversation is desultory and concerned largely with the advertisement and fashion comments in the papers—"Hat'll be worn off the heads this Winter." . . . "Where're they going to put 'em?" . . . "Two-piece Schiaparelli suits—$5.98. You cannot tell the model from the copy." . . . "The hell you can't." . . .

The theatre news includes an announcement that the management of a new Lord Byron play can't find a young and handsome leading man for the name part. Which to Pat is unimportant. Looks don't count any more. It's good old sex appeal.

"Would you rather go out with a handsome man without sex appeal, or a homely one *with* it?" asks Kendall.

"I'd rather go out with the handsome one," says Bernice.

"Sure, and stay *in* with the other one," adds the incorrigible Judith.

There is news about Keith Burgess, too. He's coming back. One of the new girls would know who Keith is.

"He's one of those fellows who started out on a soapbox and ended up in a swimming pool," explains Judith.

There is some dispute as to whether or not Terry is still interested in Keith, now that she has been seeing so much of David Kingsley. Terry, it appears, having failed to land a stage job has gone to selling blouses in Macy's. Which, according to Madeleine, is better than trouping in a No. 3 "Horse on You" company that goes through to the coast. But this isn't true to Bobby Melrose. At least Madeleine will be making money trouping—

"Look at Sam and me," pouts Bobby. "We can't make enough to get married. Ah declare Ah'm so bored with livin' in sin."

The event of the day is to be the arrival of Jean Maitland, the big movie star. Even Terry gets up for that. Otherwise she would have spent the day in bed. She is down now and the target for many questions. The girls find it hard to understand how she ever can stand clerking, but Terry finds it possible. She keeps thinking that the part will come along next week. And she spends her lunch hour preserving both her hopes and her contacts visiting managers' offices. . . .

One of the girls has spied Jean getting out of a car in front of the house. And what a car! She is wearing red foxes, too. There is a mad scramble to tidy the room against Jean's arrival and then a rush for the door as the great movie star enters, followed by explosions of "DAR-ling!" and "WON-derful!" Now Jean is in Terry's arms, and then in the arms of Mrs. Orcutt and Mattie and Frank, too, and there is much laughter.

Jean, in the excitement, has forgotten that she has brought along her firm's resident publicity man and his assistant, who is to snap a few pictures. This is exciting news. The girls rush pell-mell to their rooms to get fixed up. . . .

Jean has come East to have a part in a play. The star part, in fact, which frightens her a little. They all think she will be fine in it, and she is to meet Mr. Kingsley and Mr. Gretzl, the President of her company, today.

"Terry, darling, when am I going to see you?" demands Jean, suddenly. "I've got loads to tell you and I want to hear all about you. Rehearsals start Wednesday. How about lunch tomorrow?"

"Oh, not tomorrow, Miss Maitland," objects Larry. "You're lunching with the press."

"Oh, dear. Let's see—David Kingsley is taking me to that opening in the evening. . . . How about tea?"

"Not tea! You've got the magazine people. And you've got photographs all day Tuesday."

"But I want to see her. How about Wednesday? I'll get away from rehearsal and we'll have lunch. One o'clock?"

"You won't believe it, but my lunch hour's eleven-thirty to twelve-thirty."

Jean can't understand that, but before she can get an explanation the picture activities engulf them all.

Jean has brought a little surprise for the girls—for all the girls and the dear old Footlights Club. It is a picture of herself "all eyelashes, golden hair and scarlet lips," and it creates something very like a sensation. There is no place to hang it—unless—the Bernhardt—

But at the moment Jean's picture must serve as a background for a picture of the star surrounded by her old pals of the club. Then they all romp upstairs for a few human interest shots of Terry's wash on a line in Jean's old room. Only Terry and Judith are left below.

"If I'm going to work as an extra I want my five dollars a day," is Judith's argument.

"I do hope I left my room looking sordid enough," hopes Terry.

"Say, what about that play they've got her doing? Do you suppose it's really something?"

"Oh, it is. David Kingsley told me about it. He says it's a really fine and moving play."

"Then why does he let her do it?" Judith is looking at Jean's portrait.

"He couldn't help it," explains Terry. "They got it into their heads out on the coast. It's Gretzl's idea. What do they care about the theatre? They think the stage is something to advertise pictures with."

"Listen, Jean can't act. If the play's as good as all that, she'll kill it. It doesn't make sense!"

The next moment Keith Burgess is standing in the arch. He has barged right in, as though it were a daily custom, yet he has been away a year. "He still wears the sweater, but it is an imported one; the trousers are beautifully tailored, the shirt probably cost eighteen dollars; no necktie, and, of course, no hat."

Keith is glad to see Terry again, and quick to notice that she is looking thin and hasn't any color. He is only in the East for three days, then he is going back. They wouldn't let him go after his year was up. Yes, he's writing another play, but he hasn't finished it yet. He'll get to that later. Just now he's tied up with pictures. Keith also has an idea. The idea concerns Terry. He can't believe she is clerking in Macy's, and if she is she's got to quit—

"Good God! Listen, darling!" Keith is quite excited. "You spend years on Broadway and finish up in Macy's. And look at Jean! Two years in Hollywood and she's a star."

"They speed up everything in Hollywood. In two years you're a star, in four you're forgotten, and in six you're back in Sweden."

"That's the kind of reasoning that's put you where you are! From now on I'm going to take charge of you. You're going to be—"

The doorbell has announced David Kingsley. Terry is glad to see David, but Keith has a time being gracious. He isn't gracious very long. Not after Kingsley has pointedly congratulated him on getting away from pictures after he had served his year.

"It always amuses me to hear a fellow like you, who makes his living out of pictures, turn on Hollywood and attack it," sneers Keith. "If you feel that way about pictures, why do you work in them?"

"Well, we can't always do what we want to, Keith. After all, you're working in Hollywood, and I'm selling blouses, and David Kingsley is—"

"No, Terry," protests Kingsley. "He's right. I shouldn't talk that way, and I don't very often. But I'm a little worked up this morning. I reread Jean's play last night. (*A gesture toward* JEAN's *portrait.*) And I realized more than ever what a beautiful play it is. That's what's got me a little low. When picture people come into the theatre—when they take a really fine play and put a girl like Jean in it—when they use a play like this for camera fodder, that's more than I can stand. The theatre means too much to me."

Keith isn't satisfied with the explanation. He would have Kingsley know that Hollywood has changed. They don't even talk about pictures at their parties any more. They talk art, and politics and books. Keith likes pictures. He's going back—and he's going to take Terry with him—

"It's time somebody took her in hand, and I'm going to do it," announces Keith. "I'm going to marry her."

KINGSLEY (*turning to* TERRY)—Terry, you can't do that!

TERRY (*hopefully*)—Why not, David?

KEITH—Look here, you—

KINGSLEY—I've told you why a hundred times. You belong in the theatre.

TERRY—Is that the reason! You certainly *have* told me a hundred times. A thousand! I've sat across a table from you and heard it with the soup and the meat and the coffee. Actress! Actress! Actress!

KINGSLEY—Of course I've told you. Because you *are* an actress.

TERRY—And I've just realized why. Because you quit the theatre yourself, and you've been salving your own conscience by preaching theatre to me. That made you feel less guilty, didn't it?

KINGSLEY—Terry, that's not true.

TERRY—Oh, yes, it is. *So* true. Funny I never thought of that before.

KEITH—Look, I've got to get out of here. . . . If I may have just a moment. (*He steps between* TERRY *and* KINGSLEY.) When are we going to get married?

TERRY (*in a deadly tone*)—When are we going to get married? We are going to get married, Mr. Burgess, when Hollywood to Dunsinane doth come. That's Shakespeare—you know, the fellow they're digging up out there.

KEITH (*stunned*)—Huh?

TERRY—It's too late, Keith. When you walked out on me a year ago, you walked out on yourself, too. That other Keith was cocksure and conceited, but he stood for something. What was it—"thunder and lightning and power and truth?" Wasn't that what you said? And "if you believe in something you've got to be willing to starve for it." Well, I believed in it, Keith. (*She turns her gaze to* KINGSLEY, *then her look includes both of them.*) So—I guess that leaves me just a young lady with a career. Or, shall we say—just a young lady?

She goes slowly up the stairs as the curtain falls.

The living room of the Footlights Club is in semi-darkness. It is midnight two weeks later. For a moment no one appears. Then the two Marys let themselves in. They have been to the theatre and they didn't like the show. Judith Canfield arrives next, very tired but still trying to be polite to Mr. Milhauser of Seattle, who happens to be in town again. Mr. Milhauser will also be in town for a week, he announces, but unhappily all Judith's time will be taken up, what with her gymnasium work and everything.

Frank is making a last tour of inspection prior to closing for the night when David Kingsley appears a little excitedly bringing with him a "short, thickset man who carries himself with great authority in order to make up for his lack of stature." This would be Adolph Gretzl, the manager.

Kingsley, it transpires, has brought Gretzl to meet Terry. There has been a rehearsal tonight and it has been definitely decided that Jean is not up to the part. Kingsley has grabbed the chance to urge Mr. Gretzl to give Terry a chance. Gretzl resents the interference and is pretty sore about the whole thing. However, he will see Terry if Kingsley insists, though he is personally convinced that good actresses don't live in places like the Footlights Club. Besides, even if Jean can't make the grade as an actress, she is at least a beautiful girl. When she comes on the stage audiences will gasp. However—let this other actress come—

"She's got presence and authority and distinction!" promises Kingsley. "And a beautiful, mobile face. She's exactly right for the play."

"If she's such a great beauty and such a wonderful actress, where's she been keeping herself?" demands Gretzl.

"She's been learning her business," answers David.

Presently Terry appears on the stairs. Frank had wakened her and she has thrown a "loose, flowing robe over her nightgown. Her hair falls over her shoulders; her feet are in low scuffs. She is anything but the dazzling figure described by Kingsley."

Introductions over, Gretzl having mumbled his forced greeting, Kingsley explains the emergency that has brought them. He wonders if Terry could start rehearsals in the morning—

But Gretzl isn't so sure. He has been giving Terry a fairly thorough examination and it isn't easy for him to accept her as the person described by David. He would like to hear Terry read a couple of speeches from the play.

The idea is terrifying to Terry, but Kingsley has brought the part and is sure she can do it. Just to let Mr. Gretzl see what she can do—

Terry starts to read: "Look, boys, I haven't got any right to stand up here and tell you what to do. Only maybe I have got a right, see, because, look—"

She stumbles there, and asks Gretzl if he minds if she starts over. Gretzl doesn't mind. Terry starts again—

"Look, boys, I haven't got any right to stand up here and tell you what to do. Only maybe I have got a right, see, because, look, I'm engaged to be married. We were going to be married tomorrow. You all know who it is. He's right here in this hall."

Gretzl has left his chair and is pacing up and down the room. Terry goes on, stumblingly. . . . Now Gretzl has picked up a match box, struck a match and lighted a large cigar.

"That's why I'm telling you—strike! Strike! Str—"

Terry has quit. She throws the part to the floor. She won't go on. She would be a fool if she did, agrees Kingsley, angrily.

Gretzl has arisen and started buttoning his coat with a gesture of finality.

"You must excuse me. I am a plain-speaking man. I don't want to hurt anybody's feelings, but in my opinion this young lady is not anything at all. Not anything."

TERRY—But, Mr. Gretzl, nobody could give a reading under these conditions. It isn't fair. It isn't possible for an actress—you don't understand.

GRETZL—All right. I don't understand. But I understand my business and I know what I see. So I will say good night, and thank you. Come on, Kingsley.

KINGSLEY—I'm sorry, Terry. No one could look a great actress in bathrobe and slippers. And Mr. Gretzl only knows what he sees.

GRETZL—Are you working for me or against me, Kingsley?

KINGSLEY—I'm working *for* you. What are you going to do about your play tomorrow?

GRETZL—I'm going to throw it into the ash can. All I wanted it for was Jean Maitland. So she could make a picture of it. All right. She'll do something else. I can get plenty of material.

KINGSLEY—It's incredible that anyone should be so stupid.

GRETZL (*rising to his full height*)—Mr. Kingsley, you are *out!* You will hear from our lawyers in the morning.

TERRY—Oh, David!

KINGSLEY—It's all right, Terry. Gretzl, if you've lost your interest in the play, how about selling it to me?

GRETZL—I see. You're going back into the theatre, eh?

KINGSLEY—I might. Will you sell it to me?

GRETZL—How much?

KINGSLEY—Just what it cost you.

GRETZL—All right. See Becker in the morning. He'll fix it up. Good night.

KINGSLEY—Good night.

GRETZL (*as he goes*)—And *I* am the stupid one? Huh!

TERRY—David! David, oh, my dear, you mustn't do this just for me.

KINGSLEY—No, I'm not one of those boys who puts on a play just so that his girl can act in it. . . . By the way, you *are* my girl, aren't you?

TERRY (*brightly*)—Oh, yes, sir.

KINGSLEY—I just thought I'd ask. (*He takes her in his arms and kisses her.*) You know, I had a couple of nasty weeks, Terry, after you drove me out into the cold.

TERRY—Weeks? It seemed like years. (*Again he embraces her—just as* MRS. ORCUTT *enters, in bathrobe and slippers.*)

MRS. ORCUTT—I'm sorry, Mr. Kingsley, but this is against the rules.

TERRY—Mrs. Orcutt, it's the play!

KINGSLEY—My apologies, Mrs. Orcutt. This may look a little strange. But I came up on business.

MRS. ORCUTT—Frank said there was another gentleman.

TERRY (*gaily*)—But he's gone! And oh, Mrs. Orcutt! I'm going to do the play! (*At the end of this announcement, as she says "play," her hand goes to her mouth, like a little girl's; she is surprised to find herself crying.*)

MRS. ORCUTT—Terry, my child!

KINGSLEY—Darling, you're tired. You must get your sleep. (*There is a farewell kiss, with the full approval of* MRS. ORCUTT.) Good night.

TERRY—Good night.

KINGSLEY—Eleven in the morning, at the Lyceum.

TERRY (*in a low voice*)—I'll be there. (KINGSLEY *is gone.*)

MRS. ORCUTT—Terry, dear, I'm so happy for you. Aren't you thrilled?

TERRY (*her eyes glowing*)—It was like Victoria. When they came to tell her she was Queen.

MRS. ORCUTT—Dear child! But now you must run along to bed and get your sleep.

TERRY—No, no. I must learn my part. And I must be alone. I want a room by myself tonight. Please, Mrs. Orcutt.

MRS. ORCUTT—I'll see what I can do. (*She goes, first switching off the main light.*)

Terry (*standing alone in the semi-darkened room. A light from a street lamp shines through the window and strikes her face. For a moment she stands perfectly still. Then the realization of her new position comes over her. She seems to take on height and dignity.*)—Now that I am Queen, I wish in future to have a bed, and a room, of my own.

She stands transfixed as

THE CURTAIN FALLS

THE WOMEN

A Comedy in Three Acts

BY CLARE BOOTHE

CLARE BOOTHE, whose writing urge carried her through and out of a society career into the columns of the smarter magazines and finally into the theatre, frankly tells her readers in a preface to the published volume of "The Women" that she harbors nothing resembling illusions regarding either the play's character as an exposure of her sex or its quality as contemporary literature.

"'The Women' is a satirical play about a numerically small group of ladies native to the Park Avenues of America," she writes, a firm if not defiant note sounding between the lines. "It was clearly so conceived and patently so executed. The title, which embraces half the human species, is therefore rather too roomy. It was chosen, ungenerously it may seem, from a host of more generic titles—'Park Avenue,' 'The Girls,' 'The Ladies'—simply because it was laconic, original and not altogether too remote. Moreover, its very generality seemed to hold a wide audience appeal, a consideration which few commercial dramatists are required to ignore. This having been frankly stated, I am sure that few readers will be distracted by the width of the title from the narrowness of the play's aim: a clinical study of a more or less isolated group, projected, perhaps in bad temper, but in good faith. The reader, who, warned of this, nevertheless claims to discover in it a portrait of *all* womankind, is obviously bound to experience the paradoxical discomfort which ensues to the wearer when the shoe unexpectedly fits."

With that clarifying statement of the case for the defense we may move on to a consideration of "The Women" as distinctly a feature of the theatre season of 1936-1937, in which it shared popularity with the best of the season's productions.

It was a Christmas week offering favorably received by drama reviewers whose praise was as generous as their blushes were strange. When a critic blushes, that's news. These, however, were not blushes induced by the drama's boldnesses so much as by its intimacies. Miss Boothe not only removes the traditional fourth walls of her houses, but likewise the partitions that hide

to by Lucas-Pritchard Studio, New York.

"THE WOMEN"

Sylvia: A wonderful new manicurist. Olga's her name. She's marvelous. Look! Jungle red!
Nancy: Looks as if you'd been tearing at somebody's throat.

(*Margalo Gillmore, Jane Seymour, Phyllis Povah, Ilka Chase, Adrienne Marden*)

bathrooms, powder rooms and maternity wards. Which serves to put the men a little uncomfortably in the position of so many listening if not peeping Thomases.

The first reaction of playgoers was one of interest but without marked enthusiasm. After about three weeks, however, women patrons began to crowd the matinees. They evidently enjoyed being witness to the exposure of these selected feminine types. Soon the men were drawn in, and for many months there was a succession of capacity audiences at the theatre presenting the comedy. Miss Boothe, somewhat overwhelmed by the success, and admittedly frightened at the prospect of having to make further explanations to the income tax collectors, announced that she would devote her royalties to charity.

The opening scene in "The Women," appropriately enough, shows four of them playing bridge in Mary Haines' living room. They are: "Nancy, who is sharp, but not acid; sleek, but not smart; a worldly and yet virginal 35—Peggy, who is pretty, sweet, 25, whose character has not, will never quite 'jell'—Sylvia, who is glassy, elegant, feline, 34—and Edith, who is a sloppy, expensively dressed matron of 33 or 34; indifferent to everything but self; incapable of either deliberate maliciousness or spontaneous generosity."

The room itself is not another of those "Park Avenue living rooms decorated with a significant indifference to the fact that ours is still a bi-sexual society;" not a "period peacock alley" or a "crystal-hung prima-donna roost." Mary's living room "would be thought a comfortable room by a man. This, without sacrificing its own subtle, feminine charm."

The girls are waiting for Mary, whose place Peggy has taken temporarily. The conversation is catty and bright. One of the trends is keynoted by Sylvia's opening remark—

"So I said to Howard," she reports to her fellow bridgers, "What do you expect me to do? Stay home and darn your socks? What do we all have money for? Why do we keep servants?"

"You don't keep them long, God knows," counters Nancy.

After that it ranges from frequent observations to the effect that Peggy's atrocious bridge is probably due to her still being naively in love with her husband; that Edith's pregnancy is so unpleasant she is determined this shall be the last time she will ever "go through this lousy business for any man;" and (*while* EDITH *is out of the room*) that her (Edith's) husband, Phelps Potter, is constantly "making passes at all the women of his acquaintance."

Finally they reach the important item of the afternoon, and that concerns the smug complaisance and apparent domestic happiness of their hostess, Mary Haines. This bit does not begin to boil properly until Mary, called to the telephone, and the others disappearing, Edith and Sylvia are left alone for a moment. Then Sylvia becomes really informative—

SYLVIA—Edith, I've got to tell you! I'll burst if I wait!

EDITH—I *knew* you had something! (*She brings her well-laden plate and tea-cup and settles herself happily beside* SYLVIA *on the sofa.*)

SYLVIA—You'll die!

EDITH—Mary?

SYLVIA—No, Stephen. Guess!

EDITH—You couldn't mean . . . ?

SYLVIA (*nodding*)—Stephen Haines is cheating on Mary!

EDITH—I don't believe you; is it true?

SYLVIA—Wait till you hear. (*Now she is into it.*) You know I go to Michael's for my hair. You ought to go, pet. I despise whoever does yours. Well, there's the most wonderful new manicurist there. (*Shows her scarlet nails.*) Isn't that divine? Jungle Red—

EDITH—Simply divine. Go on.

SYLVIA—It all came out in the most extraordinary way, this morning. I tried to get you on the phone—

EDITH—I was in the tub. Go on.

SYLVIA—This manicurist, she's marvelous, was doing my nails. I was looking through *Vogue,* the one with Mary in the Beaux Arts Ball costume—

EDITH—In that white wig that flattered her so much?

SYLVIA (*nodding*)—Well, this manicurist: "Oh, Mrs. Fowler," she said, "is that that Mrs. Haines who's so awfully rich?"

EDITH—Funny how people like that think people like us are awfully rich.

SYLVIA—I forget what she said next. You know how those creatures are, babble, babble, babble, babble, and never let up for a minute! When suddenly she said: "I know the girl who's being *kept* by Mr. Haines!"

EDITH—No!

SYLVIA—I swear!

EDITH (*thrilled*)—Someone *we* know?

SYLVIA—No! That's what's so awful about it. She's a friend of this manicurist. Oh, it wouldn't be so bad if Stephen had picked someone in his own class. But a blond Floosie!

EDITH—But how did Stephen ever meet a girl like that?

SYLVIA—How do men ever meet girls like that? That's what they live for, the rats!

EDITH—But—

SYLVIA—I can't go into all the details, now. They're utterly fantastic—

EDITH—You suppose Mary knows?

SYLVIA—Mary's the kind who couldn't help showing it.

EDITH (*nodding, her mouth full of her third cake*)—No self-control. Well, she's bound to find out. If a woman's got any instincts, she feels when her husband's off the reservation. I know *I* would.

SYLVIA—Of course you do, darling. Not Mary— (*Rises and walks about the room, wrestling with* MARY'S *sad problem.*) If only there were some way to *warn* her!

EDITH (*horrified, following her*)—Sylvia! You're not going to tell her?

SYLVIA—Certainly not. I'd *die* before I'd be the one to hurt her like that!

EDITH—Couldn't someone shut that manicurist up?

SYLVIA—A good story like that? A lot those girls care whose life they ruin.

EDITH—*Isn't* it a dirty trick?

SYLVIA—Isn't it *foul?* It's not as though only Mary's friends knew. We could keep our mouths shut.

EDITH—I know plenty that I never *breathe* about my friends' husbands!

SYLVIA—So do I! (*They exchange a sudden glance of sharp suspicion.*) Anyway, the whole thing's disgustingly unfair to Mary. I feel like a disloyal skunk, just knowing about it—

EDITH—I adore her—

SYLVIA—I *worship* her. She's my dearest friend in all the world.

The others are coming back. Sylvia and Edith become suddenly pre-occupied with solitaire. Which doesn't fool Nancy Blake.

"Must have been choice. You both look so relaxed," suggests Nancy.

The phone call was for Mary from Stephen, her husband. He wanted to tell her that he would not be able to get home to dinner. He will have to work—

"Are you sure it's *work*, darling, and not a beautiful blonde?" inquires Sylvia sweetly.

Mary laughs, perhaps a little smugly, at the suggestion. Yet, admitting that Stephen is an attractive man, she sometimes wonders that he hasn't deserted her for some glamorous creature long ago. One can't ever be too sure, even of what she believes in most.

Nancy would clear the air by forcing Sylvia into a confession of what she meant by saying that Mary was living in a fool's paradise. But Sylvia is too smart to be caught—

"Mary, I was just trying to make a typical Nancy Blake wisecrack about marriage," she explains. "I said, 'A woman's paradise is always a fool's paradise!' "

MARY—That's not bad, is it, Nancy? Well, Sylvia, whatever I'm living in, I like it. Nancy, cut.

SYLVIA (*examining her nails minutely—suddenly shows them to* MARY)—Mary, how do you like that?

NANCY (*not looking*)—Too, too adorable.

SYLVIA—You can't imagine how it stays on. I get it at Michael's—you ought to go, Mary!

EDITH (*protestingly*)—Oh, Sylvia—

SYLVIA—A wonderful new manicurist. Olga's her name. She's marvelous.

EDITH—Will you cut, Sylvia?

SYLVIA—Look, Jungle Red.

NANCY—Looks as if you'd been tearing at somebody's throat.

SYLVIA—I'll be damned, Nancy, if I'll let you ride me any more!

MARY—Now, Sylvia, Nancy's just being clever too.

SYLVIA—She takes a crack at everything about me. Even my nails!

MARY (*laughing*)—Well, I like it. I really do! It's new and smart. (*Pats her hand.*) Michael's, Olga, Jungle Red? I'll remember that. (*Cuts cards.*) You and I, Sylvia. I feel lucky today.

SYLVIA (*with a sweet, pitying smile*)—Do you, darling? Well, you know they say, "Lucky in cards—"

The curtain falls.

A few days later, in a hair-dressing booth at Michael's, the fat Mrs. Wagstaff is being generously attended. She is suffering the closing moments of an operation for a permanent. "Wires and clamps, Medusa-like, rise from her head" to the cap of a machine hung from an aluminum arm above her. "Olga, at her right, is doing her nails. Her fat, bare feet rest in the lap of a pedicurist." Two hairdressers are circling her, one with a watch, keeping count of the time, the other with a hand drier with which she cools the patron's steaming locks.

Mrs. Wagstaff is having a trying time. Neither the magazine in her lap, which she is trying to read, nor the cigarette she is trying to smoke, nor the sandwiches which the second hairdresser passes her from time to time can divert her mind from the scorching the machine is giving her nor her general uncomfortableness in these last moments. Still, she is a glutton for punishment. They have no sooner got her out from under the permanent machine than she decides she will have a mud-mask treatment. That, the chorus of attendants assure her, is all she will need to be really beautiful. She has Jungle Red on her nails, and a bright smear is drying on her beautiful big toe. . . .

They have sent Mrs. Wagstaff on to be unwound in the shampoo. The girls are having their fun laughing at "the old gasoline truck" and the torture she has taken on since she married a man ten years younger than she, when Mary Haines and Nancy Blake are ushered into the room. Mary has come to have a manicure by the girl who does Sylvia Fowler's nails, though not with Nancy's endorsement.

"God, I'd love to do Mrs. Fowler's nails, right down to the wrist, with a nice, big buzzsaw," snaps Nancy.

"Sylvia's all right," protests Mary. "She's a good friend underneath."

"Underneath what?"

Mary does not answer. She has caught a glimpse of herself in the mirror. It reminds her of a recent worry, also hinted at by Sylvia.

Is she getting old? The little wrinkles are creeping in. And that first gleam of white in the hair— It's a scary thought.

"There's only one tragedy for a woman," says Nancy, abruptly.

"Growing old?"

"Losing her man."

"That's why we're all so afraid of growing old," sighs Mary.

"Are you afraid?"

"Well, I was very pretty when I was young. I never thought about it twice then. Now I know it's why Stephen loved me."

Olga has started the manicuring operation. Nancy is ready to leave. She has brought her newest book, "the book my readers everywhere have been waiting for with such marked apathy," she explains, to give it to Mary. "All the Dead Ladies" is the title. Nancy is leaving next day for Africa. The book is her parting shot. She did not want any parties, or steamer baskets, or witty cables, so she's just slipping away. . . .

Olga is bursting with gossip about several of Mrs. Fowler's friends. She knows that the Herbert Parrishes are being divorced. (Mr. Parrish *simply refused to explain the lipstick on his undershirt.*) She knows that Mrs. Potter is awfully pregnant. And she has heard that Mrs. Stephen Haines—

"I guess Mrs. Fowler's told you about that," guesses Olga. "Mrs. Fowler feels awfully sorry for her."

"Oh, she does!" Mary is laughing. "Well, I don't—"

Olga—You would if you knew this girl.

Mary—What girl?

Olga—This Crystal Allen.

Mary—Crystal Allen?

Olga—Yes, you know. The girl who's living with Mr. Haines. (Mary *starts violently.*) Don't you like the file? Mrs. Potter says it sets her unborn child's teeth on edge.

Mary (*indignant*)—Whoever told you such a thing?

Olga—Oh, I thought you knew. Didn't Mrs. Fowler—?

Mary—No—

Olga—Then you will be interested. You see, Crystal Allen is a friend of mine. She's really a terrible man-trap. Soak it, please. (Mary *dazed, puts her hand in the dish.*) She's behind the perfume counter at Saks'. So was I before I got fi—left. That's how she met him.

Mary—Stephen Haines?

Olga—Yeah. It was a couple a months ago. Us girls wasn't busy. It was an awful rainy day, I remember. So this gentleman walks up to the counter. He was the serious type, nice-looking, but kind of thin on top. Well, Crystal nabs him. "I want some perfume," he says. "May I awsk what type of woman for?" Crystal says, very Ritzy. That didn't mean a thing. She was going to sell him Summer Rain, our feature anyway. "Is she young?" Crystal says. "No," he says, sort of embarrassed. "Is she the glamorous type?" Crystal says. "No, thank God," he says. "Thank God?" Crystal says and bats her eyes. She's got those eyes which run up and down a man like a searchlight. Well, she puts perfume on her palm and in the crook of her arm for him to smell. So he got to smelling around and I guess he liked it. Because we heard him tell her his name, which one of the girls recognized from Cholly Knickerbocker's column— Gee, you're nervous— Well, it was after that I left. I wouldn't of thought no more about it. But a couple of weeks ago I stopped by where Crystal lives to say hello. And the landlady says she'd moved to the kind of house where she could entertain her gentleman friend—"What gentleman friend?" I says. "Why, that Mr. Haines that she's had up in her room all hours of the night," the landlady says— Did I hurt? (MARY *draws her hand away.*) One coat, or two? (*Picks up a red bottle.*)

MARY—None.

OLGA—But I thought that's what you came for? All Mrs. Fowler's friends—

MARY—I think I've gotten what all Mrs. Fowler's friends came for. (*Puts coin on the table.*)

OLGA (*picks up coin*)—Oh, thanks— Well, good-by. I'll tell her you were in, Mrs.—?

MARY—Mrs. Stephen Haines.

OLGA—Mrs.—? Oh, gee, gee! Gee, Mrs. Haines—I'm sorry! Oh, isn't there something I can do?

MARY—Stop telling that story!

OLGA—Oh, sure, sure, I will!

MARY—And please, don't tell anyone— (*Her voice breaks.*) that you told it to *me*—

OLGA—Oh, I won't, gee, I promise! Gee, that would be kind of humiliating for you! (*Defensively.*) But in a way. Mrs. Haines, I'm kinda *glad* you know. Crystal's a terrible girl—I mean, she's terribly clever. And she's terribly pretty, Mrs. Haines— I mean, if I was you I wouldn't waste no time getting Mr. Haines away from her— (MARY *turns abruptly away.*) I mean, now you *know*, Mrs. Haines! (OLGA *eyes the coin in her hand distastefully, suddenly puts it down on the table and exits.* MARY, *alone, stares blankly in the mirror, then suddenly focusing on her image, leans forward, searching her face between her trembling hands. A drier goes into the next booth. A shrill voice rises above its drone.*)

VOICE—Not too hot! My sinus! So *she* said: "I wouldn't want anybody in the world to know," and I said: "My dear, you know you can trust *me!*"

The curtain falls.

In her boudoir, a charming room, an hour later, Mary Haines has called her maid, Jane, and ordered tea. Jane is unhappy and trying to keep back her tears. There has been a row with cook, it appears, in which cook has accused Jane of leading cook's husband on. Cook comes in now to speak for herself. She will have to give up her place again and take her husband away. It is always that way with him. He can't leave the girls alone. But cook had rather have him the way he is than not have him at all, so she does what she can to remove him from temptation.

There is also a problem with the children to be adjusted. Little Mary has slapped little Stevie, and Nurse thinks she should be punished. Nurse, being English, is inclined to take Stevie's part. Girls aren't spoiled so outrageously in England. "After all, this is a man's world," suggests Miss Fordyce. "The sooner our girls are taught to accept the fact graciously—"

Little Mary has her own defense. She had slapped Stevie because of an awful thing he said. Stevie said that little Mary was getting bumpy. In the hips and chest. Little Mary thinks maybe she is, and she doesn't like it. Even if it is because she's a girl. She doesn't want to be a girl. She doesn't want even to be a lady. Ladies don't have any fun. They don't even take care of their families, as Mother tries to point out. The servants do that. And there is always the time when ladies get the "lovie-dovies," like in the movies. After which they are practically no good at all.

"Darling, you're too young to understand," protests Mary.

"But, Mother—"

"'But, Mother, but, Mother!' There's one thing a woman can do, no man can do."

"What?"

"Have a child. (*Tenderly.*) Like you."

"Oh, that! Everybody knows that. But is that any fun, Mother dear?"

"Fun? No. But it is—joy. (*Hugging her.*) Of a very special kind."

"Well, it's never sounded specially exciting to me," says Little Mary, squirming away from her mother. "I love you, Mother. But I bet you anything you like, Daddy has more fun than you! (*She slips away from* Mary. *Then, seeing her mother's dispirited face, turns and kisses her warmly.*) Oh, I'm sorry, Mother. But you just *don't understand!*"

Little Mary agrees finally that she should be punished and she will punish herself by not going down to breakfast with her Daddy for two mornings. . . .

Mrs. Morehead, Mary's mother, has arrived. "She is a bourgeois aristocrat of 55." She has come at Mary's suggestion and she has decided from the tone of Mary's voice that there is something wrong. Probably Stephen. Probably another woman. It usually is. If that is it Mary will be wise to forget it.

MARY—But, Mother, you don't really mean I should say nothing?

MRS. MOREHEAD—I do.

MARY—Oh, but, Mother—

MRS. MOREHEAD—My dear, I felt the same way twenty years ago.

MARY—Not Father?

MRS. MOREHEAD—Mary, in many ways your father was an exceptional man. (*Philosophically.*) That, unfortunately, was not one of them.

MARY—Did you say nothing?

MRS. MOREHEAD—Nothing. I had a wise mother, too. Listen, dear, this is not a new story. It comes to most wives.

MARY—But Stephen—

MRS. MOREHEAD—Stephen is a man. He's been married twelve years—

MARY—You mean, he's tired of me!

MRS. MOREHEAD—Stop crying. You'll make your nose red.

MARY—I'm not crying. (*Patting tonic on her face.*) This stuff stings.

MRS. MOREHEAD (*going to her*)—Stephen's tired of himself. Tired of feeling the same things in himself year after year. Time comes when every man's got to feel something new—when he's got to feel young again, just because he's growing old. Women are just the same. But when we get that way we change our hair dress. Or get a new cook. Or redecorate the house from stem to stern. But a man can't do over his office, or fire his secretary. Not even change the style of his hair. And the urge usually hits him hardest just when he's beginning to lose his hair. No, dear, a man has only one escape from his old self: to see a different self—in the mirror of some woman's eyes.

MARY—But, Mother—

MRS. MOREHEAD—This girl probably means no more to him than that new dress means to you.

MARY—But, Mother—

MRS. MOREHEAD—"But, Mother, but, Mother!" He's not giving anything to her that belongs to you, or you would have felt that yourself long ago.

MARY (*bewildered*)—Oh, I always thought I would. I love him so much.

MRS. MOREHEAD—And he loves you, baby. (*Drawing* MARY *beside her on the chaise-longue.*) Now listen to me: Go away somewhere for a month or two. There's nothing like a good dose of another woman to make a man appreciate his wife. Mother knows!

It is also Mother's idea that Mary should banish all thought of "forgiving" Stephen. Or of accusing him, either. That would be the quickest way to lose him. It is being together at the end that really matters. Furthermore, let Mary be careful not to confide in her girl friends. Even if they know let them think she (Mary) doesn't know.

"If you let them advise you they'll see to it, in the name of friendship, that you lose your husband and your home. I'm an old woman, dear, and I know my sex."

Mrs. Morehead has gone. She will get tickets for Bermuda on her way home. . . . The phone is ringing. It's Stephen. He won't be able to take Mary to the theatre as they had planned. Mary has a struggle to be pleasant, but manages a graceful deception—

". . . It's all right— Have a good time— Of course I know it's just business— No, dear—I won't wait up— Stephen, I love—"

Stephen has hung up. The maid has returned.

"Jane— The children and I will have dinner alone—"

Mary has turned her back that her face may not belie the calmness of her voice. The curtain falls.

The scene changes to a dressmaker's shop. It is two months later. We are facing two identical dressing rooms, separated by a mirrored partition. In one two salesgirls are busy recovering gowns that have been submitted to a customer recently departed—the kind of customer who makes the salesgirls "drag out everything in the damned store and doesn't even buy a brassiere."

Presently a petite and attractive young woman is shown into one of the booths, followed by a salesgirl. Their conversation is in relation to the customer's opening a charge account. She gives name and address as Miss Crystal Allen of the Hotel Waverly. She has no other charges, but is anticipating establishing a number.

Neither has she a bank account at the moment—

There is a stir in the adjoining room. Mary Haines, followed by a fitter and a salesgirl, has entered and begun to undress. She is trying on a gay evening gown, with which the fitter is having some trouble. The investigation in Miss Allen's booth continues.

"I'm sorry Miss Allen. But we *must* ask for one business reference—" the salesgirl is saying.

"Oh, of course. Mr. Stephen Haines, 40 Wall. He's an old friend of my family."

"That will do. Mrs. Haines is a very good client of ours."

Crystal is a bit shocked at that revelation. She has never met Mrs. Haines, she admits, nervously, and she would prefer, until she does meet her socially, that nothing should be said as to the reference. The salesgirl understands—

Sylvia Fowler has appeared in Mary's booth. Sylvia is waiting to be called for her own fittings. Meantime she has time to criticize whatever Mary is trying on, and also to make a few subtle inquiries regarding Stephen Haines. Her husband, Mary is pleased to report, has not spent an evening in the office since she got home. He has not been seen much at the club in the afternoons, either, from what Sylvia has heard.

The Princess Tamara, a Russian model of regal bearing, is showing an extreme evening gown. The Princess and Sylvia are old and suspicious friends. At least Tamara is a very good friend of Sylvia's Howard. Or thinks she is. It is Sylvia's idea, however, knowing Howard as she does, that Tamara is simply wasting her time—

"Girls, show in Number 3 to Miss Allen," a saleswoman is calling from the corridor.

"Did you say Miss Allen?" demands the alert Sylvia. "Not Crystal Allen?"

"Why, yes—I just saw her on the floor. She's so attractive I asked her name."

"Oh, so Crystal Allen gets her things here?" Sylvia is watching Mary closely.

"She's a new client— Why, Mrs. Haines, are you ill?" Mary has sat down suddenly. In the mirror she catches a triumphant gleam in Sylvia's eye.

In the adjoining booth Miss Allen is extravagantly admiring the extreme evening gown Princess Tamara is modeling. "I'm going to have that, if I have to wear it for breakfast," she is saying.

The saleswoman has sent for a glass of sherry for Mary. Sylvia is deeply sympathetic now. If Mary knew, why hadn't she confided in her friend? "Stephen is a louse. Spending your money on a girl like that."

"Sylvia," Mary is saying, "please mind your own affairs."

SYLVIA—She's already made a fool of you before all your friends. And don't you think the salesgirls know who gets the bills?

MARY (*distraught*)—I don't care, I tell you. I don't care!

SYLVIA—Oh, yes, you do. (*Pointing to* MARY's *stricken face in the mirror.*) Don't be an ostrich, Mary. (*A pause.*) Go in there.

MARY—Go in there? I'm going home. (*She rises and begins to dress.*)

FIRST SALESWOMAN (*half enters*)—Mrs. Haines' sherry—

SYLVIA (*taking it from her, and closing the door in her face*)—All right.

SYLVIA—You've caught her cold. It's your chance to humiliate her. Just say a few *quiet* words. Tell her you'll make Stephen's life *hell* until he gives her up.

MARY—Stephen will give her up when he's tired of her.

SYLVIA—When he's tired of her? Look where she was six months ago. Look where she is now.

MARY—Stephen's not in love with that girl.

SYLVIA—Maybe not. But you don't know women like that when they get hold of a man.

MARY—Sylvia, please let me decide what is best for me, and my home.

SYLVIA—Well, she may be a perfectly marvelous influence for Stephen, but she's not going to do your children any good.

MARY (*turning to her*)—What do you mean?

SYLVIA (*mysteriously*)—Never mind.

MARY (*going to her*)—Tell me!

SYLVIA—Far be it from *me* to tell you things you don't care to hear. I've known this all along. (*Nobly.*) Have I *uttered?*

MARY (*violently*)—What have my children to do with this?

SYLVIA (*after all,* MARY's *asking for it*)—It was while you were away. Edith saw them. Stephen, and that tramp, and your children—together, lunching in the Park.

MARY—It's not true!

SYLVIA—Why would Edith lie? She said they were having a hilarious time. Little Stevie was eating his lunch sitting on that woman's lap. She was kissing him between every bite. When I heard that, I was positively *heart-sick,* dear!

In celebration of having scored this point Sylvia inadvertently tosses off the sherry that has been brought for Mary. She is ready to leave now, turning at the door for a parting shot: "No doubt that girl will make a perfectly good step-mamma for your children!"

For a moment Mary stares at the partition separating her from "the other woman." She knows she should go home, but she hesitates. Suddenly, the decision made, she goes into the hall. A moment later she is facing Crystal Allen.

Miss Allen is surprised to meet Mrs. Stephen Haines, but not particularly unnerved by the meeting. She is quite willing to talk with Mary and orders the saleswoman to keep out of the room. The saleswomen do, signaling their sisters and tiptoeing into the adjoining room, where they plaster their ears to the partition—

"I wanted to spare Stephen," Mary is saying, excitedly; "but you've gone a little too far— You've been seeing my children. I won't have you touching my children!"

"For God's sake, don't get hysterical," answers Crystal. "What do I care about your children? I'm sick of hearing about them."

"You won't have to hear about them any more. When Stephen realizes how humiliating all this has been to me, he'll give you up instantly. . . . Stephen doesn't love you."

CRYSTAL—He's doing the best he can in the circumstances.

MARY—He couldn't love a girl like you.

CRYSTAL—What do you think we've been doing for the past six months? Crossword puzzles? What have you got to kick about? You've got everything that matters. The name, the position, the money—

MARY (*losing control of herself again*)—Nothing matters to me but Stephen—!

CRYSTAL—Oh, can the sob-stuff, Mrs. Haines. You don't think this is the first time Stephen's ever cheated? Listen, I'd break up your smug little roost if I could. I have just as much right as you have to sit in a tub of butter. But I don't stand a chance!

MARY—I'm glad you know it.

CRYSTAL—Well, don't think it's just because he's *fond* of you—

MARY—*Fond?*

CRYSTAL—You're not what's stopping him— You're just an old *habit* with him. It's just those brats he's afraid of losing. If he weren't such a sentimental fool about those kids, he'd have walked out on *you* years ago.

MARY (*fiercely*)—That's not true!

CRYSTAL—Oh, yes, it is. I'm telling you a few plain truths you won't get from Stephen.

MARY—Stephen's always told me the truth—!

CRYSTAL (*maliciously*)—Well, look at the record. (*A pause.*) Listen, Stephen's satisfied with this arrangement. So don't force any issues, unless you want plenty of trouble.

MARY—You've made it impossible for me to do anything else—!

CRYSTAL (*rather pleased*)—Have I?

MARY—You haven't played fair—!

CRYSTAL—Where would any of us get if we played fair?

MARY—Where do you hope to get?

CRYSTAL—Right where *you* are, Mrs. Haines!

MARY—You're very confident.

CRYSTAL—The longer you stay in here, the more confident I get. Saint or no saint, Mrs. Haines, you are a hell of a *dull woman!*

MARY (*staring at her wide-eyed at the horrid thought that this may be the truth. She refuses to meet the challenge. She equivocates*)—By your standards, I probably am. I— (*Suddenly ashamed that she has allowed herself to be put so pathetically on the defensive.*) Oh, why am I standing here talking to you? This is something for Stephen and me to settle. (*Exits.*)

CRYSTAL (*slamming the door after her*)—Oh, what the hell!

SECOND SALESWOMAN (*in* MARY'S *booth*)—So that's what she calls meeting Mrs. Haines *socially*.

FIRST SALESGIRL—Gee, I feel sorry for Mrs. Haines. She's so nice.

NEGLIGEE MODEL—She should have kept her mouth shut. Now she's in the soup.

FIRST SALESWOMAN—It's a terrible mistake to lay down ultimatums to a man.

FIRST MODEL—Allen's smart. She's fixed it so anything Mr. Haines says is going to sound wrong.

FIRST SALESGIRL—She'll get him sure.

FIRST FITTER—Look at that body. She's got him now.

SECOND SALESGIRL—You can't trust any man. *That's* all they want.

CORSET MODEL (*plaintively, her hands on her lovely hips*)—What else have we got to give?

The curtain falls.

ACT II

Two weeks later we meet Sylvia in an exercise room in Elizabeth Arden's beauty salon. She is lying on her back on a wadded pink satin mat. A Victrola under an open window is playing a tango. A pretty instructress in a pink bathing suit is doing what she can to put Sylvia through her exercises. Sylvia is doing what *she* can to take as little exercise as possible and give the instructress as much of the current gossip as possible while she is doing it.

"Up—over—up—down! Up—stretch—up—together! Up—stretch—up!" drones the instructress.

"Of course, my sympathies are for Mrs. Haines," runs Sylvia's obbligato. "They always are—for a woman against a man—"

It is Sylvia's expressed conviction that Mary has acted like an idiot, as most women do when they lose their heads. She does wish Mary would make up her mind about the divorce. For the children's sake a woman should stay. On the other hand, she should give a man time to taper off an affair of long standing—

The instructress has managed to get Sylvia sitting alongside a rear wall, where she is supposed to "rotate on her buttocks." After which she is to "crawl slowly up the wall," neither of which exercises is at all pleasing to Sylvia.

Peggy Day has arrived. She is also in an exercise suit and joins Sylvia on the floor with some eagerness.

"Please, ladies. Let us begin with posture," the instructress is saying, briskly. "A lady always enters a room erect."

"Lots of my friends exit horizontally," mumbles Sylvia.

"Now—knees apart. Sit on the wall," continues the instructress. They sit on imaginary seats. "Relax!" They bend forward from the waist, finger-tips brushing the floor. "Now, roll slowly up the wall . . . pressing each little vertebra against the wall as hard as you can . . . shoulders back, and where they belong. Heads back. Mrs. Fowler, lift yourself behind the ears. Pretend you're just a silly little puppet dangling on a string. Chin up. (*She places her hand at the level of* PEGGY's *straining chin.*) No, Mrs. Day, your chin is resting comfortably on a little table. Elbows bent—up on your toes—arms out—shove with the small of your back—you're off!"

Sylvia and Peggy have gone mincing across the room in some sort of imitation of what the instructress had in mind. They are much more interested in their accompanying conversation. Sylvia is trying to convince Peggy that she should not give her husband, John, money. Peggy has a small income and she should keep it.

She is simply robbing John of his "manly sense of responsibility."

They are in the middle of the next exercise, which has something to do with bends and bumps, when Edith Potter appears on the scene. "She is draped in a white sheet. Her head is bound in a white towel. Her face is undergoing a 'tie-up'—that is she wears broad white straps under her chin and across her forehead." And she is plainly distressed.

Edith has been looking for Sylvia to tell her of the most ghastly thing she has, quite unintentionally done: She has told a newspaper woman, without ever remembering she was a newspaper woman, all about Stephen and Mary—

"Oh, Edith! It will be in all those dreadful tabloids!" cries Peggy.

"I know—I've been racking my brains to recall what I said—I think I told her that when Mary walked into the fitting room, she yanked the ermine coat off the Allen girl—"

"You didn't!"

"Well, I don't know whether I said ermine or *sable*—but I know I told her that Mary *smacked* the Allen girl!"

"Edith!"

Mrs. Potter's defense is simple: She has told no more than Sylvia had told her. Sylvia's defense is simple, too. Mary Haines could not broadcast her domestic difficulties and not expect them to wind up in a scandal.

"Mary didn't broadcast them!" protests Peggy.

"Who did?"

"*You* did. You—you're all making it impossible for her to do anything now but get a divorce!"

"You flatter us. We didn't realize how much influence we had on our friends' lives!"

"Everybody calling her up, telling her how badly she's been treated—"

"As a matter of fact, I told her she'd make a great mistake. What has any woman got to gain by a divorce? No matter how much he gives her, she won't have what they have together. And you know as well as I do, he'd marry that girl. What he's spent on her, he'd have to, to protect his investment. (*Sorrowfully.*) But, I have as much influence on Mary as I have on *you*, Peggy."

Sylvia's paraffine bath is ready. The instructress from whom Edith has escaped has come to take her back to where she belongs. Sylvia's parting promise is that she will call up the newspaper writer and tell her Edith had been lying to her. That should fix it. Peggy is the only one who is really concerned. She thinks something should be done about Sylvia, she's such a dreadful woman—

"Oh, she can't help it, Peggy," Edith explains. "It's just her tough luck she wasn't born deaf and dumb. But what can we do about it? She's always gotten away with murder. Why, she's been having an affair for a year with that young customers' man in Howard's office."

"Edith!"

"Right under Howard's nose! But Howard doesn't care! So what business is it of yours or mine? (*Earnestly.*) Peggy, take a tip from me—keep out of other women's troubles. I've never had a fight with a girl friend in all my life. Why? I hear no evil, I see no evil, I speak no evil!"

The curtain falls.

A few days later, in the Haines' pantry, Jane, the maid, and Maggie, the new cook, are having a midnight snack. Jane is relating, with gestures, the story of the quarrel she had just overheard between Mr. and Mrs. Haines and Maggie, "a buxom, middle-aged woman, wearing a wrapper and felt bedroom slippers," is furnishing such comment and conclusions as she deems appropriate.

There had been, according to Jane, both accusations and denials. It was Mr. Haines' defense that he had been faithful for twelve years; that the girl was a very nice girl who wouldn't take anything from him for months, and that it just happened one night unexpectedly in her room. It was the madam's reply that she could not be sure he ever had been faithful, and that the girl was interested in nothing but his money—

"Well, then they both got sore," reports Jane.

"I knew it," says Maggie, drawing closer.

Jane—So, he began to tell her all over, what a good husband he'd been. And how hard he'd worked for her and the kids. And she kept interrupting with what a good wife she'd been and how proud she was of him. Then they began to exaggerate themselves—

Maggie—Listen, anybody that's ever been married knows that line backwards and forwards. What happened?

Jane—Well, somewhere in there the madam says, "Stephen, you do want a divorce. Only you ain't got the courage to ask it." And he says, "Oh, my God, no I don't, Mary. Haven't I told you?" And she says, "But you don't love me!" And he says, "But oh, my God, Mary, I'm awful *fond* of you." And she says, very icy, "Fond, fond? Is that all?" And he says, "No, Mary, there's the children." Maggie, that's the thing I don't understand. Why does she get so mad every time he says they've got to consider the children? If children ain't the point of being married, what is?

MAGGIE—A woman don't want to be told she's being kept on just to run a kindergarten.

JANE—Well, the madam says, "Stephen, I want to keep the children out of this. I haven't used the children. I ain't asked you to sacrifice yourself for the children." Maggie, that's where he got so terrible mad. He says, "But why, in God's name, Mary? You knew about us all along. Why did you wait until now to make a fool of me?"

MAGGIE—As if he needed her help.

JANE—So then, suddenly, she says, in a awful low voice, "Stephen, oh, Stephen, we can't go on like this. It ain't worthy of what we've been to each other!" And he says, "Oh, no, it's not, Mary!"

MAGGIE—Quite an actress, ain't you?

JANE—My boy friend says I got eyes like Claudette Colbert's.

MAGGIE—Did he ever say anything about your legs? Have a cup of coffee. (*Pours coffee.*)

JANE—That's when the madam says what you could have knocked me down with a feather! The madam says, "Stephen, I want a divorce. Yes, Stephen, I want a divorce!"

MAGGIE—Tch! Tch! Abdicating!

JANE—Well, Maggie, you could have knocked me down with a feather!

MAGGIE (*waving coffee pot*)—I'd like to knock him down with this.

JANE—"My God! Mary," he says, "you don't mean it!" So she says, in a funny voice, "Yes, I do. You've killed my love for you, Stephen."

MAGGIE—He's just simple-minded enough to believe that.

JANE—So he says, "I don't blame you. My God, how can I blame you?"

MAGGIE—My God, he can't!

JANE—So then she said it was all over, because it was only the children he minded losing. She said that made their marriage a mockery.

MAGGIE—A mockery?

JANE—Something funny.

MAGGIE—I ain't going to die laughing.

JANE—He said she was talking nonsense. He said she was just

upset on account of this story in the papers. He said what else could she expect if she was going to spill her troubles to a lot of gabby women? He said she should go to bed until she could think things over. He was going out for a breath of fresh air.

MAGGIE—The old hat trick.

JANE—So the madam says, You're going to see that girl." And he says, "Oh, for God's sake, Mary, one minute you never want to see me again, the next I can't even go out for an airing!"

MAGGIE—You oughtn't to let none of 'em out except on a leash.

JANE—And she says, "Are you going to see her, or ain't you?" And he says, "Well, what difference does it make, if you're going to divorce me?" And she says, "It don't make no difference to you, I guess. Please go, Stephen. And don't come back *ever*."

Stephen had left after that, Jane reports, wiping the tears from her eyes with the memory of the scene. The madam is going to get a divorce and Jane is very sad for her. But not Maggie—

"She's indulging a pride she ain't entitled to," insists Cook. "Marriage is a business of taking care of a man and rearing his children. It ain't meant to be no perpetual honeymoon. How long would any husband last if he was supposed to go on acting forever like a red-hot Clark Gable? What's the difference if he don't love her?"

"How can you say that, Maggie?"

"That don't let her off her obligation to keep him from making a fool of himself, does it?"

"The first man who can think up a good explanation how he can be in love with his wife *and* another woman, is going to win that prize they're always giving out in Sweden!" concludes Maggie, as the curtain falls.

The start for Reno has begun. A month later Mary Haines, dressed for traveling, is pacing up and down her living room. The place has been denuded of pictures, books, vases, etc. The furniture is covered with slips. The rug is rolled up. Mrs. Morehead, dressed for the street, sits patiently on a sofa, observing her daughter. They are waiting for Stephen Haines' secretaries and the papers that will have to be signed.

It is her lawyers' idea that Mary is getting what they call a "raw deal" but Mary is content. Stephen, she insists, has been very generous. He owes her no more than he is giving. And it is too late to change things now, even if, as Mrs. Morehead insists, they are both making a terrible mistake.

"It's never too late when you love," repeats Mother. "Mary, why don't you call this thing off? I'm sure that's what Stephen's waiting for."

"Is it? He hasn't made any sign of it to me. Isn't he the one to come to me?"

"You're the one, Mary, who insisted on the divorce."

"But don't you see; if he hadn't wanted it, he'd have fought me—"

"Stephen's not the fighting kind."

"Neither am I."

It is Mrs. Morehead's further opinion that it is the damned modern laws that are to be blamed. In the old days, when women couldn't get divorces, they made the best of such situations, and often made very good things indeed out of them.

There is still the problem of Little Mary. The child will have to be told. Her mother will have to tell her. She has been putting it off, because—

"Because you hope at the last minute a miracle will keep you from making a mess of your life. Have you thought: Stephen might marry that girl?"

"He won't do that."

"What makes you so sure?"

"Because, deep down, Stephen does love me— But he won't find it out, until I've—really gone away— (*At the door.*) You'll take good care of the children, Mother? And make them write to me in Reno, once a week? And please, Mother, don't spoil them so."

The secretaries have arrived—a Miss Watts and a Miss Trimmerback. Tailored, plain girls, carrying brief cases. Mary has left the room and Mrs. Morehead goes in search of her.

Miss Trimmerback feels a little sorry for Mrs. Haines. Miss Watts, however, doesn't feel sorry "for any woman who thinks the world owes her breakfast in bed." Furthermore, Miss Watts, while she doesn't hold any brief for the Allen woman, is bound to say that Stephen Haines' interest in his work, which had been slipping, was greatly revived by his new interest in Miss Allen.

"I wish I could get a man to foot my bills," ventures Miss Trimmerback, quite honestly. "I'm sick and tired, cooking my own breakfast, sloshing through the rain at 8 A.M., working like a dog. For what? Independence? A lot of independence you have on a woman's wages. I'd chuck it like that for a decent, or an indecent, home."

And as for Miss Watts, she is defiantly sure that Mr. Haines could get along without either his wife or the Allen girl better than he could without her.

"You're very efficient, dear. But what makes you think you're indispensable?" inquires Miss Trimmerback.

"I relieve him of a thousand foolish details. I remind him of things he forgets, including, very often these days, his good opinion of himself. I never cry and I don't nag. I guess I *am* the office-wife. And a lot better off than Mrs. Haines. He'll never divorce me!"

"Why, you're in love with him!"

"What if I am? I'd rather work for him than marry the kind of a dumb cluck I could get—just because he's a *man*—"

Secretarial confessions are interrupted by the return of Mary. The papers are in perfect order—insurance papers; transfer papers for the car; power of attorney for the transaction of such business as may come up regarding the apartment, and a new will—

"If anything were to happen to you in Reno," Miss Watts explains, "half your property would revert to Mr. Haines. A detail your lawyers overlooked. Mr. Haines drew up a codicil cutting himself out. . . . You can always make changes, in the event of your re-marriage. And don't hesitate to let me know at the office if there is anything *I* can ever do for you."

Jane has brought a box containing an orchid corsage. Mr. Haines had left word that Mary was to wear it on the train. Mary opens the box and finds a card reading: "What can I say? Stephen!" She has just thrown the box and the flowers violently into a corner when Mrs. Morehead brings Little Mary into the room. A moment later mother and daughter are alone—

"You know, darling, when a man and woman fall in love what they do, don't you?" begins Mary, drawing her daughter to her.

"They kiss a lot—"

MARY—They get married—

LITTLE MARY—Oh, yes. And then they have those children.

MARY—Well, sometimes, married people don't stay in love.

LITTLE MARY—What, Mother?

MARY—The husband and the wife—fall out of love.

LITTLE MARY—Why do they do that?

MARY—Well, they do, that's all. And when they do, they get unmarried. You see?

LITTLE MARY—No.

MARY—Well, they do. They—they get what is called a divorce.

LITTLE MARY (*very matter of fact*)—Oh, do they?

MARY—You don't know what a divorce is, but—

Little Mary—Yes, I do. I go to the movies, don't I? And lots of my friends have mummies and daddies who are divorced.

Mary (*relieved, kisses her*)—You know I love you very much, don't you, Mary?

Little Mary (*a pause*)—Of course, Mother.

Mary—Your father and I are going to get a divorce. That's why I'm going away. That's why— Oh, darling, I can't explain to you quite. But I promise you, when you are older you will understand. And you'll forgive me. You really will! Look at me, baby, please!

Little Mary (*her lips beginning to tremble*)—I'm looking at you, Mother— Doesn't Daddy love you any more?

Mary—No, he doesn't.

Little Mary—Don't you love him?

Mary—I—I—no, Mary.

Little Mary—Oh, Mother, why?

Mary—I—I don't know— But it isn't either Daddy's or Mother's fault.

Little Mary—But, Mother, when you love somebody I thought you loved them until the day you die!

Mary—With children, yes. But grown-ups are different. They can fall out of love.

Little Mary—I won't fall out of love with you and Daddy when I grow up. Will you fall out of love with me?

Mary—Oh, no, darling, that's different, too.

Little Mary—I don't see *how*.

Mary—You'll have to take my word for it, baby, it is. This divorce has nothing to do with our love for you.

Little Mary—But if you and Daddy—

Mary (*rising and drawing her daughter up to her*)—Darling, I'll explain it better to you in the taxi. We'll go alone in the taxi, shall we?

Little Mary—But, Mother, if you and Daddy are getting a divorce, which one won't I see again? Daddy or you?

Mary—You and Brother will live with me. That's what happens when—when people get divorced. Children must go with their mothers. But you'll see Daddy—sometimes. Now, darling, come along.

Little Mary—Please, Mother, wait for me downstairs.

Mary—Why?

Little Mary—I have to go to the bathroom.

Mary—Then hurry along, dear— (*Sees the orchids on the floor, and as she moves to the door stoops, picks them up, goes out.*

LITTLE MARY *stands looking after her, stricken. Suddenly she goes to the back of the chair, hugs it, as if for comfort. Then she begins to cry and beat the back of the chair with her fists.*)

LITTLE MARY—Oh, please, please, Mother dear— Oh! Daddy, Daddy darling! Oh, why can't you do something—*do something*—Mother dear!

The curtain falls.

A month has passed. We visit for a moment with Edith Potter in her room in a lying-in hospital where she has recently become the mother of a son. Son, at the moment, is deep in a sea of lace which surrounds his mother, propped up in a hospital bed. This is the fourth infant that Edith has nursed and this one, she insists, a little querulously, has "got jaws like a dinosaur." A white-uniformed nurse is drooped a little wearily in a chair at the window. Nurse's expression is not altogether respectful as Edith calls for a cigarette.

Peggy Day is a caller. She brings a box of flowers and is all enthusiasm for the evidence of nature's miracle in Edith's arms. Edith has a letter from Mary Haines in Reno. A depressing letter to Peggy, but nothing more than might be expected to Edith. Getting a divorce is what Mary wanted to do and evidently she has become reconciled to the whole idea. Edith has told her husband to be sure to tell Stephen Haines that Mary is perfectly happy. Stephen, it seems, has been "going around like a whipped dog." . . .

Baby Potter has completed his feeding and Peggy has been allowed to hold him briefly. The experience is quite thrilling to Peggy. "Oh, I *like* the feeling so!" she exclaims, hugging the bundle in the crook of her arm.

"You wouldn't like it so much if you'd just had it," says Edith, a little whimperingly. "I had a terrible time, didn't I, Nurse?"

"Oh, no, Mrs. Potter. You had a very easy time," answers Nurse, going suddenly angry. "Why, women like you don't know what a terrible time is. Try bearing a baby and scrubbing floors. Try having one in a cold filthy kitchen, without ether, without a change of linen, without decent food, without a cent to bring it up—and try getting up the next day with your insides falling out, to cook your husband's—! (*Controls herself.*) No, Mrs. Potter, you didn't have a terrible time at all—I'll take the baby, please. (*Sees the reluctant expression on* PEGGY'S *face.*) I hope some day you'll have one of your own, Mrs. Day."

Nurse has taken the baby and flounced out of the room. Peggy bursts into tears. Edith can't understand that. Certainly she mustn't think the nurse has hurt her feelings. "They're all the same," Edith explains. "If you don't get peritonitis or have quintuplets, they think you've had a picnic. What's the matter?"

"Oh, Edith—John and I are getting a divorce!"

"Well, darling—that's what I heard."

PEGGY (*surprised*)—But—but we didn't decide until last night.

EDITH (*cheerfully*)—Oh, darling, everybody could see it was in the cards. Money, I suppose?

PEGGY (*nodding*)—Oh, dear! I wish Mary were here—

EDITH—Well, she'll be there. (*Laughs.*) Oh, forgive me, dear. I do feel sorry for you. But it is funny.

PEGGY—What's funny?

EDITH—It's going to be quite a gathering of the clan. (*Sitting up in bed, full of energy to break the news.*) Howard Fowler's bounced Sylvia out right on her ear! He's threatened to divorce her right here in New York if she doesn't go to Reno. And name her young customer's man—

PEGGY—But—Howard's always known—

EDITH—Certainly. He hired him, so he'd have plenty of time for his own affairs. Howard's got some girl he wants to marry. But nobody, not even Winchell, knows who she is! Howard's a coony cuss. (*Laughing.*) I do think it's screaming. When you remember how Sylvia always thought she was putting something over on us girls! (*She laughs so hard, she gives herself a stitch. She falls back among her pillows, limp and martyred.*)

PEGGY (*bitterly*)—Life's awfully unattractive, isn't it?

EDITH (*yawning*)—Oh, I wouldn't complain if that damned stork would take the Indian sign off me.

The curtain falls.

Looking out the windows of the living room in Mary's hotel suite in Reno a view of the town's squat roof-tops and the distant Nevada ranges can be had. It is a very drab and ugly room, otherwise. At the moment, a few weeks later, the chairs are strewn with clothes and the center of the room is filled with trunks and bags. Mary is leaving. Lucy, "a slatternly middle-aged, husky woman in a house dress," is doing the packing and singing in a nasal falsetto as she works:

"Down on ole Smokey, all covered with snow,
I lost my true lov-ver, from courtin' too slow.

Courtin' is pul-leasure, partin' is grief,
Anna false-hearted lov-ver is worse thanna thief—"

Lucy pauses briefly in her work when Peggy Day comes into the room. Peggy is dejected and unhappy. She could do with a little cheering, even from Lucy. Lucy has little more to offer than the philosophy of a defeatist. She has been cooking and working for divorcees for ten years. Mrs. Haines is about the nicest one she's seen, and Mrs. Haines is going back tomorrow. Lucy had contemplated divorce once, being right there in Reno, but she couldn't go through with it because she found she was in a family way. . . .

The Countess de Lage has called. The Countess "is a silly, amiable, middle-aged woman, with carefully waved, bleached hair. She wears a gaudily checked riding habit, carries an enormous new sombrero and a jug of corn liquor." The liquor, the Countess explains, is to celebrate Mrs. Haines' divorce. Peggy doesn't think divorces are anything to celebrate, but the Countess disagrees. She has had several and she knows. The Countess has long been a victim of l'amour. Her third husband was a Swiss, and she was quite shocked the day she realized he had forced her to climb an Alp just so he could push her off. Fortunately, after she slid half-way down the mountain she found herself practically in the arms of her fourth, who was the Count de Lage. Now she had found it imperative to divorce the Count. What else could she do, the Countess demands, after she found out that he was putting arsenic in her headache powders? . . .

Peggy has temporarily fled the room. Miriam Aarons, "a breezy, flashy red-head, about 28 years old," has succeeded her. Miriam "is wearing a theatrical pair of lounging pajamas," and is in a mood to join the Countess in a snort of corn liquor. She is one, too, who can sympathize with the Countess' adventures with l'amour and is willing to suggest, if not to predict, that when the Countess is free from the Count she will fly directly into the arms of a certain cowboy at the dude ranch. True, Miriam admits, she might have some trouble with him at Newport, but even Mrs. Astor would have to admit that Buck Winston is handsome, and if the Countess were to take him to Hollywood first— That's a thought— She might make Buck a picture star—

Sylvia Fowler has arrived. Sylvia has been taking a turn around the town with a boy friend. She doesn't intend to mope, like Mary. Mary, they are all agreed, would take her husband back in a minute, even on the flimsiest excuse. But Sylvia—she'd roast in hell before she would take Howard Fowler back! After what she, a faithful wife, had sacrificed—

"Of course I was a faithful wife!" shrilly protests Sylvia, as Miriam bursts with laughter. "What are you laughing at?"

"Two kinds of women, Sylvia, owls and ostriches." Miriam raises her glass. "To the feathered sisterhood! To the girls who *get* paid and paid. (*Parenthetically.*) And you got paid plenty!"

"You bet I got plenty! The skunk!"

"I never got a sou from any of my husbands, except my first husband, Mr. Straus," interjects the Countess. "He said the most touching thing in his will. I remember every word of it. "To my beloved wife, Flora, I leave all my estate in trust to be administered by executors, because she is an A No. 1 *schlemeil.*" (*Touched anew.*) Wasn't that sweet?"

Mary arrives with her hand full of mail. She greets them severally. Her last official Reno act has been to cook them a supper with her own hands—all except the steak, tomatoes and dessert. She is pleasant, even to the still catty Sylvia, but she will not drink with them.

As Sylvia opens her letter several newspaper clippings drop out. The Countess recovers these and reads them casually as Sylvia finishes her letter. They are interesting clippings. From a certain New York newspaper column, two of them.

"Miriam, you sly puss, you never told us you even knew Sylvia's husband," the Countess suddenly explodes. "Sylvia, listen to this: 'Miriam Vanities Aarons is being Renovated. Three guesses, Mrs. Fowler, for whose Ostermoor?' . . . 'Prominent stockbroker and exchorine to marry.' "

Sylvia, flaming with anger, has turned upon the lightly flustered Miriam. "Why, you little hypocrite!" she cries.

"Oh, Sylvia, why do you care?" interposes Mary. "You don't love Howard—"

"That has nothing to do with it," shouts Sylvia, brushing Mary aside, and facing Miriam, fiercely. "How much did he settle on you?"

"I made Howard pay for what he wants; you made him pay for what he doesn't want," sneers Miriam.

"You want him for his money."

"So what do you want him for? I'll stay bought. That's more than you did, Sylvia."

"Why, you dirty little trollop!"

"Don't start calling names, you Park Avenue push-over!"

They are at each other now, Sylvia smacking Miriam soundly

in the face, Miriam clutching wildly at Sylvia's hair. The Countess and Mary are trying to separate them. Lucy has come in, observed what is going on with a professional air, and gone back for the smelling salts. Mary finally gets the combatants apart, but not before Miriam has got in a good kick on Sylvia's shins, and another that serves to straighten Sylvia up when she leans over to rub the shins. Now Sylvia has caught hold of Miriam's arm and sunk her teeth in it, and Miriam has run screaming for the iodine. She can't take any chances with hydrophobia—

Sylvia, reduced to a wild hysteria, turns finally on Mary, accusing her of having taken Miriam's side.

"Listen to me, you ball of conceit," she screams. "You're not the object of pity you suppose. Plenty of the girls are tickled to death you got what was coming to you. You deserved to lose Stephen, the stupid way you acted. But I always stood up for you, like a loyal friend. What thanks do I get? You knew about that woman, and you stood by, gloating, while she—"

"Get out of here!" orders Mary. And Sylvia gets out, but not before she has grabbed an assortment of ash trays, glasses and cigarette boxes and, screaming with rage, hurled them viciously against the wall.

Peggy Day has returned to the room, just in time to see the last of the battle. She is disturbed by that, but more by her own problem. She has come to Mary for advice. Peggy is going to have a baby—and—what shall she do?

Mary knows what she'll do. She has already reached for the telephone, getting John Day's New York number over her shoulder as she does so. Peggy would protest. She couldn't tell John—

"Why, isn't it his?" demands Mary, waiting an answer to her call.

"Oh, of course!" answers Peggy. "I always wanted it. But what can I do with it now?"

MARY—Peggy, you've shared your love with him. Your baby will share your blood, your eyes, your hair, your virtues—and your faults— But your little pin-money, that, of course, you could not share.

PEGGY—Oh, Mary, I know I'm wrong. But, it's no use—you don't know the things he said to me. I have my pride.

MARY (*bitterly*)—Reno's full of women who all have their pride.

PEGGY—You think I'm like them.

MIRIAM—You've got the makings, dear.

MARY—Love has pride in nothing—but its own humility.

MIRIAM (*at telephone*)—Mr. Day, please. Reno calling—Mr. Day? My God, he must live by the phone. Just hold the—(PEGGY *leaps to the phone.*)

PEGGY—Hello, John. (*Clears her throat of a sob.*) No, I'm not sick. That is, I am sick. That is, I'm sick to my stomach. Oh, John! I'm going to have a baby— Oh, darling, are you?—Oh, darling, do you?—Oh, darling, so am I! So do I! Course, I forgive you.—Yes, precious. Yes, lamb. On the very next train! John? (*A kiss into the phone. It is returned.*) Oh, Johnny, when I get back, things are going to be so different—! John, do you mind if I reverse the charges? (*Hangs up.*) I can't stay for supper. I've got to pack.

MARY—When you get back—don't see too much of the girls.

PEGGY—Oh, I won't, Mary. It's all their fault we're here.

MARY—Not—entirely.

PEGGY—Good-by! Oh, I'm so happy, I could cry.

Miriam is amused that Mary has grown so wise. Now she knows all the answers. But why is *she* here? It wasn't for lack of advice, Mary insists. It's Miriam's opinion that Mary is there because she was a coward, like most women. Miriam lost her man because she was a coward, too, a coward with ideals, a too nice sense of morals. When she wouldn't play, her Romeo quickly found himself another girl—

MARY—A good argument, Miriam. So modern. So simple. Sex the cause, sex the cure. It's too simple, Miriam. Your love battles are for—lovers—or professionals. (*Gently.*) Not for a man and woman who've been married twelve quiet years! Oh, I don't mean I wouldn't love Stephen's arms around me again. But I wouldn't recapture, if I could, our—young passion. That was the wonderful young thing we had. That was part of our youth, like the—babies. But not the thing that made him my husband, that made me his wife—Stephen needed me. He *needed* me for twelve years. Stephen doesn't need me any more.

MIRIAM—I get it. (*Phone rings.*) That's why I'm marrying this guy Fowler. He needs me like hell. If I don't marry him he'll drink himself to death in a month, the poor dope.

MARY (*at the telephone*)—Yes? No, operator, we completed—you say, New York is calling Mrs. Haines? I'll take that call—(*To* MIRIAM.) Stephen!

MIRIAM—Listen, make him that speech you just made me!

MARY (*radiant*)—I knew he'd call. I knew when the last moment came, he'd realize he needed me.

MIRIAM—For God's sake, tell him that *you* need him!

MARY—Hello—hello? Stephen? Mary. Yes. I'm very cheerful. It's so good to hear your voice, Stephen. I—why, yes, it's scheduled for tomorrow at 12—but, Stephen, I can—(*Frightened.*) but, Stephen! No—of course—I haven't seen the papers. How could I, out here? (*There is a long pause.*) Yes, I'd rather *you* told me. Of course I understand the position you're both in. No, I'm not bitter, not bitter at all— I—I hope you'll both be very happy. No, I have no plans, no plans at all— Stephen, do you mind if I hang up? Good-by, Stephen— Good-by—

MIRIAM—He's marrying her?

MARY—Oh, God, why did I let this happen? We were married. We were one person. We had a good life. Oh, God, I've been a *fool!*

MIRIAM—Sure you have. Haven't we all, sister?

MARY—But she doesn't love him. I *do.* That's the way it is. (*She goes to the window, and looks out. There is a pause. Then, violently.*) But it's not ended if your heart doesn't say so. It's not ended!

The curtain falls.

ACT III

It is two years later. Crystal Allen Haines is in her bath, an ornate affair with a black marbleized tub and frilled shower-curtains. A gilded French telephone rests in a niche back of the tub. A satin-skirted dressing table is covered with glittering toilet bottles and cosmetic jars.

Crystal is lolling in a sea of suds, reading a magazine and smoking a cigarette. She has been there an hour. Downstairs Stephen Haines has been having supper with his daughter, Little Mary. The child is about to go now, Helene, the maid, reports, and her father is anxious she should come and say good-by to Crystal—

"Listen, that kid doesn't want to bid me beddy-by any more than I do," exclaims Crystal. "He's tried for two years to cram us down each other's throats. Let her go home to her mommer."

Helene has gone to deliver the message. The phone bell rings. Crystal picks up the receiver with lively enthusiasm—

"Hello, darling, I'm in the tub. I'm shriveled to a peanut waiting for this call. No, I'm not afraid of shock. You ought to know— Oh, Buck, I'm going to miss you like nobody's business. I can't tell you what it did to me, locking the door on our little apartment—I'll say we had fun! Coma ti-yi-yippy, what? Oh, no, say anything you like. This is the one place where I have some privacy— (CRYSTAL'S *back is to the door. She does not hear a brief rap.*) Listen, baby, must you really go to the coast? Oh, the hell with Mr. Goldwyn. (*Enter* LITTLE MARY. *She stands hesitantly against the door.*) Listen, you don't have to tell me what you sacrificed to have a movie career. I've seen that cartoon you married. If Flora was ever a countess, I'm the Duchess of Windsor. Well, Buck, maybe she's not such a half-wit, but— (*Sees* LITTLE MARY.) Oh—call me back in two minutes. I've had a small interruption. (*Hangs up.*) Who told you to come in here?"

Little Mary has come, dutifully, to say good night. She would say that and get out. No, she doesn't want to tell her Daddy what she has heard of Crystal's telephone conversation. Grown-ups are always silly on the telephone. Neither does she want to sit down, as Crystal orders. It's hot and she has her coat on— Why doesn't she like Crystal? Mary never said she didn't like Crystal. Maybe she doesn't, but she has never said so. Neither does Daddy think Crystal's so wonderful any more—

"Did he tell you that?" demands Crystal.

"No. Daddy always pretends you're all right, but he's just ashamed to have Mother know what a mean, silly wife he's got. And I don't tell Mother what *we* think, because you've made her cry enough, Crystal. So I'm not going to co-operate, *ever!*"

"Get out!"

"And *another* thing, I think this bathroom is perfectly ridiculous! Good-night, Crystal," adds Little Mary, as she turns at the door.

The telephone is ringing. Crystal, still muttering angrily, grabs the receiver and immediately resumes her melting tone. "Yes, darling— That Haines brat. God, she gets under my skin! No, she didn't hear anything. What good would it do her anyhow? You're off in the morning, and Lord knows we've been discreet— What? You are? (*Giggling.*) Dining with the first Mrs. Haines?—Well, darling, lay off the gin. It makes you talk too much— Well, just be careful, darling."

With a light "Yoohoo," followed by a quick "May I come in?" Sylvia Fowler is in. And just in time to hear Crystal snarl into the telephone: "No, this is not the Aquarium. It's the Grand Central Station!" She had, she explained, got a wrong number.

Sylvia is both inquisitive and informative. Inquisitive as to what Crystal has been doing, and with whom, and informative as to what she has learned from a new psycho-analyst. Stephen Haines, says the analyst, has a Guilt Complex, as most men have. He grew up in a generation that was taught to believe infidelity a sin. That is why he allowed Mary to divorce him and why he married Crystal. Crystal, on the other hand, has a Cinderella Complex. She was taught to believe that marriage to a rich man should be her aim in life—

"He says we neither please the men nor function as child-bearing animals," repeats Sylvia.

"Will you function yourself into the bedroom?" angrily demands Crystal.

Sylvia is hurt. After all she has done for Crystal; taking her up when the rest of Mary's friends had dropped her! But she manages to stay on. Now she confirms Crystal's report that Mary Haines is having a dinner party that night and that the Potters and the Winstons are going—

"The Countess de Lage—Mrs. Buck Winston," chortles Sylvia. "My God, I have to laugh when I think of Flora actually turning that cowboy into a movie star. Of course he's not my type, but he's positively the Chambermaid's Delight—"

"Will you shut up?" shouts Crystal.

"But, Crystal—"

"I said shut up—"

Crystal has called Helene and drawn the curtains for her shower. Sylvia has time to snoop a little about the dressing table, finding among other things that Crystal does touch up her hair, that her perfume is a brand favored by all the tarts in town and that she has a key to the Gothic apartments, of all places. That, chirps Sylvia, is where her husband had had her followed and the door-man of the Gothic is nothing but a blackmailer, really—

Crystal, out of the bath, has grabbed the key from Sylvia. It happens to be to the apartment she and Stephen used before the divorce. She has kept it for sentimental reasons—

"Poor Stephen!" sighs Sylvia. "My dear, I thought tonight how tired he looked, and old. Crystal, I've told you everything. Tell me: how long do you think you can be faithful to Stephen?"

"Well, life plays funny tricks. The urge might hit me to-morrow."

"I doubt it, pet. You're a typical blonde."

"So what?"

"Most *blondes* are frigid."

"Really? Well, maybe that's just a dirty piece of *brunette* propaganda!"

The curtain falls.

At 11 o'clock that night, after Mary has given a dinner for the old Renoites, Nancy Blake and Miriam Fowler are in Mary's bedroom to recover their wraps. They are going on to a party. Peggy Day follows them and then Edith Potter, complaining a little petulantly about the stairs—

"Mary, I wish you had an elevator in this house. It's so difficult to walk upstairs in my condition," pouts Edith.

"Edith, are you Catholic or just careless?" demands Miriam. . . .

They have all gone on to the party, now. It is to be the Countess' farewell to all Manhattan worry. She has come to suspect Buck Winston is cheating her. She wants to get him back in Hollywood where Will Hays will protect her, at least from Dietrich and Harlow.

Mary has started to undress. Jane has come to turn down the bed. And to report that Little Mary is back from her visit with her father, and brooding, as usual after such visits. . . . Mrs. Morehead stops in to say good night—and to wonder a little how Mary can stand that crowd of Renoites, even once a year. She does wish Mary could find—

"Some nice man!" Mary knows the speech so well she finishes it for her mother. "We've been all over that before, Mother. I had the only one I ever wanted. I lost him—"

"It wasn't entirely your fault."

"If I hadn't listened to everyone, everything but my own heart!"

"He loved her."

"He still does. Though you know, Mother, I'm just beginning to doubt it."

"Why?"

"Because so many people, like Edith, make a point of telling me how much he loves her. Oh, Mother, I'm terribly tired."

"Well, do cheer up, darling. Living alone has its compensations. You can go where you please, wear what you please and eat what you please. I had to wait twenty years to order the kind of meal I liked! Your father called it bird-food— And, heaven knows, it's marvelous to be able to sprawl out in bed, like a swastika. Good night, darling."

"Good night, Mother."

Mary is in bed reading when Little Mary, in her nightgown and barefooted, comes wandering sleepily into the room. Mary has had a bad dream and is seeking comfort. She wants to crawl in with her mother—

"I don't mind if you kick me," Little Mary protests. "You know, that's the only good thing about divorce; you get to sleep with your mother."

Little Mary has snuggled down, but it isn't easy for her to get to sleep. She remembers so many things, or tries to. She remembers that she told her Daddy how silly Crystal is, and—

"Mother?"

"Sssh!"

"I think Daddy doesn't love her as much as you any more."

MARY—What makes you think so, Mary?

LITTLE MARY—He told me so after I saw Crystal.

MARY—What?

LITTLE MARY—But he said I mustn't tell you because, naturally, why do you care how he feels. Mother?

MARY—Yes?

LITTLE MARY—What's anyone want with a telephone in the bathroom?

MARY—I don't know. Sssh!

LITTLE MARY—Crystal has one. She was awful mad when I walked in on her while she was talking.

MARY—Sleep, Mary!

LITTLE MARY—Mother, who's the Duchess of Windsor?

MARY—What a question!

LITTLE MARY—Well, Crystal said on the telephone if somebody else was a Countess, she was the Duchess of Windsor!

MARY—Really!

LITTLE MARY—Good night, Mother.

MARY—Good night, baby.

LITTLE MARY (*after a pause*)—I wonder if it was the same man you had for dinner.

MARY—Maybe, ssh!

LITTLE MARY—I thought so.

MARY (*curiously*)—If who was the same man?

LITTLE MARY—Crystal was talking to, so lovey-dovey.

MARY (*protestingly*)—Oh, Mary!

LITTLE MARY—Well, the front part was the same, Mother.

MARY (*a pause*)—The front part of what?

LITTLE MARY—His name, Mother!

MARY (*taking her by the shoulders*)—What are you talking about?

LITTLE MARY—That man Crystal was talking to in the bathtub.

MARY (*half shaking her*)—Mary, what do you mean?

LITTLE MARY—I mean his front name was *Buck,* Mother! (MARY *gets quickly out of bed, rings bell on table.*) Oh, Mother, what are you doing?

MARY—Go to sleep, darling. (*Begins to pull on stockings.*)

LITTLE MARY—Grown-ups are so sudden. Are you dressing?

MARY—Yes, Mary.

LITTLE MARY—You forgot you were invited to a party?

MARY—Almost, Mary.

LITTLE MARY—What are you going to do when you get there, Mother?

MARY—I don't know yet. But I've got to do something.

LITTLE MARY—Well, have a good time! (*Rolls over. Then suddenly sit up.*) Mother!

MARY—Yes?

LITTLE MARY—I remember now I had something to tell you!

MARY (*eagerly*)—Yes?

LITTLE MARY (*dolefully*)—I was awfully rude to Crystal.

MARY—I'll forgive you this time.

JANE (*entering*)—You ring, ma'am?

MARY—Yes. My evening dress, Jane, and a taxi—and don't stand there gaping! Hurry! Hurry!

The curtain falls.

The Powder Room of the Casino Roof is "rich, tawdry and modernistic." Swinging doors let into it from the supper and dance floor, and out of it into adjoining washrooms. A wide window at back overlooks "the glitter of midnight Manhattan."

A screen near the door hides a coatrack, guarded by "a little old woman in a black maid's uniform and apron." Her name is Sadie. Between checkings Sadie reads a tabloid. There is, however, not much time for reading. The feminine traffic is pretty heavy. Two flashily dressed young women, leaving their wraps, report the place crowded. A Dowager and a Debutante brush through the room, the Dowager laying down maternal law governing the kind of dancing the boys are doing, as well as wine guzzling and all the rest of it.

"It's one thing to come out. It's quite another to go under the table!" snaps mother, as the swinging doors of the washroom close behind her.

Presently Miriam and Nancy, piloting the Countess de Lage that was, the Mrs. Buck Winston that is, arrive. The Countess is "tight and tearful." By the time her guides get her to a sofa she has told nearly all. Buck has insulted her. Of her five husbands he is the only one who has ever told her what he really thought of her in public. Buck had even boasted that he had been deceiving her for months.

"Flora, did he tell you the lady's name?" asks Nancy.

"Certainly not, Nancy. He's not that drunk. He wouldn't tell me her name because she's a married woman. Buck is very proletarian, but he's not a bounder. He just said *she* was a natural blonde."

"That ought to narrow down the field considerably," thinks Nancy.

"He said she was pretty as a painted wagon."

"Oh, you're not such a bad calliope. Snap out of it, Flora. You know, you're going to forgive him."

"I'd forgive unfaithfulness, but not base ingratitude. I rescued him from those prairies. I married him. What thanks do I get? (*Wailing.*) He says he'll be a cockeyed coyote if he'll herd an old beef like me back to the coast!"

"Let this be your lesson. Don't let your next husband become financially independent of you."

"Now, don't lecture me, Nancy. Every time I marry I learn something. This has taught me once and for all—you can't expect *noblesse oblige* from a cowboy— (*Sitting up.*) Ohhh, my eyes! They're full of mascara."

The room is empty, except for Sadie and the cigarette girl when Miriam and Mary arrive. Mary is quite excited. She hasn't any plan in particular, but she feels that she must find Crystal tonight. Buck Winston is leaving for Hollywood in the morning. Mary has no proof, but if Buck is as drunk as reported he is pretty sure to give something away.

Mary and Miriam have gone back to the supper room when Peggy and Edith arrive. They have come for their wraps. The party has broken up. The Countess, according to Peggy, was quite disgusting. Edith thought the whole thing rather funny. Even the kettle drummer was laughing—

"My dear," Edith philosophizes, "who could stand the life we lead without a sense of humor? But Flora is a fool. Always remember, Peggy, it's matrimonial suicide to be jealous when you have a really good reason."

"Edith, don't you ever get tired of giving advice?"

"Listen, Peggy, I'm the only happy woman you know. Why? I don't ask Phelps or any man to understand me. How could he?

I'm a woman. (*Pulls down her corset.*) And I don't try to understand them. They're just animals. Who am I to quarrel with the way God made them? I've got security. So I put my faith in the law. And I say: 'What the hell?' And let nature take its course—it's going to, anyway."

A few moments later Crystal and Sylvia have arrived. They check their wraps. Crystal is in a defiant mood. Stephen, she admits, is in a mood, too, but he "can take it and like it." Having adjusted their make-ups they are about to return to the supper room when Mary and Miriam return.

Mary does not hesitate. She moves forward resolutely and faces Crystal. Crystal would ignore the greeting if she could. Mary introduces the others, sweetly: "Mrs. Fowler, Mrs. Haines, Mrs. Fowler, Mrs. Fowler." Crystal is disgusted. Mary, she suspects, has been drinking. Mary has—or says she has—been drinking all evening with Mr. Winston. Surely they know Mr. Winston? He is in the lobby at the moment, waiting for someone, and quite drunk. Mary is afraid Crystal may have a difficult time handling him, especially in front of Stephen.

Crystal, having denied even knowing Mr. Winston, gives up going to the lobby, and would retire to the washroom. That, too, would be dangerous, advises Mary. Mrs. Winston is in the washroom having hysterics. She has just found out that Buck has been deceiving her—

"Really!" sneers Crystal. "What has that to do with me?"

"A good deal, I'm afraid. You seem to be the woman."

"Why, Crystal!—*Are* you?" Sylvia is eager to know.

"If he used my name, it's a lie!" explodes Crystal. "He's just the cheap sort— I'll tell my husband."

"You'll have to. Tomorrow it will be common gossip. I don't think Stephen will like it."

Crystal's anger is boiling, but she is not beaten yet. They have been trying to pin something on her, she charges, and they are quite without evidence. If Mary knows what she intimates she knows, why isn't she outside telling it to Stephen? Mary thinks that might be good advice, and starts for the door.

"Oh, he wouldn't believe you," calls Crystal.

"Oh, you can't tell, Crystal," puts in Sylvia. "He's terribly fond of Mary."

Crystal—Now get this straight, Mrs. Haines. I like what I got, and I'm going to keep it. You handed me your husband on a silver platter. (*Enter* Nancy.) But I'm not returning the compliment. I can't be stampeded by gossip. What you believe and what Stephen believes will cut no ice in a divorce court. You need proof and you haven't got it. When Mr. Winston comes to his senses, he'll apologize. And Stephen will have no choice, but to accept—my explanations. Now that's that! Good night!

MARY (*desperately*)—I hope Mrs. Winston will accept your explanations.

CRYSTAL—What have I got to explain to her?

MARY (*with a conviction she does not feel*)—What about the apartment?

CRYSTAL—What apartment?

MARY—You know as well as I do.

CRYSTAL—Oh, stop trying to put two and two together—

MARY—Oh, Mrs. Winston did that. She had you watched—she's seen you both.

CRYSTAL (*defiantly*)—Where?

MARY—Going in, and coming out!

CRYSTAL—Going in and coming out *where?* (*A pause.*) You're lying!

MARY (*warningly*)—I wouldn't be so sure, Crystal!

MIRIAM—Sounds like the McCoy to me, Crystal.

CRYSTAL—Shut up!

SYLVIA—Oh, Crystal, why didn't you confide in me? (CRYSTAL *turns to the door again, triumphantly.*)

MARY (*dismayed*)—Sylvia, didn't she?

SYLVIA—Certainly *not!* (CRYSTAL *smiles, very pleased with herself.*) She's the cat that walks alone. (*Goes to* CRYSTAL.) Why, Crystal, I could have told you some place *much safer* than the Gothic Apartments!

CRYSTAL (*exploding*)—Why, you big, loud-mouthed idiot!

SYLVIA—How dare you!

CRYSTAL—I'd like to slap your stupid face.

SYLVIA (*backing up*)—Oh, Mary, how dare she?

MIRIAM—Oh, I've got a job to do on Flora. (*She pats* SYLVIA *affectionately.*) Kiss you when I get back, Sylvia. (*Exits.*)

NANCY—And I'll explain the facts of life to Stephen. (NANCY *exits.*)

CRYSTAL (*to* MARY, *fiercely*)—You're trying to break up my marriage!

SYLVIA—The way you did hers, you floosie!

CRYSTAL (*nasty*)—Well, maybe you're welcome to my—left-overs.

MARY (*calmly*)—I'll take them, thank you.

SYLVIA—Why, Mary, haven't you any *pride?*

MARY—That's right. No, no pride; that's a luxury a woman in love can't afford. (*Enter* COUNTESS *and* MIRIAM. MIRIAM *gets their wraps.*)

COUNTESS (*rushing for* CRYSTAL)—Oh, mon Dieu, mon Dieu!

MARY (*stopping her*)—Flora, it's really too bad—

COUNTESS (*to* CRYSTAL)—You—you painted wagon!

CRYSTAL—So you're determined to have a scandal, Mrs. Haines.

COUNTESS—I'm the one who's going to have the scandal. Why, Mary, she's no more a blonde naturelle than I am. What's the creature's name? Miriam forgot to tell me.

MARY—Mrs. Stephen Haines, currently.

COUNTESS—Is that the thing Stephen left you for? Well, chérie, all I can say is, you're an idiot! I hope I never live to see the day when an obvious piece like that conquers *me* on the champs d'amour! (*She exits, followed by* MIRIAM.)

CRYSTAL (*to* MARY)—That damn fool didn't know. (SADIE *gives* MARY *her wrap.*)

MARY—I'm afraid she didn't. (*Enter* NANCY.)

NANCY—There's a gentleman called Mr. Haines. He says he's been waiting a long time for his wife— (CRYSTAL *moves to get her wrap.*)

MARY (*stepping between her and* SADIE)—Tell him, I am coming. (*Exit* NANCY *quickly.*)

SYLVIA—Mary, what a dirty female trick!

CRYSTAL—Yes! From the great, noble little woman! You're just a cat, like all the rest of us!

MARY—Well, I've had two years to sharpen my claws. (*Waves her hand gaily to* SYLVIA.) Jungle-red, Sylvia! Good night, ladies!

THE CURTAIN FALLS

ST. HELENA

A Drama in Three Acts

By R. C. Sherriff and Jeanne de Casalis

CHARLES MORGAN, dramatic correspondent of the New York *Times,* was writing of the production of "St. Helena" at the Old Vic Theatre in London. This was in February, 1936. "If our commercial theatre is too dead or too hidebound to receive it," he wrote, "I have little doubt that the United States will prove our error to us."

In October of that same year Max Gordon, the American producer, did his best to prove Mr. Morgan a sound prophet. He imported "St. Helena" and produced it in New York with Maurice Evans playing the role of Napoleon Bonaparte. The play, admittedly one of the superior biographical dramas of the time, had much the same experience in New York that it had in London.

In London, after having been denied production by a majority of the West End producers, it was given a hearing at the comparatively obscure Old Vic Theatre, which is on the wrong side of the Thames. An actor named Keneth Kent played Napoleon and the play struggled through a discouraging fortnight. Then Winston Churchill, among other enthusiasts, wrote to the London *Times* to call attention to the fact that here was a fine drama that was being deliberately neglected by those who prided themselves upon their good taste and superior sense of selection in such matters. Business at the Old Vic improved immediately. "St. Helena" was transferred to Daly's Theatre on the right side of the river and there achieved a run of proportions.

Mr. Gordon, accepting the play from a script study, had been impressed by Mr. Evans' performance as the Dauphin in Katharine Cornell's production of "St. Joan." Mr. Evans, an Old Vic favorite, knowing of "St. Helena," and regretting that he had missed a chance to play the role in London, was keenly eager to play it in America. Adding the one circumstance to the other it was easy enough to bring about the engagement of Mr. Evans for the New York production.

"St. Helena" was well received, and Mr. Evans' personal performance was generously acclaimed. Still business lagged. It was early in the season, the temper of the playgoing crowd favored the broader comedies and biographical drama is always a little handicapped. Yet, each time Mr. Gordon was ready to withdraw "St. Helena" the house would fill with protesting enthusiasts and there would be a minor demonstration following each performance. So it continued for eight weeks, jumping from one announced closing to another.

Written by the R. C. Sherriff whose "Journey's End" was a sensation of other years, and Jeanne de Casalis, a London actress, "St. Helena" is an honest and generally unbiased report of the Napoleonic exile.

It is an exile, and this is a Napoleon, seen through English eyes and visualized by an English actor. But one feels that such historical liberties as may have been taken and such exaggerations as may have crept into the text serve to soften and refine the character of the military genius of France rather than to distort it in any important particular.

"St. Helena" opens late on that December day in 1815 when Napoleon Bonaparte and his small staff of loyal officers and servants were brought to the island of their exile. We are standing in the dining-room of Longwood House, to which English workmen are just putting the finishing touches of repair preparatory to turning it over to the Emperor's party.

A large dining table is the principal article of furniture in sight. Much of the space is filled with packing cases, boxes and bales containing the goods of the incoming tenants. A door to the right leads to Napoleon's suite, that to the left to the library and other parts of the house.

Cipriani, a swarthy and bustling Corsican, the maître d'hôtel and majordomo of the household, is doing most of the directing. Cipriani was with Napoleon at Elba. The Emperor depends greatly upon him as a source of news and a retailer of the gossip of his entourage.

The fact that parts of Longwood House had formerly been used as a stable is causing a good deal of criticism. The floors are new and serve to brighten the picture but they do not lessen the pungency of the odors emanating from the manure underneath. . . .

Three of the Emperor's party have arrived. They are General Bertrand, the Grand Marshal, "a man of medium height and hatchet-faced, bald and rather gloomy looking;" Count Montholon, "handsome, easygoing and elegantly dressed," and General Gourgaud, "tall and ungainly, rough in manner but childish at heart."

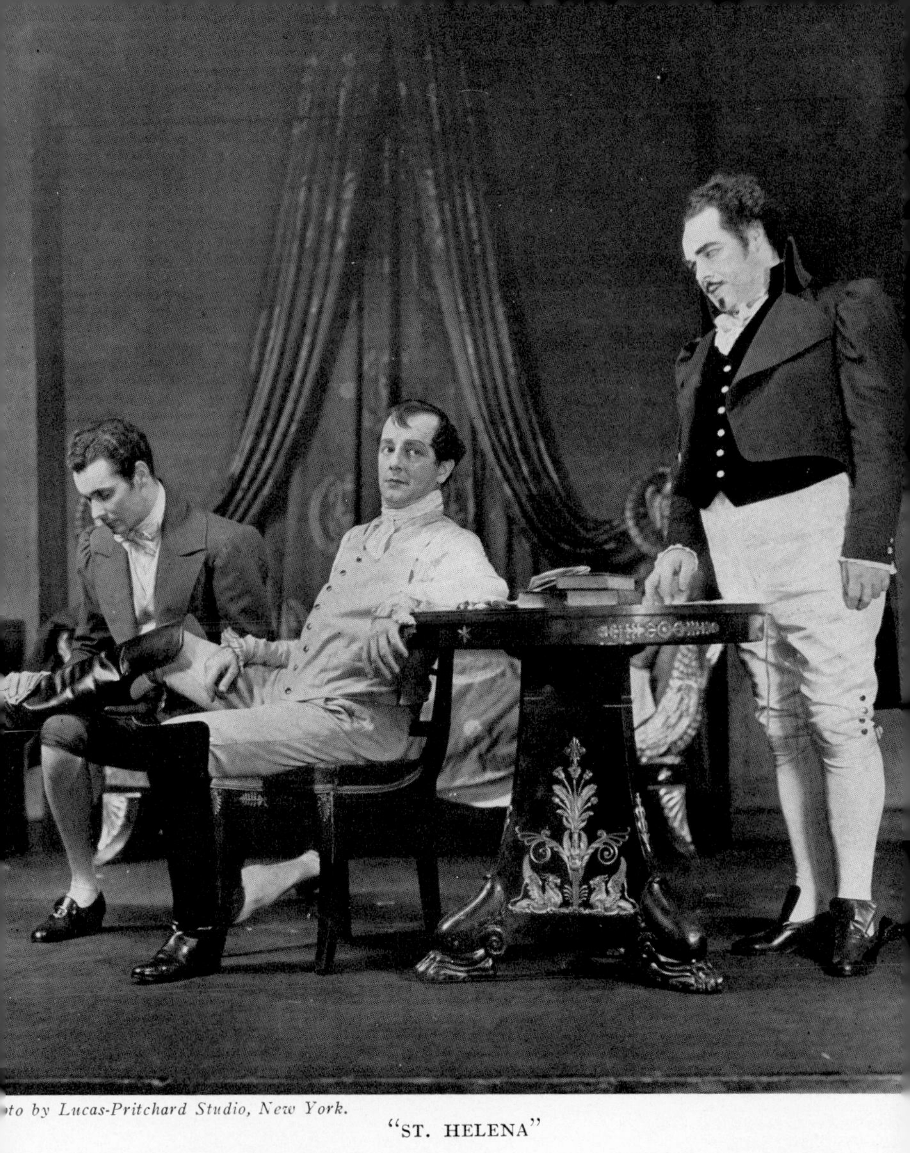

oto by Lucas-Pritchard Studio, New York.

"ST. HELENA"

Napoleon: Good! Let him stand them (the guards) shoulder to shoulder along the cliff, if it uses him . . . but let him leave us in peace up here.

(*Barry Sullivan, Maurice Evans, Jules Epailly*)

It is Bertrand's idea that, whatever conditions they have found, they will have to make the best of them. Gourgaud admits as much, but, being irritable, resents the fact that everybody seems to be making the best of things at his expense. The room assigned him, for instance, is good enough as a room but it reeks of horses. The one satisfaction Gourgaud is able to extract from the situation is that Las Cases, Napoleon's secretary, has been assigned a room over the kitchen. "Very hot—like an oven," Cipriani reports. "Good!" explodes Gourgaud. "That will give the little beast something to think about!"

The problem of arranging places at table is also shouldered by Bertrand. When Mme. Bertrand and he are dining, they will sit at the Emperor's right and left. When they are absent the seats of honor shall fall to the Count and Countess Montholon. Las Cases will have a place at the farther end of the table. This arrangement stands until Las Cases, "a small, sleek little dandy, with quick, bird-like movements," arrives and undertakes to alter it. The place at the Emperor's right shall be his. Let there be no mistake about that. . . .

The Emperor has arrived with Admiral Cockburn of the British Navy, temporarily responsible for the exile's welfare. This is a first tour of inspection. Learning the direction of his suite the Emperor disappears hurriedly in that direction followed by most of his party. Presently Cipriani is back with word that the Emperor must have a bath. And there is no hot water. The single stove in the establishment is at the moment covered with dishes being prepared for dinner. There is considerable excitement over that bath, but it is finally composed. A fire will be built and the hot water carried down the hall. . . .

Napoleon, having seen his suite, would gruffly thank Admiral Cockburn for what he has done.

"I have endeavored to carry out my Government's instructions," modestly replies the Admiral. "Kindly inform me through the official channels if you have any further requests."

"I am not in the habit of making requests," answers the Emperor, with a slight increase of stature. "If I had been content to live the life of a prisoner I could have remained in Europe. Either I command or I am silent. . . . Good morning."

Napoleon is content with the quarters furnished him. "It's not the Tuileries—but we'll manage," he says. His rooms are small, but he likes small rooms. And he is not at all interested in a new house for which the English have drawn plans. "It would take the English six months to build a new house," declares the Emperor, with conviction. "We shall all be back in Europe by then." At the moment he is most concerned with getting the bath of which he had spoken—

"Posterity will never forgive the English for leaving me in a single room for two months without the possibility of having a bath," he prophesies, moving to the window. Across the yard he sees several men standing against a fence.

"Sentries," explains Gourgaud. "The Admiral has ordered the house surrounded at dusk."

"The Admiral's even got sentries on the goat-paths in the mountains," reports Montholon.

NAPOLEON—He flatters me! When are we to see the last of that imbecile?

BERTRAND—The new Governor, Sir Hudson Lowe, is reported to be sailing shortly, Your Majesty.

NAPOLEON—Well, let's hope he has a quick voyage. At least he's a soldier. This Admrial's nothing but a shark. We'll sketch a nice portrait of him in our Memoirs, hey, Las Cases?

LAS CASES—We certainly will, sir!

NAPOLEON (*noticing a note in* BERTRAND'S *hand*)—What's that?

BERTRAND—An invitation to dine with the Admiral at Plantation House tomorrow night.

NAPOLEON—Whom is it for?

BERTRAND (*reluctantly*)—For Your Majesty!

NAPOLEON—Tear it up! (BERTRAND *is about to do so.*) No! Wait! Let me see . . . "Requests the pleasure of General Bonaparte . . ." "*General* Bonaparte?"

NAPOLEON (*raises his head and looks out of the windows, where the quick, tropic twilight is gathering behind the mountains. Then throws the card on the table*)—For eleven years the Emperor of France—chosen by the French nation and consecrated by the Pope—was acknowledged ruler of the destiny of Europe—I accept no other title. (*Tossing card on table.*) Send this card to General Bonaparte. The last news I had of him dates from the battlefields of the Pyramids. (*He turns away and looks around the room.*) Is there any means of removing this smell of paint?

They are all looking vaguely at the walls and sniffing the paint as the lights fade and the curtain falls.

It is early next morning and a beautiful day. We are still in the dining room. With the assistance of Marchand and Novarrez, his two valets, Napoleon is shaving. Shaving and giving a few instructions as to the routine that shall be adopted at Longwood House. It is important that none of his party in exile shall allow himself to become flabby, declares the Emperor. Each morning, while he is having his ride, he suggests that his valets take to the air for a run. Let them run down to Fisher's Valley and back, even if it is two miles.

Cipriani follows the shaving. Cipriani is a little shy on news, but he has heard that the new Governor will not arrive until April and that the Admiral still in charge has ordered the thorough searching of every vessel that leaves the harbor and the posting of guards to patrol the coast day and night.

The careful watching does not bother Napoleon, so long as he is left in peace, but he is considerably irritated by the fact that his milk, brought all the way from Jamestown in the sun, is frequently sour. Let them deliver it at night, or let them have a cow of their own. . . .

General Gourgaud is lightly troubled. He cannot sleep, thinking of his poor old mother in France and her fight against poverty. Napoleon had provided 50,000 francs for the old lady, but it never had been given her. Now he agrees that she shall be paid 1,000 francs a month. That should cheer Gourgaud—

"You're famous, Gourgaud," declares the Emperor, encouragingly. "If you'd stayed in France, you wouldn't have been anybody—but now, when we get back, you'll have all the lion-hunters in Paris after you! Then we'll find you a little wife! That's what you said—a nice little wife."

"In the meantime, it's not easy to lead this monastic existence, sir. It's not to be wondered at that I'm ill and out of sorts."

"Well, we must find you something to go on with. I'll tell Cipriani to make inquiries."

"I've already asked him, Your Majesty, but so far he's been unsuccessful."

"Don't worry, we'll find you someone. If I allowed myself to think of women—in five nights I should be in a state of revolt. You're a slave to your imagination."

Another cause for complaint with Gourgaud is the Emperor's recent preference for Las Cases as an assistant in the preparation of his memoirs. Napoleon is not particularly interested. Las Cases is older and he knows England. Napoleon would learn all he can about England. He may be living there some day—

"I'm not interested in your feelings, Gourgaud," he admits. "I don't read hearts; I hear words, that's all. You can look cheerful, no matter how you feel. . . . Don't you think that sometimes when I wake up in the night I have my bad moments too? When I think of what I was and what I am now? A soldier must have a soul of marble, Gourgaud. I could listen to the news of the death of my wife or my son without a change of feature. Later the feelings of the man burst forth—but only when I am alone with myself."

"Your Majesty knows I would blow my brains out for you."

"All right," replies the Emperor, absently, "I'll keep that in mind. In the meantime I want you all to live as a family, happily. Then I shall be happy, too."

Count Montholon is a second visitor. He is happier than Gourgaud. Partly because the mail has arrived and there are reports of rioting in Paris. "Crowds have shouted: 'Long live the Emperor!' under the King's windows," reports Montholon, excitedly.

Napoleon quickly takes the paper from him and reads it intently. He is staring thoughtfully into space when the sound of the arrival of horses outside recalls the morning ride.

"This morning we take the road to Hutts Gate," announces Napoleon, with a show of spirit; "then the mountain road 'round the Punch Bowl, you see? Cipriani tells me there are fields around here, with a fine gallop down to Sandy Bay. . . . Come on, let's be off. . . ."

He has taken his riding crop from Marchand and is ready when he glances again through the window and sees something that arrests his attention.

"Who's that man in uniform beside the horses?" he demands.

"The English orderly officer, Your Majesty," answers Montholon, uneasily.

NAPOLEON—The English orderly officer? Why is he there?

MONTHOLON—Instructions from the Admiral. An English officer is to accompany Your Majesty when you go riding outside the Longwood boundaries.

NAPOLEON (*silent, then speaking quickly, in a low voice*)—So that's the latest insult! It isn't enough that they have me here like a rat in a trap. They must humiliate me as well. I'm to be followed step by step, like a convict at exercise? (*He paces up and down.*) You'll see! They'll find an excuse to run me through with a bayonet next—or poison me! (*He flings his hat off and sits down.*) We shall need all our courage to tolerate life under these conditions, gentlemen!

MONTHOLON (*feebly*)—Sir, may I . . . ?

NAPOLEON (*rising abruptly*)—They haven't put sentries in my rooms yet. Very well, we shall remain indoors. Their insults can't reach me here. Send the horses back to the stables, Gourgaud!

GOURGAUD—But, sir, I . . .

NAPOLEON (*thundering*)—Send them back! Let the Englishman follow his own shadow! We remain indoors! . . . They're determined to force on me a martyr's crown of thorns. Let them do it! If we can't ride, at least we can read and write. (*He is calm again.*) Yes. We must re-organize our lives, Montholon. There's plenty to do indoors. Our Memoirs; the battles. We'll spend our time like this. From 9 till 12 we'll read and work at our English. From 4 till 8 we'll work on the campaigns of 1812-13-14. 8 till 10, dinner and conversation. Ten till midnight . . . (*His voice trails away. He begins again in a new, casual tone.*) Riots in Paris, you said? Give me that newspaper! (MONTHOLON *hands him the paper.* NAPOLEON *hums to himself, then raises his head for a moment.*) All right, Marchand, come back presently; you can have the coat and turn the cloth.

Marchand goes out. Montholon stands waiting. Napoleon's head is lowered once more over the newspaper as the lights fade out.

It is early afternoon of an April day some weeks later. Lunch is over and Napoleon, the Montholons and Gourgaud are playing cards, as the servants clear the table. Napoleon is talkative. He inquires amiably for Mme. Bertrand, who is expected to be absent for some time. Why the modern woman cannot have her babies as easily and as expeditiously as the women of other days had them is more than the Emperor can understand. His own mother was running over the Corsican hills a few days before he was born. "She just had time to get home and drop me on the mat," confides Napoleon. He is, however, in favor of large families. Six children to every marriage, at least.

"You've got to allow for say three to die and three to live," figures the Emperor. "That's two to replace the father and mother —and one in reserve for accidents. . . . If a wife will not supply a man with a large family, he is entitled to have concubines—as in the olden days. . . . Today you have mistresses instead of concubines. A great mistake. They have too much influence and upset fortunes far too easily."

The game is over and the Emperor has won, as usual. Three hundred francs, and he insists on cash in hand. If Mme. Montholon has forgotten her purse, as she insists she has, he is prepared to send for it. . . .

Dr. O'Meara, an amiable Irishman attending the Emperor's household, reports the approach of the new Governor and the imminent departure of Admiral Cockburn, whom Napoleon has come to detest. The Doctor is anxious about his distinguished patient's health, and Napoleon is free to admit a good deal of pain. That would be his liver, the Doctor is convinced, for which riding is the best cure. The Emperor could, if he would, ride within the boundaries of Longwood without an orderly escort, but he will not think of that.

"I need to ride eight leagues a day," thunders Napoleon. "I will stay in this house and die in this house until they withdraw the guard."

"You are a very bad patient, sir," protests O'Meara. "You have only been out once in the last fortnight, and then Las Cases tells me you worked into the night again."

"We worked until three o'clock this morning."

"You can't expect to feel better, sir."

"Work is my element. Eight hours in the saddle and then half the night in dictating. That was my life, O'Meara. Now I spend my days caged up in these stables. No wonder I am ill."

The new Governor's party is approaching. Preparations are made for the reception. The Emperor and Bertrand retire to the library. The others dispose themselves in expectant groups. Presently the visitors arrive, led by Sir Hudson Lowe, "a man of medium height, slight and alert, a bleakness in his cold, gray eyes and sandy, gray-shot hair." Sir Hudson is accompanied by Admiral Cockburn and members of his staff. Introductions completed, Bertrand announces formally that he will advise the Emperor of their presence.

There is an embarrassed silence, broken finally by obvious attempts on the part of the Montholons, Gourgaud and Las Cases to start a conversation. There is a good deal of comparing voyages and weather conditions. It had taken the Lowe party sixty-six days to come from England. The others had made it from France in sixty-four days. Sir Hudson is a fairly good sailor, but—

Bertrand is back to announce that while the Emperor is closely engaged upon important business, he sends his compliments and will be able to see Sir Hudson Lowe directly he is free.

Again the silence is rather strained. There isn't much more to be said about either the weather or the adventure of sailing. Las Cases thinks to help a little by recalling the ten years he had lived in England during the revolution. He had taught French, Las Cases explains, and written a book, *The Atlas Historique et Genealogique*. It was, Las Cases is convinced, an admirable work.

Now Novarrez, the Emperor's giant Swiss valet, has come to summon Sir Hudson to the library. Admiral Cockburn would follow, but Novarrez suddenly blocks the way. He was instructed to announce only Sir Hudson Lowe. The Admiral is furious, almost beyond expression.

"You've given me happy memories to take back to England, gentlemen," he sneers.

"You've made them for yourself," answers Gourgaud.

ADMIRAL—I'm told that General Bonaparte intends to destroy my reputation and ruin my career.

MONTHOLON—You'll excuse my saying so, Admiral, but I think you've accomplished that without the Emperor's intervention.

ADMIRAL—From the day we landed, you've done everything in your power to make my efforts on your behalf impossible. You accuse me of forbidding sealed correspondence to Europe; I did so upon my Government's orders.

MONTHOLON—If the Emperor gives a coin to a negro, you think the peace of Europe is being disturbed!

ADMIRAL—You complain that I keep news from you. I've sent you every newspaper; my own even, before I've read them. You complain of your food; you get the best; I've denied you nothing.

GOURGAUD—No one's accusing you. . . .

MONTHOLON—You've often denied us things we need.

ADMIRAL—Yes, once! When your man demanded the brains of three bullocks for a single dish.

GOURGAUD—Pooh! Absurd!

ADMIRAL—You continually abuse me for withholding from General Bonaparte the title of Emperor. My Government never acknowledged that title!

MONTHOLON—The Emperor's not the prisoner of your Government!

GOURGAUD—He's not a prisoner at all!

ADMIRAL—At your own request I ordered the officer to ride sixty paces behind the General. Then he plays a childish trick. He gallops off and hides in a ditch—and has the whole island searching for him!

GOURGAUD—Well, you can't blame him for trying to get a little amusement.

ADMIRAL—He created for himself an imaginary France—an imaginary Spain—now he wants to create an imaginary St. Helena!

Admiral Cockburn has turned on his heel and stalked out of the room. He will do the rest of his waiting outside. The Napoleon party think it a great joke. So, too, when Sir Hudson suddenly reappears, apparently quite annoyed, and also leaves promptly. He is so mad, Las Cases, at the window, reports, that he has difficulty getting on his horse. . . .

Bertrand has come from the library. He carries a legal looking document and wears a worried expression. The document, it seems, is a declaration for them to sign. Either they must each promise to remain in attendance upon "General" Bonaparte for such time as the "general" is there at His Britannic Majesty's pleasure, or they will be taken in custody to the Cape, and there held as prisoners. They also must sign the document as it is written, with the word "Emperor" omitted. The ship is being held in harbor awaiting their decision.

The Emperor has re-entered. He paces nervously across the room before he speaks. Then he turns and faces them—

NAPOLEON—Well, my friends, I see you've heard the news. It seems that this is to be our last evening together. (*Pause.*)

MME. MONTHOLON (*crying*)—We can't let you stay here alone, sir!

LAS CASES—I . . . we . . . perhaps if Bertrand were to see the Governor again or if . . .

BERTRAND—We have only until midnight to make up our minds!

NAPOLEON—You needn't worry, my friends. I order that none of you shall sign that form! You must all go. I'll stay here alone. Bertrand, return this form. You will all be better off away from here.

GOURGAUD (*fiercely*)—No! I'll sign anything, rather than dishonor myself by deserting you. I've been at Your Majesty's side for six years; I followed you in your victories!

NAPOLEON—Yes, Gourgaud—I know—but I refuse to allow any of you to bind yourselves to my Fate.

GOURGAUD—You order me not to sign, unless that form includes the title word of "Emperor"; I shall sign because you are more to me than that: The word "Emperor" may not be written on that paper, but it's written here! Give me the paper, Bertrand!

Gourgaud signs the paper with a flourish. The others silently follow. Napoleon sits quietly without a sign of his feelings. The paper signed, Bertrand passes it to Novarrez—

Bertrand—Novarrez! Take this form to the Orderly Officer, and instruct him to deliver it to the Governor tonight.

Napoleon—Tell him to inform the Governor that it was signed against my orders. . . .

They have all bowed and left the room. Napoleon is alone. He raises his head with a smile of triumph as the lights fade.

It is August 15, 1816, the night of Napoleon's birthday. In the dining room at Longwood the anniversary is being celebrated by a dinner. The room is ablaze with candles, the servants are wearing their green velvet liveries, and everybody is at least a little gay. The toast being drunk at the moment is to the Emperor. A moment later the party resumes its seats with a mingling of congratulations and many "A happy birthday, Your Majesty."

The Emperor is pleased. He regrets that Mme. Bertrand could not be with them, and he would, if he could, have an orchestra. He always enjoyed an orchestra—if it were properly muffled.

"Well, a lot of secret toasts will be drunk tonight in France," ventures His Majesty.

"A lot of open ones in Italy and Germany," adds Las Cases.

"Not many in Germany, a few perhaps. I shouldn't be surprised if we are dining together at Malmaison this night next year! (*He pauses.*) Still we must not be carried away by our imagination."

There is some discussion as to which book the party shall read on this occasion. Or what play. But before a decision can be arrived at the Emperor has grown reminiscent. He remembers this anniversary night a year ago—

"It was the fourth night of our voyage," he says. "I left dinner early to allow the Admiral and his officers to get drunk without formality. I walked alone on deck. It was a clear sunset and I could just see the Coast of Spain. Cape Finisterre. The last we saw of Europe. Two years ago today I was at Elba. I might have been happy there. I was creating a new kind of sovereignty. (*He pauses.*) In any case they wouldn't have let me stay—even then they were talking about St. Helena. No. I ought to have died at Moscow. (*Thoughtfully.*) Eh, Gourgaud? Come on! *You* always say what you think."

"No—no—no!" they cry out in chorus.

NAPOLEON—Yes, I ought to have died at Moscow.

MONTHOLON—And deprive history of its finest chapters? Your Majesty should not in any case have died until Waterloo.

NAPOLEON—I wonder. What do you think, Bertrand?

BERTRAND—Jena would have been a fine moment.

CIPRIANI (*who cannot resist*)—No—no!

NAPOLEON—No, Cipriani? Where do you suggest, then?

CIPRIANI (*shrugging his shoulders*)—Not Jena—Your Majesty, not Jena.

LAS CASES (*a sudden idea*)—Wagram! After that magnificent victory, when they spread a bearskin for Your Majesty on the battlefield!

NAPOLEON—Yes— (*Smiles.*) —a fine subject for a picture, eh?

LAS CASES (*carried away*)—If at that moment Your Majesty had died! What a moment!

NAPOLEON—No, I still think Moscow. Although a sword-thrust at Borodino—just before reaching my greatest days—would have given me a death like Alexander's. No, I don't think death matters so much; it's birth that sets our destiny. Everything depends on coming into the world at the right moment.

MME. MONTHOLON—No one ever chose a more fortunate moment than Your Majesty.

NAPOLEON—No. I came into the world too late. There was nothing great left for me to do. Look at Alexander, for instance. After he had conquered Asia he declared himself to be the son of Jupiter. The whole world believed him, except his mother.

Gourgaud would recall the time his Emperor might easily have died at Brienne, had it not been for Gourgaud—but it is an old story and the party is inclined to spoof the General for its repetition. Asked when she thinks he should have died, Mme. Montholon is quick to reply—

"I think Your Majesty should die on his birthday in 1849—at the ripe old age of eighty. Thirty-three years after he returns from St. Helena to rule France—again—"

There are shouts of "Bravo!" and the party is gay again. The party is gay but conversation lags. Napoleon would know of a race meeting of the day before, but Mme. Montholon can recall no incident of interest. He would inform Bertrand that the reason his child is not doing well is directly traceable to the quality of his wife's milk, a suggestion that Bertrand politely resents. His wife is quite well and his child is perfectly normal, as Dr. O'Meara will attest.

Speaking of milk, the Emperor would like to know when they may expect to have fresh milk from their cow again, and is disturbed to hear that the cow has, for two nights now, broken her halter and returned to her old friends of the pasture. The news infuriates the Emperor. How dare anyone look upon such a happening as a joke? Let the grooms be summoned. He will inform them that if the cow is not brought back by dawn the value of the animal will be deducted from their wages. What do they imagine he bought a cow for if—Napoleon does not finish what he was saying.

"A low growling rumble is heard far away deep and ominous. Suddenly the whole room quivers—a vase falls from the mantelpiece and crashes in the fireplace; a picture falls from the wall. Mme. Montholon cries out in terror; the men start forward; someone shouts 'Earthquake!' and there is a sudden scramble towards the doors. Napoleon blocks the rush by moving into the door frame."

In the midst of the agitation Napoleon remains calm. They will all be safer in the house. Let them stay there. Only Bertrand is allowed to leave, to go to his wife. For the rest—Cipriani will serve coffee in the dining room, after he has quieted the servants.

Anyway, the shocks are over. And an earthquake is just what they needed to make the island really and completely enjoyable! There is a book on the Lisbon earthquake of 1775 in the library. Let Gourgaud fetch that. For the others, let them return to their places at table and let the doors be shut—

"An earhquake is just what we needed to make us really happy," repeats the Emperor, resuming his place at table. "This island's an old volcano. If it becomes active again, we shall be submerged in molten lava and the Governor can withdraw his sentries. (*To* GOURGAUD, *who has returned with the book.*) "You've got it? All right, Gourgaud, let's hear what it says."

GOURGAUD (*stands, reading*)—"For many centuries the City of Lisbon has suffered from earthquakes. On November, the first, 1755 . . ."

NAPOLEON—'55 . . . you see?

GOURGAUD (*looking up, but going on when* NAPOLEON *nods to him*)—". . . the greater part of it was reduced almost in an instant to a heap of ruins. A tidal wave . . ."

NAPOLEON (*aware of* NOVARREZ *coming in*)—What is it, Novarrez?

NOVARREZ (*again at his place behind the* EMPEROR'S *chair*)—Archambault is waiting upon Your Majesty. Your Majesty summoned him.

NAPOLEON (*absently*)—Tell him the cow must be caught by dawn!

NOVARREZ—The cow has returned, Your Majesty, on its own.

NAPOLEON—All right. See if you can milk it! (NOVARREZ *bows and retires.* NAPOLEON *nods once more to* GOURGAUD.)

GOURGAUD—"A tidal wave at the same time broke over the Quays and wrecked the shipping in the Tagus. Fire broke out to complete the work of destruction.

The curtain falls.

ACT II

It is a wet, cheerless morning in 1816. In the dining room Montholon is trying, with little success, to balance his budget. He is in charge of the household accounts and hates the job. The fact that General Gourgaud keeps interrupting his figuring with heavy sighs and querulous remarks adds to Montholon's irritations.

Gourgaud is unhappy, as usual. For two hours and twenty minutes the Emperor has been shut up in his room with Las Cases, working on the journal. Whereas he (Montholon) had been told to reserve the mornings for the Italian campaign, the Emperor has not referred to them for a week. It is a disgusting experience Gourgaud is suffering. . . .

Dr. O'Meara has arrived from Government House with his instruments. Being informed that the Emperor is suffering from his liver, his legs and his teeth he is not at all surprised. Considerable mail, the Doctor reports, has arrived, but he has no idea when they will be allowed to see it. The Governor, when last observed, was sniffing and tapping and holding the envelopes to the light. There is also a box of books for the Emperor and a case containing a bust of the Emperor's son—

"Between ourselves, I hear they wanted to break it up to see if there were any secret letters in it," reports O'Meara. "They're frightened out of their wits about this rumor of smuggling him off the island in a dirty-linen basket. Is he disengaged?"

"Of course he's not," sharply answers Gourgaud. "Las Cases is with him. He's never out of the Emperor's room nowadays;

he's dined alone with him three nights running."

"Nothing left for you, eh?"

"I keep a journal, but I would die before I allowed it to be published. Las Cases reckons he'll make a fortune out of his memoirs."

"Why not do the same?"

"The Emperor's words to me are sacred. Half our troubles on this island are due to Las Cases. He's always urging the Emperor on to complain. The Governor's a difficult man, but, to do him justice, he does try to make things more comfortable for us."

"He's got a peculiar way of doing it," chips in Montholon.

"He's had his knuckles rapped pretty badly over those letters you people got through to the English papers," answers O'Meara. "I've an idea Monsieur Las Cases may have a slight shock this morning." . . .

The Emperor has summoned the Doctor and his instruments. He would have another tooth pulled this morning. Precious souvenirs, the Emperor's teeth. The one O'Meara is now carrying in his pocket, when he is not tossing it up and down in his hand, would probably fetch fifteen pounds in a London auction room. And more in Paris.

Las Cases would like to have a tooth. So would Gourgaud. Gourgaud, in fact, has been promised one. He thinks perhaps he will take the one O'Meara is playing with, but when he tries to take it from the Doctor there is a scuffle which might have had consequences if O'Meara had not been called in the middle of it. He grabs his instruments and departs, retaining the tooth. . . .

Las Cases is plainly elated. He has enough material to finish his third volume with what the Emperor has given him this morning. Gourgaud is furious at the thought and bitterly sarcastic in his references to the secretary's work. The two would-be biographers are soon quarreling at the tops of their voices.

"What was it you reckoned your Diary would bring you in? A hundred thousand francs?" Gourgaud sneeringly inquires.

"What are you insinuating?" demands Las Cases, advancing belligerently.

"For God's sake! Go and quarrel somewhere else!" shouts Montholon.

"I've no idea, General Gourgaud, what financial value may be attached to my Book," Las Cases is saying, sententiously; "but I don't think I'm exaggerating when I say it is a work that will go down to history as the basis of all future biographies!"

At which moment a British officer and two troopers appear at the door. They have come to arrest Las Cases. Ten days ago a letter which the secretary was trying to smuggle to Europe with the aid of a servant was discovered. Now a second letter, written on satin, has been found in the same servant's waistcoat. It contains false reports of the Napoleon party's treatment on the island.

"What does this mean, exactly?" quietly demands the secretary.

"It means that you will be transported from the island," answers the officer.

"To Europe?"

"I presume so."

"Very well, then," agrees Las Cases, with a shrug. "I admit the letter and the means I took. Very well, then. I took the risk for the sake of the Emperor. I will come now, if you will first allow me to go to my room."

"The orderly officer is in your rooms arranging the packing of your property."

"But my books!" Las Cases' face is blanched with fear. "My journals! I must pack them myself. They're my *private* property—"

"Your property will be respected, but the Governor orders that your journals must be confiscated."

"You can't take my books! They're mine!"

With a wild rush Las Cases has tried to recover that part of his journal which is on the table. The officer is before him. Now the troopers have seized the struggling and infuriated secretary. He is kicking and screaming his rights to his books as the troopers drag him from the room.

For a moment there is general excitement. The news of Las Cases' arrest spreads rapidly, bringing other members of the party to the house. The anxiety is insistent. What has happened? And why? Does the Emperor know? Yes, the Emperor knows. He saw them carrying Las Cases away!

They are staring anxiously at each other as General Bertrand, resuming a wonted calm, goes into the Emperor's rooms. The lights fade.

Some weeks later, in the study of Longwood, which looks out on a garden to which entrance is made through French windows, Napoleon and Gourgaud have been working on their journal. They have paused now to read a letter that Cipriani has brought. A cordial but apparently anonymous letter from Europe that gives no news of the Empress, nor of the donor of the bust of the King of Rome that is now at Government House. Not a very hopeful letter in that it reports a growing feeling in Europe that though Napoleon is not expected ever to return to power, there is a chance the King of Rome may succeed him. England, however, is reported as favoring the Duke of Orléans. That thought is a sobering one—

"He's right," announces the Emperor, pacing the room. "My career is over."

"He means that anything might happen, sir . . . at any time . . ."

"I doubt it! No! Let's put these thoughts away. What children we are! To allow our imaginations to soar away with us too easily."

Napoleon is convinced that it is the Empress who has sent the bust. He is eager to see it. Let Cipriani bring it at once. Meanwhile he will continue with his dictation to Gourgaud—

"If I am accused of despotism, they can claim that dictatorship was necessary in the circumstances," reads Gourgaud—

"Is it freedom I attacked?" continues Napoleon, resuming his pacing. "They can answer that Anarchy was beating at our doors. Striving for world dominion? Too ambitious? That may be true. But my ambitions were of the sublimest. I wanted to found a European system. Universal laws. There would have been but one people throughout Europe—Frenchmen, Italians, Germans. A united national whole: the United States of Europe. What visions of strength, greatness and prosperity that opens up! . . . Whoever troubled the peace of such a Europe would ask for civil war! (*He stops pacing.*) Have you got that?"

GOURGAUD (*writing hard*)—Er . . . almost, sir.

NAPOLEON—One cannot criticize a work that is only half completed. (*Digging* GOURGAUD *in the back.*) How did we begin that paragraph?

GOURGAUD—Er . . . "I closed up the chasm of anarchy; I cleansed the Revolution from the filth it had accumulated; I stabilized thrones . . ."

NAPOLEON (*quickly*)—Did I say that?

GOURGAUD—Yes, sir.

NAPOLEON—M'm. (*He smiles.*) It verges on the mountebank! That isn't how I put it in the notes I made during the night, is it?

GOURGAUD (*picking up another paper*)—No. . . . Er . . . er . . .

NAPOLEON (*impatiently*)—Can't you read it?

GOURGAUD—Not very well.

NAPOLEON—Why can everybody read my writing except you?

It's quite clear. Give it to me. (*But he can make nothing of it himself. He throws the paper down.*) Let it stand as it is for a moment. (*Going through the French window into the Courtyard just a step.*) No, my fame won't rest on my forty victorious battles, Gourgaud. Waterloo will wipe out the memory of all those victories.

GOURGAUD—Never, sir.

NAPOLEON—Yes. The last act makes one forget the first. (*He begins to stride the room again.*) But what will never pass away is my Book of Laws—my Code— (*Coming back into the Study.*) the harbors of Antwerp and Flushing—put that down—with room for the largest fleets in the world. The port of Venice. The high-roads from Antwerp to Amsterdam, from Marne to Metz, from Bordeaux to Bayonne, from the Pyrenees to the Alps. The pass over the Simplon, Mount Cenis, the Corniche, opening up the Alps in four directions. The water-supply of Paris—the Louvre—the Museums—all erected without loans being raised to pay for them. Those are the Monuments that will defy calumny! (*He stops by the window.*) Cipriani is a long time with that case. (GOURGAUD *writes hard. There is a pause.*) Waterloo! With 20,000 men less, I ought to have won the battle!

GOURGAUD—I have finished my account of Waterloo, if Your Majesty would care to read it over.

NAPOLEON—Your account? You mean my account?

GOURGAUD—I thought you meant me to write it, sir?

NAPOLEON (*impatiently*)—We will see. A comma or a full stop by me changes everything. Yes— (*Leaning against the table.*) —if I had delayed my attack I should have had 12,000 extra men. Perhaps it was a mistake to have attacked at all. (*He sighs.*) When I close my eyes, all my mistakes parade before me like figures in a nightmare. But don't let's talk of all that. What will be, will be. It is all written there! No one can escape his fate.

Cipriani has arrived with the case containing the bust. The dictation is abandoned while the Emperor himself, with chisel and hammer and no little excitement, proceeds to open the case. He has just begun, however, when there is a sound of voices outside the garden. Sir Hudson Lowe has arrived, with General Bertrand, and is insisting loudly that he must see General Bonaparte, and see him in person. The voices first interest and then irritate Napoleon. How dare anyone raise his voice so close to his (the Emperor's) windows? Nor will he see Governor Lowe. If the

Governor has anything to say, let him say it to Bertrand—

"He declines to deal with the matter through me," protests the unhappy go-between.

"Then he can keep it to himself," snaps the Emperor. "Tell him so."

"Yes, sir."

"I never want to see him again. Each time I've received him, he's made me lose my temper."

Napoleon has resumed his work on the packing case. Bertrand returns to Sir Hudson Lowe, who has entered the garden, and made his report of the Emperor's decision. The Governor is insistent. This is his fourth visit. He is tired of being told that General Bonaparte is either engaged or indisposed. He refuses to convey his message through General Bertrand or anyone else. He—

Napoleon has picked up his hat, put it under his arm and stepped through the French window into the garden. The Governor's voice ceases abruptly. Seeing Napoleon, he removes his own hat and produces a curt bow to match that of the Emperor.

LOWE—Good evening, sir. (*He pauses, but* NAPOLEON *makes no reply.*) The obstructive attitude of Count Bertrand makes it necessary for me to see you.

NAPOLEON—Within these boundaries Count Bertrand still acts under my orders. By what right do you presume to criticize him?

LOWE—I am not here to answer questions. The only orders I recognize are those of my Government. Instructions have come from—England concerning the expenses of your establishment. I wish to discuss this with you personally. I've come here on four occasions, and each time Count Bertrand has informed me that you were in your bath.

NAPOLEON (*nodding*)—I had one directly I heard you were coming.

LOWE—It's my wish to do everything in my power for your comfort, but I am deliberately obstructed. (NAPOLEON *is silent for some moments. He looks the* GOVERNOR *up and down, thoughtfully and impersonally.*)

NAPOLEON—Count Bertrand is famous in Europe; he's commanded armies, and you treat him like a Corporal. I know the names of every distinguished English General, but I've never heard of you. We've had nothing but trivial, humiliating annoyances since you arrived here! (EMPEROR *turns and walks down the path outside the house.* SIR HUDSON *falls in beside him. The whole interview takes place in this manner.*) I had reason to be displeased with some things the Admiral did—but he never stuck pins in our backs as you do. You're a Lieutenant-General, but you behave like a spy!

LOWE—I'm quite indifferent to your attacks, sir. I never sought this appointment. I accepted it as a duty and would gladly resign it tomorrow.

NAPOLEON—That's the best thing you can do!

LOWE—The expenses of this house in twelve months reached 17,000 pounds, an impossible figure. My Government has fixed the allowance at 8,000 pounds. On my own responsibility, I am prepared to raise this to 12,000 pounds, providing—

NAPOLEON— Discuss these details with my cook!

LOWE—I must discuss them with you, if I am to do anything to make your situation more agreeable. That's my chief desire.

NAPOLEON—And for that reason you publicly discuss the contents of my private letters! A letter came from my mother, and its contents were told round the whole island, before I was allowed to see it.

LOWE—Not by me!

NAPOLEON—Yes, by you! I was told by Dr. . . . (NAPOLEON *checks himself.*)

LOWE—By Dr. O'Meara?

NAPOLEON—I am an Emperor in my own circle, and will be as long as I live. You can make my body prisoner, but my soul's as free as when I ruled Europe! Try and starve me! Do you see the camp there—where the troops are? I shall go there and tell them the first soldier in Europe begs to share their meal.

LOWE—I should forbid anything so theatrical. I repeat that I have my orders and shall carry them out!

NAPOLEON—If you were ordered to assassinate me, would you do so?

LOWE (*obstinately*)—My instructions are that you are to be seen once a day by my orderly officer.

NAPOLEON—Supposing I'm ill? Are you going to assault the privacy of my rooms? If you try that, I shall use my sword and your orderly can enter over my dead body. Why don't you hang me—or poison me—and be done with it?

LOWE—Concerning your new house; timber arrived on the boat last week.

NAPOLEON—You can use it for my coffin! I want to be left alone. You've kept the statue of my boy in your house for three weeks before sending it here. You would have destroyed it if you hadn't been afraid. . . .

LOWE (*heatedly*)—I didn't come here to be insulted! It's your policy to get false stories back to Europe. But my Government is fully aware of your schemes. And will attach no importance to them whatever. Good morning.

During the interview, Cipriani, outraged by what he considers the succession of insults put upon his Master, has gone into the house, found a gun and is at the window, prepared to kill the Governor when Gourgaud sees what is happening and wrests the gun from him. Now they have hustled the weeping Cipriani out of the room before Napoleon storms in from the garden, furious with Governor Lowe and determined never to see him again.

"He's a common jailer—a hangman, he poisons the very air," mutters Napoleon, as he returns to the opening of the case. But now he lets Novarrez oversee the job, and soon he has the bust in his hands. His face aglow, he places it now on the table and gazes at it raptly. For a silent moment or two he continues to gaze, and then calls the others. Let them send for the Montholons. And Dr. O'Meara.

With the party gathered Napoleon invites his friends' opinion. The Montholons find the bust perfect. O'Meara is sure it is worth much more than they were quoting at the Government House. The English didn't think it was worth more than 100 pounds—

"Bertrand, trace the man who brought this and give him 300 pounds, d'you hear?" orders Napoleon. "It's worth a million pounds to me!" And then, turning to Mme. Montholon, he asks, anxiously: "The neck—just a little slender, don't you think?"

"I don't think so."

"He's like his mother. Look at that face! A man would have to be a monster to harm a face like that. (*He pauses.*) If Lowe had destroyed it, I would have raised such a storm that every woman in Europe would have execrated his name. . . ."

Gourgaud has recovered the gun that Cipriani had brought in and is seeking surreptitiously to get it out of sight when Napoleon notices him. Immediately he demands an explanation. Soon he has the story from Gourgaud. He is greatly disturbed by it. Cipriani must be spoken to, and firmly—

"The madman! The fool! Does he want to destroy all our hopes? O'Meara, not a word about this!"

O'MEARA—Of course not, sir!

NAPOLEON—Where is he now?

GOURGAUD—Marchand and St. Denis are with him.

NAPOLEON—All right. Leave him. I'll speak to him presently. (*He turns to the bust, examines it, then looks up at the others with an indulgent smile, and shrug of his shoulders.*) We Corsicans are all like that. (*He examines the bust again.*) To have a son like that and not to be able to see him, guide him! (*With a sudden burst of anger.*) Caged up in Vienna like an animal! (*He bangs the table with his fist.*) And to think I spared that city three times! (*Pause. He turns to* MME. MONTHOLON.) Is that a crack or a scar, there on the side?

MME. MONTHOLON—No, sir. It's only a fault in the marble—it's nothing.

They stand round the Emperor in a little group as the lights fade.

It is New Year's Day, 1817. Below the veranda of Longwood House Bertrand and Mme. Bertrand, Montholon and Mme. Montholon, Gourgaud and Dr. O'Meara are gathered, evidently waiting expectantly for what is about to happen. They are chatting amiably—all except Gourgaud, who stands a little apart, apparently a lonely man.

Presently voices are heard, followed by the appearance of the Emperor on the veranda. He is followed by Cipriani carrying an armful of packages. The party calls out a merry "Happy New Year, Your Majesty," to which Napoleon responds with a smile and a wave of the hand, as he comes down the steps to join them. Evidently his leg is paining him. He walks with a slight limp. Now he has turned to Cipriani and the packages. They are little gifts to make his friends happy. A box of beautifully carved chessmen for Bertrand. A handsome gold snuff-box for Dr. O'Meara. A pair of field glasses for Gourgaud. A jeweled cross for Montholon.

For the ladies Napoleon has produced a square box of beautifully colored silk shawls, which he proceeds to divide between them, punctuating their exclamations of delight with comments of his own as to the essentially barbaric tastes of the feminine sex—

"They are nothing but savages at heart," declares the Emperor, observing Mmes. Montholon and Bertrand preen themselves in the gay colors. "We ought to keep them locked up, like the Arabs do."

The present-giving over, Napoleon would have his friends gather around him for a little New Year's talk, and also a surprise. From the Cape a few oranges have arrived and he would share these also with the others—

"We used to pick them straight from the tree in Corsica," Napoleon is reminded; "but they never cultivated them properly; they were full of pips."

"That's better than getting them rotten, as we do in England," says O'Meara.

"A botanist once brought me a plan for growing them without pips," continues the Emperor, "but I told him it was contrary to nature. I told him you could no more grow pipless oranges than you could give birth to eunuchs." . . .

"Well, it's the New Year. We must make some good resolutions today," the Emperor is saying a moment later. "We must try to live together as a family and forget all our little troubles. We must be able to look back on these days and only remember the happy times. (*He pauses.*) Happy times? When was I ever happy, I wonder?"

"Weren't you happy at the time of your marriage, sir?" asks Mme. Montholon.

"Which one?"

"With the Empress Marie Louise."

"Yes, I was pleased."

"I should say at the birth of the King of Rome," ventures Mme. Bertrand.

"Yes. I was happy at the birth of the King of Rome," admits the Emperor. And then, after a pause, he adds: "No. The best time of all was after my welcome in Italy. The enthusiasm! The cries of 'Long live the Liberator!' It was then that I knew what I would become. I saw the world beneath me. I felt myself carried in the air as though I had wings! And I was only twenty-five. . . ."

Napoleon has given the signal for the party to disperse. They are to meet again at dinner. There will be champagne then. They have all made their formal adieux and retired—all save Gourgaud, whom the Emperor has called back.

There have been reports of a duel between Gourgaud and Montholon. The Emperor would know about that. It is difficult for him to believe such nonsense. He wants it stopped. Gourgaud is acting like a child. He knew what he was coming to when he followed his Emperor. Let him face it like a man—

"I could face a thousand times more hardship if I had Your Majesty's friendship," Gourgaud is muttering—

"But that's not enough for you," interrupts Napoleon. "You want more than that: you want to be my familiar, my equal! I accept that from nobody. You'd make my life a burden here, with your continual jealousy. You hated Las Cases because I found pleasure in his conversation, you hate O'Meara because as my Doctor I allow him into my rooms. You hate Bertrand! Now you hate Montholon!"

GOURGAUD—I hate his wife more than I hate him!

NAPOLEON—Why?

GOURGAUD—Because she has stolen the regard you had for me! Because . . .

NAPOLEON (*fiercely*)—Be quiet! That's enough! (*More quietly.*) What a child you are! Do you expect me to send you love-letters? (*He pats him on the shoulder.*) Come on, Gourgaud: your whole life's ahead of you.

GOURGAUD—For three weeks now Your Majesty has never sent for me—at dinner you ignore me: I sit alone in my miserable room, my hovel—waiting—

NAPOLEON—Because, if I send for you, you do nothing but argue and contradict—

GOURGAUD (*fiercely*)—Because I'm the only one of your—

NAPOLEON (*breaking in*)—I know—the only one who's frank and honest! Why is it that the others can always think of something pleasant to say?

GOURGAUD—Because they say the rest behind your back!

NAPOLEON—What do I care what people say behind my back? I defy any man to deceive me. He can never be as bad as I imagine him.

GOURGAUD—I sacrificed everything to follow you, and yet you suggest to Bertrand that if I were to commit suicide it would arouse sympathy for you in Europe!

NAPOLEON—Are you mad, sir?

GOURGAUD—It's the truth. My dead body is all that would be of any value!

NAPOLEON (*livid with anger*)—It's of no value—living or dead! You're afraid of this life, because you are a coward; and cowards are no use to me!

GOURGAUD (*leaping up*)—By God, then, I'll go!

NAPOLEON—Yes! Go! I owe you nothing for following me here—if you'd stayed in France you would have been hanged! (*There is a long pause.*) Sometimes I think it would be best if you all went—the whole lot of you! You're a wretched lot. So many funeral mutes! Go! I'll stay here alone—waited on by a solitary Negro. (*He turns to* GOURGAUD *and sees that he is crying.*

Suddenly his anger leaves him. He speaks quietly.) Write me a letter saying that you are ill. I will endorse it and send it to the Governor. (*Pause. Gently.*) I shall miss you, Gourgaud. But you are right; it's useless for you to stay. We shall meet again in another world. Good-by, Gourgaud! Leave me now.

GOURGAUD—Accept my farewell, sir, and my wishes for your happiness. When thinking of me sometimes, may Your Majesty say, "He at least had a good heart."

"Gourgaud takes the Emperor's hand: He kisses it and goes away. The Emperor is alone. He looks round at the remnants of paper that covered his presents—at the little dish of oranges. He limps slowly up the steps on to the veranda and into the shadows of the room beyond" as the curtain falls.

ACT III

It is nearing sunset on July 18, 1818. The windows looking out on the veranda at Longwood are closed and the curtains drawn. A British sentry is pacing up and down in front of the house. Occasionally he pauses and tries to peer in a window. Now he has completed his tour and left.

Immediately there are signs of life inside the house. Marchand comes through the French window and disappears in the garden. Montholon comes out on the steps and looks about. The servants are seen in the house behind him. Novarrez is at the door, St. Denis at the window. They have all been waiting for the sentry to leave.

They are barely outside the house when Captain Nicholls of the Governor's staff is seen approaching. Immediately Novarrez and St. Denis dash back into the house and lower the curtains. Montholon follows and locks the door. When Captain Nicholls, followed by a young subaltern officer, arrives the place is deserted.

After repeated knocks Novarrez half opens the door. He is not extremely communicative. General Montholon, reports Novarrez, is not in. All communications for His Majesty will have to be delivered through the Grand Marshal. The Grand Marshal is ill. Novarrez will see if he can find Monsieur Marchand.

"They're a slippery lot," observes the subaltern when Novarrez has gone. "When did you see him last?"

NICHOLLS—Five days ago. And then just a glance through the toilet window. He hasn't put his nose out of doors since they took

O'Meara away and Cipriani died. I'd rather deal with Marchand than with any of them. Here's somebody coming. (*The door is unlocked.* MARCHAND *appears.*) Monsieur Marchand, I am ordered by the Governor to hand these communications to the Emp—to General Bonaparte.

MARCHAND—Only Marshal Bertrand can do that. I have not the power to take on the Marshal's duties. If I were to hand these to the Emperor, he would only throw them into the fire. (NICHOLLS *looks at the* OFFICER *in despair.*)

OFFICER—The Governor will be here himself in a minute. If General Bonaparte won't see him, he would like an interview with General Montholon.

MARCHAND—We have looked for General Montholon, but he must be out. He is not indoors.

NICHOLLS (*ingratiatingly*)—Monsieur Marchand, can't you help me? You know my orders are to see General Bonaparte every day—even if it's only a glimpse. Five days have passed since anyone saw him. I warn you that if I fail to see the General the Governor will have to insist upon seeing him himself. Now if you could just let me . . .

MARCHAND—I'm sorry, Captain Nicholls. I can only tell you the Emperor is in his bath. I told you to look through his bathroom window yesterday.

NICHOLLS—I know, but I couldn't see anything for steam.

MARCHAND—He won't see anyone. I can't help you.

OFFICER—At least you will tell him that the Governor is coming, and wishes to see him?

MARCHAND—I'll tell him, but I know it is useless. (MARCHAND *goes in and locks the door.*)

NICHOLLS—What the devil's one to do? I'm damned if I . . .

OFFICER—Look out! Here comes the Governor. (SIR HUDSON LOWE *enters accompanied by an orderly.*)

LOWE (*quickly and peremptorily*)—Have you seen anyone?

NICHOLLS—No one, sir. Monsieur Marchand opened the door, but refused to take the message.

LOWE—Knock again. (NICHOLLS *does so.*) Knock louder. (*He comes halfway up the steps.*) I've had enough of this game of hide and seek. I'm going to stop it. (LOWE *goes up on the veranda.*)

NICHOLLS—The moment our backs are turned they'll all be out like lizards in the sun.

MARCHAND (*re-appearing at the door*)—Sir?

LOWE—Will you advise General Bonaparte that I am here and

wish to see him? I have important communications to make to him.

MARCHAND—I have advised the Emperor that you were here, sir. The Emperor has had a bad night and is at present in his bath. He orders me to tell you that the dead do not receive visitors.

LOWE—Nonsense! If he's so ill, why did he refuse to see Dr. Verling?

MARCHAND—The Emperor declines to see any but his own doctor.

LOWE—Dr. O'Meara's duties with General Bonaparte are at an end. He sails for England tomorrow. I wish to see the General to explain the nature of some orders I've received.

MARCHAND—The Emperor is in his bath.

LOWE—We will wait in the billiard-room until he has finished his bath.

MARCHAND—The Emperor will be in his bath for two or three hours.

LOWE—Kindly allow us in. (MARCHAND *comes out on to the steps and closes the door behind him.*)

MARCHAND—General Montholon is somewhere in the grounds. If I could find him for you he might be able to . . .

LOWE—We will wait indoors, if you please. (MARCHAND *makes a pretense at opening the door.*)

MARCHAND—I'm afraid I've locked myself out—it's an automatic lock and . . . If you would come around to the back, sir, and wait in Captain Nicholls' quarters . . .

LOWE (*angrily*)—Come on, Nicholls! I'm sick of this farce. You will return every half-hour until you can report that you have seen General Bonaparte. If he hasn't been seen by this time tomorrow, I shall take other measures.

The enemy has retired and there is again activity inside the house, threatened again by the approach of Dr. O'Meara. O'Meara, however, is like one of their own. Which is the reason he has been ordered away. He has been seeing the Bertrands and has stopped by to say his farewells to the others.

The Emperor, Marchand reports, has been suffering a lot of pain in his side. He has missed Dr. O'Meara, but he refuses to see his successor, Dr. Verling. A Corsican doctor is being sent out by Napoleon's mother, they understand, but it will be months before he can arrive. Montholon wishes O'Meara might stay for a bit—

"The Governor won't let me stay on this island another day," reports O'Meara.

"But you've done nothing wrong."

"That's not his opinion. If I don't report every word I hear in the Emperor's rooms, the Governor considers I'm taking the Emperor's side against him. He practically told me I was a spy. Well, I won't be sorry to leave this rock."

It is O'Meara's opinion that the Emperor is undoubtedly suffering from an affliction of the liver and is in need of constant care. This is disturbing news to Montholon, though there seems nothing can be done about it.

"He won't let any of us near him since Cipriani died," sighs Montholon, wearily.

"I hear two priests are coming out with this Corsican doctor."

"Yes. Cipriani had to be buried without a priest and that upset the Emperor. I believe Cipriani meant more to him than any of us."

The sentry re-appears, takes note of their presence and passes on. It is growing rapidly darker. Napoleon appears in the window. He is leaning on Mme. Montholon's shoulder. She finds him a chair and places a lamp on the table beside him. O'Meara is witness to the scene over Montholon's shoulder. He sees Mme. Montholon lay her hands upon the Emperor's brow. The Emperor takes her hands in his and kisses them.

"I should have liked to say good-by to Mme. Montholon again," says the Doctor.

"She'll be leaving soon," answers Montholon. "It's four years now since we've seen our two eldest children. We can't go on like this."

"Yes. She needs to get away," agrees the Doctor.

Mme. Montholon has moved away from the window. Napoleon sits alone with a book in his hand. O'Meara repeats his good-by and is gone, Montholon walking with him as far as the stables.

There is a faint sound of bugles from the camp. Napoleon lowers his book, listens, and resumes his reading. The sound of footsteps is followed by the appearance of Captain Nicholls. Napoleon puts out his hand and quietly draws the blind. Nicholls stands staring at the vague shadows on the blind as the lights fade.

The scene changes to Napoleon's bedroom. It is a late afternoon in September, 1819, and Napoleon, "older, more unkempt," is sitting at a table reading. "His uniform is unbuttoned, he looks physically and mentally oppressed."

The books he has tried have not pleased His Majesty. He has thrown most of them aside, both table and floor being littered with them. The patient Marchand is picking them up.

This is to be a day of audience for the new people who have arrived. Napoleon has been waiting a year for them, a doctor and two priests. He is anxious now to see them.

The first to be ushered in by General Bertrand is the Abbe Buonavita, "a trembling old man, fat, kindly and almost completely inarticulate." The Abbe is quite deaf and very uncertain of his directions in the dimly lighted room. Novarrez manages finally to guide him to Napoleon, where he would kneel at his Emperor's feet but is not quite able to make it. At first he is unable to hear anything the Emperor says, but manages to report that he had seen the Emperor's mother before he had left Corsica and that she had sent her son many messages as well as an embroidered altar-cloth, with the expressed hope that he would hold Mass every Sunday.

"And she herself—is she well?" asks the Emperor.

"God be praised, sir, God be praised!" answers the Abbe, a little ambiguously.

"He's as deaf as a door-post," observes His Majesty in an aside to Bertrand. He raises his voice— "Where did you take Holy Orders?"

"Rome, Your Majesty, Rome."

"How old are you?"

"Sixty-five."

"Is that all? What complaint do you suffer from?"

"A little gout, sir, but it is nothing . . . the journey was very tiring for an old man. A long journey . . . the horses particularly. . . ."

"Horses? What horses?"

"Coming through Germany."

"They drove through Germany, sir," Bertrand explains.

"I see. He'll be lucky if he sees France again," concludes Napoleon, as he dismisses the Abbe. They will have Mass in the morning in the dining room. . . .

The second priest, the Abbe Vignali, "is very young, painfully stupid and uncouth. Like the old man, he is nervous and over-awed. Napoleon takes him in at a glance and wastes little time in the interview."

The young man's name in Angel Paul and he has, in addition to taking Holy Orders, studied medicine in Rome. He promises, however, to confine his services to his ecclesiastical duties and not to try his medical skill on anyone on the island.

"Why did you come here?" Napoleon would like to know of Vignali.

"I . . . er . . ."

"You probably don't know. Well, you won't find life easy here. We must all try and make the best of each other. You may go now. We will meet at Mass tomorrow."

Vignali also finds his way to the door. The Doctor is next. He is, as Bertrand promises, at least different. Antommarchi is the name. "He also appears rough and uncouth, but carries himself with an air of insolent assurance."

Past the preliminary information of his having studied medicine at Pisa and that he is thirty years old, Napoleon would also know of the Doctor's reasons for accepting this particular call to duty. He is forced on two occasions to reprimand Antommarchi, once for fidgeting, once for talking out of turn, but the Doctor is in no marked degree dismayed.

"You know that I am not sympathetic towards doctors," Napoleon is saying. "What good is a doctor to a starving man, when all he needs is a loaf of bread? Exercise was all I needed. The English made that impossible for me. It has resulted in a chronic affection of the liver—and the heart. . . ."

ANTOMMARCHI—There are other ways of getting the exercise Your Majesty needs.

NAPOLEON—Would you have me turn somersaults in my bedroom?

ANTOMMARCHI (*laughing boldly*)—No, sir. But there are games; exercises. My father added years to his life by digging up his lands every morning.

NAPOLEON—Yes, that's an idea. We might start digging our graves. (ANTOMMARCHI *laughs.*) What was the matter with your father? Is he still alive?

ANTOMMARCHI—No, sir; he died of old age.

NAPOLEON—My father died of a glandular tumor when he was a young man. (*He rises from his chair with the assistance of a small billiard-cue.*)

ANTOMMARCHI—I am glad to see Your Majesty is able to walk. I was led to understand that . . .

NAPOLEON—I will see you in your capacity as doctor this evening, after dinner. You will bring O'Meara's reports with you—although they're ancient history now. It is a year since he left.

ANTOMMARCHI—Yes, sir.

NAPOLEON—Yes. You will need philosophy and resignation to live here, Doctor. You're too young to have either.

ANTOMMARCHI (*smiling*)—I think Your Majesty will find . . .

NAPOLEON—I recommend Buonavita to your care. Look after him; he is a very sick man. Madame Bertrand sees the English doctor, but she may want your opinion as well. She specializes in miscarriages. (ANTOMMARCHI *laughs.*) She has just had one. (BERTRAND *stirs uncomfortably.*) Count Montholon also needs looking after. He's ill, too. You'll have plenty to occupy your time. (*He makes a gesture of dismissal.*) All right—you may go now.

ANTOMMARCHI (*kissing* NAPOLEON'S *hand*)—Your Majesty!

There is a note of distress in the Emperor's voice when the last of the newcomers has disappeared.

"A charming trio, Montholon," the Emperor observes. "A paralytic, a cretin and a lout! And these are the men who have come to take the place of Las Cases, Cipriani, O'Meara, even poor Gourgaud! We didn't realize how fortunate we were! . . . Well, misfortune has its good sides. It teaches us the truth. Resignation—that is the dominion of reason, the real triumph of the soul."

MONTHOLON—It is indeed, sir!

NAPOLEON—Are you feeling any better, Montholon?

MONTHOLON (*miserably*)—No, sir. (*He puts his hand on his chest.*) God knows I don't want to leave Your Majesty, but it's very hard for me to stay on, sir.

NAPOLEON (*quickly*)—I know, I know. But wait, wait, Montholon. Let me get used to these new arrivals. This Corsican doctor may be better than he appears.

MONTHOLON—Let's hope so, sir.

NAPOLEON—He recommends exercise. He suggests we dig the earth!

MONTHOLON—He may be right. But I don't think it would suit me, sir!

NAPOLEON (*rises, goes and looks out of the window; pauses*)—I wonder, could one make some sort of garden here?

MONTHOLON—I doubt it, sir. Look at the trouble the Bertrands had with those miserable little shrubs.

NAPOLEON—Yes, but they *have* grown a few shrubs! We might do the same . . . more . . . why not? We could have a lawn down there in front of the windows . . . an Avenue up to the porch. D'you see what I mean? Come here . . . look . . . there . . . d'you see? (MONTHOLON *joins* NAPOLEON *at the window. Warming to his subject.*) . . . and then perhaps an orchard down there . . .

MONTHOLON (*incredulously*)—An orchard?

NAPOLEON—Why not? Yes, an orchard down there . . . a fountain in that corner . . . a vegetable garden round there . . . and we might even grow oranges, peaches, grapes . . .

Their voices fade with the lights. The curtain is down.

We are in the garden that runs along one side of Longwood House. It is just after dawn has broken on a fine sunlit day in January, 1820. A strip of flower bed parallels the house. At back there is a bit of lawn, and a few recently planted trees can be seen.

Presently Napoleon appears, coming from his sitting room. He wears a dressing gown, red slippers and a broad-brimmed straw hat. "Although he walks with difficulty he whistles cheerfully as he goes to the bell (fastened to the house) and rings it vigorously."

There is still no sign of life in the house. Napoleon is soon tapping the windows with a short billiard cue which he carries to assist him in walking. He would have everybody up and at work. They are a set of lazybones, he shouts.

Marchand is the first one out, and the first to get the brunt of the Emperor's keen disappointment and disgust. The seeds that they had planted yesterday have all been scratched up by Novarrez' chickens. The Emperor wants his gun brought, and at once. He had warned Novarrez of what would happen to his chickens, if—

Now the others begin to appear. Montholon with ruffled hair and heavy eyes coming from the house; Bertrand appearing through the garden is none too alert. St. Denis and Novarrez, followed by two or three Chinese gardeners carrying an assortment of garden tools, gather at the back. They are none of them in a mood for work. Bertrand reports that Mrs. Bertrand is in bed with a sore back due to her exertions with a heavy rake the day before. Montholon reports a temperature and would be excused. But the Emperor is obdurate. All any of them needs is a good perspiration. Also he has thought out an entirely new plan for the planting. The fruit trees they had put out yesterday will be moved today to where they had thought to have a lawn. The lawn will have to be put farther down the slope—

"Montholon and Marchand can roll the turf up and move it," directs Napoleon. "No! Let the Chinese dig the holes. Ali and Novarrez move the turf—and Montholon and Marchand move the trees. . . . Now, to work! We'll break at 9 o'clock for a cup of coffee, for five minutes."

They all go dutifully but reluctantly to work. Napoleon's own task is to plant seeds in a furrow drawn by Bertrand. He thinks perhaps the ground should be worked over again by Bertrand, digging is such good exercise. Now he has caught sight of three of Novarrez' chickens headed that way. In an instant he has his gun and, as soon as he can get Montholon out of range, he lets fly.

"That'll teach them to scratch up our seeds," mutters the Emperor, with satisfaction. "Not a bad shot, eh, Bertrand? We might have some good sport up here. Chickens are no good; see if we can get some wild goats in Jamestown. We could put them in the meadow and pop at 'em from the summer house. Now then—the seeds—draw the furrow . . . I'll lay the seed."

His Majesty knows exactly how it should be done, but he has planted but few seeds when a pain in the side catches him and he is forced to quit. He would keep at it until the muscles get hard, but soon he has sought a chair and sunk into it with a sigh of relief. He continues his direction of the others from that point of vantage. Suddenly he stops talking and listens.

"Was that the sound of a bell?" he inquires of Bertrand.

"A bell? No, sir, I didn't hear it."

"A sound came into my head just then like the ringing of a bell. I shall be hearing voices next—like Joan of Arc! I miss the sound of bells here. My first memories of childhood were the bells that rang in the villages round home. Sometimes my courtiers thought I was planning new campaigns or new laws; I was just allowing the sound of a bell to take me back to Corsica . . . all those early days and peaceful dreams. . . . I'd like to write a history of Corsica . . . (*He yawns.*) Come on, come on, don't stand about talking—get to work!"

The Emperor has drawn his hat over his eyes. Gradually, as the others look on warily, he falls into a slumber. Quietly they deposit their tools in a tidy pile and prepare to quit work.

"I'll get back to bed," whispers Montholon. "Tap on my window if he wakes up."

One by one they quietly steal away. Only Marchand is left. He sits on the steps leading to Napoleon's bedroom, places a handkerchief under his hat, drawing it over his eyes as he begins his vigil in the sun. There is a moment of complete silence before the lights fade and the curtain falls.

It is a Sunday morning in May, 1821. Napoleon is lying on the bed in his room. He is wearing a white shirt, breeches and felt slippers. His eyes are closed. St. Denis sits motionless beside him. Through a half-opened door Vignali may be heard intoning Latin prayers. Marchand tiptoes quietly in to relieve St. Denis.

The Emperor stirs slightly, without opening his eyes. He senses what is going on. It is, they tell him, 6 o'clock. He is tired of Vignali's prayers. Let him be stopped. Yes, he will see the priest for a moment. Let them help him into his chair. . . .

Vignali is deeply moved, prayerfully hopeful. A comet had been seen in the sky, and that is a happy omen. Perhaps, if it is visible another night, agrees the Emperor, he will see it.

"A comet was seen in the sky when Caesar died," Napoleon remarks to Marchand, when the tearful Vignali has left.

"The people at the observatory say this wasn't a comet, it was a meteor," declares Marchand reassuringly.

"Ah, well, we shall have to die without a comet, that's all," muses Napoleon.

The pain in his side has gripped him again, but he will have no more of Antommarchi's poisonous medicine, even disguised in lemonade. The attack passes.

Now Count Montholon has been summoned. There are paragraphs that the Emperor would like to add to his will. He has, he makes sure, put Vignali down for 100,000 francs. Now he would like to add 10,000 francs for the subaltern officer Cantillon who had tried to assassinate Lord Wellington—

"Cantillon had as much right to assassinate that oligarch as the latter had to send me to perish upon this rock of St. Helena. Is that not right, Montholon?"

"Yes, sir."

NAPOLEON—And now, after paragraph 47, insert . . . (*He pauses.*) "I demand that a post-mortem should be made after my death. I believe I am dying of the same illness as my father. I wish the truth to be known, so that my son should be spared my sufferings." (*There is a pause.* MONTHOLON *writes hard.*) What paragraph follows?

MONTHOLON (*in an unsteady voice*)—"It is my wish that my ashes repose on the banks of the Seine, in the midst of the French people I have loved so well."

NAPOLEON—Yes. (*To* MARCHAND.) Call St. Denis; let him come in and copy this now—in here. (*To* MONTHOLON.) I think the billiard room is the best place for the post-mortem—they can make use of the table—there's plenty of room, and it's light in there.

MONTHOLON (*overcome*)—Sir! . . .

NAPOLEON—It would be a pity not to die after tidying up everything so nicely!

MONTHOLON—Your Majesty, you talk as though your career lay three hundred years behind you. How can we tell what will happen? You are better today than you were yesterday. Yesterday you were better than the day be—fore. . . .

NAPOLEON—No man can escape his Fate, Montholon. It's written in the stars . . . that I am to die here. . . . (*Pause.*) Perhaps it's just as well. In America I should have been assassinated! It's a free country—or, worse still, I might have been forgotten! (*He pauses.*) No. This martyrdom may save my dynasty. Now, regarding my son. . . . My son should not think of avenging my death: he should profit by it. The aim of all his efforts should be to reign by peace. To do my work all over again would be to suppose that I had done nothing. I was obliged to daunt Europe by arms; the way to convince her today is by reason. (*Pause.*) Let my son study history well, and ponder on it; for there alone he will learn the true philosophy. (MARCHAND *returns with* ST. DENIS, *who has a book.*) St. Denis—there are three paragraphs for you to copy here.

ST. DENIS—Yes, sir.

MONTHOLON—Can you read it?

ST. DENIS—I think so.

NAPOLEON—All right, Montholon. (MONTHOLON *exits.*) Have those books arrived, Ali?

ST. DENIS—Yes, sir. I think you'll be pleased, Your Majesty—The Hannibal was amongst them. I've got it here.

NAPOLEON—Ah! We've been crying for that book for the last six months—give it to me! Sit down, Marchand!

MARCHAND (*sitting on the chair beside the bed*)—Thank you, sir!

NAPOLEON—The wars of Hannibal? (*He weakly turns over the pages of the book.*) War is a simple art, you know, Marchand, like everything beautiful! (*He smiles.*) I used to argue with myself for hours, concerning the plan of a battle—magnifying every incident, every danger. When I appeared the most calm I was vibrating with the greatest excitement! Like a girl about to have a baby! (*He laughs.*) Taking it all in all, what a ballad my life has been! (*He hands the book to* MARCHAND.) Read it to me— (MARCHAND *clears his throat and turns over the leaves of the book. A bugle is heard faintly in the distance.*)

MARCHAND (*reading*)—"The Wars of Hannibal occupy a page in history that has no counterpart in antiquity. As a boy of nine, Hannibal was taken by his father to Spain . . ."

THE CURTAIN FALLS

YES, MY DARLING DAUGHTER

A Comedy in Three Acts

By Mark Reed

THE arrival of a success in a Broadway theatre after the Christmas holidays is invariably a matter of expressed surprise. It is a fixed impression that all observing producers of plays are most eager to get their best scripts into action early in the season, while theatre interest is keen and the playgoer appetite is whetted. The matter of eagerness is true enough, but there are many reasons why a play success might be conceivably delayed.

It happens that in the case of "Yes, My Darling Daughter" the delayed February opening was quite reasonable. The producer who first held it could not raise the money necessary for its staging. Once it was turned over to a producer who had the money it was placed quickly in rehearsal, with something very like an inspired selection of players (Lucille Watson, Peggy Conklin and Violet Heming) and rode gaily toward a rousing first-night reception.

"Yes, My Darling Daughter" is another modern comedy in the planning and writing of which sophistication's artful aid has been a factor. Mr. Reed confesses having had the idea of bringing a pioneer liberal mother face to face with the concrete result of her early propagandizing as long ago as the early post-war years.

"Disregarding the little experiment in the Garden of Eden," he has written, "sex emancipation may be said to have started, at least in America, with the group of liberals who began snipping the laces of prudery in the so-called Greenwich Village movement of 1908." Thinking along which line in play terms he evolved a plot: "My mother could be a pioneer suffragist and feminist of the old Village days, while a younger woman could bring in a touch of the Scott Fitzgerald tradition. . . . A sympathetic and understanding feminist mother, an erstwhile flaming and still glowing aunt, and a straight-thinking, college-bred daughter of 1937." These three representing definite points of view: "Rebellion, license and a growing sanity toward sex."

And so we come to a meeting with this interesting trio at the Murray summer home near New Canaan, Connecticut. The Murray place bears no fancy name. It is old and rambling because of additions built to join the original plain rectangular stone manor house. The living room into which we are ushered at the rise of the curtain is "dignified and hospitable." . . . "The furnishings and ornaments are the accretion of taste and travel." . . . "Above all else, you feel the room has been lived in; the furniture has been hauled about for charades, the fireplace has known a thousand fires, while men and women have gathered around, sipped good liquor, and talked out their thoughts vigorously, if not always intelligently. In brief, a room which has associated long enough with human beings to acquire a mellow and gracious humanity of its own."

We discover Ellen Murray, "an alert, slender, well-built girl of twenty-two," sprawled over a couch consulting references in a scholarly looking book. "She wears blue denim overalls, red sandals, tortoise-shell glasses. Her bobbed hair is at loose ends."

Ellen is still at the business of research when Lewis Murray joins her. Lewis "is genial, well-tanned, tall and about forty-eight." A genial and hearty person but one who, being a banker, can also become on occasion an amiable bore.

Lewis is looking for Ellen's mother and is inclined to be both fretful and peeved because his daughter will not tell him where she is.

"What you reading?" he suddenly demands.

"I'm brushing up on my Constitution," answers Ellen. "You know, Dad, those fifteen judges have me worried. Do you think he can get away with it?"

"I suppose so. He generally does," admits Lewis. To which he adds, with considerable feeling: "I wish he'd spend more time on his stamp collection."

People are expected for the week-end. That's why Ann Murray is hiding, trying to get a love story finished. A Mr. Jaywood is even now on his way from the station. Mr. Jaywood is an important international literary agent. Aunt Connie also is coming. Aunt Connie, as a matter of fact, is there, hoo-hooing from the hallway at practically this very moment. Aunt Connie is Constance Nevins, "stylish, chic, still young-looking at thirty-five. Basically a gay, affectionate, fun-loving sort of woman, she has not let a rather embittering marital career get her down."

Connie is just back from Reno and happily free. She had a nice judge, but the Reno food was terrible. No, she doesn't know just who she will marry next. And she is glad Ann has gone back to writing about love.

"I never can understand her articles about Women in Business, and Women in Marriage, and Women out of Marriage . . . except I've a vague idea they're all aimed at me," admits Connie. "What made her go back to fiction after all these years?"

"That!" explains Ellen, pointing to her father. "He felt Mother was getting too independent, so he's disciplining her."

"Ellen! Play fair!"

"Why not tell the truth? You are."

"Connie, it's this way. Last week my own sweet, dutiful, loving Annie ordered our duck pond made into a swimming pool. After I expressly told her we couldn't afford it. So this week she's writing a love story to pay the bill."

"Can't you afford a swimming pool?"

"This is a matter of principle. I don't have to be firm with my Annie very often; but when I am firm, by God! I'm granite."

"One minute you men go broke to give up a pearl necklace, the next you tell us our extravagance has ruined you . . . a woman doesn't know where she gets off."

"My Annie knows where she gets off . . . don't forget that!"

"I'll admit you two seem to get along."

"We're celebrating our twenty-third anniversary next week. Drop around."

"Think of it! Remember Father said you and a woman like Ann wouldn't last it out a month. . . ."

"My father was an old-fashioned man."

"Lord, Father, what's so modern about you?"

"The brilliant way I handle the modern woman."

There is some discussion as to where Aunt Connie is to be put, seeing that the approaching Mr. Jaywood and other expected guests have been assigned most of the available space. Yet Lewis insists that any sister of his, just back from Reno, rates the best room in the house, and he is prepared to tell his wife so, too. Whereupon Martha, the housekeeper, having been told where Mrs. Murray is hiding ("between the vegetable garden and the pump house under a beach umbrella") is sent to fetch her mistress.

The talk turns to Ellen and her school work. Connie is surprised, and a little distressed, to discover that Ellen has been duly graduated and handed a diploma without having had a single man at commencement to dance attendance upon her. To Connie that just isn't normal, but Ellen is content—

"Connie, you worry about *your* love life and I'll worry about *mine,*" Ellen snaps. But she apologizes a second later.

"I daresay I *am* peculiar," she admits. "Personally I think a woman's a fool to try and build her happiness around a man."

"Really, Ellen, do tell me," begs Connie, a little too sweetly. "I'm in a position this minute where I yearn to know. What else can the average woman build her happiness around?"

"Plenty of things!"

Before these can be enumerated, however, Ann Murray has come from the garden. "The name 'Ann Whitman Murray' has for years carried considerable prestige in the newspaper and feminist world; but in appearance Ann looks merely a very comfortable, human, motherly sort of person . . . with a growing tendency to be stout. At the moment she wears a cotton blouse and garden skirt, neither any too clean, a large sun hat and old straw sandals. Her face is streaked with dirt, and strands of loose hair tend to get in her eyes. Yet despite this external untidiness, she strikes one instantly as a personality and a profoundly charming woman."

Ann's greeting of Connie is sincere and affectionate. She quite ignores the others, particularly her husband. Soon she has sent him on his way to Larchmont in his boat with the pious wish that he will get a good ducking. Ellen has gone to see her father off, which leaves Connie and Ann a chance to have a good talk.

ANN—Light yourself a cigarette, Connie, and tell me everything.

CONNIE (*lighting cigarette*)—Ann, it's been a tremendous experience. Tremendous! I've come back full of ideas. You know during my first divorce how I got all weepy and hurt; then the next time when Ted went off with that mouse-colored blonde, of course I got bitter and drank a lot, and was all kinds of a damn fool. Well, this time I took myself in hand and did some thinking.

ANN—Grand!

CONNIE—I studied those women out there. Ann, ninety percent of them, one look and you'd see why they couldn't hold a man six months unless they had money. There was even more drinking this time than last.

ANN—Really?

CONNIE—I said to myself: Connie Nevins, you don't belong in this gang.

ANN—You don't, you know, Connie.

CONNIE—That's why it's been such an experience. I've found myself. At last I know what I want and why I haven't been happy. From now on I'm going to simplify my life.

ANN—I see.

CONNIE—I'm going to live in the country and have a garden and enjoy all the simple pleasures the way you do. Look, Ann, you and Lewis haven't had a row?

ANN—Not a serious one.

CONNIE—He's a beast to make you write a love story.

ANN—It was my own mistake.

CONNIE—He has money enough for fifty swimming pools. I wouldn't stand for it.

ANN—Well, he said he couldn't afford it . . . we've had extra expenses with both Roger and Ellen . . . then I saw Jim Bamberra weeping around without any work and nine children, and got soft-hearted.

CONNIE—All the same, I'd be furious with Lewis.

ANN—I'd been furious with him if he had let himself be coaxed into paying the bill . . . when I was wrong. I wouldn't want a husband I could twist around my little finger.

CONNIE—If he's around your little finger, you know where he is. (*She consults her wrist watch.*) Ann, is it all right if I fly . . . shortly?

ANN—Of course.

CONNIE—I'm having tea at the club . . . with Glen.

ANN (*trying to be enthusiastic*)—Are you? Glen Williams?

CONNIE—You've probably guessed I would anyway . . . but I want you to be the first to know. Glen and I are going to be married next week.

ANN—Next week? I thought you were going to simplify your life?

CONNIE—I am.

ANN—But you said you'd found yourself?

CONNIE—I have.

ANN—Suppose you lose yourself again?

CONNIE—It isn't as though I didn't know Glen awfully well. . . . I mean *awfully well.*

ANN—I know you mean *awfully well.* So why the rush? Wait a bit before you marry again. Take a trip. Enjoy a vacation from the masculine sex.

CONNIE—I've just had a six months' vacation. If I dangle Glen any longer, I might lose him.

If she could be married there, in Ann's happy home, Connie thinks it might bring her luck, and Ann agrees it is certainly worth a try. So that's arranged. . . .

Connie's next worry is Ellen. She can't understand the girl's glasses for one thing, nor her general untidy appearance for another. In addition to which Ellen's lack of interest in men is, to Connie, quite incredible—

"If she were my daughter I'd rush her tomorrow to some good beauty consultant, then to a really intelligent dress-maker."

"I think she has several Schiaparelli's."

"You'd never guess it to look at her. After all, our family does have some position. Why shouldn't Ellen have the benefit of it? Seriously, Ann, why don't you have her come out?"

There is, Ann agrees, probably something in what Connie says. She will make a note of it, and does, when Ellen comes back to warn her that she will simply have to get herself into some other clothes—Mr. Jaywood has arrived—

It is agreed hurriedly that for the present Connie is to take Ellen's room—Ellen having planned to be away over Sunday—and the two have gone to change. Not, however, until Ellen has begged her mother to let her have fifteen minutes alone with Mr. Jaywood. Ellen has always wanted to meet an International Literary Agent and this is her chance.

When Titus Jaywood appears he seems "a quietly alert Englishman in his early forties. He wears a conservative business suit." He graciously accepts Ellen's suggestion that they introduce themselves. He is happy to be there. No, he is not really an old friend of Ellen's mother's—having met her only five weeks before at a literary tea. Yes, he will have a little whiskey and soda. Certainly he would like to have Ellen come straight to the point, if there is a point—

"Mr. Jaywood, I've just graduated from college," begins Ellen, with enthusiasm. "The customary thing would be for me to play up to you all this week-end, put myself across as hard as I could . . . then just before you leave, ask you to help me get a job."

JAY—I wish, Miss Murray, you'd stick to your American customs. I'd much prefer to be "played up to" till Monday.

ELLEN—But I'm not going to be home this week-end.

JAY—Oh, that's too bad.

ELLEN—I've got to visit a classmate in Hartford. Her father runs a paper there. I'd a lot rather stay here and talk with you. I've a million questions to ask you about Maugham, and Priestley and all the other authors you handle. Unfortunately I made this date before I knew Mother had asked you out.

JAY—Naturally you can't look for work in two places the same week-end.

ELLEN—No, not very well. Will you excuse me if I talk about myself?

› by Lucas-Pritchard Studio, New York.

"YES, MY DARLING DAUGHTER"

›ug: You can't expect a woman to wait around forever.
ın: Yes, the girls today are extremely impatient.
len: Some of them were impatient in your day, too, Mother.
ın: Imprudent was the word then, dear.

(*Nicholas Joy, Peggy Conklin, Lucile Watson, Boyd Crawford*)

JAY—I think it would be charming.

ELLEN—Of course, I was editor of the "Lit" and all that sort of junk, and of course, I've learned all I can from Mother. You see, I want to be one of the best all-round newspaper women that ever drew breath, like Anne O'Hare McCormick or Dorothy Thompson.

JAY—Splendid.

ELLEN—You needn't if you don't want to, but I thought perhaps you'd give me letters to two or three editors. I wouldn't mind going on a magazine . . . anything to get a start. You don't have to say anything very good about me . . . just enough so I can get one foot inside an editor's door.

JAY—That will make it easier.

ELLEN—I wish you'd stop looking so amused. After all, I have already sold stuff.

JAY (*surprised*)—You have? What?

ELLEN—Oh, a few poems . . . at the large sum of two dollars each. I wish there was money in poetry.

JAY—A lot of poets wish that.

ELLEN—Then, of course, I've sold quite a few articles on education and politics.

JAY—Politics? How's your thousand-page novel?

ELLEN—Fine. How's yours? (JAY *smiles.*) Really, it's no credit to me. Mother and I get into awful arguments. She sells what she says to liberal papers, and I sell what I say to conservatives.

JAY—Haven't you your viewpoints reversed?

ELLEN—When it comes to being liberal, Mother's got me licked six ways. She's just as radical as when she wrote for the *Masses* in Greenwich Village and headed Suffrage Parades. You know, she used to be a famous feminist when she was young. Incidentally, Mr. Jaywood, Mother's been in jail nineteen times.

JAY—That's a very nice record.

ELLEN—I suppose the reason I'm conservative is on account of Father. He's half Dutch. Have you ever met him?

JAY—No, I never have.

ELLEN—I think you'll like him. Can you imagine? Mother an Iowa hog and corn farmer and Father Dutch Social Register! What do you suppose that makes me?

JAY—Let's hope it makes you a good all-round newspaper woman.

There is one question that Mr. Jaywood would like to ask before he starts his series of introductory letters. Is Ellen engaged? Ellen should hope not. Neither is there any danger that she will be compelled to leave a job within a year because she is going to have a child, which has been a common experience with Mr. Jaywood's other protégés. Ellen is quite positive—

"There's a Mr. Douglas Hall outside that says . . ." announces Martha at this juncture.

"What's *that* man doing here?" demands Ellen, angrily.

"He's waiting on the steps," frankly admits Martha.

"Tell him I can't see him. I have to leave the house immediately," announces Ellen. She has lost her poise, and her one desire is to flee. "I simply must go," she explains to Mr. Jaywood. "You've been awfully helpful. I wish I could stay and get really well acquainted."

Douglas Hall has not waited to be ushered into the room. He is there now, calling a defiant "Hi, Ellen!" as he enters. "Doug" is an attractive, forceful young man of around twenty-five. His clothes are of good material and cut, but well worn.

"Mr. Jaywood, much as I regret the necessity, may I introduce Mr. Hall?" queries Ellen.

The men have shaken hands and Mr. Jaywood has discreetly withdrawn. Then the real battle is on. It appears that Douglas had discovered that he would not be able to leave Boston the week before, and Ellen had telegraphed him twenty-five dollars. The suggestion that he was a paid escort had insulted Doug and he had promptly wired the money back. The letter he had had from Ellen in return was even more insulting than the telegram. If Ellen had any understanding of people's psychology she would have realized that Doug could not come to her Commencement because he wasn't in the mood.

"I'd have been a gloom in all that Commencement gaiety," Doug protests, spiritedly. "It wasn't the actual carfare. Lord, I'd have pawned my watch and hitch-hiked."

"Exactly! You didn't want to come."

"Sure I wanted to come."

"Then why didn't you?"

"I told you."

"You were too proud."

"Damn right I was too proud. Think I'd humiliate you?"

"I'd rather be humiliated than . . . than disappointed."

Now the truth comes out. Doug has come to say good-by. He has chucked architecture. "The hell with it! What do I want with that profession? After six years' study and work, it won't pay me enough even to go and see the girl I love graduate!"

Doug had not meant to say so much—but there it is. Ellen had not expected to hear so much—but now she's happy. So Doug takes her in his arms and they kiss, shyly, and then more eagerly.

Everything should be all right now, but it isn't. Doug is sailing Monday night! Ellen is taking a train in less than an hour for Hartford! All the time they'll have to see each other, or talk over things, will be lost to them. Doug might go with Ellen—but there would be a crowd. They might stay home but there would be a crowd there, too. Then Ellen has an idea—

"Suppose I start for Hartford, then you join me, and I won't go."

"Won't they expect you?"

ELLEN—I'll wire them I can't come. That would give us three whole days together.

DOUG (*uneasily*)—Together? Er, where?

ELLEN—I don't know. Somewhere! Some little cottage maybe . . . with a lake and a canoe. We could cook our own meals, and smoke and talk, and plan our whole life together.

DOUG—I don't know about that. (*He crosses to left, worried and uncomfortable.*)

ELLEN—What's the matter? Have I shocked you?

DOUG—No, it's not that.

ELLEN—In marriage everything depends on getting off to a right start.

DOUG—This might not be such a swell start.

ELLEN—I mean we've been separated so much and had so many misunderstandings. Before you go, I think it's terribly important we settle every point we could possibly fight about after you're gone.

DOUG—Something to that.

ELLEN—I know a little lake outside Lanesville. We used to drive over from college. There are several darling cottages on it. I know we could hire one. The season doesn't start till the Fourth. There wouldn't be three people around the entire lake.

DOUG—Three people is plenty sometimes. I don't want you to lose your reputation.

ELLEN—I won't . . . if we plan things carefully.

DOUG—I still don't quite like the idea.

ELLEN—Maybe you think I've done something like this before.

DOUG—Of course not.

ELLEN (*solemnly*)—Doug, this is an emergency measure.

Doug—God, I wish we could marry.

Ellen—Well, if we can't, we can't! And I do think we're entitled to something . . . something beautiful and set apart. Something we can cling to after you're gone! Don't you?

Doug—Yes, but . . .

Ellen—Doug, be frank. What do you really feel? Does . . . does my willingness to go like this make me seem cheap?

Doug—What do you think I am? (*He rises and takes her by the shoulders affectionately.*) Makes you seem precious. What I don't like is . . . it's a bit underhanded.

Ellen—Whose earthly business is it, except yours and mine?

Doug—You've got a mother, you know.

Ellen—I don't think she'd mind particularly. . . .

Doug (*surprised*)—Why not?

Ellen—I mean, under the circumstances. Mother's tremendously advanced. Not, of course, that I'd want her to know. . . .

Doug—I wish we had more time to think it over.

Ellen—So do I, but we haven't. Well, what shall we do?

Doug—I think you're right, Ellen. We'll go.

Ellen—Oh, I'm glad.

Doug—So am I.

Doug has decided to drive over to a place called Silver Mine, six miles away, and sell a Yale man his drafting instruments. He'll be back in time for Ellen's train to Hartford. He will, cautions Ellen, if he drives carefully. They haven't time to get arrested!

Ellen is gazing wistfully after the departed Doug when her mother comes down the stairs. Ann has changed into afternoon dress and done her hair. "The result is a well-groomed, much more sophisticated-looking woman."

Ann is pleased that Ellen has had a pleasant visit with Mr. Jaywood, but a little disturbed that she had taken advantage of the visit to ask for letters of introduction. She says as much to her friend after she has welcomed him to her home.

"I'm out of patience with this current mania for frankness," says Ann. "It's just a cold-blooded excuse to say what you please, do what you please, and get what you please, without regard for the common decencies."

"Mother, there's an article in that," Ellen cuts in, eagerly. "Here I am, just out of college. It's terribly hard to get a job. A nice important person like Mr. Jaywood comes along . . . should I, or should I not, tell him frankly how good I am and ask his help? And if I don't tell him how good I am, and ask his help, would I, or would I not, be a spineless idiot who ought to end her days in the gutter?"

"Suppose you change your clothes and start for Hartford."

"Okay. By the way, Mother, I've altered my plans slightly." Ellen's manner is most innocent and casual. "Doug Hall showed up just now out of the blue. . . . He said he'd come back and take me to the train." So Ellen will not be using the family car.

A new warmth has come into the meeting of Ann and Titus Jaywood when they are left alone. It is apparently quite pleasant to Ann, but a little disturbing to Jay. He has a feeling the week-end is going to be something of an ordeal—

"It's not easy to visit an old sweetheart," muses Jaywood. "A chap looks about, and realizes this happy home, this gracious wife and lovely daughter might . . . with better luck . . . have been his. It makes for melancholy in a single man at times."

"I imagine it might."

JAY (*brightly*)—On the other hand, it may work the other way. A man realizes what he has escaped. Why only last Monday morning, I left a home over in Jersey . . . laughing like a hyena.

ANN—Don't you start any hyena laughs around here!

JAY—No danger!

ANN—You said you never married, didn't you?

JAY—Yes. I've had a few flutters, but you were the big palpitation.

ANN—I must have been. I meet you accidentally at a tea, and find you've been in America three years . . . without looking me up.

JAY—I made inquiries the day I landed. Unfortunately, not in the right social sphere. I asked around Washington Square. One person told me positively you were dead.

ANN—What did I die of?

JAY—It was no joke, I can tell you. I walked slowly under the Arch and started up Fifth Avenue. The next I knew I was on Riverside Drive. There, in the twilight, I buried my youth . . . and my love . . . right next to Grant's Tomb! Later on, of course, I heard you'd married a wealthy banker. It seemed better to let go at that.

ANN (*with faint sarcasm*)—Oh, much better.

JAY (*after a pause*)—Er, you never got to England?

ANN—Several times.

JAY—Without looking me up?

ANN—I tried to. I decided probably you didn't get through the war.

JAY—Yes, I got through.

ANN—When we were in London, several years ago, Lewis dragged me to the Tomb of the Unknown Soldier. Know what I thought as I stood there?

JAY—I can't imagine.

ANN—I thought: "My heavens! For all I know, this may be Jay!" I burst into tears. Lewis was thoroughly irritated. He made me walk ten paces behind . . . so I wouldn't disgrace him.

JAY (*drily*)—We both seem to have shed some unnecessary tears.

They have started for a stroll over the farm. Someway it reminds them of the corduroy pants Jay used to wear—wore, in fact, as he recalls them, from 1908 to 1913 inclusive. "They used to moan when I walked," says Jay. "And whistle when you ran," adds Ann.

Now they have decided to wait and say good-by to Ellen before they stroll the farm. The talk turns to Ann's husband. Jay is rather eager to meet the man who domesticated Ann Whitman. Ann would deny the impeachment, but she is quite sure Jay will like Lewis Murray. . . .

Connie Nevins is down and ready to start for town. She hears of Ellen's changed plans, and of the boy from Boston who is to drive her to the train. It gives Connie an idea she would like to talk over with Ann. Jay promptly offers to withdraw, but Ann will not have that—

"Nonsense, Mr. Jaywood," she promptly protests. "Connie's always being mysterious."

"Ann, please!"

ANN—It can't be as important as all that!

CONNIE—There's no time to argue. Ann, you've simply got to do something. I'm sure Ellen isn't going to Hartford at all. She's going off somewhere with this boy . . . right now!

ANN—Connie Nevins, do you know what you're saying?

JAY (*starting to go*)—If you'll excuse me . . .

ANN—No, you've heard part. I prefer that you hear the rest.

CONNIE—When I came back into Ellen's room just now, she had started to re-pack her bags completely.

ANN—What of it? I always pack the things I don't want first.

CONNIE—She'd taken out her party dresses and her white

evening coat, and was putting in riding breeches and heavy shoes. She said she thought she'd probably do more hiking than dancing.

ANN—Why get suspicious over that?

CONNIE—I didn't, until I put this boy and the breeches together . . . well, er, you know what I mean.

ANN—I still see nothing to justify . . .

CONNIE—Ann, I may not know much, but I do know a week-end date when I see one. Her expression had completely changed. Her eyes were all shining and starry. She had that look, you know . . .

ANN—I know. Anticipatory.

CONNIE—Exactly. I felt you ought to know about it at once. (*She turns to* JAY.) No doubt you think I'm a meddling old aunty.

JAY—Quite the contrary.

CONNIE (*to* ANN)—I've got to fly. I don't know when I'll be back. I imagine Glen will want to go on somewhere for dinner. (*Turning back in archway.*) Good-by, Mr. Jaywood. Don't wait up for me, Ann.

ANN (*calling after her*)—You know where the key is?

CONNIE (*outside*)—Yes, I know. Good-by.

ANN (*turning to* JAY, *after a pause*)—You must have seen this boy. Did he look like a week-ender?

JAY—He looked like a very decent chap.

ANN—This thing does have a kind of plausibility to it. An affair's the one subject on earth on which Connie is a final authority. (*Getting worked up, she rises.*) Maybe Ellen thinks she's being modern. Maybe she's just a love-sick child. Jay, what shall I do?

JAY—I'm hardly qualified to say. . . .

ANN—You've been around, haven't you?

JAY—My dear Ann, not to the point of being a mother.

ANN—I'm going upstairs to ask a few questions. Make yourself comfortable. (*She turns in archway.*) And pray for me.

"She goes out. Jay shrugs his shoulders expressively," as the curtain falls.

ACT II

Ann has come to her "office," a comfortable and much-used upstairs room. There are many shelves of books and bound volumes of magazines, a large desk with two telephones and a typewriter on it, and a touch of hominess in a fireplace with a couch in front of it. Sunlight is filtering through green trees outside and through open dormer windows into the room.

Ann has called to Ellen asking her to stop in and say good-by before she goes. Before Ellen comes her mother does a bit of pacing and pondering up and down the room. She nervously watches the door, and as Ellen's coming is delayed, calls again.

Now Ellen is there. "She wears a light Summer traveling suit and appears extremely piquant and self-possessed." She kisses her mother, and with a gay: "Think you'll be able to protect yourself from interruptions without me?" would hurry on her way. Ann asks her to close the door and wait there until Mr. Hall calls for her. Ann has something to say to Ellen, something serious. And she finds the saying of it difficult.

At first Ellen would deny that she has made an unexpected change in her plans, as her mother suggests, but when she learns of the report her Aunt Connie has made she admits the charge. She is pretty angry with Connie. "Every time she looks at a man her I.Q. goes down ten!" snaps Ellen. "The way she flits from one male to another is positively biological. Finally facing the charge she declares her intentions in one pentup outburst—

"Mother, Doug and I've had a terrible time. We've both been at cross purposes and only making each other miserable, then suddenly we got a complete understanding and realized how much we mean to each other . . . and bang! Just like that, Doug announced that Monday he had to go away and I wouldn't see him for two years!"

ANN—Where has he got to go?

ELLEN—Belgium.

ANN—Why Belgium?

ELLEN—He has a job there.

ANN—Two years is not so long.

ELLEN—Sometimes it's forever.

ANN—Of course, there is the quaint old custom of marriage.

ELLEN—How could *we* marry? Mother, there's just no use discussing it. My mind is made up. We talked it over. This is absolutely the only chance we may ever have to be together . . . and nothing's going to stop us. I'm sorry if you're going to let yourself get upset, but you have Connie to blame for that, and really, deep down in your heart, Mother, I think you do understand, don't you?

ANN—Suppose you meet someone who recognizes you?

ELLEN—We'll look out. We're going to a little lake in Lanesville. There won't be a soul there.

ANN—Ellen, it's not as simple for you as you make it sound, unless . . .

ELLEN—Unless what?

ANN—Unless this is not the first time. . . .

ELLEN—Put your mind to rest. It is.

ANN (*rising*)—That makes my duty all the more clear to me. I'm sorry, I know how miserably unhappy it will make you at first.

ELLEN (*interrupting*)—Mother, I simply won't be stopped by you or anybody else!

ANN—What do you think your father would say?

ELLEN—Does he have to know?

ANN—We have shared your virtues and your sins equally so far.

ELLEN—I know I must sound awfully underhanded and tricky but, you know, I did intend to tell you eventually.

ANN (*gently sarcastic*)—Oh, did you?

ELLEN—Sometime when we were alone and feeling confidential over a cocktail, or late some night by the fire. . . .

ANN—That would have been considerate. You could tell me too, if I didn't like it, I could lump it!

ELLEN—After all it's none of your business.

ANN—You just get that idea out of your head, Ellen. You are my business. You and Roger. True, I've puttered around a little the past twenty years at writing and lecturing; but my real thought and my real concern have been over you and Roger. You're all I have to show for my life. That's why, when half my business gets it into its head to go into bankruptcy, I feel I do have something to say about it.

That Ann should become sentimental strikes Ellen as a little odd. Of all persons, she never thought her mother would turn hypocrite. Yet Ellen knows of a certain poem in a certain book—She has found the book now and is reading—

"It was a blustering March, but a song of Spring
Piped high through the Village. Our hungering
Hearts revolted from sidewalk meetings;
From park-bench trysts; from corner greetings.
All we asked of the gods above
Was a place we could be alone with our love.
  Yet there's always a moment the fates relent.

Some optimistic editor sent
Me thirty dollars . . . enough for rent.
Oh, that was the moment our fortunes were blessed,
For Twenty-one Barrows Street got dispossessed!
While I bearded the landlord, you hurried to borrow,
Tony the Iceman's two-wheeled barrow,
And we trundled my Japanese prints and your chair,
Clothes, books and brass candlesticks over the Square. . . .
Oh, yes, I smile now that I write of it,
Only . . . I'll never forget the delight of it,
How you'd come rushing in of nights
Burning with zeal for Woman's Rights,
To find me probably, just as hot
Over Capital's errors and Labor's lot.
We took our life strong, in Barrows Street.
And did we love it? And wasn't it sweet?
For the Spring Song piped high, while our busy tongues flew,
That you were with me and I was with you!
Ah, we had it all, then, all of Love's delight;
Good talk, good food, good fire bright,
And peace . . . and a kind bed at night."

"It's still alive and beautiful, isn't it?" demands Ellen, eyeing her mother intently to note her reaction. "I think it's one of John Bliss's best poems. The Village meant something in those days, didn't it? Oh, Mother, I can imagine what it must have been! You all together for a table d'hôte at the Griffou . . . John Reed, and Max, and maybe Dreiser and "Jig" Cook or perhaps you were all broke so you were at Polly's . . . or maybe they were all there except you . . . and someone rushes in and says: 'What do you know? John Bliss just called up from Paterson! The police knocked Ann Whitman down and they've thrown her in jail!' Then everybody got as excited as anything, and they all rushed around trying to borrow money to bail you out!"

Ann (*sharply*)—Where'd you hear all this?

Ellen—I didn't hear it. I imagined it.

Ann—You didn't imagine those names.

Ellen—Oh, I had to read up, of course.

Ann—What do you mean: you had to read up, *of course?*

Ellen—For my thesis in Senior English.

Ann—I don't quite get the connection, Ellen.

Ellen—You see, I didn't want to write about one of the conventional cut-and-dried literary topics, so I talked it over with

Chop-sticks . . . of course he knows you're my mother . . .

ANN—Chop-sticks?

ELLEN—Professor Lingley. He always carries his own chop-sticks in a little case when he goes to a Chinese restaurant. He said by all means write about what I was most interested in.

ANN—Did he, indeed?

ELLEN—So I wrote on "The Contribution of Greenwich Village to the Cause of Freedom in American Art and Morals." It's a lousy title, don't you think?

ANN—Extremely lousy.

ELLEN (*excitedly*)—I've been dying to talk it over, but you've been so busy since I came home. You know, I got thrill after thrill. Almost everything we've got now, that we take as a matter of course . . . bobbed hair, tearooms, better art, poetry, votes for women, freedom of speech and sex . . . is due to you pioneer women.

ANN—Maybe not all to our credit!

ELLEN—That's what I meant . . . it's so ridiculous for you to start going back on yourself.

ANN—At my age we know more about the world's limitations than at twenty.

Ellen can see no difference between the problem that she and Doug are facing today and that which Ann and John Bliss faced "in a prudish Victorian society." She thinks Ann and her poet were absolutely justified, and she is quite confident that her sources of information were entirely reliable—

"John Bliss wrote 'Twenty-one Barrows Street' in 1911 at the time he was living there," she has checked; "and from other sources I found at least a dozen references to John and Ann. There was no other important Ann in the Village but you, and his name was never linked with that of any other girl."

Ann thinks it wasn't cricket for Ellen to go prowling around in her mother's past with a college professor, but Ellen insists she didn't do that. She isn't that kind of an egg. And all she is asking now is that her mother should be consistent.

Consistent or not, Ann is determined that Ellen is not going to do what she is planning to do. She is still dependent upon her father's support. When Ann lived in the Village she was a reporter on the old *World*. Let Ellen get a job—

ELLEN—Mother, of all the illogical poppycock! If I was two years older, and you were dead, and I had a job . . . ! (*The horn sounds outside.*) Yes, yes, I'm coming!

ANN (*moving between* ELLEN *and the door*)—Ellen, you're not to stir one step out of this room.

ELLEN—It . . . it's going to be awful if we quarrel, isn't it?

ANN—It is!

ELLEN—When I'm so in love and have been so unhappy, how you can be so utterly, inhumanly lacking in sympathy . . . !

ANN—I do sympathize.

ELLEN—You don't! You're like all the other blue-noses. Everything is just ducky for you to do, but all wrong for everybody else!

ANN—Ellen, please!

ELLEN—If there's one thing I loathe it's a hypocrite . . . and now you . . . I thought you stood for something! Plenty of mothers would be stupid, I know, but I . . . (*She breaks down, sits in desk chair and begins to cry.*) I counted on you.

ANN (*also near tears*)—Please, dear, please . . . don't cry! We . . . we'll work this out together some way.

ELLEN—Sorry . . . I said . . . what I said.

ANN—Forget it.

ELLEN (*horn again.* ELLEN *wipes her eyes and blows her nose.*)—How are my eyes?

ANN—Fine. How are mine?

ELLEN (*coldly, ignoring this invitation to fraternize*)—I'll call up Monday. Meanwhile you and Dad talk it over and decide whether you ever want me in the house again.

ANN (*putting hand on* ELLEN'S *shoulder and forcing her back into chair*)—Ellen, you're running the risk of a terrible disillusionment. I wonder if I can explain. You know, we women have considerable moral sense when we *don't* love a man. Mighty little when we *do*. With a man, it's the opposite. If he doesn't care for a girl, he's without scruples. If he *does* care, he is likely to develop a moral code only the angels can live up to. Suppose Doug gets moral and turns against you?

ELLEN—He won't!

ANN—How do you know he isn't just taking advantage of . . . of your generosity?

ELLEN (*rising impatiently*)—Oh, that's old-fashioned! He's not taking advantage of me any more than I'm taking advantage of him.

Ann makes one last plea. She never has even seen Doug Hall. Let Ellen bring him up for five minutes. Nothing shall be said that will embarrass Doug, on Ann's word of honor. And nothing that is said need make any difference in Ellen's intentions.

With this understanding Ellen goes to call Doug in and Ann orders tea. Also she asks Martha to ask Mr. Jaywood to come upstairs. When he comes Ann feverishly asks his advice. Hurriedly she outlines the situation. What is she to do? Her husband is in the middle of Long Island Sound, and of no help from there.

Ellen, Ann explains, knows of her mother's "unhallowed moments." She even knows about "Twenty-one Barrows Street." Fighting for time Ann has induced Ellen to bring her friend in. The four of them are to have tea—

"It's to be a perfectly respectable tea," Ann explains. "I promised. Nobody knows anything about anyone. I thought maybe some way we could show him up, or show free love up, or show something up!"

Soon they are, a little tensely, it may be, having tea. Douglas has explained that he is staying at the home of a cousin because it is central and he has a number of errands to do before Monday—

"I'm sort of liquidating my education," explains Doug. "I've already sold my Encyclopaedia Britannica and my drafting instruments. And I still have two pairs of skis, a Phi Beta Kappa key, and about a thousand architectural plates that I hope to cash in on before Monday night."

"Doesn't an architect need plates?"

"I'm through with that trade. Two years ago I got fifteen dollars a week; this spring I'm working for nothing; next year my boss admitted he'd expect me to pay him a salary."

In Belgium, Doug admits with some embarrassment, he is taking up the sale of razor blades, which Jay thinks should be a good business in Belgium. There is no use depending on architecture if a man ever expects to have a home and a wife. "You can't expect a woman to wait around forever," Doug insists.

"Yes, the girls today are extremely impatient," agrees Ann.

"Some of them were impatient in your day, too, Mother," counters Ellen.

"Imprudent was the word then, dear."

Ellen and Doug get away finally, but not until Ellen, called back for a last good-by and her mother's blessing, settles a little mystery of her own to her own great satisfaction. Ann has spoken quite freely before Mr. Jaywood, assuring Ellen that she believes in her and will stand by her, whatever the issue of her adventure. Ellen has protested that her mother should not speak so freely of her (Ellen's) affairs before their visitor, even if he had heard her Aunt Connie's revealing tattle. This prompts Jay to protest:

"I assure you, Ellen, your romance will lie, er . . . tenderly and close within my breast."

Ellen is struck by the phrase.

"That line scans," says she, her lips and forefinger accentuating the words. "Several of the things you said downstairs . . . ! You're a poet! You're John Bliss."

"Nonsense!" interjects Ann.

ELLEN—I might have known it. I felt you two had known each other a long time!

JAY—My name is Titus Jaywood. Want to see my baptismal certificate?

ELLEN—Who'd write poetry under a name like Jaywood! (*To* ANN, *with simple frankness.*) I certainly am glad to get this point cleared up. You know, I worked my head off trying to find out what had become of him. I bet I wrote a dozen letters.

JAY—What did they reply?

ELLEN—They said you were missing.

JAY—I am . . . poetically.

ELLEN—Why'd you change your name back?

JAY—You were on the correct scent. No New York editor would bother to read poems of American mines and steel mills written by an Englishman named Titus Jaywood; whereas, he would jump at the opportunity to buy an English novel from Jaywood, Ltd.

ELLEN—Naturally. Mother, you don't intend to stop me now, do you?

ANN—I told you I didn't. Besides, this boy may never come back. Anything may happen in Europe in the next two years.

ELLEN—That's what I meant.

ANN—Well, then go quickly before I regain my common sense. Go. Climb hills. Walk hand in hand under the stars. Make love. This may be your one great hour on earth. Go. I'll stand by you.

ELLEN—Oh, Mother, I won't go . . . if you say I shouldn't!

ANN—Get out of here . . . quick!

ELLEN (*to* JAY)—It's been grand meeting you . . . especially since I know who you really are.

JAY—I've enjoyed meeting you.

ELLEN (*to* ANN, *kissing her*)—Good-by. (*Then, impulsively.*) Oh, Mother, I never realized how much I loved you!

ANN (*clasping her fiercely in her arms*)—Ellen, dear . . . it's all right. It's all right. Don't let a thing worry you. I'll stand by you.

ELLEN—Don't *you* worry.

ANN—I won't. Good-by. (ELLEN *goes. A pause.* ANN *looks at* JAY.) Say it, say it! I'm not a fit mother to bring up a decent girl.

JAY—Now, Ann, I wouldn't go as far as that.

ANN—But you think it.

JAY—On the contrary, I think you did the wise thing. The boy's good stuff. He won't let her down.

ANN (*sitting*)—Jay, give me a cigarette. I'm going to bawl.

JAY—Pull yourself together. (*He lights cigarette for her. She takes handkerchief from his breast pocket, dabs her eyes.*) You know perfectly well that a high-minded romance, conceived more in the spirit of poetry than of legality, is just about the noblest work of man . . . and woman! If this had to come, I think you are to be congratulated that when it did come, your daughter acted with so much dignity and fine feeling.

ANN—Oh, shut up your Mayfair cynicism! Now it's all over, I realize I haven't acted as I have just because I'm a liberal thinker. More likely it's because I'm a selfish coward.

JAY—Now, really, Ann . . . !

ANN—When we first talked she got angry. She called me a hypocrite and a look came into her eyes. I couldn't endure the thought of losing her respect . . . of deliberately shoving myself off the pedestal on which she had placed me!

JAY (*with a protesting gesture*)—Now, Ann . . .

ANN (*from behind her handkerchief*)—She's like her father. When she turns, she turns hard! Oh, it's all such a mess! I'm such a mess! You're such a mess!

JAY (*sharply, in a gay tone*)—I resent that. I'm a well-ordered human being, thinking clearly, a good judge of correct artistic values . . . both in fiction and in life! And so are you!

ANN—Oh, stop trying to cheer me up . . . !

Connie is back. Her friend Glen had left word at the club that he was tied up in court and would phone later. Just now Connie is more interested in Ellen's affair than in her own. She does hope Ann was able to persuade Ellen not to make a fool of herself. She is quite upset when she learns what has happened, though she tries desperately to get back her liberal point of view and agrees with them that the news of Ellen's adventure should be kept from her father. . . .

Now the phone has rung. The call is for Connie. The others listen to her end of the conversation—

"Hello. Hello, dear. Oh, that's quite all right. Of course! I can't wait to see you. (*Pause.*) Your voice does sound tired. (*Pause; during next speeches,* CONNIE's *tone changes from enthusiasm to a dull, stunned quality.*) Glen, you're joking. I see. I've heard that alibi before. Oh, much better not to see each other at all. A real inspiration on your part, and so much easier for you. (*Long pause.*) Well, you might have been man enough to meet me as you promised and tell me to my face! Oh, you're right! The telephone does lessen the shock. Yes. Good-by. (*Mechanically she hangs up the phone. A pause. Her lips quiver, as she fights for self-control, then she laughs.*) Well, well, Connie, take that on the chin!"

"You poor dear! That's a rotten dirty trick to play!" sympathizes Ann.

"God, Ann! And I thought this was the real thing at last!"

"Perhaps it's better to find it out now than later."

"It saves flying to Reno," ruefully admits Connie, wiping her eyes and trying to recover poise. "Ann, it just can't be done. You can't give your love to too many men. They hold you cheap. (LEWIS *appears in the doorway. Her voice begins to get shrill and hysterical.*) That's why I know I was so absolutely right in telling you about Ellen. You ought to have stopped her. You ought to have prevented her making the damn fool stinking mess of her life that I have made of mine!"

Lewis would know just what kind of a tea party this happens to be but Connie rushes from the room.

Briefly both Ann and Lewis try to accept the situation with great casualness. Jay, being introduced to Lewis, feels the awkwardness of the moment and would withdraw as gracefully as possible. Lewis, however, is for asking a few questions. He is interested to learn that Mr. Jaywood is the chap who hopes to sell his Annie's story, and that they have known each other only since May. He would like to know, also, just why he finds his Annie upset and Connie in tears. As for Mr. Jaywood's begging off to dress for dinner, that isn't necessary. There is no formality in the Murray home. But if their guest would like to give Lewis five minutes alone with his wife, that would be fine.

Jay retires with a pantomimic warning to Ann to tell no more than she has to—a warning he has to change abruptly into a wave of farewell as Lewis turns around suddenly.

Lewis is not content with a skeletonized account of what has happened from Ann. He would like to know all. Nor can Ann's graceful fencing lessen his interest. Lewis knows that something serious has happened. If Ann doesn't want to tell him, perhaps Connie will. He had heard what Connie had said about Ellen.

If the truth is to be wrung out of anyone, Ann prefers that she should be that one. She would like to preface what she is going to say, however, by reminding Lewis that the one thing she has found most endearing in him throughout their married life has been his broadmindedness. She would like to remind him of that—

"Lewis, that Boston boy who failed Ellen at Commencement turned up this afternoon," begins Ann, in some desperation. "They've gone off together for the week-end."

"Well, what of it? Whose house? Someone we know, isn't it?

ANN—They're not going to anybody's house. They're just going off together alone. (*Pause. He looks blank.*) You know the meaning of the phrase, don't you, Lewis?

LEWIS—You mean they're going off *together* . . . *alone?*

ANN—That's what I mean.

LEWIS—Ellen's not that kind. A vulgar cheap week-end!

ANN—This is on a very high plane. Really, it is, dear. They didn't find out they loved each other till this afternoon . . . and the young man's leaving for two years.

LEWIS—How did *you* learn so much about it?

ANN—The young man called for a moment. His name is Hall.

LEWIS—Oh, you're imagining this! He probably took her to the train.

ANN—Ellen told me they were going.

LEWIS—Why didn't you stop her?

ANN—I did try.

LEWIS—You mean she defied you?

ANN—Why, no . . . not exactly. Naturally I tried to talk it over calmly with her.

LEWIS—Ann, we've got to find them . . . before it's too late. (*He starts for the door.*)

ANN (*going to him hastily*)—Lewis, you can't go rushing after her. You'd only be ridiculous. . . .

LEWIS (*stopping*)—Well, we must do something.

ANN—Dear, I know how you love to spring into action, but this is one occasion where if nothing is done, nothing will happen.

LEWIS—Do you mean Ellen deliberately told you, and then

walked out of the house?

ANN—Lewis, will you please stop feeling you've got to do something about it? I think our duty is to be sympathetic and understanding, and let them work out their own destiny . . . !

LEWIS—Don't tell me you were sympathetic!

ANN—Not at first, perhaps!

LEWIS—Ann, are you crazy? Did you let a girl of twenty-two talk you into a thing like this? You should have stopped her, if you had to tie her. Don't you love her?

ANN—Of course I love her.

LEWIS—That's a pretty way to show it.

ANN (*quietly*)—Ellen has exactly as much right to love as you have yourself. All we can do, as parents, is prepare her to exercise that right intelligently and decently. In fact, our work is over.

Lewis' anger mounts. The more he demands to know the less is he satisfied with the little Ann is prepared to tell him. Again he threatens to go to Connie. Ann does not approve. They have always faced everything together. Let them go on. When they were married Lewis had no idea that he was the first man in Ann's life. He admits that. Therefore, when it came to Ellen's taking the stand she did Ann could not very consistently oppose her. It's much wiser, thinks Ann, for a parent to be consistent with a girl of Ellen's mentality, and Ellen knew more about her mother than her mother knew herself—

"She's been writing a thesis on 'The Contribution of Greenwich Village to the Cause of Freedom in American Art and Morals,' " explains Ann. "Naturally she discovered that I, among others, had contributed my bit."

"This is a hell of a time to be funny," explodes Lewis.

ANN—I didn't mean to be.

LEWIS—But you admit it's right.

ANN—Right or wrong, I don't know. Justifiable anyway!

LEWIS (*exploding*)—By God, my father spoke the truth! He warned me. He was a wiser bird than I was.

ANN—You know your father was a conservative old fool. You've told me so a hundred times.

LEWIS—Huh! I can hear him now. (*Quotes in severe hard tone.*) "So, Lewis, you don't mind if the mother of your children is a woman of loose morals!" (*He strides to couch and back.*)

ANN (*angrily, following him*)—My morals aren't loose. I've

never looked at another man since I married you. You've got to be fair. You're not going to take any high and mighty attitude with me and get away with it.

LEWIS—I can't understand. I should think when Ellen found she had a mother like you . . .

ANN (*interrupting, coolly*)—I took care I had a rather beautiful love affair. . . .

LEWIS (*savagely*)—I don't want to hear about it.

ANN—I don't intend to tell you. It's pretty late in the day, Lewis, for you to be jealous over a twenty-five-year-old romance!

LEWIS—I suppose you helped your daughter pick out a pleasant place to go.

ANN—I wasn't consulted in the matter.

LEWIS—She told you where she was going though, didn't she? (ANN *does not answer.*) I see she did.

ANN—Lewis, they won't be discovered. I don't think there's a chance.

LEWIS—Where is this place? (*A pause.*) I said: Where is this place?

ANN—I don't know . . . exactly. I won't tell you anyway.

LEWIS—Naturally, I suppose not! (*Balked, he crosses to the desk. He stands for a moment, thinking, then he returns to* ANN.) I'll ask you once more. Will you tell me where Ellen was going?

ANN—No, I won't. At least, not till you've cooled off.

LEWIS—Very well. (*He turns to go.*)

ANN—Where are you going? Dinner's at seven.

LEWIS—I certainly don't intend to sit opposite *you* at dinner tonight.

ANN (*running to him, seizing his coat by both lapels furiously, as though to shake him*)—Darling, you big fool, will you come to your senses! I didn't want to tell you. You insisted. Now the least you can do is stand by me, so we can help Ellen over this tough spot . . . !

LEWIS (*freeing himself from her grasp*)—I'm going to talk with Connie . . . after that I can be reached at my Club.

ANN—Oh, don't be such a stuffed shirt! Run off to your Club to sulk! I'm ashamed of you!

LEWIS—With your perverted moral sense, I daresay you are. (*He goes out, slamming the door. For a moment* ANN *stands motionless, then she mutters a disgusted "Oh!" She sees the untidy tea tray. Mechanically she picks it up and starts for the door.*)

Ann (*angry and unhappy, through a suggestion of tears*)—Oh, goddamn sex anyway!

The curtain falls.

ACT III

At 10 o'clock the following Monday morning the terrace outside the Murray living room is flooded with sunshine. A rather stiff breeze is blowing the curtains, and it is the breeze that has, in a way, blown Titus Jaywood indoors. He is wearing a blue coat, gray trousers and a vivid crimson scarf around his throat.

Martha, the maid, following Jay with his coffee, sets the tray down and manages to find him a copy of the *Times*. For a moment, with coffee and paper, Jay is "a picture of unruffled contentment." Then Connie discovers him. Connie is wearing a "smart white costume with trousers and bolero jacket effect. She looks cheerfully seductive."

Connie *is* cheerful. And as seductive as she knows how to be. She would, if Jay would permit her, be as solicitous as a mother and wife combined, pouring him more coffee, making sure of his comfort and contributing a line of bright and interesting conversation. She is wondering now whether or not Ellen will bring her young man home with her—

"This younger generation is too much for me," sighs Connie. "In my day we had at least a shred of decency." (*She has removed her outer jacket and revealed a well-tanned back.*) "At least we *knew* we were kicking over the traces. But Ellen apparently thinks what she is doing is all in the day's work. (Jay *smiles.*) Frankly, don't you find it rather shocking?"

"Other people's affairs of the heart never shock me. Sometimes they bore me; sometimes they nauseate me; but they never shock me."

Connie finds it very difficult to understand how Jay has solved his love life. She really is envious. Here, the rest of them find themselves "embroiled in sex up to their necks," while Jay calmly lolls about and enjoys life. How does he get that way? Hasn't he really ever married?

No, Jay has never married. He manages to struggle along, he says, even without wifely admiration, in a small penthouse in the East Fifties, and with no more than a Filipino chap to cook for him. As for love, he finds plenty of that in the twenty to thirty love stories he reads every day. Finishing that task he is ready for a prizefight. He may be missing a lot, Jay admits, but, "one pays a price for everything . . . even contentment."

Connie thinks there may be something in Jay's philosophy. She would like very much to come up to Jay's penthouse some time and talk it over. If he will just take her telephone number and give her a ring some time—

"It's very easy to remember," says Connie, archly. "Four times three. It's the only four of a kind in the book that adds up to an even dozen. You can't forget it."

"I'm sure I can't," agrees Jay, gloomily.

Ann comes and Connie goes. Ann "appears gay and casual, but underneath she is heavy hearted and worried." She trusts that Jay's breakfast has been properly looked after and is amused to hear his report of Connie's solicitude, and the telephone number that adds up to an even dozen. But she is somewhat disturbed by Jay's report that Lewis has gone to Greenwich to see about a marriage license.

"The dear, befuddled lamb! And I suppose in case Ellen refuses to be made a good woman, he'll bring along a snowstorm, too, to cast her out into!"

"I don't think he means it that way. He feels . . ."

"He feels moral, that's what he feels . . . superior, capable of leading the entire female sex back to the Gay Nineties. The idea of his trying to marry Ellen off like some wanton! (*She begins to walk back and forth.*) I feel the old militant spirit surging within! I'm going to strike a blow for feminine emancipation on the top of Lewis' head that will . . ."

"Ann!"

"You're right. Whacking Lewis won't help Ellen." . . .

Ann is of the opinion that Jay should go back to town. It would not be unlike Ellen to blurt out something to her father and not unlike Lewis to make a fool of himself—but Jay thinks he will stay.

Now Lewis is back, appearing very busy and self-righteous. He has seen the mayor, had the five-day ruling overlooked and is prepared, as Ann puts it, to insult his daughter as soon as she enters his house.

"What do you mean? Insult my daughter?" angrily demands Lewis.

"A clergyman and a marriage license waiting on the doorstep sounds like an insult to me."

But Lewis is convinced he is merely helping Ellen out and bringing her young man to a realization of the responsibilities he has assumed.

"Lewis, dear, don't you realize Ellen has undergone a rather . . . how shall I put it for your correct ears . . . a rather revolutionary physical experience since Friday?"

"I don't know anything about that."

ANN—No, I don't suppose you do. That's why I'm telling you. I think it's only fair we give Ellen a little time to . . . to brood and dream, before she takes her next step.

LEWIS—Meanwhile this young man leaves the country.

ANN—Well, what of it? Ellen can sail later . . . if she still wants to.

LEWIS—If she *still* wants to! Exactly! It's phrases like that I can't understand, Ann. You've got the god-damnedest attitude.

ANN—I'm only trying . . .

LEWIS—Know what you remind me of? The way I was last fall when Roger made the football team . . . just like his old man. By Jingo, you're proud of Ellen.

ANN—I am. She's beginning to be a person in her own right.

LEWIS—You're swaggering all over the place because she has made the free-love team.

ANN (*bursts out laughing*)—Just like her old woman! Look out, Lewis, you'll smile.

LEWIS (*refusing to smile*)—What you never did get through your head is that this is basically a conventional world. Always has been, always will be. Buck the conventions and you pay for it sooner or later.

ANN—Did I pay for it? I was rewarded.

LEWIS—How?

ANN—I got *you*.

LEWIS—There's no use arguing with you. At any rate, you know where I stand.

ANN—You don't stand anywhere. You're lying down, back in the Dark Ages.

LEWIS (*starting on a new tack*)—Damn it, Ann, take our own case. This old lover of yours bobbing up has nearly got us on the rocks, and you know it!

ANN (*startled, in a small voice*)—Which old lover?

LEWIS—I don't know. Any of 'em! All of 'em!

ANN—I don't think my old lovers need bother you.

LEWIS—They make me want to wring your neck!

ANN—Well, that's a risk a woman has to run if she marries a

man with a narrow mind.

Lewis—Thanks!

Ann—You're quite welcome.

Connie has come to warn Ann that Ellen has arrived home alone and in a taxi. A moment later, while both Lewis and Connie are trying hard to appear quite normal, Ellen bursts in, trying desperately to appear quite casual, even after she notes the presence of her father. She drops her suitcase and goes to her mother. Ann holds her protectingly and very close for a second and hears the first reports of a week-end that, says Ellen, has been deadly. The Colbys are certainly antiques—

"Prayers before Sunday dinner! Dad, can you imagine?"

"No, dear, but I see you can," drily answers Lewis.

Ellen pauses for a second, and then dashes on with further details of her trip and her deductions as to its results. She recalls suddenly that she is terribly hungry and would start for some bacon and eggs. The stern voice of her father stops her at the door.

"Why, Dad, what's the matter?"

"You didn't go to Hartford."

Ellen stands looking at them for a moment, then comes slowly back into the room.

"Does Dad know?" she asks Ann.

"He does, I regret to say."

Ellen—But, Mother, you said you'd stand by.

Ann—And I intend to. But you see, dear, after you left things became so involved. . . .

Ellen—Connie, you ought to be taken out and shot!

Lewis—That's enough of that attitude.

Connie—Ellen, I'm frightfully sorry. I felt . . .

Ellen—Couldn't you think back a bit? In your day you did a little pioneering yourself.

Connie (*trying to laugh it off*)—I've never even seen a covered wagon in my life.

Ellen—You're a fine one to talk! If you weren't rich, and Dad's sister, and too old, you'd have been put in a home for delinquent girls years ago!

Connie (*explosively*)—Well . . . !

Ann—Ellen Murray . . . !

Ellen—She had it coming to her.

Lewis—Ellen, I told you . . . !

Ellen—Okay, I see my mistake. I just shouldn't have come back to this house. I had too much confidence in my family, that's all! (*She starts to go.*)

Lewis (*stopping her and putting his arm around her waist*)—Now, Ellen, hold on. No, you didn't. Your old Dad wants to help. He's taking all the circumstances into consideration. In fact, he is mighty sympathetic.

Ellen (*looking at him doubtfully*)—Are you sure you are?

Lewis—Positive. Now, tell me . . . deep down in your heart . . . are you quite happy about this situation?

Ellen—Yes, I am.

Lewis—You two are both deeply in love, aren't you?

Ellen—Of course we are. (*Indignantly.*) What do you think?

Lewis—I think maybe I can help you.

Ellen—I don't know what you can do . . . unless you start rebuilding the economic system, and a lot of people are ahead of you on that already.

Lewis—Have you considered marrying this Mr. Douglas . . . ?

Ann (*helpfully*)—Mr. Hall, Lewis.

Lewis—Mr. Hall . . . before he sails?

Ellen—Of course I haven't! We don't even dare consider it until after he gets back.

Lewis—By the way, where is your, er . . . friend?

Ellen—You mean Doug? He stopped in Stamford for a shave. He still doesn't know that any of you know, and he's terribly sunk over leaving. Will you all be generous enough to act as though our miserable little romance hadn't been flaunted before the general public?

Lewis—Huh!

Ellen—Mother, do make Father behave himself, won't you?

Ann—I hope we can all behave.

Ellen—I've got to dress. I'm going in town to help Doug shop. You know, that man hasn't but two pairs of socks to his name. . . .

There is a call on the phone for Mr. Jaywood. It is, as it transpires, from the *Paris Herald* man and he is quite sure he can promise a position to the young woman Jay describes. And that, as Lewis accepts the news, fits right into his plan—

"We'll all motor to Greenwich about four and have a quiet family wedding. Dr. Whittacker is available, he tells me, at that hour. Then a nice quiet little supper which your loving mother will arrange . . . and you're off on the 'Queen Mary' at midnight! Now isn't that neat?"

"Very neat. Doug is sailing *steerage* on the 'Laconia.' " The sarcasm in Ellen's tone is not even slightly veiled.

Then Lewis has another plan: He will give them a bridal suite as a wedding present. He is eager to do everything to make Ellen happy, and see her happily married. If it is a matter of money—

But Ellen is set in her mind. She cannot hang herself about Doug's neck and she cannot submit to the ignominy of having her father support her after she is married. No, if Mr. Jaywood can get her a job she is of a mind to take it. But not as a married woman. She'll take it on her own, and she has the backing of her mother in that decision.

The women have gone. Connie is getting her car out to drive Jay to town, somewhat to Jay's discomfiture and Ann has followed Ellen. It is Lewis' chance to suggest a further conspiracy with Jay. Let Jay see that Ellen does not get the Paris job. Let him—

Douglas Hall is calling. Lewis, with mounting anger, has told the maid to show him in.

"Easy does it, old boy," cautions Jay.

"I intend to be diplomatic," snaps Lewis.

Doug is frightened at the sight of Lewis, but he recovers himself and is casually grateful that Jay is there. It is Jay who negotiates the introductions and Doug explains that he has dropped in to see if Ellen had returned from Hartford. Oh, yes, Ellen is back. Been back about twenty minutes, they'd say. In that case Doug is wondering whether or not Ellen has had time to tell them—

"You see, Mr. Murray," explains Doug, "I've fallen pretty deeply in love with Ellen, and before I left Friday, we decided to become engaged . . . of course with your consent. . . ."

LEWIS—Frankly, Mr. Hall, in your particular case don't you feel the word engagement is a slight, er . . . error in terminology?

DOUG—You mean on account of my going away for so long?

LEWIS—I had in mind the fact you'd been away.

DOUG—Been away?

LEWIS—I said "been away."

JAY (*with warning gesture*)—Easy.

LEWIS—Mr. Hall, unfortunately I wasn't at home when you dropped in for tea.

DOUG (*politely*)—I was disappointed to find you away.

LEWIS (*explosively*)—How in the name of heaven can a well-born, clean-cut, apparently decent young chap like you stand there and look me in the eye. . . . (*Noticing* JAY'S *worried expression.*) No, suppose we drop that phase of the matter. . . .

DOUG—I'd prefer you continue.

LEWIS—I . . . you . . . (*The subject is too difficult for him. He gives up.*) Nothing important, my boy. Some other time . . . when we're better acquainted.

DOUG (*coolly*)—I'm driving in town directly with Ellen, sir, and I sail at midnight. If you have anything to say, I wish you'd say it now.

LEWIS—Er, Mr. Hall, my daughter's happiness means a great deal to me. I don't want to jeopardize it. Probably I am, as my wife frequently reminds me, narrow-minded. Anyway, my personal opinion is that you have behaved like a . . .

JAY (*warningly*)—Easy does it.

LEWIS (*in a milder tone*)— . . . damn cad.

JAY (*to* DOUG)—In brief, he knows you spent the week-end with his daughter.

DOUG—I thought that was what he was driving at.

LEWIS—Correct! That's it.

DOUG—Did Ellen just tell you?

LEWIS—No, I've known it for some time.

DOUG—Some time? That's impossible.

LEWIS—I knew it last Friday.

DOUG—Then why didn't you stop us?

LEWIS—I didn't get the news until after you had gone.

DOUG (*thoroughly mystified*)—But Ellen assured me . . . why, we all had tea together . . . nobody knew then.

JAY—A few of us were in on it.

DOUG—Did Mrs. Murray know?

JAY—Oh, definitely.

DOUG—Before we started?

JAY—Yes.

DOUG—Do you mean to say that Mrs. Murray sat there all the time, served tea and talked nonsense . . . ?

JAY—That's right.

DOUG—Did *you* know?

JAY—Oh, yes!

DOUG—What kind of a family is this?

JAY—They're extremely nice people, Mr. Hall.

DOUG (*to* LEWIS)—Say, why didn't some of you raise a row? Then, naturally, I wouldn't have thought of going.

LEWIS—Not much courage, eh?

DOUG—Oh, I've plenty of courage. I admit if a person didn't know the facts, my conduct might seem kind of rotten; but frankly, I think you have only yourselves to blame. You know I'm beginning to get pretty good and sore about this!

LEWIS—By God! *You* needn't get sore . . . !

Connie breaks in upon them. She has come for her cigarette case and, noting the general air of suppression, would go right away again. She has to remain, however, and be introduced to Mr. Hall. And to learn from Mr. Hall that he is getting pretty mad at any family that could invite him in to tea, knowing that he was about to go away with the daughter of the family, and not try to stop him.

When Ann comes Doug centers his anger on her. He can hardly be polite to Ann—

"What kind of a woman are you to serve a man tea when all the time you know he is running off with your daughter? Where were your motherly instincts?"

"Under control, Mr. Hall!"

"Don't you think it's pretty tough for Ellen and me to be let in for any such exhibition as this?"

"Of course I do, bless your heart. Lewis! Ellen begged you not to tell him we knew."

And now Ellen comes in, furious at what she discovers and ready to turn on her family—

"So you have told him . . . the moment my back was turned! Oh, darling, they're just trying to spoil everything. I'm ready. Let's get out of here. . . ."

But Doug is in no mood to leave. Nor will he let anyone else leave until the whole thing has been talked out.

"Why, Doug, what's come over you?" demands Ellen, anxiously.

"I want them to hear me propose to you," answers Doug, firmly.

ELLEN—But, Doug, you ought to know you don't have to propose to me.

DOUG—Darling, they think I've misled you.

ELLEN—What do you care what they think?

DOUG—Don't you understand, it's the wrong way to look at it. I care too much for you to . . . to . . . to . . .

ELLEN—We don't need to go into that now. Listen, Doug, we've had a grand piece of luck. Through Mr. Jaywood, I may be able to get a job on the *Paris Herald*. Isn't that a break? A newspaper job one week out of college! Aren't you excited?

DOUG—Say, it might work out at that. (*He turns to* LEWIS.) We could get married and Ellen could come over later.

LEWIS—We thought she might even sail with you.

DOUG—I see no objection.

ELLEN—I see plenty. It's out of the question. Anyway, we can talk it over on the boat.

DOUG—Ellen, I'm sorry. I can't let you take the same boat with me. . . .

ELLEN—Why not? You didn't buy it, did you?

DOUG—Ellen, you and I are going to be married here, right now, today, where your family can watch . . . or you're not going to see me for two years. . . .

ELLEN—Darling, you're just having a moral spasm. It'll pass.

DOUG (*making gesture of protest*)—Ellen, I'll have to insist. Either you marry me today, or it's good-by for *more* than two years.

ELLEN—I won't be forced . . . by you, or any of the rest of you. I know: you've all been working on him.

CONNIE—I'd say he's been working on us.

ELLEN (*turning back*)—Doug, I can't marry you like this.

DOUG—Ellen!

ELLEN—In fact, I *won't* marry you like this.

DOUG (*weakly, overwhelmed*)—That sounds final.

ELLEN—It is.

DOUG—Then good-by.

ELLEN—Good-by.

DOUG (*turning to* LEWIS)—Sorry. At least you'll admit I've tried. . . .

LEWIS—Hall, you've acted mighty fine. No father could ask more.

DOUG (*backs toward archway; takes final look at* ELLEN *to see if there is chance of her relenting; then awkwardly*)—Pleased to have met you all. (*He hurries out.*)

CONNIE—Good-by, Mr. Hall.

JAY—Good-by, old boy. (*A pause. No one knows what to say.*)

ELLEN (*miserably unhappy, turns to* ANN *in appeal*)—Mother, what do you think?

ANN (*in pleasantly vigorous tone*)—I think, when a man makes such a fuss over being seduced . . . a nice girl ought to marry him. (*It is the tiny filip needed to decide* ELLEN.)

ELLEN—Maybe you're right. (*Calling.*) Doug! Doug, wait a minute! (*She turns and runs out.*)

"Ann turns to Lewis and gives a nod of profound satisfaction, a nod that says: 'There you are, I handled her in my own way. What are you kicking about?' She extends her arms. He hesitates, then extends his. They embrace in hearty congratulation" as

THE CURTAIN FALLS

EXCURSION

A Comedy in Three Acts

By Victor Wolfson

THERE were two quite heartening new play surprises uncovered during the last weeks of the 1936-37 theatre season. One was the April production of Victor Wolfson's "Excursion." The other a May production by George Abbott of the Murray-Boretz "Room Service."

The Wolfson comedy was, perhaps, the greater surprise of the two. Its author had had some contact with the progressive theatre through the Theatre Union, but was known only for a dramatization of Dostoievsky's "Crime and Punishment" and an equally somber version of Silone's "Fontamara," which he called "Bitter Stream." This placed him definitely with the radical theatre and nothing as essentially simple and sentimental, human and heart-warming as "Excursion" was expected from his pen.

This is a comedy that happily possesses a majority of the virtues looked for in a popular success—including those of novelty of idea, an incisive genuineness in characterization, frank audience appeal in story, an abundance of honest humor, and a touch of propaganda.

"'Excursion' is the most effective propagandist play of the season," wrote Richard Watts, Jr., "because it is so gently persuasive. It is not a mere futile drama of futile escape, but is, in its modest way, a sort of exultant paean to the essential gallantry of the battered human spirit."

The production of "Excursion" was followed by an almost fulsome critical endorsement and such public support as follows those plays that make their appeal to limited in place of limitless publics. It ran out the season, with a little help from a confident management and a loyal cast.

In the cabin of the S.S. "Happiness" Captain Obadiah Rich is reading the Bible. It is Sunday morning and the Captain, "a gentle, naive man of fifty-five, immaculately uniformed, as though he were Captain on a Cunarder," is surrounded by his crew, caps in hand.

"'And they were in jeopardy, and they came to him and awoke

him, saying, Master, master, we perish,'" sonorously intones the Captain. "'Then He arose and rebuked the wind and the raging of the water: and they ceased, and there was a calm. And he said unto them, Where is your faith? And they, being afraid, wondered, saying one to another, What manner of man is this! for he commandeth even the winds and water, and they obey him. And they arrived at the country of the Gadarenes, which is over against Galilee.'"

The reading finished a hymn is sung. Then the formal meeting is closed with Captain Obadiah's hearty Amen. There is a collection for the Seaman's Institute and the men are prepared to return to their posts. This is to be the last trip of the "Happiness," after thirty years of service, and she must be left as spick and span as she was the day they took her over. They are all agreed on that.

Three bells are struck. By a stout pull at the whistle cord Obadiah warns whatever listeners there may be among prospective passengers ashore that the "Happiness" is about to cast off. Then it occurs to him that it is time to begin worrying a little about his brother Jonathan and old Zenas Hopkins. These two are on their way down from New Bedford to make this last trip on the "Happiness." They're not lost— Obadiah's not thinking that. But—

There is something of a commotion outside and a moment later Matson and Pop of the crew have maneuvered a huge wreath into the cabin. Straight from the main office it has come, and from Mr. Pitman himself.

"'To Captain Obadiah Rich—In recognition of thirty years of faithful service,'" reads the Captain from a card attached. He has taken off his specs and straightened up. A queer look of loneliness and apprehension has come into his eyes. "Thirty years—dead years crowned by a funeral wreath," he mutters. "I s'pose that's as it should be. But I don't know what I'm gonna do. Doggone it, I always had some sort of a ship."

Now there is an anxious call from the other side of the cabin door. A hearty "Ahoy, there!" A second later Jonathan Rich has burst into the room, his arms full of bundles. "He is a dry, taut, humorous little man."

The meeting is hearty, with a "Hello, Obadiah!" and a "Y' ol' bluenose y'! How y' been!" And then Jonathan's bundles are stowed and the crew is introduced and dismissed. But where is Zenas Hopkins? Well, it seems Zenas is dead. Jonathan was with him when he died—

"He was awfully tired, Obadiah," Jonathan explains. "We

been preparin' f' weeks t' come down f' y' last trip. The excitement wasn't too good f' him. Y'd think it was his first voyage he was plannin'—hoppin' around the way he was like a young one. He was close on t' four score."

"He left half his things t' me an' half t' you, Obadiah," Jonathan explains a moment later, untying one of his bundles. "Here. Here's his ship's clock f' y'. An' his spy-glass. An' his charts. An' here's a cup he made outa rope sittin' on the deck quiet afternoons sunnin' himself."

"His spy-glass—his clock—his charts—" Obadiah shakes his head solemnly. "God A'mighty. Funny how these things kin make y' rip through the years like a Sou'easter. Zenas taught me all I knew 'bout ships an' sailin'. I used these things when I was a youngster, Stevens. Sailin' t' Rennel Island outa Singapore f' trade with the natives. Pearls."

"Now let's not talk any more about that, Obadiah," puts in Jonathan, quickly. "A man as close t' heaven or hell as I am don't like to talk too much about it. Let's have a splice at the main brace, eh?"

Jonathan has taken a bottle from his pocket and Stevens has fetched three glasses. They drink to Davy Jones and to the ship—

"Aye! To our ship!" echoes Obadiah. "She's been in service since before this century was born. Used t' make the journey down t' Savannah, Georgia—'fore she took over this here run."

JONATHAN—That so?

OBADIAH—Aye, been battling the winds an' the rain, the cold an' the sleet! For thirty years an' now she's through. Through like an old circus horse. They're goin' t' make a garbage scow outa her.

JONATHAN (*sympathetically*)—No—

OBADIAH—Aye. They're sellin' her off when she comes back from this trip. She ain't payin' her own way no more, they said at the bank.

JONATHAN (*drinking rum, smacking lips*)—What kind a cargo y' carry, Obadiah? (*Silence.* OBADIAH *stares a moment at* JONATHAN, *then at* STEVENS.)

OBADIAH—Cargo?

JONATHAN—Aye.

OBADIAH—Well, what kind a cargo would y' say we carried, Stevens?

STEVENS—Well, would y' say humans, sir?

by Vandamm Studio, New York.

"EXCURSION"

e: Obadiah, darling, listen! All this is for you—as well as for us! You mustn't listen to what say! People who do new things, think new thoughts, are always called names—outlaws and :s! Obadiah, what does it matter? You and I—all of us—are sailing out of the old lanes. nave our eyes fixed on a new world. That's what matters.

(*Whitford Kane, Flora Campbell*)

JONATHAN—Humans, Obadiah! A slaver are y'?

OBADIAH (*grinning*)—No, Jonathan. No. Well—in a way—maybe. (*The buzzer rings.* OBADIAH *goes to it, picks up the tube.*) The quarter hour blast, Mr. Stevens. Yes, Mr. Linton—Yes. He's here, Mr. Linton. Start warmin' y' engines. We'll let her slip in quarter of an hour. Right, Mr. Linton. (*He drops the tube.* STEVENS *pulls the whistle cord.*)

JONATHAN—That's a nice blast y' got, Obadiah. Heard it half way t' New Bedford.

OBADIAH—Aye? An' where y' been so late, Jonathan? Get lost?

JONATHAN—Aye. Wanderin' around. Askin' f' Captain Rich's ship. No one seemed t' know. I tol' 'em y' sailed f' the islands—but I couldn't remember what islands, Obadiah. What islands do y' sail for?

OBADIAH—The Coney Islands, Jonathan, 'tain't far— (*The lights begin to fade.*)

JONATHAN—The Coney Islands. Hmn. Y' goin' t' have another splice with me, Obadiah?

OBADIAH—No. Don't think I will, Jonathan. (*He sits quietly staring before him.* JONATHAN *pours out another drink for himself as the scene changes.*)

The side walls of the cabin have been swung inward, which reveals the rear of the lower passenger deck. There is a circular railing and side seats for passengers. Two steep side ladders rise to the upper deck. There is a pile of canvas chairs in the center of the deck, and at the side rails two huge life-preserver cases bearing the legend: "S.S. Happiness, New York, Coney Island." From a dance hall somewhere back of the salon wall, which is plastered with advertisements, a small orchestra is playing quite badly. Occasionally distant steamer whistles can be heard, but it is Sunday morning and river traffic is not heavy.

Passengers are beginning to arrive. Mrs. Geasling, with her arms full of Marie, the baby, and her attention taken largely by Mike, her freckled son of ten, is the first. She has a time of it, does Mrs. Geasling, trying to get Mike to help arrange the chairs so she can change Marie. Mike is only an hour away from home but he is already hungry.

Mac Colman, a voluble young man, and Miss Dowdie, a pleasant old maid, are making an inspection of the ship. Miss Dowdie has just won a *Daily News* contest—"Why I Should Like to Visit New York City in Three Hundred Words—By One Who

Has Never Been There." It is Mr. Colman's present job to see that Miss Dowdie gets a good view of the city. Also one of Brooklyn.

Martha, who is big and blond, and Lollie, who is attractive in spite of horn-rimmed glasses, have come to this part of the boat hoping to grab a couple of chairs "before the rest of the animals get on." Martha and Lollie work in Gimbels—Martha in wall paper and Lollie in books. Just now Martha is full of a recent adventure with a man from Flatbush who bought wall paper for his little girl's bedroom and then wanted Martha to come out to his house and advise him about the other rooms. Martha went, of course, and was she surprised when that man never even made a pass at her!

The Winches drift by—Mr. and Mrs., little Pauline and Stanley—but they do not stay. Pauline and Stanley manage to drop a pail, a rake and a shovel on one trip across the deck. It is probably just as well they went on.

Martha has got as far in her story as her second trip to Flatbush and her discovery that whatever else her wall paper patron may be he certainly is no fairy. Mrs. Geasling has managed to discourage young Michael's effort to prove that his baby sister is cockeyed by sticking his finger between her eyes. And Lollie, having listened to Martha's Flatbush romance with both curiosity and amusement, has gone a bit romantic herself—

"I guess I must feel older than you, Martha," laughs Lollie. "But the first time I came on this boat I was young. Do you know what happens when you're young, Martha? You get all excited and all the smells smell good and you love everyone you see and even the city you're leaving behind. That doesn't happen when you're old."

"Now don't keep sayin' that!"

"When you're young you just sit down next to a man, and he turns out to be the son of the owner of the line—"

"That never happened to me."

"It did to me. And then you go to Steeplechase and the owner's son takes your arm and you ride high up on the ferris wheel—way above the lights—and he touches your hand to keep you from being frightened. . . ."

"Gee, Lollie!"

". . . then you come on the boat again and go sailing up to the city in the dark, watching the lights on shore. The next day you're in Economics B, and you never see the owner's son again. After a while, of course, things happen to you and you find you're not so young any more. So you put on glasses and take excursions—to get the air. (*Puts on her glasses.*)"

"Y' sound so romantic, Lollie—I'll go find Tessie an' see about the lunch!"

Things are not altogether harmonious with the Fitchels and the Geaslings. Young Michael Geasling has found Mr. and Mrs. Fitchel and has herded them with some enthusiasm to where his mother is still attending the baby Marie. Mike is particularly interested in the Fitchel lunch basket. Much more interested than Mr. Fitchel, who is inclined to resent Mrs. Fitchel's idea that an excursion is a fine rest for papa when she loads him down with a hundred-pound basket and asks him to carry it from Washington Heights to Coney Island. Mike has also heard that the Fitchels have brought a lot of hard-boiled eggs, like Mrs. Geasling, and he hates boiled eggs. Nothing but a nickel finally quiets Mike. . . .

The activities of the crowd increase with the new arrivals. A boy shouting bargains in souvenirs wanders from group to group. A trio of kodak enthusiasts pose each other for atmospheric snapshots. A candy butcher peddles his wares raucously. Lollie has found Tessie, and Tessie has lost the lunch of which she had been made custodian. No lunch and no money to buy more doesn't promise a very successful day for Lollie, Martha and Tessie. . . .

Now "Red" Magoon, a husky man of thirty, has followed Mrs. Loschavio, an alert, quick-moving young matron, onto the deck. Their acquaintance is recent and they are looking for a quiet spot to continue a flirtation. They manage to find a secluded corner of the deck but hardly a passionate kiss has been exchanged before Mrs. Loschavio's little girl has found them. Mrs. Loschavio is pretty mad about being spied upon. What she would like to do to her offspring is plain, but what she does is no more than to scold her loudly and send her away in tears. "Red" offers a nickel by way of a bribe, but still the girl is not content.

"I'm goin' t' tell Daddy on y' when we get home," she shrieks at her blushing mother. "You wuz kissin' him. I saw y'. Yes. I did. You wuz kissin' him—"

Now Mrs. Loschavio is in tears and disgusted. She is not going back to the lousy wop who is her husband, she declares. He's going to be a celery king, it may be, but she can't stand him. "Works all day down in the markets—comes home stinkin' a rotten vegetables—an' wants t' lay down in bed with me—tell me how—a—some day he's gonna be celery king," wails Mrs. Loschavio. "I tell y' I just can't stand him no more! What should I do, Magoon?"

"How should I know?" answers Magoon, with a shrug of his shoulders.

Red and his lady have settled again to the routine of their flirtation when the Loschavio child dashes back. Now they have darted down the deck in a second attempt to avoid her, as the crowd moves in. . . .

Aikens, a confessed Communist, has moved into the group. Aikens is searching for evidence against the representatives of the capitalist system. He would question Tessie. And Lollie. They work hard, don't they? And they get damned little for it, don't they? Lollie knows the Aikens type. He's a writer. She knows them, being in the book department.

"And you'd better be careful," Martha warns him. "Lollie's smart—went t' college an' everything."

"Martha!" protests Lollie, as Aikens laughs. "All right. Go on. Make a crack about my glasses now."

"Bryn Mawr or Smith?"

"Hunter. (*A pause.*) "Hunter night school, studyin' my head off so I can work for fifteen dollars a week at Gimbels. I better warn you, Aikens, I hate books. And I hate the people that write them! Cause I have to stand on my feet all day long and sell 'em."

"Well, y' needn't hate me," protests the Communist. "Gosh, the things I write—have—I don't know if you'll understand me exactly—they've got social content. A point of view."

"Oh, poor thing," comments Martha.

"What have they got, Martha?" Tessie wants to know.

"Social content, y' dumb cluck, didn't y' hear him? 'Bout Park Avenue—Myrna Loy—y' know—"

All of which doesn't make much sense to Tessie, but Lollie and Aikens are agreed that there isn't much need of worrying about the sale of the Aikens books. . . .

The first whistle has blown. It is nearing time to cast off. Captain Obadiah is making a circuit of the deck to speak to the passengers, many of whom he knows by name. They have been taking these excursions with him for many years and he thinks it particularly loyal that they should have come to go on this last trip.

Suddenly there is a commotion farther down the deck, topped by the laughing voice of a young girl. Lee Pitman, handsome, in evening clothes, and a cheerful twenty in years, is greeting her old friends of the crew. Gilchrist! Matson! (*who gets a kiss*). Pop! (*who is terribly excited by the visitation*). And Obadiah himself! Lee has thrown her arms about the Captain and kissed him soundly—

"That's because you're so handsome and you didn't sail without me and I love you!" announces Miss Pitman.

And now Richard Pitman, an attractive boy of twenty-four, follows his sister to the deck. He, too, is in evening clothes and breathing hard. With Richard come explanations—

They had had to run a block from where they parked the car; they had forced Pat, the chauffeur, to drive them all the way from Watch Hill in four hours; they did not even have time to change—

"We just couldn't let you get off on your last trip without us!" pants Richard.

"It's good of you to come like this!" beams Obadiah, as he links his arms in theirs and turns to face the passengers. "M' friends—I want y' to know my favorite passengers! They've traveled many a trip with me. Since they were little ones, eh? This is Lee an' Richard Pitman, m' friends. Their father owns the line."

There are many scattered greetings and a good deal of friendly waving of hands. Suddenly Lee discovers Lollie and remembers her. Pretty soon Richard has also discovered Lollie—Lollie Popps, the girl from Hunter—

"The girl who was scared to death up in a ferris wheel."

"Are you sure?"

"What y' talking about, Lollie—y' told me you were," protests Martha.

"Well, this is swell! Say, what are you doing here?" Richard is laughingly inquisitive.

"Oh, I just came for the air," says Lollie.

"Take off your glasses!" orders Martha, under her breath.

The whistle blows hard and the band strikes up "Anchors Aweigh" in quite a military fashion as the curtain falls.

ACT II

It is just past eight o'clock that night. Captain Obadiah is in his cabin sadly taking his pictures off the walls, wrapping and packing them. It is very quiet, save for the sounds of Coney

Island coming from the shore; carousels, barkers, music, etc. When the door opens to admit Jonathan this noise swells to a din.

Jonathan is a little excited. He has been all over the ship and found her in good shape. Now he has gone to the window and is staring out at the lights of Coney. An amazing island, Jonathan finds it. Reminds him of a time when he and Obadiah were alyin' off shore while the natives ashore were havin' a big roast.

"Looks like a birthday cake for a Zulu king—don't it?—blazin' away!" muses Jonathan. "Never seen anythin' like it before in m' life."

"Probably the last time we'll see it, Jonathan," sighs Obadiah.

Stevens of the crew is missing. This worries Obadiah. Worries him terribly when he discovers that Stevens has gone ashore. "He won't be fit t' steer a rowboat when he comes aboard again," mutters Obadiah. It isn't the liquor that gets Stevens. It's hot dogs. "And relish—and onions! An' soda pop an' popcorn! An' all kinds a poison." Stevens' stomach is awful weak!

They are at the window again—Jonathan and Obadiah—listening to the carousels. "Lord, that's a nice heathen sound!" Jonathan is saying. "Makes me remember—oh, a lot of things. A lot of things!"

OBADIAH—Aye, Jonathan. A lot of things. Just look at them swarm out there! Like bees suckin' honey from a flower. Funny—how anxious they are t' set foot on that island. An' what is Coney Island, when y' think of it, Jonathan? Y' know, f' thirty years I've watched m' passengers come aboard the S.S. "Happiness." Watched 'em back there in the city, come down the narrow dark alleys between the buildings—watched 'em scramble for a place on the S.S. "Happiness"—white-faced girls, tired-out men and women, sickly-lookin' young men—all rushin' for this here boat that's goin' t' give 'em a day at the Island. An excursion outa their *real* life. God A'mighty! (*He shakes his head again.*) Aye. I've had thirty long summers t' stand up here an' watch 'em down below there. An' sometimes, Jonathan—I feel—well, it's hard t' put in words— I feel sometimes it just ain't right—if y' know what I mean.

JONATHAN—I don't believe I do, Obadiah.

OBADIAH—Well, I feel like I been foolin' m' passengers into somethin'.

JONATHAN (*laughing*)—Likely, they wanted t' be fooled, Obadiah.

OBADIAH—Aye. But it ain't right, Jonathan. It ain't the thing m' passengers are lookin' for. They don't want just a coupla hours in a day changed, they don't want a coupla hours a fun, a coupla hours a excitement, a coupla hours a—magic. M' passengers want their whole sorry life t' change, Jonathan, an' I don't know how t' do that.

JONATHAN (*nodding understandingly*)—Aye. I see how it is.

OBADIAH—Listen. For years I been goin' down on passenger deck an' talking t' 'em on the home trip. They're the saddest crew y' ever saw in y' life, Jonathan! They don't know what's the matter with them. But I do. They've been cheated.

JONATHAN—Cheated?

OBADIAH—Aye! Excursions for my passengers down there are lies! Cause every Sunday morning, they come rushing down to this old boat—just as eager—! An' every Sunday night they come back—just as sad! (*He pauses, listening to the carousels.*) Maybe I don't know what I'm talkin' about, Jonathan—but some day—

JONATHAN (*gently*)—Some day what, Obadiah?

OBADIAH—Some day m' passengers— (*He stops.*) Doggone it, I don't know how t' say it—but some day m' passengers are goin' t' be happy goin' *an'* comin'—aye—'cause the things back there they're takin' an excursion from—is goin' t' be happier—if y' know what I mean.

JONATHAN—I guess y' get plenty a time t' do y' thinkin' up here, Obadiah.

OBADIAH—Aye. Plenty. I know I'm a sentimental old fool, Jonathan, but some day—

The missing Stevens has turned up. He is about as shaky as Obadiah feared, but still able to go about his part of the packing. Now he has found his concertina and swung a little mournfully into "I wish to God I'd never been born—"

"Jonathan, if you watch my passengers getting off this ship tonight you'll see a lot of tired, disappointed backs going up the streets into the dark—and it'll remind you of that song," says Obadiah.

It is nearing time to cast off. Mr. Linton is given his orders through the speaking tube to start warmin' her up. There is a loud blast of the whistle as a warning for those still ashore.

Jonathan has picked up Zenas Hopkins' charts and is studying them intently, curiously. Now he's found a cross markin' Zenas' favorite island—

"That's where *he* was goin' when his seafarin' days was over—"
"Aye—an' he never got there."

JONATHAN—I've never been able to forget what an island that was. Food aplenty—peaceful—like the picture of Eden in the big Bible on the table in the settin' room up in Yarmouthport.

OBADIAH—Aye—

JONATHAN—Obadiah—you been doin' a lot a thinkin' an' dreamin' up here 'bout your passengers— You thought a lot about what they be wantin'. Have you ever thought about givin' it t' 'em?

OBADIAH—What?

JONATHAN—I say, have you ever thought a givin' it t' 'em?

OBADIAH (*quietly*)—Jonathan!

JONATHAN—An' there she lays. I figured it out t' be two hundred and fifty miles south by southeast a Trinidad.

OBADIAH (*tensely*)—Figured what out? What are y' talkin' about, Jonathan?

JONATHAN (*fearfully*)—What's the matter, Obadiah? (*They stare at each other strangely a moment.*)

OBADIAH—I don't know. I don't know. (*There's a long pause. The carousels keep playing gaily.* JONATHAN *sits quietly, in deep thought.*) What's that mark, Jonathan? Way up there on the coast.

JONATHAN—That's Norfolk, Virginia.

OBADIAH (*taking map*)—Norfolk!

JONATHAN—We could stop there an' pick up a little seafarin' food— Y' got nothin' but a coupla stale tea sandwiches an' candy down the lower deck, likely. Y' can't feed seagoin' passengers on that sort a nonsense, Obadiah.

OBADIAH (*suddenly losing voice, whispers hoarsely*)—Jonathan Rich! What are y' drivin' at?

JONATHAN (*rising*)—An' Norfolk's a good place f' fuelin'.

OBADIAH (*gathering himself together*)—I'll hear no more of this, Jonathan. (*Starts to rise.*)

JONATHAN (*pushing* OBADIAH *back in chair*)—Now don't go shootin' off y' mouth at me, Obadiah! I know the kind of man you are! Can't do anythin' but dream—dream—

OBADIAH—Aye, but Jonathan—

JONATHAN—That's your trouble. Always was, always will be. You don't know how to act.

OBADIAH (*sitting down helplessly*)—Y' gonna worry me t' m' grave, I know it.

JONATHAN (*continuing in fine form*)—An' I tell y' when a man's satisfied with dreamin'. Obadiah—before y' know it, his time's up an' his ship ain't even out of harbor—if y' know what I mean.

OBADIAH—Aye, I know.

JONATHAN—Didn't y' say y'd like t' do somethin' f' y' passengers after all these years? Didn't y' say y'd like t' give 'em the things they're lookin' for?

OBADIAH—Aye, aye, but—

JONATHAN—An' there y' sit! A map before y'—an island t' go t'—a ship t' sail in—an' there y' sit!

OBADIAH—Aye, I know.

JONATHAN—An' tomorrow y' have no ship t' sail in. T'morrow it's too late! (OBADIAH *picks up the map.*) Go on, Obadiah! Go on, study it hard, Obadiah, so y' know the way!

OBADIAH (*suddenly crying out; rising*)—I can't, Jonathan! I can't! Doggone it, I tell y', I can't!

A loud knock at the door announces the arrival of three members of the crew. They enter a little hesitantly. Matson finally finds words to tell Captain Obadiah that so long as the company had sent a wreath the boys wanted to give him something, too. So, they chipped in and here it is. A pair of bedroom slippers!

Obadiah is properly touched and greatly appreciative. He'll be rememberin' them and the things they've said when he is sittin' alone up there in Yarmouthport. Now let them get along and get the "Happiness" started!

The men have gone. Obadiah is standing in the doorway staring after them. Jonathan is still intent upon Zenas' charts. "If y' turn y' course south by southeast when we get t' Trinidad—" Jonathan is saying. But Obadiah doesn't answer. He has closed the door and is standing meditatively staring at the bedroom slippers. "I just know they ain't goin' t' fit y', Obadiah," Jonathan concludes, gently.

"No. I'm afraid I just can't wear 'em, Jonathan—ever," Obadiah agrees.

"An' if we go back t'night, Obadiah, t'morrow y'll have t' squeeze int' 'em, somehow."

Stevens is back feeling "a lighter man and a better sailor." There is decision in Obadiah's voice as he gives him his orders—

"If we take our ship back t'night—there's no tomorrow for us, is there, Stevens? No more ship, no more excursions, no more passengers, no more work—no more nothin'. I been thinkin' an' dreadin' this moment like the plague—an' here it is. If we go back t'night, Stevens—the S.S. 'Happiness' becomes a garbage scow. Our white an' gold ship, Stevens. Me—a retired seafarin' man in bedroom slippers settin' on the porch at Yarmouthport, tellin' kids an' summer folks about things I used to do. An' you —God knows what becomes of a man like you, Stevens—once y' start driftin' again—like y' did—well, I decided for the sake of all of us, you, me, the crew and my passengers—we're not goin' back. D' y' see?"

"I see. (*Suddenly.*) What did you say, sir?"

"We're not goin' back."

"I see, sir. It's just that I feel so bad in m' stomach. Is it t' be a long voyage, sir?"

"To another island, Stevens."

"An' back, sir?"

"I don't know. I don't know." Obadiah is plainly disturbed.

"Just one way, Stevens," puts in Jonathan, quietly.

"Thank y', sir."

Now Obadiah is at the speaking tube receiving reports and giving orders. Soon the "Happiness" has cleared the pier. Stevens is at the wheel. Now, let him turn her, and whistle as he turns—headin' the other way.

"Out there, sir? Out there in the dark, away from the lights?" Stevens is plainly anxious.

"Out there—past Sandy Hook light," answers Obadiah, with gentle defiance.

"Out there t' the open water," chimes in Jonathan.

"We're goin' t' Zenas Hopkins' Island."

"Aye, sir."

Stevens is slowly turning the wheel in the opposite direction. Jonathan is studying the map. Obadiah is slowly tying up the bedroom slippers. The sound of Coney Island's carousels grows fainter and fainter. All three are singing "Around Cape Horn in the month of May. . . . Around Cape Horn in the sleet and the spray a long time ago" as the curtain falls.

The scene has changed and we are back on the lower deck. There are strings of lights and the atmosphere is gay and festive. The orchestra is playing a sentimental waltz for the dancers in the salon. Several of the passengers we have met before are strolling about. The others, according to Gilchrist of the crew, are downstairs stuffing themselves at the candy bar. "They'll be up as soon as they're sick enough," predicts Gilchrist.

Except for the sand in his teeth from his lunch on the beach Mr. Fitchel might be happy. Young Mike Geasling has bought himself a watersnake that uncoils as he blows it on Mrs. Fitchel's neck. The souvenir boy is back, refreshed and raucously insistent. Red Magoon and Mrs. Loschavio are still trying to shake little Eileen. They haven't had a minute alone, according to Red. Still, Eileen isn't sleepy and she doesn't want to lie down. She wants to walk.

Aikens, Tessie, Lee Pitman and Pat, the Pitman chauffeur, would be singing the "Internationale" if they knew it. They make two or three fairly sour starts and then get into an argument as to the words. As it turns out Lee, the capitalist's daughter, is the only one who knows it is "justice," not "freedom" —"for *justice* thunders condemnation—"

Aikens can't quite get Lee. A daughter of Pitman and practically a member of the Communist party— But Aikens hasn't even read Karl Marx. How could he understand? . . .

There is a rushing through the door and a good deal of laughter. Richard and Lollie are finishing a race for the deck. They have been seriously debating the merits of the ferris wheel and the shoot-the-chutes as thrill experiences. Then, as they stand by the rail, "the night has a completely sobering effect upon them."

"Gosh, this is beautiful!" Richard is saying. "You know, this is the one thing I can remember. Ever since we were kids, Dad's let us go down to the Island with Obadiah, the one thing I remember is standing on the bench up in his cabin—staring at the stars. I used to think the lights of Coney Island stretched all the way home, followed me, do you know? (*A silence.* LOLLIE *is staring up at the sky. He turns to her.*) What's the matter, Lollie?"

"Oh, I don't know—it almost makes me feel ashamed," answers Lollie, with a sweeping gesture that vaguely takes in the universe.

"Of what?"

"Oh, the life I've got to start in living again in the morning, for instance—"

It is a time for confessions. Lollie admits that once she had wanted to be a landscape gardener and build parks for people. Richard can't see why she didn't go ahead and do it, with or without Mr. Gimbel's approval. Richard is finding Lollie increasingly interesting, and decidedly different. His sister Lee used to bring home girls like her, but Lee's a Red. Lee goes to all sorts of queer meetings and comes home to argue wildly with her father. And the names she calls him: Exploiter! Capitalist!

And even worse. Father took it from Lee—but Richard could never try it. Richard is afraid that he may be a little soft. . . .

What was only a mist has turned into a fairly thick fog, but they still stand there staring at the horizon. Suddenly Richard has broken a long silence with the declaration that he likes Lollie. And Lollie, accepting the declaration quite matter-of-factly, agrees that she likes him, too, though she knows Martha would never advise her admitting it. Richard has taken her hands and as they stand looking intently and deeply into each other's eyes he says:

"Take off your glasses."

"What?"

RICHARD—What's the matter? Take off your glasses.

LOLLIE (*disappointed, laughing it off, puts up her fists*)—What do you want to do—fight?

RICHARD (*shaking his head solemnly, then quietly*)—Kiss you.

LOLLIE (*seriously*)—Oh. (*She turns away, disturbed. Stares out at the horizon a moment, looks up at the sky, thinking—then finally speaks quietly.*) All right, Richard—kiss me, if you want.

RICHARD (*just too matter-of-fact*)—Well, take 'em off!

LOLLIE (*romantic mood shattered, turns on him*)—Why? Why should I?

RICHARD—Well, for the love of Pete, you don't expect me to kiss you in—

LOLLIE (*hurt, tears welling to her eyes*)—Well, why not, why not!

RICHARD—Well, I can't, that's all!

LOLLIE (*tears in her voice now*)—Why can't you! I don't like you!

RICHARD—Oh, you're acting like a baby. (*Suddenly one hand of his takes off her glasses, the other goes about her waist.*)

LOLLIE (*weeping, hurt*)—Stop it! Stop it, you! (*He kisses her into complete silence. We hear the gentle snoring of* MR. FITCHEL; *we hear the orchestra playing a jazzed version of the "Internationale."* RICHARD *still kisses* LOLLIE, *the glasses dangling in one hand. Finally he lets her go. Suddenly* LOLLIE *buries her head against him and cries softly.*)

RICHARD (*after a while, gently*)—Lollie—what's the matter?

LOLLIE—Richard! (*They kiss.*)

RICHARD (*laughing quietly, then after a moment, seriously*)—You know when I first knew, Lollie? When we were walking along out there on the boardwalk. You were eating a hot dog and you had mustard smeared all over your face—and—

LOLLIE (*laughing through her tears—props her elbow on the rail, rolls her eyes to the sky*)—Gee, you're romantic, Mr. Pitman! (*After a moment—through her tears.*) Oh, I'll never wear them again, Richard, never. Never so long as I live. I swear it. (*She blows her nose. He laughs quietly. Their eyes come to focus on the glasses in* RICHARD'S *hand. He twirls them carelessly around a second. She takes them, holds them out over the water, then lets them drop. They lean over the rail watching the glasses sink.*) A fog's coming up, darling, you better kiss me while you can still find me.

RICHARD (*laughing appreciatively as he takes her in his arms*) —Gosh, Lollie! You're wonderful! Where does a girl like you come from anyway?

LOLLIE (*quietly, as he kisses her*)—The Bronx, darling.

From a distance a boat whistle is heard. Then a foghorn blows. Suddenly from the salon Lee Pitman appears, happily excited. How would they feel, Lee wants to know, if something nice would happen. Suppose they weren't going home! Suppose— Lollie is quite thrilled with the thought. And then Lee lets them share her secret. The "Happiness" is heading out to sea!

There is more excitement now. Surely the lights on shore would seem to prove Lee right. The fog is thick, but the stars are bright above them. They should be following the shore, but they're not! Isn't it wonderful?

For a moment it is wonderful and with subdued hysteria all three are of a mind to cheer. But suddenly there is a chilling blast of the whistle and they begin to realize what might be happening. It might not be so wonderful for Obadiah! Supposing Obadiah doesn't know which way he is going?

"We've got to find out what's happened to him before they do in there," warns Lollie. "There'll be a panic!"

There is the beginning of a panic when Mac Colman arrives. He, too, has noticed the lights. There's something screwy about those lights and, by God, Mac Colman wants to know what it is. He wakens Fitchel, but Fitchel doesn't know. So Mac dashes away to find out.

Richard decides that he had better go up to Obadiah's cabin and discover what actually has happened. He is no more than at the top of the stairs before the passengers, headed by Red Magoon, come swelling out of the salon. Mac Colman's doubts have spread.

"There! He's right!" shouts Mrs. Loschavio, pointing wildly toward the shore.

"What d' y' mean, he's right! I kin see a light!" growls Magoon. "Over there, d' y' see?"

MRS. LOSCHAVIO—Yes, but we're movin' away from it! Can't y' see, Red! We're movin' away from it! (MRS. FITCHEL *enters.*)

TESSIE—Oooh, look how dark!

EILEEN (*running to her mother*)—Mamma!

MRS. FITCHEL—Papa! Papa! Did you hear what they're saying?

FITCHEL—Why don't you let me alone already?

MRS. FITCHEL—Alone, he wants to be left alone. The boat is going to Europe, but he wants to be left alone!

FITCHEL—What? (*Pleading.*) Mamma, please, what are you talking about?

MRS. FITCHEL (*deliberate*)—The boat! The boat! It's going the wrong way! Yes, don't look at me like that—go see for yourself!

AIKENS—Lee, what's happening?

LEE (*smiling idiotically*)—Oh, hello, Aikens, hello. Isn't it fun? We're going abroad!

AIKENS—Now don't get hysterical, Lee. It'll be all right!

LEE (*angrily*)—Well, I like that!

TESSIE—Oh, Martha, what'll I do? If I'm not in the basement by nine o'clock in the mornin', I'll lose m' job. (MIKE *blows the paper snake at his mother. She grabs the snake from him and throws it away.*)

MRS. GEASLING—Now stop it! Stop it, I say! Even when the boat's sinking he's got to make a nuisance of himself!

MAGOON—I'm going to find out what this is all about! I'm going up to see the Captain!

LEE—No, you can't do that!

MAGOON—Who says so? Why the hell can't we?

LEE—Don't be a fool! He's an old man, don't you see?

MAGOON—So what!

LEE—Suppose you frighten him?

MAGOON—So what!

LEE—Suppose he's crazy!

MAGOON—Crazy! We're all going up there. Come on.

Richard Pitman stands at the head of the stairs. He orders Magoon and the others back. There's no reason for their going up. The Captain is coming down. He wants to talk to them. The passengers shuffle back toward the salon doors. The candy boy is swinging through the crowd calling his stuff.

Now Obadiah is among them. He has come, as usual, to have a little visit with them. He calls several by name. There is the booming of a strange bell, and that gives Obadiah his cue—

OBADIAH—Aye, we're swinging wide of the channel tonight, m' friends. That's what I've come down to talk to you about. But first, I want you to know my brother Jonathan, 'cause he's a good sailor, a mighty fine sailor.

JONATHAN—Howdy, shipmates.

PASSENGERS—Hello.

MAGOON—Say, what the hell is all this?

OBADIAH—We don't allow swearing on this boat, mister, if you don't mind. Now then, m' friends, let's get down to the hull of it, as Zenas Hopkins used to say. You got Jonathan here to thank, mates. He thinks you should have an explanation now. Oh, I was going to tell you too, only not so soon, that's all.

MAGOON—What the hell are you driving at?

OBADIAH—I'm sorry, mister, but if you insist on swearing, I'll just have to ask you to take yourself down to the men's smoking room. Well, seeing as you and me is going to be partners in this here venture—

RICHARD—Venture, Obadiah?

OBADIAH—That's right, son. Jonathan, here, and me, we got up—now how shall I put it?—Say a little more excursion for you folks.

JONATHAN—Aye, that's it.

TESSIE—Oh, Captain, that's wonderful. I was so worried. A moonlight cruise. Oh, he's sweet.

OBADIAH—Moonlight cruise? Yes, yes, in a way. You know, I been watching you folks go on excursions for years, and I've seen how you've been fooled, 'cause Coney Island's not a real happy island, you know that, and I been noticing how you hated to go back to the things you had to go back to— Well, me mates, passengers, friends, we're all on our way now to a real happy island, where we can be really happy. (*The fog-horn blows.*)

TESSIE—Oh, Captain, what are you making such speeches for? Where's the island? I'll bet it's that one near City Island, Martha.

MARTHA—You mean near the Bronx there? Why, that's practically in my back yard, Captain.

OBADIAH—I don't happen to know the island you're talking of, girls, but the one I'm thinking of is (*He takes out a little piece of paper on which he has jotted down some information.*) 1650 nautical miles sou', sou'east of Cape Hatteras.

TESSIE—What!

OBADIAH—Latitude 8 point 9, longitude 53 point . . .

MARTHA—1650?

MAGOON—God dammit, he's crazy, I tell you!

RICHARD—Sit down, you!

MAGOON—What are you all standing here listening to him for?

LEE—Sit down, and let him finish!

MAGOON—And let him talk a lot of halfwits into taking this boat God knows where? Can'tcha see what he's driving at? He's nuts!

MRS. GEASLING—He's right. I don't know what's got into you, Captain Rich.

OBADIAH—Now, hear me, hear me.

JONATHAN—Now, take it easy, miss.

MRS. GEASLING—Don't "miss" me. I'm married, God help me, and you get me home right away, do you hear? I got to get Mike off to school in the morning. I can't go to no fancy island.

OBADIAH—Now hear me, hear me; if you don't want to go, you don't have to go.

All those who are opposed to the excursion, Obadiah explains, will be put ashore at Norfolk, Virginia. Magoon doesn't think the old tub will ever reach Virginia, but Jonathan assures him the "Happiness" is a sturdy craft and seaworthy. Tessie begins to weep. What is she going to do about her job? Obadiah is sympathetic but he still thinks everybody should leave the sheltered waters at least once in his life. This island they are planning to go to, Obadiah explains to Lee and Lollie, who are plainly anxious for him, is 1600 miles sou' sou'east in the Caribbean. He had been there thirty-two year' ago—and a fine island it is—

"Strong black soil. Fit for growin' things," says Obadiah.

"Sun up high and bright all the year through," promises Jonathan.

"What are we going to eat?" young Mike wants to know.

"There's hunting and fishing, and acres of blue grapes growing wild. They'll be wine aplenty. I tell you it's Eden, mates," chips in Jonathan.

"Aye, Eden," agrees Obadiah, with shining eyes, "and there'll be no one there to work you until you're tired in the spirit, no fear, no poverty and greed, no hatred, but peace and plenty. All yours, the whole magic island. Yours, to plow and plant and build anew. Laws such as y' need, no more. You'll be free and happy, mates. Free t' be men and women, in all your parts. I mean, your brain, your heart, your body and soul! Oh, m' passengers, it's the place for you!"

"Well, what do you say, mates?" Jonathan is facing the crowd expectantly.

Lollie is the first one to declare for going. Lollie is ready to go any place where she will be free from drudgery and fear of losing her job. Tessie and Martha think she is quite crazy. Mrs. Loschavio is next. She wants to go too—any place where she won't have the smell of the markets in her nose all day; any place to get away from everything she has back there.

But Magoon is on his feet again and protesting vigorously. They're all nuts. It may be fun now, but what about two hours from now—with the fog comin' up? An' maybe a storm?

"What about a sinkin' an' drowndin'?" Magoon wants to know.

"Jesus, Mary and Joseph!" mutters Mrs. Geasling, crossing herself.

Well, Magoon doesn't want to go, not even to Norfolk. So, what about it? Only this, so far as Obadiah is concerned: If his passengers want to go then Magoon will have to ship along as far as Norfolk. It practically comes down to a vote.

It is probably Aikens who turns the tide. What have they got to go back to? Any of them? That's what Aikens wants to know. Why shouldn't they be happy for a chance to start out building a new kind of society? Lee is very proud of Aikens.

After due deliberation Mr. Fitchel thinks perhaps he would like to go, despite the horrified protests of Mamma Fitchel. "For once in mine life let me talk," exclaims Fitchel. "I'm so sick and tired of struggling to make a living. I'm so sick and tired of worrying about my name! I'm so sick and tired of worrying about being a Jew! I'm so tired of everything back there that I'll go along with anybody that will show me how to get out of it."

Now Obadiah would like to hear from Richard. Richard's father owns the boat, but his son hasn't said a word. That is because Richard can't think of anything to say. He would like them to have the trip and all, but—

"Oh, Richard's an old conservative," interrupts Lee.

"Richard—listen—just think of that lovely island lying there in the Caribbean waiting for us— Think, Richard, we can show the entire world how to live again. We'll live in human comradeship, we'll live in peace. Just think, Richard!"

It is the practical side that Richard cannot overlook. The thing they plan is illegal and violent. They're seizing property that belongs to someone else. Richard has some respect for law and order.

"Oh, Richard, is there nothing else in your mind but words like law and order, legal and illegal?" demands Lollie. "What about words like man, woman, love for one another? That's what we see on our island, Richard; that's why we want to go."

Richard is won over finally and there are general congratulations. But Obadiah still isn't satisfied. He must be sure that most of them really want to go before he decides what to do. He calls for a showing of hands—hands held high that they may be counted. Slowly, one by one, they come up, under the exhorting of Jonathan.

Mrs. Geasling is one of the last to join. She can't quite forget that her ol' man will give her hell. But young Mike wants to go—so she joins.

Now everyone has voted for the excursion except Mrs. Fitchel. She is still holding back on account of Sarah, and the store. But Papa Fitchel helps her decide—

"Ai, Mamma! So in the last years you're going to leave me? You're going to leave me alone, ha?"

"No, Papa, no—"

"So, for God's sake, put up y' hand already! I'm getting a cramp standing like this!"

And Mrs. Fitchel, weeping softly, raises her hand. There is a loud blast of a boat whistle as the curtain falls.

ACT III

Later that night the fog had closed in around the rear deck of the S.S. "Happiness." The whistle is blowing intermittently and a little nervously. The boat is deathly still. Mrs. Geasling, Mike and Mrs. Fitchel are asleep on deck chairs. Mr. Fitchel is parading up and down the deck with military stride and an air of professional importance. Mr. Fitchel is the watch.

Mrs. Fitchel stirs uneasily, opens a sleepy eye and inquires the ship's location. Sandy Hook light? What, not Asbury Park yet? So Mrs. Fitchel goes back to sleep.

"All is well!" calls Mr. Fitchel, resuming the watch.

Now Martha, Tessie, Pat, Lee, Aikens, Lollie and Richard come in. They are in the midst of what evidently has been a heavy argument, and if they don't calm down, Richard tells them, they'll be waking the whole boat.

Aikens, it appears, is for starting right in building a factory as soon as they reach the island. They will be needing an industry. Lollie is for building everything except department stores. But Lee is firm: The first thing they'll be needing will be a nursery school for the children. What children, Martha would like to know.

"Well, of course! You've got to have children—and right away, too!" Lee explains. "Look at Russia! What's the first thing they want? Children! How are you going to build a new society unless you have children?"

Still Martha is puzzled. Who is going to have all these children? She? The suggestion gives Martha pause. She is not sure she is going to like that job. When they explain that the others, too, are prepared to do their bit she feels better about it.

The whole idea, Lee explains, will be to bring up the children so they'll be creative men and women and not go after money—like her father. Which gives Aikens the idea of teaching. He will teach the children to write for the masses— But they're not going to have any masses, Tessie reminds him, unless they have gone and changed the idea again. Without any masses to worry about it looks as though it might be pretty dull for Aikens.

They have all gone now, except Richard and Lollie. These two are happy to be alone and grateful to Obadiah and Jonathan for what they are doing for them. "Suddenly—in a few hours everything is easy, everything is possible," reports Richard. "In all this excitement did I have time to tell you, Miss Popps, you're really quite lovely without those—balloon tires?" If Lollie had a reply it is smothered in kisses.

Richard has gone to fetch a wrap for Lollie. Red Magoon and Mrs. Loschavio find their way to the deck. They have given little Eileen the slip at last. Mrs. Loschavio is thrilled with the experience. Red is quite normal. He doesn't see any reason for getting excited about what's happened or what is likely to happen. They have done what they wanted to do. So far as Red is concerned he and Mrs. Loschavio are quits, and he's going his way alone. He doesn't relish getting his guts ripped open by any greasy wop.

"So that's why y' won't take y' chance at comin' to the island, huh?" sneers Mrs. Loschavio. "That's why y' gettin' off at Norfolk! It's the yella in y'! That's the whole stinkin' reason!"

"Now, listen. I like *me,*" growls Magoon. "I still got a long stretch of good times inside a me. I ain't ready t' die yet—f' any little tart, see?"

For that Mrs. Loschavio slaps Red a stinging blow in the face. He hesitates a moment, then dashes away, bumping into Eileen as he reaches the door. . . .

Mrs. Loschavio has taken Eileen into her arms and is comforting her. Complaining to Lollie between times that she can never go back to her husband—a murderous, jealous wop. Once, on a Fourth of July, he had thrown a kitchen knife at her. He'd kill her sure if she were to go home after staying out all night.

Richard has come back with Lollie's wrap, and Lollie puts it over the sleeping Eileen. Pretty soon Captain Obadiah and Jonathan, followed by Martha and the others, come back to the deck. It is peaceful there—quiet and calm.

It doesn't take more than Mrs. Loschavio's question as to what the island they're going to is like to set the Captain and Jonathan talking. "It's a place a wonder—aye, an' wonderment's gone out that world, back there, mate," says Obadiah.

"In days gone by when we dropped anchor in Yarmouth harbor," adds Jonathan; "home from a voyage t' Zealand, say, or China, we brought fresh wonders t' the town—made 'em shine with it, eh, Obadiah?"

"Made Yarmouthport folks proud an' glad t' be in the world! Made 'em shine with somethin' y' don't see much of nowadays—back there. Aye, it comes from lookin' at the world afresh, m' mates!"

The salon door has burst open and Mac Colman rushes in, followed by one or two others. They have news—news from the Radio Press Bureau. Just heard it over the radio. At eleven o'clock all harbor police had been sent to search for the S.S. "Happiness" and reported no trace of her could be found in the lane between Coney Island and New York City. She had been reported lost—perhaps sunk! Then, at midnight, a fishing boat going into New York reported sighting something that might have been an excursion boat headed for the ocean at 2 A.M. And they're still broadcasting every ten minutes!

Now a flash has come through that a Coast Guard cutter is on the way out. That would be the elder Pitman's work, of course. "He's a hard man but I never thought he'd send a battleship after me," muses Obadiah.

"What are we going to do?" queries Lollie, anxiously.

"They'll spot our lights," ventures Richard, plainly disappointed.

LOLLIE—Why don't we turn them off?

OBADIAH—With our lights out, we might have a chance in this

fog. (*Runs to foot of steps, calls up.*) Stevens! Oh, Stevens! Lights out! All over the ship!

STEVENS—Lights out! Aye, aye, sir! (*Suddenly the lights all over the ship go out.*)

MRS. LOSCHAVIO—What do we do now?

RICHARD—Wait and hope the fog will keep us covered up.

MARTHA (*quietly*)—A fine time a night t' be playin' hide an' seek with a cruiser.

JONATHAN—Look! Look!

AIKENS—Where?

JONATHAN—Dead to leeward—coming straight at us.

AIKENS—Look at that light.

OBADIAH—It's a searchlight—swingin' round like a wild-eyed thing.

RICHARD—It's the cutter, all right.

LOLLIE—They're right on top of us! (*A pause. Suddenly a powerful beam of light flashes across the deck nervously, then focuses and becomes still. The passengers stand trapped in the glare of the searchlight. The fog-horn blows. Then a far-off voice through a megaphone is heard.*)

VOICE (*off stage*)—Ahoy there! Ahoy! What's the trouble? (*Silence.*) United States Coast Guard Cutter "Cayuga" speaking —stop your engines!

OBADIAH—Richard, he's talkin' t' me.

VOICE—S.S. "Happiness"— What's the trouble? Stop y' engines! (*An ominous silence. The fog-horn moans— Suddenly the loud boom of a cannon is heard.*)

TESSIE—What's that?

OBADIAH—They're shooting at us. (*Sings out.*) A warnin' shot across our bow, Richard! They want me t' stop! Up t' my cabin, quick!

Another cannon report as the curtain falls.

We are back in Captain Obadiah's cabin. It is early morning. The radio is on and the passengers are huddled around it listening intently.

"Ladies and gentlemen, we have been bringing you news of the S.S. 'Happiness,' excursion steamer which left New York City yesterday morning for Coney Island but has not returned and is now—at this very moment, slowly but surely proceeding down the Jersey coast. The U. S. Coast Guard Cutter 'Cayuga' has been sent in pursuit of the runaway excursion boat but as yet we have no report—"

"Two points to starboard, Mr. Stevens," calls Obadiah. "Keep her hid in the fog bank there."

"Aye, sir."

Now there is an excited flash that the Coast Guard Cutter "Cayuga" has fired a warning shot across the bow of the runaway steamer.

A tremor of excitement runs through the passengers. Lee Pitman resents the authorities classifying the "Happiness" as a runaway. They are where they are following a free discussion, deliberate and calm. Jonathan, alas, is excited. This sneakin' cutter is no better than Rusty Morgan's pirates.

There is the boom of a cannon. The cutter is firing on them now. That calls for further decision. Richard is for going on. Lollie is against giving in. Let them fight for their rights. Obadiah changes course again and moves farther into the fog bank.

"We're like a country that votes to change its government and then is stopped from making that change by people like Magoon—like my father—with guns and radios and things like that!" declares Lee, firmly.

It is decided to fight. Over in the corner stand Zenas Hopkins' guns. Jonathan calls attention to them. Excitement mounts. But Obadiah would put a stop to that foolishness—

"Now, Jonathan Rich, you've come down out of Yarmouthport an'—an'—by God A'mighty I think you've done about enough f' one night," protests Obadiah.

"D'you think we'd fight Rusty Morgan's men off with a lot a hot words, Obadiah? Y' need guns!"

"I'm tellin' y' to mind y' tongue, Jonathan Rich! Comin' in here with y' charts and y' guns an'—an' I don't know what else y' got hatchin' up there in that crow's nest o' yours."

"Obadiah, y' never did have anythin' but love in y' heart—y' never could act. But here are some as wants to fight, am I right?"

The feeling is for fighting, all right, but just then Pop rushes in to announce that the cutter has lowered a motor dory, which is headed for the "Happiness" and is full of men.

Now Jonathan is excited and having a fine time. He passes out the guns—one to Richard, one to Mr. Fitchel, one to Aikens. Again Obadiah demands that they leave the guns alone. He won't have that—

"We have just received word that Captain Donald Woods of the Coast Guard Cutter 'Cayuga' has received orders from Federal authorities to board the S.S. 'Happiness,' seize Obadiah

Rich, captain of the vessel, and hold him as an outlaw, subject to investigation by Federal authorities on his return to New York," booms the radio. "According to the New York *American News* Captain Rich is criminally liable for detaining passengers against their will."

Obadiah is crushed beyond any help from Lee Pitman's sympathy. "How kin they go and say a thing like that?" he demands, with wounded pride. "Lord—Lord—here I am—leadin' y' outa the wilderness t' a promised land—an' they go and call me an outlaw."

The dory is closing in now. The men in her can be seen with their guns. Richard is for putting on more speed, but the old "Happiness" is doing about the best she can.

"Fast as old 'Happiness' ever had t' go—'fore Jonathan there came down outa Yarmouthport an' started—all this," mumbles Obadiah.

"Obadiah, darling, listen! All this—is for you—as well as for us! You mustn't listen to what they say! People who do new things, think new thoughts, are always called names—outlaws and things! Look—even me, they call me a Red—all sorts of horrible things! Obadiah! What does it matter? You and I—all of us—are sailing out of the old lanes, don't you see, darling! We have our eyes fixed on a new world! That's what matters, darling! Don't you see?"

Obadiah can't see, but he agrees Lee is a mighty sweet girl.

The dory has pulled alongside and the Federals have thrown a rope aboard and are climbing up. Now the engines are slowing down and Mr. Linton doesn't answer the signals. A moment later there is a pounding on the door of Obadiah's cabin and an order that he open up. Obadiah doesn't answer at first. Jonathan does the talking, and he warns whoever is interferin' with them goin' to Zenas Hopkins' Island that they'd better look out.

Outside there is a shot, and Jonathan promptly answers it. A moment later the door flies open and Captain Woods, pistol in hand, orders them all to put their hands up. One of his men collects the guns and the fight is over.

"Well, who the hell's pullin' off this shindig?" demands Captain Woods, turning on Stevens. "You?"

"No, sir," weakly answers Stevens.

WOODS—Well, y' needn't look so scared!

STEVENS (*rises; apologetically*)—I'm not scared, sir. It's just that I've been sort of sick, sir—in the gut.

WOODS—Oh, maybe that's why y' been floundering around out here in the dark all night long! Y'r tub's a menace t' navigation.

STEVENS—Oh, no, sir.

WOODS—Circling round an' round till I'm so dizzy I can't see straight!

OBADIAH—Circlin' round! Stevens! You mean—

STEVENS—I'm sorry, sir. It must a been m' stomach. (MRS. LOSCHAVIO *appears in the doorway. A sudden silence. She looks around strangely.*)

MRS. LOSCHAVIO (*standing silent a moment, then in a dull even tone*)—Are we goin' back? Is that what's happenin'? (*No answer.*) Is it? Is that what he's makin' us do? (*No answer. Suddenly she shrieks.*) For the love of God—answer me some-one!! (*Pleading with a whimper in her voice.*) Tell me, tell me—is he makin' us go back? Is he?

LOLLIE—Yes. We all have to go back.

MRS. LOSCHAVIO (*suddenly begins to laugh hysterically*)—That's funny! Jesus, that's funny! (*Suddenly she lashes out at the entire group.*) Then go on! Go on back! But I'm not, see! I'm not goin' back! No one kin make me go back! Not me!

WOODS—Come on now.

MRS. LOSCHAVIO—Leave me alone, d' y' hear!! D' y' think I'm goin' back t' that dirty little flat!! D' y' think I'm goin' down into the stink a' the markets again! Well, y' got another think comin', d' y' hear!! I'm gonna have things like I was picturin' out there last night! I'm gonna have things like y' said they was gonna be on the island! Y' can't get me t' go back there! Not me! Not me! (*She turns quickly, rushes off suddenly.*)

WOODS (*stopping* LOLLIE)—You stay here, sister.

The lights fade.

We are back on the lower deck. The lights are partly on. In the half darkness Eileen Loschavio comes dashing through the salon door calling frantically for her mother. "Mamma! Ma—where are y'?" cries the child as she runs back into the salon.

Afar off there is the whistle of a passing boat. Matson and Gilchrist of the crew come in and stop to compare time. It is around five o'clock they decide. In the half darkness Mrs. Loschavio appears on the stairs and waits for the men to go. Seeing the deck free she rushes for the rail and is starting to climb over when her daughter again appears, calling wildly.

Mrs. Loschavio has come down from the rail to quiet both the cries and the fears of her child in a voice choking with emotion. She has broken down completely now and is weeping. Eileen would comfort her mother if she could.

"Ma—don't. I won't tell Daddy y' wuz kissin' him. Honest."

"Listen, baby, Mamma can't go back there. She just can't." The hysteria has passed and Mrs. Loschavio is quiet and serious. "I don't like Daddy the way you do, baby. I don't like nothin' I get—but you."

"Me? You like me, Ma?"

"A course, baby. What should we do, Eileen? What should we do?"

"Gee! I don't know, Ma."

"Gee! Neither do I. Neither do I."

The others are beginning to gather. Martha and Tessie are still a little dazed. Tessie feels as though she had been drunk or somethin'. Martha just don't feel nothin' no more. Captain Woods of the "Cayuga" is running the ship now, he announces from the upper deck, and he wants them all down on the passenger deck till the "Happiness" gets in.

Obadiah, Aikens, Lee and Jonathan come down the stairs. Obadiah is pretty low. It hurts him to bring his passengers back into harbor this way. The others would comfort him if they could.

"This is the way it has to be, Obadiah," Lee tells him. "Excursions must end."

"We can't escape," adds Aikens.

"Aye, I see that now."

"The sun's coming up."

"Look, you can see the city."

"Our island seems a long way off now, Obadiah," sighs Jonathan.

"Aye, Jonathan," answers Obadiah, simply and gently. "But let our white and gold ship come sailin' into harbor again—bearin' on her decks a new crew of men and women—y' topsails shinin' in the mornin' sun and y' innards blazin' with the spirit we found last night, out there—an' our excursion'll mean something, mates. Aye. Take the courage and the vision back there with you. Fight for the things y' want back there, like y' fought for your far away island last night. Be men an' women armed with love an' wonder, mates, an' make y' life a glowin' thing. Will y' do that?"

There is a long silence, and then reactions are registered. Mrs. Loschavio has turned to Eileen to make sure her little girl had heard. Fitchel decides in that moment not to change his name but to live and die the Jew he was born.

Now there is a great blowing of whistles, as though the ships of the harbor were welcoming the "Happiness" home. And now Stevens has rushed down from the Captain's cabin to report that great news has just come over the radio. Mr. Pitman says he is goin' to keep the "Happiness" in service another year! Obadiah can hardly believe that.

STEVENS—Yes! It's true. The whole city's been calling him up wanting to go on a trip like us too! So he's not going to sell her off!

OBADIAH—Well, bless me!

PASSENGERS—Wonderful! Oh, Obadiah!

OBADIAH (*laughing*)—Thank y', mates! Y' ain't gonna use that dirty ol' nickel subway next year, are y'? Y' just come aboard the S.S. "Happiness" f' a nice quiet trip! Nice day, Stevens!

STEVENS—Yes, sir! Sun up high an' bright!

OBADIAH—That's the way I like it f' my passengers!

JONATHAN—I been thinkin', Obadiah—

OBADIAH—Yes, Jonathan?

JONATHAN—He said y' was goin' t' be Captain a this ship next year, didn't he?

OBADIAH (*proudly*)—That's what he said, Jonathan!

JONATHAN (*nudging him*)—Don't y' see, Obadiah, m' mate! We got another chance t' try it again! We might get there—next year!

"The band has struck up 'Auld Lang Syne.' The passengers have caught the tune and are singing. The whistles are blowing loudly—as the boat steams up the river."

THE CURTAIN FALLS

TOVARICH

A Comedy in Three Acts

BY JACQUES DEVAL

(English Adaptation by Robert E. Sherwood)

"TOVARICH," which on the authority of a press staff and a variety of Russian volunteers is pronounced "Toe-*varr*-itch," with the accent on the "varr," is one of those interesting theatrical exhibits—a play with a history. A simple history, but filled with excitement. It was written by Jacques Deval, a French dramatist of standing, in what he was pleased to describe as his off moments. It was produced in Paris at practically the same time as a second Deval opus, a tragic drama entitled "Priere pour les Vivants," which was decidedly not written in off moments, but to which the author had devoted two years of serious thought. In Paris "Priere pour les Vivants" was a quick failure and "Tovarich" ran for eight hundred performances. By the end of the season of its production it had been shown in translated versions in practically every country of Europe and had proved an outstanding success in each of them.

Adapted for the English-speaking stage by Robert Emmet Sherwood, "Tovarich" ran a year and a day in London with Sir Cedric Hardwicke and Eugenie Leontovich playing the leads. When Gilbert Miller, the producer, realized that the London run promised to continue indefinitely he organized a second company, with John Halliday and Marta Abba, an Italian actress with a Continental following, in the leading roles. This company played for five weeks in the British provinces. Its leading members were then brought to America. "Tovarich" opened in October, 1936, in New York, immediately duplicating its European success, and ran through the season.

This is, by the frank confessions of all concerned, a truly simple comedy builded on one of the oldest of romantic, dramatic and comic situations, that of members of nobility forced into service to the consequent embarrassment of many persons. It is what a majority of drama critics refer to as a theme that is "well-worn" if not "trite." But it is also, they fairly admit, usually sure-fire. No attempt is made, either by M. Deval or Mr. Sherwood, to violate the conventions associated with the use of this theme, save in the particular of the play's ending. In this instance the high-borns are not returned to the aristocracy from which they sprung, but are permitted to continue a normal way among the bourgeoise with whom, in their dilemma, they had happily mingled.

The opening scene of "Tovarich" is a room in the Hôtel du Quercy in the Rue de la Glaciere in Paris. It is about 11 o'clock of a winter morning, a bright, fresh day from the limited glimpse we have of it through a side window. This is a good-sized bedroom, with bed, washstand and chest of drawers of the cheaper grade. A table, an armchair, a bedstand complete the fairly meager furnishings.

The Prince Mikail Alexandrovitch Ouratieff is lying on the bed, partially dressed, polishing a boot, an occupation of which he soon tires. He is a youngish man of prepossessing address. The Grand Duchess Tatiana Petrovna, his wife, is occupied in an adjoining bathroom with a bit of washing. A wadded sample of the washing which she shortly appears to display with some pride to His Highness represents what is left of his only shirt. The tails are very short. Her Highness has been obliged to sacrifice them to His Highness' need of handkerchiefs. She had used her own chemises as long as they held out, but when they were gone the shirt tails were all that remained.

Prince Mikail is willing to admit that the Grand Duchess Tatiana is, even as her august cousin had announced at their wedding, a saint. But the compliment, he adds, was to her devotion and not to her manners.

"You were born a Grand Duchess," he says, with mock seriousness, "and you lacked the opportunity for social contacts that was given the rest of us. You had too *many* English governesses. They gave you the wrong start in life."

For which aspersion upon her character the suddenly angered Tatiana commands Mikail to stop whatever he is doing and appear before her. She is using the foot of the bed as a throne when he arrives. He makes a rather sorry attempt to click his bare heels and bow low.

"Prince Mikail Alexandrovitch Ouratieff, aide-de-camp to His Imperial Majesty," Mikail intones, solemnly, "offers Her Highness the Grand Duchess Tatiana Petrovna, his humble apologies."

He bows even lower, and when he straightens up Tatiana slaps him soundly across the face.

"Ouch!" exclaims the Prince.

"How dare you say 'ouch'? demands Her Highness, angrily. "You're an officer. You are not permitted to feel pain."

"Very well, Highness. The ouch is withdrawn."

And now Tatiana, with a little rippling squeal, has thrown her arms about Mikail and drawn him down on the bed beside her, kissing him fiercely, shouting that he is forgiven completely as she kisses him again.

"And you'll let me be just a little bit sad if I want to?"

"I shall be sad with you—always. Always!"

"Ah, God! How good it is to be Russian!" exclaims Mikail, drawing Tatiana to him wildly.

"And insane!" she adds.

"Life for us is so sad, and so beautiful."

"And so tiresome—"

Tatiana is hungry. So is Mikail, for that matter. Tatiana would go shopping. Mikail would be ever so glad if she did, but what would she shop with? There is no money. At least there is but a hundred francs left, and eighty of that they owe for rent.

Still, Tatiana is not discouraged. She will take the hundred francs. She will pay the landlord his eighty francs and the next day she will borrow two hundred. She already has collected fifty francs from the landlord for making him the Duke of Courlande. This time she will make him a Prince, so he will be entitled to precede himself into dinner.

"Darling, do you trust me?" Tatiana suddenly demands.

"Within reason, my love," guardedly admits Mikail.

TATIANA—Then believe me. I swear, by Saint Peter and Saint Paul—I swear to bring back eighty-five francs. I shall bring back ninety francs! I shall buy some cutlets of horse and some potatoes, and I shall bring back ninety-five francs and two artichokes!

MIKAIL—You're very fond of artichokes, aren't you?

TATIANA—No, I hate them, but while the grocer is selecting the poorest potatoes, I shall be left alone among the artichokes.

MIKAIL (*reverently*)—I reverently beg that the Father of all living may look the other way, that he will not see the Grand Duchess Tatiana Petrovna . . . cousin to the Czar . . . (*He makes the sign of the cross.*) . . . arrested for stealing artichokes.

Tatiana—Nonsense! I am never arrested!

MIKAIL—You have been incredibly lucky.

TATIANA—It is more than luck, Mikail. It is the intervention of God—the God of all the Russians. Why—the other day, the grocer almost saw me as I was letting a bunch of radishes fall into this bag, but his eyes were miraculously diverted to the ceiling.

MIKAIL—Tatiana—give me that bag. I shall go myself!

TATIANA—By St. Christopher, no! A general of cavalry to be seen in the streets of Paris with cutlets of horse!—Never!

MIKAIL—But it is quite all right for a Grand Duchess, eh?

TATIANA—A Grand Duchess is above appearances!

MIKAIL (*with resignation*)—Very well—go on and commit your pathetic thieveries. But what of tomorrow—and all the tomorrows that follow? The Russian God may grow weary of elevating grocers' eyes.

TATIANA—Then we will find something to sell. We have always found . . .

MIKAIL—There's not much left. (*He looks about the room with a sigh.*) Except my sword . . .

TATIANA—The sword of Alexander the Third! Never!

MIKAIL—And the flag . . .

TATIANA—The flag of the Imperial Guard. Better let us die together, wrapped in its folds!

MIKAIL—Then that leaves nothing but the icon.

TATIANA—May heaven forgive you. (*She faces the icon and crosses herself.*) I would sooner sell my ears.

Tatiana is at the door ready to go when there is a loud knock. Mikail opens and admits a dark, pretty, but savage looking midinette. She carries a hat box and enquires for a Mme. Courtois. They tell her there is no such person in that apartment. She spies the icon and knows they are Russian. A moment later she is curtseying before Tatiana and begging her pardon for her stupidity in not recognizing Her Highness immediately.

It is, thinks Mikail, a pretty gesture, but a moment later, when Tatiana picks up the hat box and finds it empty the ruse is discovered. The young woman's name is Olga. She is a spy for the Soviet. Cornered, she turns upon them viciously and demands to know what they are going to do with the money they have stolen from Russia—

"It came from the blood and the sweat of the millions, and now you hold it for yourselves . . ." screams Olga.

Tatiana would have Mikail throw the intruder out, but Mikail would get a little information first. Who is Olga? Was she sent by one Gorotchenko? What did she hope to gain? Is she a real Communist, or just another French imitation?

To all of which queries Olga repeats a snappy "I don't know."

"You can tell Tovarich Gorotchenko we'd be grateful if some day he would honor us with his own presence," says Tatiana.

"And tell him that you found us still in good health, though slightly undernourished," adds Mikail. "Tell him we're prepared, at any moment, to be caught in one of the traps which he is thoughtfully laying for us. And when he has caught us he can burn us, by slow degrees, in the scorching flames of Red Terror—but our policy will remain unchanged: not a billion, not a million, not a thousand, not a sou!"

"Fine talk—you white-livered thieves!" sneers Olga. "You think you're safe, with your money, because you're in Paris, in the bourgeois fortress, with gendarmes to guard you. But we know how to take back what was stolen from us. And when we do, we'll also take your miserable, worthless, evil lives."

Olga has picked up her box and, with a vicious blast, blown out the light under the icon. She slams the door as she goes out. Tatiana, disturbed and angry, relights the candle. Mikail is serious. It is quite possible that one day one of these spies will kill them both. Is Tatiana afraid? Is he? There is a silent renewal of their faith as they seek each other's arms. . . .

Now Tatiana is ready for her shopping tour and Mikail has gone back to bed. He is expecting visitors, but he feels that he can cope with them quite satisfactorily in bed. They will come as representatives of the French bankers, and for bankers Mikail has but the one unvarying reply:

"Not a billion, not a million, not a thousand, not a sou! . . ."

Tatiana has gone and the bankers have arrived. They are Chauffourier-Doubieff, governor of the Bank of France, and General Count Brekenski, aide-de-camp to the current pretender to the Russian throne, both quite impressively formal. To meet their formality Mikail jumps out of bed, finds his monocle, adjusts it with care and bows from the waist with dignity. He can, however, stand the monocle no longer than it takes Chauffourier-Doubieff to introduce Count Brekenski, whose name is long and his titles even longer. In the presence of so distinguished a compatriot Mikail is dissuaded with some little difficulty from putting on what is left of his white shirt.

The visitors would assure Mikail of their great sorrow over the deplorable situation in which they find him. Chauffourier-Doubieff speaks for the Minister of Finance of France and Brekenski for His Imperial Highness, the pretender to the throne of Russia. The banker, having ascertained the exact amount of Mikail's account with the Bank of France, would like permission to reveal the sum to the Count Brekenski, which Mikail readily grants—

"With all compound interest included," reports Chauffourier-Doubieff, "the account of Prince Ouratieff amounts to exactly three billion, eight hundred and eighty-three million, two hundred thousand and sixty-two francs, sixty-five centimes. In round figures, four billion francs."

Brekenski, after moistening his lips with some effort, finds the sum truly impressive. Mikail admits as much, but insists that it is possible for one to get used to anything—even the possession of four billion francs.

CHAUFFOURIER—Excellency, how long must we continue with this absurd situation? That vast sum of money is lying idle, doing no good to you nor to anyone. Can you forget that France, the unshakable ally of your lamented sovereign, is today struggling amidst the most bitter difficulties?

MIKAIL—I know, my dear Governor . . . I regret it with all my heart . . . France's sorrows are my sorrows . . . France has given sanctuary to me and to many of my countrymen. At great risk to her national security, she has even allowed some of us to drive taxis. She is Queen among realms—mistress of all mankind—but that money is not mine; it belongs to the Czar.

CHAUFFOURIER—Yes—but it could so easily be converted into French Government bonds. We can offer you any one of twelve state loans, each one more . . .

BREKENSKI (*interrupting*)—Without forgetting either, that our holy Russia is groaning under its tyrants, that His Imperial Highness is ready to put himself at the head of his generous loyalists, to reconquer the sacred soil . . . whenever the funds for this campaign are forthcoming.

CHAUFFOURIER (*vehemently*)—Millions which the Bank of France is perfectly ready to advance, against the conversion into any one of twelve state loans . . . if . . .

BREKENSKI—You will be the liberator of Russia, the restorer of the throne. . . .

CHAUFFOURIER—Need I add that my Government will be happy to render—homage, as extensive as it would be discreet, to your affectionate confidence?

MIKAIL—Gentlemen . . . gentlemen . . . this is all very fine . . . but can't we be more precise? You are about to offer me something. What is it?

CHAUFFOURIER (*quickly*)—Five millions.

BREKENSKI (*quickly*)—Ten millions.

ɔ by Vandamm Studio, New York.

"TOVARICH"

ikail: What is your Christian name?
ɔrotchenko: Dmitri.
ikail: Dmitri Gorotchenko! . . . One of the most heartless, soulless, ruthless blackguards that desecrated the God-formed surface of this earth. . . .

(Cecil Humphreys, John Halliday, Marta Abba)

CHAUFFOURIER—Think of it, Excellency, financial security to the end of your days.

MIKAIL—Fifteen millions, to a man who can order four billion buns for his breakfast! Gentlemen, it is ludicrous! However, my dear Count, I authorize you to say to His Highness that my person and my fortune are entirely his . . . (*Exclamation of joy from* BREKENSKI *and the* COUNT. *Both rise.*) And that I ask no compensation either from his High Highness, or from the French Government.

The joy of the visitors would know no bounds if Mikail had not quickly added that he referred only to his services as a soldier and to a personal fortune of twenty francs. With that realization they are quite disgusted. Mikail, however, tries again to convince them that the four billion francs are not his to give. He had received them from the hands of a czar, it is into the hands of a czar he will give them back, and neither the threats of Brekenski to invoke the law, nor the continued cajoleries of the pleading Chauffourier-Doubieff have the least effect upon him.

"But, Excellency, what does our bank ask?" repeats Chauffourier-Doubieff. "A simple conversion into state loans . . . a mere matter of bookkeeping."

"Prince Ouratieff, you doubtless have your own reasons for your arrogant stubbornness," adds Brekenski, with some sign of anger; "but permit me to say that in my eyes your refusal . . . suggests not only bad faith but down-right treason. And I feel sure that His Highness will agree . . ."

MIKAIL (*arising with considerable show of spirit*)—Great God! If I refuse to agree to this mere matter of bookkeeping, I'm a traitor. So be it, gentlemen. But . . . I must remain free to make my own mistakes in my own way. That was my master's wish. The Czar of Russia trusted me. In his wisdom, he knew that calamity was at hand, and a few weeks before the revolution he caused those colossal sums to be placed in the Bank of France in my name and at my disposal. His only stipulation to me was that I should administer it in the best interests of my sovereign. Make careful note of those words, Count Brekenski,—the best interests of my sovereign. I am serving those interests—perhaps stupidly—but with all the devotion at my command. I see no reason to squander that money in the financing of a counter-revolution which will be doomed to grotesque and horrible failure. It would take far more than four billion francs to wreck the Soviet

Government. We shall accomplish that only when we can prove to the world and to ourselves that we're more fitted to govern than they are.

BREKENSKI—You are speaking for yourself, Prince Ouratieff.

MIKAIL—Precisely. And for myself I say to you—not a billion, not a million (BREKENSKI *is annoyed*), not a thousand, not a sou! It was a crowned Czar, not a pretender, who gave it to me. To a crowned Czar it will be returned. I tell you this, gentlemen, in the hope that it will relieve you of the necessity for further visits to this dismal quarter of Paris.

CHAUFFOURIER—Have you considered the possibility of your death?

MIKAIL—I am reminded of that frequently. But God is a Russian. He will take care of the money—and me—after I have been murdered.

CHAUFFOURIER—*Murdered?*

MIKAIL (*calmly*)—Yes.

BREKENSKI—Your life has been threatened?

MIKAIL—The representatives of the other Russia are also concerned about those four billion francs. I think they will spare no effort to get them.

BREKENSKI—But—it is unthinkable that they might . . .

MIKAIL—Don't worry, my dear Count. They may seize me; they may get my right hand—but they will not obtain my signature.

CHAUFFOURIER—And don't *you* worry, Excellency. Our police are excessively vigilant. Why—would you believe it?—in this district, not so much as an artichoke is stolen, without their knowing of it at once.

Now it is revealed that Tatiana's small but consistent abstractions from the vegetable marts have all been duly noted and reported upon by the police. The Government has been quite content to assist the Ouratieffs, if this is the way they prefer to live. Therefore salesmen have been instructed to look the other way whenever Tatiana has been observed to have her eye on a particular artichoke or other vegetable, and report the same to the authorities. The Government would even be willing to do a great deal more—

At which embarrassing moment Tatiana returns with a shopping bag bursting with supplies, a bottle of champagne under one arm and a huge bundle of flowers under the other.

Tatiana is pleased to accept the homage of the distinguished visitors, but during the introductions she is obliged to apologize while she extracts from the top of her blouse the two artichokes she has placed there. They scratch. Mikail is naturally disturbed and eager to end the interview. Which he does with a dignity that is only lightly put aside when he calls Chauffourier-Doubieff back from the door and places in his hat the two artichokes Tatiana has taken from her blouse. . . .

Further investigation of Tatiana's bag discloses a pound jar of caviare. For Mikail this is a little too much. Caviare at 200 francs a pound! Tatiana must be spoken to. Tatiana *is* spoken to, but with practically no result. She had, it is true, failed to pay the rent, because she could not find the landlord. She had spent the entire 100 francs for the food and the wine. She had to. This happens to be an anniversary. Five hundred years ago today Feodor the Third had vanquished Solimar at Samarcand, and that victory calls for a celebration. What are five hundred years to eternal Russia? It also happens that this time she had paid for the artichokes which Mikail had so nobly returned to their host. The caviare and wine? Well, they're different.

There is nothing left for them to do now except to move, Mikail insists. From the hotel certainly and probably from France. They simply cannot remain as the wards of the Government. Tatiana, too, is agreed that they must go. The French are swine to put them thus in their debt. They must be paid back, even if Mikail is obliged to draw from the bank—

"It would only be a little bit, to save our honor," pleads Tatiana. "Surely heaven would forgive us for that."

"I would not trust myself," answers Mikail. "If I touch a penny of that money, we're lost. I don't do things by halves. In a fortnight we should be living at the Ritz. No, my darling,—our honor has been lost and I see no prospect of regaining it this side of the grave."

"We must never again submit to their treacherous charity," Tatiana agrees. "We will go to the ends of the earth. But when we get there . . . what shall we have to eat?"

Mikail has no answer. He can think of but one other solution: He will have to work! Tatiana is horrified at the thought. Even in fun Mikail should not say such things. But Mikail is firm. After all, Admiral Soukhomine works. The Admiral navigates a taxi. And Colonel Trepanoff works. The Colonel does a dagger dance at the Kasbeck. Mikail could do a dagger dance, as he tries to illustrate with a kitchen knife. It looks much too dangerous to Tatiana.

No, Mikail should not do any dagger dance. Rather than that Tatiana would pose for an artist. One had asked her. He would like to paint her in the nude, he said. Mikail would not permit anything so degrading, even though they should be condemned to misery and hunger all their days—

"Yes—misery and hunger—the greatest luxuries of our race!" repeats Tatiana, soulfully, clinging the harder to Mikail. "We were born to suffer and to love it. Life for us is so beautiful and so sad."

There is a knock at the door. They bid the visitor enter without changing their positions. He is revealed as Martelleau, "a little man, poorly but neatly dressed." Martelleau has come in the interests of a little woman in Room 16, whose baby had been born two days before and who is in dire straits. He knows their Highnesses will be glad to give a little something, and he knows they are Highnesses from the gossip of the house.

Tatiana and Mikail would be ever so willing to give as much as a thousand francs, if they had a thousand francs, but having nothing—

Martelleau can quite understand. He, too, has been without work for a long time. But he has not lost hope. When the little woman upstairs is again well enough to work they will find a place. The little woman is not Martelleau's wife, but they will do very well together without disturbing Mme. Martelleau, who has a place as nurse in Amiens. There are frequently calls for married couples in newspaper advertisements of domestic situations vacant.

"You know, my pigeon," says Tatiana, sitting beside Mikail on the bed, "it sounds like an ideal existence." Then, turning to Matelleau, she asks: "Are there many such opportunities?"

"Oh, yes, you hear of them now and then. There is a most excellent one in the paper today." Martelleau produces the paper to prove it. "Number four, Avenue de Tourville, Butler and Housemaid. Two rooms of their own on the sixth floor . . . with servants' lift. Luxurious surroundings. Use of motor car to go shopping in. One Sunday out of two. Absolute Paradise!"

TATIANA (*sadly*)—And you and the little woman will have all that?

MARTELLEAU—No—they won't wait for her recovery. But—I must be getting on with the collection. Good day, Madame.

TATIANA (*bundling up the food*)—No—wait! You are not going away empty-handed. Give this to the little woman and the brat.

MARTELLEAU—But will you have anything left?

TATIANA—That doesn't matter. Go on—take it all.

MIKAIL (*resignedly*)—Don't hesitate, my friend. She is a saint.

MARTELLEAU—Oh, I can see that. Madame, I can never repay you for this.

TATIANA—Oh—yes, you can. Give me that newspaper.

MARTELLEAU—But of course . . .

TATIANA—No—don't go yet. (*She takes the champagne and gives it to him.*) Tell the little woman to drink to the health of Russia.

MARTELLEAU (*overcome with emotion*)—Thank you—thank you— God bless and preserve you. . . .

TATIANA (*closing the door and turning to* MIKAIL)—It doesn't really matter if the victory of Samarcand is celebrated in Room 4 or in Room 16. You weren't really hungry, were you, darling? Tell me you weren't.

MIKAIL—I was not.

TATIANA—No more was I. (*She looks at the paper.*) Two well-heated rooms—luxurious surroundings—servants' lift—one Sunday out of two. . . . Absolute Paradise!

MIKAIL—Are you trying to tell me that we might be "a married couple"?

TATIANA (*exultantly*)—Yes, yes, yes! (*She goes to him and throws her arms about him.*) You the butler and I the housemaid!

MIKAIL—But are we fitted for such grandeur?

TATIANA—Why not? You have been a chamberlain and I a lady-in-waiting.

MIKAIL—That was in Petersburg, for the Czar!

TATIANA—And this is in Paris—but still for the Czar!

MIKAIL (*excitedly*)—My sainted darling! (*He sees an opportunity for some grandiose acting.*) I believe it is possible! I see myself again, throwing open the windows of the Imperial chamber and announcing: "Majesty, this morning there is snow." (TATIANA *is properly appreciative of his performance.*) And then, with perfect grace presenting belt and tunic to Nicholas Alexandrovitch. And you doing the fair hair of your Imperial mistress, fetching her gloves, telling poor Frederiks that Her Majesty will not be visible today. We were good servants, Tatiana. We will be good servants again.

The matter of references is quickly settled. They write their own. At least Tatiana writes a reference at Mikail's dictation, recommending Michel Dubrovsky and his wife Tina most highly as having been, while in the employ of Grand Duchess Tatiana Petrovna, Princess Ouratieff, "faithful, loyal, exceptionally intelligent, skillful, unobtrusive and honest." Also they do not drink.

"Do you think we've said enough about our good points?" questions Tatiana.

"We mustn't exaggerate," protests Mikail. "Go and put on your hat."

"You know the Duke of Courlande may object to us leaving so abruptly."

"We're not leaving officially. We are going for a little walk."

Mikail starts the packing. The flag and the sword must go with them. And the icon. Tatiana has gone to fetch the clothes from the other room when Martelleau returns. He had come to tell them that the little woman had gobbled up everything except the caviare, and that he had managed to put that away, just to show the little woman how harmless it was.

"Oh, Madame, you *are* a saint," declares Martelleau, with feeling, as Tatiana reappears. "And this day you have earned a higher place in heaven."

"With a servants' lift, I hope," fervently adds Mikail.

Mikail has taken the flag and draped it about Tatiana's shoulders. The sword he places down one trousers leg, wincing comically as the cold steel strikes his bare leg.

"Does it show much?" he would know, as he takes a few limping steps in front of Tatiana.

"You will become used to it," she comforts him. "It is a long walk to the Avenue de Tourville."

MIKAIL (*looking round*)—Is there anything else?

TATIANA (*looking round*)—No.

MIKAIL—Then we must go. We mustn't keep our employers waiting.

TATIANA—Wait! Let us finish the vodka. (*She gets bottle off the washstand, fills two glasses, gives him one.*) This is for courage! (*They drink Russian fashion, link arms.*)

MIKAIL—A life for the Czar, Tatiana.

TATIANA—A life for the Czar, Mikail. (*When they finish they throw the glasses onto the floor.* MIKAIL *limps to the door, throws it open.*)

MIKAIL—Proceed, Highness! (*He starts to bow, but the sword catches him.*)

TATIANA—Don't try to bow!

Mikail follows with shopping bag as the curtain falls.

ACT II

Both the Charles Duponts are dressing in Fernande Dupont's boudoir. It is an interesting room, "chic—modernistic—but containing an unuttered confession of bourgeoise bad taste."

Charles Dupont, a quite average banker type of middle years, is irritated at the moment because he cannot find his other shoe. If Fernande would give a little more attention to the servant question they would have a proper staff and Charles would be able to complete his dressing in peace.

Fernande is unruffled. The servant problem is a difficult one. Servants are "a vanishing race, dying out, like the buffaloes," she insists. "The only ones I've seen in the last week are either escaped convicts or congenital idiots."

"Well, if you see any more escaped convicts engage them," snaps Charles. "Either that or we'll move to a hotel."

Charles is in a state of mind. In addition to the problem of the shoe, he is suffering a splitting headache which a bottle of aspirin has failed to relieve. "I think I'll have to go away somewhere," wails Charles; "if there's any place on earth where you don't hear endless talk about economic chaos—threats of war—and the collapse of civilization—and where I won't ever have to dress for dinner."

At which psychological moment Louise, the maid, appears to announce that there is another married couple below and that they believe in monarchy. Madame had told Louise always to find out the political opinions of applicants for positions. . . .

Tatiana and Mikail are dressed as they were when they left their hotel. Mikail walks a bit stiffly, which is entirely in keeping with their formal attitude during the investigation.

"You're looking for a place?" Fernande begins, pleasantly.

"Yes, Madame; we saw your esteemed advertisement and so we have come. . . ."

TATIANA—We are eager to serve you, Madame.

FERNANDE (*suspiciously*)—Weren't you happy in your previous place?

TATIANA (*eagerly*)—Ah, yes, madame. We have always been divinely happy—even when . . .

MIKAIL (*interrupting*)—But our employers went abroad.

CHARLES—Are you Swiss?

MIKAIL—We are Russian, sir.

TATIANA—White Russian, sir.

FERNANDE—Who were your previous employers?

MIKAIL—His Excellency General Prince Ouratieff.

TATIANA—And his wife, Her Imperial Highness the Grand Duchess Tatiana Petrovna.

CHARLES (*impressed*)—Really!

FERNANDE—You have references, of course?

TATIANA—Oh, yes, Madame. (*She hands it to* FERNANDE.)

CHARLES—Where else have you been in service?

TATIANA—For a while we were with the Duke of Courlande.

MIKAIL (*silencing her*)—That was merely a visit.

FERNANDE—This reference is most encouraging—"faithful—loyal—exceptionally intelligent—unobtrusive." Evidently you pleased the Grand Duchess. I shall ask for an interview with her.

TATIANA—Oh, no, Madame. Her Highness is in—in—where *is* Her Highness?

MIKAIL (*thinking very hard*)—Let me see . . .

FERNANDE—This is written from Spoletto.

MIKAIL—Spoletto! Of course.

FERNANDE (*handing back the reference*)—Did you have another place before you were with Her Highness?

TATIANA—Yes, Madame. We had another master in Russia.

CHARLES—Who?

TATIANA—He is dead. (*Both she and* MIKAIL *cross themselves.*)

CHARLES—Yes, yes . . . That's all right. Killed in the Revolution?

MIKAIL—Yes, sir.

FERNANDE—I can see that you *are* loyal. What wages do you expect?

MIKAIL (*vaguely*)—Wages, Madame?

FERNANDE—How much do you expect to be paid?

TATIANA (*helplessly*)—We don't know, Madame. We don't know at all.

FERNANDE—Well—what did you receive in your last place?

MIKAIL—Just what was it, Tati— Tina?

TATIANA—I can't quite remember—not a billion—not a million—not a thousand—

FERNANDE—I should hope not.

CHARLES (*helpfully*)—Perhaps you're not very familiar with *French* money.

MIKAIL—That's it, sir! That's it exactly!

FERNANDE (*with some impatience*)—Whatever it was—I shall give—seven hundred francs to the butler and four hundred to the maid.

TATIANA—That will not do!

FERNANDE—I consider it a very good wage.

MIKAIL—It is a most admirable wage!

TATIANA—No! Four hundred for the butler and seven hundred for the maid.

FERNANDE—You may arrange that between yourselves.

CHARLES—When can you come to us?

MIKAIL (*with a glance at* TATIANA)—Well, sir—

CHARLES—We are in a great hurry.

MIKAIL—Then we could arrange to start—let us say—now.

CHARLES—Splendid!

Charles and Fernande, having withdrawn to the end of the room for a conference, shortly return to announce that Mikail and Tatiana may consider themselves engaged—on a temporary basis, of course.

It is a little difficult for the new servants to account for their lack of luggage. They have no other clothes, they explain, having worn their native Russian costumes in their last place. Luckily the Duponts have clothes worn by former servants, and these will do for the present. There are four in the Dupont family, Fernande and husband and their two children, Monsieur Dupont and Mademoiselle Helene.

Monsieur Dupont, being a banker, is extremely particular about accounts with trades people. Mikail is visibly shocked at the discovery of his employer's business, but he attributes his reaction to the fact that his former employer, the Prince Ouratieff, loathed bankers with a deep loathing. He will, of course, make every effort to overcome the prejudices of Ouratieff.

Charles is somewhat worried about Mikail's stiff-legged rheumatism, and Fernande is a little anxious about the looks she had observed her husband casting in the direction of the new maid. But, on the whole, it is agreed that "Michel" and "Tina" will do. . . .

George and Helene Dupont have burst into the room. "They are as formal and snobbish as their parents; devoid of all apparent youthfulness, although she is about 18 and he is 20." The younger Duponts would know about the funny looking couple they passed in the hall. The new servants? Incredible! "He looks more like a waiter than a butler," says George. "She seems a cheap, impudent little thing," adds Helene.

"Perhaps you two superior beings will be interested to know

that they worked for sixteen years for Prince Ouratieff and his wife, the Grand Duchess Tatiana," counters Fernande.

Their mother would also have George and Helene treat the new servants with more consideration and respect than they had shown their predecessors. Mikail will not be expected to take Helene's Pekinese for a walk every hour, and if George has insulting remarks to make about them he can at least wait until they have left the room. . . .

Mikail, having found Charles Dupont's shoe, brings it in on a little cushion. With extreme suavity he manages to ease the master's foot into the shoe, calmly smoothing the ruffled nerves caused by the headache as he does so. Now Mikail has called the Banker Chauffourier-Doubieff on the phone, at the somewhat sharp insistence of Charles, and a business engagement of some importance has been arranged. Mikail's distaste for bankers is still apparent, and not at all pleasing to his employer.

Tatiana, returned a little stealthily to the room, frankly adds to what she hears of their conversation that there would have been no Russian revolution had it not been for the bankers. Charles is ready to explode. He is of a mind to send his new servants away forthwith, but is temporarily deterred by the extravagant and dramatic pleading of Tatiana. She is on her knees, with both arms about her master's legs, and Charles is not only moved to compassion but to considerable embarrassment as well. He manages finally to convince Tatiana that she is forgiven, and even submits, as she leaves, to kissing her perfunctorily upon the brow, which she tells him, is the Russian kiss of reconciliation. . . .

Mikail has brought the headache medicine. It is, he confides, after Charles has downed the draught, concocted of "pure gin—with twenty drops of ether, a hundred grains of salt and a hundred and fifty grains of gunpowder."

"Gunpowder!" cries Charles.

"Yes, sir;—I took the liberty of opening one of your cartridges."

"Gunpowder! Good God! If I light a cigarette will I explode?"

"No, sir. The powder is damp. And—may I enquire after your headache, sir?"

"Headache?" repeats Charles, absently. "Oh! It—it seems to have gone."

"It never fails, sir."

By the time Mikail has readjusted his master's tie, and refolded the handkerchief he carries in the breast pocket of his coat, Charles has become convinced that he is going to like his new servant. He is not inclined, however, to indorse either the kiss of gratitude, which Mikail is at pains to implant on his shoulder, or any of the other kissing customs which appear to be excessively common to Russians. If Mikail doesn't mind, they will leave kissing out of the daily routine.

For a moment, after the Duponts have left them, Mikail and Tatiana happily express to each other their gratitude at the good luck that has found them this Dupont Paradise. Their bed is wonderful! The view from the window is of the Orthodox church! That is almost like being in Russia. The whiff of chicken they have had from the pot Louise, the cook, is preparing for them is heavenly—

"We'll be good servants, won't we, Tatiana?" feelingly demands Mikail.

"There will be none to compare with us in the whole land of France. We have been blessed with a home—at last—after all these long years. . . . A bed of our own—and a window that looks upon Russia. We will be worthy of such blessings."

Mikail has taken Tatiana in his arms as George Dupont comes in. They are not in the least disturbed.

George has brought his fencing foils, which he wishes Mikail to clean. Mikail, examining the foils, suggests that while he is about it he will also improve the points. George is a little surprised that Mikail, too, has played at fencing. He is even more surprised when, having induced Mikail to illustrate a valuable defensive point to employ against a rushing adversary, he finds himself beaten at every turn by his servant.

"Oh, please, Michel, let Monsieur George hit you once," pleads Tatiana, who has been watching the combat.

"No," answers George, with more spirit than breath; "I don't want any favors. Go and get the cocktails."

Now Helene has come with a guitar she wants tuned. She is startled to find George fencing with the butler. George, however, is greatly satisfied. Mikail is a marvel. A point that is visibly proved as the Russian manages not only to hold his young opponent at bay, but also to work around the room to where he can place a chair for Helene while he is doing it.

Tatiana, returning with the cocktails, has offered to help Helene tune the guitar. Helene pours the cocktails. Tatiana is playing and singing. Mikail and George are fencing furiously as the curtain falls.

It is two weeks later. In the Duponts' large drawing room Helene and George are studying Russian, she repeating a list of words, he supplying their Russian equivalents. The word that is interesting them most at the moment is "Tovarich," which means "Comrade." Both Michel and Tina, they admit, hate "Tovarich." It's Bolshevik. George is also greatly intrigued with the phrase "Ia wass loublou," meaning "I love you."

George and Helene have not only acquired a Russian vocabulary, but a great liking for their new friends. They had played poker with them the night before until 3 in the morning, George acknowledging a loss of 2,050 francs and Helene a loss of 800. Mikail has protested that George plays too high, and too often, but the young man is not impressed.

The elder Duponts are giving a dinner party this evening. The younger Duponts are to clear out and return later and go with Michel and Tina to a Russian party—a fete that will "bring out all the homesick émigrés in Paris."

"There will be a great deal of exquisite sobbing," promises Mikail; "I hope that it will amuse you."

George and Helene are thrilled at the prospect. They are thrilled, in fact, with everything that brings them closer to Mikail and Tatiana. Helene has followed Mikail to the pantry when Tatiana finds George waiting and eager to help with the distribution of the flowers she brings for the decoration of the room. Suddenly George has grown quite romantically serious and insists on his Tina's listening. He would practice his Russian on her by proclaiming with passion, "Ia wass loublou! Ia wass loublou!" It means "I love you!" thinks George, but Tatiana corrects him. The way he says it it means "little sick dog!"

"Tina! I love you!" declares George, impetuously.

"And it's right that you should," agrees Tatiana, calmly. "The master must love the servant! And the servant the master! I love you, too, Monsieur George."

George—Oh! But don't you see?—I love you passionately. Can't you understand that? Passionately! Wildly! It's the first time in my entire life that I've known what it is—I mean to feel *real* love!

Tatiana (*tenderly*)—Monsieur George—you are a dear little delightful boy—but you must not have wicked thoughts.

George—Is love wicked? Is there anything wrong or unnatural about—

Tatiana (*softly*)—Yes! Because if you love me, you want to sleep with me!

George (*rebelliously*)—Oh—no!

TATIANA—Oh—yes! You couldn't have any other idea in declaring your passion for me, a housemaid.

GEORGE—You are not like any other housemaid that ever lived.

TATIANA—No—I'm superior— I realize that. But it isn't right for a beautiful, distinguished young gentleman like you to think like that about even the best housemaid. You know it isn't.

GEORGE—I know that I am only happy at night, when Mother and Father have gone to bed, and Helene and I come down to the kitchen, on tip-toe . . . and when you sing, and deal the cards with those exquisite little hands . . .

TATIANA—And Michel pours out the vodka. Don't forget Michel! He cleans your boots and brushes your clothes and teaches you fencing. . . .

GEORGE—That's his job. . . .

TATIANA—But it is not his job to be a deceived husband!

GEORGE (*stopping her*)—Tina! I have got money! I can make you as happy as a princess.

TATIANA (*gently*)—A princess! I only want to be as happy as a housemaid.

GEORGE—Haven't you any ambition?

TATIANA—Oh, yes, sir. To be a good and faithful servant.

GEORGE (*taking her hands and looking into her eyes*)—Have you ever been unfaithful to Michel?

TATIANA—Never. . . . (*Putting her hand through his hair.*) Once I was violated . . .

GEORGE—Tina!!!

TATIANA (*with supreme detachment*)—By one of the Bolsheviks.

GEORGE (*furious*)—The swine!

TATIANA—Oh—no! Not a swine. He was just a man who happened to have the advantage. It was the usual thing at the time. It didn't matter.

GEORGE—You can stand there and say that . . .

TATIANA—Yes, little Monsieur George—I can stand here and say it didn't matter. And I also can say that you're a nice, darling boy. . . . (*All of a sudden she kisses him very quickly on the mouth.*)

GEORGE (*in ecstasy*)—Oh!

TATIANA (*kisses him again very quickly on the mouth*)—You mustn't think about me any more.

GEORGE (*trying to take her in his arms*)—Tina!!

TATIANA (*freeing herself furiously*)—Because this kind of foolishness tires me—it tires me very much indeed.

George—Tina! (*Follows her.*) I won't stand for it. I tell you—I won't stand for it!

Charles Dupont appears suddenly in the doorway. He is interested in knowing what it is George will not stand for. George, explains Tatiana, hurriedly, was objecting to the way she made Martini cocktails. She had stupidly used the wrong vermouth. Which satisfies Charles as an explanation, but not as an excuse. If he ever hears his son addressing Tina as rudely as that again he will find ways to make life extremely unpleasant for him.

With George gone Charles would like to continue his apologies. He is extremely humiliated and would like Tina to forgive him for having so ill-mannered a son. Tina should forgive him in the Russian manner, the kiss upon the brow. During the ceremony Charles manages to hold Tina very close. He is telling her something about her melting eyes and kissing her hands with a good deal of fervor when Mikail appears. Charles is at immediate pains to explain that he was apologizing to Tina in the Russian manner. . . .

The Duponts find it a little difficult to instruct Mikail and Tatiana as to their duties at the dinner. Chiefly because they are forced to confess that their guest of honor will be Soviet Commissar Gorotchenko. Mikail and Tatiana receive the news without apparent protest, but there is an oppressive pause.

"You've doubtless heard of him?" ventures Charles.

"Yes, sir. We have heard of Commissar Gorotchenko," answers Mikail, in a dull tone.

Fernande—We want to be sure that your behavior during dinner will give us no cause for anxiety.

Mikail—Has our behavior ever given such cause, Madame?

Charles—Of course not! Never!

Mikail—Then tonight will be no different.

Fernande—I've never met this Gorotchenko, but I suppose he's pretty much of a boor. However, he is our guest and we must do everything we can to put him at his ease.

Mikail—He is a most cultivated man, Madame, with a very lively wit. A bit malicious, perhaps—but keen. It was he who composed that immortal sentence which was engraved on the door of the Loubianka Prison. "Four walls for punishment are three too many."

Charles—He has never done you any personal harm? Has he?

MIKAIL (*slowly*)—None, sir.

TATIANA—Less than none, sir.

CHARLES—We, then, can all forget the past; Gorotchenko is now representing oil interests, and *oil,* as we all know, is most effective in smoothing out differences of opinion.

MIKAIL—Yes, sir, of course. He was not always in oil, sir. He was chief of the investigating staff of the Tcheka. At that time, my former master, Prince Ouratieff, had some dealings with him.

CHARLES—Really.

MIKAIL—Yes, sir. The conversation between them wasn't progressing as smoothly as Commissar Gorotchenko wished—so—to enliven matters—he placed the end of his cigarette—the lighted end, of course—between Prince Ouratieff's fingers. You'll find him very interesting, monsieur.

FERNANDE—How horrible!

TATIANA—Oh, Madame, you also will find him very entertaining. When he was Commissar of the Fort of Kronstadt, the Grand Duchess was imprisoned there. I've heard her speak of him often. (*Turns away.*) Women always found him irresistible.

CHARLES—You mean, he—he made . . . ?

TATIANA (*levelly*)—Advances, yes, sir.

FERNANDE—But he must be an appalling person!

CHARLES—Nonsense! Michel and Tina have only heard of him from people with a very prejudiced point of view.

FERNANDE (*rising*)—But I hope—you're not going to think about these awful things when you're serving the soup?

TATIANA (*soberly*)—Madame—we shall think only that we're your servants and that we must be worthy of your trust.

Mikail and Tatiana are permitted to withdraw. They are, the Duponts are agreed, perfect treasures. But they will have to be nice to Gorotchenko. He represents the vastly rich and undeveloped Baku oil fields. He must sit at Fernande's right and Chauffourier at her left. Madame van Hemert, who represents the Anglo-Dutch interests, should be placed at Charles' right—

"If all works out as I hope, we'll be swimming in oil—liquid gold," enthuses Charles. "There's a fortune involved, my dear. But, of course, everything depends on Gorotchenko. . . ."

Madame van Hemert is the first to arrive. "She is thin, hard, sharp, rather chic, very elegant." And a widely traveled lady. "I'm a sort of vestal virgin," reports Madame Hemert. "I am one of those whose duty it is to keep the lamps of the world filled with oil. It necessitates a great deal of travel."

A moment later Tatiana has come to ask if she shall serve the cocktails. One look at Tatiana and Madame van Hemert rises and approaches her. With dignity she sweeps into a deep ceremonial curtsey, greatly to Tatiana's confusion, as she hurries from the room.

The Duponts are astounded. They demand to know why Madame van Hemert should do such a thing, and Madame is as curious to know why the Grand Duchess Tatiana Petrovna is there. She had known Her Highness well in Petersburg. And her husband, the Prince Ouratieff—

Now the Duponts are both astounded and disgusted. If Tina and Michel should indeed be of the Russian nobility their employers will be the laughing stock of Paris! Before they can think of anything to do about it the Chauffouriers have arrived. And no sooner has Chauffourier caught a glimpse of Mikail than he is offering to shake hands with his High Highness as a fellow guest. Mikail goes calmly about his work.

"It *is* a joke, isn't it?" demands Chauffourier.

"The best joke in years," laughs van Hemert.

MME. CHAUFFOURIER—Are you going to explain it now—or must we wait?

CHARLES—It makes no difference when we explain it. Tomorrow—it will be in every newspaper.

FERNANDE (*rising*)—And Gorotchenko! Why, they'll be at each other's throats! (*Imploringly to her guests.*) I'm horribly sorry—but—will you mind awfully if we dine at a restaurant?

VAN HEMERT—Not at all.

CHAUFFOURIER—But why? With Prince Ouratieff on hand, the situation is ideal. We might persuade him to join the combine. He might agree to finance the whole scheme.

CHARLES—Him—finance us?

CHAUFFOURIER—Why not? As a Russian, he'd appreciate the value of the oil concession. . . .

CHARLES—But—forgive me, Governor—I'm a little bewildered. . . .

CHAUFFOURIER—You evidently don't know that Ouratieff is probably the only man living who can write his check on the Bank of France for four billion francs.

CHARLES—Four billion. . . .

CHAUFFOURIER—Yes—and have it honored! So—when you've

finished your little joke, whatever it is, we'd better sit down with His Excellency and talk a little business.

Monsieur Gorotchenko is announced. "He is strongly built, with a humorous, saturnine expression—a civilized barbarian with keen perceptivity and a great appreciation of life."

Gorotchenko gracefully greets his host and hostess and his fellow guests. When Mikail enters with the cocktails the Commissar gives no indication that he recognizes him, nor does he take conscious note of Chauffourier's efforts to attract his attention to Mikail. When Tatiana follows with the sandwiches he is as studiedly unperturbed, while the others indulge in all manner of artificial small talk to cover the situation.

"But what a charming room this is, Madame," observes Gorotchenko, accepting a light for his cigarette from the ubiquitous Mikail. "Isn't it a replica of the Hôtel de Landouzy?"

"Why, yes, it is," answers Fernande, with an apprehensive eye on the retreating Mikail. "Did you know the Hôtel de Landouzy?"

GOROTCHENKO—I am an old Parisian, Madame. For three years I was a dishwasher in the Quai de Bourbon.

FERNANDE—A dishwasher! How very interesting!

GOROTCHENKO—Yes—literally! I washed dishes. That was when I was studying for my philosophical degree.

CHARLES—In addition to everything else—you're a Doctor of Philosophy?

GOROTCHENKO—That was a long time ago, Monsieur Dupont. I'm afraid I've forgotten most of it now.

CHAUFFOURIER (*chuckling*)—Yes—you've passed on from pure theory to impure fact.

GOROTCHENKO (*laughing*)—That's it, my dear Governor. I was captivated by the concept of the Perfect State. Where every man has the brain of Socrates in the body of Adonis, and every woman—but I'm sure you ladies have already achieved the Platonic ideal.

VAN HEMERT (*to* FERNANDE)—He's poisonous, isn't he? He'll make Communists of us all.

CHAUFFOURIER—I see, Commissar. You learned about the Perfect State and then went home to Russia and built it.

GOROTCHENKO—No—when I returned to Russia, I was careful to leave my idealism behind. That was a bad time for Idealists, you know. A few of them escaped into Finland. But the majority were submerged in rivers of blood.

MME. CHAUFFOURIER—How shocking!

CHAUFFOURIER—And how necessary! That's the one point on which Capitalism and Communism agree; the idealists must be drowned.

GOROTCHENKO—The Governor is a realist! You know Plato himself likened all of us to prisoners, chained in a cave. Behind us a fire is burning—and we're forced to contemplate our own shadows, magnified horribly on the wall. We're terrified of them. They awaken in us race memories, and we shrink from them, as though they were prehistoric monsters. We of the Soviet Union have tried to break the chains, and escape from the cave into the world of clear reality. You may feel that we have failed, but even so we have provided a fascinating chapter of history for the dishwashers of the future. But I am afraid I am becoming much too talkative, madame. It's a Russian failing.

CHAUFFOURIER—Oh—no—Commissar. I'm sure we've all greatly enjoyed your little lecture.

Mikail has returned to tell Fernande that dinner is served. With the usual polite confusion the guests are herded toward the dining room, continuing the small talk in which they are engaged.

"You know—it's a very bad thing for a Communist to dine in a French house," Gorotchenko is saying, as he crosses to Fernande; "a shamefully corrupting influence."

"You're in a good mood, Commissar."

"Why not, Madame? I'm not often privileged to enjoy such charming company."

There is a buzz of conversation and a scraping of chairs from the dining room. "Mikail looks at Tatiana, then goes to her and takes her in his arms. For a moment they are close together, silent. Then she pats his shoulder, as much as to say, 'Go serve the dinner.' He lets go of her and crosses to the door, then pauses, turns to her and bows."

"After you, Highness," he says.

Tatiana crosses to the door, her head held high, as the curtain falls.

ACT III

Three hours later, in the kitchen of the Duponts' house, Mikail, Tatiana and Louise, the cook, are having their dinner. There are many embarrassing silences. Louise is inquisitive as to how the other dinner had come off, and neither Mikail nor Tatiana is in a mood to talk about it. Everything was all right—but they have been fired. Following dinner Madame Dupont had informed them, ever so elegantly, that the usual notice would be dispensed with. "We receive our wages and depart in the morning," reports Mikail.

Louise is disappointed. It has seemed to her that Michel and Tina have done more than enough. She is further surprised when the cause of dismissal is explained to her, but the discovery that her companions of the kitchen are Highnesses in disguise, as it were, does not disturb Louise.

"Princes and Highnesses have to live somewhere, like other people," says the cook. "They may as well live here as anywhere else."

"Godly woman! You understand things," answers Tatiana.

Louise is still puzzled. If Tina and Michel like their work so much, and are really fitted for nothing else, as Michel says, why don't they drop their titles and join the union? The union will solve their troubles—

"It will protect you from this very thing—I mean being dismissed for no good reason," explains Louise. "Why—if your employers say or do anything you don't like, you'll only have to go to the Union and lodge a protest. And then the Union will send an officer round to the house—and those officers use the front door, not the back door, believe me. And he'll say a few things to Monsieur and Madame—and the next thing you know, they'll be apologizing to you, and raising your wages, and putting a wireless set in your room."

"But that—that sounds like Bolshevism," protests Mikail.

"Call it anything you please, Michel. It makes life a lot easier for the likes of us."

Louise has gone. Mikail and Tatiana are left to finish up the work for the last time; to put away the ugly china of which they have grown so fond and been so careful. Never in their lives have they labored so honestly. Surely God knows. He will find them another place. Still, Tatiana thinks it might not be a bad idea for them to join the union.

"It's useless," declares Mikail. "Wherever we go—here in France—they'll know all about us. How much money have we?"

Tatiana has eleven francs. The rest she has spent for a dress for the fete. Mikail has his poker winnings, two thousand and fifty francs. Perhaps that would be enough to take them to South America. Desperate people always go to South America.

Mikail—Ah—my darling! How can we go to that party tonight, with those two young monkeys? How can we pretend to be gay when we've lost bread and bed and central heating?

TATIANA (*sweeping below table*)—We've promised, Mikail. The Archduke Alexis would never forgive us. He saved up for two years to give this party. And everyone else there will have no more reason for rejoicing than we have. And then poor little Monsieur George. He has been very good to us.

MIKAIL—The amorous puppy!

TATIANA—And Mademoiselle Helene—she's been good to us, too—and—(*with a malicious smile*)—for the same reason. We mustn't disappoint them.

MIKAIL (*sitting on end of table*)—Very well—we'll go. We'll make the last gruesome pretense.

TATIANA (*putting her arms about him*)—My poor, tragic pigeon. You weren't nearly so depressed when they burned down our palace at Barchevia—and destroyed all your beautiful horses in the stable and the twelve Rembrandts in the library.

MIKAIL—That was in Russia, Tatiana.

TATIANA—And you laughed when they arrested us, and imprisoned you in the Loubianka, and me in the Kronstadt prison, and we were so certain we were going to die . . .

MIKAIL—That, too, was in Russia, Tatiana.

TATIANA—Well—and where are we now?

MIKAIL—In the kitchen of the house of a banker named Dupont.

TATIANA—It is *our* kitchen, Mikail. Breathe the air, my darling. . . . It smells of onions and coal gas and brown soap—but when you breathe it in, it becomes the air of Russia—cold and clean. Wherever we may go, it will be the same. In our lungs, and our eyes, and our hearts will be Russia.

They are clinging to each other now, and shouting "Nitchevo!" lustily. By repeating this Russian equivalent of "Don't worry!" or "What does it matter?" they pull themselves out of their depression and are happy again. Soon Mikail has gone to return the Dupont service clothes while Tatiana finishes up the work. As she works she sings a Russian song, "A Life for the Czar."

Softly the pantry door is opened. Commissar Gorotchenko enters. He stands for a moment watching her. Tatiana, suddenly aware of his presence, quickly throws a dishcloth over the silver. It may be he has come for that. If not, what has he come for?

Gorotchenko suavely insists that he has come hoping to see Prince Ouratieff. He has left the party in the drawing room to think over in solitude an agreement they want him to sign. The bankers think he is in the study. He prefers the kitchen. Does

Tatiana mind? Not so long as he remains sitting down, she tells him. Perhaps he does not remember their last meeting. . . .

"You were sitting behind your enormous desk, smoking a cigarette, just as you are now," she recalls. "Then you stood up and walked around the desk, put down your cigarette and took hold of my wrist."

"I see no reason to refer to that, Madame," Gorotchenko replies, calmly. "It was something that happened in another world, a very long time ago."

TATIANA—Oh, I hold no grudge, Gorotchenko.

GOROTCHENKO—I'm sure you don't.

TATIANA—But I'd like to have you know that when I get back, I shall have your eyes burned out and the sockets filled with Siberian salt.

GOROTCHENKO—If you do come back, Madame, the most horrible retribution you can think of will be no more than I deserve. Because I was guilty of the most unpardonable of crimes.

TATIANA—It does me no good to hear you admit it.

GOROTCHENKO—I was guilty of sentimentality.

TATIANA (*laughing*)—Sentimentality! That's a rather quaint way of describing it, Commissar.

GOROTCHENKO—I was referring to the moment of weakness when I permitted you to go off in that motor boat, through the darkness.

TATIANA—You knew that the motor boat was there?

GOROTCHENKO—Yes, Madame . . . The man who took you was shot, but not until after he had delivered you safely in Finland.

TATIANA—You killed that godly man?

GOROTCHENKO—Somebody had to be punished for your escape. Had it not been he, it would have been the governor of the prison. The revolution was young then,—and I was not quite ready to die.

TATIANA—Why did you let me go?

GOROTCHENKO—There was something in you that impelled me to neglect my obvious duty. I suppose that something can best be described as gallantry . . . and furthermore—I could not rid myself of the belief that your usefulness to Russia had not ended.

For a long moment Tatiana stares at the Commissar, then sharply dismisses him for a second time. Let him go and drink brandy with the bourgeoisie. But Gorotchenko prefers to stay. He would help her with the dishes if she would permit. He would—

Mikail interrupts the scene. He, too, would quickly be rid of this intruder. Monsieur and Madame Dupont may have had their own reasons for inviting him into their drawing room, but the kitchen folk are more particular.

Gorotchenko is not impressed. He would remind them that Tatiana was a Grand Duchess in Russia. She must know that as a Grand Duchess she is hostess in any house that is graced by her presence. He is, therefore, Madame's guest—

"The dog is right," admits Tatiana.

"Very well," Mikail submits. "You may remain and derive what enjoyment you can from the spectacle of your former commanding officer cleaning his master's boots."

Gorotchenko has come, he says, to ask Mikail a question. But first he would refresh his memory of the last time he (Mikail) drew his sword and charged with his three thousand Preobjenski.

"There were not three thousand on that day, Gorotchenko," Mikail corrects him. "There were three hundred. The rest had put red bands on their sleeves and deserted. It was the Austrians who were three thousand. But we charged, anyway. (*He waves his shoe brush as though it were a saber.*) And we routed them. The next day the command was taken from me. It was given to a student of chemistry. That day it was two hundred Austrians who routed twenty thousand Russians."

"Ah—yes. That was the day of the chemistry students," recalls Gorotchenko. "It happens in all revolutions. The chemistry students must have their little moment of glory. . . . But the next year it was I who commanded the Russian cavalry."

It was a very real admiration that he bore his General in those days, Gorotchenko would have Mikail believe. The compliment is not appreciated. Gorotchenko was thoroughly objectionable even then. And Mikail finds his story very dull.

Gorotchenko is still unmoved. He has come, he now declares, to ask General Prince Ouratieff to do him a slight favor, a favor that will cost him little in the way of effort and nothing in the way of money. He would like to have Prince Ouratieff write him a check for four billion francs. That is the object and the purpose of his visit. It was he who had arranged the Dupont dinner. Not once has he lost touch with Mikail and Tatiana since they sent him word by the last of his agents to call upon them—a stupid, violent little girl—urging him to call in person.

"We acknowledge the visit, Commissar," says Mikail, preparing to take a tray of lemonade to the guests in the drawing room.

"But first you'll sign the check," persists Gorotchenko. "It won't take a moment." Mikail has walked over to the sink and is watching Gorotchenko over his shoulder. The Commissar continues: "General Ouratieff—for *two hours* I have been closeted in there with Chauffourier, of the Bank of France, and Madame van Hemert, whose name is Anglo-Dutch Oil, and Dupont, who represents United Petrol. Can you imagine why they are so cordial to me, a despised Bolshevist,—a potential destroyer of the whole system of civilization, to which their lives are dedicated? I shall tell you. They want me to sign the transfer of the Baku and Petrovolsk oil fields for the next fifty years."

MIKAIL (*drying his hands*)—And will you sign?

GOROTCHENKO—I've been fighting to avoid it. For it would mean fifty years of English, Dutch, French and Americans—digging Russian soil, capitalizing Russian resources, drawing life blood from the veins of our country.

MIKAIL (*calmly*)—Keep up the fight, Commissar. Don't sign.

GOROTCHENKO—I'm afraid—I must, General. For I have been commissioned to find credits in gold for the Sokols of the Ukraine and the Ural, for the manufacture of tractors and agricultural machines. If I don't find that money, and at once, some five million wretched peasants will starve to death—without mentioning those we shall have to shoot so that they won't make a fuss about it. . . . When I asked you for your last memory as a general, I wanted to remind you, that more than a sword can be wielded in behalf of Russia. There is another weapon—money.

MIKAIL—I have no money.

GOROTCHENKO—You have four billion francs.

MIKAIL—It is not mine.

GOROTCHENKO—It was given to you, unconditionally, by Nicholas Romanoff.

TATIANA (*crossing herself*)—It was given him by the Czar.

GOROTCHENKO—Yes, Madame. That was in the year 1917. And now—

MIKAIL—You needn't continue, Gorotchenko. If you have watched me so closely, you will know that I have held on to that money as I have held on to my immortal soul. And I was not saving it for you.

GOROTCHENKO—I know, General. I know all about the offer of Count Brekenski to equip an army of Latvians and Lithuanians to invade the Soviet Union. You showed wisdom in rejecting that absurdity. It would be a tragic farce. . . . But it is not a farce to give Baku and Petrovolsk into the hands of foreigners.

MIKAIL—Don't worry, Gorotchenko. When the time comes, we shall take them back again.

GOROTCHENKO—You are a fine officer, General. But in that case you would be engaging too many enemies at once.

TATIANA—Who did you say these people are—who want you to sign?

GOROTCHENKO—It is a combination of interests, Madame—French, Dutch, American, English!

MIKAIL—I don't care who they are! I have denied that money to all the scavengers who have tried to take it from me. I have denied it to myself.

GOROTCHENKO—No one has questioned your integrity, General Ouratieff.

MIKAIL—And don't think you can flatter me out of it.

GOROTCHENKO—I should not so far insult your intelligence.

MIKAIL—You wouldn't hesitate to do anything, Gorotchenko. Once you even tried to torture me.

GOROTCHENKO—I know, General. My conduct was then both unworthy and unwise. But now, our relative positions are very different.

MIKAIL—Nothing is different. What was then the Czar's remains the Czar's. . . .

GOROTCHENKO—Yes, General. But—I wish I could take you now into the Czar's room at Tsarkoe Selo.

TATIANA—Is it still there?

GOROTCHENKO—Intact, Madame. Largely through my own efforts, if I may say so. It has been preserved precisely as it was.

TATIANA—Is my photograph still there—in a white dress, with a high collar and ruffles?

GOROTCHENKO—Yes, Madame. And—it pains me to say it—you have a mustache supplied by a barbarous visitor. He was condemned to ten years' penal servitude.

TATIANA—For lèse-majesté?

GOROTCHENKO—For damaging the workers' property. (*He turns to* MIKAIL.) Do you remember in that room, on the wall, behind the Czar's desk, a big map of all the Russias?

MIKAIL—Yes—I remember the map.

GOROTCHENKO—At the top of it, to the right, are marked Baku and Petrovolsk. Of all the undeveloped oil fields on earth—they are the richest. If I sign that agreement with the foreigners—a part of that map will have to be torn away.

MIKAIL (*fiercely*)—Then don't sign! (*Turns to* GOROT-

CHENKO.) Are you such a weakling that you'll allow them to rob you—and Russia? Where is your devotion to the workers' property?

GOROTCHENKO—The people of the Ukraine and the Ural must have tractors for their Spring planting.

MIKAIL (*resisting desperately*)—Not from me! The money belonged to the Czar. To the Czar it will be returned.

GOROTCHENKO—And who was the Czar, General?

MIKAIL—He was beyond your degraded comprehension.

GOROTCHENKO (*to* TATIANA)—I ask it of you, Madame. Who was the Czar?

TATIANA (*rising*)—He was Russia!

GOROTCHENKO (*gravely*)—Yes—he was Russia. And therefore—he is not dead.

MIKAIL (*suddenly, to* TATIANA)—I can tell you—the day will come when we can strike back—when Russia will need us. And —on that day—no foreigner will be allowed to remain in possession of so much as a square centimeter of our soil. . . .

TATIANA—No, no, my darling! You are wrong. We may take back that which belongs to France, or to America. But no one has ever taken back anything from England.

MIKAIL (*stares at her—then goes close to her*)—You want me to do it, Tatiana?

TATIANA (*dropping a plate that is in her hand*)—Yes, Mikail . . . Look, I've broken a plate.

MIKAIL—The first one. (*They stoop to pick up the pieces.* MIKAIL *turns to* GOROTCHENKO.) You may tell Chauffourier and the others that Baku and Petrovolsk are not for sale.

Tatiana has found Mikail a pen and some ink. Louise had put them with the onions. She is sure he is doing right. She is sure her sovereign would never have let Baku and Petrovolsk go, even at the cost of his throne or his life. Yes, Mikail is doing right—

"From the depths of his grave he sees you, and says that you are fulfilling his trust," Tatiana says, reassuringly. "From the very height of the skies he is reaching down, to guide your hand."

It is only the onions that are making her cry, she says, as Mikail holds the pen poised.

"Four billion francs! I've lived with them so long—I—I've grown used to them. They're all we have left of what *he* gave us. . . ."

"We have the sword, and the flags, and the icon, Mikail—and ourselves."

"And ourselves!"

Mikail has written in the date and turned to Gorotchenko: "What is your Christian name?"

"Dmitri."

"Dmitri Gorotchenko . . . one of the most heartless, soulless, ruthless blackguards that ever desecrated the God-formed surface of this earth . . . you know . . . I can't fill in the exact sum. Now I must sign. Mikail Alexandrovitch Ouratieff."

The check is signed. Mikail has taken the check book and tossed it into the fire. He will have no more use for that. Now Tatiana has picked up the signed check and turned to Gorotchenko.

"To whom will this check be given?" she asks.

"It will be deposited in Paris to the credit of the Soviet Government," replies Gorotchenko. And then, as he faces them, he adds: "Tatiana Petrovna Romanoff—Mikail Alexandrovitch Ouratieff . . . the flag of the Romanoffs no longer flies over Soviet territories. But I shall arrange with the Central Committee that it shall be affixed twice into the map in the room that once was the Czar's. It shall mark the spot that is Baku and the spot that is Petrovolsk."

Gorotchenko would have made a speech of thanks also, if Mikail had not shut him up. He stands at the door staring at Tatiana. Mikail has gone to serve the lemonade in the drawing room.

"Good-by, Serene Highness."

"Good-by, Tovarich!"

He has crossed the floor rapidly and kissed Tatiana's left shoulder. At the door he turns again.

"Good-by, Russia!" he says, very gravely and magnificently.

For a moment Tatiana stands staring after him. Then she slowly shrugs her shoulders and returns to the sink. She is continuing with the dishes when George Dupont comes bounding into the room.

George is greatly excited. He would, with any encouragement, repeat his love for Tatiana, but this, she tells him, is not the moment. She will let him know if the moment should ever arrive. Meantime she must dress. . . .

Mikail is back and he, too, has his preparations to make. He is glad of their enthusiasm for the party, and he will do what he can to help them enjoy it. He doubts, however, that it will be possible to pass them off as long lost cousins, as Helene suggests. There are, Mikail points out, "essential racial differences."

"I know. We're congenitally dull," ventures George.

"It isn't that, Monsieur," corrects Mikail. "The trouble is—we're congenitally savage. That's what makes us the fools that we are. Sentimental barbarians! You can't emulate that. You have within you too great an accumulation of common sense. Your civilization goes back too far—all the way to Romulus and Remus, I suppose. We've had only two hundred years of the blessings of culture. And that isn't enough. We may wear the same clothes that you do, and read the same books, and know which fork to use at dinner—and be superficially presentable. But our souls are still roaming the steppes, wildly—baying with the wolves at the moon."

"Ah, Michel—when I hear you talk like that—I—wish . . ."

"When you hear me talk like that, Mademoiselle, you may be sure that I, too, am listening, enraptured, to the sound of my own voice."

Mikail has adjusted his coat and found a half dozen of his decorations. They are, he is quick to assure George, such baubles as could be bought at any pawnbroker's. He is pinning on the Order of St. Christopher, which is awarded for extreme valor, when Charles Dupont comes into the kitchen.

Charles is visibly disturbed. First to find his children there and, second, to note that Mikail has already resumed his identity. The plans for the fete are explained to the elder Dupont, and he is forced to listen to his son defend with great vehemence the dignity and charm of servants such as Michel and Tina. Charles is only slightly mollified. He would have the children clear out of the room. He wants to talk to Michel.

"I never dreamed that you could do such a cruel thing to me," says Charles.

"Perhaps some day you'll forgive me, sir," answers Mikail, humbly. "But we understand perfectly that you and Madame have every reason to detest us and wish to be rid of us."

CHARLES—No, Prince Ouratieff. Madame and I . . .

MIKAIL—I beg of you, sir. My name to you remains Michel.

CHARLES—Michel, then. We do not detest you.

MIKAIL—Ah—thank you, sir.

CHARLES—In fact, we—well—we respect and admire you. But where will you go now?

MIKAIL—To South America, sir. To dwell among apes and

cobras.

CHARLES—South America, eh? And what will you do there?

MIKAIL—This same work, we hope, sir.

CHARLES—Then—if that is what you wish . . . (*He is fumbling for the words he wants to utter.*) Madame and I have been talking it over. We—we like you—you and Her Highness. . . .

MIKAIL—Tina, sir.

CHARLES—Tina. And we think you like us.

MIKAIL (*with simple sincerity*)—We love you, sir.

CHARLES—Well, then . . . if you could forget . . . (TATIANA *comes in, beautifully dressed.* CHARLES *turns and sees her and bows.*) Your Highness.

MIKAIL—No, sir—no—please. You were saying?

CHARLES—I was about to say—if you are determined to continue with this sort of work, then why not continue with it here . . . ?

TATIANA—Ah—godly man—you wish us to stay?

CHARLES—Well—that is—I mean, it's for you to say. . . .

MIKAIL—Before all the saints, sir, I swear to you that never by word or deed should we remind you that we have ever been other than Michel and Tina. You may reduce our wages to nothing—you may beat us with whips—you may cancel the every other Sunday we have free . . .

CHARLES (*nervously*)—Very well—very well. (*Turns to* TATIANA.) Then, it's settled. . . . (TATIANA *smothers him with kisses.*) Now—no, my dear—that's enough of that for the time being. And—and—thank you. . . .

TATIANA (*as the door closes after* CHARLES)—We are saved! *Saved*—from South America!

MIKAIL—Never have two poor Russians had greater cause for celebration. Come, my sweet love.

TATIANA (*at the door*)—Our kitchen! Our dear, darling kitchen! (*She crosses to the window and looks out.*)

MIKAIL—What are you looking at, Tatiana?

TATIANA—Look, my pigeon! It is snowing! (*He goes to her. His arm about her.*) How beautiful it is!

MIKAIL—How beautiful—and how sad!

TATIANA—Yes—everything is sad, isn't it? Even happiness!

MIKAIL—Especially happiness. (*He takes her in his arms and kisses her.*)

TATIANA—Your eyes are full of tears.

MIKAIL—They're only a reflection of yours, Tatiana.

TATIANA—We're fools, aren't we, Mikail?

MIKAIL—Yes, my darling. Fools! Now and forever! Come on! (*She breaks away from him. He goes to hold open the door. She goes hastily to the sink and picks up two empty milk bottles.*)

TATIANA—If I don't leave these for the milkman, the Russian God won't do it for me.

THE CURTAIN FALLS

THE PLAYS AND THEIR AUTHORS

"High Tor," a comedy in three acts by Maxwell Anderson. Copyright, 1937, by the author. Copyright and published, 1936, by Anderson House, Washington, D. C. Distributed by Dodd, Mead & Co., New York.

Maxwell Anderson, who has made five previous appearances in the Year Book, established a new record last season by having three plays of his authorship running successfully in New York simultaneously. These were "High Tor," which was awarded the Drama Critics' Circle prize as the best play of the season by an American author; "The Masque of Kings," a dramatization of the tragic romance involving Prince Rudolph and the Baroness Mary Vetsera, of Bavaria, and "The Wingless Victory," in which Katharine Cornell appeared the better part of the season. Mr. Anderson's biography is well known to readers of "The Best Plays." After graduation from the University of North Dakota he took more or less unwillingly to teaching, drifted into newspaper work as an editorial writer and wrote his first successful play in collaboration with Laurence Stallings. That was "What Price Glory." He is the son of a minister and was born in Atlantic, Pa.

"You Can't Take It with You," a comedy by Moss Hart and George S. Kaufman. Copyright, 1936, by the authors. Copyright and published, 1937, by Farrar & Rinehart, Inc., New York.

Both Mr. Hart and Mr. Kaufman are repeaters, so far as the year books are concerned, Mr. Hart making his debut with "Once in a Lifetime," also written with Mr. Kaufman, in the issue of 1930-31, and repeating with "Merrily We Roll Along," another Kaufman collaboration, in 1934-35. Born and educated in New York, Mr. Hart got a start as a playwright when he was an office assistant to a producing manager and wrote a comedy for him as a surprise. It lasted five weeks in Chicago as "The Hold-up Man." He got further practice with Irving Berlin when he worked on the books for "As Thousands Cheer" and "Face the

Music."

Mr. Kaufman came to us in 1921-22 with "Dulcy," the first of several happy collaborations with Marc Connelly. He has been represented in practically every volume since then, and all but once with a collaborator. His solo contribution was "The Butter and Egg Man" in 1925-26. Born in Pittsburgh, Kaufman tried salesmanship, drifted into newspaper work and graduated from journalism with honors after he became the most successful playwright of the last decade.

"Johnny Johnson," a drama in three acts by Paul Green. Copyright, 1936, 1937, by the author. Copyright and published, 1937, by Samuel French, New York.

Paul Green continues to follow playwriting as an avocation. He is on the faculty of the University of North Carolina, as he has been practically since his graduation in 1921, though he did do some post-graduate work at Cornell. He was born near the seat of his alma mater and won the Pulitzer prize with "In Abraham's Bosom" the season of 1926-27. He left college to go to war, came out a second lieutenant and shows the results of his military experience in "Johnny Johnson."

"Daughters of Atreus," a tragedy in three acts by Robert Turney. Copyright, 1936, by the author. Copyright and published, 1936, by Alfred A. Knopf, New York.

Robert Turney's grandfather was Governor Turney of Tennessee. Robert was born in Nashville, February 17, 1900. He always had the urge for dramatics, and when he got as far as Columbia he took up the study seriously. Did some work also at the University of Toronto, had a season with Jacques Copeau in Paris, and did a bit of studying in Salzburg. Finally he went with Lawrence Langner in Westport. He played small parts and looked after the stage. Did the same for the Theatre Guild's production of "End of Summer." He toured with a WPA unit and took a job as dramatic coach at Madison Settlement House. He liked that. Found the East Side children marvelously receptive. He had been writing "Daughters of Atreus" on and off for the better part of fifteen years when Dame Sibyl Thorndike read it and liked it. Her enthusiasm fired others and the Delos Chappell production was the result.

"Stage Door," comedy by Edna Ferber and George S. Kaufman. Copyright, 1936, by the authors. Copyright and published, 1936, by Doubleday, Doran & Co., Garden City, N. Y.

Here, again, are two familiars of the Best Play list. Miss Ferber and Mr. Kaufman were represented in the issue of 1924-25 by "Minick," a dramatization of one of Miss Ferber's novels; by "The Royal Family" in 1927-28; by "Dinner at Eight" in 1932-33. Miss Ferber spaces her playwriting activities so that they stimulate and do not interfere with her regular job as a popular novelist. She was born in Kalamazoo, Michigan, and had some experience as a contributor to newspapers before the magazine editors discovered her. From the magazines to the ranks of the novelists proved but a short step.

The Kaufman career may be checked elsewhere in this volume, or in any one of fourteen other volumes of "The Best Plays."

"The Women," a comedy in three acts by Clare Boothe. Copyright, 1936, by the author. Copyright and published, 1937, by Random House, Inc., New York.

She does not like to be called Clare Boothe Brokaw Luce, and there is no reason why she should. She had made her way in society as Clare Boothe before she married George T. Brokaw, of the haberdashery Brokaws, and she had made her way in literature before, having divorced Mr. Brokaw, she married Henry R. Luce, the publisher of *Time, Fortune* and a couple of other successful magazines. Miss Boothe has always been a revealing writer. She startled her society friends with an early opus called "Stuffed Shirts," and when she was managing editor of *Vanity Fair* it was the best informed of the society-minded publications. She has written five plays and had two produced, one called "Abide with Me," which didn't last, and "The Women," which threatens to last forever. She is still in her early thirties and smartly decorative.

"St. Helena," a drama in three acts by R. C. Sherriff and Jeanne de Casalis. Copyright, 1936, by the authors. Copyright and published, 1937, by Gollanz, Inc., London, England.

Mr. Sherriff is the young man who came out of the war to write one of the greatest of the war plays, "Journey's End," which was included in the Year Book covering the season of 1928-29. His literary output has been light since then, his first play to achieve attention being the "St. Helena" that is here included. Thanks to the international success of "Journey's End" he is under no compulsion to write if he lacks the inspiration to do so.

Miss de Casalis was born in South Africa and educated in Paris. It was the idea at first that she should become a professional pianist, but she liked the stage better and trained for a career under Mme. Thenard of the Comédie Française and Theodore Komisarjevsky of the Moscow Art. She has made many appearances in London and Paris, and was in America in the Theatre Guild's production of "The Tidings Brought to Mary" at the Garrick Theatre in 1922. She has taken an active part in many of the independent productions made by the Stage Society and the Renaissance Society in London.

"Yes, My Darling Daughter," a comedy in three acts by Mark Reed. Copyright, 1936, by the author. Copyright and published, 1937, by Samuel French, Inc., New York.

Ask Mark Reed and he will tell you that he went to Dartmouth to study football, to Massachusetts Institute of Technology to study architecture and to Harvard to study playwriting with Prof. George Pierce Baker. He did very well in football, and very well in architecture, too, but it was the detail of the latter that got him down. His last job as an architect was working out the marble jointure details for the sixty bathrooms of a New York hospital and that is where he quit. He had a fine time at Harvard and not long after he left English 47 he sold a piece called "She Would and She Did" to Grace George, who produced it in 1919. He wrote a couple of others, one called "Let's Get Rich" and one "The Skyrocket," but nothing happened until Dennis King played in one called "Petticoat Fever" in 1935. That was what might be called a moderate success. "Yes, My Darling Daughter" and real success followed two years later. Mr. Reed is a bachelor and spends a lot of time down Cape Cod way. He was born in Chelmsford, Mass., near Boston and has a home in white Plains, N. Y.

"Excursion," a comedy in three acts by Victor Wolfson. Copyright, 1937, by the author. Copyright and published, 1937, by Random House, N. Y.

Mr. Wolfson is one of the newer New York playwrights, having stepped to the left with the Theatre Union and similar groups last season. His first produced play was an adaptation of Dostoevsky's

"Crime and Punishment," which he did with Victor Triva. His second was a dramatization of the Ignazio Silone novel, "Fontamara," which he called "Bitter Stream." Neither of these got far. Suddenly out came "Excursion," a gentle and heart-warming comedy as it reached the stage, whatever may have been Mr. Wolfson's more radical tendencies regarding it originally. Mr. Wolfson was born in New York and went to the University of Wisconsin to complete his education. They are very proud of him out Madison way.

"Tovarich," a comedy in three acts by Jacques Deval, adapted by Robert E. Sherwood. Copyright, 1936, by the authors. Copyright and published, 1936, by Random House, New York.

Robert E. Sherwood (the E. being for Emmet, though he doesn't use it any more) made his bow as a Best Play author in the 1926-27 volume, when his first produced play, "The Road to Rome," was included. After that he earned a second inclusion with "Reunion in Vienna," and since then has been represented by "The Petrified Forest" and last season's "Idiot's Delight." He is a New Rochelle, N. Y., boy and was being educated at Harvard when he decided to go to war in 1918. Back from the trenches he went in for magazine writing and editing, serving *Vanity Fair* and *Life,* writing both motion picture and dramatic criticism, and becoming an editor of Scribner's finally. He has spent a good deal of time in England the last few years. And a little time in Hollywood.

Jacques Deval is a prolific writer of dramas in Paris. It is related that he wrote "Tovarich" in a state of pique because a play that he considered the best thing he had done, and on which he had spent a good deal of time, had been turned down by his producers. He dashed off "Tovarich" in an "if this is the sort of thing they like I'll give it them" spirit, and it was not only an immediate success in Paris, but ran through a season in London, has had long engagements in all the European capitals and is in its ninth month of continuous playing in New York.

PLAYS PRODUCED IN NEW YORK

June 16, 1936—June 15, 1937

(Plays marked with asterisk were still playing June 15, 1937)

THE KICK BACK

(16 performances)

A play in three acts by Edwin Harvey Blum. Produced by Paul Groll and George L. Miller at the Ritz Theatre, New York, June 22, 1936.

Cast of characters—

Mrs. Muller....................Jane Marbury
Joy Mallon....................Diane Tempest
Margie Wilson....................Mary Hutchinson
Pat Malone....................G. Swayne Gordon
Jack Williams....................Cleve Garrett
Prof. Mark Adams....................Maurice Burke
Dr. Siska....................Walter Scott Weeks
Dean Chipes....................Robert Harrison
Prof. Bidwell....................Harold Smalley
Rexford....................Donald McMillan

Acts I, II and III.—Living Room and Study in Home of Dr. Siska and Professor Adams, Campus of Heath University.

Staged by Carl Hunt; setting by Rollo Wayne.

Dr. Siska and Prof. Adams, members of the faculty of a midwestern college, are vitally interested in clearing up the murder of a girl student found strangled in a lonely cabin. Dr. Siska, at the request of Prof. Adams, has helped to exonerate a suspected student. Circumstantial evidence points to the guilt of Prof. Adams himself. Dr. Siska, forced finally to denounce his friend, is pretty startled himself when certain discoveries reveal the real culprit as a former high-minded patron of the university.

DORIAN GRAY

(16 performances)

A drama in three acts adapted by Jeron Criswell from Oscar Wilde's "The Picture of Dorian Gray." Produced by Groves Quigley at the Comedy Theatre, New York, July 20, 1936.

Cast of characters—

Dorian Gray....................David Windsor
Basil Hallward....................Robert Carlyle
Lord Henry Wotton....................Oscar Stirling
Sibyl Vane....................Winifred Q. Fothergill

Lady Fermor.......................................Vera Hurst
Hetty.......................................Flora Sheffield
James Vane.......................................Clement O'Loghlen
Allen Campbell.......................................Malcolm Soltan
Parker.......................................Leslie King

Acts I, II and III.—Drawing Room.
Staged by Edwin O'Hanlon.

Dorian Gray, falling under an evil spell, sells his soul to the Devil on condition that he shall remain forever young while his painted portrait takes on the ravages of the years he wastes. Living sinfully for thirty years Dorian's mind is affected by the knowledge of his guilty secret. He plunges a knife through the portrait. His friends find him a hideous old corpse lying beside the picture.

THE LIFE AND LOVES OF DORIAN GRAY

(32 performances)

A comedy in three acts adapted from the Oscar Wilde novel by Cecil Clarke. Produced by Annette Schein at the Comedy Theatre, New York, August 17, 1936.

Cast of characters—

Basil Hallward.......................................Frederic Albee
Meadows.......................................Eric Tarbet
Sir Henry Watton.......................................Henry Schact
Dorian Gray.......................................Jeron Criswell
Allan Cameron.......................................John B. Culbertson
Lady Gwendolyn Ferrol.......................................Stella Dean Alda
Sybil Dane.......................................Doris Reed
James Dane.......................................Bruce Bancroft
Flora.......................................Vera Patten

Acts I, II and III.—Living Room of Dorian Gray, 20 Belgrave Square, London.
Staged by Edwin O'Hanlon.

A revised version of the play done originally as "Dorian Gray," record of which has been made a few pages to the rear.

D'OYLY CARTE OPERA COMPANY

(156 performances)

Presenting a repertory of Gilbert and Sullivan operettas at the Martin Beck Theatre, New York, beginning August 20, 1936.

THE MIKADO

(28 performances)

Cast of characters—

The Mikado of Japan.......................................Darrell Fancourt
Nanki-Poo.......................................Derek Oldham

Ko-Ko....................................Martyn Green
Pooh-Bah....................................Sydney Granville
Pish-Tush....................................Leslie Rands
Go-To....................................Radley Flynn
Yum-Yum....................................Sylvia Cecil
Pitti-Sing....................................Marjorie Eyre
Peep-Bo....................................Elizabeth Nickell-Lean
Katisha....................................Evelyn Gardiner
Chorus of School Girls, Nobles, Guards and Coolies
Act I.—Courtyard of Ko-Ko's Official Residence. Act II.—Ko-Ko's Garden.
Orchestra Under the Direction of Isidore Godfrey.

On August 19, 1886, a half century before this revival, "The Mikado" was presented for the first time in America by the original D'Oyly Carte Company at Stetson's Fifth Avenue Theatre, New York.

TRIAL BY JURY

(August 31)

(20 performances)

Cast of characters—

The Learned Judge....................................Sydney Granville
Counsel for the Plaintiff....................................Leslie Rands
The Defendant....................................Robert Wilson
Foreman of the Jury....................................T. Penry Hughes
Usher....................................Richard Walker
Associate....................................C. William Morgan
The Plaintiff....................................Ann Drummond-Grant
First Bridesmaid....................................Kathleen Naylor
Scene—A Court of Justice.

Followed by—

THE PIRATES OF PENZANCE

(20 performances)

Cast of characters—

Major-General Stanley....................................Martyn Green
The Pirate King....................................Darrell Fancourt
Samuel....................................Richard Walker
Frederic....................................John Dean
Sergeant of Police....................................Sydney Granville
Mabel....................................Brenda Bennett
Edith....................................Marjorie Eyre
Kate....................................Elizabeth Nickell-Lean
Isabel....................................Kathleen Naylor
Ruth....................................Evelyn Gardiner
Act I.—Rocky Seashore on Coast of Cornwall. Act II.—A Ruined Chapel, by Moonlight.

THE GONDOLIERS

(September 7)

(20 performances)

Cast of characters—

The Duke of Plaza-Toro....Martyn Green
Luiz....John Dean
Don Alhambra Del Bolero....Sydney Granville
Marco Palmieri....Derek Oldham
Giuseppe Palmieri....Leslie Rands
Antonio....Richard Dunn
Francesco....Robert Wilson
Giorgio....Radley Flynn
Annibale....Frank Steward
The Duchess of Plaza-Toro....Evelyn Gardiner
Casilda....Brenda Bennett
Gianetta....Sylvia Cecil
Tessa....Marjorie Eyre
Fiametta....Ann Drummond-Grant
Vittoria....Elizabeth Nickell-Lean
Giulia....Margery Abbott
Inez....Josephine Curtis

Act I.—Venice. Act II.—Pavilion in the Palace of Barataria.

THE YEOMEN OF THE GUARD

(September 14)

(20 performances)

Cast of characters—

Sir Richard Cholmondeley....Leslie Rands
Colonel Fairfax....Derek Oldham
Sergeant Meryll....Darrell Fancourt
Leonard Meryll....Robert Wilson
Jack Point....Martyn Green
Wilfred Shadbolt....Sydney Granville
First Yeoman....Bernard Maher
Second Yeoman....Mansel Dyer
First Citizen....C. William Morgan
Second Citizen....Frank Steward
Elsie Maynard....Sylvia Cecil
Phoebe Meryll....Marjorie Eyre
Dame Carruthers....Evelyn Gardiner
Kate....Margery Abbott

Acts I and II.—Tower Green.

IOLANTHE

(September 21)

(20 performances)

Cast of characters—

The Lord Chancellor....Martyn Green
Earl of Mountararat....Darrell Fancourt
Earl Tolloller....Derek Oldham
Private Willis....Sydney Granville
Strephon....Leslie Rands
Queen of the Fairies....Evelyn Gardiner

Iolanthe....................................Elizabeth Nickell-Lean
Celia....................................Ann Drummond-Grant
Leila....................................Ivy Sanders
Fleta....................................Kathleen Naylor
Phyllis....................................Brenda Bennett
Chorus of Dukes, Marquises, Earls, Viscounts, Barons and Fairies.
Act I.—An Arcadian Landscape. Act II.—Palace Yard, Westminster.

COX AND BOX

By Maddison Morton, F. C. Burnand and Arthur Sullivan

(September 28)

(16 performances)

Cast of characters—

Cox....................................Richard Dunn
Box....................................John Dean
Bouncer....................................Richard Walker
Scene—A Room in Bouncer's House.

Followed by—

H.M.S. "PINAFORE"

(21 performances)

Cast of characters—

The Rt. Hon. Sir Joseph Porter, K.C.B....................Martyn Green
Captain Corcoran....................................Leslie Rands
Ralph Rackstraw....................................Derek Oldham
Dick Deadeye....................................Darrell Fancourt
Bill Bobstay....................................Richard Walker
Bob Becket....................................Radley Flynn
Josephine....................................Sylvia Cecil
Hebe....................................Marjorie Eyre
Little Buttercup....................................Evelyn Gardiner
First Lord's Sisters, His Cousins, His Aunts, Sailors, Marines, etc.
Scene: Quarter-Deck of H.M.S. "Pinafore," off Portsmouth.

PATIENCE

(October 5)

(12 performances)

Cast of characters—

Colonel Calverley....................................Darrell Fancourt
Major Murgatroyd....................................Frank Steward
Lieut. The Duke of Dunstable....................................John Dean
Reginald Bunthorne....................................Martyn Green
Archibald Grosvenor....................................Leslie Rands
Mr. Bunthorne's Solicitor....................................Wynn Dyson
The Lady Angela....................................Marjorie Eyre
The Lady Saphir....................................Elizabeth Nickell-Lean
The Lady Ella....................................Brenda Bennett
The Lady Jane....................................Evelyn Gardiner
Patience....................................Sylvia Cecil
Chorus of Rapturous Maidens and Officers of the Dragoon Guards.
Act I.—Exterior of Castle Bunthorne. Act II.—A Glade.

PRINCESS IDA

(October 12)

(12 performances)

Cast of characters—

King Hildebrand....Sydney Granville
Hilarion....Derek Oldham
Cyril....John Dean
Florian....Leslie Rands
King Gama....Martyn Green
Arac....Darrell Fancourt
Guron....Richard Walker
Scynthius....Radley Flynn
Princess Ida....Sylvia Cecil
Lady Blanche....Evelyn Gardiner
Lady Psyche....Ann Drummond-Grant
Melissa....Marjorie Eyre
Sacharissa....Kathleen Naylor
Chloe....Marjorie Abbott
Ada....Elsie Winnall

Act I.—Pavilion in King Hildebrand's Palace. Act II.—Gardens of Castle Adamant. Act III.—Castle Adamant Court.

RUDDIGORE

(October 22)

(8 performances)

Cast of characters—

Sir Ruthven Murgatroyd....Martyn Green
Richard Dauntless....John Dean
Sir Despard Murgatroyd....Sydney Granville
Old Adam Goodheart....Radley Flynn
Sir Roderic Murgatroyd....Darrell Fancourt
Rose Maybud....Brenda Bennett
Mad Margaret....Marjorie Eyre
Dame Hannah....Evelyn Gardiner
Zorah....Ann Drummond-Grant
Ruth....Kathleen Naylor

Act I.—Fishing Village in Cornwall. Act II.—Picture Gallery in Ruddigore Castle.

VICTORIA REGINA

(Return engagement 314 performances. Total 517.)

A play in three acts by Laurence Housman. Engagement resumed by Gilbert Miller at the Broadhurst Theatre, New York, August 31, 1936.

Cast of characters—

A Footman....Alfred Helton
Lord Conyngham....E. Bellenden-Clarke
Archbishop of Canterbury....Harry Plimmer
A Maidservant....Mary Austin
Duchess of Kent....Babette Feist
Victoria....Helen Hayes
Lord Melbourne....Charles Francis

Prince Albert....................Vincent Price
Prince Ernest....................George Macready
Mr. Richards....................Albert Froom
Mr. Anson....................Oswald Marshall
1st Queen's Gentleman....................Arthur Gould-Porter
Royal Footman....................Alan Bandler
A Court Usher....................Edward Martin
Lady Muriel....................Mary Heberden
Lady Grace....................Renee Macredy
Lady-in-Waiting....................Mary Newnham-Davis
2nd Queen's Gentleman....................Fothringham Lysons
Mr. Oakley....................James Bedford
Duchess of Sutherland....................Cherry Hardy
Lady Jane....................Helen Trenholme
General Grey....................Tom Woods
3rd Queen's Gentleman....................Edward Jones
John Brown....................James Woodburn
Benjamin Disraeli (Earl of Beaconsfield)....................Abraham Sofaer
A Footman....................Robert Von Rigel
Sir Arthur Bigge....................Herschel Martin
An Imperial Highness....................Felix Brown
His Royal Highness....................Gilbert McKay
1st Princess....................Mary Forbes
2nd Princess....................Shirley Gale
3rd Princess....................Elizabeth Munn
Members of the Royal Family, Footman and Court Officials: Jean Stephenson, Willis Duncan, Guy Moneypenny, Shirley Poirier, Buddy Buehler.

Act I.—Scene 1—Entrance Hall, Kensington Palace. 2 and 3—Sitting Room, Windsor Castle. 4—Prince Albert's Dressing Room, Windsor Castle. Act II.—Scenes 1 and 4—Prince Albert's Writing Room at Buckingham Palace. 2—Room in Buckingham Palace Overlooking Park. 3—Ante-Chamber at Windsor Castle. Act III.—Scene 1—Garden Tent at Balmoral Castle. 2—Buckingham Palace.

Staged by Gilbert Miller; settings by Rex Whistler.

The engagement of "Victoria Regina," begun December 26, 1935, was interrupted June 20, 1936, that Miss Hayes and her company might enjoy a Summer vacation. With two major changes in cast, Abraham Sofaer replacing George Zucco as Disraeli and Charles Francis taking over the role of Lord Melbourne, played originally by Lewis Casson, the engagement was resumed August 31, 1936. See "Best Plays 1935-36."

IDIOT'S DELIGHT

(Return engagement 179 performances. Total 300.)

A drama in three acts by Robert E. Sherwood. Engagement resumed by the Theatre Guild at the Shubert Theatre, August 31, 1936.

Cast of characters—

Dumptsy....................George Meader
Signor Palota....................Stephen Sandes
Donald Navadel....................Gilmore Bush
Pittaluga....................S. Thomas Gomez
Auguste....................Edgar Barrier
Captain Locicero....................Edward Raquello
Dr. Waldersee....................Sydney Greenstreet
Mr. Cherry....................Bretaigne Windust
Mrs. Cherry....................Jean Macintyre

Harry Van..Alfred Lunt
Shirley..Jacqueline Paige
Beulah..Connie Crowell
Edna..Frances Foley
Francine..Edna Ross
Elaine..Marjorie Baglin
Bebe...Ruth Timmons
1st Officer.................................Georgio Monteverde
2nd Officer..Winston Ross
3rd Officer ....John Allen
4th Officer......................................Tomasso Tittoni
Quillery...Richard Whorf
Signor Rossi.......................................Le Roi Operti
Signora Rossi...............................Ernestine De Becker
Major...Joseph Della Malva
Anna...Una Val
Irene...Lynn Fontanne
Achille Weber....................................Francis Compton
Musicians: Gerald Kunz, Max Rich, Joseph Knopf.

Acts I, II and III.—Cocktail Lounge in Hotel Monte Gabrielle in the Italian Alps, Near Frontiers of Switzerland and Austria.

Staged by Bretaigne Windust under supervision of Alfred Lunt and Lynn Fontanne; settings by Lee Simonson; dance directed by Morgan Lewis.

With minor changes in cast the engagement of the Sherwood drama, interrupted July 4, 1936, when the Lunts decided to have a rest, was resumed August 31, 1936. See "Best Plays 1935-36."

SPRING DANCE

(24 performances)

A comedy in three acts adapted by Philip Barry from a play by Eleanor Golden and Eloise Barrangon. Produced by Jed Harris at the Empire Theatre, New York, August 25, 1936.

Cast of characters—

Mildred..Mary Wickes
Walter Beckett.......................................Philip Ober
Miss Ritchie..Marie Bruce
John Hatton...Jack Warren
The Lippincot..Jose Ferrer
Doc Boyd..Tom Neal
Buck Buchanan....................................Brooks Bowman
Mady Platt...Tookie Hunter
Frances Fenn.....................................Peggy O'Donnell
Alex Benson..Louise Platt
Kate McKim..Ruth Matteson
Sally Prescott.....................................Martha Hodge
Sam Thatcher....................................Richard Kendrick

Acts I, II and III.—Small Living House Near the Campus of a Girls' College in New England.

Staged by Jed Harris; settings by Steward Chaney.

Alex Benson has a secret hope that Sam Thatcher, coming to the Spring dance at her college, will propose marriage, Alex being admittedly in love with Sam. Sam, influenced by The Lippincot, arrives at the dance but only to tell Alex good-by. Sam has decided that he wants to devote the next few years to studying the world's problems, especially in Russia, and doing what he can to set them right. Alex takes the blow meekly, but her dormitory pals, led by Kate McKim and Sally Prescott, refuse to see her let down. They "gang up" on Sam, inspire him with jealousies and unrest, and finally lead him to grab Alex and hasten with her to the magistrate's office.

ZIEGFELD FOLLIES OF 1936-1937

(112 performances)

A revue in two acts by Ira Gershwin and David Freedman; music by Vernon Duke. Engagement resumed at the Winter Garden, New York, September 14, 1936.

Principals engaged—

Fannie Brice
Ruth Harrison
Gypsy Rose Lee
Jane Pickens
Cass Daley
James Farrell
Bobby Clark
Alex Fisher
Stan Kavanagh
Hugh Cameron
Marvin Lawler
Ben Yost's Varsity Eight
Cherry and June Preisser

Staged by John Murray Anderson; settings and costumes by Vincente Minnelli; dances directed by Robert Alton; sketches by Edward Clarke Lilley and Edward D. Dowling.

The first edition of this particular "Ziegfeld Follies" was produced at the Winter Garden January 31, 1936, with Fannie Brice, Josephine Baker, Bob Hope, Harriet Hoctor, Gertrude Niesen, Hugh O'Connell and Herb Williams the chief principals. See "Best Plays 1935-36."

THE GOLDEN JOURNEY

(23 performances)

A comedy in three acts by Edwin Gilbert. Produced by the Messrs. Shubert at the Booth Theatre, New York, September 15, 1936.

Cast of characters—

Julian Verney....................Alan Bunce
Ivan Black....................Hugh Rennie
Clayton Herrick....................Alan Hewitt
Williams....................Aldrich Bowker
Violet Freely....................Leona Powers
Elinor Knightsbridge....................Joan Tompkins
Nancy Parrish....................Eleanor Lynn
Sorrel Freely....................Raymond Bramley
Miss Faber....................Jane Bancroft

Acts I, II and III.—Flat of Julian Verney and Clayton Herrick in the East Fifties, New York City.

Staged by Harry Wagstaff Gribble; setting by Watson Barratt; costumes by Helene Pons.

Julian, Ivan and Clayton, novelist, poet and playwright respectively, are living on their wits and such dates as they can negotiate with daughters of the rich and wives of the successful. Julian has a manuscript accepted by Publisher Freely through the influence of Violet Freely, the publisher's amorous wife. Clayton sells a play to a producer when Nancy Parrish, his fiancée, agrees to put up the cost of production if she can play the lead. Julian's manuscript is proved a plagiarism from the French and Clayton's play is a flop, although Nancy is a hit. Julian is absolved when it is discovered he had inherited the script and Clayton agrees to marry Nancy. Leaving Ivan, the poet, for Violet, the restless wife.

SEEN BUT NOT HEARD

(60 performances)

A comedy in two acts by Marie Baumer and Martin Berkeley. Produced by D. A. Doran in association with International Productions, Inc., at the Henry Miller Theatre, New York, September 17, 1936.

Cast of characters—

Duke Winthrop	Frankie Thomas
Elizabeth Winthrop	Anne Baxter
Tommy Winthrop	Raymond Roe
Harriett	Grace Fox
Romney	John Winthrop
John Clyde	Paul McGrath
Reverend Clifford Winthrop	Ernest Woodward
Senator Howard Winthrop	Boyd Davis
Ruth Winthrop	Lulu Mae Hubbard
Celia Winthrop	Ann Winslow
Bob Winthrop	Kent Smith
Thelma Barker	Eleanor Phelps
Jeffreys	Ralph Theadore
Lowell	Anthony Blair
Dr. Paley	Dean Raymond

Acts I and II.—Living Hall of Winthrop Home in New England Village.

Staged by Arthur Sircom; setting by John Root.

Duke Winthrop, 15, Elizabeth, 13, and Tommy, 10, brought to the funeral of a favorite aunt, Mrs. John Clyde, grow increasingly suspicious of the dead woman's husband as a party to the automobile accident which had resulted in her death. Clyde, unpopular with the Winthrops, had loosened a nut on the wheel of his wife's automobile. In a brush with Bob Winthrop Clyde falls, strikes his head on an iron staple and is killed. The children, continuing their investigations, expect to fasten that crime on a butler whom they also dislike. At the moment they are ready to hand their evidence over to the Sheriff they realize that they will convict their Uncle Bob. Hysterically they seal their lips and take an oath never to tell anybody anything.

ARREST THAT WOMAN

(7 performances)

A melodrama in three acts by Maxine Alton. Produced by A. H. Woods at the National Theatre, New York, September 18, 1936.

Cast of characters—

Go-Go	Gertrude Short
Marie Smith	Doris Nolan
Tom Thornton	Mervyn Williams
Donald Drake	Hugh Marlowe
Madlyn Harcourt	Lillian Emerson
Judge Marvin Drake	George Lessey
Brown	Frank Andrews
Police Telephone Operator	Francis Roberts
Police Radio Announcer	Roger Hundley
Davis	Gerald Kent
Officer McCarthy	Charles Wiley, Sr.
Sailor	Dave Mallen
Marine	Walter Kinsella
Buddy	Merle Clayton
Robert Dorgan, District Attorney	Walter N. Greaza
Kelly	Harry Hanlon

Act I.—Scene 1—Marie Smith's Room. 2—Judge Drake's Study. Act II.—Office of District Attorney. Act III.—Judge Drake's Study.
Staged by Ira Hards; settings by Nicholas Yellenti.

Marie Smith, having quit prostitution and gone to modeling so she can marry Tom Thornton and live respectable, tries to help Tom restore a thousand dollars which he has stolen to help his ailing mother. Marie goes to the home of her father, an upright Judge, who was never married to her mother, and threatens to scandalize his name by shooting herself in his house unless he helps her. In a struggle for the gun the Judge is killed. Marie is arrested. The case goes to Assistant District Attorney Donald Drake, son of the slain Judge. Marie is forced to confess that Drake is her half brother. He promptly goes over to the defense, helping Marie to escape the law.

TIMBER HOUSE

(1 performance)

A melodrama in three acts by John Boruff. Produced by Charles E. Fiske and Paul Hammond at the Longacre Theatre, New York, September 19, 1936.

Cast of characters—

Edward Brinold	Donald Cameron
Mohena	Ann Dere

Miriam Brinold....................................Lenita Lane
Markam Walling....................................Thomas Louden
Al Roberts....................................Melvin Benstock
Martin Winnow....................................Edward Marr
Ralph Miller....................................Robert Shayne
Alvina Glouster....................................Frieda Altman
Allen Garver....................................Paul Hammond

Acts I, II and III.—Living Room of Timber House, Edward Brinold's Summer Home in Vermont.

Staged by J. Edward Shugrue; setting by Donald Oenslager.

Edward Brinold, insanely jealous of his wife and knowing that he is dying of a brain cancer, plots a suicide that shall make it appear he has been killed by Miriam, the wife, and Ralph Miller, her lover. He fires a bullet from a revolver into a sack of flour, recovers the bullet and puts it in the cartridge of another gun. He plants the first revolver on the lover, turns out the lights, shoots himself and leaves the rest to the police. Things look bad for lover and wife. Ballistic authorities trace the bullet to the lover's gun. But Alvina Glouster, investigating Brinold's life insurance policy, unravels the plot and exposes the conspiracy.

REFLECTED GLORY

(127 performances)

A comedy in three acts by George Kelly. Produced by Lee Shubert, in association with Homer Curran and Joseph M. Gaites, at the Morosco Theatre, New York, September 21, 1936.

Cast of characters—

Mr. Hanlon....................................Clay Clement
Hattie....................................Elizabeth Dunne
Miss Sloane....................................Ann Andrews
Miss Flood....................................Tallulah Bankhead
Mr. Wall....................................Phillip Reed
Mr. Howard....................................Alden Chase
Bruno....................................Robert Bordoni
Stage Door Man....................................William H. Turner
Mrs. Howard....................................Madeline Holmes
Mr. Omansetter....................................William Brisbane
Irene....................................S. T. Bratton

Act I.—Miss Flood's Suite, Lorraine Hotel, Rochester. Act II.—Scene 1—Dressing Room in New York Theatre during Last Act of Saturday Matinee. 2—Miss Flood's Suite in New York Hotel. Act III.—New York Theatre Dressing Room.

Staged by George Kelly; settings by Norman Rock.

Muriel Flood, popular emotional actress, is torn between a desire to leave the theatre, marry and settle down, and an artist's urge to go on with her career. She turns down a Mr. Howard of Baltimore and takes up with a Mr. Wall of Chicago, who turns out to be a cheater. In which dilemma Muriel decides to go on with her career.

SO PROUDLY WE HAIL

(14 performances)

A drama in two acts by Joseph M. Viertel. Produced by James R. Ullman in association with International Productions, Inc., at the 46th Street Theatre, New York, September 22, 1936.

Cast of characters—

Plebe Cadet	Charles Walters
Plebe Cadet	Eddie Bracken
Mrs. Thornton	Ethel Jackson
Tom Newton	Edwin Philips
Anne Greer	Jean Rouverol
Jim Thornton	Richard Cromwell
Cadet	Robert Angevine
Cadet Sergeant	James Keogan
Cadet Lieut. Atkins	Angus Duncan
Major Cooper	Charles Dingle
Captain Tremont	Gordon Nelson
Miss Benson	Blanche Haring
Rodney Burns	Edward Andrews
William McDost	John Call
Cadet Sergt. Sherman	Ronald Brogan
Orderly	Peter Johnston
Officer of the Day	Stanley Hughes
Cadet	Norman Williams
Cadet Lieutenant	Reed Smith
Cadet Wilson	Vernon Crane
Major Prall	Jack Davis

Acts I, II and III.—Stone Ridge Military Academy.
Staged by Anton Bundsmann; settings by John Root.

Jim Thornton enters Stone Ridge Military Academy with boyish enthusiasm and high hopes. He is roughly hazed by the upper classmen, rigidly disciplined by his teachers. In six months he tries to desert, is caught and sentenced to thirty days in the guard house. During his incarceration his best friend dies of pneumonia, induced by drill exposure during a fever he was ashamed to report. Thornton threatens to make an issue of his friend's death and is subtly bribed by the promise of a sergeantcy his second year. He comes out of his confinement determined to accept the school for what it is. He will become as hard as the others. Thoroughly brutalized he takes his resentment out on a friend who comes to school to be near him, seeing him viciously thrashed for a minor delinquency. At graduation they award Thornton the medal of honor as a model student.

BRIGHT HONOR

(17 performances)

A comedy in three acts by Henry R. Misrock. Produced by Jack Kirkland and Sam H. Grisman at the 48th Street Theatre, New York, September 27, 1936.

Cast of characters—

Mrs. Thompson....................................Kathleen Wallace
Mary Manning...Renee Terry
Cadet George (Red) Johnson..................Charles R. Duncan
Cadet Jack MacLean......................................Edwin Mills
Cadet Michael Fenner...................................Junior Bealin
Cadet James T. Kingston..........................George Makinson
Cadet Steve Berkhofer.....................John Drew Devereaux
Cadet Bob "Dixie" Tyler.............................Robert Scott
Cadet Alfred "Fatso" Symonds.......................Jack Maher
Cadet Juan Bustillo.......................................John Foster
Cadet Bruce "Smoothy" Barclay................Arthur C. Scanlon
Cadet Roger "Peanuts" Bendix.......................Roy Le May
Cadet Morris "Moe" Greenblatt...............Neal Vernon Buhler
Cadet Joe Allen.......................................Edward Wragge
Joan Clark...Dorothy Tree
Cadet Herbert Selton...................................Walter Ward
Gordon Reese..Leon Ames
Captain John J. Stocker.........................James Spottswood
Chaplain Arthur Manning..............................Bram Nossen
Thomas Briggs, Jr....................................Charles Powers
Peter Thompson...................................Foster J. Williams
Cadet Elmer Gardeuer..............................Frederic Stange
Cadet Raymond Fleming..................................John Cort
Cadet Tom Horn......................................John D. Coons
Cadet Henry Metchik........................Marshall L. Buchwald
Cadet Walter Willard................................Ralph Welliver
Cadet Anthony Mazetti...................................Perry Meyer
Mr. Thomas Briggs....................................Frank Harvey
Mr. Herbert Selton....................................Otis Sheridan
Mrs. Herbert Selton.......................................Aileen Poe
Agnes Fenner...Elinor Queen
Vivian Caldwell..................................Florence Sundstrom
Mildred Shotwell..Ruth Gilbert
General Dayton M. Warren..........................John T. Dwyer
Mrs. Dorothy MacLean..............................Helen Peabody
Guest at Dance..Patricia Howell
Guest at Dance..Claire Maynard
Guest at Dance...Jewel Hart
Guest at Dance...Claire Harvey
Guest at Dance...Ann Sherry

Acts I, II and III.—Newtown Military Academy.
Staged by Anthony Brown; settings by W. Oden Waller.

Thomas Briggs, Jr., is sent to Newtown Military Academy because his parents wanted to be rid of him. He enters school rebelliously, is taken down by the "old boys" and forced finally to a choice between supporting the *esprit de corps* as dictated by his fellows or remaining loyal to Gordon Reese, his English professor and only friend on the faculty. Thomas chooses the *esprit de corps* and sees his friend dismissed.

NIGHT MUST FALL

(64 performances)

A drama in three acts by Emlyn Williams. Produced by Sam H. Harris at the Ethel Barrymore Theatre, New York, September 28, 1936.

Cast of characters—

The Lord Chief Justice.............................Ben Webster
Mrs. Bramson.............................May Whitty
Olivia Grayne.............................Angela Baddeley
Hubert Laurie.............................Michael Shepley
Nurse Libby.............................Shirley Gale
Mrs. Terence.............................Doris Hare
Dora Parkoe.............................Betty Jardine
Inspector Belsize.............................Mathew Boulton
Dan.............................Emlyn Williams

Before the Play—The Court of Criminal Appeal, London. Acts I, II and III.—Sitting Room of Forest Corner, Mrs. Bramson's Bungalow, Essex, England.

Staged by the author, with a bow to Miles Malleson of London.

Dan is a bellboy in a resort hotel remotely located in Essex, England. Having seduced Dora Parkoe, maid at Mrs. Bramson's, Dan is summoned to the Bramson cottage. Such is his charm that Mrs. Bramson is immediately taken with him, adding him to her household servants. The murder of a guest at the hotel is traced to Dan by Olivia, an unhappy niece of Mrs. Bramson's, who elects to shield the boy. Dan, grateful but powerless in the grip of his homicidal instincts, plots the murder of Mrs. Bramson for her money. The police take him away to be hanged, leaving Olivia relieved but desolate.

LOVE FROM A STRANGER

(31 performances)

A drama in three acts by Frank Vosper. Produced by Alex Yokel at the Fulton Theatre, New York, September 29, 1936.

Cast of characters—

Louise Garrard.............................Minna Phillips
Mavis Wilson.............................Olive Reeves-Smith
Cecily Harrington.............................Jessie Royce Landis
Bruce Lovell.............................Frank Vosper
Nigel Lawrence.............................Leslie Austen
Hodgson.............................A. G. Andrews
Ethel.............................Mildred Natwick
Dr. Gribble.............................George Graham

Act I.—Cecily's and Mavis' Flat, Bayswater, England. Acts II and III.—The Cottage.

Staged by Auriol Lee; settings by Kate Drain Lawson.

Cecily Harrington and Mavis Wilson, winning $20,000 in the sweepstakes, rent their Bayswater apartment to an engaging young man named Bruce Lovell. Cecily also falls in love with Bruce on sight. They are married and are honeymooning in a forest cottage when it develops that Lovell is a psychopathic case, a murderer impelled to crime by an unconquerable passion of periodic recurrence. He has the cellar set for Cecily's extinction when she goads him into a paralytic stroke.

MIMIE SCHELLER

(29 performances)

A drama in three acts by Alfred L. Golden. Produced by Ned Jakobs at the Ritz Theatre, New York, September 30, 1936.

Cast of characters—

Frank Healy....................................Edward Blaine
Joe Matthews....................................Calvin Thomas
Mike Pratt....................................Morgan Conway
Deputy Warden....................................John Vosburgh
Warden....................................Herbert Warren
Hank Fisher....................................Conrad Cantzen
Matron Marsh....................................Marie Curtis
Len Shay....................................Bigelow Sayre
Williams....................................Gordon McCracken
Matron Winthrop....................................Ann Williams
Prison Physician....................................Richard Allen
Chaplain....................................John Davis
Mimie Scheller....................................Ara Gerald
Acts I, II and III.—Death House, Mid-Western Penitentiary.
Staged by Dickson Morgan; setting by Cirker and Robbins.

Mimie (My-mee) Scheller, as tough a lady as ever headed a gang of bank robbers, disguises herself as the aged sister of Frank Healy, who had been her chauffeur, and visits him in the death house of a Mid-Western penitentiary, intending to stage a jail delivery. Frank squeals and Mimie finds herself jailed. There is a bet between two of the guards as to whether Mimie will break or not before she marches through the little green door to the electric chair. Mimie breaks, but not before she has shaken most of the rattles out of that old death house, and shivered the rest of it with her curses.

STORK MAD

(5 performances)

A farce in three acts by Lynn Root and Frank Fenton. Produced by James R. Ullman at the Ambassador Theatre, New York, September 30, 1936.

Cast of characters—

Harry Dever....................................Lynn Root
Hank Dever....................................Marion Willis
Granpap Dever....................................Carlton Macy
Mary Dever....................................Dortha Duckworth
Peter Dever....................................Jackie Grimes
Matthew Dever....................................Percy Kilbride
Annie Prestor....................................Ann Thomas
Dr. Guthrie....................................Arthur Griffin
Jed Peters....................................Edward F. Nannary
Sam Peters....................................Alfred Herrick
Cedric Prestor....................................Walter Jones
Preacher Perkins....................................George Glass

Judas Dever....................................Warren Mills
Melinda Dever....................................Patsy Roe
Paul Dever....................................Donald Brown
Sheriff Higgins....................................Hale Norcross
Emma Peters....................................Mary McQuade

Acts I, II and III.—Dever Home in the Hill Country of Southern Ohio.

Staged by William Schorr; setting by S. Syrjala.

Natives of the hill country in Southern Ohio have heard of the "baby derby," by the terms of which a certain rich man has willed a fortune of half a million dollars to the wife and mother who produces the greatest number of offspring in ten years. Matthew Dever and his long time enemy, Jed Peters, figure themselves chief contestants, with Matthew off to a head start when Mrs. Dever enters with triplets, one born the wrong side, two born the right side of the starting hour of midnight, as against Mrs. Peters' single. Matthew continues to lead with Mrs. Dever's annual contribution until Jed frames an assault charge against him and keeps him in jail the better part of a year. If Matthew hadn't got his jailer drunk and got home for a few hours Peters might have beaten him. It didn't really matter. In the end Harry Dever's wife comes through with quadruplets to add to her other eight entries and win.

WHITE HORSE INN

(223 performances)

A musical comedy in three acts by Hans Mueller, suggested by Oskar Blumenthal and G. Kandelburg and adapted by David Freedman; lyrics by Irving Caesar; music by Ralph Benatsky. Produced by Laurence Rivers, Inc., at the Center Theatre, New York, October 1, 1936.

Principals engaged—

William Gaxton	Kitty Carlisle
Robert Halliday	Carol Stone
Billy House	Melissa Mason
Tommy Gavin	Marie Marion
Oscar Ragland	Almira Sessions
Robert Williamson	Mme. Reverelly
Arnold Korff	Frederick Graham
Buster West	Nelson Clifford
Milton Gill	Native Tyroleans

Act I.—Scenes 1, 2 and 6—White Horse Inn. 3—The Forest. 4—The Cow Shed. 5—The Garden Restaurant. Act II.—Scene 1—Village Market. 2—White Horse Inn. 3—Railway Station. 4—The Solarium. 5, 7 and 9—The Forest. 6—Alpine Plateau. 8—Town Hall. 10—On the Landing Stage. Act III.—Scenes 1 and 7—White Horse Inn. 2, 4 and 6—The Forest. 3—Tyrolean Wine Garden. 5—Hill Top.

Staged by Erik Charell; settings by Ernst Stern; modern costumes by Irene Sharaff; dances by Max Rivers.

LEND ME YOUR EARS!

(8 performances)

A comedy in three acts by Philip Wood and Stewart Beach. Produced by Leo Peters, Leonard Field and Robert Weenolsen at the Mansfield Theatre, New York, October 5, 1936.

Cast of characters—

Junior Beam..........Robert Mayors
Wallace Titcomb..........Cliff Heckinger
Willa Beam..........Jane Seymour
Marjolaine Beam..........Lynn Mary Oldham
Jasper Beam..........Walter C. Kelly
Fred Carpenter..........John F. Kirk
Daphne Wayne..........Mary Holsman
Steve Delaney..........Bertram Thorn
Ed Flanagan..........Robert Williams
Clayton Sommers..........McLain Gates
Herman Pratt..........Frederick Kaufman
Clifford Pine..........Jack Harwood
Mrs. Sterling Tutt..........Lida Kane
Ann Harmon..........Ann Winthrop
Polly Andrews..........Lucille Conrad
Mrs. Willoughby..........Sara Floyd
Mike McCartney..........Clyde Franklin

Acts I, II and III.—Living Room of Jasper Beam's Home in Fair River, Near New York.

Staged by Leo Bulgakov; setting by Cirker and Robbins.

Jasper Beam is an oratorical small town politician with a fondness for quoting the classics. Daphne Wayne, a New York newspaper woman, conceives the idea of running Beam for a village office on a New Deal platform, hoping to help her paper's country circulation. The Beam boom gains local importance early, spreads to the county and then to the state. The candidate is going strong until he invites a nudist convention to the town. For this Willa Beam, his wife, leaves him. Jasper breaks down in a sentimental broadcast, which brings Willa home and elects him to office. They are thinking of running him for Governor at the curtain.

ST. HELENA

(63 performances)

A drama in three acts by R. C. Sherriff and Jeanne de Casalis. Produced by Max Gordon at the Lyceum Theatre, New York, October 6, 1936.

Cast of characters—

A Marine..........Lewis Dayton
A Ship's Carpenter..........Paul Porter
Cipriani..........Jules Epailly
A Sailor..........Charles F. O'Connor

General Count Bertrand....Reginald Mason
General Baron Gourgaud....Joseph Macaulay
General Count Montholon....Stephen Ker Appleby
Novarrez....Robert Ansteth
St. Denis....Barry Sullivan
Napoleon....Maurice Evans
Admiral Sir George Cockburn....Edward Fielding
Count Las Cases....Alan Wheatley
Marchand, Napoleon's Valet....Marc Loebell
Countess Montholon....Kay Strozzi
Sir Hudson Lowe....Percy Waram
Dr. O'Meara....Whitford Kane
Captain Nicholls....Stephen Courtleigh
Tristan Montholon....Jack Kelly
Napoleon Bertrand....Edward J. Ryan, Jr.
Hortense Bertrand....Joyce Walsh
Countess Bertrand....Rosamond Pinchot
Orderly Officer....Paul Adams
A Sentry....Samuel Danzig
The Abbe Buonovita....Francis Pierlot
The Abbe Vignali....Harry Bellaver
Dr. Antommarchi....Joseph De Santis
Sailors, Troopers, Staff Officers, Chinese Gardeners.

Act I.—Dining Room and Bedroom, Longwood House, St. Helena, 1815. Act II.—Scene 1—Dining Room. 2—Study and Courtyard. 3—Veranda. Act III.—Scene 1—Veranda. 2 and 4—Napoleon's Bedroom, 1821. 3—Garden.

Staged by Robert B. Sinclair; settings and costumes by Jo Mielziner.

See page 257.

HAMLET

(132 performances)

A tragedy in two parts by William Shakespeare. Revived by Guthrie McClintic at the Empire Theatre, New York, October 8, 1936.

Cast of characters—

Francisco....Murvyn Vye
Bernardo....Reed Herring
Horatio....Harry Andrews
Marcellus....Barry Kelly
Ghost of Hamlet's Father....——
Claudius, King of Denmark....Malcolm Keen
Cornelius....Whitner Bissell
Voltimand....James Dinan
Laertes....John Emery
Polonius....Arthur Byron
Hamlet....John Gielgud
Gertrude, Queen of Denmark....Judith Anderson
Ophelia....Lillian Gish
Reynaldo....Murvyn Vye
Rosencrantz....John Cromwell
Guildenstern....William Roehrick
The Player King....Harry Mestayer
Prologue....Ivan Triesault
The Player Queen....Ruth March
Lucianus....Whitner Bissell
Fortinbras....Reed Herring
A Captain....George Vincent
A Sailor....William Stanley
First Grave-Digger....George Nash
Second Grave-Digger....Barry Kelly
Priest....Ivan Triesault
Osric....Morgan Farley

Lords, Ladies, Officers, Sailors, Messengers and Other Attendants: Evelyn Abbott, Neal Barry, James Dinan, John Galland, Stanley Gould, Peter Gray, Henry Hull, Jr., Mary Lee Logan, Donaldson Murphy, Sydna Scott, Kurt Steinbart.

The Ghost's Lines are Read by Malcolm Keen.

Scenes 1 and 4—Sentinel's Platform before Royal Castle, Denmark. 2, 6 and 16—Council Chamber. 3 and 5—Polonius' House. 7, 8, 12, 14 and 19—Great Hall. 9 and 11—King's Dressing Room. 10—Queen's Private Apartment. 13—A Plain in Denmark. 15—Horatio's House. 17—Churchyard. 18—Corridor in Castle.

Staged by Guthrie McClintic; settings and costumes by Jo Mielziner.

Three previous revivals of "Hamlet" have achieved long runs on Broadway, that of Edwin Booth in 1880, John Barrymore in 1922 and John E. Kellerd (at popular prices) in 1912. Johnstone Forbes-Robertson last played Hamlet in America in 1913. The Forbes-Robertson Hamlet was also filmed in 1912.

AND STARS REMAIN

(56 performances)

A comedy in three acts by Julius J. and Philip Epstein. Produced by the Theatre Guild, Inc., at the Guild Theatre, New York, October 12, 1936.

Cast of characters—

Lucy Trenchard	Claudia Morgan
Overton Morrell	Clifton Webb
Faith Feible	Mary Sargent
Perry Feible	Richard Barbee
Grandfather Trenchard	Charles Richman
Mrs. Trenchard	Suzanne Jackson
Cynthia Hope	Helen Gahagan
Frederick Holden	Ben Smith
Nichols	Edgar Kent

Acts I, II and III.—Cynthia Hope's Apartment in Sutton Place.

Staged by Philip Moeller; setting by Aline Bernstein.

Cynthia Hope, convicted as an accessory in the illegal conduct of her husband's bank, is sent to jail for five months. Her husband commits suicide. Cynthia comes out of jail with a changed point of view. Her capitalistically minded grandfather would reopen the case in the hope of vindicating the name of his dead son. Frederick Holden, assistant prosecutor, advises strongly against a second sacrifice of Cynthia. She discovers her sympathies to be with the champion of the people rather than with her Bourbon grandfather. Her family loyalties hold her as grandfather's defender for a time. When grandfather also determines to work for the abolishment of all relief work she turns and threatens to reveal the real story of the bank's closing unless he gives over. After which she takes Holden for better or worse.

THE LAUGHING WOMAN

(23 performances)

A play in prologue, two acts and epilogue by Gordon Daviot. Produced by James R. Ullman in association with the Messrs. Shubert at the Golden Theatre, New York, October 13, 1936.

Cast of characters—

A Young Man	Richard Speer
Attendant	William Cragin
1st Chit	Edna Ramsey
2nd Chit	Ruth Frank
A Man	Fred Leslie
Mr. Honeymoon	Neville Percy
Mrs. Honeymoon	Patricia Morgan
Rene Latour	Tonio Selwart
Ingrid Rydman	Helen Menken
Madame Grumier	Beverley Sitgraves
Smith	Wilfred Seagram
Mrs. Smith	Elizabeth Valentine
Hazel Graham	Lora Baxter
Laura Gadd	Marga Ann Deighton
Marion Slade	Teresa Guerini
O'Brien	Lloyd Gough
Burched	Roland Bottomley
Sir Cuthbert Graham	J. W. Austin
Butler	Gerald Corbet
Doll Simmons	Mary Howes
Hergesheimer	A. J. Herbert
Miss Casson	Cynthia Sherwood
1st Schoolgirl	Minelda Lange
2nd Schoolgirl	Patricia Waters
3rd Schoolgirl	Lois Hall

Prologue and Epilogue—London Art Gallery Corridor. Act I.—Scene 1—Cheap Apartment House Room in Paris. 2 and 3—Room in London Tenement. Act II.—Scene 1—Drawing Room in Graham's House, Queen Ann Street. 2 and 3—London Tenement.

Staged by Alexander Dean; settings by Watson Barratt.

Ingrid Rydman, a Swedish novelist, meets and admires Rene Latour, a young French artist, several years her junior. Ingrid agrees to live with Rene as his sister and help him in his work. Rene develops into a genius and the sisterly passion into something more intimate, to the distress of Ingrid. Society snubs the pair. Rene goes to war and is killed. Ingrid lives on with his memory her dearest possession.

DAUGHTERS OF ATREUS

(13 performances)

A tragedy in three acts by Robert Turney. Produced by Delos Chappell at the 44th Street Theatre, New York, October 14, 1936.

Cast of characters—

Polymnia	Maria Ouspenskaya
Nepthis	Elizabeth Young
Nerissa	Carla Ogle
Euterpe	Ann Freschmann

Thetis..Barbara Adams
Fria..Eileen Burns
Sharadha..Clara Mahr
Elektra, as a Child....................................Gilda Oakleaf
Iphegeneia..Olive Deering
Klytaimnestra..............................Eleonora Mendelssohn
Vortigern..John Boruff
Cheops..Edgar Stehli
A Messenger..Leslie Gorall
Agamemnon..Gale Gordon
Achilles..Edward Trevor
Kalchas..Harry Irvine
Elektra..Joanna Roos
Orestes, as a child....................................Howard Sherman
Orestes' Attendant....................................Robert Stewart
Aegisthos..Hal Conklin
Hippolytos..Tom Neal
Phaon..Cornel Wilde
Hero..Helen Walpole
Melissa..Eleanor Powers
Orestes..Eric Wollencott
Pylades..Edmond O'Brien
Aesculapios....................................Thomas Coffin Cooke
Soldiers of Klytaimnestra, Kalchas, Achilles, Agamemnon and Aegisthos: James Larmore, Franklyn Webb, William Van Gundy, Ben Edwards, Richard Burdette, Sidney Bryson, John Grimshaw, Arthur Sachs, Carl Rodgers, Louis Varca, Michael Sage, Melvin Parks, Gordon Peters, Robert Stewart, Vincent Gardner.

Act I.—Scene 1—Courtyard of Klytaimnestra's Palace at Mycenae. 2—Before the Temple at Aulis. Act II.—The Palace. Act III.—Scene 1—The Courtyard. 2—The Palace.

Staged by Frederic McConnell; settings by Jo Mielziner; costumes by James Reynolds.

See page 142.

* TOVARICH

(285 performances)

A comedy in two acts by Jacques Deval; English version by Robert E. Sherwood. Produced by Gilbert Miller at the Plymouth Theatre, New York, October 15, 1936.

Cast of characters—

Prince Mikail Alexandrovitch Ouratieff...............John Halliday
Grand Duchess Tatiana Petrovna......................Marta Abba
Olga..Irina Feodorova
Count Feodor Brekenski.......................Frederic Worlock
Chauffourier-Dubieff.................................Ernest Lawford
Martelleau....................................Aristides de Leon
Fernande Dupont....................................Margaret Dale
Charles Dupont....................................Jay Fassett
Louise..Barbara Gott
Georges Dupont....................................James E. Truex
Helene Dupont....................................Amanda Duff
Concierge....................................J. Colville Dunn
Madame Van Hemert....................................Leni Stengel
Madame Chauffourier-Dubieff.....................Adora Andrews
Commissar Gorotchenko.........................Cecil Humphreys

Act I.—Scene 1—Room in Hotel du Quercy, Paris. 2—Fernande Dupont's Boudoir. Act II.—Scene 1—Duponts' Drawing Room. 2—Duponts' Kitchen.

Staged by Gilbert Miller; settings by Raymond Sovey.

See page 357.

WHITE MAN

(7 performances)

A drama in three acts by Samson Raphaelson. Produced by Sam Byrd at the National Theatre, New York, October 17, 1936.

Cast of characters—

Paul Grimm.....Sam Byrd
Mary Nile.....Louise Campbell
Lucy Arlington.....Patsy Ruth Miller
Richard Arlington.....George Baxter
Pansy Washington.....Sylvia Field
Countess Fillipe.....Jessamine Newcombe
Rufus Nile.....Harold Gould
Greta.....Nancy Cushman
A Nurse.....Mary Jeffery
Archie.....William Coley Grant
His Wife.....Marietta Warren
Stanley.....William Walker
A Negro Minister.....Leigh Whipper
Negroes of Harlem: Louise Reynolds, Eddie Bear, Clarence Evans, Adolph Aikens, Frank Swift, Edward Mathews.

Act I.—Scene 1—Deck of an Ocean Liner. 2—Arlington Suite in Paris Hotel. 3—Nile Suite in same hotel. Act II—Living Room in Paul's Apartment, New York City. Act III.—Scene 1—Paul's Apartment, New York. 2—A Courtyard in Harlem.

Staged by Melville Burke; settings by Nat Karson.

Paul Grimm, born in North Carolina of a white father and an octaroon mother, reared as a white man, determines to "pass" as white when he falls in love with Mary Nile. Mary assures him that she does not want children. When Paul is married, against the advice of his sister Lucy and other "passers," he is happy until Mary tells him she is to have a baby. Paul flies into a rage and confesses his Negro blood. Mary's father takes his daughter away. Her child is given to Pansy Washington, a Negress, to rear. Paul goes back to Harlem, but discovers the Negroes don't want him either.

SWING YOUR LADY

(105 performances)

A comedy in two acts by Kenyon Nicholson and Charles Robinson. Produced by Milton Shubert at the Booth Theatre, New York, October 18, 1936.

Cast of characters—

Shiner Ward.....Henry Norell
Popeye Bronson.....Matt McHugh
Joe Skopapoulos.....John Alexander
Mabel.....Ruth Chorpenning
Cookie McGinn.....Dennie Moore
Ed Hatch.....Joe Laurie, Jr.
Sadie Horn.....Hope Emerson

Rufe Horn....................................Junior Eric Burtis
Viney Horn....................................Teresa Keane
Roscoe Horn....................................Billie Redfield
Waldo Davis....................................Walter Baldwin
Ollie Giffen....................................Eddie Hodge
Noah Wulliver....................................Al Ochs
Sheriff Tude Scott....................................Eugene Keith
1st Legionnaire....................................Jack Reynolds
2nd Legionnaire....................................Frank Harvey
Mort Larkin....................................Charles Niemeyer
Referee Smith....................................Jack Byrne
Peanut Man....................................Warren Parker
A Girl....................................Gloria Doray
A Young Man....................................Al Bartolot

Act I.—Scene 1—Room in Excelsior Hotel, Joplin, Mo. 2 and 4—Sadie Horn's Smithy, Plunkett, Mo. 3—The American Legion Clubrooms. Act II.—Scenes 1 and 2—Legion Clubrooms. 3—The Arena.

Staged by Bertram Harrison; settings by S. Syrjala.

Ed Hatch and a crowd of New York promoters of the "ras'lin' racket," stranded in Joplin, Missouri, frame a wrestling match between their boy, Joe Skopapoulous, and an unknown in the interior of the state. The unknown turns out to be Sadie Horn, a large girl and the village smithy. Sadie, needing the money, is willing to wrestle Joe, but Joe is afraid to trust himself. The more Sadie tries to break down his resistance the more determined Joe becomes. He loves Sadie and will not endanger her charms. The promoters substitute a man mountain, Noah Wulliver, who is the father of one of Sadie's offspring. Joe and Noah fight it out on the mat and Joe wins.

IRON MEN

(16 performances)

A drama in three acts by Francis Gallagher. Produced by Norman Bel Geddes at the Longacre Theatre, New York, October 19, 1936.

Cast of characters—

Joe....................................Frank Jaquet
Mustard....................................John F. Hamilton
Cookie....................................Marion Stephenson
Scratch....................................Richard Taber
Kid....................................Clark Twelvetrees
Andy....................................William Haade
Nils....................................Harold Moffet
Pusher....................................Josef Draper
Whitey....................................W. Dana Hardwick
Monk....................................Jack Carr
Windy....................................Paul Randall
Jigg....................................Harris Wishart
Insurance Man....................................D. J. Hamilton
Sadie....................................Jeanne Marlowe
Mrs. Murphy....................................Mary Perry
Dutch....................................Fritz Gerlach
Kate....................................Kathleen Fitz

Plumber....................................Edward V. Bracken
Fred....................................Gerald Kent
Smallens....................................Harry Horner
Ida....................................Johnne Barrie
Mabel....................................Gloria Blondell
Collins....................................Carl Cleator
Barney....................................William E. Morris
Taxi Driver....................................Yale Okun
Smith....................................Meyer Berenson
Kelly....................................John Quartell

Act I.—Scene 1—Lower East Side Barroom. 2—63rd Floor of Skyscraper Under Construction. Act II.—Scene 1—Atop the Skyscraper. 2—The Barroom. Act III.—Scene 1—The Barroom. 2—The Skyscraper.

Staged by Norman Bel Geddes who also designed settings.

Andy is the head of a gang of steel workers. His men worship Andy and Andy worships himself, with occasional reservations. His best pal and greatest help is Nils. Nils is going to quit working on skyscrapers and bridges and get a job on the ground. His wife is scared and Nils loves the little woman. Andy resents the skirt's interference. When he is in liquor he sends a fellow up to see her and sends Nils after him. Nils will think his wife is unfaithful, reasons Andy, and quit her. But Nils kills his wife and then himself. Andy crumbles under the shock.

STAGE DOOR

(169 performances)

A comedy in three acts by George S. Kaufman and Edna Ferber. Produced by Sam H. Harris at the Music Box, New York, October 22, 1936.

Cast of characters—

Olga Brandt....................................Sylvia Lupas
Bernice Niemeyer....................................Janet Fox
Susan Paige....................................Lili Zehner
Mattie....................................Dorothea Andrews
Mary Harper (Big Mary)....................................Beatrice Blinn
Mary McCune (Little Mary)....................................Mary Wickes
Madeline Vauclain....................................Grena Sloan
Judith Canfield....................................Lee Patrick
Ann Braddock....................................Louise Chaffee
Mrs. Orcutt....................................Leona Roberts
Kaye Hamilton....................................Frances Fuller
Pat Devine....................................Virginia Rousseau
Linda Shaw....................................Jane Buchanan
Jean Maitland....................................Phyllis Brooks
Bobby Melrose....................................Juliet Forbes
Louise Mitchell....................................Catherine Laughlin
Kendall Adams....................................Margot Stevenson
Frank....................................William Andrews
Terry Randall....................................Margaret Sullavan
Sam Hastings....................................Robert Thomsen
Jimmy Devereaux....................................Alex Courtney
Fred Powell....................................Walter Davis
Lou Milhauser....................................Edmund Dorsay

David Kingsley............Onslow Stevens
Keith Burgess............Richard Kendrick
Mrs. Shaw............Helen Ray
Dr. Randall............Priestly Morrison
Ellen Fenwick............Judith Russell
Tony Gillette............Draja Dryden
Larry Westcott............Tom Ewell
Billy............William Atlee
Adolf Gretzl............Ralph Locke

Act I.—Scene 1—Main Room of Footlights Club, Somewhere in the West Fifties, New York. 2—One of the Bedrooms. Acts II and III.—Main Room.

Staged by George S. Kaufman; settings by Donald Oenslager.

See page 182.

TEN MILLION GHOSTS

(11 performances)

A drama in three acts by Sidney Kingsley. Produced by the author at the St. James Theatre, New York, October 23, 1936.

Cast of characters—

Foreman............Howard Solness
Peter............Martin Gabel
Andre............Orson Welles
Ryan............Otto Hulett
Madeleine............Barbara O'Neil
German Worker............Joseph Singer
French Worker............David Leight
Zacharey............George Coulouris
Balkan............Lester Alden
Louis............Myles Geoffrey
Armed Guard............Felton Bickley
Francois de Kruif............Lee Baker
Otto von Kruif............Dodson L. Mitchell
Secretary............Meg Mundy
Dr. La Marr............John Walker
Messenger Boy............Charles Bowden
Messenger Boy............George Justin
Telegraph Boy............Peter Barry
General Louvet............J. Carroll Ashburn
Aide to Louvet............Myles Geoffrey
Orderly............John Harding
General Dumont............Russell Sage
Soldier............Stuart Ferguson
Butler............David Leight
Gabry............Ray Harper
Bonnard............Felton Bickley
Lessay............Philip Bourneuf
Intelligence Officer............Kurt Stall
Schmidt............Robert X. Williams
Muller............Alfred A. Hesse
Red Cross Sergeant............Bernard Lenrow
Shore............Stanley Jessup
Spewack............Dave Arthur
Anderson............James Sidney
Jones............Russell Sage
Roberts............John Walker
Thomas............David Merrill
Waiter............Lester Alden

Act I.—Scene 1—Gun Works of Universal Forges, Inc. 2—Office of Francois de Kruif. 3—Paris Pension. Act II.—Scene 1—Nissen Hut Back of French Lines, Briey Sector. 2—General Louvet's Headquarters. 3—The de Kruif Home, Paris. Act III.—Scene 1—

Nissen Hut. 2—Shack Behind German Lines. 3—France, Portugal, England. Citations. 4—Geneva. Ballroom of Hotel International.
Staged by the author; settings by Donald Oenslager.

Before the Great War Andre and Madeleine love each other and want to marry. Andre is a French poet, Madeleine the daughter of the De Kruifs, largest munitions manufacturers in France. A second suitor for Madeleine's hand is Zacharey, super-salesman of war munitions to all the world. Comes the war. Andre enlists as an aviator. At the front he becomes distressingly conscious that the iron mines of the Briey basin, furnishing Germany with ore, are being spared by French bombers, as those of Dombasle, similarly servicing France, are also being protected. Andre undertakes a private bombing party hoping to call the attention of the world to this seeming conspiracy on the part of Germany and France to prolong the war. Andre is killed. Madeleine marries Zacharey. A new war impends.

SWEET RIVER

(5 performances)

A drama in two acts by George Abbott, adapted from Harriet Beecher Stowe's "Uncle Tom's Cabin." Produced by George Abbott at the 51st Street Theatre, New York, October 28, 1936.

Cast of characters—

Hagar....Gertrude McBrown
Tisha....Ethel Purnello
Ben....Allen Lewis
Juba....Eulabelle Moore
Hesper....Assotta Marshall
Eliza....Margaret Mullen
Marie St. Clare....Kathryn March
Edward St. Clare....Bartlett Robinson
Topsy....Inge Hardison
Eva....Betty Philson
Uncle Tom....Walter Price
Gabe....Juan Hernandez
General Jim Jones....John T. L. Bunn
Deeter....Ray Yeates
Simon Legree....Matt Briggs
Sam....John Marriott
Hedda....Anna Franklin
Aunt Ophelia....Lora Rogers
Queenie....Harriett Jackson
Jasper....Allen Lewis
Phineas....Charles Dingle
Waiter....Roy Johnson
Sheriff....Marion Willis
Deputy Sheriff....Herbert Duffy
Auctioneer....Foster Williams
Assistant Auctioneer....LaMar King
Major Putnam....Tom Morgan
Colonel Jenks....William Crimans
Charlotte....Vivian Collier
Mort....James E. Lightfoot

Dan....John Taylor, Jr.
Jonah....Paul L. Johnson
Luke....Julian Miles
Sheriff....Wylie Adams
Deputy Sheriff....Philip Wood

Merchants, Slaves, Deputy Sheriffs, etc.

Slaves: Birleanna Banks, G. Harry Bolden, Orange Cox, John Diggs, Darlean Duval, Estelle Floyd, George F. Hall, Clinton Holland, Mildred Lassiter, Richard McMyers, Dorothy Marks, May Peebles, Iona Reynolds, James Sparks, Louise Twyman, Charles Welch, Irma Williams, Musa Williams, Haas Woodlin, Regina Williams, Jean Williams, Gerald Williams, Earl Burke, Leslie Phipps.

Act I.—Scenes 1, 3 and 4—Slave Quarters on St. Clare Plantation. 2—In St. Clare House. 5—A Forest. 6—A Tavern. 7—The River. Act II.—Scene 1—St. Clare House. 2—Auction Mart. 3 and 5—Slave Quarters. 4—The St. Clare's New Home Across the River.

Staged by the author; choral work arranged and directed by Juanita Hall; settings by Donald Oenslager.

A version of "Uncle Tom's Cabin" reducing the story to a straight narrative, minus a few of the characters and a number of the features traditionally associated with the old "Tom" show. Marks, the lawyer, is missing; Topsy is an impish slave girl without vaudeville specialty; Eliza is married to a stalwart young slave, named Gabe; Simon Legree's hatred of Uncle Tom is born of Tom's aiding Eliza's escape; Little Eva is a healthy and not too precocious child robbed of a death scene. There is a colored choir to represent the St. Clare slaves. The play ends with the death of Uncle Tom just as St. Clare arrives with enough of Aunt Ophelia's money to buy his freedom.

RED, HOT AND BLUE

(183 performances)

A musical comedy in two acts by Cole Porter, Howard Lindsay and Russel Crouse. Produced by Vinton Freedley at the Alvin Theatre, New York, October 29, 1936.

Cast of characters—

Reporters.... { Geoffrey Errett, Karl Kohrs, Bill Houston, Norman Lind, Eleanor Wallace, Arnita Wallace }
Deputy Warden Mulligan....Lew Parker
Warden of Larks Nest Prison....Forrest Orr
"Nails" O'Reilly Duquesne....Ethel Merman
"Policy" Pinkle....Jimmy Durante
Vivian....Vivian Vance
Anne Westcott....Dorothy Vernon
Grace....Grace Hartman
Lucille....Lucille Johnson
Cecile....Cecile Carey
Kay....Kay Picture
Irene....Ethelyne Holt
Betty....Betty Allen
"Fingers"....Paul Hartman

Bob Hale..Bob Hope
Sonny Hadley.......................................Thurston Crane
Peaches La Fleur.....................................Polly Walters
"Ratface" Dugan...Bill Benner
"Sure-Thing" Simpson...............................Prentiss Davis
"Flap-Ears" Metelli...................................Leo Schippers
"Louie the Louse"...............................Bernard Jannsen
Mrs. Peabody...May Abbey
Tiny..Anne Wolf
Louella...Jeanette Owens
Senator Musilovitch......................................Lew Parker
Senator Malvinsky....................................Robert Leonard
Senator O'Shaughnessy...................................Forrest Orr
Senator Del Grasso...............................Houston Richards
Sergeant-at-Arms...Norman Lind
First Expressman.....................................Geoffrey Errett
Second Expressman...Karl Kohrs
Girl..Gloria Clare
First Marine...Frank Archer
Second Marine...Bruce Covert
Decorator...Houston Richards
Debutantes and Guests: Ruth Bond, Jeanette Bradley, Dorothy Jackson, Jean Scott, Dorothy Schwank, Stella Bailey, Charlene Tucker, Nancy Lee, Althea Elder, Prudence Hayes, Peggy Oden, Mary Joan Martin, Grace Gillern, Ruth Gormley, Marguerite James, Muriel Downey, June Le Roy, Hazel Nevin, Frances Stewart, Gloria Clare, Beverly Hosier, Joanne Allen, Marquita Nicolai, Evelyn Kelly, Ruth Ernst, Annette Nine, Eve Sorel, Helen Hudson, Jessica Pepper.

Act I.—Scene 1—Warden's Office at Larks Nest Prison. 2—Mrs. Duquesne's Penthouse in New York City. 3—Street Corner in Washington, D. C. 4—Committee Room in the Senate. 5—Lottery Headquarters. 6—Pinkle's Bedroom in the Dolly Madison House. 7—Garden of the Dolly Madison House. Act II.—Scene 1—Room in the White House. 2—Courtyard in the Marine Barracks. 3—White House Lawn.

Staged by Howard Lindsay; dances and ensembles by George Hale; settings by Donald Oenslager; costumes by Constance Ripley.

Mrs. "Nails" Duquesne, inheriting a million, seeks to assist a Junior League charity by the conduct of a lottery. As assistants in the raising of funds she impresses into service four of the best money getters in Larks Nest prison, through the co-operation of the parole board. The leader of the four is "Policy" Pinkle. "Policy" resents being paroled, having recently achieved the captaincy of the prison polo team. The lottery's first prize is to go to the discoverer of the childhood sweetheart of Bob Hale, now grown to young womanhood. The only known mark of identification is the imprint left by a hot waffle iron upon which the young woman had inadvertently sat when she was aged four. The sweetheart is found but disqualified.

FORBIDDEN MELODY

(32 performances)

A musical comedy in two acts by Otto Harbach; music by Sigmund Romberg. Produced by Jack Kirkland and Sam H. Grisman at the New Amsterdam Theatre, New York, November 2, 1936.

Cast of characters—

Thedor..Bela Lublov
Tosk..Leo Chalzel
Kuzdu..Daniel A. Harris
Katcha..Lillion Clark
Alexis Constantine..Charles Bryant
Doma..Joseph Greenwald
Gregor Fiorescu..Carl Brisson
A Waiter..Herman Williams
Col. Geza..Arthur Vinton
Mme. Geza..Ruth Weston
Nicholas Constantine..Jack Sheehan
Rozsa..June Havoc
Elene Constantine..Ruby Mercer
Mitzi..Nitza Vernille
Butler..Tomes Chapman
Frederic..Harry Raine
A Streetwalker..Marie Louise Quevli
A Policeman..Richard Tolk
A Girl..Dolores Flanders
Another Girl..Muriel Muth
Capt. Fedovitch..Gladstone Waldrip
Lt. Czenyi..Clark Kramer
Dancer..Helen Gray

Staged by Macklin Megley; dialogue directed by Jose Ruben; music directed by Robert Dolan; settings by Sergei Soudeikine; gowns and costumes by Ten Eyck.

Act I.—Scene 1—Private Dining Room, Hotel Roumania, Bucharest. 2—Elene's Dressing Room, National Variety Theatre, Budapest. 3—Stage of National Variety Theatre. 4—Backstage. 5—Elene's Villa, Budapest. Act II.—Scene 1—Street outside Hotel Buda, Budapest. 2—Garden Gate of Hotel Buda. 3—Royal Suite. 4—Backstage. 5—Elene's Dressing Room. 6—Gardens of Roumanian Embassy, Budapest.

Gregor Fiorescu, attractive to the ladies, has been photographed with a certain lady in the window of a hotel. The lady happens to be the wife of a prominent politician. To shield her it is proposed that a popular actress assume the responsibility of the affair with Gregor. The actress, proving more attractive to Gregor than the lady friend he had compromised, he finds himself in trouble with a jealous woman and threatened by the jealous woman's husband. The story is presumed to circle an escapade indulged by Carol of Roumania.

DON'T LOOK NOW

(16 performances)

A comedy in three acts by John Crump. Produced by Gustav Blum at the Bayes Theatre, New York, November 2, 1936.

Cast of characters—

Tom MacDonald..Edward Marr
James Cabot..Robert Shayne
Winters..Oscar Stirling
Ernest Johnson..Ferdi Hoffman
Fred Luden..Robert Leslie
Mrs. Jones..Kathryn Harris

Elaine Jones....................................Queenell Tucker
Sam Stern....................................Joseph Buloff
Nina Gay....................................Beverly Phalon
T. T. Lawrence....................................Forbes Dawson
Rodney Fletcher Schloss....................................Jack Hasler
Colonel Vance....................................Carleton Macy
Acts I, II and III.—James Cabot's Apartment in a Mid-Town New York Hotel.
Staged by Gustav Blum; setting by Lou Bromley.

Sam Stern, a producer of pictures on the Pacific coast, has lost Nina Gay, his most valuable star, because Nina has left a picture to hunt up a lover in New York. Nina finds her lover, an author, about to marry a lady who has offered to back his play. Sam is forced to buy off the angel in order to get Nina her lover and, through the lover, back to the picture lot.

GREEN WATERS

(5 performances)

A drama in three acts by Max Catto. Produced by Lee and J. J. Shubert at the Masque Theatre, New York, November 4, 1936.

Cast of characters—

Michael Fraser....................................Dennis O'Dea
Joey Fraser....................................Jackie Jordan
Ian McRuvie....................................Dennis Hoey
Richard Fraser....................................Reginald Bach
Jennifer Fraser....................................Doris Dalton
Edgar Fraser....................................Terence Neill
Father Roffe....................................Ralph Cullinan
Mrs. McFaden....................................Alice John
Acts I, II and III.—The Frasers' House on the West Coast of Scotland.
Staged by Reginald Bach and Milton Shubert; setting by Watson Barratt.

Richard Fraser is living with his two sons, Michael and Joey, on the west coast of Scotland. The boys are the illegitimate offspring of a woman with whom the father had lived for some years but was prevented from marrying because her first husband would not release her. The taint of bastardy has embittered the older boy, Michael, until he has become a brooding neurotic. Edgar Fraser, an elder son, both legitimate and smug, brings his young wife, Jennifer, from London for a visit. Jennifer is drawn to Michael and he to her. Tragedy threatens. Edgar, after thrashing Michael, orders Jennifer back to London. She leaves with him, but changes her mind at the station and returns to Michael.

PLUMES IN THE DUST

(11 performances)

A drama in three acts by Sophie Treadwell. Produced by Arthur Hopkins at the 46th Street Theatre, New York, November 6, 1936.

Cast of characters—

Mrs. Frances Allan	Fredrica Slemons
Miranda	Laura Bowman
Lizzie	Artie Belle McGinty
John Allan	Charles Kennedy
Rosalie Poe	Barbara Fulton
Edgar Allan Poe	Henry Hull
Moncure Harrison	Don Shelton
Elmira Shelton	Ruth Yorke
Mrs. Maria Clemm	Mary Morris
Virginia Clemm	Amelia Romano
Miss McNab	Iris Whitney
John P. Kennedy	Earl Fleischman
Anne Lynch	Eleanor Goodrich
Sarah Anne Lewis	Hedwig Schoch
Mr. Lewis	Maurice Lavigne
N. P. Willis	William C. Jackson
Elizabeth Ellet	Gertrude Coghlan
Margaret Fuller	Portia Morrow
Frances S. Osgood	Dorothea Petgen
Dr. Griswold	Donald Willson
Mrs. Sutherland	Ada Potter
Lou	Pauline Myers
Dr. Snodgrass	Palmer Ward
An Attendant	Bernard Kisner
Dr. Moran	Edwin Cushman
Nurse	Julia Fremont

Act I.—Scene 1—Sitting Room in Home of John Allan, Poe's Foster Father, Richmond, Virginia, December 24, 1926. 2—Living Room in Lodgings of Mrs. Clemm, Baltimore, 1833. Act II.—Scene 1—Living Room in Poe's Home, Fordham, 1847. 2—Parlor in Home of Miss Anne Lynch, Waverly Place, New York. Act III.—Scene 1—Sitting Room in Home of Mrs. Shelton, Richmond, 1849. 2—Room in Washington Hospital, Baltimore.

Staged by Arthur Hopkins; settings by Woodman Thompson.

Edgar Allan Poe, at 17, returns to the home of his adoptive parents, the John Allans of Richmond. His foster father, angered by the boy's extravagance at school, including a gambling debt of some size, orders him from the house, despite the pleading of the gentle Mrs. Allan. Poe, already crushed by the discovery that Elmira, the romance of his youth, has married, is glad to go. Seven years later he is living with the Clemms in Baltimore, where he meets the sad little Virginia Clemm whom he married when she was 13. The scene changes to Fordham, N. Y., in 1847. Poe, having had some little success with editing and writing, is again in distress. Virginia, his wife, dies after he has left her to thrash an editor who has made a public appeal for Poe. Poe returns to Richmond in 1849, finds and is disillusioned by the now widowed Elmira and starts back to New York. For four days he is lost to his friends. When they find him he is dying in a Baltimore hospital.

BLACK LIMELIGHT

(64 performances)

A drama in three acts by Gordon Sherry. Produced by George Bushar and John Tuerk at the Mansfield Theatre, New York, November 9, 1936.

Cast of characters—

Bishop	Frederick Voigt
Jemima Barrett	Brenda Forbes
Naomi Charrington	Winifred Lenihan
Williams	A. P. Kaye
Mrs. Chandler	Olive Reeves Smith
Mr. Tanner	J. Malcom Dunn
Mr. Traynor	Herbert Standing
Lawrence Manfred	George Curzon
Peter Charrington	Alexander Kirkland
Lily James	Kate Warriner
1st Policeman	Harold Thomas
2nd Policeman	John Trevor
Mr. Chandler	Bruce Evans
Lewis	R. Birrell Rawls

Acts I, II and III.—Sitting Room in Suburban Villa near London.
Staged by Robert Milton; setting by Watson Barratt.

Naomi Charrington, convinced that her husband, Peter, is innocent of the brutal murder of Lily James, of which he has been accused, is holding the fort at home while Peter remains in hiding hoping that the real murderer will be arrested. Peter has admitted that Lily had been his mistress and that he kept a week-end tryst with her the time she was killed. He had gone to the store for supplies and found the girl hacked to pieces when he returned. Naomi, uncovering a clew that implicates the family lawyer, maneuvers the suspect into a position from which he is glad to escape by confessing. He was a moon-crazed victim of an obscure eye disease known as nyctalopia. He could see clearly in the dark, but must protect his eyes from the light with glasses.

HAMLET

(39 performances)

A tragedy by William Shakespeare. Produced by Leslie Howard at the Imperial Theatre, New York, November 10, 1936.

Cast of characters—

King Claudius of Denmark	Wilfrid Walter
Queen Gertrude	Mary Servoss
Ghost of King Hamlet	John Barclay

Prince Hamlet....................Leslie Howard
Lord Polonius....................Aubrey Mather
Laertes....................Clifford Evans
Ophelia....................Pamela Stanley
Horatio....................Joseph Holland
Marcellus....................Wesley Addy
Bernardo....................John Parrish
Francisco....................Paul Genge
Rosencrantz....................Denis Green
Guildenstern....................Winston O'Keefe
First Player....................Herbert Ranson
Player King....................Alexander Scourby
Player Queen....................Mary Meyer
Prologue....................Madelyn Phillips
First Gravedigger....................Stanley Lathbury
Second Gravedigger....................O. Z. Whitehead
A Chaplain....................Eric Mansfield
Osric....................Albert Carroll
A Gentleman....................Edward Potter
Prince Fortinbras of Norway....................John Barclay
Norwegian Captain....................Paul Genge
Courtiers: Vernon Tanner, John Byrd, James Hayes, Arthur Zwerling, Paul Foster, Richard Ogden, Richard Cameron, Edward Potter.
Court Ladies: Gay Adams, Janet Hill, Toni Sorel, Daphne Bayne, Mary Shower, Hope Spingarn, Daphne Sylva, Joan Adrian.
Pages: Eugene Francis, Philip Sudana, Richard Clayton, Tileston Perry.
Soldiers: George Ingham, George Volk, Henry Leonard, Keith Randall, Hugh Norton, William Blood.

Act I.—Scenes 1 and 3—The Ramparts of Elsinore. 2 and 5—Interior of the Castle. 4—The Royal Crypt. Act II.—Scene 1—Interior of the Castle. 2—A Wharf. Act III.—Scenes 1 and 3—Interior of the Castle. 2—A Churchyard.

Staged by Leslie Howard and John Houseman; settings by Stewart Chaney.

The version of "Hamlet" used by Mr. Howard was prepared with the help of Schuyler Watts. Principal addition is a scene of Hamlet's departure from England in which he speaks from the prow of a Viking ship the soliloquy beginning "How all occasions do inform against me, and spur my dull revenge!" Additional cuts and additions are a matter of lines and a readjustment of scene.

DOUBLE DUMMY

(21 performances)

A farce-satire in two acts by Doty Hobart and Tom McKnight. Produced by James Ullman and Mark Hellinger at the Golden Theatre, New York, November 11, 1936.

Cast of characters—

Hymie....................Teddy Bergman
Clancy....................Albert G. West
Brains McGill....................Charles D. Brown
Principal Keeper....................William F. Nugent
Milton Weintraub....................Joseph Kleema
Warden William DuBose....................Dudley Clements
Mrs. Graham....................Carrie Weller
Lou....................Barbara Weeks
Professor Christian Gideon....................John McGovern

Mrs. Nussbaum.................................Adelaide Klein
Carol Griswold.................................Martha Sleeper
Nullo Sykes.................................Hanley Stafford
Leo Rothstein.................................Sanford Bickart
Miss Willis.................................Lesley Woods
Dr. James Starr Jameson.................................Owen Coll
Edith Jameson.................................Cynthia Rogers
Sergeant Winchell.................................Robert J. Mulligan
Izzy.................................William Call
Moe.................................Archer Landon
Radio Announcer.................................Paul Douglas
Colonel Growler.................................G. Albert Smith
A Bum.................................Marvin Blackstone
Ted Husing (On the Air).................................Ted Husing

Act I.—Scene 1—A Prison Corridor. 2—Warden's Office. 3, 6, 9 and 11—Professor Gideon's Room. 4—A Pullman Sleeper. 5—Carol Griswold's Room. 7—Warden DuBose's Address. 8—Nullo Sykes' Office. 10 and 12—The McGills' Room. Act II.—Scenes 1 and 8—Police Station. 2 and 4—The McGills' Room. 3—Nullo Sykes' Office. 5, 6 and 9—Stage of the Golden Theatre. 7—A Taxi.

Staged by Edith Meiser; settings by S. Syrjala.

Brains McGill, serving a term in the penitentiary, is bored stiff by the contract bridge pep-talks radioed by the expert, Nullo Sykes, and forced on the prisoners by Warden DuBose, a bridge fiend. Promoting bridge, says McGill, is a racket. Released on parole, Brains decides to take a hand in the game. He organizes a bridge tournament, promotes Warden DuBose as an unknown and challenges Sykes to meet him. When Sykes sets gangsters on the Warden, sending him to a hospital, McGill substitutes Prof. Gideon, a timid mathematical wizard who masters bridge overnight, and wins the tournament.

MATRIMONY PFD.

(61 performances)

A comedy in three acts by Louis Verneuil; adapted by Grace George and James Forbes. Produced by William A. Brady at the Playhouse, New York, November 12, 1936.

Cast of characters—

Victor Gustav Martineau.................................A. E. Matthews
Andre Lorre.................................Jose Ruben
Linda Lessing.................................Grace George
Pauline.................................May Marshall
Mrs. Robert Levy-de Coudray.................................Sylvia Field
Baroness von Geldern.................................Rosemary Ames
Colonel Jouvet.................................A. J. Herbert
Florist.................................Victor Morley
Dr. Robert Levy-de Coudray.................................Rex O'Malley

Acts I, II and III.—Linda Lessing's Country House, Near Paris.

Staged by Jose Ruben; setting by Donald Oenslager.

Linda Lessing, having had and lost three lovers in her day, is not quite certain as to the parentage of her son, whom she has called Robert Levy-de Coudray to be on the safe or alkaline side. Robert, having married a puritan, it seems fitting to Linda that she should also marry and provide a background of legitimacy for her son. She is about to become Mrs. Victor Martineau when the younger Baroness von Geldern vamps the prospective bridegroom. It becomes necessary in the crisis to send son Robert to entertain the Baroness while Linda is edging Victor toward the altar.

HEDDA GABLER

(32 performances)

A drama in four acts by Henrik Ibsen. Revived by Sam Levey at the Longacre Theatre, New York, November 16, 1936.

Cast of characters—

Miss Julia Tesman....................Leslie Bingham
Bertha....................Grace Mills
George Tesman....................Harry Ellerbe
Hedda Tesman....................Mme. Nazimova
Mrs. Elvsted....................Viola Frayne
Judge Brack....................McKay Morris
Eilert Lovborg....................Edward Trevor

Acts I, II, III and IV.—George Tesman's House.
Staged by Alla Nazimova; setting by Stewart Chaney.

A lightly modernized version of Ibsen's "Hedda Gabler," prepared and staged by Mme. Nazimova. Played by that actress as a highly sensitized neurotic in a closely set red wig and a cast much more youthful than any previously employed. Tesman is here presented as a youthful scholar wrapped up in post-graduate work. Lovborg is a husky young poet, Brack a sinister and lustful gentleman of early middle age and Mrs. Elvsted a worried ingénue.

JOHNNY JOHNSON

(68 performances)

A comedy with music in three acts by Paul Green; music by Kurt Weill. Produced by The Group Theatre at the 44th Street Theatre, New York, November 19, 1936.

Cast of characters—

The Mayor....................Bob Lewis
The Editor....................Tony Kraber
Minny Belle Tompkins....................Phoebe Brand
Grandpa Joe....................Roman Bohnen
A Photographer....................Will Lee
A Boy....................Curt Conway
Johnny Johnson....................Russell Collins
Anguish Howington....................Grover Burgess
Aggie Tompkins....................Susanna Senior
Captain Valentine....................Sanford Meisner

Dr. McBray....................................Lee J. Cobb
Private Patrick O'Day..........................Curt Conway
Sergeant Jackson..................................Art Smith
A Camp Doll.............................Eunice Stoddard
Corporal George........................Albert Van Dekker
Private Fairfax..........................William Challee
Private Goldberger....................................Will Lee
Private Harwood................................Tony Kraber
Private Kearns....................................Elia Kazan
Private Svenson..............................Herbert Ratner
A West Point Lieutenant.......................Joseph Pevney
An English Sergeant.............................Luther Adler
A British Soldier................................Judson Hall
Johann Lang.....................................Jules Garfield
A French Nurse..................................Paula Miller
An Orderly...Paul Mann
A Doctor...Art Smith
A Sister from the O. D. S. D. L. D..................Ruth Nelson
Chief of the Allied High Command...............Morris Carnovsky
His Majesty, a King..............................Orrin Jannings
Belgian Major-General...........................Luther Adler
British Commander-in-Chief...........................John Most
A French Major-General............................Lee J. Cobb
French Premier..Bob Lewis
American Commander-in-Chief.....................Roman Bohnen
Scottish Colonel..............................Thomas C. Kennedy
A Liaison Officer..............................Jack Saltzman
American Priest.....................................Alfred Saxe
German Priest...Paul Mann
Military Policeman............................Herbert Ratner
Dr. Mahodan..................................Morris Carnovsky
His Secretary..Kate Allen
Dr. Frewd..Elia Kazan
Brother Thomas..Art Smith
Brother Claude....................................Roman Bohnen
Brother George...Lee J. Cobb
Brother William......................................Curt Conway
Brother Hiram................................Albert Van Dekker
Brother Jim...Robert Joseph
Brother Theodore.....................................Tony Kraber
Brother Henry...Luther Adler
A Doctor...William Challee
An Attendant......................................Herbert Ratner
Anguish Howington, Jr...................................Eddie Ryan
Soldiers....................Peter Ainsley, James Blake, Judson Hall
Song...Jean Burton

Act I.—Scene 1—Hill-Top, 1917. 2—Tompkins Home. 3—Recruiting. 4 and 5—Camp Drill Ground. 6—New York Harbor. Act II.—Scene 1—Road in France. 2—Front Line Trench. 3—Churchyard. 4—Hospital. 5—Château de Cent Fontaines. 6—Edge of Great Battlefield. 7—Battle. 8—No Man's Land. 9—New York Harbor. Act III.—Scene 1—Superintendent's Office, State Hospital. 2—Forensic Arena in House of Balm. 3—A Street, Today.

Staged by Lee Strasberg; settings by Donald Oenslager; costumes by Paul Du Pont.

See page 96.

200 WERE CHOSEN

(35 performances)

A drama in three acts by Ellsworth Prouty Conkle. Produced by Sidney Harmon and The Actors Repertory Company at the 48th Street Theatre November 20, 1936.

Cast of characters—

Tom Johnson	Anthony Ross
Mrs. Lulu Johnson	Kathryn Grill
Henry	Royce Blackburn
Tommy	Ramon Blackburn
Mrs. Nicoll	Dorothy Brackett
Ola	Rose Keane
Jim Chandler	Robert Williams
Bill Day	Douglas Parkhirst
Herb Collins	Fred Stewart
Farley Sprinkle	Will Geer
Mickey Nicoll	Robert Porterfield
Hodges	Aldrich Bowker
Beatrice Cole	Lesley Stafford
Don Bliss	Eric Walz
Luke Cole	Gordon Nelson
Mrs. Ella Cole	Norma Chambers
Birdie	Patricia Roe
Cleve Walters	Charles Jordan
Jennie Walters	Paula Bauersmith
Jim Conwell	Neill O'Malley
Hannan	David Clarke
Mrs. Hannan	Lucille Strudwick
Shaw	John O'Shaughnessy
Paulsen	Richard Allen
Amick	Richard Fredericks
Lindstrum	Edward Mann
Mrs. Lindstrum	Herta Ware
Riley	William H. Chambers
A Colonist	Robert Reeves
Per Solum	Frank Tweddell
Inspector Ingraham	Bertram Thorn
Guard	Everett A. Perez

Acts I, II and III.—U. S. Government Camp at Matanuska Valley, Alaska.

Staged by Worthington Miner and J. Edward Shugrue; setting by Donald Oenslager.

The Tom Johnsons, the Luke Coles, the Cleve Walters and a hundred or more others, taken off relief in the Middle West and transported to Matanuska, Alaska, as the vanguard of a colonizing project organized by the United States government, arrive in Alaska and bump into the familiar problems attending such enterprises. The Army men in charge, hampered by red tape, have failed to provide the promised living quarters or clear the way to a proper starting of crop planting. The colonists, led by Johnson, organize a "sit down" strike when they are ordered to pull down shacks they have erected which do not comply with government specifications. A fever epidemic breaks out among the children and tragic failure threatens the colony. Order is restored and the colonists are won over to an agreement to co-operate with the government, largely through the efforts of Jim Conwell, an upstanding civil employe of the government, and Jennie Walters, a sane worker among the women of the camp.

TONIGHT AT EIGHT-THIRTY

(118 performances)

Three groups of short plays by Noel Coward. Produced by John C. Wilson at the National Theatre, New York, beginning November 24, 1936.

First Group

HANDS ACROSS THE SEA

A Comedy in One Scene

Walters..Moya Nugent
Lady Maureen Gilpin (Piggie)....................Gertrude Lawrence
Com. Peter Gilpin, R.N.................................Noel Coward
Lieut. Com. Alastair Corbett, R.N..............Edward Underdown
Mrs. Wadhurst...Joyce Carey
Mr. Wadhurst..Alan Webb
Mr. Burnham...Kenneth Carten
The Hon. Clare Wedderburn.........................Joan Swinstead
Major Gosling (Bogey)...........................Anthony Pelissier

Drawing Room of the Gilpins' Flat in London.

Lady Maureen Gilpin has invited friends met on a world cruise to look her up in London. They do. But Lady Gilpin is at some loss to place them, resulting in amusing confusion.

THE ASTONISHED HEART

A Play in Six Scenes

Barbara Faber..Joyce Carey
Susan Birch..Joan Swinstead
Tim Verney...Anthony Pelissier
Ernest...Edward Underdown
Sir Reginald French......................................Alan Webb
Leonora Vail.......................................Gertrude Lawrence
Christian Faber...Noel Coward

Drawing Room of the Fabers' Flat in London.

Christian Faber, psychiatrist, having helped many patients out of mental difficulties, discovers when he falls desperately in love with Leonora Vail that he cannot help himself, even with the assistance of his sympathetic and understanding wife.

RED PEPPERS

An Interlude with Music

Lily Pepper..Gertrude Lawrence
George Pepper..Noel Coward
Alf...Kenneth Carten
Bert Bentley.......................................Anthony Pelissier
Mr. Edwards...Alan Webb
Mabel Grace...Joyce Carey

Stage and in a Dressing Room of the Palace of Varieties in One of the Smaller English Provincial Towns.

Lily and George Pepper, touring the provincial music halls of England, have their dressing-room spats which threaten the act with disintegration, but present a united front when they are attacked by the manager of the house, a common enemy.

Second Group

(November 27)

WE WERE DANCING

A Comedy in Two Scenes

Ippaga.....Kenneth Carten
George Davies.....Edward Underdown
Eva Blake.....Moya Nugent
Louise Charteris.....Gertrude Lawrence
Karl Sandys.....Noel Coward
Clara Bethel.....Joyce Carey
Hubert Charteris.....Alan Webb
Major Blake.....Anthony Pelissier

Scenes 1 and 2—Veranda of the Country Club at Samolo.

Louise Charteris and Karl Sandys find themselves swept off their feet in the dance. They want to elope immediately. Louise's husband, however, interposes a mild objection which results in an overlong conference. By the time the conference is ended the spell is broken.

FUMED OAK

An Unpleasant Comedy in Two Scenes

Doris Gow.....Gertrude Lawrence
Mrs. Rockett.....Joyce Carey
Elsie.....Moya Nugent
Henry Gow.....Noel Coward

Scenes 1 and 2—Sitting Room of the Gows' House in South London

Henry Gow, having, he feels, been tricked into marriage, has resented his home life for fifteen years. Having secretly held out enough from his salary to give him independence for the moment he proceeds to tell his wife, his mother-in-law and his daughter what he thinks of them and departs.

SHADOW PLAY

A Play with Music

Lena.....Moya Nugent
Victoria Gayforth.....Gertrude Lawrence
Martha Cunningham.....Joyce Carey
Simon Gayforth.....Noel Coward
Hodge.....Kenneth Carten
A Young Man.....Anthony Pelissier
George Cunningham.....Alan Webb

Sibyl Heston....................................Joan Swinstead
Michael Doyle....................................Edward Underdown
Scene—The Gayforths' House in Mayfair.

Victoria and Simon Gayforth, having quarreled, are ready to talk divorce. Victoria has taken an extra bromide to quiet her headache. When Simon comes for a conference Victoria drifts off into a bemused delirium in which she and Simon dance and sing their way back to their honeymoon. With Victoria's recovery comes Simon's apology and all is well again.

Third Group

(November 30)

WAYS AND MEANS

A Comedy in Two Scenes

Stella Cartwright....................................Gertrude Lawrence
Toby Cartwright....................................Noel Coward
Gaston....................................Kenneth Carten
Lord Chapworth (Chaps)....................................Alan Webb
Olive Lloyd-Ransome....................................Joan Swinstead
Princess Elena Krassiloff....................................Moya Nugent
Murdoch....................................Anthony Pelissier
Nanny....................................Joyce Carey
Stevens....................................Edward Underdown
Scene—Bedroom in the Lloyd-Ransomes' House, Villa Zephyre, Côte d'Azur.

Stella and Toby Cartwright find themselves strapped after having overstayed their welcome at a house party. When their room is invaded by a burglar they conspire with the lad to rob a fellow guest and split with them.

STILL LIFE

A Play in Five Scenes

Laura Jesson....................................Gertrude Lawrence
Myrtle Bagot....................................Joyce Carey
Beryl Waters....................................Moya Nugent
Young Man....................................Charles Peters
Stanley....................................Kenneth Carten
Albert Godby....................................Alan Webb
Alec Harvey....................................Noel Coward
Bill....................................Edward Underdown
Johnnie....................................Anthony Pelissier
Mildred....................................Betty Hare
Dolly Messiter....................................Joan Swinstead
Scene—Refreshment Room of Milford Junction Station.

Laura Jesson and Alec Harvey are married, but not to each other. On successive Thursdays they meet in a lunch room and furtively exchange sympathy that drifts into love. Still they can find no solution to their problems and are forced again to go their separate ways.

FAMILY ALBUM

A Comedy of Manners to Music

Jasper Featherways....................Noel Coward
Jane....................Gertrude Lawrence
Lavinia Featherways....................Joyce Carey
Richard Featherways....................Edward Underdown
Harriet Winter....................Joan Swinstead
Charles Winter....................Anthony Pelissier
Emily Valance....................Moya Nugent
Edward Valance....................Kenneth Carten
Burrows....................Alan Webb

The Action of the Play Passes in the Drawing Room of the Featherways' House in Kent in the Autumn in the Year 1860.

Orchestra Under the Direction of John McManus.

The Featherways and their kin have gathered, following the funeral of Papa Featherways, to mourn respectfully for the dead. A spot or two of Madeira, a tune from an old music box, and a lot of reminiscences remind the Featherways and kin that, after all, Papa was an old bounder, and the party gets a bit rough but very gay.

All nine plays staged by Noel Coward; settings by Gladys E. Calthrop.

PRELUDE TO EXILE

(48 performances)

A drama in three acts by William McNally. Produced by The Theatre Guild, Inc., at the Guild Theatre, New York, November 30, 1936.

Cast of characters—

Countess Marie D'Agoult....................Lucile Watson
Adolph....................Roland Hogue
Cosima Liszt Von Bulow....................Miriam Battista
Hans Von Bulow....................Manuel Bernard
Richard Wagner....................Wilfrid Lawson
Mathilde Wesendonck....................Eva Le Gallienne
Otto Wesendonck....................Leo G. Carroll
Malwina Schnorr....................Beal Hober
Ludwig Schnorr....................Arthur Gerry
Minna Wagner....................Evelyn Varden
Gottfried....................Henry Levin

Acts I and III.—Richard Wagner's Study in the "ASYL." Act II.—Scene 1—Small Entrance Hall in the Wesendonck Villa. 2—Wagner's Study.

Staged by Philip Moeller; settings and costumes by Lee Simonson.

Richard and Minna Planer Wagner, his actress wife, are living at Green Hill, Zurich, as the guests of Otto and Mathilde Wesendonck. Richard is irritated by Minna's lack of appreciation of his genius and desperately enamored of Mme. Wesendonck, whom he feels is the inspiration of his "Tristan and Isolde." He would run away with Mathilde on money borrowed from her husband.

The day she decides to make the sacrifice Richard captures the rapture theme for Tristan. Then Mathilde changes her mind and Richard goes away alone.

THE COUNTRY WIFE

(89 performances)

A comedy in two acts by William Wycherley. Revived by Gilbert Miller in association with Helen Hayes, at the Henry Miller Theatre, New York, December 1, 1936.

Cast of characters—

Mr. Horner...Roger Livesey
Quack...George Carr
A Boy..Raymond Johnson
Sir Jasper Fidget..............................George Graham
Lady Fidget.......................................Irene Browne
Mrs. Dainty Fidget............................Edith Atwater
Mr. Harcourt.....................................Anthony Quayle
Mr. Dorilant..............................Stephen Ker Appleby
Mr. Sparkish.......................................Louis Hector
Mr. Pinchwife.....................................Percy Waram
Mrs. Pinchwife....................................Ruth Gordon
Alithea...Helen Trenholme
Mrs. Squeamish.................................Helena Pickard
Lucy...Jane Vaughn
Old Lady Squeamish...........................Violet Besson
A Parson..Louis Dayton
Ladies in Exchange Scene: Frances Greet, Alice Thompson, Flora Campbell, Elizabeth Malloch, Catherine Emburie, Linda Lee.
Footmen, Linkman, and Gentlemen in Exchange Scene: Warren Reid, Donald Stevens, Roger Blankenship, Lewis Sealy, Salo Douday, Reginald Stanborough, David Gray, William Justus.

Act I—Scene 1—Horner's Lodging. 2, 4 and 6—Garden. 3 and 5—Room in Pinchwife's House. 7—The New Exchange. Act II.—Scene 1—Alithea's Dressing Room. 2—Bedroom in Pinchwife's House. 3 and 8—Horner's Lodgings. 4 and 6—Horner's Dressing Room. 5—Room in Pinchwife's House. 7—Piazza of Covent Garden.

Staged by Gilbert Miller; settings by Oliver Messel.

Mr. Pinchwife, being a careful husband and knowing his London, hesitates to bring Mistress Pinchwife, his newly married country girl, to town. Having her there he does his best to keep her at home and away from temptation. Mrs. Pinchwife goes to the play, however, and hugely admires the actors. Also a certain Mr. Horner, who allows the report to spread that he has been a victim of a Paris surgeon and is altogether a harmless young man. The evening offers circumstantial evidence to the contrary.

THE HOLMESES OF BAKER STREET

(53 performances)

A comedy in three acts by Basil Mitchell, adapted by William Jourdan Rapp and Leonardo Bercovici. Produced by Elizabeth Miele at the Masque Theatre, New York, December 9, 1936.

Cast of characters—

Shirley Holmes.................................Helen Chandler
Williams..John Parrish
Dr. Watson.................................Conway Wingfield
Inspector Withers...............................Stuart Casey
Mr. Holmes...Cyril Scott
Mr. Canning.....................................Don Dillaway
Mrs. Watson......................................Cecilia Loftus
Inspector Laker...............................Raymond Bramley
Maid...Beatrice Graham
Joe Murray.....................................Arthur Marlowe
Tom Braggs...Jack Lee
Arthur Singer..................................Murray Stephens

Act I.—The Study at Baker Street, London. Act II.—Sitting Room at Eastmill, Surrey. Act III.—Scene 1—An Attic in Bloomsbury. 2—Study at Baker Street.

Staged by Reginald Bach; settings by Kate Drain Lawson.

Sherlock Holmes, having retired and taken to raising bees in the country, will have nothing to do with Scotland Yard when its best men come to urge him to help them run down the newly active White X gang. A queen bee in a cage is received as a gift to Holmes. Shirley, Holmes' daughter, to keep her father from running to the country with the bee before she is ready to go, steals the cage. Comes Scotland Yard with the report that the White X gang has hidden the Medici pearl in with the queen bee. The gang, to recover the pearl, grabs Shirley as a hostage. Shirley, who has inherited her father's gifts, outwits the gang, puts the Yard in touch with them, and becomes a detective on her own, much to her father's disgust.

* YOU CAN'T TAKE IT WITH YOU

(215 performances)

A farcical comedy in three acts by Moss Hart and George S. Kaufman. Produced by Sam H. Harris at the Booth Theatre, New York, December 14, 1936.

Cast of characters—

Penelope Sycamore.............................Josephine Hull
Essie...Paula Trueman
Rheba...Ruth Attaway
Paul Sycamore..................................Frank Wilcox
Mr. De Pinna....................................Frank Conlan
Ed...George Heller
Donald...Oscar Polk
Martin Vanderhof...............................Henry Travers
Alice..Margot Stevenson
Henderson.......................................Hugh Rennie
Tony Kirby...Jess Barker
Boris Kolenkhov................................George Tobias
Gay Wellington....................................Mitzi Hajos
Mr. Kirby......................................William J. Kelly
Mrs. Kirby..................................Virginia Hammond
Three Men..{ George Leach, Ralph Holmes, Franklin Heller }

Olga..Anna Lubowe
Acts I, II and III.—Home of Martin Vanderhof, New York.
Staged by George S. Kaufman; setting by Donald Oenslager.

See page 70.

DAYS TO COME

(7 performances)

A play in three acts by Lillian Hellman. Produced by Herman Shumlin at the Vanderbilt Theatre, New York, December 15, 1936.

Cast of characters—

Hannah..Clare Woodbury
Lucy..Muriel Gallick
Cora Rodman..Frieda Altman
Henry Ellicott..Ned Wever
Andrew Rodman..William Harrigan
Julie Rodman..Florence Eldridge
Thomas Firth..Joseph Sweeney
Leo Whalen..Ben Smith
Sam Wilkie..Charles Dingle
Mossie Dowel..Jack Carr
Joe Easter..Thomas Fisher
Acts I and III.—Living room of the Rodman House in a Small Town in the Middle West. Act II.—Scenes 1 and 3—Rodman Living room. 2—The Strike Office.
Staged by Herman Shumlin; settings by Aline Bernstein.

For generations the Rodmans have owned the brush factory and most of the working people of the small Mid-Western town in which they live have worked for them. The time comes when the workers organize and ask for increased wages. Andrew Rodman thinks he cannot pay more than he is paying. The workmen strike. Old friendships are engulfed, old traditions wiped out. Rodman is badly advised to import strike breakers. Mrs. Rodman, victim of a loveless marriage, takes a fancy to the leader of the organizers and offers herself to him. A strikebreakers' murder is made to appear a workers' murder. The strike is lost. The Rodmans are crushed. There are days and days to come.

* BROTHER RAT

(213 performances)

A comedy in three acts by John Monks, Jr., and Fred F. Finklehoffe. Produced by George Abbott at the Biltmore Theatre, New York, December 16, 1936.

Cast of characters—

Mrs. Brooks.............................Curtis Burnley Railing
Joyce Winfree.............................Wyn Cahooh
Jenny.............................Anna Franklin
Claire Ramm.............................Mary Mason
Harley Harrington.............................Richard Clark
Bing Edwards.............................Eddie Albert
Billy Randolph.............................Frank Albertson
Kate Rice.............................Kathleen Fitz
Dan Crawford.............................Jose Ferrer
A. Furman Townsend, Jr.............................Robert Foulk
"Newsreel" Scott.............................Gerard Lewis
"Tripod" Andrews.............................Robert Griffith
Grant Bottome.............................Ezra Stone
Slim.............................David Hoffman
Lieut. "Lace Drawers" Rogers.............................Vincent York
Colonel Ramm.............................Carroll Ashburn
Member of the Guard.............................James Monks
Member of the Guard.............................Walter Wagner
Member of the Guard.............................Robert O'Donovan

Acts I and II.—Scene 1—Porch of Mrs. Brooks' Home Adjoining Parade Grounds. 2—Barracks Room. Act III.—Scene 1—Front of Barracks. 2 and 3—Barracks Room.

Staged by George Abbott; settings by Cirker and Robbins.

Bing Edwards, the best pitcher V.M.I. has had in a long time, is having trouble with his studies, but his hope is pinned on graduating and being awarded a special prize of $200 as the best athlete of his class. The day before the crucial game Kate Rice tells Bing he is to be the father of an infant. Kate and Bing have been secretly married for months. The fear of exposure, and a resulting expulsion, as well as the worry over Kate, tosses Bing into a field of jitters. His roommates, Billy Randolph and Dan Crawford, try to help him out and just push him in deeper and deeper. He loses the game, but he wins his diploma and Kate's child gets $300 for being the first baby in the class.

IN THE BAG

(4 performances)

A comedy in three acts by Don Carle Gillette. Produced by Mack Hilliard at the Belmont Theatre, New York, December 17, 1936.

Cast of characters—

Sam Budwesky.............................Philip Van Zandt
Suzie.............................Ruth Lee
Bud Graham.............................Morgan Conway
Gus.............................Don Anthony
Allan Van Dycke.............................Reed McClelland
Jamaica Jones.............................Dudley Clements
Sybil.............................Tonia Lawton
Ned Crane.............................Teddy Jones
Tony.............................Charles La Torre
Dolly Martin.............................Joan Churchill
Detective Harrigan.............................Frank McCormack

Mr. Burton....................................Henry Antrim
Acts I, II and III.—A Broadway Producer's Office.
Staged by Frank McCormack; setting by P. Dodd Ackerman.

Bud Graham is running a play producing business and looking for backers. Jamaica Jones has a play written by his niece. Bud agrees to produce the play if Jamaica can raise the money. Jamaica borrows two thousand from a bootblack and three thousand from an Italian restaurateur. The play is produced and, bad as it is, it fools the critics. Which is more than "In the Bag" did.

BLACK RHYTHM

(6 performances)

A negro musical comedy in two acts by Donald Heywood. Produced by Earl Dancer and J. H. Levey at the Comedy Theatre, New York, December 19, 1936.

Cast of characters—

Jenny....................................Jeni LeGon
Laura....................................Maude Russell
Mr. Heydon....................................William Walker
Cornbread....................................Alex Lovejoy
Babe....................................Babe Matthews
David Songbird....................................Walter Richardson
Rhythm....................................Avon Long
Mr. Feinstein....................................Franklin Klien
Dusty....................................Joe Byrd
Bodidly....................................Speedy Wilson
Eva....................................Geneva Washington
Slim....................................Eddie Baer
Eugene....................................John Foss
Toby....................................Sammy Gardner
Swing....................................Sinclair Brooks
Ghichi....................................Walder Davis
Money....................................Clarence Albright
Joe Michaels....................................Eddie Matthews
Wardrobe Sal....................................Ina Duncan
Van Bugg....................................Woodrow Wilson
Sonny....................................Barrington Guy
Staged by Earl Dancer and Donald Heywood.

An amateur night in Harlem detached and moved into Broadway with some sort of loose-jointed plot to hold the various acts together.

AGED 26

(32 performances)

A romantic drama in two acts by Anne Crawford Flexner. Produced by Richard Aldrich at the Lyceum Theatre, December 21, 1936.

Cast of characters—

Charles Armitage Brown....................................Kenneth MacKenna
John Taylor....................................Matthew Boulton

Mrs. Brawne....................................Leona Powers
William Gifford....................................Fred Leslie
John Lockhart....................................Lloyd Gough
Lord Byron....................................Charles Trexler
Shelley....................................Anthony Kemble Cooper
John Keats....................................Robert Harris
Joseph Severn....................................William Whitehead
Mr. Hart....................................H. Cooper Cliffe
Fanny Brawne....................................Linda Watkins
Dr. Sawrey....................................A. G. Andrews
Hannah....................................Sally Fitzpatrick

Act I.—Scene 1—Reading Room of Taylor and Hessey, Fleet Street, 1818. 2—Keats' Study, Wentworth Place, Hampstead. Act II.—Scene 1—Keats' Study. 2—Deck of the "Maria Crowther."

Staged by Harry Wagstaff Gribble; settings by Steward Chaney.

John Keats, having written "Endymion" among other poems, is beginning to attract some attention in London. Both Byron and Shelley are quite inclined to approve of him. His publisher, John Taylor, is optimistic as to his future, and his best friend, Charles Armitage Brown, insists that the young poet should live at his house. It is while he is with Brown that Keats meets and falls desperately in love with Fanny Brawne, a sweet girl in this biography. As his health continues to fail Brown and Taylor make it possible for Keats to go to Italy for the Winter. His separation from Fanny is difficult for both. They spend their last night together. A point is made of a legacy that should have been given Keats when he came of age. His guardian withheld it on a technicality, thereby denying him the comforts and medical attention he should have had.

ALL EDITIONS

(23 performances)

A comedy in three acts by Charles Washburn and Clyde North. Produced by Juliana Morgan at the Longacre Theatre, New York, December 22, 1936.

Cast of characters—

Miss Colson....................................Gladis Griswold
Mortimer Caldwell....................................Clyde Franklin
Rollo Hepplesworth....................................Franklyn Dae
Page....................................Eric Udo
Clarence Class....................................Walter N. Greaza
Drake....................................John Zoller
Bernie Head....................................Jerry Sloane
Carlotta....................................Ruth Holden
Dot Melrose....................................Nancy Evans
The Rhinoceros....................................John Ravold
Radio Actress....................................Claire Nolte
Radio Actor....................................Carrington Lewis
Spike Hennessy....................................Joseph Vitale
Nicky Hanlon....................................Frederick Howard
Danny Dowd....................................Albert Bergh

Acts I, II and III.—Private Office of Clarence Class, Counsel on Public Relations, New York City.

Staged by Clyde North; setting by Cirker and Robbins.

Clarence Class, a former circus spieler become the most colorful and probably the most dynamic of public relations counsels, finds himself in a spot when his ex-wife, Carlotta, shows up as Carlotta, the Anointed, a fake evangelist, and demands publicity for herself and her racket. Clarence is busy trying to find a homely man who wants to die and become handsome in death for a client who is a mortician. He is also trying to return a kidnaped baby in the interests of another client, Nicky Hanlon, the gangster. Even when he restores the baby with the divine guidance of Carlotta things don't go so well. Dot Melrose, his girl, walks out on him; Carlotta blasts him utterly and he hasn't a friend in the world. So he goes back to his regular wife.

THE WINGLESS VICTORY

(110 performances)

A tragedy in three acts by Maxwell Anderson. Produced by Katharine Cornell at the Empire Theatre, New York, December 23, 1936.

Cast of characters—

A Girl	Mary Michael
Reverend Phineas McQueston	Kent Smith
Jared Mungo	Arthur Chatterton
Winston Urquhart	John Winthrop
Mrs. McQueston	Effie Shannon
Ruel McQueston	Myron McCormick
Venture	Lois Jameson
Faith Ingalls	Ruth Matteson
Happy Penny	Barry Kelly
Letty	Theodora Pleadwell
Nathaniel McQueston	Walter Abel
Oparre	Katharine Cornell
Toala	Helen Zelinskaya
Durian	Claire Howard
Harry	John Winthrop
Van Zandt	Victor Colton
Longshoreman	Franklyn Davis

Acts I and II.—Living Room of House in Salem, Massachusetts in 1800. Act III.—Cabin in the "Wingless Victory."

Staged by Guthrie McClintic; settings by Jo Mielziner.

Nathaniel McQueston, who sailed out of Salem harbor in 1773 with the curses of his family ringing in his ears, sails back in 1800 in the "Wingless Victory," loaded down with spices. Oparre, a Malay princess, is in the cabin. Nathaniel has married Oparre and she has borne him two children. The Salem McQuestons, God-fearing Puritans, hesitate to accept Nathaniel and his dark-skinned wife, but would compromise on his fortune. It is agreed by the Rev. Phineas McQueston, Nathaniel's sanctimonious brother, and Mrs. McQueston, his mother, that Nathaniel and his family shall stay more or less on probation. Within a year the plan has failed. The Princess has been snubbed and Nathaniel has been badly treated. Oparre, sensing the defeat, goes back to the "Wingless Victory," and in its cabin kills herself and her children. Nathaniel is free.

* THE SHOW IS ON

(197 performances)

A revue in two parts assembled by Vincente Minnelli, with David Freedman, Moss Hart, Vernon Duke, Ted Fetter, Howard Dietz, Arthur Schwartz, Richard Rodgers, Lorenz Hart, chief contributors. Produced by the Messrs. Shubert at the Winter Garden, New York, December 25, 1936.

Principals engaged—

Bert Lahr	Beatrice Lillie
Charles Walters	Mitzi Mayfair
Paul Haakon	Evelyn Thawl
Robert Shafer	Gracie Barrie
Reginald Gardiner	Vera Allen
Jack McCauley	Marie Carroll
Ralph Riggs	Roy Campbell's Continentals

Staged by Vincente Minnelli; sketches directed by Edward Clarke Lilley; choreography by Harry Losee; settings by Minnelli.

* THE WOMEN

(202 performances)

A comedy in three acts by Clare Boothe. Produced by Max Gordon at the Ethel Barrymore Theatre, New York, December 26, 1936.

Cast of characters—

Jane	Anne Teeman
Sylvia (Mrs. Howard Fowler)	Ilka Chase
Nancy Blake	Jane Seymour
Peggy (Mrs. John Day)	Adrienne Marden
Edith (Mrs. Phelps Potter)	Phyllis Povah
Mary (Mrs. Stephen Haines)	Margalo Gillmore
Mrs. Wagstaff	Ethel Jackson
Olga	Ruth Hammond
First Hairdresser	Mary Stuart
Second Hairdresser	Jane Moore
Pedicurist	Ann Watson
Euphie	Eloise Bennett
Miss Fordyce	Eileen Burns
Little Mary	Charita Bauer
Mrs. Morehead	Jessie Busley
First Saleswoman	Doris Day
Second Saleswoman	Jean Rodney
Head Saleswoman	Lucille Fenton
First Model	Beryl Wallace
Third Saleswoman	Martina Thomas
Crystal Allen	Betty Lawford

A Fitter....................................Joy Hathaway
Second Model....................................Beatrice Cole
Princess Tamara....................................Arlene Francis
Exercise Instructress....................................Anne Hunter
Maggie....................................Mary Cecil
Miss Watts....................................Virgilia Chew
Miss Trimmerback....................................Mary Murray
A Nurse....................................Lucille Fenton
Lucy....................................Marjorie Main
Countess de Lage....................................Margaret Douglass
Miriam Aarons....................................Audrey Christie
Helene....................................Arlene Francis
Sadie....................................Marjorie Wood
Cigarette Girl....................................Lillian Norton

Act I.—Scene 1—Mary Haines' Sitting Room. 2—Hairdresser's. 3—Mary Haines' Boudoir. 4—Fitting Room. Act II.—Scene 1—Exercise Salon. 2—Mary Haines' Pantry. 3—Mary Haines' Sitting Room. 4—Hospital Room. 5—Reno Hotel Room. Act III.—Scene 1—Crystal's Bathroom. 2—Mary Haines' Bedroom. 3—Ladies' Powder Room, Casino Roof.

Staged by Robert B. Sinclair; settings by Jo Mielziner; costumes by John Hambleton.

See page 218.

AROUND THE CORNER

(16 performances)

A comedy in three acts by Martin Flavin. Produced by Lodewick Vroom at the 48th Street Theatre, New York, December 28, 1936.

Cast of characters—

Ephraim Clark....................................Dodson Mitchell
Sarah Clark....................................Zamah Cunningham
Fred Perkins....................................Charles Coburn
Mary Perkins....................................Merle Maddern
Amos Perkins....................................Cyrus W. Wendall
Sally....................................Lillian Emerson
Joe....................................Milburn Stone
Dave....................................Boyd Crawford
Mac....................................Edwin Cushman
Mr. Peterson....................................Frank Tweddell

Acts I, II and III.—Living Room of the Perkins Home. Small Middle Western Town.

Staged by Bertram Harrison; setting by Yellenti.

Fred Perkins was a prospering hardware merchant in a small Middle Western town until the depression struck. Fred couldn't collect his accounts or pay his bills. He took to fishing. His son Joe, out of a job, went in for gin and pool. His daughter, Sally, home from Chicago where her husband, Dave, is also out of work, helps with the housework and waits for Dave. Dave comes and grows bitter under the pressure of idleness and his mother-in-law's criticism. Joe, in gin, decides to become a thief and a stick-up man. Dave, thinking Sally is going to have a baby, agrees to help with a hold-up of the station agent. Joe gets too drunk and

Dave loses his nerve. The sheriff, being Joe's uncle, overlooks the evidence. Better times, says Fred, are just around the corner.

PROMISE

(29 performances)

A drama in three acts by Henry Bernstein; English version by H. M. Harwood. Produced by Gilbert Miller at the Little Theatre, New York, December 30, 1936.

Cast of characters—

Toni Flammery....................................Thomas Collins
Emile Delbar....................................Cedric Hardwicke
Therese Delbar....................................Irene Browne
Solange....................................Louise Platt
Thierry Keller....................................Frank Lawton
Catherine....................................Jean Forbes-Robertson
Gustave....................................Henry Vincent

Acts I, II and III.—Salon of Delbars' Apartment, Paris.
Staged by Gilbert Miller; setting by Raymond Sovey.

Emile Delbar, married a second time, finds himself facing a family crisis when Mme. Delbar, a vain, ambitious and neurotic woman, lavishes her affections and attentions upon her own daughter, Solange, leaving her step-daughter, Catherine, to pine and suffer the fate of an ugly duckling. Thierry Keller, engaged to Solange, gradually becomes convinced that it really is Catherine whom he loves. He boldly proclaims his change of heart, takes Catherine away with him and leaves Mme. Delbar to fume and curse and make herself generally miserable in her defeat. M. Delbar accepts it all philosophically and is much happier than his wife in the end. "L'Espoir" was the French title.

THE PEPPER MILL

(6 performances)

An intimate revue in two acts with skits by W. H. Auden, Klaus Mann, Erich Muhsam, Ernst Toller and Erica Mann; English adaptation by John Latouche and Edwin Denby; music by Magnus Henning, Aaron Copland, Peter Kreuder, Herbert Murril and Werner Kruse. Produced by F. C. Coppicus in association with the Columbia Concerts Corporation at the Chanin Auditorium, New York, January 5, 1937.

Principals engaged—

Erica Mann
Lotte Goslar
Sybille Schloss
Therese Giehse
Wallace Rooney
John Latouche
John Beck

Staged by Therese Giehse; settings by Anton Refregier.

OTHELLO

(21 performances)

A tragedy by William Shakespeare. Revived by Max Gordon at the New Amsterdam Theatre, New York, January 6, 1937.

Cast of characters—

Othello..Walter Huston
Desdemona..Nan Sunderland
Emilia..Natalie Hall
Iago...Brian Aherne
Cassio...G. P. Huntley, Jr.
Roderigo...Arthur Pierson
Brabantio..Edward Fielding
Duke of Venice...A. P. Kaye
Lodovico..Walter Beck
Gratiano...Joseph Roeder
Paulo...William E. Morris
Montano...Leo Chalzel
A Herald...George Spaulding
Messenger...Philip Foster
A Gentleman...Elliott C. Brown, Jr.
Senators: George W. Masters, Al Bayfield, G. B. Kingston, Henry Walters, Edward James.
Officers, Gentlemen, Messengers, Sailors and Attendants: Burton Bowen, Hudson Shotwell, Charles Campbell, Nicholas Warwick, Robert Selman, Bernard Goodman, Howard Kelder, Charles Brunswick, Vincent Manz, Leslie Ostrander, Sidney Palmer, Ralph Scharff, Arthur Rosen, Clark Butler, Michael, Arthur Mack, Joseph Rustad, John Morley, Lloyd Bridges, Alexander Micone, Robert Stewart, David Dittmer, Michael Brodkin, Marvin Hansen.

Act I.—Scene 1—Before Brabantio's House, Venice. 2—Before the Sagittary. 3—Council Chamber. 4—Arrival at Cyprus. 5—Tavern, Cyprus. 6—Hall in Castle at Cyprus. Act II.—Scene 1—Hall in Castle, Cyprus. 2—Another Room in Castle. 3—Cyprus Wharf. 4—Bedchamber in Castle.

Staged and designed by Robert Edmond Jones.

A version of the tragedy arranged by Robert Edmond Jones for presentation at Central City, Colorado, in 1934. The last previous revival of "Othello" in New York was that of Philip Merivale in September, 1935, with Gladys Cooper his Desdemona.

THE ETERNAL ROAD

(153 performances)

A Biblical spectacle by Franz Werfel, adapted by William A. Drake from a Ludwig Lewisohn translation; music by Kurt Weill. Produced by Meyer W. Weisgal and Crosby Gaige at the Manhattan Opera House, New York, January 7, 1937.

Cast of characters—

A SYNAGOGUE

The Rabbi...Myron Taylor
The Adversary...Sam Jaffe

The Timid Soul....................................Mark Schweid
The Rich Man.....................................Anthony Blair
The Estranged One..............................Harold Johnsrud
The Estranged One's Son........................Sidney Lumet
President of the Congregation................David A. Leonard
First Pious Man................................Robert Harrison
Second Pious Man...............................Charles Adler
Third Pious Man................................Baruch Lumet
Fourth Pious Man...............................Leslie Austen
Fifth Pious Man................................Bennett Challis
Sixth Pious Man................................Cassius C. Quimby
Seventh Pious Man..............................Harry Hamill
Eighth Pious Man...............................Hal Kingsley
Ninth Pious Man................................Kurt Kasznar
Fanatic..Roger De Koven
Adversary's Follower...........................Abner Biberman
Watchman.......................................David Kurlan
Elders..................Al Clifford, Charles Homer, Gustav Stryker
Jesse—A Young Man..............................Herbert Rudley
The Alien Girl.................................Olive Deering
An Ancient.....................................Charles Hale

The Voice of God Is Sung by Ben Cutler.

Act I

ABRAHAM

Abraham..Thomas Chalmers
Sarah..Bertha Kunz-Baker
Isaac..Dickie Van Patten
Eliezer..Carl Formes
The White Angel................................John Uppman
First Dark Angel...............................Edward Kane
Second Dark Angel..............................Ben Cutler
Voice of a Cherub..............................Tommy Mott

JACOB AND RACHEL

Jacob..Ralph Jameson
Rachel...Sarah Osnath-Halevy

JOSEPH AND HIS BROTHERS

Joseph...Earl Weatherford
Reuben...Robert Warren Bentley
Shimon...Noel Cravat
Levi...Paul Hammond
Judah..Joseph Macaulay
Issachar.......................................Starr West Jones
Zebulon..Kurt Kasznar
Dan..Carl Formes
Naphtali.......................................Edward Fisher
Gad..Leonard Mence
Asher..Edward Vermonti

JOSEPH IN EGYPT

Benjamin.......................................Walter Elliott
The Steward....................................Blake Scott
The Juggler....................................Florence Meyer

Act II

MOSES IN EGYPT

Moses..Samuel Goldenberg
Miriam...Lotte Lenya
The Taskmaster.................................Raymond Miller

A Hebrew Slave.......................................Paul Marion
Aaron...Noel Cravat

IN THE WILDERNESS

The Adversary's Follower........................Benjamin Zemach
The Priestess of the Golden Calf..................Florence Meyer
Joshua...Robert Bentley
White Angels.........................Edward Kane, John Uppman
The Angel of Death.............................Joseph Macaulay
Soul of Moses...Tommy Mott

Act III

THE SYNAGOGUE

RUTH

Ruth...Katherine Carrington
Naomi...Bertha Kunz-Baker
Boaz..Ralph Jameson
Head Reaper.......................................Kurt Kasznar

SAUL

King Saul...Walter Gilbert
Samuel..Bennett Challis
Jonathan..Hal Kingsley
David..Earl Weatherford
A Henchman..Fred Barrie
David's Comrade.................................Paul Hammond
The Witch of Endor...................................Lotte Lenya

DAVID

King David.....................................Earl Weatherford
Bath-Sheba.....................................Rosamond Pinchot
Uriah...Raymond Miller
The Dark Angel.................................Joseph Macaulay
A Courtier..Fred Barrie
A Sentinel.......................................Starr West Jones
The Ghost of Ruth.........................Katherine Carrington

SOLOMON

King Solomon..John Uppman

THE SYNAGOGUE

The Ghost of Rachel..........................Sarah Osnath-Halevy
The Voice...Tommy Mott
The King's Messenger..........................Starr West Jones

Prologue.—Synagogue. Act I.—Scene 1—Abraham. 2—Jacob and Rachel. 3—Joseph and his Brothers. 4—Joseph in Egypt. Act II.—Scene 1—Moses in Egypt. 2—In the Wilderness. Act III.—Scenes 1 and 6—The Synagogue. 2—Ruth. 3—Saul. 4—David. 5—Solomon.

Staged by Max Reinhardt, assisted by Francesco von Mendelssohn, Harry Horner and Charles Alan; dances directed by Benjamin Zemach; settings, costumes and lighting by Norman Bel Geddes.

Frightened Jews are gathered in the synagogue of a village in Eastern Europe. A mob outside is threatening them. A ruler in a distant castle is debating their extinction or their banishment.

Their rabbi quiets and comforts them by reading the stories of the Old Testament, which are acted in a March of Time sequence.

HIGH TOR

(171 performances)

A comedy in three acts by Maxwell Anderson. Produced by Guthrie McClintic at the Martin Beck Theatre, New York, January 9, 1937.

Cast of characters—

The Indian.....Harry Irvine
Van Van Dorn.....Burgess Meredith
Judith.....Mab Maynard
Art J. Biggs.....Harold Moffet
Judge Skimmerhorn.....Thomas W. Ross
Lise.....Peggy Ashcroft
Captain Asher.....Byron McGrath
Pieter.....John Philliber
First Sailor.....William Casamo
Second Sailor.....Will Archie
Third Sailor.....Harold Grau
DeWitt.....Chas. D. Brown
Dope.....Leslie Gorall
Elkus.....Hume Cronyn
Buddy.....John Drew Colt
Patsy.....Charles Forrester
A. B. Skimmerhorn.....John M. Kline
Budge.....Jackson Halliday

Acts I, II and III.—Sections Near and at the Summit of High Tor.
Staged by Guthrie McClintic; settings by Jo Mielziner.

See page 29.

A HOUSE IN THE COUNTRY

(7 performances)

A comedy in three acts by Melvin Levy. Produced by Murray Queen at the Vanderbilt Theatre, New York, January 11, 1937.

Cast of characters—

Frankie Lotzgazel.....Tom Powers
President, his dog.....Puck Powers
Gramma Alladay Lotzgazel.....Fredrica Slemons
Herman Sigafoos.....Alfred Herrick
Delphine Lotzgazel.....Louise Campbell
Mr. Mooney.....Will Geer
"Mr. Knox".....Roy Gordon
Joe.....Teddy Bergman
Mac.....Leon Ames
Bean.....Elmer Brown

Acts I, II and III.—House Occupied by the Lotzgazel Family at Jugtown, Pa., Just Across the Delaware River from New Jersey.
Staged by Melville Burke; settings by P. Dodd Ackerman.

Grandpa and Grandma Lotzgazel, poor folk in Pennsylvania, are living in an abandoned farm house near Jugtown. A racketeer trio from New York, headed by "Mr. Knox," invades the place. Knox had used the farm house as a hideout during prohibition. The Lotzgazels are suspicious but shrewd. With the help of the local game warden they finally corner the crooks and turn them over to the law.

BUT FOR THE GRACE OF GOD

(42 performances)

A drama in three acts by Leopold L. Atlas. Produced by the Theatre Guild by arrangement with Sidney Harmon at the Guild Theatre, New York, January 12, 1937.

Cast of characters—

Josey	James McCallion
Eddie	Gene Lowe
Petey	Joey Brown, Jr.
Mickey	Leslie Klein
Snowball	Theodore McKnight
Uncle Louis	Harry Levian
Fotzo	Robert Mayors
Mooch	Arthur Bruce
Sharkey	Edgerton Paul
Bugsey	Jack Arnold
Ralphey	Melbourne Ford
Charley	Robert J. Mulligan
Frank Adamec	James Bell
Mrs. Sullivan	Beatrice Moreland
Hannah Adamec	Kathryn Grill
Wilson	Anthony Ross
Rusek	Clem Willenchik
Stanley	Maurice Burke
Kababian	Joseph Greenwald
Zhlub	John Call
Julius	Stanley Povich
Rosey	Gilda Oakleaf
Bertha	Harriet Caron
Bosco	P. A. Xantho
Whitey	Lester Lonergan III
Marty	Robert Reeves
Mac	Clem Willenchik
George Shay	Frank Gabrielson
Bert	Philip Sheridan
First Woman	Dorothy Scott
Second Woman	Blossom MacDonald
Interne	Sidney Packer
Steve	Philip Sheridan
York	Robert Gordon

Act I.—Scene 1—Street Corner in Medium-sized Industrial City. 2—The Adamecs' Home. 3—Kababian's Shop. Act II.—Scenes 1 and 3—Roof-Top of Adamecs' Tenement. 2—Adamecs' Home. 4—Back Room of Police Station. Act III.—Scene 1—Street Corner. 2—Kababian's Shop. 3—Adamecs' Home.

Staged by Benno Schneider; settings by Stewart Chaney.

Frank Adamec has been out of work for two years. His son, Ralphy, is working in a factory and suffering from insipient tuberculosis. His son, Josey, is shining shoes, running errands and hating his father as an incompetent. Ralphy has to give up and go to a hospital. Josey takes his place. Ralphy can't get well without treatment. Josey decides to go in for crime to get money. Josey and two of his pals steal a copper's revolver, stick up the proprietor of the factory and shoot him dead when he can only give them $8. Ralphy dies. Josey goes to prison.

BEHIND RED LIGHTS

(177 performances)

A drama in three acts by Samuel Shipman and Beth Brown, adapted from Beth Brown's novel "For Men Only." Produced by Jack Curtis at the Mansfield Theatre, New York, January 13, 1937.

Cast of characters—

Joe Burke	Bruce MacFarlane
Lily White	Maida Reade
F. Reid Singleton	Murray Bennet
Ben Miller	Richard Taber
Teddy	Ruth Edell
Ruby	Blanche Gladstone
Jerry Wilkins	George Lewis
Mona	Lucille Beaumont
Gracie	Jane Johns
Fay	Barbara Fulton
Ned Stone	George Baxter
Laura Taylor	Marjorie Lytell
Peggy	Thelma Shaw
Gladys	Barbara Brown
Winnie	Wilma Drake
Frank Moran	Arthur Hughes
Dan O'Connor	Edward Andrews
Jim Donovan	George N. Volk
Samuel J. Armstrong	Hardie Albright
Lucy Gray	Beatrice Kaye
Norma King	Dorothy Hall
Wendy	Betty Lee
Billie	Jane Moxon
Myrtle	Marion Crosson
Jean	Eileen Wenzel
Connie	Jerrie Maxwell
Emma Good	Mary Morris
Kitty	Mitzi Haynes
Eddie	Don Ostrander
Delight	Georgette Harvey
Three College Boys	David Pelham Alan Dinehart, Jr. Stephen Wilson
Dick Jackson	Richard Sterling
Mrs. Taylor	Katherine Grey
Tony	Earl Ebi
Nick	Henry Antrim
George	Edgar Mason
Policemen	John Kearney Randolph Preston

Act I.—Scene 1—An Office. 2—Office of Special Prosecutor Samuel J. Armstrong. Acts II and III.—Living Room in Norma King's Apartment, Park Avenue, New York.

Staged by A. H. Van Buren; settings by Nicholas Yellenti.

Norma King is running a high-class call house in New York. The vice ring tries to force her to join the organization. Sam Armstrong, special prosecutor hoping to round up the under-cover leaders of the vice ring, tries to induce Norma to come in with him and help the state. Norma is a good sport and refuses both invitations. A murder in her house finally forces her to take sides with the prosecutor to protect her girls. The ring is smashed. Norma is in love with the prosecutor, but Armstrong is not for her. Norma is shot by one of the ring.

HOWDY STRANGER

(77 performances)

A farce in three acts by Robert Sloane and Louis Pelletier, Jr. Produced by Theodore J. Hammerstein and Denis Du-For in association with Robert Goldstein at the Longacre Theatre, New York, January 14, 1937.

Cast of characters—

Tex	Tex Fletcher
1st Dude	Peter Hues
Miss Martin	Jean McCoy
Ma Hardy	Mary Horne Morrison
Jane Hardy	Dorothy Libaire
Panthia	Tonia Lawton
Jeff Hardy	Marion Willis
Professor Landis	Walter Scott Weeks
2nd Dude	Anthony Gray
Pa Hardy	Royal C. Stout
Sam Thorne	Arthur L. Sachs
Elly Jordan	Frank Parker
Roy Chadwick	Louis Sorin
Miss Semple	Francetta Malloy
Pat Dunn	Russ Brown
Bell Boy	Thomas Todd
Mrs. Jordan	Catherine Proctor
Mr. Jordan	Hans Robert
From *The Star*	Arthur Uttry
From *The Chronicle*	Peter Van Buren
From *The Transcript*	Joseph Kleema
From *The Beacon*	Rudulf Brooks
Camera Man	Al Waldron
Gibson Girls	Sandra Waring Elaine Adams Monica Klopping Kay Thorne

Act I—Hardy's Dude Ranch Near Cody, Wyoming. Acts II and III.—Living Room in New York Hotel Suite.
Staged by Carl Hunt; settings by Karle O. Amend.

Elly Jordan, a Brooklyn tenor, starts on a hike for Hollywood. In Wyoming he stops at a dude ranch, sings for the natives, attracts the attention of a Jewish theatrical agent, is engaged for radio, brought back to New York and exploited as a singing cowboy. Frank's chief phobia is a fear of animals. All animals, large and small. When his rivals would expose him as a fake cowboy, he is given the privilege of entering a rodeo at Madison Square Garden and proving his quality. With the help of a hypnotist Frank wins the medal for bulldogging and keeps his radio job.

TIDE RISING

(32 performances)

A drama in three acts by George Brewer, Jr. Produced by Richard Aldrich and Richardson Myers at the Lyceum Theatre, New York, January 25, 1937.

Cast of characters—

Joe Peabody....Oliver Barbour
Mrs. Tanner....Elinor Hopkinson
Tony....John Guy Sampsel
Sam....Charles Howard
Jim Cogswell....Grant Mitchell
Jane Cogswell....Peggy O'Donnell
Mary Cogswell....Alice Ann Baker
Pete....Francis Grover Cleveland
Graham Hay....Clyde Fillmore
Terry....Howard Miller
Fred MacKay....Edward Marr
Spike Webb....Charles Jordan
Mrs. Perkins....Irene Cattell
Dan....Larry Johns
Galoot Wilson....Tom Fadden
Tom Stevens....Cameron Prud'homme
Eric....Jack Harling
David Cogswell....John D. Seymour
Ruth Cogswell....Tamara
Mr. Kelly....Frank McCormack
Judge Choate....Irving Locke
Bill....Sandy Strouse
Hank....Fred Sears
Jack....Whitefield Cook
Edgar Lawrence....Joaquin Souther
Chief-of-Police Olson....Scott Moore
Mill Workers, passers-by: Dee Lowrance, John de Angelis, Richard Allen, Alan Gilbert, Edwin Gordon, Richard MacKay, George Miller, Frederick Olmsted, Richard Ross, Warren Young.

Acts I, II and III.—Jim Cogswell's Drug Store and Office.
Staged by Arthur Sircom; setting by Hugh Willoughby.

Jim Cogswell is an honest citizen of a milltown in the Middle West. He manages a chain drug store, lives contentedly for several years and then eats up all his surplus during the depression. When the millhands strike to better their $12-a-week wage Jim tries not to take sides. His son, who has been in New York, comes home with a Communist wife, Ruth. Ruth goes into the mills and organizes the strikers at a time they were beginning to weaken. The citizens meet, elect Jim sheriff and order him to stop the strike. Jim arrests the millowner and the strike leader. He sends all strikebreakers back where they came from. When he is attacked, a half-wit he has befriended kills his attacker. A compromise is in sight when rioting is resumed and Jim's son is killed.

NAUGHTY NAUGHT '00

(173 performances)

A musical drama by John Van Antwerp; lyrics by Ted Fetter; music by Richard Lewine. Produced by John and Jerrold Krimsky at the American Music Hall, New York, January 23, 1937.

Cast of characters—

P. De Quincy Devereux..........................Alexander Clark
Spunky..Percy Helton
Frank Plover..................................Bartlett Robinson
Jack Granville.................................Leslie Litomy
Stub...Phil Eppens
Fred..Howard Fischer
Claire Granville..............................Eleanor Phelps
Jim Pawling....................................Alan Handley
Joe..Lee Berkman
Tom..Douglas Rowland
Bartender.....................................Harry Meehan
Tough...Isham Keith
Cathleen.....................................Gerrie Worthing
Pugsy..Howard Sullivan
A Student.......................................Kermit Love
Gibson Girls: Eleanora Dixon, Anna Erskine, Julie Hartwell, Jane Hammond, Barbara Hunter, Lucille Rich.

Act I.—Scene 1—Yale Campus. 2—Frank and Jack's Dormitory Room. Act II.—Scene 1—Dormitory Room. 2—Moriarity's Saloon. 3—Railroad Station, New Haven. Act III.—Scenes 1 and 3—Boathouse on the Thames. 2 and 4—River Bank. 5—On the Thames.

Staged by Morgan Lewis; settings by Eugene Dunkel.

Frank Plover, Yale '00, was the best stroke the crew ever had until P. De Quincy Devereux engineered a conspiracy that (1) slipped gin into Plover's lemon squash the day before the big race, and (2) arranged to have Cathleen, a hussy, kiss him frankly upon the mouth just as Claire Granville came around a corner of the scenery. It was Claire whom both Plover and Devereux loved. Yale, however, won the race. After which everybody sang the old songs.

AND NOW GOOD-BYE

(25 performances)

A drama in three acts by Philip Howard based on the novel by James Hilton. Produced by John Golden at the Golden Theatre, New York, February 2, 1937.

Cast of characters—

Rev. Howat Freemantle....Philip Merivale
Mary Freemantle....Margaret Anderson
Ellen....Marie de Becker
Aunt Viney....Kathryn Collier
Dr. Ringwood....Richie Ling
Mrs. Freemantle....Hilda Plowright
Mrs. Trevis....Horace Sinclair
Mr. Garland....Edgar Kent
Mrs. Garland....Ruth Vivian
Elizabeth Garland....Marguerite Churchill
Waiter....Thomas Bate
Miss Potts....Eda Heinemann
Acts I and III.—Rev. Freemantle's Study, Browdley. Act II.—Scenes 1 and 3—Studio in Chelsea, London. 2—Restaurant in Soho.
Staged by Reginald Bach; settings by Raymond Sovey.

The Rev. Howat Freemantle, a godly man and faithful to his calling, despite a nagging wife and a variety of petty irritations, goes to London hoping to induce Elizabeth Garland of his parish to return to the home from which she has fled. Elizabeth wants to study music in Vienna. The Rev. Freemantle is sympathetic and understanding. He and Elizabeth attend a symphony. He brings her home. She induces him to visit until she can call a taxi. When the taxi (which Elizabeth had forgotten to order) doesn't come the Rev. Freemantle decides to stay the night. Next morning, as they are on a train planning an elopement, there is a collision. Elizabeth is killed. The Rev. Freemantle, assisting in the rescue work, is injured. At home he is welcomed as a hero.

THIRSTY SOIL

(13 performances)

A drama in three acts by Raymond Bond. Produced by E. John Brandeis in association with Leila Bliss and Harry Hayden at the 48th Street Theatre, New York, February 3, 1937.

Cast of characters—

Silas Warner....Raymond Bond
Mrs. Warner....Maude Allen
Matt Warner....George Makinson
Milly Warner....Ann Meril
Luke Warner....Leon Ames
Mr. Hurd....Robert Thorne
Primrose Hurd....Greta Granstedt
Acts I, II and III.—Living Room of Nebraska Farmhouse.
Staged by Harry Hayden; setting by Louis Bromberg.

The Silas Warners, formerly of Vermont, have moved onto a Nebraska prairie farm. It is a bleak farm, in the drought and tornado country. Old Silas becomes a religious fanatic through brooding. Luke Warner, the oldest boy, runs away to become a peddler of fake medicine. Matt, his brother, with an urge for education, works his way through school and dreams of teaching and planting trees. Milly Warner is an adopted daughter suffering the need of companionship through the years of adolescence. Only Mother Warner, beset with all the family problems as well as a few of her own, is able to hold an even course. Silas loses his mind and his life. Luke seduces Milly. Matt falls in love with Priscilla Hurd, and she not of his social strata. A tornado practically wrecks the farm, but Ma works on, still hopeful. Luke comes back and marries Milly. Matt is still dreaming of Priscilla.

FREDERIKA

(95 performances)

An operetta in three acts by Franz Lehar; American adaptation and lyrics by Edward Eliscu. Produced by the Messrs. Shubert at the Imperial Theatre, New York, February 4, 1937.

Cast of characters—

PROLOGUE

Miss Hotchkiss....................................Edith Gresham
Mrs. Thorne....................................Edith King
Mr. Linker....................................George Dobbs
Mrs. Linker....................................Mary Jane Barrett
Jessica Thorne....................................Mildred Schroeder
Arthur Benson....................................William Newgord
Dr. Bauer....................................Wheeler Dryden
Guide....................................Fred Sherman

PLAY

Parson Brion....................................J. Arthur Young
Magda Brion....................................Rose Winter
Salomea....................................Doris Patston
Postillion....................................Fred Sherman
Countess Scholl....................................Ulita Torgerson
Frederika....................................Helen Gleason
Jung-Stilling....................................George Dobbs
Meyer....................................Charles Columbus
Engelbach....................................William Newgord
Lenz....................................Ernest Truex
Weyland....................................George Trabert
Goethe....................................Dennis King
Herr Gruenwald....................................Earl McDonald
Captain Knebel....................................Arthur Vinton
Countess Hahn....................................Edith King
Liselotte....................................Diana Gaylen
Lackey....................................Wesley Bender
Count Hahn....................................Wheeler Dryden
Hortense....................................Mary Jane Barrett
Karl August, Duke of Weimar....................................Ralph Magelsson

Act I.—Scene 1—Prologue. 2—Parsonage at Sesenheim, 1771. Act II.—Countess Scholl's Salon, Strasburg. Act III.—Scene 1—Goethe's Study. 2—The Parsonage.

Staged by Hassard Short; settings by Watson Barratt; costumes by William Weaver; choreography by Chester Hale.

Johann Wolfgang von Goethe was in love with Frederika when she was a town belle of his student days and he a penniless student. He wooed her with his scribblings, and as his fame grew so did his love. Finally Goethe was summoned to the court of the Duke of Weimar. He would not go without Frederika, so, at the second act finale, she told him that she was going to marry the other fellow who was rich. A year later Goethe came again for Frederika, but again she sent him away. She simply would not be a hindrance to his career.

KING RICHARD II

(133 performances)

An historical drama by William Shakespeare; incidental music by Herbert Menges and Rupert Graves. Revived by Eddie Dowling and Robinson Smith at the St. James Theatre, New York, February 5, 1937.

Cast of characters—

King Richard, the Second....Maurice Evans
John of Gaunt, Duke of Lancaster....Augustin Duncan
Edmund of Langley, Duke of York....Lionel Hogarth
Henry, Surnamed Bolingbroke, Duke of Hereford, Son to John of Gaunt: Afterwards King Henry IV....Ian Keith
Duke of Aumerle....Sherling Oliver
Thomas Mawbray, Duke of Norfolk....William Post, Jr.
Bushy....John Halloran
Bagot....Everett Ripley
Green....Robert K. Adams
Earl of Northumberland....Charles Dalton
Henry Percy, Surnamed Hotspur....Randolph Echols
Lord Ross....Bram Nossen
Lord Willoughby....Stephen Courtleigh
Lord Marshall....Reynolds Evans
First Herald....Lawrence Murray
Second Herald....Rhys Williams
Earl of Salisbury....Lionel Ince
Captain of a Band of Welshmen....Rhys Williams
Bishop of Carlisle....Reynolds Evans
Sir Stephen Scroop....Donald Randolph
Gardiner....Whitford Kane
Second Gardiner....Philip Truex
Duke of Surrey....Lawrence Murray
Sir Pierce of Exton....Donald Randolph
Servant to Exton....Robert K. Adams
A Groom....Rhys Williams
A Keeper....Lionel Ince
Queen to Richard....Olive Deering
Duchess of Gloucester....Irene Tedrow
Ladies Attending on Queen....{ Betty Jenckes / Julia Lathrop }
Lords, Officers, Soldiers, Monks, Messenger and Other Attendants: Philip Truex, William Howell, Neal Berry, Alfred Paschall, Samuel Danzig, Walter Williams.

Act I.—Scene 1—King Richard's Palace. 2—Duke of Lancaster's Palace. 3—The Lists at Coventry. 4—The Court. 5—Ely House. Act II.—Scene 1—Windsor Castle. 2—Wilds of Gloucestershire. 3—Camp in Wales. 4—Bristol before the Castle. 5—Coast of Wales. 6—Wales before Flint Castle. Act III.—Scene 1—Duke of York's Garden. 2 and 6—Westminster Hall. 3—London Street Leading

to the Tower. 4—Windsor Castle. 5—Pomfret Castle. April 1398 to March 1400.
Staged by Margaret Webster and Charles Alan; costumes designed by David Ffolkes.

The first revival of the tragedy in America since it was played by Edwin Booth at the Fifth Avenue Theatre, New York, in 1878.

THE MASQUE OF KINGS

(89 performances)

A tragedy in three acts by Maxwell Anderson. Produced by Theatre Guild, Inc., at the Shubert Theatre, New York, February 8, 1937.

Cast of characters—

The Countess Larisch	Claudia Morgan
A Maid	Catherine Lawrence
Count Taafe	Herbert Yost
The Emperor Franz Joseph of Austria-Hungary	Dudley Digges
A Servant	Pierre Chace
Koinoff	Glenn Anders
The Empress Elizabeth of Austria-Hungary	Pauline Frederick
Count Larisch	John Hoysradt
Marie	Bijou Fernandez
Fritzi	Alan Hewitt
Louise	Elizabeth Young
D'orsy	Benjamin Otis
Loschek	Edward Broadley
The Crown Prince Rudolph of Austria-Hungary	Henry Hull
Bratfish	Henry Hull, Jr.
The Baroness Mary Vetsera	Margo
The Archduke John of Tuscany	Joseph Holland
Sceps	Wyrley Birch
An Officer	Franklin Downing
A Soldier	Charles Holden
A Soldier	Hobart Skidmore
Count Joseph Hoyos	Leo G. Carroll

Act I.—Scene 1—Emperor Franz Joseph's Study, Hofburg, Vienna. January 1889. 2—Crown Prince Rudolph's Apartments, Hofburg, Vienna. Act II.—Scene 1—Part of Room of Crown Prince Rudolph. 2—Study of Emperor Franz Joseph. Act III.—Crown Prince Rudolph's Shooting Lodge, Mayerling.
Staged by Philip Moeller; settings and costumes by Lee Simonson.

Crown Prince Rudolph of Austria-Hungary, of liberal mind and resenting the tyranny of his father, the Emperor Franz Joseph, is ripe for revolution. Being in love with the Baroness Mary Vetsera he is also interested in divorcing his wife and marrying Mary. His application for special dispensation to the Pope is denied. His father threatens the continuance of his love for Mary. Prince Rudolph, caught in an emotional crisis, joins John of Tuscany and other revolutionists and finds himself, following a successful coup, within a short step of the throne of the dual kingdom. Two things stop him: His recoil from the thought of further bloodshed, and the suggestion that he cannot mount the throne until old Franz Joseph is out of the way. Prince Rudolph abandons the revolution and flies to his shooting lodge at Mayerling. Mary Vetsera follows. Her loyalty being doubted Mary shoots herself to release the Prince from all obligations. Rudolph, to "keep faith with a faith," kills himself with the same revolver.

BE SO KINDLY

(8 performances)

A comedy in three acts by Sara Sandberg. Produced by Richard Skinner and Hope Lawder in association with Aldrich and Myers at the Little Theatre, New York, February 8, 1937.

Cast of characters—

Mrs. Kadan	Angela Jacobs
Clarisse Kadan	Jeanne Greene
Della Kadan	Eva Langbord
Mr. Kadan	Francis Pierlot
George Herzog	Albert Hayes
Miss Payne	Jane Dewey
Bert Kadan	John Call
Shirley Lefkowitz	Edith Tachna
Edith Martinson	Judith Barry
David Friedsam	Franklin Gray

Acts I, II and III.—Living Room in Kadans' Apartment on West End Avenue, New York City.
Staged by Kenneth MacKenna.

The Kadans (née Kadansky in the Bronx) are living in West End Avenue and trying to keep up with the Lefkowitzes. There is business rivalry between Kadan and Lefkowitz in dress manufacturing. There is love rivalry between Clarisse and Della Kadan, when Clarisse's husband loses his money and Della's boy-friend wins a literary prize that brings him movie capital.

* YES, MY DARLING DAUGHTER

(149 performances)

A comedy in three acts by Mark Reed. Produced by Alfred de Liagre, Jr., at the Playhouse, New York, February 9, 1937.

Cast of characters—

Ellen Murray	Peggy Conklin
Lewis Murray	Charles Bryant
Constance Nevins	Violet Heming
Martha	Margaret Curtis
Ann Whitman Murray	Lucile Watson
Titus Jaywood	Nicholas Joy
Douglas Hall	Boyd Crawford

Acts I and III.—Living Room of the Murray Summer Home, New

Canaan, Connecticut. Act II.—Ann's Office.
Staged by Alfred de Liagre, Jr.; settings by Raymond Sovey.

See page 293.

FULTON OF OAK FALLS

(37 performances)

A comedy in three acts by George M. Cohan from a story by Parker Fennelly. Produced by George M. Cohan and Sam H. Harris at the Morosco Theatre, New York, February 10, 1937.

Cast of characters—

Ed Fulton (of Oak Falls)........................George M. Cohan
Emma..Jessamine Newcombe
Betty...Francesca Lenni
Mrs. Todd.......................................Gilberta Faust
Corey.......................................Harold Vermilyea
Rev. George Halliday..........................Brandon Peters
Harry Sheldon.....................................Robert Light
Mrs. John Tilson...............................Kathryn Givney
Elaine Tilson....................................Rita Johnson
Bobby Crawford................................Edward Craven
Mr. Douglas....................................James LaCurto
Bertha Douglas..................................Edna Holland
Sprague...William David
Mildred...Doro Merande
Simms ....Edwin Redding
Annie...Frances McHugh
Charlie...Harold Woolf

Acts I and III.—Scene 1—Living Room in Fulton Home, Oak Falls. 2—Exterior of Fulton Home. Act II.—Scene 1—Fulton's Room in Bassett Lake Hotel. 2—Exterior of Bassett Lake Hotel.
Staged by Sam Forrest; settings by W. Oden Waller.

Ed Fulton, Oak Falls' solid citizen, pleads with his wife, Emma, to let their daughter, Betty, go on a projected week-end party with Harry Sheldon, financially the town's most desirable catch. Betty, her father knows, is at the breaking point because of her mother's too strict guardianship. Later Ed takes a sentimental journey to an inn that was the scene of his first romance. At the inn Ed runs into Betty and her young man. They are there for the week-end and there is no chaperone in sight. Betty, too, is disgusted at finding her father evidently slyly interested in a youthful blonde. Betty is ordered home, Ed follows and explanations ensue. Then Betty's young man proposes marriage.

A POINT OF HONOR

(4 performances)

A drama in two acts by Jo Eisinger and Stephen Van Gluck. Produced by Luther Greene at the Fulton Theatre, New York, February 11, 1937.

Cast of characters—

Peggy Shippen Arnold............................Lillian Emerson
Mr. Chilton............................Leslie King
Punch............................Charles H. Moore
Hannah Arnold............................Florence Reed
Benedict Arnold............................Wilfred Lawson
David Franks............................A. J. Herbert
Edward Shippen............................Alexander F. Frank
John Andre............................Lloyd Gough
Joseph Reed............................Lewis Martin
Council.......Gary Mohr, Peter Mitchell, James Hurd, Robert Dean

Act I.—At the Shippens', Philadelphia. Act II.—The Arnolds' quarters, West Point.

Staged by Luther Greene.

Peggy Shippen of the Philadelphia Shippens, accepted Tories, loves Major Andre of the British forces, but marries Benedict Arnold of the Continentals, who is desperately in love with her, in the hope of turning him to the British cause. She is successful in influencing Arnold, who sells the plans of West Point to Andre but refuses to accept a cash payment. After Andre has left for New York Arnold suffers an attack of remorse, sends a rider to overtake and obliterate him and recover the plans. Andre is taken by others, thanks to the help of Hannah Arnold, Benedict's sister, and the conspiracy is revealed. Miss Shippen transfers her affections to Arnold and he rides away with "his head buzzing and his heart singing."

CALL ME ZIGGY

(3 performances)

A farce in three acts by Dan Goldberg. Produced by Michael Todd at the Longacre Theatre, New York, February 12, 1937.

Cast of characters—

Augie............................Ralph Theadore
Charlie............................W. J. Hackett
Eddie............................Tom Tully
Steve............................Charles Ellis
Harriet Gilman............................Cyrilla Dorne
Fred Thompson............................Jack Hasler
Jack Hotchkiss............................William Valentine
Walter Burton............................Jack Soanes
Joe Riley............................Robert Williams
Sidney Castle............................Joseph Buloff
Pete............................William Foran
Dorothy La Vere............................June Webster
Gloria Saunders............................Lucille Sears
Rita Phillips............................Barbara Barton
Ivan Davidson............................Sanford Bickart
Herman Gross............................Spencer Kimbell
John R. Smith............................Stanley Jessup
Harris............................Milano Tilden

Acts I, II and III.—Backstage and on Stage, Court Theatre, Chicago.

Staged by Gregory Deane; settings by Clark Robinson.

Sidney Castle is trying to continue the run of a farce called "Three in a Bed" long enough to attract the attention of motion picture promoters. He began on a shoestring and lost the string. His actors walk out, his creditors walk in on him. He is reduced to dire straits just before a bed company makes an offer for the farce for advertising purposes and the movie moguls buy it as a sop to the censors.

AN ENEMY OF THE PEOPLE

(16 performances)

A drama in four acts by Henrik Ibsen. Revived by Walter Hampden at the Hudson Theatre, New York, February 15, 1937.

Cast of characters—

Doctor Thomas Stockmann.......................Walter Hampden
Mrs. Stockmann.......................................Mabel Moore
Petra...Marjorie Jarecki
Eilif..Walter Ward
Morten...Dick Wallace
Peter Stockmann...........................C. Norman Hammond
Morten Kiil.......................................Dodson Mitchell
Hovstad...Albert Van Dekker
Billing...Allen Nourse
Horster..Albert Bergh
Aslaksen..Hannam Clark
Mr. Vik..Conrad Cantzen
Three Gentlemen.....Mortimer Weldon, Arthur Gilmour, Paul Tripp
Two Workingmen...............Murray D'Arcy, James C. Malaidy
Townsfolk: Richard E. Bowler, Wyman Kane, Richard Ross, Boris Ulmar
A Drunken Man...................................Richard Freemen
A Maid Servant...........................Elizabeth Dean Farrar
A Boy..Leslie Klein
A Lady..Constance Pelissier
Other Residents of the Town: Harvey Sayers, Herbert Treitel, John de Angelis, George Marsh, Truman Bengali, Frank Phillips, John E. Wheeler, John C. Davis, Edward M. Grace, Walter James, G. B. Kingston, Sidney Palmer, John Rustad, Walter Kapp, Albert Allen, Richard Allen, Charles Brunswick, Haakon Ogle.

Act I.—Dr. Stockmann's Sitting Room. Act II.—Editor's Room of "People's Messenger." Act III.—Room in Captain Horster's House. Act IV.—Dr. Stockmann's Study. Town on South Coast of Norway.

Staged by Walter Hampden; settings by Claude Bragdon.

Ibsen's war on hypocrisy and the willfulness and ignorance of the compact majority was first revived by Walter Hampden the season of 1927-28 and ran for 127 performances. Before that it had been revived by the Moscow Art Theatre the season of 1923-24, with Vassily Katchaloff in the role of the fighting Dr. Stockmann, who would expose the politicians of a Norwegian spa who are not averse to exploiting the polluted springs and baths of the town.

MARCHING SONG

(61 performances)

A drama in three acts by John Howard Lawson. Produced by The Theatre Union at the Bayes Theatre, New York, February 17, 1937.

Cast of characters—

Jenny Russell	Frieda Altman
Pop Fergus	Charles Kuhn
Clancy	Charles Smith
Lucky Johnson	Rex Ingram
Sunshine Sellers	Robert Reed
Parlez-vous	Lester Lonergan, Jr.
Blister Haddock	Walter Beck
Rose Graham	Gertrude Flynn
Mary McGillicuddy	Frances Bavier
Bridget McGillicuddy	Tommi Bissell
Mrs. Zilitch	Fanya Cherenko
Mrs. Malucci	Hester Sondergaard
Minerva Bliss	Maria Coxe
Pete Russell	Grover Burgess
Hank McGillicuddy	Alfred Herrick
Joe Bell	Joseph Taulane
Woody Rosenbloom	Curt Conway
Tubby Smuts	John Huntington
Bill Anderson	Martin Wolfson
Inspector Feiler	Stanley G. Wood
Mel Mosely	James Macdonald
Tony Malucci	Roy Le May
Brussels Sprouts	Lester Lonergan III
Dopey Belcher	Russell Morrison
Warren Winkle	Edward Everett Hale
Leni Throop	Lisa Markah
Toad	Theodore Corday
Binks	Manart Kippen
Giuseppa Malucci	Amelia Romano
Gunboat Gurney	Charles Smith
Doc Matthews	Richard Barrows

Sylvia Barnett, Alice Brooks, Edward Ferguson, Leonard S. Grime, Barbara Guerdon, Dorothy Howard, T. J. Hughes, Jr., Dan James, Gloria Levinge, Mildred Lewis, Ben Metz, Charles Neville, Robert Ober-Reich, Clark Robinson, Yngvi Thortelson, Mark Toby.

Acts I, II and III.—Interior of Abandoned Factory on Outskirts of Brimmerton.

Staged by Anthony Brown; setting by Howard Bay.

Pete Russell, a blacklisted striker, is evicted by the bank that holds a mortgage on his home. With his wife and baby he takes up temporary residence in an abandoned factory in which a variety of transient unemployed workers live. A second strike is ordered in the factory that has barred Russell. He is given an opportunity of getting his old job back if he will betray the leader of the labor forces. Russell refuses. The leader is discovered and shot down by hired strikebreakers.

LONDON ASSURANCE

(5 performances)

A comedy in five acts by Dion Boucicault; adapted with lyrics by Ethel Barrymore Colt; incidental music by Phyllis Flanigan. Revived by Barbara Robbins at the Vanderbilt Theatre, New York, February 18, 1937.

Cast of characters—

Cool....................Henry Vincent
Dazzle....................Mathew Smith
Young Courtly....................John Raby
Sir Harcourt Courtly....................Douglas Rowland
Max Harkaway....................Lewis L. Russell
Pert....................Darthy Hinkley
James....................Pendleton Harrison
Grace Harkaway....................Ethel Barrymore Colt
Meddle....................Jack Harling
Lady Gay Spanker....................Ellen Love
Dolly Spanker....................Don McClure

Act I.—Ante-Room in Sir Harcourt Courtly's Home, Belgrave Square, London. Act II.—Lawn before Oak Hall, Squire Harkaway's Mansion, Gloucestershire. Act III.—Morning-Room in Oak Hall. Act IV and V.—Drawing Room, Oak Hall.

Staged by Robert Bell; symphonic quartette directed by Maurice Nitke; settings by Louis Kennel.

Rose Coghlan was the great Lady Gay Spanker of the 70's and 80's, at Wallack's theatre in New York. The last previous revival in New York was made by the Yale University Dramatic association in January, 1910. The Boucicault plot revolves about the effort of the aging Sir Harcourt Courtly to marry the young and beautiful Grace Harkaway. Sir Harcourt is outwitted by his wild but handsome son, Young Courtly.

* HAVING WONDERFUL TIME

(132 performances)

A comedy by Arthur Kober. Produced by Marc Connelly, in association with Bela Blau, at the Lyceum Theatre, New York, February 20, 1937.

Cast of characters—

Mac Finkle....................B. D. Kranz
Gussie....................Mona Conrad
Rosalind....................Ann Thomas
Reba....................Irene Winston
Tiny....................Irving Israel
Maxine....................Henriette Kaye
Lois....................Connie Lent
Sammy....................Tony Kraber
Mrs. G....................Ann Brody
Hi....................Mitchell Grayson
Sophie....................Kay Loring
Itchy Flexner....................Philip Van Zandt

Abe Tobias	Wolfe Barzell
Schmutz	Solen Burry
Barney	Edward Mann
Birdie	Helen Golden
Doc	Cornel Wilde
Eli	Shimen Ruskin
The Voice of Kare-Free	William Swetland
Miriam Robbins	Muriel Campbell
Chick Kessler	Jules Garfield
Fay Fromkin	Janet Fox
Mr. G.	Hudey Block
Teddy Stern	Katherine Locke
Henrietta Brill	Loise Reichard
Charlie	Herbert Ratner
Joe	William Swetland
The Honeymooners	Herbert Vigran Sandra Gould
Pinkie Aaronson	Sheldon Leonard
Kitty	Lily Winton
Sam Rappaport	Frank Gould

Camp Guests, Waiters, Etc.—Helen Edwards, Estelle Raymond, Laura Windsor, Connie Ernst, Peggy Craven, Richard Allen, MacFarlane Roberts, Bob Strauss, Juanita Beatty, Tony Heath.

Act I.—Scene 1—Outside Writing Lodge, Camp Kare-Free, Berkshires. 2—Teddy's Bungalow. 3—Dining Room. 4—Back Porch of Social Hall. Act II.—Scene 1—Eagle Rock. 2—Teddy's Bungalow. 3—Pinkie's Bungalow. Act III.—Scene 1—Teddy's Bungalow. 2—Dining Room.

Staged by Marc Connelly; settings by Stewart Chaney.

Teddy Stern has gone for a two-week vacation to Camp Kare-Free in the Berkshires. She has just quarreled with Sam Rappaport, forty years old and her mother's choice for her husband. At camp Teddy meets Chick Kessler, a young lawyer waiting on table to pay his camp expenses. They feel a mutual attraction, which Chick would capitalize without waiting until he can afford to marry. Teddy is bitterly resentful of the suggestion. She tries to get away from Chick, finds herself in trouble with an even less scrupulous flirt and finally realizes that it is Chick who is really her man. Marriage is then made possible.

THE AMAZING DR. CLITTERHOUSE

(80 performances)

A melodrama in three acts by Barre Lyndon. Produced by Gilbert Miller, in association with Warner Brothers, at the Hudson Theatre, New York, March 2, 1937.

Cast of characters—

Nurse Ann	Helen Trenholme
Dr. Clitterhouse, M.R.C.P.	Cedric Hardwicke
Chief-Inspector Charles	Edward Fielding
Benny Keller	Clarence Derwent
"Pal" Green	Ernest Jay
Daisy	Muriel Hutchison
Sergeant Bates	Stephen Fox
A Constable	Ralph Sumpter
"Oakie"	Alexander Field
"Tug" Wilson	Ross Chetwynd

"Badger" Lee....................................Victor Beecroft
Sir William Grant, K.C...........................Frederic Worlock

Act I.—Scene 1—Dr. Clitterhouse's Consulting Room in St. John's Wood, London. 2—Keller's Club, near Theobalds Road. Act II.—Scenes 1 and 3—Ground Floor Flat, Bloomsbury. 2—On a Roof near Upper Thames Street. Act III.—Dr. Clitterhouse's Consulting Room.

Staged by Lewis Allen; settings by Raymond Sovey.

Dr. Clitterhouse is eager to make a study of the reactions suffered by criminals while they are actively engaged in law breaking. He becomes an amateur cracksman himself, negotiates a series of neighborhood robberies successfully, becomes involved with a gang of thieves under the direction of Benny Keller and helps with a huge fur robbery. When he tries to leave the gang and make use of the facts he has discovered he is trailed by Keller and would have been blackmailed back into crime had he not managed to put his menacing Nemesis out of the way.

NOW YOU'VE DONE IT

(43 performances)

A comedy in three acts by Mary Coyle Chase. Produced by Brock Pemberton at the Henry Miller Theatre, New York, March 5, 1937.

Cast of characters—

Mrs. Harlan L. Hazlett, Junior..................Barbara Robbins
Newsboy...Radley E. Collins
Harlan L. Hazlett, Junior.........................Walter Greaza
Mrs. Harlan L. Hazlett, Senior...................Evelyn Varden
Mrs. Harry Gleason...............................Jane Bancroft
Mr. Harry Gleason...............................Junior Eric Burtis
Mrs. MacDuffy.......................................Ruth Gates
Grace Dosher.....................................Margaret Perry
Mrs. William Eckley...............................Mary Howes
Lawrence Ainsworth...............................Richard Carlson
Senator Elias M. Vandergroot....................George Lessey
Sam Hellburn.....................................Ralph Chambers
E. J. McNaught..................................George L. Taylor
Muggsie..Jack Tyler

Acts I, II and III.—Living Room of House of Harlan L. Hazlett, Junior, Glorioca.

Staged by Antoinette Perry; settings by John Root.

Harlan Hazlett is a dumb politician in a Western city whose slogan when he goes into a race for a Congressional nomination is "God first, the People second, Me third." His mother, socially ambitious and superficially interested in reform work, employs Grace Dosher from a Home for Incorrigibles and makes her a maid in the Hazlett home. Having worked as a cashier in Madame Evelyn's place Grace knows all the politicians and a good many other prominent male citizens by sight. She is therefore in a position to aid the Hazlett candidacy when it is threatened by the party leaders.

STORM OVER PATSY

(48 performances)

A comedy in three acts by Bruno Frank; adapted by James Bridie. Produced by The Theatre Guild, Inc., at the Guild Theatre, New York, March 8, 1937.

Cast of characters—

Victoria Thomson	Claudia Morgan
Maggie	Valerie Cossart
Mr. Burdon	Roger Livesey
Mrs. Honoria Flanagan	Sara Allgood
Lisbet Skirving	Brenda Forbes
William Thomson, Provost of Baikie	Ian McLean
Joseph McKellar	Francis Pierlot
Horace Skirving	J. W. Austin
Court Usher	Clement O'Loghlen
Clerk of the Court	Farrell Pelly
The Judge	Leo G. Carroll
Mr. Fraser, the Prosecutor	Louis Hector
Mr. Menzies, K.C.	John Hoysradt
Junior Counsel	Kendall Clark
Stenographer	Jack Burley
Policeman	Herbert Standing
Dr. Cassidy	Jack Byrne
Patsy	Colonel

Court Spectators: Frances Kidner, Elizabeth A. Jones, Seymour Gross, Dan Rudsten, Carrie Bridewell, Harry Hermsen, Phyllis Langner.

Acts I and II.—Living Room of Provost Thomson's Home in Baikie, Scotland. Act III.—A Courtroom.

Staged by Philip Moeller; settings by Aline Bernstein.

William Thomson, provost of the small Scottish town of Baikie, is standing for the House of Parliament. At the outset of his campaign a newspaper reporter named Burdon, come to interview Thomson on the issues of the campaign, is witness to a scene in which the provost not only refuses to do anything to help save the life of a pet dog named Patsy, property of an Irish woman, Honoria Flanagan, but is quite brutally unresponsive to Honoria's plea for time. In place of writing a favorable interview with Candidate Thomson Burdon turns in a scathing criticism of Thomson, the bully. Scandal follows. Thomson is booed off the stage at a political rally. There is a trial for scandal and in the end Thomson's young wife divorces him and is ready to marry the reporter.

CANDIDA

(50 performances)

A drama in three acts by Bernard Shaw. Revived by Katharine Cornell at the Empire Theatre, New York, March 10, 1937.

Cast of characters—

James Mavor Morell....................................Kent Smith
Miss Proserpine Garnett...........................Mildred Natwick
Alexander Mill.......................................Morgan Farley
Burgess...A. P. Kaye
Candida...Katharine Cornell
Eugene Marchbanks...............................Robert Harris
Acts I, II and III.—Sitting Room in St. Dominic's Parsonage, Northeast Suburb of London.
Staged by Guthrie McClintic; setting by Woodman Thompson.

Produced first by the Stage Society in London in 1900, "Candida" has been revived many times in the world's theatrical centers. Its first American presentation was made by the late Arnold Daly, in association with the late Winchell Smith, in 1903. It became something of a sensation that season, with Dorothy Donnelly playing Candida to Daly's Marchbanks. Later revivals have been those of 1915, with Hilda Spong in the name part; 1922, with Ellen Von Volkenberg; 1924, with Katharine Cornell; 1925, with Peggy Wood.

SUN KISSED

(53 performances)

A comedy in three acts by Raymond Van Sickle. Produced by Bonfils and Somnes, Inc., at the Little Theatre, New York, March 10, 1937.

Cast of characters—

Newton Utterback.....................................John Ravold
Amy Jessup..Jean Adair
Maude Sweeney...............................Ruth Chorpenning
Ira Gilkey..Philip Wood
Mattie Bowers.....................................Jeanne Temple
Betty...Mary Fletcher
Geneva Twine...Marie Carroll
Vernon Weaver..................................Carrington Lewis
Bee Delmar...Juliette Day
Gypsy...Sylvia
Vincent Pugh.......................................Sidney Palmer
Fay Carver...Barbara Brown
Humphrey Newberry............................Charles Coburn
Frances Newberry.............................Francesca Bruning
Bill Underwood.....................................Russell Hardie
Messenger...John Albert
McTigue..Ben Laughlin
Acts I, II and III.—Living Room of Newberry Hall, South Alvardo Street, Los Angeles.
Staged by George Somnes; setting by John Root.

Humphrey Newberry is the proud and particular proprietor of Newberry Hall, in Los Angeles. His guests are mostly mid-Western folk come to California to enjoy the climate and their savings. Frances Newberry, Humphrey's daughter, has had a marital experience as the wife of Bill Underwood, a college professor, and left him. Suddenly Bill appears at Newberry Hall bent on winning Frances back. She refuses to acknowledge him as her husband. He is immediately sought after by the other ladies of the house. Complications multiply until the exposure of a variety of previously unsuspected sleeping arrangements serves to reconcile Frances and her Professor and convince Humphrey that he had better keep a sharper lookout on his guests.

ARMS FOR VENUS

(12 performances)

A comedy in three acts by Randolph Carter; incidental music by Philip James. Produced by Mary Hone at the John Golden Theatre, New York, March 11, 1937.

Cast of characters—

Caius...Alan Davis
Nero...Walter Klavun
Quartilla..Beatrice de Neergaard
Habinas...Felton Bickley
Crysis..Hortense Alden
Acts I, II and III.—A Roman Tomb.
Staged by Francis Hartman Markoe; setting by Nat Karson; costumes by Herbert Callister.

Crysis, widow of a Roman general, determines to shut herself in her husband's tomb and starve herself to death. She inadvertently leaves the door unlocked and several persons wander in. These include a handsome soldier, trying to get out of the rain, Nero, who has known Crysis for quite some time, and a group of slaves, who bring food and dainties and a lot of beds. The adventure reawakens Crysis' interest in life. She decides not to die, but to fall in love with Caius, the handsome soldier, instead.

CROSS-TOWN

(5 performances)

A comedy in three acts by Joseph Kesselring. Produced by John Dietz at the 48th Street Theatre, New York, March 17, 1937.

Cast of characters—

Bumps Malone..Joseph Downing
Mary Malone...Mary McCormack
Benny Gorden...Edgar Nelson
Jack Forde..Clarence Chase
Pops Malone...Jack Irwin
Gloria Dufresne...Ruth Holden
Helen Barton...Fraye Gilbert
Caterer..Roland Bottomley
Claire Baxter..Carmin Lewis
Granville Monmott.......................................Austin Fairman
Larry Jansen...Barry Mahool

Jim Sherman....................................Charles Ryder
Sid Stein.......................................Walter Armin
Gwendolyn Stein.................................Gloria Pierre
Beulah Crowly...................................Lois Landon
Montgomery Barton..............................Herbert Warren
Winchell Matthews..............................Vaughn Glaser
First Reporter.................................Leon E. Stern
Second Reporter...............................Clarence Chase
Delivery Boy...................................Junior Bealin
Bill Collector.................................Barry Mahool

Act I.—Living Room in Apartment of "Bumps" Malone, The West Forties, New York. Acts II and III.—Living Room in Apartment of Ronald Blackwell X. Malone. The East Fifties.

Staged by William B. Friedlander; settings by Karl O. Amend.

Bumps Malone is a prizefighter's son with an urge to write. He tries a hand at rewriting in his gutter English short stories he discovers in old magazines, and is greatly surprised when he sells them. He has, he believes, discovered a new racket. Certain literary lights, charmed with Bumps' originality, take him up, introduce him at literary teas and otherwise win him away from his blind father and Mary, his loyal wife. Then he meets one of the authors he has been plagiarizing and the jig is up. A lawsuit is settled out of court by a lady admirer who would take Bumps as payment. Before he is obliged to fulfill this contract Bumps discovers that he can also write original stories and his future looks promising.

CHALKED OUT

(12 performances)

A melodrama in three acts by Warden Lewis E. Lawes and Jonathan Finn. Produced by Brock Pemberton at the Morosco Theatre, New York, March 25, 1937.

Cast of characters—

Mrs. Stone..................................Mabel Montgomery
Madge Stone................................Katherine Meskil
Johnny Stone.....................................John Raby
Fred Burke....................................Frank Lovejoy
Frank Wilson.................................Charles Jordan
Officer Carter...................................Tom Tulley
Officer Black.................................Frank Lindsay
Andy..John M. James
Smoky.......................................Harry Bellaver
Smitty...Lex Lindsay
Scappa.......................................Maurice Burke
Chuck..Ronald Brogan
Jake.......................................Frederick Kaufman
Blimp..Sandy Strouse
Keeper Burns...................................Blair Davies
Tom...Charles Walton
Slim.......................................Philip Faversham
Tower Guard....................................Roger Combs
Sam..John Marriott
Sergeant Monahan...........................Robert J. Mulligan
Principal Keeper (P.K.)........................Leo Kennedy
Pop...Frank Jaquet

Zip....................Stephen Maley
Patsy....................David Hughes
George....................Harry Wilson
Carey....................Otto Hulett
District Attorney....................Ed Smith
Warden....................James Coots
Johnson....................Marlin Poindexter
Keeper....................Price Holmes
Doctor....................John C. Taylor

Act I.—Scene 1—Living Room of Stone Flat. 2—Prison Yard. 3—Prison Library. Act II.—Scene 1—Prison Library. 2—Conference Room in Death House. 3—Corridor in Prison. Act III.—Scene 1—Library. 2—Cell Block. 3—Prison Yard.

Staged by Antoinette Perry; settings by John Root.

Johnny Stone, out of work, runs with the Frank Wilson gang that hangs out at the corner pool room. Johnny borrows the service revolver of his sister's suitor, Fred Burke, and loans it to Wilson. Wilson kills a man with the gun, which is traced to Burke. To escape being dragged into the case Johnny and Wilson plead guilty to minor crimes. They are in prison when Burke is brought to the death house convicted of the murder. Johnny lacks the courage to tell the truth and save Burke by turning in Wilson. In an attempted jail break Johnny is mortally wounded. His dying confession frees Burke, landing Wilson in the death house in his place.

FAREWELL SUMMER

(8 performances)

A comedy in three acts by North Bigbee and Walter Holbrook. Produced by Walter Franklin at the Fulton Theatre, New York, March 29, 1937.

Cast of characters—

Mrs. Stuart....................Suzanne Jackson
Mr. Stuart....................George Spaulding
Keith Stuart....................Lois Wilson
Sally Lindsay....................Marilyn Jolie
Jane Lindsay....................Ellen Love
Professor Albert Lindsay....................Walter Gilbert
Guy Boyd....................G. Albert Smith
Freddy....................George Vigor
Dot....................Lynn Whitney
Philip Howard....................James Todd
Avis Howard....................Virginia Campbell
T. J. Green....................Richard S. Bishop
Bobo....................O. Z. Whitehead
Emma Lou....................Linda Lee Hill

Acts I, II and III.—Side Terrace of Stuart Home in Southwestern University Town.

Staged by B. F. Kamsler; setting by Frederick Fox.

Keith Stuart, a student specializing in biology, loves Professor Lindsay, with whom she works. Knowing her love is hopeless, the professor being married, she turns to Philip Todd and thinks to marry him, until she catches him flirting with another girl. Briefly she considers taking on a week-end lover, one Guy Boyd, but cannot quite bring herself to that step. Finally she decides on a life of celibacy and dreams.

RED HARVEST

(15 performances)

A drama in three acts by Walter Charles Roberts. Produced by Brock Pemberton in association with The Theatre Foundation of America at the National Theatre, New York, March 30, 1937.

Cast of characters—

Private Transky....................................Michael Carlo
Private Adams....................................Chester Stratton
Private Hawley....................................Lloyd Gough
Veronica Ellis....................................Elizabeth Love
Carol Whiting....................................Martha Hodge
Belle Smith....................................Doro Merande
Mary Luddy....................................Amelia Romano
Rose Clarkson....................................Jeanne Hart
Dorothy Bruffel....................................Margaret Mullen
Major David Allison, M.C....................................Frederic Tozere
Zinna Meek....................................Leona Powers
Corporal Topley....................................Edwin Rand
Private Breen....................................Allan Hale
Charlotte Van Worter....................................Malan Cullen
Sally Farrell....................................Frances Creel
Courier Rockman....................................Walter Burke
Holly Farrell....................................Phyllis Langner
Sergeant Bennett....................................John Alexander
Soeur Therese....................................Joan Sudlow
Major McCann, M.C., C.O....................................Carl Benton Reid
Ruth Bissley....................................Drue Leyton
Courier, G.H.Q....................................Robert Marcato
Nurses, Nurses' Aids, Orderlies, Ambulance.

Act I.—Interior of Ward-tent, Hospital at Jouy-sur-Morin, France.
Acts II and III.—Oratory of Hotel-Dieu. August 1918.
Staged by Antoinette Perry; settings by John Root.

The drama is the record of a Red Cross nurse's diary covering the first eighteen days of August, 1918, during which the American army suffered a series of blood drenchings ending in the fighting at Château-Thierry. Zinna Meek, in charge of a Red Cross unit, bravely holds her nurses together under trying circumstances, pulling them through innumerable attacks of hysteria and dilemmas created by the bungling higher-ups. A particular irritation is a brilliant but erratic surgeon, Major David Allison, who first fails but later does much to support Nurse Meek.

YOUNG MADAME CONTI

(22 performances)

A melodrama in three acts adapted by Hubert Griffith and Benn W. Levy from a play by Bruno Frank. Produced by Bernard Klawans at the Music Box, New York, March 31, 1937.

Cast of characters—

Nella Conti....................................Constance Cummings
Betty Wanniger....................................Betty Norton
Arnold Zimmermann....................................William Fox
Stephen Horka....................................Patrick Barr
Mrs. Ebersbacher....................................Ruth Vivian
Mr. Lechner....................................Tom Dillon
The President of the Court....................................William Dewhurst
Dr. Reuchlin....................................Raymond Huntley
Dr. Schonberg....................................Cameron Hall
Otto Farenthold....................................Phillip Leaver
Clerk of the Court....................................Robert Woods
Second Janitor....................................William Rolston
Judge Becker....................................G. Swayne Gordon
Third Judge....................................Courtlandt Davis
Wardress....................................Dorothy Dewhurst
The Governor....................................Charles Wellesley
Jurymen, Spectators, Witnesses, Etc.: Nell Converse, Nellie Ranson, Gertrude Magill, Mary Martin, George Miller, Edward Power, Robert Joseph, Vezey Varley, Ira Lee, Herbert Kreitel, Paul Pascoe, Joseph Burton, J. H. Emerson, Hitous Gray.

Acts I and III.—Madame Conti's Lodgings, Large Town in Austria.
Act II.—Court Room.
Staged by Benn W. Levy; settings by Ernst Stern.

Nella Conti, following an unhappy marital experience, deliberately takes to a life of prostitution to provide her with financial independence. Falling desperately in love with a client, she later overhears him boast of living pleasantly off her earnings. Determining to rid the world of the rat she awaits his coming with a loaded revolver in hand. As she waits she imagines what the outcome of her act will likely be; sees herself arrested, tried, convicted and sentenced to be hanged. The vision does not deter her. When the man she hates does come she shoots him dead.

BET YOUR LIFE

(8 performances)

A farce comedy in three acts by Fritz Blocki and Willie Howard. Produced by Ben Stein at the Golden Theatre, New York, April 5, 1937.

Cast of characters—

Luke Chance....................................John Call
Ima Chance....................................Claire Carleton
Mark Burton....................................J. Robert Haag
Ma Chance....................................Lulu McConnell
Willie Chance....................................Lew Hearn
Bruce Humberston....................................John Clarke
Wiggins....................................William Valentine
Clarice....................................Jean McCool
Marjorie....................................Blanche Haring
Telegraph Boy....................................John Foster
McCauley....................................Scott Moore
Chauffeur....................................Edgar Charles

Acts I, II and III.—The Chance Home.
Staged by A. H. Van Buren; setting by Stagecraft Studios.

Willie Chance, an inveterate gambler, wins a sweepstakes prize, splits it with the family. Family tosses the money away in a variety of extravagant ways. Whereupon Willie wins another sweepstakes. Might have gone on indefinitely, but fortunately didn't.

MISS QUIS

(37 performances)

A comedy in three acts by Ward Morehouse. Produced by Vinton Freedley at the Henry Miller Theatre, New York, April 7, 1937.

Cast of characters—

Ed Trett	Tom Fadden
Alf	Paul Porter
Liz Quis	Peggy Wood
Buster Niles	James Rennie
Crickett	Peggy Converse
Tom Anning	Calvin Thomas
Sheriff	James Lightfoot
Esau	Howard Smith
Christine Anning Lathrop	Jessie Royce Landis
Hector McBee	William David
Zuella McBee	Eda Heinemann
B. C. Calico	Walter Baldwin
Opal Calico	Mary Gildea
Sam Whittle	Charles Dow Clark
Cornwallis Moon	J. Norman Hammond
Amos Yadkin	Edwin Cooper
Tavinia Windell	Emily Ann Wellman
Henderson Lathrop	John Vosburgh

Acts I, II and III.—Parlor of Selby Manor, Town of Fancy Gap.
Staged by Bertram Harrison; setting by Donald Oenslager.

Liz Quis had done odd housekeeping jobs in Fancy Gap ever since she was forced to leave High School and go to work to help support a drunken father and a frail mother. Her principal job for six or eight years was keeping house for old Col. Selby. When the Colonel died he left a fortune of $700,000 to Liz, hoping she would be able to do a lot of things he had been obliged to leave undone. Liz invites all the Colonel's enemies, political and personal, to a party, offers to buy out their businesses and advises them to leave town on penalty of being exposed as morally unfit and criminally guilty of crimes against the town. The accidental killing of one of her planned victims stays Liz' hand. She is obliged to compromise in order to save the life of her best friend, Buster Niles, the town gambler.

HITCH YOUR WAGON

(28 performances)

A comedy in three acts by Bernard C. Schoenfeld. Produced by Malcolm L. Pearson and Donald E. Baruch at the 48th Street Theatre, New York, April 8, 1937.

Cast of characters—

Donnelly	Mary I. Wickes
Jimmy the Orderly	Keenan Wynn
Matt Conroy	Joseph Sweeney
Rex Duncan	George Curzon
Miss Schwartz	Dennie Moore
Delivery Boy	William Tracy
Constantin Yox	Robert X. Williams
Mr. Wayne	Willis Claire
Taxi Driver	Gilmore James
Geneva	Ethel Purnello
Mr. Schwartz	Joseph Greenwald
Mel Kahn	Kenneth Roberts
Mrs. Schwartz	Dora Weissman
Miss Hunt	Millicent Green
Dawson	George Hunter
Master of Ceremonies	James G. Backus
Al	Robert Kellard
Pete	John Galedon
Speedy McLane	Frank Munn
Taxi Driver	Thomas Willard

Act I.—Scene 1—Private Room, Knickerbocker Sanitarium. 2—A—New York. B—Hollywood-New York. C—Van Cortlandt Park. 3—Schwartz Apartment, West End Avenue, New York. Act II.—Scene 1—A—On the Air. B—Hollywood-New York. C—Telephone Booth. 2 and 4—The Schwartz Apartment. 3—A—New York. B—Room at Hotel Devon. 5—New Amsterdam Theatre. Act III.—Schwartz Apartment.

Staged by Garson Kanin; settings by Watson Barratt.

Rex Duncan, noted English cinema star, is taking treatment for an attack of acute alcoholism at a New York sanitarium. Slipping past his guards, Camille Schwartz brings Rex a bowl of noodle soup, further renewing his interest in living by praising him as one of the world's great actors. Rex escapes the sanitarium, resumes his spree and goes to live at the Schwartz home. Camille and her stage-struck mother cater to his alcoholic whims until he finds himself engaged to marry Camille. Also to teach her to act. Hearing her read speeches from "Antony and Cleopatra" at an Actors' Fund benefit, Rex flees the place, is recaptured by Camille's friends and finally released when Camille decides to marry a football star instead. Rex goes back to the sanitarium.

* EXCURSION

(77 performances)

A comedy in three acts by Victor Wolfson. Produced by John C. Wilson at the Vanderbilt Theatre, New York, April 9, 1937.

Cast of characters—

Obediah Rich....Whitford Kane
Linton....John Cherry
Stevens....Fred Stewart
Pop....William Foran
Gilchrist....William H. Malone
Matson....John L. Kearney
Jonathan Rich....J. Hammond Dailey
Candy Boy....Lester Wald
Mr. Boomer....Henry Clark
Mrs. Boomer....Kathryn Grace
Mrs. Geasling....Irene Cattell
Mike Geasling....Jackie Grimes
Mac Colman....Conway Washburne
Miss Dowdie....Nellie Thorne
Lollie....Frances Fuller
Martha....Connie Gilchrist
Aiken....Robert Thomsen
Mrs. Fitchel....Jennie Moscowitz
Mr. Fitchel....James R. Waters
Tessie....Sylvia Leigh
Mrs. Loschavio....Shirley Booth
Red Magoon....Robert Williams
Eileen Loschavio....Marilyn Erskine
Lee Pitman....Flora Campbell
Richard Pitman....Richard Kendrick
Pat Sloan....William H. Chambers
Woods....Anthony Ross
Tony....Joseph Olney
Other Passengers: Eric Walz, Mae Grimes, Billy Redfield, Julie Lawrence, Sylvia Weld, Dorothy Brackett, John O'Shaughnessy, Lesly Woods.

Act I.—Scene 1—Captain's Cabin. 2—The Deck. Act II.—Scene 1—Captain's Cabin. 2—Deck. Act III.—Scenes 1 and 3—Deck. 2—Captain's Cabin. Aboard the S.S. "Happiness."

Staged by Worthington Miner; settings by G. E. Calthrop.

See page 328.

* BABES IN ARMS

(71 performances)

A musical comedy in two acts by Lorenz Hart; music by Richard Rodgers. Produced by Dwight Deere Wiman at the Shubert Theatre, New York, April 14, 1937.

Cast of characters—

Maizie LaMar....Ethel Intropidi
Dan LaMar....Jere Delaney
Val LaMar....Ray Heatherton
Nat Blackstone....George E. Mackay
Emma Blackstone....Aileen Poe
Marshall Blackstone....Alfred Drake

Billie Smith..Mitzi Green
Sheriff Reynolds....................................George Watts
Gus Fielding..Rolly Pickert
Booker Vanderpool...................................Kenneth Wilkins
Pinkie..Bob Fishelson
Lee Calhoun...Dana Hardwick
Beauregard Calhoun..................................Douglas Perry
Sam Reynolds..Ray McDonald
Dolores Reynolds....................................Grace McDonald
Lincoln Vanderpool..................................LeRoy James
Peter...Duke McHale
Baby Rose...Wynn Murray
Ivor DeQuincy.......................................Harold Nicholas
Irving DeQuincy.....................................Fayard Nicholas
Rene Flambeau.......................................Aljan de Loville
Phil McCabe...Alvin Kerr
Dr. Snyder..George E. Mackay
Bobby...Bobby Lane
Elenore...Elenore Tennis
The Gang: Gloria Franklin, Mitzi Dahl, Jean Owens, Ted Gary, Don Liberto, Libby Bennett, Verna Ceders, Mickey Herson, Marjorie Jane, Betty Lee, Connie Leslie, Audrey Palmer, Claire Harvey, Davenie Watson, Stella Clausen, Tania Clell, Eleanore Fiata, Georgia Hiden, Gedda Petry, Ursula Seiler, Roy Adler, Buddy Allen, Mickey Alvarez, Jay Bee, Jack Stanton, Dan Dailey, Bronson Dudley, Alex Courtney, Clifton Darling, James Gillis, Robert Rounseville.

Fairchild and Carroll at the Steinways.

Act I.—Scene 1—Kitchen of LaMar House, Seaport, L. I. 2—Street. 3—Oscar W. Hemingway Post of American Legion. 4—Discarded Railway Box Car. 5—Calhoun Living Room. 6—Back Door of LaMar House. 7, 8 and 9—Old Barn Theatre. Act II.—Scene 1—Stable on Work Farm. 2—Ballet "Peter's Journey." 3—LaMar's Field. 4—Bedroom in LaMar House. 5—Solarium of Seaport Yacht Club.

Staged by Robert Sinclair; settings by Raymond Sovey; choreography by George Balanchine; costumes by Helene Pons.

Fifteen or twenty talented youngsters, the children of touring vaudeville performers, are threatened by the Sheriff of their County with being sent to the work farm until their parents return. They organize a show hoping to bail themselves out. The show proves an artistic success but a financial failure. It is the work farm after all. Then a famous aviator making a trans-Atlantic flight is forced down in the work farm yard and comes to their aid.

PENNY WISE

(65 performances)

A comedy in three acts by Jean Ferguson Black. Produced by Juliana Morgan at the Morosco Theatre, New York, April 19, 1937.

Cast of characters—

Jeff..Bertram Thorn
Tina..Irene Purcell
Martha..Mildred Wall
Gordon..Kenneth MacKenna
Penny...Linda Watkins
Katherine...Nancy Sheridan

Commissioner Dunn....................................Albert Bergh
Acts I, II and III.—Penny Wise Farm in Connecticut.
Staged by Arthur Sircom; setting by Cirker and Robbins.

Gordon and Penny Chase have been married for ten years. Gordon is a philandering playwright who is given to wandering away from his own fireside periodically. Martha and Tina, two young women with whom he previously has wandered, hear that he is contemplating a third trip with Katherine. Martha and Tina are determined to prevent this, out of love for Penny. Katherine, also impressed with Penny's blissful ignorance, decides to confess all. She and Gordon are, she admits, planning a trip to Brittany. Penny is delighted. That is just like Gordon. And she doesn't mind a bit. Which takes all the fun out of Gordon's plans for Gordon.

CURTAIN CALL

(4 performances)

A drama in two parts by Le Roy Bailey. Produced by Jack Quigley and Irving Schachtel at the Golden Theatre, New York, April 22, 1937.

Cast of characters—

Lackey....................................Frank Thomas
Alberto....................................Brewster Board
The Princess....................................Marie Curtis
Pietro Rizzo....................................Blaine Cordner
Alesandro Casella....................................Auguste Aramini
The Young Lady....................................Sandra Kostner
Lolo Campinili....................................Almira Sessions
Doctor Conti....................................Mortimer Weldon
Antonio Sebastiano....................................Guido Nadzo
Reno Rizzo....................................Selena Royle
Isola Casella....................................Ara Gerald
Anna....................................Michelette Burani
Ambassador....................................Arnaud de Bordes
Sister....................................Frances Reinhart
Call Boy....................................Arnaud de Bordes
The Nurse....................................Sandra Kostner
The Interne....................................Tommy Mudell
Part I.—Episode 1—Corridor Behind Boxes. In the Palace, Rome, 1894. 2—Convent near Rome. 3—Corner in Lounge, Hotel in Paris. 4—Casella's Apartment. Part II.—Episode 1—Casella's Apartment, Paris, 1900. 2—Casella's Dressing Room at Theatre. 3—Casella's Apartment in New York Hotel, 1925.
Staged by Dickson Morgan; settings by Cleon Throckmorton; costumes by Ellis Porter.

Isola Casella, a great actress of Italy, after having left the stage and prepared for service in a convent, is lured back to the stage through her love for a young genius, Antonio Sebastiano, a progressive among playwrights. For five years they are supremely happy as lovers and successful as associates in art. Then Antonio tires of Isola, indulges an affair with ambitious Reno Rizzo and writes a novel which brazenly makes copy of his life with Isola. Spiritually crushed and physically beaten Isola, on a last tour of America, dies in a lonely room in a Pittsburgh hotel.

WITHOUT WARNING

(17 performances)

A drama in three acts by Ralph Spencer Zink. Produced by A. L. Jones at the National Theatre, New York, May 1, 1937.

Cast of characters—

Sally...Claire Carleton
Private Pratt.....................................Edward Craven
Private Ferris....................................Harold Walridge
Corporal Sanger...................................Russell Morrison
Lieutenant Matthews...............................Donald Dillaway
Colonel Hackett...................................Franklyn Fox
Mr. Jevries.......................................Philip Ober
Doctor Brooks.....................................J. Arthur Young
Colonel Rodgers...................................Jack Roseleigh
Privates of the Guard—Lee Worth, Carl Carr, David Rubin, Frank Ellis.

Acts I, II and III.—Section of Experimental Shack on Powder Island Arsenal.
Staged by John Hayden; setting by Nat Karson.

A tricky army man is found butchered and pinned to the wall of an experiment shack at an army arsenal. There seems to be no possible clew to the perpetrators of the crime. Colonel Hackett of the post sends for Col. Rodgers of the Army Secret Service to conduct the investigation, which Col. Rodgers does ruthlessly and with a good deal of force. A variety of suspects are third degreed to within a quarter inch of their lives before the plot is unraveled.

ORCHIDS PREFERRED

(7 performances)

A musical comedy in two acts by Fred Herendeen; music by Dave Stamper. Produced by Charles H. Abramson at the Imperial Theatre, New York, May 11, 1937.

Cast of characters—

Gertrude Devereaux................................Hilda Knight
Violet Manning....................................Frances Thress
Billie..Doris Vinton
Elsie...Elsie Edwards
Margie..Margie Conradi
Sally...Lillian Carson
Edithe..Violet Carson
Sunny...Lucille Rich
Marion Brown......................................Vicki Cummings
Bubbles Wilson....................................Eddie Foy, Jr.
Bobbie..James Babbitt
Doorman...William Chalmers
Penelope Halchester...............................Ethel Barrymore Colt

Evangeline Landreth....................Julie Sterling
Henry Warrenton....................Jack Clifford
Hortense Chatfield....................Frew Donald
Mary Ann Miller....................Audrey Elliott
Lillian Mahoney....................Benay Venuta
Chauffeur....................Bill Pillick
Footman....................Jack Curry
Helene Windsor....................Fay Long
Goldie....................Phyllis Avery
Dr. Sommers....................Bob Borger
Dorothy Charters....................Verna Long
Teddy Barber....................Henry Russell
Henry Monroe....................Bob Rice
Eve....................Verda Twiford
Eva....................Dilys Miles
Evy....................Helen Martin
June....................Joanne
July....................Jules Walton
Richard Hope, Jr....................John Donaldson
Elmer Traum....................Jack Whittridge
Elizabeth Hope....................Helen Leftwich
Richard Hope, Sr....................Leslie Austin

Act I.—Scene 1—Suite in the Waldmore. 2—Motor Entrance. 3 and 5—Corridor. 4—Crystal Bar. 6—Dick's Apartment. Act II.—Scene 1—The Walk in the Waldmore. 2—Passageway. 3—Solarium. 4—Emergency Exit.

Staged by Alexander Leftwich; dances by Robert Sanford; sets by Frederick Fox.

Gertrude Devereaux and Violet Manning, night club hostesses, induce innocent Marion Brown to join their racket, which is that of gold digging among the richer and less wary playboys. Marion proves so stupidly innocent that she convinces her intended victim, Richard Hope, Jr., her love is sincere and worth having. Marriage threatens to overtake them before the evening is finished.

* ABIE'S IRISH ROSE

(39 performances)

A comedy in three acts by Anne Nichols. Revived by Anne Nichols at the Little Theatre, New York, May 12, 1937.

Cast of characters—

Isaac Cohen....................Bernard Gorcey
Mrs. Isaac Cohen....................Bertha Walden
Rabbi Jacob Samuels....................Jack G. Bertin
Solomon Levy....................Alfred H. White
Abraham Levy....................Richard Bond
Rosemary Murphy....................Marian Shockley
Patrick Murphy....................Billy Fay
Father John Whalen....................E. J. Blunkall
Maid of Honor....................Barbara Beech
Matron of Honor....................Shannon Dean
Bridesmaids: Ethel McKenzie, Hope Chandler, June Miley, Lorraine Teatom.

Acts I and II.—Solomon Levy's Apartment, New York City. Act III.—Abie and Rosemary's Apartment, New York City.

Staged by Anne Nichols; settings by Cirker and Robbins.

This comedy revolving about the marriage of young Abraham Levy and Rosemary Murphy, which excites and arouses the comic protest of both their families, was first produced in New York at the Fulton Theatre May 23, 1922. Following a doubtful start it achieved an enormous popularity and played for more than five years, a total of 2,532 performances being given in New York alone. "Abie" has been revived sporadically in some part of the world every year since. Alfred H. White, born Weisman, and Bernard Gorcey of the above cast were members of the original company.

DAMAGED GOODS

(8 performances)

A drama in three acts by Eugene Brieux; adapted by Henry Herbert from a translation by John Pollock. Revived by Richard Highley at the 48th Street Theatre, New York, May 17, 1937.

Cast of characters—

Georges Dupont	Staats Cotsworth
The Doctor	Henry Herbert
Henriette	Florence Barry
Madame Dupont	Marie Curtis
The Nurse	Johnne Barrie
Justin	Bruce Rogers
Hospital Nurse	Ann Sorel
M. Loches	Thomas F. Tracey
The Woman	Rose Flynn
The Man	Stapleton Kent
The Girl	Jane Bancroft

Acts I and III.—The Doctor's Consulting Room. Act II.—Home of Georges Dupont.

Staged by Henry Herbert.

The Brieux play was first produced in New York at a special matinee March 14, 1913, by Richard Bennett, Wilton Lackaye and a company of co-workers, under the auspices of the Medical Review of Reviews. It was repeated the following month with Charles A. Stevenson replacing Lackaye as the Doctor. It ran for sixty-six performances in New York and for the better part of two seasons on tour. It is a powerful dramatic tract rather than a drama. It relates the experience of a Paris physician in propagandizing the exposure of syphilis as a prevalent scourge and its proper control as a public menace.

SEA LEGS

(15 performances)

A musical comedy in two acts by Arthur Swanstrom; music by Michael H. Cleary. Produced by Albert Bannister and J. Edmund Byrne at the Mansfield Theatre, New York, May 18, 1937.

Cast of characters—

Captain Nordstrom....Charles King
Mrs. Alice Wytcherly....Mary Sargent
George W. Tuttle....Walter N. Greaza
Val Tuttle, Jr....Derek Fairman
Mildred....Rosie Moran
James McCracken....Rosco Ates
Bill Halliday....Charles Collins
Isobel West....Kathryn Mayfield
Barbara Deeds....Dorothy Stone
Deedee....Deedee
Pat....Patricia Knight

Ben Yost's Catlina Eight.

Acts I and II.—Sun Deck of Yacht "Pixie" Lying off Catalina Island.

Staged by Bertram Harrison; dances by Johnny Mattison; music directed by Frank Cork; setting by Mabel Buell assisted by Rear Admiral Yates Stirling, Jr.

Bill Halliday stows away on Mrs. Alice Wytcherly's yacht to be near Barbara Deeds. When caught he pretends to be a veterinary sent to treat Mrs. Wytcherly's cat. George W. Tuttle, a suitor of Mrs. Wytcherly's, hires the yacht steward, McCracken, to make way with the cat. Complications, including singing and dancing duets, pile up until 11 o'clock. Then the cat comes back and the romances are consummated.

* ROOM SERVICE

(31 performances)

A farce in three acts by John Murray and Allen Boretz. Produced by George Abbott at the Cort Theatre, New York, May 19, 1937.

Cast of characters—

Sasha Smirnoff....Alexander Asro
Gordon Miller....Sam Levene
Joseph Gribble....Cliff Dunstan
Harry Binion....Philip Loeb
Faker Englund....Teddy Hart
Christine Marlowe....Margaret Mullen
Leo Davis....Eddie Albert
Hilda Manney....Betty Field
Gregory Wagner....Donald MacBride
Simon Jenkins....Philip Wood
Timothy Hogarth....Jack Byrne
Dr. Glass....Hans Robert
Bank Messenger....William Mendrek
Senator Blake....Ralph Morehouse
Senator Blake's Secretary....William Howard

Acts I, II and III.—Room in White Way Hotel.

Staged by George Abbott; setting by Cirker and Robbins.

Gordon Miller, a shoestring promoter, has a play, a cast of actors, a mechanical staff and a promise of a theatre, but no money. He has sold a 10 percent interest in the play to the resident manager of a chain hotel and moved the company in.

His problem is to keep the company together until he can negotiate a production of the play. An investigator of the hotel company threatens to evict the actors. Miller and his associates induce the play's author to play sick to hold the hotel room. When this ruse threatens to fail they have the author fake a suicide and finally are obliged to announce his death and conduct a service over him to stave off eviction. The play turns out a hit and everybody is happy.

MONEY MAD

(1 performance)

A comedy in three acts by Fritz Blocki. Produced by Edwin A. Relkin at the 49th Street Theatre, New York, May 24, 1937.

Cast of characters—

Milton Chance	David Milton
Bernice Chance	Bernice Caryl
Lane Burton	Lane Allan
Ma Chance	Doris Underwood
Lou Chance	Ludwig Satz
Telegraph Boy	John Foster
Bruce Humberston	John Clarke
Gladys	Gladys Shelley
Wiggins	William Valentine
Juliette	Juliette Howell
Baxter	Walter Fenner
McCauley	Scott Moore
Cyrus P. Watts	Leslie King

Acts I, II and III.—The Chance Home.
Staged by Rowland G. Edwards.

A rewritten version of "Bet Your Life" (see page 476). Disagreement as to the cause of the original failure induced Fritz Blocki, co-author with Willie Howard, comedian, of "Bet Your Life," to submit a second script. Reviewers agreed that the rewritten play showed definite improvement, but not enough. Chief alteration in story was in the play's conclusion. In "Bet Your Life" the improvident winners of an Irish sweepstake ticket, after wasting one fortune, won another. In "Money Mad" it is the son's investment in Texas oil wells that provides a happy ending.

THE BAT

(18 performances)

A mystery melodrama in three acts by Mary Roberts Rinehart and Avery Hopwood. Revived by Ben Lundy and B. F. Kamsler at the Majestic Theatre, New York, May 31, 1937.

Cast of characters—

Lizzie Allen	May Vokes
Cornelia Van Gorder	Minnette Barrett
Billy	Arvid Paulson
Jack Brooks	Norman Stuart
Dale Ogden	Linda Lee Hill
Doctor Wells	Robert Ober
Detective Anderson	Hermann Lieb
Richard Fleming	Matthew Smith
Reggie Beresford	Eric Kalkhurst
Unknown Man	Richard Barrows

Acts I and II.—Living Room and Library of a Country House. Act III.—Trunk Room on Third Floor.

Staged by B. F. Kamsler; settings by Frederick Fox.

"The Bat" was produced originally August 23, 1920, at the Morosco theatre, New York, and ran for a total of 867 performances. The cast included May Vokes, Effie Ellsler, Edward Ellis, Harrison Hunter, Kenneth Hunter, Anne Morrison and Richard Barrows. See "The Best Plays, 1920-21."

* THE CAT AND THE CANARY

(1 performance)

A mystery melodrama in three acts by John Willard. Revived by Ben Lundy and B. F. Kamsler at the Majestic Theatre, New York, June 14, 1937.

Cast of characters—

Mammy Pleasant	Ethel Purnello
Roger Crosby	Robert Ober
Harry Blythe	Eric Kalkhurst
Cicily Young	Jeanette Chinley
Susan Sillsby	Jeanne Temple
Charles Wilder	Matthew Smith
Paul Jones	Howard Miller
Annabelle West	Helen Claire
Hendricks	Hermann Lieb
Dr. Patterson	Richard Barrows

Acts I and III.—Library at Glencliff Manor on the Hudson. II.—The Next Room.

Staged by B. F. Kamsler; settings by Barney Turner.

"The Cat and the Canary" was produced originally at the National Theatre, New York, February 7, 1922. The cast included the author, John Willard, playing Harry Blythe. Henry Hull was the Paul Jones and Florence Eldredge the Annabelle West. At the end of the season a total of 148 performances had been recorded, and these were added to those of the season following. See "Best Plays, 1921-22."

* TOBACCO ROAD

(1516 performances)

A play in three acts by Jack Kirkland based on a novel by Erskine Caldwell. Produced by Anthony Brown at the Masque Theatre, New York, December 4, 1933.

Cast of characters—

Dude Lester....................Robert Rose
Ada Lester....................Ann Dere
Jeeter Lester....................James Barton
Ellie May....................Ruth Hunter
Grandma Lester....................Kate Morgan
Lov Bensey....................Tilden Davis
Henry Peabody....................Ashley Cooper
Sister Bessie Rice....................Vinnie Phillips
Pearl....................Cynthia Arden
Captain Tim....................Del Hughes
George Payne....................Edwin Walter

Acts I, II and III.—Farm of Jeeter Lester, Tobacco Road, Georgia.
Staged by Anthony Brown; setting by Robert Redington Sharpe.

Produced originally December 4, 1933, "Tobacco Road" has run through three seasons with numerous changes of cast. There have been two replacements in the Jeeter Lester role in New York, James Barton succeeding Henry Hull, who created the part, in June, 1934, and James Bell replacing Barton in December, 1934. Barton resumed the role in August, 1935, and has played it ever since. Maude Odell, the original Sister Bessie, died in her dressing room in February, 1937, and was succeeded by Vinnie Phillips. Sam Byrd, the original Dude Lester, retired after a thousand performances and Robert Rose took up the role. Three members of the original cast are still playing, Ruth Hunter, Ashley Cooper and Edwin Walter. On the road Jeeter has been played by Taylor Holmes, James Kirkland and Charles Timblin.

FEDERAL THEATRE PROJECT FOR NEW YORK

(Important Activities June 15, 1936—June 15, 1937)

THE LIGHTS O' LONDON

(11 performances)

A play in five acts by George Robert Sims. Revived by the Federal Music Project at the Palm Garden, New York, June 23, 1936.

Principals engaged—

Squire Armytage....................Edwin Redding
Marks....................Emmet Shackelford

Bess Marks....................................Dorothy de Becker
Harold Armytage....................................Donald Foster
Hetty Preen....................................Winifred Dean
Clifford Armytage....................................William McGurn
Seth Preen....................................Gordon Hamilton
Joe Jarvis....................................Philip Bishop
Eliza....................................Edith Shayne
Jim....................................Albert Watson
Philosopher Jack....................................William Barrow
Shakespeare Jarvis....................................Gertrude Guyer

Act I.—Armytage Hall, a Manor House in Sussex. Act II—. Armystage Arms, an English Inn. Act III.—Scene 1—Sussex Roadside. 2—Exterior of Police Station, London. 3—The Jarvis Living Room. Act IV.—Scene 1—Drawing Room at Clifford Armytage's Home, St. John's Wood, London. 2—Exterior of The Boro Workhouse, London. 3—Waterloo Bridge, the Embankment, London. Act V.—Scene 1—A Poor Street, London. 2—The Jarvis Living Room. 3—The Boro Market at Night. 4—Police Station Interior.

Staged by Louis M. Simon and Earle Mitchell; music conducted by Mildred Howard; settings by Nels Astner and Cleon Throckmorton; costumes by Emily Stoner.

Harold Armytage was honest, upright, loving and out of luck. Squire Armytage, his cousin, was a dastard as well as a villain four shades deeper than the deepest dye. But, although the Squire put it over for several acts and a great many scenes, Harold, thanks to the friendship of two good old troupers, Joe Jarvis and his buxom missus, Eliza, was a tired but happy victor in the end.

HELP YOURSELF

(82 performances)

A farce in three acts adapted by John J. Coman from the Viennese by Paul Vulpius. Produced by the Popular Price unit of the Federal Theatre Project at the Manhattan Theatre, New York, July 14, 1936.

Cast of characters—

Frederick Bittlesby....................................Walter Burke
Uncle John....................................George Probert
Fanny Keane....................................Mary Roth
Messenger....................................Huntly Weston
Miss Breckenridge....................................Jenny Wren
Miss Oglesby....................................Martha Skeen
Tony, the barber....................................Alan Wilson
Christopher Stringer....................................Curt Bois
A Job Hunter....................................Charles Burrows
Schuyler Danforth, President of the Mutual Trust.....George LeSoir
A. B. Alexander, Chairman of the Board of Directors..Edward Forbes
Peggy Danforth....................................Camelia Campbell
Philip Nichols....................................Charles McLean Savage
John C. Holman....................................Clay Cody
Henry Williams, of the R. F. C.................Stephen Courtleigh
Nicholas B. Bradley, President of the Park Avenue Bank..Doan Borup
An Office Boy....................................William Vaughn
A Woman....................................Barna Ostertag

Act I.—Reception Room Outside President's Office in Mutual Trust Company. Act II.—Conference Room of Mutual Trust. Act III.—Christopher Stringer's Office in Mutual Trust.

Staged by Lucius Moore Cook; settings by Tom Adrian Cracraft.

Christopher Stringer, out of work, finds himself one of a street crowd being photographed for a motion picture. When the extras get in line to collect their pay checks Christopher follows them and is paid. This convinces him that jobs are to be had by those with the courage to take them. He tries out the theory by walking into a bank where a timid school friend is employed as assistant to the President. Finding an unoccupied desk Chris establishes himself as a new executive, dictates a letter to the President of a rival bank inquiring what has been done about the "Kubinsky business" and induces an absent-minded chief to sign it. When a reply demands more particulars about the Kubinsky business it is turned over to Chris to answer. With this start he manages to work himself into a job and a successful flirtation with the President's daughter.

IT CAN'T HAPPEN HERE

(95 performances)

A drama in three acts by John C. Moffitt and Sinclair Lewis, from the novel by Sinclair Lewis; incidental music composed by Hans Bruno Meyer. Produced by the Federal Theatre Project of the WPA at the Adelphi Theatre, New York, October 26, 1936.

Cast of characters—

Doremus Jessup....................................Seth Arnold
Lorinda Pike....................................Helen Morrow
David Greenhill....................................Larry Garden
Mary Greenhill....................................Camelia Campbell
Dr. Fowler Greenhill....................................Robert Perry
Shad Ledue....................................Edwin Cooper
Henry Veeder....................................Halliam Bosworth
Francis Tasbrough....................................Gustave Gordon
Mrs. Veeder....................................Minnie Stanley
Clarence Little....................................George Henry Trader
Julian Falck....................................Ben Starkie
Mrs. Whitcomb....................................Georgia Harvey
Corporal Nickerson (of the Corpos.)....................Tom Greenway
Effingham Swan....................................Frederic Tozere
Telephone Operator....................................Viola Swayne
Pastor Paul Peter Prang....................................Robert Harrison
Pastor Prang's Secretary....................................Alan Wilson
Lee Sarason....................................Maurice Burke
Berzelius "Buzz" Windrip....................................John Adair
Dan Wilgus....................................Robert Lawrence
Mr. Dimmick....................................Robert Bruce
Private Brown (of the Corpos.)....................Raymond Southwick
Lieutenant Peabody (of the Corpos.)....................Jack Foss

Act I.—Scene 1—Hilltop near Ft. Beulah. 2—Clarence Little's Grocery Store. 3 and 6—Doremus Jessup's Living Room. 4—Telephone Switchboard of Little Brown Church in the Vale, Zenith. 5—Broadcasting Chapel. Act II.—Editorial Sanctum of "Ft. Beulah Informer." Act III.—Scenes 1 and 2—Doremus Jessup's Living Room. 3—Corpo Immigration Post, Vermont-Canada Border.

Staged by Vincent Sherman; settings by Tom Adrian Cracraft; costumes by Charles Hawkins.

Doremus Jessup, the honest editor of the Fort Beulah, Vermont, *Informer,* will not believe the United States can be taken over by Dictator "Buzz" Windrip and his "Corpo" guards following Windrip's election to the presidency. When he finally is convinced, when his friend, the grocer, is beaten to death and his son-in-law is shot down, Jessup undertakes to stem the tide of fascism. He is seized by the Corpos, thrown into a concentration camp, brutally mistreated and saved from death only by his escape to Canada. From Canada he continues to work for the restoration of his country's liberties.

DR. FAUSTUS

(128 performances)

A comedy by Christopher Marlowe; music by Edward Bowles. Revived by Federal Theatre Project "891" at the Maxine Elliott Theatre, New York, January 8, 1937.

Cast of characters—

The Pope....Charles Peyton
Cardinal of Lorrain....J. Headley
Faustus....Orson Welles
Valdes....Bernard Savage
Cornelius....Myron Paulson
Wagner, Servant to Faustus....Arthur Spencer
First Scholar....William Hitch
Second Scholar....Joseph Wooll
Third Scholar....Huntly Weston
Clown....Harry McKee
Robin....Edgerton Paul
Ralph....Wallace Acton
Vintner....George Smithfield
Old Man....George Duthie
First Friar....Edward Hemmer
Mephistopheles....Jack Carter
Good Angel....Natalie Harris
Evil Angel....Blanche Collins
Spirit in the Shape of Helen of Troy....Paula Laurence
Seven Deadly Sins—
Pride....Elizabeth Malone
Covetousness....Jane Hale
Wrath....Helena Rappaport
Envy....Cora Burlar
Gluttony....Della Ford
Sloth....Nina Salama
Lechery....Lee Molnar
Baliol....Archie Savage
Belcher....Clarence Yates
Staged and designed by Orson Welles.

A restaging of the Marlowe legend of Faustus and Mephistopheles in modernesque fashion on a bare stage with the characters picked out in lights at their entrance and during their scenes.

* POWER

(99 performances)

A series of news sketches by Arthur Arent; music by Lee Wainer. Produced by the Living Newspaper unit of the Federal project at the Ritz Theatre, New York, February 23, 1937.

Principals engaged—

Announcer.....Charles Dill
Consumer.....Norman Lloyd
Electric Co. Manager.....Allan Tower
Samuel Insull.....H. H. McCollum
Senator Norris.....Burton Mallory

Staged by Brett Warren under supervision of Morris Watson; settings by Howard Bay.

An analysis and graphically pictured statement of the enormous importance of electricity as power and as a people's need. The rapaciousness of the more ruthless interests and the apparent helplessness of the consumer public is traced from the early development of electricity, in the days of Edison, Faraday, Ohm and Gramme, to those of the great mergers and the prevailing holding companies. This leads naturally into the governmental experiments with TVA and an expressed desire for governmental supervision of power in the people's interest.

NATIVE GROUND

(17 performances)

A cycle in two parts by Virgil Geddes. Produced by the Experimental Theatre of the Federal Theatre Project at the Venice Theatre, New York, March 23, 1937.

Cast of characters—

Lora Bentley.....Georgiana Brand
Lars Bentley.....William Burbridge
Tod.....Wade Dent
Myrtle Bentley.....Alfreda Sill
Hawkins.....Alan MacAteer
Milton Rogers.....Josef Draper
Oscar Holm.....Michael Cisney

Part 1.—"Native Ground"—Act I.—Scene 1—Shanty of Bentley Farmhouse in Nebraska. 2—At Supper Table. Act II.—Scene 1—Granary. 2—Edge of Grove. 3—Watering Trough and Pump.

Part 2—"The Plowshare's Gleam"—Act I.—Scene 1—Edge of Prairie in Dakota. 2—Dining Room of Rogers Farmhouse in Dakota. Act II.—Scene 1—Front Yard. 2—Rogers' Dining Room.

The third part of the original trilogy was omitted.

Staged by James Light; settings by Howard Bay; lighting by Feder.

Lora and Lars Bentley have reached their later middle years dragging out their lives on a Nebraska farm. Milton Rogers, a former hired hand, comes back from Oklahoma hoping to marry their daughter, Myrtle. Lora, herself an old flame of Milton's, opposes the match, finally confessing to both Milton and Myrtle that Milton and not Lars is Myrtle's father. The lovers refuse to believe the story and defiantly marry. In Oklahoma they live secretly as brother and sister. After some years Myrtle takes up with another hired hand. The play ends with her announcement to her father that he is at last to have his wish. She is to make him a grandfather. Which, as news, is more surprising than pleasant to her husband.

TOBIAS AND THE ANGEL

(22 performances)

A fantasy in three acts by James Bridie. Produced by the Studio Theatre of the Federal Theatre Project at the Provincetown Theatre, New York, April 28, 1937.

Cast of characters—

Tobit..Harry Brooks
Tobias..Edwin Michaels
The Archangel Raphael..Kirk Lucas
Anna..Dorothy Chesmond
Bandit..David Gnessin
Kish..Anne Weiss
Azorah..Maya Riviere
Shera..Lydia Balsam
Timkah..Esther Goodman
Sara..Florence Eames
Raguel..Claude Thalmore
Sam..William Simmons
Asmoday..Edwin McKenna
Toby..Himself
Staged by Ellen van Volkenburg; settings by Samuel Leve; costumes by Mary Merrill.

Tobias, son of Tobit, undertakes a pilgrimage having as its object the collection of a debt owing his blind father. Tobias is accompanied by the Archangel Raphael in disguise and during the pilgrimage he is not only cured of his timidities and strengthened greatly in character, but he is brought back to his home a successful man of the world with money in his purse. The story's foundation is an item of the Apocrypha.

* PROFESSOR MAMLOCK

(74 performances)

A drama in four acts by Friedrich Wolf; translated from the German by Anne Bromberger. Produced by the Jewish Theatre

Project of the Federal Theatre at Daly's Sixty-third Street Theatre, New York, April 13, 1937.

Cast of characters—

Dr. Inge Ruoff	Frances Beck
Nurse Hedwig	Greta Karnot
Mrs. Ruoff	Augusta Durgeon
Dr. Hellpach	Herb Breakstone
Orderly Simon	William Dansker
Dr. Hirsh	Emil Hirsch
Dr. Seidel	Wayne Arey
Dr. Carlsen	Tom Morrison
Prof. Mamlock	Morris Strassberg
Wounded Worker	Harry Lessin
Rolf Mamlock	Joseph Anthony
Mrs. Mamlock	Edith Angold
Ruth Mamlock	Mary George
Ernest	Louis Brandt
1st Nurse	Eleanor Gillmore
2nd Nurse	Mary Adams
3rd Nurse	Izella Phenice
1st Storm Troper	Abe Barso
2nd Storm Troper	Lawrence Clark
3rd Storm Troper	Maurice Lazarus
Nurse	Molly Buchsbaum
Patient	Jeanette Klein
Nurse	Shifra Baraks

Acts I and IV.—Ante-Room of Operating Room of Professor Mamlock's Surgical Clinic. Acts II and III.—Mamlock Living Room.
Staged by Harold Bolton; settings by George Phillips.

Professor Hans Mamlock, a Jewish surgeon of standing in post-war Germany, is permitted for years to continue his activities because of a fine war record. Following the burning of the Reichstag the Hitler fanatics close in upon him, publicly humiliating him, stripping him of his clinic and his associate surgeons; insulting and degrading his daughter and hounding his son into exile. Realizing that any continued opposition means additional misery for his family and friends the professor kills himself.

* THE CASE OF PHILIP LAWRENCE

(8 performances)

A drama in three acts by George MacEntee. Produced by the WPA Negro Theatre at the Lafayette Theatre, June 7, 1937.

Cast of characters—

Half Pint	William Brown
Heavy Head	Louis Sharp
Jim	Milton Lacey
Racy Green	Gerald De LaFontaine
Martha "Mom" Robbins	Alberta Perkins
Nancy	Frauline Alford
Mrs. Jenkins	Estelle Hemsley
Phil Lawrence	Maurice Ellis
Sue Wilkins	Dorothey Paul
Dancers: Ollie Simmons, Arthis Savage, Frederic Gibson, Zola King.	
Blues Singer	Frances Smith
Accordion Player	Clarence Brown

Chick Turner....................................Thomas Mosely
Dreamy Dale....................................Robert Veritch
Marian..Eleanor Scher
Cigarette Girl...................................Bebe Townsend
Matron...Mabel Thorne
First Bodyguard...................................Sidney Easton
Second Bodyguard..................................Walter Duke
Prosecuting Attorney...........................Bertram Miller
Defense Attorney.................................George Nixon
Judge...Fritz Weller
Detectives.................James Williams and Edward J. Fleischer
College Professor...........................William Melville
Rev. Stowe.....................................J. Louis Johnson
First Guard..Steve Horn
Second Guard................................Pat McCullough
Children............Wanda Macey, Bertram Holmes, Shirley Macey

Act I.—Mom Robbins' Restaurant in Basement of Her Home Somewhere in Harlem. Act II.—Scenes 1, 3 and 5—Chick Turner's Cabaret. 2 and 4—Sue Wilkins' Dressing Room. Act III.—Scene 1—Cell in Tombs Prison. 2—Chick Turner's Room. 3—Street Corner. 4—Rev. Stowe's Study. 5—District Attorney's Office.

Staged by J. A. Smith; settings by WPA Federal Theatre Workshop and WPA Negro Theatre Workshop.

Philip Lawrence, just out of college, rebels at taking a red-cap porter job at Grand Central station and facing a future without hope of cultural progress. He wants to marry Nancy Robbins and, to get money, takes a job as a master of ceremonies in Chick Turner's night club. Chick shoots a down-town racketeer and frames Philip for the murder. Philip is about to be convicted on circumstantial evidence when newly discovered evidence releases him and sends him into Nancy's arms.

OTHER FEDERAL THEATRE ACTIVITIES

"Macbeth" (Negro Unit) which ran from April 14 to June 20, 1936, in Harlem with 64 performances, moved uptown to the Adelphi Theatre for 11 more performances beginning July 6, 1936. "Class of '29" finished its run at the Manhattan July 4, bringing the number of performances to 50, and "Battle Hymn," which had opened at the Experimental Theatre May 22, closed July 25, 1936, with 72 performances to its credit. "Injunction Granted," the third offering of the Living Newspaper (not counting the ill-fated "Ethiopia") opened July 24, was revised August 6 and closed October 20, 1936, with 76 performances. "Cherokee Night" the first production of the Teaching Theatre Technique Unit, opened July 20 and closed August 1.

"The Emperor's New Clothes" of the Children's Unit returned from the portable theatre July 22, 1936, and played three matinees a week until September 4, reopening at the Heckscher Theatre for the Christmas-New Year holiday, giving 63 performances in all. "The Path of Flowers," third offering of the Experimental

Theatre, gave 57 performances from September 17 to November 11, 1936, at Daly's Theatre.

The Classic Theatre Branch gave 61 performances of "Horse Eats Hat" at the Maxine Elliott and the Negro Unit's fifth production was "Noah" presented at the Lafayette in Harlem with 46 performances from October 7 to November 28. The Irish Theatre's first production was "Mr. Jiggins of Jigginstown," with 21 performances at Labor Stage, starting December 17, 1936. "Bassa Mona," a dance drama staged by Momodu Johnson at the Lafayette, ran from December 8 to January 9, reopened at the Ritz January 12, closing January 23, 1937, and was then presented at Daly's from February 9 to the 27th.

"Flight," the Theatre of Youth's first production, opened at the Heckscher December 26, 1936, and ran for 22 performances, directed by Ira Silberstein. Sierra's "Holy Night" was given a series of 10 matinees around Christmas holiday at the Labor Stage. There were 35 performances of "Sweet Land" by Conrad Selier at the Lafayette Theatre from January 19 to February 28 and 74 of "The Sun and I," staged by the Popular Price Theatre at the Adelphi from February 26 to May 22, 1937.

The Negro Theatre's revival of "The Show Off" at the Lafayette opened March 5 and closed May 8, 1937. A trio of "museum pieces" was presented at Daly's 63rd Street Theatre from March 9 to April 10, 1937, directed by M. Verdi. They were "Love in Humble Life" by John Howard Payne; "Clock on the Stairs," by Colin H. Hazelwood, and "A Regular Fix" by John Maddison Morton. Other revivals were "Hymn to the Rising Sun" and "Unto Such Glory," by Paul Green, presented at the Ritz beginning May 6, 1937, giving ten performances to the end of the season and promising a continuance.

The Children's Theatre presented "The Revolt of the Beavers" at the Adelphi four times a week from May 20, 1937, to June 19, 1937. "How Long Brethren" and "Candide," two dance dramas, at the Nora Bayes Theatre were still running at the end of the 1936-37 season. Of the Gilbert and Sullivan operas presented, "H.M.S. Pinafore," "Trial by Jury" and "Iolanthe" led with 12 performances each, "Pirates of Penzance" had 8, "The Mikado" 5.

OFF BROADWAY

In early July at the Heckscher Theatre the Metropolitan Players presented "Nine O'Clock Revue," with music by Arthur Jones and Paul Stackpole and sketches by Jay Strong, Dorothy Quick, Kerry Shaw, and Richard Fehr. The staging was in the hands of Mabel Rowland and John P. Ludlum was responsible for the settings. Allen Kearns and Mabel Rowland were in the cast.

Robert Porterfield brought his Barter Theatre up from Virginia and gave a single performance of Henry Porter's "Two Angry Women of Abingdon" under the auspices of the New School for Social Research, tickets being bartered for serviceable produce in the lobby of the theatre, September 13, 1936.

September 29 "The Years of the Locusts," a war-time convent play by C. M. O'Hara, was brought to Broadway and produced at the Comedy Theatre by Lee Marion.

Paul Gilmore's Cherry Lane Theatre in Greenwich Village had a long run of "The Bishop Misbehaves" with Gilmore and his daughter Virginia in the cast.

John Wexley's "Steel," readapted, was revived by Labor Stage, Inc., and acted by a cast recruited largely from the Lady Garment Workers' Union at the old Princess Theatre in the early Spring, and the Rebel Arts Players at the Labor Stage presented Michael Blankfort's "The Brave and the Blind" March 21, 1937.

Catherine A. Bammer started her fifth season and eighth edition of "Sunday Nights at Nine" at the Barbizon-Plaza Theatre December 6, 1936, and continued through the season.

The Irish Repertory Players under the direction of J. Augustus Keogh presented at Lincoln Square Studios, Shaw's "The Man of Destiny" and "O'Flaherty, V. C.," "The Far-Off Hills," Synge's "Riders to the Sea," "The Workhouse Ward" and "The Rising of the Moon" by Lady Gregory.

The Artef Players, a collective group handling social themes, revived "Recruits," Sholem Aleichem's "200,000," and H. Leivick's "Chains." "Chains," which was directed by Joseph Buloff and designed by M. Solotaroff, began a run January 21, 1937.

The New Theatre School's Studio Unit produced Chekhov's "The Marriage" and Cervantes' "The Cave of Salamanca." The New Theatre League's musical revue satire, "Pink Slips on Parade," with music by Earl Robinson, book and lyrics by Muni

Diamond, Ben Ross, Kenneth Hunter and Peter Martin, was presented at the Adelphi Theatre, January 30, 1937.

Monodrama

Cornelia Otis Skinner gave four performances at the Lyceum, March 28, 30, April 2 and 4, 1937, including "Loves of Charles II," "Empress Eugenie," "Wives of Henry VIII" and "Mansion on the Hudson." Ruth Draper under the aegis of the Actor-Managers, Inc., gave 8 performances in December and January first at the Guild and then the Morosco Theatre. Her program included among others "The Miner's Wife," "In County Kerry," "In a Church in Italy," and "Love in the Balkans." Beatrice Herford appeared at the Hotel Pierre April 28, 1937, and Helen Howe presented "Characters and Caricatures" at the Little Theatre in March. Her program included "Mañana" and "The Lesser Breed." Dorothy Gordon had a program of songs and stories at Town Hall, Sheila Barrett a repertoire of comedy sketches at the Paramount and Mrs. Richard Mansfield gave several Shakespearian readings.

Puppets

The Bufano Marionettes presented at the MacDowell Club "Alice in Wonderland," "The Pig and the Pepper," "In the Circus Parade," "Alice at the Mad Hatter's Tea Party," "The Spanish Dancers," "Little Black Sambo," "The White Way," "Cinderella," etc., in January and February.

The Yale Puppeteers were at the Barbizon-Plaza in February and Tony Sarg's puppets played "Mikado" "Tom Sawyer" and "Huck Finn" in December and January. Ellen Van Volkenburg's marionettes came from the Pacific Coast for an engagement at the Master Institute in late January and Sue Hastings was at the Plaza Theatre with her company in late December showing "Robin Hood" and "Snow White."

Children

The Children's Art Theatre gave four one-act plays:—"Hansel and Gretel," "Red Riding Hood," "The Fourth Kingdom" and "The Black Cat." Claire Tree Major, at the Barbizon-Plaza during the holidays, presented "Pinocchio." The Lilliput Theatre, seeking to establish a permanent and national stage for children in early February, presented "The Wonder Hat," by Ben

Hecht, and "Two Slatterns and a King" by Edna St. Vincent Millay, together with folk songs and dances in early February at 5 East 19th Street. The Juvenile Theatre of Art produced "What Happened to Jones?" at the Morosco Theatre in November with a cast recruited from professional child-actors of the New York stage, screen and radio. "The Second Hurricane," a play opera by Edwin Denby with music by Aaron Copland, depicting adventures in the Ohio Valley flood, was presented at the Neighborhood Playhouse.

College Plays in New York

The Hasty Pudding Club of Harvard put on their annual Spring show at Mecca Temple, New York, April 9, 1937. The play was called "Come Across" and was written by Arnett McKennan, Gaspar Bacon, Jr., Benjamin Welles and Cammann Newberry. In the cast were Nathaniel Benchley, son of Robert Benchley, and George H. Earle, 4th, son of the Governor of Pennsylvania. The advisory committee back of the show included Brock Pemberton, John Golden, Burgess Meredith, Peggy Ashcroft, Margaret and Antoinette Perry, Vincent Freedly and Robert Benchley.

The Mask and Wig of the University of Pennsylvania gave its annual presentation at the Hippodrome in January, producing "The Mad Whirl" by Louis C. Maderia and George Hess. It was staged by Frederick J. Hake. The Barnard College students presented "It Doesn't Happen Here" at Brinckerhoff Theatre, March 12, 1937.

Foreign Language Plays

The French Theatre of New York, directed by Guy de Vestel, opened its 1936-37 season November 11, 1936, at the Barbizon-Plaza Theatre with the premiere of "L'Heure du Berger," by Eduard Bourdet. This was followed by "Martine" by Bernard, "Un Dejeuner D'Amoureux" by Birabeau, "Si Je Voulais" by Paul Geraldy and Robert Spitzer, "Bichon" by Jean Letraz, "Dans Le Noir" by Michel Dulud and "Christian" by Yvan Noe.

Paulina Singerman and her Argentine Players presented a repertoire of Spanish plays at the Ambassador Theatre beginning April 18, 1937. Among them were "Todo Un Hombre" by Miguel Unamuno, "Amor" by Vianna, "Terra Baja" by Gulmera and "Cuando Los Hijos de Eva no son Lo Hijos de Adan" by Benevente.

The Italian Teatro d'Arte gave Ibsen's "Ghosts" under the

direction of Giuseppa Sterni at the Vanderbilt, March 21, 1937. Other plays presented during the season were "Feudalism or the Lowland" by Guimera, Henry Bernstein's "Sansone," Giacometti's "La Morte Civile," "La Sera del Sabato" by Personaggi, "L'ora di Diana" by Boggia and d'Ennery's "The Two Orphans."

The Deutsche Schauspiel-Buehne launched a German-language theatre at the New York Turnhalle, November 19, 1936, with Gerhart Hauptmann's "Die Versunkene Glocke." The Ukrainian Theatrical Company presented the American premiere of Simon Artemowsky's operetta, "Cossacks Beyond the Danube," April 16, 1937.

Among other plays the Yiddish Art Theatre, Maurice Schwartz directing, presented Albert Ganzert's "Borderline" at the 49th Street Theatre, February 9, 1937, and "The Water Carrier" a musical show by Jacob Prager, with music by Alexander Olshanetsky, which opened December 24, 1936, and had an unusually long run.

STATISTICAL SUMMARY

(LAST SEASON PLAYS WHICH ENDED RUNS AFTER JUNE 15, 1936)

Plays	*Number Performances*	*Plays*	*Number Performances*
Bury the Dead	97	Mulatto	373
Call It a Day	194	New Faces of 1936	193
Children's Hour	691	On Your Toes	315
Dead End	687	Pre-Honeymoon	255
End of Summer	153	Prelude	97
First Lady	246	Three Men on a Horse	835
Idiot's Delight	300	To My Husband	24
Love on the Dole	145	Victoria Regina	517

LONG RUNS ON BROADWAY

To June 15, 1937

(Plays marked with asterisk were still playing June 15, 1937)

Plays	*Number Performances*	*Plays*	*Number Performances*
Abie's Irish Rose	2,532	Adonis	603
*Tobacco Road	1,516	Street Scene	601
Lightnin'	1,291	Kiki	600
The Bat	867	Blossom Time	592
Three Men on a Horse	835	Show Boat	572
The Ladder	789	The Show-Off	571
The First Year	760	Sally	570
Seventh Heaven	704	Strictly Dishonorable	557
Peg o' My Heart	692	Good News	551
Children's Hour	691	The Music Master	540
Dead End	687	The Boomerang	522
East Is West	680	Blackbirds	518
Irene	670	Sunny	517
*Boy Meets Girl	660	Victoria Regina	517
A Trip to Chinatown	657	The Vagabond King	511
Rain	648	The New Moon	509
The Green Pastures	640	Shuffle Along	504
Is Zat So	618	Personal Appearance	501
Student Prince	608	Bird in Hand	500
Broadway	603	Sailor, Beware!	500

DRAMA CRITICS' CIRCLE AWARD

Meeting in late March, 1937, the Drama Critics' Circle took eleven ballots before the reviewers could decide which of the season's new plays was entitled to the annual award as "the best new play written by an American playwright and produced in New York." On the eleventh ballot the choice fell to Maxwell Anderson's fantastic comedy, "High Tor," which received the necessary fourteen of the eighteen votes cast. On the last ballot the runner up was Paul Green's "Johnny Johnson," with three votes. A single vote was cast for Robert Turney's "Daughters of Atreus."

Other plays by American authors that received votes during the balloting were Moss Hart's and George Kaufman's "You Can't Take It with You," Mark Reed's "Yes, My Darling Daughter," Arthur Kober's "Having Wonderful Times," John Howard Lawson's "Marching Song" and two additional entries by Mr. Anderson, "The Wingless Victory" and "The Masque of Kings."

The Drama Critics' Circle awards to date have been:

1935-36—Winterset, by Maxwell Anderson
1936-37—High Tor, by Maxwell Anderson

PULITZER PRIZE WINNERS

"For the original American play performed in New York which shall best represent the educational value and power of the stage in raising the standard of good morals, good taste and good manners."—The Will of Joseph Pulitzer, dated April 16, 1904.

In 1929 the advisory board, which, according to the terms of the will, "shall have the power in its discretion to suspend or to change any subject or subjects . . . if in the judgment of the board such suspension, changes or substitutions shall be conducive to the public good," decided to eliminate from the above paragraph relating to the prize-winning play the words "in raising the standard of good morals, good taste and good manners."

The committee awards to date have been:

1917-18—Why Marry? by Jesse Lynch Williams
1918-19—None
1919-20—Miss Lulu Bett, by Zona Gale
1920-21—Beyond the Horizon, by Eugene O'Neill
1921-22—Anna Christie, by Eugene O'Neill
1922-23—Icebound, by Owen Davis
1923-24—Hell-bent fer Heaven, by Hatcher Hughes
1924-25—They Knew What They Wanted, by Sidney Howard
1925-26—Craig's Wife, by George Kelly
1926-27—In Abraham's Bosom, by Paul Green
1927-28—Strange Interlude, by Eugene O'Neill
1928-29—Street Scene, by Elmer Rice
1929-30—The Green Pastures, by Marc Connelly
1930-31—Alison's House, by Susan Glaspell
1931-32—Of Thee I Sing, by George S. Kaufman, Morrie Ryskind, Ira and George Gershwin
1932-33—Both Your Houses, by Maxwell Anderson
1933-34—Men in White, by Sidney Kingsley
1934-35—The Old Maid, by Zoe Akins
1935-36—Idiot's Delight, by Robert E. Sherwood
1936-37—You Can't Take It with You, by Moss Hart and George S. Kaufman

PREVIOUS VOLUMES OF BEST PLAYS

Plays chosen to represent the theatre seasons from 1909 to 1934 are as follows:

1909-1919

"The Easiest Way," by Eugene Walters. Published by G. W. Dillingham, New York; Houghton Mifflin Co., Boston.

"Mrs. Bumpstead-Leigh," by Harry James Smith. Published by Samuel French, New York.

"Disraeli," by Louis N. Parker. Published by Dodd, Mead and Co., New York.

"Romance," by Edward Sheldon. Published by the Macmillan Co., New York.

"Seven Keys to Baldpate," by George M. Cohan. Published by Bobbs-Merrill Co., Indianapolis, as a novel by Earl Derr Biggers; as a play by Samuel French, New York.

"On Trial," by Elmer Reizenstein. Published by Samuel French, New York.

"The Unchastened Woman," by Louis Kaufman Anspacher. Published by Harcourt, Brace and Howe, Inc., New York.

"Good Gracious Annabelle," by Clare Kummer. Published by Samuel French, New York.

"Why Marry?" by Jesse Lynch Williams. Published by Charles Scribner's Sons, New York.

"John Ferguson," by St. John Ervine. Published by the Macmillan Co., New York.

1919-1920

"Abraham Lincoln," by John Drinkwater. Published by Houghton Mifflin Co., Boston.

"Clarence," by Booth Tarkington. Published by Samuel French, New York.

"Beyond the Horizon," by Eugene G. O'Neill. Published by Boni & Liveright, Inc., New York.

"Déclassée," by Zoe Akins. Published by Liveright, Inc., New York.

"The Famous Mrs. Fair," by James Forbes. Published by Samuel French, New York.

"The Jest," by Sem Benelli. (American adaptation by Edward Sheldon.)

"Jane Clegg," by St. John Ervine. Published by Henry Holt & Co., New York.

"Mamma's Affair," by Rachel Barton Butler. Published by Samuel French, New York.

"Wedding Bells," by Salisbury Field. Published by Samuel French, New York.

"Adam and Eva," by George Middleton and Guy Bolton. Published by Samuel French, New York.

1920-1921

"Deburau," adapted from the French of Sacha Guitry by H. Granville Barker. Published by G. P. Putnam's Sons, New York.

"The First Year," by Frank Craven. Published by Samuel French, New York.

"Enter Madame," by Gilda Varesi and Dolly Byrne. Published by G. P. Putnam's Sons, New York.

"The Green Goddess," by William Archer. Published by Alfred A. Knopf, New York.

"Liliom," by Ferenc Molnar. Published by Boni & Liveright, New York.

"Mary Rose," by James M. Barrie. Published by Charles Scribner's Sons, New York.

"Nice People," by Rachel Crothers. Published by Charles Scribner's Sons, New York.

"The Bad Man," by Porter Emerson Browne. Published by G. P. Putnam's Sons, New York.

"The Emperor Jones," by Eugene G. O'Neill. Published by Boni & Liveright, New York.

"The Skin Game," by John Galsworthy. Published by Charles Scribner's Sons, New York.

1921-1922

"Anna Christie," by Eugene G. O'Neill. Published by Boni & Liveright, New York.

"A Bill of Divorcement," by Clemence Dane. Published by the Macmillan Company, New York.

"Dulcy," by George S. Kaufman and Marc Connelly. Published by G. P. Putnam's Sons, New York.

"He Who Gets Slapped," adapted from the Russian of Leonid Andreyev by Gregory Zilboorg. Published by Brentano's, New York.

"Six Cylinder Love," by William Anthony McGuire.

"The Hero," by Gilbert Emery.

"The Dover Road," by Alan Alexander Milne. Published by Samuel French, New York.

"Ambush," by Arthur Richman.

"The Circle," by William Somerset Maugham.

"The Nest," by Paul Geraldy and Grace George.

1922-1923

"Rain," by John Colton and Clemence Randolph. Published by Liveright, Inc., New York.

"Loyalties," by John Galsworthy. Published by Charles Scribner's Sons, New York.

"Icebound," by Owen Davis. Published by Little, Brown & Company, Boston.

"You and I," by Philip Barry. Published by Brentano's, New York.

"The Fool," by Channing Pollock. Published by Brentano's, New York.

"Merton of the Movies," by George Kaufman and Marc Connelly, based on the novel of the same name by Harry Leon Wilson.

"Why Not?" by Jesse Lynch Williams. Published by Walter H. Baker Co., Boston.

"The Old Soak," by Don Marquis. Published by Doubleday, Page & Company, New York.

"R.U.R.," by Karel Capek. Translated by Paul Selver. Published by Doubleday, Page & Company.

"Mary the 3d," by Rachel Crothers. Published by Brentano's, New York.

1923-1924

"The Swan," translated from the Hungarian of Ferenc Molnar by Melville Baker. Published by Boni & Liveright, New York.

"Outward Bound," by Sutton Vane. Published by Boni & Liveright, New York.

"The Show-off," by George Kelly. Published by Little, Brown & Company, Boston.

"The Changelings," by Lee Wilson Dodd. Published by E. P. Dutton & Company, New York.

"Chicken Feed," by Guy Bolton. Published by Samuel French,

New York and London.

"Sun-Up," by Lula Vollmer. Published by Brentano's, New York.

"Beggar on Horseback," by George Kaufman and Marc Connelly. Published by Boni & Liveright, New York.

"Tarnish," by Gilbert Emery. Published by Brentano's, New York.

"The Goose Hangs High," by Lewis Beach. Published by Little, Brown & Company, Boston.

"Hell-bent fer Heaven," by Hatcher Hughes. Published by Harper Bros., New York.

1924-1925

"What Price Glory?" by Laurence Stallings and Maxwell Anderson. Published by Harcourt, Brace & Co., New York.

"They Knew What They Wanted," by Sidney Howard. Published by Doubleday, Page & Company, New York.

"Desire Under the Elms," by Eugene G. O'Neill. Published by Boni & Liveright, New York.

"The Firebrand," by Edwin Justus Mayer. Published by Boni & Liveright, New York.

"Dancing Mothers," by Edgar Selwyn and Edmund Goulding.

"Mrs. Partridge Presents," by Mary Kennedy and Ruth Warren. Published by Samuel French, New York.

"The Fall Guy," by James Gleason and George Abbott. Published by Samuel French, New York.

"The Youngest," by Philip Barry. Published by Samuel French, New York.

"Minick," by Edna Ferber and George S. Kaufman. Published by Doubleday, Page & Company, New York.

"Wild Birds," by Dan Totheroh. Published by Doubleday, Page & Company, New York.

1925-1926

"Craig's Wife," by George Kelly. Published by Little, Brown & Company, Boston.

"The Great God Brown," by Eugene G. O'Neill. Published by Boni & Liveright, New York.

"The Green Hat," by Michael Arlen.

"The Dybbuk," by S. Ansky, Henry G. Alsberg-Winifred Katzin translation. Published by Boni & Liveright, New York.

"The Enemy," by Channing Pollock. Published by Brentano's,

New York.

"The Last of Mrs. Cheyney," by Frederick Lonsdale. Published by Samuel French, New York.

"Bride of the Lamb," by William Hurlbut. Published by Boni & Liveright, New York.

"The Wisdom Tooth," by Marc Connelly. Published by George H. Doran & Company, New York.

"The Butter and Egg Man," by George Kaufman. Published by Boni & Liveright, New York.

"Young Woodley," by John Van Druten. Published by Simon and Schuster, New York.

1926-1927

"Broadway," by Philip Dunning and George Abbott. Published by George H. Doran Company, New York.

"Saturday's Children," by Maxwell Anderson. Published by Longmans, Green & Company, New York.

"Chicago," by Maurine Watkins. Published by Alfred A. Knopf, Inc., New York.

"The Constant Wife," by William Somerset Maugham. Published by George H. Doran Company, New York.

"The Play's the Thing," by Ferenc Molnar and P. G. Wodehouse. Published by Brentano's, New York.

"The Road to Rome," by Robert Emmet Sherwood. Published by Charles Scribner's Sons, New York.

"The Silver Cord," by Sidney Howard. Published by Charles Scribner's Sons, New York.

"The Cradle Song," translated from the Spanish of G. Martinez Sierra by John Garrett Underhill. Published by E. P. Dutton & Company, New York.

"Daisy Mayme," by George Kelly. Published by Little, Brown & Company, Boston.

"In Abraham's Bosom," by Paul Green. Published by Robert M. McBride & Company, New York.

1927-1928

"Strange Interlude," by Eugene G. O'Neill. Published by Boni & Liveright, New York.

"The Royal Family," by Edna Ferber and George Kaufman. Published by Doubleday, Doran & Company, New York.

"Burlesque," by George Manker Watters. Published by Doubleday, Doran & Company, New York.

"Coquette," by George Abbott and Ann Bridgers. Published by Longmans, Green & Company, New York, London, Toronto.

"Behold the Bridegroom," by George Kelly. Published by Little, Brown & Company, Boston.

"Porgy," by DuBose Heyward. Published by Doubleday, Doran & Company, New York.

"Paris Bound," by Philip Barry. Published by Samuel French, New York.

"Escape," by John Galsworthy. Published by Charles Scribner's Sons, New York.

"The Racket," by Bartlett Cormack. Published by Samuel French, New York.

"The Plough and the Stars," by Sean O'Casey. Published by the Macmillan Company, New York.

1928-1929

"Street Scene," by Elmer Rice. Published by Samuel French, New York.

"Journey's End," by R. C. Sheriff. Published by Brentano's, New York.

"Wings Over Europe," by Robert Nichols and Maurice Browne. Published by Covici-Friede, New York.

"Holiday," by Philip Barry. Published by Samuel French, New York.

"The Front Page," by Ben Hecht and Charles MacArthur. Published by Covici-Friede, New York.

"Let Us Be Gay," by Rachel Crothers. Published by Samuel French, New York.

"Machinal," by Sophie Treadwell.

"Little Accident," by Floyd Dell and Thomas Mitchell.

"Gypsy," by Maxwell Anderson.

"The Kingdom of God," by G. Martinez Sierra; English version by Helen and Harley Granville-Barker. Published by E. P. Dutton & Company, New York.

1929-1930

"The Green Pastures," by Marc Connelly (adapted from "Ol' Man Adam and His Chillun," by Roark Bradford). Published by Farrar & Rinehart, Inc., New York.

"The Criminal Code," by Martin Flavin. Published by Horace Liveright, New York.

"Berkeley Square," by John Balderstone. Published by the Macmillan Company, New York.

"Strictly Dishonorable," by Preston Sturges. Published by Horace Liveright, New York.

"The First Mrs. Fraser," by St. John Ervine. Published by the Macmillan Company, New York.

"The Last Mile," by John Wexley. Published by Samuel French, New York.

"June Moon," by Ring W. Lardner and George S. Kaufman. Published by Charles Scribner's Sons, New York.

"Michael and Mary," by A. A. Milne. Published by Chatto & Windus, London.

"Death Takes a Holiday," by Walter Ferris (adapted from the Italian of Alberto Casella). Published by Samuel French, New York.

"Rebound," by Donald Ogden Stewart. Published by Samuel French, New York.

1930-1931

"Elizabeth the Queen," by Maxwell Anderson. Published by Longmans, Green & Co., New York.

"Tomorrow and Tomorrow," by Philip Barry. Published by Samuel French, New York.

"Once in a Lifetime," by George S. Kaufman and Moss Hart. Published by Farrar and Rinehart, New York.

"Green Grow the Lilacs," by Lynn Riggs. Published by Samuel French, New York and London.

"As Husbands Go," by Rachel Crothers. Published by Samuel French, New York.

"Alison's House," by Susan Glasgow. Published by Samuel French, New York.

"Five-Star Final," by Louis Weitzenkorn. Published by Samuel French, New York.

"Overture," by William Bolitho. Published by Simon & Schuster, New York.

"The Barretts of Wimpole Street," by Rudolf Besier. Published by Little, Brown & Company, Boston.

"Grand Hotel," adapted from the German of Vicki Baum by W. A. Drake.

1931-1932

"Of Thee I Sing," by George S. Kaufman and Morrie Ryskind; music and lyrics by George and Ira Gershwin. Published by Alfred Knopf, New York.

"Mourning Becomes Electra," by Eugene G. O'Neill. Published by Horace Liveright, Inc., New York.

"Reunion in Vienna," by Robert Emmet Sherwood. Published

by Charles Scribner's Sons, New York.

"The House of Connelly," by Paul Green. Published by Samuel French, New York.

"The Animal Kingdom," by Philip Barry. Published by Samuel French, New York.

"The Left Bank," by Elmer Rice. Published by Samuel French, New York.

"Another Language," by Rose Franken. Published by Samuel French, New York.

"Brief Moment," by S. N. Behrman. Published by Farrar & Rinehart, New York.

"The Devil Passes," by Ben W. Levy. Published by Martin Secker, London.

"Cynara," by H. M. Harwood and R. F. Gore-Browne. Published by Samuel French, New York.

1932-1933

"Both Your Houses," by Maxwell Anderson. Published by Samuel French, New York.

"Dinner at Eight," by George S. Kaufman and Edna Ferber. Published by Doubleday, Doran & Co., Inc., Garden City, New York.

"When Ladies Meet," by Rachel Crothers. Published by Samuel French, New York.

"Design for Living," by Noel Coward. Published by Doubleday, Doran & Co., Inc., Garden City, New York.

"Biography," by S. N. Behrman. Published by Farrar & Rinehart, Inc., New York.

"Alien Corn," by Sidney Howard. Published by Charles Scribner's Sons, New York.

"The Late Christopher Bean," adapted from the French of René Fauchois by Sidney Howard. Published by Samuel French, New York.

"We, the People," by Elmer Rice. Published by Coward-McCann, Inc., New York.

"Pigeons and People," by George M. Cohan.

"One Sunday Afternoon," by James Hagan. Published by Samuel French, New York.

1933-1934

"Mary of Scotland," by Maxwell Anderson. Published by Doubleday, Doran & Co., Inc., Garden City, N. Y.

"Men in White," by Sidney Kingsley. Published by Covici, Friede, Inc., New York.

"Dodsworth," by Sinclair Lewis and Sidney Howard. Published by Harcourt, Brace & Co., New York.

"Ah, Wilderness," by Eugene O'Neill. Published by Random House, New York.

"They Shall Not Die," by John Wexley. Published by Alfred A. Knopf, New York.

"Her Master's Voice," by Clare Kummer. Published by Samuel French, New York.

"No More Ladies," by A. E. Thomas.

"Wednesday's Child," by Leopold Atlas. Published by Samuel French, New York.

"The Shining Hour," by Keith Winter. Published by Doubleday, Doran & Co., Inc., Garden City, New York.

"The Green Bay Tree," by Mordaunt Shairp. Published by Baker International Play Bureau, Boston, Mass.

1934-1935

"The Children's Hour," by Lillian Hellman. Published by Alfred Knopf, New York.

"Valley Forge," by Maxwell Anderson. Published by Anderson House, Washington, D. C. Distributed by Dodd, Mead & Co., New York.

"The Petrified Forest," by Robert Sherwood. Published by Charles Scribner's Sons, New York.

"The Old Maid," by Zoe Akins. Published by D. Appleton-Century Co., New York.

"Accent on Youth," by Samson Raphaelson. Published by Samuel French, New York.

"Merrily We Roll Along," by George S. Kaufman and Moss Hart. Published by Random House, New York.

"Awake and Sing," by Clifford Odets. Published by Random House, New York.

"The Farmer Takes a Wife," by Frank B. Elser and Marc Connelly.

"Lost Horizons," by John Hayden.

"The Distaff Side," by John Van Druten. Published by Alfred Knopf, New York.

1935-1936

"Winterset," by Maxwell Anderson. Published by Anderson House, Washington, D. C.

"Idiot's Delight," by Robert Emmet Sherwood. Published by Charles Scribner's Sons, New York.

"End of Summer," by S. N. Behrman. Published by Random House, New York.

"First Lady," by Katharine Dayton and George S. Kaufman. Published by Random House, New York.

"Victoria Regina," by Laurence Housman. Published by Samuel French, Inc., New York and London.

"Boy Meets Girl," by Bella and Samuel Spewack. Published by Random House, New York.

"Dead End," by Sidney Kingsley. Published by Random House, New York.

"Call It a Day," by Dodie Smith. Published by Samuel French, Inc., New York and London.

"Ethan Frome," by Owen Davis and Donald Davis. Published by Charles Scribner's Sons, New York.

"Pride and Prejudice," by Helen Jerome. Published by Doubleday, Doran & Co., Garden City, New York.

WHERE AND WHEN THEY WERE BORN

Abba, Marta	Milan, Italy	1907
Abbott, George	Hamburg, N. Y.	1895
Abel, Walter	St. Paul, Minn.	1898
Aborn, Milton	Marysville, Cal.	1864
Adams, Maude	Salt Lake City, Utah	1872
Adler, Stella	New York	1904
Aherne, Brian	King's Norton, England	1902
Akins, Zoe	Humansville, Mo.	1886
Alexander, Katherine	Arkansas	1901
Alexander, Ross	Brooklyn, N. Y.	1904
Allanby, Peggy	New York	1905
Allen, Adrianne	Manchester, England	1907
Allen, Viola	Huntsville, Ala.	1869
Allgood, Sara	Dublin, Ireland	1883
Ames, Robert	Hartford, Conn.	1893
Ames, Winthrop	North Easton, Mass.	1871
Anders, Glenn	Los Angeles, Cal.	1890
Anderson, Judith	Australia	1898
Anderson, Maxwell	Atlantic City, Pa.	1888
Andrews, Ann	Los Angeles, Cal.	1895
Anglin, Margaret	Ottawa, Canada	1876
Anson, A. E.	London, England	1879
Anspacher, Louis K.	Cincinnati, Ohio	1878
Arling, Joyce	Memphis, Tenn.	1911
Arliss, George	London, England	1868
Arthur, Julia	Hamilton, Ont.	1869
Ashcroft, Peggy	Croydon, England	1907
Astaire, Fred	Omaha, Neb.	1899
Atwell, Roy	Syracuse, N. Y.	1880
Atwill, Lionel	London, England	1885
Bainter, Fay	Los Angeles, Cal.	1892
Baker, Lee	Michigan	1880
Bankhead, Tallulah	Huntsville, Ala.	1902
Banks, Leslie J.	West Derby, England	1890
Barbee, Richard	Lafayette, Ind.	1887
Barrett, Edith	Roxbury, Mass.	1904

Barrie, James Matthew	Kirriemuir, N. B.	1860
Barry, Philip	Rochester, N. Y.	1896
Barrymore, Ethel	Philadelphia, Pa.	1879
Barrymore, John	Philadelphia, Pa.	1882
Barrymore, Lionel	London, England	1878
Barton, James	Gloucester, N. J.	1890
Bates, Blanche	Portland, Ore.	1873
Baxter, Lora	New York	1907
Beatty, Roberta	Rochester, N. Y.	1900
Beecher, Janet	Chicago, Ill.	1884
Behrman, S. N.	Worcester, Mass.	1893
Bell, James	Suffolk, Va.	1891
Ben-Ami, Jacob	Minsk, Russia	1890
Bennett, Richard	Cass County, Ind.	1873
Bennett, Wilda	Asbury Park, N. J.	1894
Bergner, Elizabeth	Vienna	1901
Berlin, Irving	Russia	1888
Best, Edna	Sussex, England	1900
Binney, Constance	Philadelphia, Pa.	1900
Blackmer, Sidney	Salisbury, N. C.	1896
Boland, Mary	Detroit, Mich.	1880
Bolger, Ray	Dorchester, Mass.	1906
Bondi, Beulah	Chicago, Ill.	1892
Bordoni, Irene	Paris, France	1895
Brady, Alice	New York	1892
Brady, William A.	San Francisco, Cal.	1863
Brady, William A., Jr.	New York	1900
Braham, Horace	London, England	1896
Brent, Romney	Saltillo, Mex.	1902
Brian, Donald	St. Johns, N. F.	1877
Brice, Fannie	Brooklyn, N. Y.	1891
Broadhurst, George H.	England	1866
Broderick, Helen	New York	1891
Bromberg, J. Edward	Hungary	1903
Bruce, Nigel	San Diego, Cal.	1895
Bryant, Charles	England	1879
Buchanan, Jack	England	1892
Buchanan, Thompson	Louisville, Ky.	1877
Buckler, Hugh	Southampton, England	1886
Burke, Billie	Washington, D. C.	1885
Burton, Frederick	Indiana	1871
Byington, Spring	Colorado Springs, Colo.	1898
Byron, Arthur	Brooklyn, N. Y.	1872

Cabot, Eliot	Boston, Mass.	1899
Cagney, James	New York	1904
Cahill, Lily	Texas	1885
Cahill, Marie	Brooklyn, N. Y.	1871
Calhern, Louis	New York	1895
Cantor, Eddie	New York	1894
Campbell, Mrs. Patrick	England	1865
Carle, Richard	Somerville, Mass.	1871
Carlisle, Alexandra	Yorkshire, England	1886
Carminati, Tullio	Zara, Dalmatia	1894
Carpenter, Edward Childs	Philadelphia, Pa.	1871
Carr, Alexander	Russia	1878
Carroll, Earl	Pittsburgh, Pa.	1892
Carter, Mrs. Leslie	Lexington, Ky.	1862
Catlett, Walter	San Francisco, Cal.	1889
Cawthorne, Joseph	New York	1868
Chandler, Helen	Charleston, N. C.	1906
Chaplin, Charles Spencer	London	1889
Chase, Ilka	New York	1900
Chatterton, Ruth	New York	1893
Cherry, Charles	England	1872
Christians, Mady	Vienna, Austria	1907
Churchill, Burton	Toronto, Can.	1876
Claire, Ina	Washington, D. C.	1892
Clarke, Marguerite	Cincinnati, Ohio	1887
Cliffe, H. Cooper	England	1862
Clifford, Kathleen	Charlottesville, Va.	1887
Clive, Colin	St. Malo, France	1900
Coburn, Charles	Macon, Ga.	1877
Coghlan, Gertrude	England	1879
Coghlan, Rose	Petersborough, England	1850
Cohan, George M.	Providence, R. I.	1878
Cohan, Georgette	Los Angeles, Cal.	1900
Colbert, Claudette	Paris	1905
Collier, Constance	Windsor, England	1882
Collier, William	New York	1866
Collinge, Patricia	Dublin, Ireland	1894
Collins, Charles	Frederick, Okla.	1904
Collins, José	London, England	1896
Colt, Ethel Barrymore	Mamaroneck, N. Y.	1911
Colt, John Drew	New York	1914
Conklin, Peggy	Dobbs Ferry, N. Y.	1912
Connolly, Walter	Cincinnati, Ohio	1888

Conroy, Frank	London, England	1885
Cook, Joe	Evansville, Ind.	1890
Cooper, Gladys	Lewisham, England	1888
Cooper, Violet Kemble	London, England	1890
Cornell, Katharine	Buffalo, N. Y.	1900
Corrigan, Emmett	Amsterdam, Holland	1871
Corthell, Herbert	Boston, Mass.	1875
Cossart, Ernest	Cheltenham, England	1876
Courtenay, William	Worcester, Mass.	1875
Courtleigh, William	Guelph, Ont.	1869
Coward, Noel	England	1899
Cowl, Jane	Boston, Mass.	1887
Craven, Frank	Boston, Mass.	1880
Crews, Laura Hope	San Francisco, Cal.	1880
Crosman, Henrietta	Wheeling, W. Va.	1865
Crothers, Rachel	Bloomington, Ill.	1878
Cumberland, John	St. John, N. B.	1880
Cummings, Constance	Seattle, Wash.	1911
Curzon, George	Amersham, England	1898
Dale, Margaret	Philadelphia, Pa.	1880
Dalton, Charles	England	1864
Daly, Blyth	New York	1902
Danforth, William	Syracuse	1869
Daniels, Frank	Dayton, Ohio	1860
Davis, Donald	New York	1907
Davis, Owen	Portland, Me.	1874
Davis, Owen, Jr.	New York	1910
Dawn, Hazel	Ogden, Utah	1891
Day, Edith	Minneapolis, Minn.	1896
De Angelis, Jefferson	San Francisco, Cal.	1859
Dean, Julia	St. Paul, Minn.	1880
De Cordoba, Pedro	New York	1881
Dillingham, Charles B.	Hartford, Conn.	1868
Dinehart, Allan	Missoula, Mont.	1889
Dixey, Henry E.	Boston, Mass.	1859
Dixon, Jean	Waterbury, Conn.	1905
Dodson, John E.	London, England	1857
Doro, Marie	Duncannon, Pa.	1882
D'Orsay, Lawrence	England	1860
Dressler, Eric	Brooklyn, N. Y.	1900
Dressler, Marie	Cobourg, Canada	1869
Drew, Louise	New York	1884

Duncan, Augustin	San Francisco	1873
Dunn, Emma	England	1875
Dunning, Philip	Meriden, Conn.	1890
Dupree, Minnie	San Francisco, Cal.	1875
Durante, Jimmy	New York City	1893
Edeson, Robert	Baltimore, Md.	1868
Eldridge, Florence	Brooklyn, N. Y.	1901
Ellerbe, Harry	Georgia	1905
Ellis, Mary	New York	1900
Elliston, Grace	Wheeling, W. Va.	1881
Ellinger, Desirée	Manchester, Vt.	1895
Elliott, Gertrude	Rockland, Me.	1874
Elliott, Maxine	Rockland, Me.	1871
Eltinge, Julian	Boston, Mass.	1883
Emery, Gilbert	Naples, New York	1875
Emerson, John	Sandusky, Ohio	1874
Errol, Leon	Sydney, Australia	1881
Ervine, St. John Greer	Belfast, Ireland	1883
Evans, Edith	London, England	1888
Evans, Maurice	Dorchester, England	1901
Fairbanks, Douglas	Denver, Colo.	1883
Farnum, William	Boston, Mass.	1876
Farrar, Geraldine	Melrose, Mass.	1883
Faversham, William	Warwickshire, England	1868
Fenwick, Irene	Chicago, Ill.	1887
Ferber, Edna	Kalamazoo, Mich.	1887
Ferguson, Elsie	New York	1883
Field, Sylvia	Allston, Mass.	1902
Fields, Lew	New York	1867
Fields, W. C.	Philadelphia, Pa.	1883
Fischer, Alice	Indiana	1869
Fiske, Minnie Maddern	New Orleans, La.	1867
Fontanne, Lynn	London, England	1887
Forbes-Robertson, Sir J.	London, England	1853
Foster, Claiborne	Shreveport, La.	1899
Foster, Norman	Richmond, Ind.	1907
Foster, Phœbe	New Hampshire	1897
Foy, Eddie, Jr.	New Rochelle, N. Y.	1906
Franklin, Irene	St. Louis, Mo.	1878
Frederick, Pauline	Boston, Mass.	1884
Friganza, Trixie	Cincinnati, Ohio	1870
Frohman, Daniel	Sandusky, Ohio	1850

Gahagan, Helen	Boonton, N. J.	1902
Garden, Mary	Scotland	1876
Gaxton, William	San Francisco, Cal.	1893
Gaythorne, Pamela	England	1882
Geddes, Norman Bel	Adrian, Mich.	1893
George, Grace	New York	1879
Gerald, Ara	New South Wales	1902
Gershwin, George	Brooklyn, N. Y.	1898
Gershwin, Ira	New York	1896
Gielgud, John	London, England	1904
Gillette, William	Hartford, Conn.	1856
Gillmore, Frank	New York	1884
Gillmore, Margalo	England	1901
Gish, Dorothy	Massillon, Ohio	1898
Gish, Lillian	Springfield, Ohio	1896
Gleason, James	New York	1885
Glendinning, Ernest	Ulverston, England	1884
Golden, John	New York	1874
Gordon, Ruth	Wollaston, Mass.	1896
Gottschalk, Ferdinand	London, England	1869
Granville, Charlotte	London	1863
Granville, Sydney	Bolton, England	1885
Greaza, Walter	St. Paul, Minn.	1900
Green, Martyn	London, England	1899
Green, Mitzi	New York City	1920
Greenstreet, Sydney	England	1880
Grey, Katherine	San Francisco, Cal.	1873
Groody, Louise	Waco, Texas	1897
Gwenn, Edmund	Glamorgan, Wales	1875
Haines, Robert T.	Muncie, Ind.	1870
Hale, Louise Closser	Chicago, Ill.	1872
Hall, Bettina	North Easton, Mass.	1906
Hall, Laura Nelson	Philadelphia, Pa.	1876
Hall, Natalie	North Easton, Mass.	1904
Hall, Thurston	Boston, Mass.	1882
Halliday, John	Brooklyn, N. Y.	1880
Halliday, Robert	Loch Lomond, Scotland	1893
Hamilton, Hale	Topeka, Kansas	1880
Hampden, Walter	Brooklyn, N. Y.	1879
Hannen, Nicholas	London, England	1881
Hanson, Gladys	Atlanta, Ga.	1887
Harding, Lyn	Newport, England	1867

Hardwicke, Sir Cedric	Lye, Stourbridge, England	1893
Harrigan, William	New York	1893
Harris, Sam H.	New York	1872
Harrison, Richard B.	London, Ontario	1864
Hart, Vivian	Texas	1905
Hayes, Helen	Washington, D. C.	1900
Hazzard, John E.	New York	1881
Hedman, Martha	Sweden	1888
Heggie, O. P.	Australia	1879
Heineman, Eda	Japan	1891
Heming, Violet	Leeds, England	1893
Hepburn, Katharine	Hartford, Conn.	1907
Herbert, Evelyn	Brooklyn, N. Y.	1900
Herne, Chrystal	Dorchester, Mass.	1883
Hobert, Rose	New York	1906
Hodge, William	Albion, N. Y.	1874
Hopkins, Arthur	Cleveland, Ohio	1878
Hopkins, Miriam	Bainbridge, Ga.	1904
Hopper, de Wolf	New York	1858
Hopper, Edna Wallace	San Francisco, Cal.	1874
Holmes, Taylor	Newark, N. J.	1872
Howard, Leslie	London, England	1890
Howard, Sydney	Oakland, Cal.	1891
Hull, Henry	Louisville, Ky.	1893
Hunter, Glenn	Highland Mills, N. Y.	1896
Huston, Walter	Toronto	1884
Hutchinson, Josephine	Seattle, Wash.	1898
Inescort, Frieda	Hitchin, Scotland	1905
Ingram, Rex	Dublin, Ireland	1892
Irving, Isabel	Bridgeport, Conn.	1871
Irwin, May	Whitby, Ont.	1862
Janis, Elsie	Delaware, Ohio	1889
Joel, Clara	Jersey City, N. J.	1890
Johann, Zita	Hungary	1904
Jolson, Al	Washington, D. C.	1883
Johnston, Moffat	Edinburgh, Scotland	1886
Joy, Nicholas	Paris, France	1892
Kane, Whitford	Larne, Ireland	1882
Kaufman, George S.	Pittsburgh, Pa.	1889
Kaye, A. P.	Ringwood, Hampshire, England	1885

Keane, Doris	Michigan	1885
Keith, Ian	Boston, Mass.	1899
Keith, Robert	Scotland	1899
Kelly, Walter C.	Mineville, N. Y.	1875
Kennedy, Madge	Chicago, Ill.	1890
Kerrigan, J. M.	Dublin, Ireland	1885
Kerr, Geoffrey	London, England	1895
Kershaw, Willette	Clifton Heights, Mo.	1890
King, Dennis	Coventry, England	1897
Kingsford, Walter	England	1876
Kingsley, Sydney	New York	1906
Kirkland, Alexander	Mexico City	1904
Kosta, Tessa	Chicago, Ill.	1893
Kruger, Alma	Pittsburgh, Pa.	1880
Kruger, Otto	Toledo, Ohio	1895
Lackaye, Wilton	Virginia	1862
Larimore, Earl	Portland, Oregon	1899
Larrimore, Francine	Russia	1898
La Rue, Grace	Kansas City, Mo.	1882
Lauder, Harry	Portobello, England	1870
Laughton, Charles	Scarborough, England	1899
Lawrence, Gertrude	London	1898
Lawson, Wilfred	London, England	1894
Lawton, Thais	Louisville, Ky.	1881
Lean, Cecil	Illinois	1878
Lederer, Francis	Karlin, Prague	1906
Le Gallienne, Eva	London, England	1900
Leiber, Fritz	Chicago, Ill.	1884
Lenihan, Winifred	New York	1898
Leontovich, Eugenie	Moscow, Russia	1894
Levey, Ethel	San Francisco, Cal.	1881
Levy, Benn	London, England	1900
Lewis, Mabel Terry	London, England	1872
Lillie, Beatrice	Toronto, Canada	1898
Locke, Katherine	New York	1914
Logan, Stanley	Earlsfield, England	1885
Loraine, Robert	New Brighton, England	1876
Lord, Pauline	Hanford, Cal.	1890
Lorraine, Lillian	San Francisco, Cal.	1892
Lou-Tellegen	Holland	1881
Love, Montagu	Portsmouth, Hants	1877
Lowell, Helen	New York	1866
Lunt, Alfred	Milwaukee, Wis.	1893

Mack, Andrew	Boston, Mass.	1863
Mack, Willard	Ontario, Canada	1873
Macdonald, Donald	Denison, Texas	1898
Mackay, Elsie	London, England	1894
MacKellar, Helen	Canada	1896
Margo	Mexico	1918
Marlowe, Julia	Caldbeck, England	1870
Marshall, Herbert	London, England	1890
Massey, Raymond	Toronto, Canada	1896
Matthews, A. E.	Bridlington, England	1869
Matthison, Edith Wynne	England	1875
Maude, Cyril	London, England	1862
McClintic, Guthrie	Seattle, Wash.	1893
McCormick, Myron	Albany, Indiana	1906
McIntyre, Frank	Ann Arbor, Mich.	1879
Meek, Donald	Glasgow, Scotland	1880
Meighan, Thomas	Pittsburgh, Pa.	1879
Melba, Nellie	Melbourne, Australia	1866
Menken, Helen	New York	1901
Mercer, Beryl	Seville, Spain	1882
Meredith, Burgess	Cleveland, Ohio	1909
Merivale, Philip	Rehutia, India	1886
Merman, Ethel	Astoria, L. I.	1909
Miller, Gilbert	New York	1884
Miller, Marilyn	Findlay, Ohio	1898
Mitchell, Grant	Columbus, Ohio	1874
Mitchell, Thomas	Elizabeth, N. J.	1892
Mitzi (Hajos)	Budapest	1891
Moore, Grace	Del Rio, Tenn.	1901
Moore, Victor	Hammonton, N. J.	1876
Moran, Lois	Pittsburgh, Pa.	1909
Morgan, Claudia	New York	1912
Morgan, Helen	Danville, Ill.	1900
Morgan, Ralph	New York City	1889
Morris, Mary	Boston	1894
Morris, McKay	San Antonio, Texas	1890
Muni, Paul	Lemberg, Austria	1895
Nagel, Conrad	Keokuk, Iowa	1897
Nash, Florence	Troy, N. Y.	1888
Nash, Mary	Troy, N. Y.	1885
Nazimova, Alla	Crimea, Russia	1879
Nielsen, Alice	Nashville, Tenn.	1876

Nolan, Lloyd	San Francisco, Cal.	1903
Nugent, J. C.	Miles, Ohio	1875
Nugent, Elliott	Dover, Ohio	1900
O'Connell, Hugh	New York	1891
Odets, Clifford	Philadelphia	1906
Olcott, Chauncey	Buffalo, N. Y.	1862
Oldham, Derek	Accrington, England	1892
O'Neill, Eugene Gladstone	New York	1888
O'Neill, Nance	Oakland, Cal.	1875
Ouspenkaya, Maria	Tula, Russia	1876
Overman, Lynne	Maryville, Mo.	1887
Painter, Eleanor	Iowa	1890
Pawle, Lenox	London, England	1872
Pemberton, Brock	Leavenworth, Kansas	1885
Pennington, Ann	Philadelphia, Pa.	1898
Perkins, Osgood	Boston, Mass.	1892
Perry, Margaret	Denver, Colo.	1913
Philips, Mary	New London, Conn.	1901
Pickford, Mary	Toronto	1893
Pollock, Channing	Washington, D. C.	1880
Post, Guy Bates	Seattle, Wash.	1875
Power, Tyrone	London, England	1869
Powers, James T.	New York	1862
Powers, Leona	Salida, Colo.	1900
Powers, Tom	Owensburg, Ky.	1890
Pryor, Roger	New York City	1901
Quartermaine, Leon	Richmond, England	1876
Rains, Claude	London, England	1889
Rambeau, Marjorie	San Francisco, Cal.	1889
Rathbone, Basil	Johannesburg	1892
Reed, Florence	Philadelphia, Pa.	1883
Rennie, James	Toronto, Canada	1890
Revelle, Hamilton	Gibraltar	1872
Richman, Charles	Chicago, Ill.	1870
Ridges, Stanley	Southampton, England	1891
Ring, Blanche	Boston, Mass.	1876
Ring, Frances	New York	1882
Robson, May	Australia	1868
Rogers, Mary	Rogers, Ark.	1916

Roos, Joanna	Brooklyn, N. Y.	1901
Ross, Thomas W.	Boston, Mass.	1875
Royle, Selena	New York	1905
Ruben, José	Belgium	1886
Rumann, Siegfried	Hamburg, Germany	1879
Russell, Annie	Liverpool, England	1864
Sanderson, Julia	Springfield, Mass.	1887
Sands, Dorothy	Cambridge, Mass.	1900
Santley, Joseph	Salt Lake City	1889
Sawyer, Ivy	London, England	1897
Scheff, Fritzi	Vienna, Austria	1879
Schildkraut, Joseph	Bucharest, Roumania	1896
Scott, Cyril	Ireland	1866
Segal, Vivienne	Philadelphia, Pa.	1897
Selwyn, Edgar	Cincinnati, Ohio	1875
Serrano, Vincent	New York	1870
Shannon, Effie	Cambridge, Mass.	1867
Shepley, Ruth	New York	1889
Sherman, Lowell	San Francisco, Cal.	1885
Sherwood, Robert Emmet	New Rochelle, N. Y.	1896
Sidney, George	New York	1876
Sidney, Sylvia	New York	1910
Sinclair, Arthur	Dublin, Ireland	1883
Sitgreaves, Beverly	Charleston, S. C.	1867
Skelly, Hal	Allegheny, Pa.	1891
Skinner, Cornelia Otis	Chicago	1902
Skinner, Otis	Cambridgeport, Mass.	1857
Smith, Ben	Waxahachie, Texas	1905
Smith, Queenie	New York	1898
Sondergaard, Gale	Minnesota	1899
Sothern, Edward H.	New Orleans, La.	1859
Spong, Hilda	Australia	1875
Stahl, Rose	Montreal, Canada	1872
Standing, Sir Guy	London	1873
Starr, Frances	Oneonta, N. Y.	1886
Stickney, Dorothy	Dickinson, N. D.	1903
Stone, Fred	Denver, Colo.	1873
Stone, Dorothy	New York	1905
Strudwick, Sheppard	North Carolina	1905
Sullavan, Margaret	Norfolk, Va.	1910
Sunderland, Nan	Fresno, Cal.	1898
Sydney, Basil	London	1894

Taliaferro, Edith	New York	1892
Taliaferro, Mabel	New York	1887
Tanguay, Eva	Middletown, Conn.	1878
Taylor, Laurette	New York	1884
Tearle, Conway	New York	1878
Tell, Alma	New York	1892
Tell, Olive	New York	1894
Terris, Norma	Columbus, Kansas	1904
Thomas, Augustus	St. Louis, Mo.	1859
Thomas, Frankie	New York	1922
Thomas, John Charles	Baltimore, Md.	1887
Thorndyke, Dame Sybil	Gainsborough, England	1882
Tobin, Genevieve	New York	1901
Tobin, Vivian	New York	1903
Toler, Sidney	Warrensburg, Mo.	1874
Tone, Franchot	Niagara Falls, N. Y.	1907
Travers, Henry	Berwick, England	1874
Truex, Ernest	Red Hill, Mo.	1890
Tynan, Brandon	Dublin, Ireland	1879
Ulric, Lenore	New Ulm, Minn.	1897
Vallée, Rudy	Island Pond, Vermont	1902
Varesi, Gilda	Milan, Italy	1887
Victor, Josephine	Hungary	1891
Waldron, Charles	New York	1877
Walker, June	New York	1904
Walker, Charlotte	Galveston, Texas	1878
Walter, Eugene	Cleveland, Ohio	1874
Warfield, David	San Francisco, Cal.	1866
Warwick, Robert	Sacramento, Cal.	1878
Ware, Helen	San Francisco, Cal.	1877
Waterous, Herbert	Flint, Mich.	1863
Watkins, Linda	Boston, Mass.	1908
Watson, Minor	Marianna, Ark.	1889
Webb, Clifton	Indiana	1891
Weber, Joseph	New York	1867
Welford, Dallas	Liverpool, England	1874
Welles, Arson	Kenosha, Wisc.	1915
Westley, Helen	Brooklyn, N. Y.	1879
Westman, Nydia	White Plains, N. Y.	1906
Whiffen, Mrs. Thomas	London, England	1845

White, George	Toronto, Canada	1890
Whiteside, Walker	Logansport, Ind.	1869
Whorf, Richard	Winthrop, Mass.	1908
William, Warren	Aitkin, Minn.	1896
Williams, Emlyn	Mostyn, Wales	1905
Williams, Hope	New York City	1901
Wilson, Francis	Philadelphia, Pa.	1854
Wiman, Dwight Deere	Moline, Ill.	1895
Winwood, Estelle	England	1883
Witherspoon, Cora	New Orleans, La.	1891
Wood, Peggy	Brooklyn, N. Y.	1894
Worlock, Frederick	London, England	1889
Wright, Haidee	London, England	1868
Wycherly, Margaret	England	1883
Wyndham, Olive	Chicago, Ill.	1886
Wynyard, Diana	London, England	1906
Wynn, Ed.	Philadelphia, Pa.	1886
Young, Roland	London	1887
Yurka, Blanche	Bohemia	1893
Zabelle, Flora	Constantinople	1885
Ziegfeld, Florenz, Jr.	Chicago, Ill.	1868

NECROLOGY

June 15, 1936—June 15, 1937

Aarons, A. E., producer, composer, 71. Started in Philadelphia, later joining Koster and Bials, then Klaw and Erlanger; wrote music for and produced "Mlle. 'Awkins"; also produced "Yama," "His Honor the Mayor," etc. Born Philadelphia, Pa., died New York City, November 16, 1936.

Abbott, Marion, actress, 70. Debut in 1893 with Sol Smith Russell, later joining Charles Frohman; supported Maude Adams, E. H. Sothern, Otis Skinner, William Gillette, Virginia Harned, William Hodge and Frank Craven. Born Danville, Kentucky; died Philadelphia, Pa., January 15, 1937.

Aldrich, Richard, drama critic, 73. American reporter, editorial writer, music and drama critic; with Providence *Journal,* New York *Tribune* and New York *Times.* Born Providence, R. I.; died Rome, Italy, June 2, 1937.

Alexander, Ross (Ross Alexander Smith), actor, 29. First appearance with Blanche Yurka in "Enter Madame"; later in many Broadway plays including "That's Gratitude," "Let Us Be Gay" and "After Tomorrow." Born Brooklyn, N. Y.; died Hollywood, January 2, 1937.

Anson, Albert Edward, actor, 56. British actor widely known in America; member of Sir Herbert Tree's repertory company in 1904; toured United States with Viola Allen; prominent in support of Doris Keane, Laurette Taylor and others; last screen play "Arrowsmith"; last Broadway performance in "That's the Woman" in 1930. Born England; died Monrovia, Calif., June 25, 1936.

Arcaro, Flavia, actress and singer, 61. Prominent in Western stock companies; sang in first production of "Parsifal" in English; in original company of "Chocolate Soldier." Born Minonk, Illinois; died New York City, April 8, 1937.

Balieff, Nikita, actor, impresario, 59. Famous as director of "Chauve Souris"; started in Moscow; last appearance as commentator for "Continental Varieties." Born Russia; died New York City, September 3, 1936.

Barnes, T. Roy, actor, 57. Teamed in vaudeville with wife, Bessie Crawford; prominent in "Katinka," "The Red Canary,"

"The Passing Show," etc.; finished in motion pictures. Born England; died Hollywood, Calif., March 30, 1937.

Barnum, George W., actor, 84. Veteran of American and English stage; supported Mrs. Leslie Carter, Ethel Barrymore, William J. Scanlon, De Wolf Hopper, etc.; last appearance in "The Noose." Born Newark, N. J.; died Philadelphia, Pa., March 30, 1937.

Boleslawski, Richard, actor and director, 47. Assistant director of Moscow Art Theatre, 1909-1915; came to America 1920; assisted Reinhardt with "The Miracle"; staged "Vagabond King," "Mr. Moneypenny," etc.; director American Laboratory Theatre; in pictures wrote with Helen Woodward "The Way of a Lancer." Born Warsaw, Poland; died Hollywood, Calif., January 17, 1937.

Booth, Sydney Barton, actor, 60. Last of male line of famous American theatrical family; nephew of Edwin Booth; son of Junius Brutus 2nd and Agnes Booth; debut with Marie Wainwright at Wallack's 1892; subsequently supported long list of American stars including Sol Smith Russell, James Herne, Henrietta Crosman, Henry E. Dixey, Lillian Russell, Maude Adams and William Gillette. Born Boston, Mass.; died Stamford, Conn., February 5, 1937.

Browne, W. Graham, actor and director, 67. Debut London, 1891; supported Beerbohm Tree, F. R. Benson, Forbes-Robertson, George Alexander and Olga Nethersole, with whom he came to America; married Marie Tempest; wife's leading support for years. Born Ireland; died Hampstead, England, March 11, 1937.

Buckler, Hugh, actor, 66. Prominent many years in England, South Africa, Australia, New Zealand and America; supported Eva Le Gallienne in "L'Aiglon?" Ethel Barrymore in "The Constant Wife," Helen Hayes in "Mary of Scotland"; killed in auto accident with his son, John. Born Southampton, England; died Lake Malibu, Calif., October 31, 1936.

Buckler, John, actor, 40. Son of Hugh Buckler. Prominent in support of Katharine Cornell in "The Green Hat" and "Barretts of Wimpole Street"; recently in Hollywood in "Tarzan" pictures. Born London, England; died Lake Malibu, Calif., October 31, 1936.

Caldwell, Anne, playwright and lyricist, 60. Wrote many successful musical stage productions including "Top of the World," "The Nest Egg," "Chin-Chin" and "Hitchy-Koo" with Glen

McDonough. Born Boston, Mass.; died Beverly Hills, Calif., October 22, 1936.

Coburn, Ivah Wills (Mrs. Charles), actress, 57. Debut 1900 with E. H. Sothern; co-producer with husband of "The Yellow Jacket," "The Farmer's Wife" and "Lysistrata"; helped establish Mohawk Drama Festival. Born Appleton, Mo.; died New York City, April 27, 1937.

Cort, Harry Linsley, producer author, 44. Son of the late John Cort; wrote "Listen Lester," "Jim Jam Jems," "China Rose," etc.; with Charles H. Abramson produced "Veneer" and "All the King's Horses." Born Seattle, Washington; died New York City, May 6, 1937.

Coulter, Frazer, actor, 88. Supported Mrs. Sheridan Shook in "School for Scandal" in the seventies; last appearance in 1931 as the Judge in "Oh, Promise Me"; played at Noblo's Garden; supported Lawrence Barrett, Fanny Davenport, Stuart Robson, William Crane, Rose Coghlan and Richard Mansfield; in original production of "Hazel Kirke." Born Smith Falls, Ontario, Canada; died East Islip, N. Y., January 26, 1937.

Damerel, George, tenor, 57. Forty year stage career included five years of "The Merry Widow" with Lina Abarbanell; retired in 1929. Born Hastings, Minn.; died Glendale, Calif., July 10, 1936.

Drinkwater, John, author, actor, poet, 54. Best known in America for his "Abraham Lincoln"; wrote "Mary Stuart," "Oliver Cromwell," "Robert E. Lee," "Bird in Hand," etc.; adapted Mussolini's "Napoleon" receiving decoration; last work scenario for "The King and His People," tracing history of British Royal Family. Born Leytonstone, England; died London, March 25, 1937.

Durbin, Maud (Mrs. Otis Skinner) actress author, 66. Joined Mme. Modjeska's company in 1893; supported Otis Skinner in repertory; collaborated with Jules Eckert Goodman writing "Pietro"; last stage appearance with her husband in "The Silent Voice," 1915. Born Hannibal, Mo.; died New York City, December 25, 1936.

Eustace, Jennie, actress, 69. With A. M. Palmer Stock Company in "Jim the Penman," "Caste," "Alabama," etc.; toured with Richard Mansfield, Sir Henry Irving, E. H. Sothern and Forbes-Robertson; last appearance with Mrs. Fiske in "Mrs. Bumpstead-Leigh," 1929. Born Troy, N. Y.; died Dobbs Ferry, N. Y., July 10, 1936.

Fagan, Barney, actor author, 87. Famous minstrel and vaudeville headliner; team of Fagan and Fenton; co-organizer of Sweatnam, Rice and Fagan's Minstrels; wrote song, "My Gal's a Hign-born Lady," and comedy, "Paradise Alley." Born Boston, Mass.; died Bay Shore, N. Y., January 12, 1937.

Fenwick, Irene (Frizzel), actress, 49. Wife of Lionel Barrymore whom she supported in "The Claw" and other plays; first appearance in "Peggy from Paris"; played in "The Zebra," "The Fortune Teller," "Song of Songs," "Laugh, Clown, Laugh" and "The Co-Respondent." Born Chicago, Ill.; died Beverly Hills, Calif., December 24, 1936.

Gibson, Preston, playwright, 57. Wrote "The Turning Point," "Fate," "Mrs. Erskine's Devotion," "The Vacuum," "Lola Montez" and others. Born Washington, D. C.; died New York City, February 15, 1937.

Gorky, Maxim (Alexis Maximovitch Pieshkov), author, 68. Last of the great pre-Revolution Russian writers; wrote "Mother," "Lower Depths," etc.; many novels, books of reminiscences, short stories, etc. Born Nizhni, Novgorod, Russia (now called Gorky); died Moscow, Russia, June 18, 1936.

Granville, Bernard, actor, 50. Dancing comedian in "Marriage à la Carte," "Ziegfeld's Follies," "Vanities of 1923," "No, No, Nanette," etc.; last Broadway appearance "Whistling in the Dark" in 1932. Born Chicago, Ill.; died Hollywood, Calif., October 5, 1936.

Harlow, Jean (Harlean Carpenter), screen actress, 26. Became famous in "Hell's Angels"; followed "Red-Headed Woman," and "Red Dust" with Clark Gable; "Dinner at Eight," "Wife Versus Secretary," "Suzy," etc. Born Kansas City, Mo.; died Hollywood, Calif., June 7, 1937.

Harrison, Louis, comedian and playwright, 70. Started with Mrs. John Drew in Philadelphia; supported Henry Dixey, Lillian Russell, Fritzi Scheff; wrote "The Isle of Champagne," "Princess Nicotine," "Broadway and Tokio," rewrote "Mlle. Modiste"; last appearance in "Sonny." Born Philadelphia, Pa.; died New York City, October 23, 1936.

Hassell, George, actor, 56. Veteran character actor widely known in England, Australia and America; appeared in "Countess Maritza," "The Chocolate Soldier," "The Student Prince," etc.; to motion pictures in 1934. Born Birmingham, England; died Chatsworth, Calif., February 17, 1937.

Helton, Alf, actor, 78. Came from England in 1892; supported De Wolf Hopper, Lillian Russell, Maude Adams and Otis

Skinner; last appearance in "Victoria Regina." Born England; died Forest Hills, N. Y., March 6, 1937.

Heron, Bijou (Mrs. Henry Miller), actress, 75. Mother of Gilbert Miller and daughter of Matilda Heron; famous child actress playing in 1874 Adrienne in "Monsieur Alphonse," Fanfan in "The First Family," and Oliver Twist to Fanny Davenport's Nancy Sikes; complimentary testimonial given at Union League Theatre, January 20, 1875; youngest actress to play Juliet. Born New York City; died New York City, March 18, 1937.

Higgins, David, actor playwright, 78. Known for "His Last Dollar," "The Scallawag," "Piney Ridge," "Up York State," etc. Born Chicago, Ill.; died Brooklyn, June 30, 1936.

Hope, Adele Blood, actress, promoter, 50. Toured world with Shakespearian stock company; once called "most beautiful blonde on American stage." Died Yonkers, N. Y., September 13, 1936.

Ince, Ralph W., actor director, 50. Started with Richard Mansfield after doing cartoons on New York papers; pioneer screen actor and director, starting with Vitagraph. Born Boston, Mass.; died Kensington, England, April 11, 1935.

Jennings, Dewitt C., actor, 65. Stage career of 42 years started with James O'Neill; joined motion picture colony in 1920; outstanding appearance in "Mutiny on the Bounty." Born Cameron, Mo.; died Hollywood, Calif., March 1, 1937.

Kingdon, Frank, actor, 72. Forty years on stage; debut in "Richard III" with Richard Mansfield; supported Sothern and Marlowe, Kelcey and Shannon, H. B. Warner and Marilyn Miller. Born Providence, R. I.; died Englewood, N. J., April 9, 1937.

Laughlin, Anna (Mrs. Dwight V. Monroe), singer, 52. Greatest success in "Wizard of Oz" with Montgomery and Stone; also remembered in "Top of the World"; early success in vaudeville. Born Sacramento, Calif.; died New York City, March 6, 1937.

Ling, Richie, actor and singer, 70. Prominent for fifty years in operetta and as leading man for Lillian Russell, Fritzi Scheff, Viola Allen, Eva Le Gallienne, Jane Cowl, Peggy Wood and others. Born England; died Lambs Club, New York, March 5, 1937.

Long, Mary Elitch, theatre owner and manager, 86. Widow of John Elitch, old time showman; developed Elitch Gardens and theatre in Denver, Colorado; oldest stock company enterprise in the West, entertaining many famous stars since 1890—Sarah Bernhardt, Minnie Maddern Fiske, Blanche Walsh, Rose Coghlan, Blanche Bates, Douglas Fairbanks, etc. Born Philadelphia, Pa.; died Denver, Colorado, July 16, 1936.

Marquis, Marjorie Vonnegut, actress, 44. With Theatre Guild in "The Apple Cart" and "Ah, Wilderness"; prominent in Summer and Little Theatre movements. Born Indianapolis, Ind.; died New York City, October 25, 1936.

Martin, Mrs. Jacques (Lillian Gerome), actress, 73. Toured England and America 20 years before her New York debut with Nazimova in "Hedda Gabler" in 1906; once English music hall favorite; played many prominent roles in America. Born Michigan; died New York City, July 11, 1936.

McClendon, Rose, actress, 51. One of the best known Negro players on American stage; an organizer of Negro People's Theatre in 1935; remembered in "Deep River," "In Abraham's Bosom," "Porgy," "The House of Connelly" and "Mulatto." Born New York City; died New York City, July 12, 1936.

Meighan, Thomas, actor, 57. Began in stock company in Pittsburgh with Henrietta Crosman; later with William Collier in "The Dictator," all-star "Two Orphans" and "The College Widow"; film debut in "Fighting Hope" with Laura Hope Crews; greatest film success "The Miracle Man." Shepherd of Lambs Club in 1924. Born Pittsburgh, Pa.; died Great Neck, N. Y., July 8, 1936.

Mellish, Fuller, actor, 71. Member of famous LeClercq theatrical family in England; began career in Edwin Booth's London company; supported Mary Anderson, Beerbohm Tree, Annie Russell, Mrs. Pat Campbell, Viola Allen, Henry Irving and Mrs. Fiske. Born England; died New York City, December 7, 1936.

Miltern, John, actor, 67. Prominent for more than 30 years; debut in "Chinatown Charlie"; remembered as Professor Moriarity in "Sherlock Holmes." Born New Britain, Conn.; died Los Angeles, Calif., January 15, 1937.

Odell, Maude, actress, 65. Broadway debut in Daniel Frohman's production of "Nerves"; supported James K. Hackett in "The Prisoner of Zenda" and James O'Neill in "The Count of Monte Cristo"; died in dressing room while playing Sister Bessie in "Tobacco Road." Born Beaufort, S. C.; died New York City, February 27, 1937.

Parker, Lottie Blair, actress author, 78. Started with Boston Theatre Stock Company; supported John McCullough, Mary Anderson and Dion Boucicault; toured with Janauschek, Lawrence Barrett and others; name part in "Hazel Kirke"; wrote "White Roses," "Way Down East" and "Under Southern Skies." Born Oswego, N. Y.; died Great Neck, N. Y., January 5, 1937.

Pickford, Lottie, actress, 41. Sister of Mary Pickford; before screen career toured with Mary in "Little Red School House" and "The Two Orphans." Born Toronto, Canada; died Beverly Hills, Calif., December 9, 1936.

Pirandello, Luigi, author producer, 69. Wrote forty-one plays. Won Nobel prize for literature in 1934; best known in America for "Six Characters in Search of an Author," and "As You Desire Me." Born Girgenti, Sicily; died Rome, Italy, December 10, 1936.

Pitt, Fanny Addison, actress, 93. Active on stage for 45 years playing in support of Ethel Barrymore, John Drew, E. H. Sothern and Julia Marlowe; last appearance with Margaret Anglin; retired in 1929. Born England; died Philadelphia, Pa., January 7, 1937.

Rice, Fanny, actress, 77. Debut with Ideal Opera Company, Boston, 1880; sang original roles in "Ermine" "The Brigands," "Poor Jonathan" and "Nadjy"; headed own farce-comedy company; last appearance in "The Barker," Los Angeles, 1930. Born Lowell, Mass.; died New York City, July 10, 1936.

Sale, Chic, comedian author, 51. Vaudeville headliner for years; appeared in revues at Winter Garden, on Amsterdam Roof and in Shubert revues, "Gay Paree" and "Hello, Paris"; with films since 1931. Born Huron, S. D.; died Los Angeles, Calif., November 7, 1936.

Schumann-Heink, Ernestine Roessler, dramatic contralto, 75. Debut at Dresden in "Il Trovatore"; American debut in 1898 at Metropolitan as Ortrud in "Lohengrin"; famous in World War work of entertaining soldiers. Born Prague, Bohemia; died Hollywood, Calif., November 17, 1936.

Shipman, Samuel, playwright, 53. First play "Kreutzer Sonata," adapted with Clayton Hamilton, 1904; last play, "Behind Red Lights" with Beth Brown, 1937; others included "Friendly Enemies," "East is West," "Lawful Larceny," "Crime" and "Alley Cat." Born New York City; died New York City, February 9, 1937.

Standing, Sir Guy, actor, 63. Son of Herbert Standing, British actor; prominent in support of Annie Russell, Mrs. Pat Campbell and Alla Nazimova; with Charles Frohman company in "Sowing the Wind," "The Little Minister," "The Conquerors," etc.; toured in "Cynara" before entering films in 1933. Born London, England; died Hollywood, Calif., February 24, 1937.

Truesdell, George Frederick, actor, 64. Leading man in many plays including "Our Betters," "The College Widow," "East is West" and "Maggie Pepper"; last New York engagement in "The Apple Cart" in 1930. Died New York City, May 3, 1937.

Tyler, Odette (Mrs. R. D. Shepherd), actress, 67. Long a member of Charles Frohman's Empire Theatre Stock Company; appeared with William Gillette in command performance of "Sherlock Holmes" before Queen Victoria; last New York appearance with William Faversham in 1913; organized Los Angeles Philharmonic Orchestra; wrote "The Red Carnation"; married R. D. MacLean, Shakespearian actor. Born Savannah, Ga.; died Hollywood, Calif., December 8, 1936.

Walthall, Henry B., actor, 60. Started in New York in "Under Southern Skies" and "The Great Divide"; became famous in early silent films; first picture "Ramona" with Mary Pickford; remembered best as the Little Colonel in "Birth of a Nation" filmed in 1915. Born Shelby City, Ala.; died Monrovia, Calif., June 17, 1936.

Whiffen, Blanche (Mrs. Thomas), actress, 91. Played over 400 roles in 63-year career on stage; daughter of Mary Galton, British opera singer; came to America with Galton Opera Company; was original "Little Buttercup" in "H.M.S. Pinafore"; with Daniel Frohman company in "The Wife," "Charity Ball," etc.; later supported Mary Mannering, Eleanor Robson, Margaret Anglin and many other stars; last appearance in 1930 in "Trelawney of the Wells." Born London, England; died Montvale, Va., November 25, 1936.

Williams, Herb, comedian, 52. Internationally known in vaudeville in comedy team of Williams and Wolfus; appeared in Earl Carroll's "Vanities," "Farmer Takes a Wife," and "At Home Abroad." Born Philadelphia, Pa.; died Freeport, N. Y., October 1, 1936.

Williams, Malcolm, actor, 67. Remembered in "The Wisdom Tooth," "Beyond the Horizon," "Little Accident"; married

Florence Reed. Born Spring Valley, Minn.; died New York City, June 10, 1937.

Winter, Banks, balladist, 81. Minstrel comedian and singer for 50 years; toured with Chauncey Olcott; wrote the song "White Wings." Died Reseda, Calif., December 13, 1936.

Vosper, Frank, actor author, 37. Started with Ben Greet in England; toured with Basil Dean and H. B. Waring in India and Far East; with Old Vic Company in 1926; last play "Love from a Stranger" written with Agatha Christie, produced in 1936 in London and New York. Born London; died at sea March 6, 1937.

THE DECADES' TOLL

(Persons of Outstanding Prominence in the Theatre Who Have Died in Recent Years)

	Born	*Died*
Aborn, Milton	1864	1933
Bacon, Frank	1864	1922
Baker, George Pierce	1866	1935
Belasco, David	1856	1931
Bernhardt, Sarah	1845	1923
Coghlan, Rose	1851	1932
Crabtree, Charlotte (Lotta)	1847	1924
Crane, William H.	1845	1928
De Koven, Reginald	1861	1920
De Reszke, Jean	1850	1925
Dillingham, Charles Bancroft	1868	1934
Ditrichstein, Leo	1865	1928
Dressler, Marie	1869	1934
Drew, John	1853	1927
Drinkwater, John	1883	1937
Du Maurier, Sir Gerald	1873	1934
Duse, Eleanora	1859	1924
Fiske, Minnie Maddern	1865	1932
Galsworthy, John	1867	1933
Goodwin, Nathaniel	1857	1920
Gorky, Maxim	1868	1936
Greet, Sir Philip (Ben)	1858	1936
Hawtrey, Sir Charles	1858	1923
Herbert, Victor	1859	1924
Hopper, De Wolf	1858	1935
Lackaye, Wilton	1862	1932
Mantell, Robert Bruce	1854	1928
Miller, Henry	1858	1926
Morris, Clara	1848	1925
O'Neill, James	1850	1920
Patti, Adelina	1843	1919
Pinero, Sir Arthur Wing	1855	1934
Pirandello, Luigi	1867	1936
Rejane, Gabrielle	1857	1920

	Born	*Died*
Rogers, Will	1879	1935
Russell, Annie	1864	1936
Russell, Lillian	1861	1922
Schumann-Heink, Ernestine	1861	1936
Sembrich, Marcella	1859	1935
Shaw, Mary	1860	1929
Smith, Winchell	1862	1933
Sothern, Edwin Hugh	1859	1933
Terry, Ellen	1848	1928
Thomas, Augustus	1857	1934
Warde, Frederick	1851	1935
Whiffen, Mrs. Thomas	1845	1936
Wilson, Francis	1854	1935
Ziegfeld, Florenz	1869	1932

INDEX OF AUTHORS

INDEX OF PLAYS AND CASTS